Routledge Handbook of the Business of Women's Sport

Combining knowledge from sport management, marketing, media, leadership, governance, and consumer behavior in innovative ways, this book goes further than any other in surveying current theory and research on the business of women's sport around the world, making it an unparalleled resource for all those who aspire to work in, or understand, women's sport.

Featuring international perspectives, with authors from North America, South America, Europe, Asia, and Oceania, and insightful, in-depth profiles of real leaders within different sectors of women's sport in the global sport industry, the *Routledge Handbook of the Business of Women's Sport* offers an integrated understanding of the ways traditional media and social media impact both the understanding and the advancement of women's sport properties, businesses, teams, and athletes. Innovative case studies show how societal issues such as gender, power, and framing impact the business of women's sports and those who work in women's sport.

An essential reference for any researcher or advanced student with an interest in women's sport or women in business, and useful supplementary reading for researchers and advanced students working in sport business, sport management, mainstream business and management, or women's studies.

Nancy Lough is Graduate Coordinator and Director of the Higher Education graduate degree programs in the College of Education at the University of Nevada, Las Vegas, NV, USA, where she is also Professor and Chair of the Intercollegiate Athletics Council. She has received the Stotlar Award for outstanding contributions to the field of Sport Marketing, been recognized as a Sport Marketing Research Fellow by the Sport Marketing Association, and named as an affiliate scholar with the Tucker Center for Research on Girls and Women in Sport.

Andrea N. Geurin is Reader in the Institute for Sport Business at Loughborough University, UK. She is on the Executive Council for the North American Society of Sport Management (NASSM), serving as the organization's secretary and she serves on the editorial boards of eight academic sport management journals. In 2015 she was named a NASSM Research Fellow.

Routledge Handbook of the Business of Women's Sport

*Edited by Nancy Lough and
Andrea N. Geurin*

Routledge
Taylor & Francis Group
LONDON AND NEW YORK

First published 2019
by Routledge
2 Park Square, Milton Park, Abingdon, Oxon OX14 4RN

and by Routledge
52 Vanderbilt Avenue, New York, NY 10017

Routledge is an imprint of the Taylor & Francis Group, an informa business

© 2019 selection and editorial matter, Nancy Lough and Andrea N. Geurin; individual chapters, the contributors

The right of Nancy Lough and Andrea N. Geurin to be identified as the authors of the editorial material, and of the authors for their individual chapters, has been asserted in accordance with sections 77 and 78 of the Copyright, Designs and Patents Act 1988.

All rights reserved. No part of this book may be reprinted or reproduced or utilised in any form or by any electronic, mechanical, or other means, now known or hereafter invented, including photocopying and recording, or in any information storage or retrieval system, without permission in writing from the publishers.

Trademark notice: Product or corporate names may be trademarks or registered trademarks, and are used only for identification and explanation without intent to infringe.

British Library Cataloguing-in-Publication Data
A catalogue record for this book is available from the British Library

Library of Congress Cataloging-in-Publication Data
A catalog record has been requested for this book

ISBN: 978-1-138-57161-7 (hbk)
ISBN: 978-0-203-70263-5 (ebk)

Typeset in Bembo
by Swales & Willis Ltd, Exeter, Devon, UK

Printed in the United Kingdom
by Henry Ling Limited

Contents

List of contributors	x
Introduction *Nancy Lough and Andrea N. Geurin*	1

PART I
History and evolution of women's sport business   9

1 History and evolution of women's sport *Elizabeth A. Gregg and Elizabeth Taylor*	11
2 The impact of Title IX and other equity laws on the business of women's sport *Ellen J. Staurowsky*	23
3 Sociological perspectives of women in sport *Nicole M. LaVoi, Anna Baeth, and Austin Stair Calhoun*	36
4 Women trailblazers in sport business *Lynn L. Ridinger and Donna L. Pastore*	47
5 The history of women in sport management academe and the treatment of female faculty members in sport management higher education *Elizabeth Taylor and Elizabeth A. Gregg*	65

PART II
Management of women's sport   81

6 The role of bias in the under-representation of women in leadership positions *George B. Cunningham and Na Young Ahn*	83

Contents

7   The delivery and management of women-only sport events and their
    future sustainability   95
    Brianna L. Newland

8   Women in leadership positions within Canadian sport   106
    Guylaine Demers, Lucie Thibault, Sophie Brière, and Diane Culver

9   Professional women's sport in Australia   124
    Emma Sherry and Chelsey Taylor

10 From the battlefield to the board room: the place of gender
    in sex-integrated sport   134
    Donna de Haan and Lucy Dumbell

11 Migratory process of Brazilian Olympic women   151
    Katia Rubio, Neilton Ferreira Junior, and Gislane Ferreira de Melo

12 Management of professional women's golf in the United States   161
    Melissa Davies and Eric Hungenberg

13 Socio-historical development of Korean women's golf   178
    Hyun-Duck Kim, Hongyoung Kim, and Colleen McGlone

PART III
Economics and financial aspects of women's sport   **189**

14 The relative success story of the WNBA   191
    David Berri

15 Public expenditure on women's sport and gender equality among
    recipients of public expenditure in European sport   204
    Pamela Wicker

16 The new gender equity in elite women's sports   217
    Dionne Koller

17 Social entrepreneurship   228
    Carrie W. LeCrom and Allison B. Smith

18 Business analytics in women's professional sports   239
    Ceyda Mumcu

PART IV
Leadership and governance   253

19 Under-representation of women in leadership roles in women's sport   255
    Laura J. Burton

20 Women's roles and positions in European sport organizations:
    historical developments and current tendencies   269
    Gertrud Pfister

21 Socio-political context in which the business of women's sport
    takes place in Latin America   280
    Rosa López de D'Amico

22 National sporting organizations and women's sport participation:
    an Australian focus   292
    Katie Rowe

23 Governance of women's sport in China   303
    Hanhan Xue and Joshua I. Newman

24 Women's involvement in sport governance: a case study of
    New Zealand rugby   316
    Gaye Bryham, Lesley Ferkins, Katie Dee, and Jacqueline Mueller

25 Governance of college sport   329
    Erianne A. Weight and Molly P. Harry

26 The evolution of women's rugby   341
    Brittany Jacobs and Nicole Sellars

27 Women and elite coaching in New Zealand: challenges, benefits,
    and opportunities   352
    Sarah Leberman and Jane Hurst

PART V
Marketing and consumer behavior   365

28 Authentically communicating with women consumers: examining
    successful (and non-successful) branding and marketing efforts   367
    Brandon Brown and B. Nalani Butler

29 Team identification in women's sport: what little we know   380
    Elizabeth B. Delia

30 Women are sport fans! An examination of female sport fandom   391
    Michelle Harrolle and Katie Kicklighter

31 Marketing women's professional tennis   403
    Ashleigh-Jane Thompson

32 Sexism in marketing women's sport and female athletes:
    ineffective and harmful   418
    Janet S. Fink

33 You're just not our type: an examination of the obstacles faced
    by women athlete endorsers   429
    Ted B. Peetz

34 Sponsorship of women's sport   439
    Nancy Lough and Greg Greenhalgh

PART VI
Media and technology   **453**

35 Social media and women's sport: what have we learned so far   455
    Ann Pegoraro, Katie Lebel, and Alanna Harman

36 Female athletes find a place for expression on Instagram   468
    Lauren M. Burch and Matthew H. Zimmerman

37 Transforming sporting spaces into male spaces: considering
    sports media practices in an evolving sporting landscape   480
    Erin Whiteside

38 Netball: carving out media and corporate success in the
    game for all girls   492
    Margaret Henley and Toni Bruce

39 Deserving of attention: traditional media coverage and the
    use of social media by female athletes with disabilities   504
    Erin McNary and Michael Cottingham

40 Sport, sponsors, and sponsor fit: media presentations of
    Norwegian women athletes in Olympic events   515
    Elsa Kristiansen, Birgit Andrine Apenes Solem,
    and Mikael Lagerborg

41 Media coverage of women athletes during the Olympic Games   529
    Andrea N. Geurin

    Conclusion   540
    Andrea N. Geurin and Nancy Lough

Index   *544*

Contributors

Na Young Ahn is a doctoral student in the Division of Sport Management in the Department of Health and Kinesiology at Texas A&M University, College Station, Texas, USA. She also works in the Center for Sport Management Research and Education. Previously, Ahn worked as a research assistant in the Division of Policy R&D in the Department of Policy Development and a program coordinator for Women's Sports Leadership Academy at the Korea Institute of Sport Science.

Anna Baeth is a PhD student in kinesiology, studying Sport Sociology, at the University of Minnesota, MN, USA. Her focus is on gender and coaching, resiliency in the coaching profession, coach development, masculinity in sport, and socially responsible sport practices.

David Berri is professor of economics at the Southern Utah University, Cedar City, Utah, USA, and has spent the last two decades researching sports and economics. His research covers a wide variety of topics including the evaluation of players and coaches, competitive balance, the drafting of players, labor disputes, the National Collegiate Athletic Association (NCAA), and gender issues in sports.

Sophie Brière is an associate professor in the management department of the Faculty of Business Administration at Université Laval, Quebec City, Canada. She holds the Chair for academic coordination of a graduate program about Women and Organization, international development and humanitarian action, and project management. During her career, she has worked as a consultant, trainer, and researcher with organizations and universities in various countries in Latin America, Africa, and Asia.

Brandon Brown is a clinical assistant professor of sport management in the School of Professional Studies at New York University, NYC, USA. In addition to serving as a marketing consultant for several professional sport entities, Brown has spent a number years working with the New York Mets in Queens, New York. His current line of study focuses on sport marketing, consumer behavior, and minority consumption habits.

Gaye Bryham has over 20 years' experience in the sport and recreation industry. Her work has focused on advancing educational opportunities for students, and building successful relationships and partnerships between Auckland University of Technology, New Zealand, and industry organizations. Bryham is currently Department Head of Sport Leadership and Management, and the Deputy Head of School, Sport, and Recreation at Auckland University of Technology. Her research and teaching focus is in the area of sport leadership and the social construction of leadership.

Contributors

Toni Bruce is professor of sociology of sport and sports media in the Faculty of Education and Social Work at the University of Auckland, New Zealand. Drawing primarily from cultural studies and feminism, her main research focus is the interrogation of sports media discourses, with particular emphasis on how "difference" is produced and manifests itself in media coverage, especially of sportswomen. Her recent work explores the rise of the pretty *and* powerful female athlete, through a third-wave feminist lens.

B. Nalani Butler is assistant professor of sport management at the University of Tampa, Downtown Tampa, FL, USA, where she is the faculty advisor for the Sport Women of Tampa (SWOT) and the President for the Honor Society of Phi Kappa Phi. At the University of Tampa she teaches History of the Modern Olympics, Stadium and Arena Management, and Media Relations and Sport Communications. She volunteers with the Tampa Bay Paralympic community, playing beach tennis, or paddle boarding. Butler's research in the discipline of sport studies includes: globalization and sport, sport labor migration, and sport for development.

Lauren M. Burch is an assistant professor of marketing and the MBA Program Director at Indiana University–Purdue University Columbus (IUPUC), Columbus, IN, USA. She teaches courses in business, marketing, and statistics. Her research interests include digital media, brand equity, and personal branding. Before, and concurrent with returning to academia, Burch spent four years working in industry as a business development analyst for Lockheed Martin Corporation, and as a public relations specialist at Hirons & Company Communications.

Laura J. Burton is a professor of sport management in the Department of Educational Leadership within the Neag School of Education at the University of Connecticut, Storrs, CT, USA. Her research interests include understanding leadership in organizations (particularly sport organizations) and exploring development, access, and success in leadership. In her work, Laura focuses on issues of gender in leadership contexts and specifically how stereotypes and discrimination impact women in sport leadership. She has served as the editor of the *Journal of Intercollegiate Sport* and serves on the editorial board of the *Journal of Sport Management and Women in Sport* and *Physical Activity Journal*.

Austin Stair Calhoun is currently the Chief of Staff in the Office of Medical Education at the University of Minnesota, MN, USA. Calhoun is a sport media scholar, technology enthusiast, and advocate for gender and GLBT issues in sport. With over a decade of public relations and higher education experience, she is the former team lead of the University of Minnesota's School of Kinesiology eLearning and Digital Strategy group, spearheading their grassroots communications and academic technology efforts. Her research concentrates on media and sport, specifically social and digital media in sport and media representations of gender in sport.

Michael Cottingham is an assistant professor of sport administration in the Department of Health and Human Performance at the University of Houston (UH), TX, USA. His research interests focus on perceptions of athletes with disabilities, as well as spectatorship and sponsorship in disability sport. In addition, he examines broader topics in sport consumer behavior. Cottingham is involved in the Sport Administration graduate program at UH and he also teaches senior level undergraduate classes. In addition, he serves as the director of adaptive athletics at UH.

Diane Culver is an associate professor in the School of Human Kinetics, the Faculty of Health Sciences at the University of Ottawa, in Ottawa, Ontario, Canada. With a practical background as an athlete, then coach, at international/Olympic levels she studies coach development, women in coaching, social learning theory, and qualitative research methods. She is on the editorial board of the *Canadian Journal for Women in Coaching*, the *International Sport Coaching Journal*, and the LASE *Journal of Sport Science*. She is a member of the International Council for Coach Excellence and the Canadian Sport Psychology Association, and is a Coach Developer for the Coaching Association of Canada. Culver also developed coaches for the Coaching Association of Canada in Haiti and Luxembourg. She consults with athletes, coaches, and sport organizations facilitating the enhancement of their performance.

George B. Cunningham is a professor of sport management at Texas A&M University, College Station, TX, USA. He serves as the director of the Center for Sport Management Research and Education, as well as the Laboratory for Diversity in Sport. Cunningham holds a faculty affiliate appointment in the Women's and Gender Studies Program. Cunningham is the former president of both the North American Society for Sport Management and Aggie Allies. He is a member of the National Academy of Kinesiology.

Melissa Davies is assistant professor of sport management at the University of the Pacific in Stockton, California, USA. Her primary research interests include understanding the recruitment and retention of sport participants, while also conducting studies related to brand and event management. Related with this text, Davies has published research that examined the role of Instagram in a Ladies Professional Golf Association's (LPGA's) brand management, as well as an investigation of the fan, volunteer, and management perceptions of the mobile device policies at a PGA Tour golf event.

Donna de Haan is an associate professor at The Hague University of Applied Sciences, The Hague, Netherlands. She has over 14 years' experience developing curricular, research, and lecturing at undergraduate and postgraduate levels, in both the UK and the Netherlands. She conducts primarily qualitative research in the field of gender equality in sport, associated with issues of participation, coaching, leadership, and governance. She is passionate about the application of research into practice, and works closely with several international sport organizations to help them improve their governance practices.

Katie Dee is a researcher with Auckland University of Technology, New Zealand. As a member of the Rugby Codes Research Group, she works on numerous rugby-related projects, has published in sport leadership, and is part of the award-winning teaching team in the area of leadership in sport and recreation.

Elizabeth B. Delia is an assistant professor in the Mark. H. McCormack Department of Sport Management in the Isenberg School of Management at the University of Massachusetts Amherst, Amherst, MA, USA. Her primary research interest is studying the meaning of sport-related consumer identities, informed by multiple disciplinary perspectives. She is also interested in understanding how consumers' identities are influenced by the marketing activities of sports organizations.

Guylaine Demers is a professor at Laval University, Quebec City, Canada. She is particularly interested in issues of women in sport and LGBT-phobia in sport. She currently serves as Chair of Égale-Action, Québec's Association for the Advancement of Women in Sport. Dr. Demers made the CAAWS's list of Most Influential Women in Sport and Physical Activity in Canada in 2007, 2010, and 2015. In 2015, she organized *Conversation 2015*, a national conference dedicated to fostering solutions to bettering the experiences of girls and women in the Canadian sport system. She is the newly appointed Women's Studies Research Chair at Université Laval.

Lucy Dumbell has worked for over 20 years in UK higher education and has led curriculum development, lectured, and worked in higher education management during that time. Her roots were, however, in equestrianism and her first career was in teaching riding and horse care. A founder member of the Equestrian Performance Research and Knowledge Exchange Arena at Hartpury, a UK post-compulsory educational institution and equestrian competition venue, she researches the role of the human equestrian athlete in equestrian sport, striving to advance knowledge and practice alongside each other.

Lesley Ferkins has 20 years' experience as an academic in sport management in Australia and New Zealand. She joined Auckland University of Technology (AUT), New Zealand, in 2015 and is currently Director of the AUT Sports Performance Research Institute New Zealand (SPRINZ). Ferkins' area of research specialization is leadership and governance within sport organizations. She is also on the board of Tennis New Zealand, Associate Editor of *Sport Management Review*, and an editorial board member of the *Journal of Sport Management*.

Gislane Ferreira de Melo is a full professor at the Catholic University of Brasília, Brazil. She has experience in physical education, with an emphasis on physical activity and health, working mainly in the following subjects: elderly, physical activity, athletes, gender, and psychological profile of gender.

Neilton Ferreira Junior is a PhD student at the Escola de Educação Física e Esporte of the Universidade de São Paulo (EEFE-USP), Brazil. He is a member of the Centro de Estudos Socioculturais do Movimento Humano and Grupo de Estudos Olímpicos (EEFE-USP) and a member of the Brazilian Olympic Academy. He studies athletic career, racism, and imaginary sports.

Janet S. Fink is a professor and Chair of the Mark H. McCormack Department of Sport Management at the University of Massachusetts Amherst, USA. Her research interests include the marketing of women's sport and female athletes, sport consumer behavior, and diversity issues in sport. Fink is the Senior Associate Editor of the *Journal of Sport Management*. She is a NASSM Research Fellow, recipient of the Dr. Earle F. Zeigler Award, and former President of NASSM.

Greg Greenhalgh is an associate professor in the Center for Sport Leadership at the Virginia Commonwealth University, Richmond, VA, USA. Greenhalgh's primary research interest focuses on the marketing of sport organizations, specifically investigating what attracts fans and sponsors to niche, or non-mainstream, sports, and how these sports can position themselves to be more sustainable in the future. His other research interests include consumer behavior, and sport and the natural environment. Greenhalgh spent several years in the sport industry. He held the position of Company Representative at FieldTurf, attending and representing the company at Super Bowl XL and the NCAA Convention.

Elizabeth A. Gregg is currently an associate professor of sport management and Chair of the Department of Leadership, School Counseling, and Sport Management at the University of North Florida, FL, USA. She teaches classes on Issues in Sport, Introduction to Sport Management, Foundations of Sport Management, and Leadership. Her research interests include issues in intercollegiate athletics, sport history, women in sport, and branding.

Contributors

Alanna Harman is an assistant professor at St. John's University, New York City, USA, in the Division of Sport Management. Harman's research interests include the construction of gender in sport, psychological contracts, and organizational behavior.

Michelle Harrolle is Director of Residency Placement and an assistant professor in the Vinik Sport and Entertainment Management Program at the University of South Florida, Tampa, FL, USA. She teaches Sales and Fundraising and Marketing Research in Sport. Harrolle, who has been published in a number of journals including the *Journal of Sport Management*, also has years of experience in the sport industry. Her research focuses on understanding how motivations, constraints, and awareness relate to sport consumption patterns and how this information can be used for effective marketing. Dr. Harrolle has conducted numerous consumer behavior and economic impact studies for international professional leagues and teams.

Molly P. Harry is a doctoral candidate at the University of Virginia, Charlottesville, VA, USA, studying higher education with a focus on intercollegiate athletics. Her research interests include education through athletics participation, academic reform for college athletics, and student-athlete rights and well-being.

Margaret Henley lectures in media sport, television production, and sports journalism in Media & Communication, School of Social Sciences, at the University of Auckland, New Zealand. She has a particular interest in the representation of women playing sport in early film and cinema newsreels, with a long-term research focus on New Zealand netball history through moving images. Her contemporary netball research is focused on the relationship between the game and television broadcasting in a domestic and international context, and the growth of online social media communities associated with the game.

Eric Hungenberg is a professor of sport, outdoor recreation, and tourism management at the University of Tennessee at Chattanooga, TN, USA. His passion for sport surrounds its ability to enrich society and promote personal well-being. His research interests involve exploring the role the physical environment plays in influencing fan and participant consumption behaviors.

Jane Hurst is a management consultant specializing in public sector policy, strategy, and governance. She has an academic background in law, media studies, and management. Hurst has a particular interest in the career and leadership development of women and has completed a doctorate researching the experiences of New Zealand women managing and being managed by women, and the influence these experiences had on their career path and decisions. She also assists in running a martial arts school and has a keen interest in helping young women develop self-confidence, self-esteem, and leadership skills through participation in martial arts.

Brittany Jacobs is assistant professor of sport management at Nichols College, Dudley, MA, USA, and has worked for USA Rugby, the national governing body for rugby in the United States. Jacobs' research focuses on the impact of organizational structures and behaviors on sport development. She sees the practical outcome of such work as enhanced effectiveness in sport program development through improved marketing, policy-making, and administration.

Katie Kicklighter is a research assistant at the University of South Florida's Vinik Sport and Entertainment Management Program, Tampa, FL, USA. She completed her undergraduate studies in business administration with a concentration in marketing at the Denver Broncos Sport Management Institute at Colorado State University, where she was a swimmer.

Hyun-Duck Kim is a professor in the College of Physical Education at Keimyung University, Daegu, South Korea, and also serves as the secretary general of Korean Society of Sports Management. Before coming to Keimyung University, Kim worked as a faculty member/coordinator of the sport management program (golf industry emphasis) of Barry University, Florida. Hyun-Duck's main research interests include, but are not limited to, sustainability of mega-sporting events, sport and physical education administration, and golf performance.

Hongyoung Kim is a former sports agent with a specialization in golf. He worked at leading sport-marketing agencies in Korea, such as Bravo & NEW and GalaxiaSM, and has served as a field agent for world-renowned golf professionals such as Inbee Park and So-Yeon Ryu.

Dionne Koller is professor of law, Associate Dean for Academic Affairs, and Director of the Center for Sport and the Law at the University of Baltimore School of Law, Baltimore, MD, USA. Koller's scholarly focus is Olympic and amateur sports Dionne has served as chair and as a member of the Executive Board for the Sports Law Section of the Association of American Law Schools and is a member of the United States Anti-Doping Agency's Anti-Doping Review Board. She is also on the editorial board for the *International Sports Law Journal*. Most recently, Professor Koller has served as part of the advisory group for the Aspen Institute's *Project Play: Baltimore* initiative.

Elsa Kristiansen is professor of management, School of Business at the University of South-Eastern Norway. Her research is in the areas of sport psychology (e.g., motivation, coping with organizational issues and media stress, coping with youth competitions) and sport management (e.g., volunteerism, Youth Olympic Games, stakeholders involved in talent development, event management).

Mikael Lagerborg is a senior librarian at the University of South-Eastern Norway. At the university, he works with research support, research documentation, providing courses in literature search and academic writing for staff and students. Lagerborg is also interested in library history and the history of arctic cartography.

Nicole M. LaVoi is a senior lecturer in the area of social and behavioral sciences in the School of Kinesiology at the University of Minnesota, St. Paul, MN, USA, where she is also the Co-Director of the Tucker Center for Research on Girls & Women in Sport. Through her multidisciplinary research she answers critical questions that can make a difference in the lives of sport stakeholders—particularly girls and women. Her seminal research includes the annual *Women in College Coaching Report Card*, which is aimed at retaining and increasing the number of women in the coaching profession, and the groundbreaking book *Women in Sports Coaching*. She also collaborates with colleagues on media representations of females in sport, including co-producing an Emmy-winning best sports documentary titled *Media Coverage & Female Athletes: Women Play Sports, Just Not in the Media*, and has a new documentary titled *Game ON: Women Can Coach*.

Katie Lebel is an assistant professor at Ryerson University, Toronto, Canada, in the Ted Rogers School of Management. Lebel specializes in the area of sport marketing, with a particular focus on digital image management strategies and consumer engagement.

Contributors

Sarah Leberman is Professor of Leadership and Dean Academic for Massey University, Palmerston North, New Zealand. Her research focus is on women in leadership within sport and academia. She was a Fulbright Senior Scholar in 2008, which she tenured at the Tucker Centre for Research on Girls and Women in Sport, at the University of Minnesota, USA. Leberman was a member of the New Zealand Olympic Committee, Women in Sport Group, and the Manager of the Women's Junior Black Sticks and Black Sticks teams. She is a co-founder member of Women in Sport Aotearoa, which was established to transform sport for the betterment of women and girls and, through sport participation, to grow future leaders and role models.

Carrie W. LeCrom is the Executive Director and Associate Professor at the Center for Sport Leadership at the Virginia Commonwealth University, Richmond, VA, USA, where she has taught since 2005. She is passionate about the use of sport for social change, and has generated over US$1.3 million in grant funding from sources such as the US Department of State and the NCAA. Her research interests focus on sport for development, leadership, and consumer behavior. She was the recipient of the 2014 Ruch Award for Excellence in Teaching and the 2016 Award of Excellence, both given by the VCU School of Education.

Rosa López de D'Amico is coordinator of the research center "Estudios en Educación Física, Salud, Deporte, Recreación y Danza" (EDUFISADRED), Maracay, Venezuela. Her research is focused on physical education, comparative studies in sport, sport policy, sport management, culture, and gender. She has participated in more than 30 projects and has contributed to the creation of undergraduate and graduate programs. She has multiple publications, is an editorial board member of various academic journals, and is the current editor of the Latin American *Journal for Sport Management*. In 2007 she received the highest research award given by the Venezuelan Universities Council (CDCHT). In her previous gymnastics career, she was a member of the Venezuelan national team, and later coach, international judge, and administrator. In 2006 she received "The Gold Medal of Honor" given by the ICHPER-SD. In 2013 she was a member of honor of the World Association for Sport Management; President of the IAPESGW (2013–2021); and board member of WASM, ISCPES, and ICSSPE. She was a Founder President of the Latin America Sport Management Association ALGEDE.

Colleen McGlone is professor and Chair of Recreation and Sport Management at the Coastal Carolina University, Conway, SC, USA. She has taught courses in intercollegiate Athletics, Organizational Culture, Sport Sociology, and Sport Marketing, as well as numerous other courses. Her research focus includes organizational culture, hazing in sport, women in sport, sport consumer behavior, and sport governance.

Erin McNary is an assistant professor of sport administration in the Department of Kinesiology and Sport Sciences at the University of Miami (UM), FL, USA. Her research interests include sport management pedagogy. In addition, she examines the promotion of and ethics in youth sport communication, as well as marketing, advertising, and promotion of youth and marginalized athletes. McNary also explores topics relating to facility and event management, an area in which she has several years of experience working in both campus recreation and a national non-profit sports physical and activity program.

Jacqueline Mueller is a doctoral researcher affiliated with the Institute for Sport Business at Loughborough University London, London, UK. She has been granted full funding for her

PhD project, which focuses on implicit leadership theories within a sporting context. Her research interests are in sport leadership, gender diversity, and leadership education.

Ceyda Mumcu is an assistant professor of sport management in the College of Business at the University of New Haven, Connecticut, USA. Her research is focused on marketing and consumer behavior in sport, the special nature of women's sports and its marketing applications, marketing research and analytics in sport, and business models of international sports. Mumcu's edited book, *Sport Analytics: A data-driven approach to sport business and management*, was published in 2017. She has been involved in research projects for Women's National Basketball Association (WNBA), National Lacrosse League (NLL), and Connecticut Open (CT Open). Before coming to the United States, she played professional basketball for eight years in the Turkish Women's Basketball League.

Brianna L. Newland is a clinical associate professor and the Academic Director for Undergraduate Programs in the Preston Robert Tisch Institute for Global Sport at New York University, New York City, USA. Newland's research explores the patterns of sport participation/delivery and the development of sport. This includes research on what fosters/hinders adult participation in sport, and how sport events can be leveraged to develop sport and tourism. In 2018, she was named a NASSM Research Fellow. She serves as the associate editor for the *Sport and Entertainment Review* and the editorial board for the *Journal of Applied Sport Management*. She also serves on the NASSM Executive Council as a Member-at-Large.

Joshua I. Newman is professor of media, politics, and cultural studies and Director of the Center for Sport, Health, and Equitable Development in the Department of Sport Management at Florida State University (FSU), Tallahassee, FL, USA. His most recent book *Sport, Spectacle, and NASCAR Nation: Consumption and the Cultural Politics of Neoliberalism* was awarded the NASSS's Outstanding Book for 2012 and was named as a Choice Outstanding Academic Title in 2013. He is on the editorial boards of the *Sociology of Sport Journal*, *Communication and Sport*, *Qualitative Research in Sport, Exercise, and Health*, *International Review for the Sociology of Sport*, and the *Journal of Global Sport Management* and he is a Distinguished Overseas Professor with the Shanghai University of Sport, China. Newman is the current NASSS President.

Donna L. Pastore is a professor at the Ohio State University in Columbus, OH, USA. Her research interests focus on faculty mentoring, diversity management within sport organizations, and the examination of current issues influencing and impacting intercollegiate athletics. She is a NASSM and NAK Research Fellow and recipient of the NASSM Earle F. Zeigler Award.

Ted B. Peetz is an associate professor and director of the sport administration program in the Department of Sport Science at Belmont University, Nashville, TN, USA. Peetz has worked in coaching, marketing and administrative positions in professional and intercollegiate athletics. He is an active member of the Sport Marketing Association (SMA) and the North American Society for Sport Management (NASSM) and serves on the editorial boards for the *Sport Management Education Journal*, *Sport Marketing Quarterly*, and the *Journal of Amateur Sport*. His research interests include celebrity athlete endorsers, fandom, and sport consumer behavior.

Ann Pegoraro is the Director of the Institute for Sport Marketing (ISM) and an associate professor in the School of Human Kinetics at Laurentian University, Greater Sudbury, Ontario, Canada. Pegoraro focuses her research on the intersection of digital media and sport.

Contributors

Gertrud Pfister is professor at the Department of Exercise and Sport Sciences, University of Copenhagen, Denmark. She serves as a member of the scientific boards in the European College of Sport Sciences (ECSS), WSI (Women's Sport International), and the International Association of Physical Education and Sport of Girls and Women (IAPESGW). She is also a member of the editorial boards of 15 scientific journals and served on several committees that evaluated sport faculties. Pfister has won four awards for her scholarly work, among others the Award of the International Society for Sport History and the Howell and Howell Distinguished Lecturer Award of NASSH. She has published more than 20 books and more than 200 scholarly articles. She is active in various sports and has served in sport clubs and federations.

Lynn L. Ridinger is a professor and Department Chair at Old Dominion University in Norfolk, Virginia, USA. Her research interests focus on psychosocial factors associated with sport involvement, consumer behavior, and women's sports. She is a North American Society for Sport Management (NASSM) Research Fellow and recipient of the NASSM Distinguished Sport Management Educator Award.

Katie Rowe is Lecturer in Sport Management, a member of the Centre for Sport Research, at Deakin University, Australia. Her research interests include sport and active recreation participation, and community development through sport, with a particular emphasis on women and girls. Her PhD focused on women's cycling participation and she regularly works with industry stakeholders regarding women's cycling participation issues. Rowe has presented her research at sport management and physical activity conferences internationally and has published in journals including the *Journal of Sport Management* and *Sport Management Review*. She is a guest editor of a special issue of *Sport Management Review* entitled "Managing Sport for Health."

Katia Rubio is an associate professor at the Centro de Estudos Socioculturais do Movimento Humano and Grupo de Estudos Olímpicos (EEFE-USP), Brazil. She serves as the Coordinator of the EEFE-USP and is a member of the Brazilian Olympic Academy. Rubio is also a member of the Instituto de Estudos Avançados of Universidade de São Paulo, where, in 2017, she participated in the Sabbatical Year Program with the project "The influence of national displacements and transnational migration in the formation of the identity of Brazilian Olympic athletes."

Nicole Sellars is a doctoral candidate at the University of Northern Colorado, Greeley, CO, USA. After working for three seasons in the National Basketball Association's Development League, she chose to move away from the sport industry toward a career in academia. Her research focuses predominately on gender issues in sport, and addresses diversity and equality in areas including coaching, management, fandom, and participation.

Emma Sherry is an associate professor at Swinburne University in Melbourne, Australia, specializing in the area of sport for development. Sherry's current research interests include community development through sport activities, undertaking a broad range of research projects with national and regional sport organizations in Australia and Oceania, including Netball Australia, National Rugby League, Australian Football League, Tennis Australia, and Hockey Victoria. Other recent research has included access and equity in sport participation, sport in correctional facilities, and sport and recreation for at-risk and marginalized communities.

Allison B. Smith is originally from Daleville, VA and now lives in Richmond, VA, USA as a postdoctoral research fellow in the Center for Sport Leadership at the Virginia Commonwealth

University. Her research focus is the holistic care of student athletes, particularly looking at their psychological and physiological state after transitioning out of sport, work–life balance of coaches and administrators in college sport, as well as the role of women in intercollegiate athletics.

Birgit Andrine Apenes Solem is associate professor at the School of Business of the University of South-Eastern Norway. Her research is in the areas of consumer behavior, branding, marketing communication, social media marketing, event management, business model innovation, and service innovation and design.

Ellen J. Staurowsky is a professor of sport management in the Center for Sport Management at Drexel University, Philadelphia, PA, USA. She is internationally recognized as an expert on social justice issues in sport, including college athletes' rights, the exploitation of college athletes, gender equity and Title IX, and the misappropriation of American Indian imagery in sport.

Chelsey Taylor is a research assistant at Swinburne University of Technology, Melbourne, Australia. She has a passion for sport and business, with a keen interest in the commercialization of women's sport. Taylor has tracked and followed the professionalization of women's leagues internationally and in Australian sport. Other research areas include fan engagement, member satisfaction, systematic review of women's sport literature, and barriers to physical activity and participation.

Elizabeth Taylor is an Assistant Professor of Sport and Recreation Management at Temple University, Philadelphia, PA, USA. Her work broadly focuses on improving diversity and inclusion within the sport industry, specifically as it relates to gender discrimination and homophobia, sexual harassment and sexual assault education, and harassment of female faculty members.

Lucie Thibault is the dean of the Faculty of Health Sciences at the University of Ottawa, Ottawa, Ontario, Canada. Thibault has taught organizational theory, ethics in sport, globalization of sport, governance, and policy, and social issues in sport. She serves on the editorial board of the *International Journal of Sport Policy and Politics* as well as the *European Sport Management Quarterly*. She is a member of the NASSM and was named a NASSM research fellow in 2001. In 2008, Thibault was awarded the Earle F. Zeigler Award (NASSM) for her scholarly and leadership contributions to the field. Her research interests lie in interorganizational relationships in sport organizations. She also investigates Canadian government involvement in sport excellence and sport participation, as well as sport policy.

Ashleigh-Jane Thompson is a lecturer in the Department of Management, Sport and Tourism at La Trobe University, Melbourne, Australia, where she teaches in the sport management program. Her research considers the (re)presentation of entities in media, digital and social media, and examines the influence and impact on the communication across sport organizations, athletes, and consumers. Thompson is a current member of the International Association for Communication and Sport (IACS) and the Sport Management Association of Australia and New Zealand (SMAANZ). She also currently serves on the SMAANZ board, and the editorial board of the *International Journal of Sport Communication*.

Erianne A. Weight is associate professor of sport administration at the University of North Carolina at Chapel Hill, NC, USA, a research consultant for collegiate sports associates, and the Director of the Center for Research in Intercollegiate Athletics. Her research is directed by a vision to increase the quality and quantity of opportunities for education through athletics.

This effort has thus far been focused on examining the financial, educational, and administrative impacts and opportunities for improvement within intercollegiate athletics. Weight has worked with university administrators and faculty senate leaders throughout the country and is an active consultant in intercollegiate athletics.

Erin Whiteside is associate professor of journalism and electronic media at the University of Tennessee (UT), Knoxville, TN, USA. Her research focuses on sociopolitical issues in communication and sport, with a special focus on the experiences of women working in sports media, discourses of gender and sexuality in sports media, and contexts and trends in relation to women's sports coverage. At UT, she teaches classes on media and diversity, sports journalism and sports, media and society. Before entering academia, she worked as an editor for Major League Baseball, and as an athletic communications director for Penn State.

Pamela Wicker is an academic councilor at the Department of Sport Economics and Sport Management at the German Sport University Cologne, Cologne, Germany. In 2011 and 2012, she was employed as a Senior Lecturer in Sport Management at Griffith University, Australia. Her main research interests include non-profit sport organizations, determinants and outcomes of sport participation, monetary valuation, and labor market research. She provides service to the academic community in various ways, including two Associate Editor positions (*Sport Management Review* and *European Sport Management Quarterly*) and seven editorial board memberships.

Hanhan Xue is an assistant professor in the Department of Sport Management at Florida State University, Tallahassee, FL, USA. Her research and teaching focus on management of international business for sport organizations, particularly in the Chinese market, as well as e-sports. She is a fellow in the FSU Center for Sport, Health, and Equitable Development, where she conducts community needs assessments for urban redevelopment projects in Tallahassee, FL. Her research has been featured in major international journals, such as *European Sport Management Quarterly*, *International Journal of Sports Marketing and Sponsorship*, *Communication and Sport*, *Sociology of Sport Journal*, and *International Review for the Sociology of Sport*.

Matthew H. Zimmerman is an assistant professor of sport studies at Mississippi State University, Starkville, MS, USA. He spent five years covering sports for two newspapers in his native Southern California, and his main research interests pertain to the use of online media by sports organizations to connect with their target publics.

Introduction

Nancy Lough and Andrea N. Geurin

The evolution of women's sports over the last four decades has been dramatic, with indicators showing reason for continued growth. In this era when women's sport is positioned to break new ground economically and socially, there is a need to focus on the value women bring to sport as athletes, managers, leaders, and scholars. Although the business of women's sport is thriving now more than ever, theory, scholarship, and education focused on women's sport are still lacking. Too often academic preparation programs neglect to focus on developing an understanding of women's sport, despite the likelihood that graduates of both genders will find employment opportunities requiring a knowledge of the unique attributes of women's sport. In this handbook we bring thought leaders together to engage in discussion on some of the key questions emerging as we highlight the untapped business potential of women's sport.

Economically, the business of women's sport continues to demonstrate viability. In 2018, the Women's National Basketball Association (WNBA) reported record increases in viewership and revenue. In 2017, three teams experienced double-digit growth as well as a new high for average attendance with 7,716 fans per game, and total attendance reaching 1,574,078 (Lough, 2018). In American college basketball, the Women's Final Four reported a 20% increase in 2017, with nearly four million viewers watching the game live on television (Hobson, 2017). Similarly, viewership of the Women's College World Series (WCWS) reached 814,000 in 2014 (Bracht, 2015) and had more viewers than the men's College World Series in 2015 and 2016 (Nyatawa, 2017). In soccer, the 2015 Women's World Cup championship game set viewership records, eclipsing ratings for other prominent mainstream sport properties.

> A survey across eight key markets around the world (U.S., U.K., France, Italy, Germany, Spain, Australia and New Zealand) found that 84% of sports fans are interested in women's sports. Of those, 51% are male, which confirms that women's sports engage a gender-balanced audience.
>
> *(Nielsen Sports Women's Sport Research, 2018).*

Noting that women are not the only consumers of women's sport is an important shift within the business of women's sport. On average, men comprise the majority of fans for the Women's Tennis Association (WTA), Ladies Professional Golf Association (LPGA), and

National Pro Fastpitch (NPF) (Mumcu, Lough, & Barnes, 2016), whereas well over a third of all major league sport fans (i.e., National Football League, Major League Baseball) in the United States are women. In terms of mainstream sport fans internationally, 47% of Australian sport fans are women according to the Australian Bureau of Statistics (ABS), and a 2015 Gallup poll revealed that 51% of females in the United States identify themselves as sport fans (Jones, 2015), whereas approximately 45% of baseball fans in South Korea are female. These are just a few examples of the popularity of sport among women sport consumers globally. Fandom starts most often with socialization from family members and sport participation.

Recent research has found that women comprise 40% of all sport participants in the United States and, since 2009, girls' sport participation has grown 50% each year (National Federation of State High School Associations, 2016). In the United States, 81% of millennial women played sport in school. In 2014 alone, 19 million girls played volleyball, basketball, and soccer (Sport & Fitness Industry Association, 2014). Female participation numbers are high in other countries as well. The Australian Bureau of Statistics (2015) reported that 59.4% of Australian females participated in sport in 2014. Sport England reported, in 2015, that the number of women playing sport in that country was increasing faster than the number of men (BBC, 2015). The growth in sport participation rates translates directly to business opportunities, either in development of new apparel and equipment for competition and training, or in marketing potential available to potential sponsors or sport properties.

In a related fashion, the business side of women's sport has continued to grow. One recent author forecasting future sport business trends stated that "prioritizing women is paramount" for all sports properties (Antoniacci, 2016, para. 10). In 2014, women spent US$15.1 billion on active wear, which represented a 7% increase year on year (Sport & Fitness Industry Association, 2014). Women spend 80% of all sport apparel dollars and account for 85% of all brand purchases. This growing value of women's sport has not been lost on those who seek beneficial business partnerships. The most recent sponsorship deal signed by the WTA was a 10-year, US$525 million media rights deal, making it the largest deal of this type in history (Sandomir, 2014). In this case, women's tennis has been the business leader due to its equal broadcasting of events for both the men's and the women's major tournaments. This momentum was also evident in a deal signed by Samsung to sponsor the Italian elite volleyball league Serie A, one of the best professional volleyball leagues in the world (Labrie, 2016). The league includes Olympians from several countries, creating worldwide appeal similar to the WTA. Increasingly, marketing investments like these are being made in women's sport by companies seeking to distinguish their brands in an increasingly cluttered environment.

Women's sports fans of both genders are progressively using new media to watch games, discuss sports, form communities, and gain insights about their favorite players and teams (Billings & Brown, 2017). As a demonstration of the growing viability of women's sport-driven business, espnW.com achieved record traffic in July of 2016, with 11.4 million unique visitors according to Omniture, up 24% from the same time the previous year (Glass, 2016). Research also indicated that ESPN Radio's female audience grew by 42% from 2015 to 2016, one of the reasons being the development of new programming, led by women contributors from espnW. Although most sports media consumption still occurs via traditional outlets (such as radio, television, and newspapers), the proportion is dropping as consumers seek emerging formats like espnW and migrate toward innovative platforms creating new ways to connect with other fans. Never before have the lines between producer and consumer, fan and athlete been more blurred, warranting a need for innovative business approaches and analysis. The internet has provided unprecedented access for fans by making virtually everything available for consumption, which has enhanced the content availability for women's sport fans while also making the understanding of the business of women's sports substantially more complex.

Yet, women's sport continues to face resistance not experienced by mainstream sports. For example, indicators show women's sport receives only about 4% of all sports media coverage in the UK, and averages less than 10% in the United States (Musto, Cooky, & Messner, 2017). Some suggest that, with men representing 90% of sports editors, and 90% of these men being white, the challenges facing women's sport to gain media attention and recognition as a viable sport product have been formidable. The Women's Media Center's 2015 report on "The status of women in the U.S. media" showed that just 10.2% of sports coverage in 2014 was produced by women. Women of color, who constitute over 70% of WNBA players, are particularly poorly represented in the media that cover them, with a 2014 report showing that just four sports editors at US newspapers were black women, and the numbers of reporters were correspondingly small. Despite the lack of coverage and representation of women in sports media, the 2015 Women's World Cup championship game set viewership records for both men's and women's soccer. With 25.4 million viewers in the United States, the final match between the United States and Japan became the most-watched soccer game – men's or women's – in US history, eclipsing the previous record of 18.7 million watching the US men's team play against Portugal (Deitsch, 2015).

Similarly, during the 2016 Olympic Games, women dominated the media coverage because they won most of the medals for the United States and were sought out by every major media outlet. Still, this pattern has occurred in previous Olympic Games, with media focused on women's sport fading as the halo of the Games diminished. In this era, when women's sport is positioned to break new ground economically and socially, there is a need to focus on communicating the value women bring to the business of sport. The momentum achieved from the support garnered during each Olympic Games needs to be sustained after the torch diminishes, because women's sport today offers tremendous opportunity. From media outlets like espnW, to professional sport organizations like the WTA, to college sport, to mass participation sporting events dominated by women (e.g., Running USA reported that women comprised 57% of all road race participants in 2015), to burgeoning new businesses such as Oiselle, a women's specialty athletic apparel company that experienced a three-year growth rate of 496% in revenues (Ryan, 2016), the opportunity for women's sport to thrive as good business is more present now than ever.

Scholarship about women's sport has evolved to demonstrate the emerging economic viability, while also pointing to the significant challenges that remain. Questions emerging include whether the antiquated approach to women's sport coverage will be altered in the digital environment in ways that will add value. What marketing distinctions relevant for women's sport are understood and what remains to be explored? How does "gatekeeping" prevent women from advancing to positions where decision-making authority could significantly impact the relationship between consumers and the product, property, or event? These questions continue to evolve along with opportunities for innovative ways to market and sell women's sports and for groups previously at the margins to be recognized and valued (Maxwell & Lough, 2009; Messner, Duncan, & Wachs, 1996; Mumcu et al., 2016).

Unique women's sport scholarship has emerged in the last decade. The significant upswing in the quantity and quality of research in this area has identified new avenues for understanding distinct aspects of women's sport (Geurin-Eagleman & Burch, 2016; Kane, LaVoi, & Fink, 2013; Mumcu et al., 2016). All seem to agree that a different approach to the business of women's sport is warranted, yet there is little agreement on what specific strategies are needed to insure a future leading to greater economic viability. In this handbook, analysis of scholarly work and industry trends will frame the discussion in each chapter to point toward strategic approaches that will continue the advancement of theory, as well as the development of women's sport as a commodity and women as leaders in the business of sport.

Editors' ambition

Few studies have focused on women sport consumers, their attitudes towards the marketing of women's sport, and the relationship of their consumption behavior to their levels of fandom. For years scholars have reported that fans with stronger attachment to a sport team attend more events, consume related media more often, and purchase more merchandise than the fans with lower fandom (e.g. Murrel & Dietz, 1992; Wann, 2006; Brown, Devlin, & Billings, 2013). However, these studies focused on mainstream sport, not women's sport. Similarly, Funk and James (2001) reported that, among sport fans, higher consumption intentions are possible with improved awareness. Increasing awareness has, however, continuously been a challenge for women's sport due to the lack of traditional media coverage. Currently, interest is emerging in millennials and Generation Z as growing consumer bases. Yet millennials, who are known to have more of an entitlement mindset with regard to gender equity (Rubin & Lough, 2015), are less likely to view their fandom as a means to support their gender or to see women's sport as a "cause," which was a centerpiece of fan identity among the Title IX generation of fans. Thus, fan development now requires strategic approaches to identify and appeal to newly emerging market segments, some of which view and consume sport differently to past generations.

Sport business scholars have initiated investigations into these inherently fluctuating questions. For example, scholars have found similarities between women's sport and mainstream sport, reporting favorable attitudes toward a sport property, whether a team or a league increases fans' and spectators' likelihood of attending events, watching games on TV, purchasing sport property products, and online consumption via social media and the internet (Dwyer, 2013; Funk & James, 2006; Lim, Martin, & Kwak, 2010). Important new women's sport scholarship has emerged in the last decade, with recent years demonstrating a significant upswing in the quantity and quality of work in this area as researchers have identified new avenues for understanding these unique aspects of women's sport (e.g., Geurin-Eagleman & Burch, 2016; Kane et al., 2013; Mumcu et al., 2016). Although there is agreement that a new approach to the business of women's sport is warranted, there remains little consensus on what specific strategies will insure a future of greater economic viability.

One solution points to the need to measure and improve the representation of women in sport executive positions, with the power to influence key decisions. The more diverse the set of leaders a business has, the more likely the success of that business (Tulshyan, 2015). Yet, in 2017 women comprised only 22% of the board directors at S&P 500 companies (Spencer Stuart, 2017). The lack of women in leadership roles is no different in sport business. From the 20% of women senior administrators in the NFL to the 13.1% of women executive committee members of International Federations of sport (Lapchick, 2016), women continue to be underrepresented in leadership positions in all levels of sport around the globe (Burton, 2015). With men dominating the decision-making roles in women's sport, and the emergence of an increasing economic value aligned with women's sport, the need for a resource to educate those who aspire to work in the business realm of women's sport is clear.

Overview of the book

The *Handbook of the Business of Women's Sport* combines knowledge bases from sport management, marketing, media, sport participation, and consumer behavior in innovative ways, and is the most comprehensive resource on women's sport business published to date. Consisting of 41 chapters organized by subject into 6 robust sections, the book provides a unique focus on the evolution and history of women's sport business, the management of women's sport, the economics and financial aspects of women's sport, leadership and governance, marketing and consumer behavior, and media and technology.

The first section (Chapters 1–5) takes a deep dive into the history and evolution of women's sport business, with chapters focusing on the historical and sociological foundations of women's sport, influential women trailblazers within the field, the impact of Title IX in the US, and a unique perspective on women in professorial roles within the sport management academic landscape. Following this, the second section (Chapters 6–13) builds on the history of women's sport business in order to examine the current management of women's sport from a variety of perspectives and contexts. This section offers insights on the biases and stereotypes within women's sport, the management of women's sport in countries such as Australia, Canada, and Brazil, the management of women's professional golf from both US and South Korean contexts, and insights into managing women's sporting events. In addition, this section features a chapter focused on a unisex sport, equestrian, providing readers with an awareness and deeper understanding of this unique sport context in which women and men compete with and against each other even at the highest levels of the sport.

The third section (Chapters 14–18) examines financial and economic aspects of women's sport business, with chapters focused on the economic demand for women's professional sport, labor issues, social entrepreneurship, sports analytics, and the public expenditure on women's sport in European nations. Following this, the fourth section (Chapters 19–27) examines the leadership and governance of women's sport, beginning with a chapter focused on the underrepresentation of women in leadership roles. Next, several chapters discuss the issue of women's leadership in sport from a wide variety of national and regional contexts, including Europe, Latin America, Australia, New Zealand, China, and the US. The truly global focus within this section provides a unique opportunity for readers to compare and contrast different countries and areas of the world, and to learn from the successes and challenges of other nations/regions.

The fifth section (Chapters 28–34) presents readers with current issues related to marketing and consumer behavior within women's sport business. These chapters provide examples of successful marketing campaigns by women's sport organizations, examples of sexism within marketing of women's sport, the profiles and behaviors of women who are fans of women's sport, and the areas of sponsorship and endorsements within women's sport. The final section of the book (Chapters 35–41) discusses media and technology as these areas relate to women's sport. Topics covered in the sixth section include traditional media representations of women athletes, promotion of women's sport and women athletes via social media, coverage of women's sport during the Youth Olympic Games and the Olympic Games, and specific examinations of media coverage of the sport of netball in New Zealand and women who compete in disability sport.

By implementing an interdisciplinary approach to the study of the business of women's sport, this handbook delivers a contemporary view of the "state of women's sport" from a business perspective. Analysis of scholarly work in each of the combined areas points toward strategic approaches to continue the advancement of theory as well as the development of women's sport as a commodity and women as leaders in the business of sport.

References

Antoniacci, M. (2016). Top 10 sports business trends to watch in 2016. Retrieved from https://www.inc.com/mandy-antoniacci/top-10-sports-business-trends-to-watch-in-2016.html.

Australian Bureau of Statistics (2015). Participation in sport and physical recreation, Australia, 2013–14, 'Table 1 Persons participating in sport and physical recreation, states and territories, by sex and age', cat. no. 4177.0. Retrieved from www.abs.gov.au/ausstats/abs@.nsf/Latestproducts/4177.0Media%20Release12013-14?opendocument&tabname=Summary&prodno=4177.0&issue=2013-14&num=&view.

BBC (2015). Sport England: Women lead increase in sport participation. Retrieved from https://www.bbc.com/sport/35061399.

Billings, A.C. & Brown, K.A. (2017). *Evolution of the Modern Sports Fan: Communicative approaches*. Lanham, MA: Lexington Books.

Bracht, W. (2015). ESPN programmers are bullish on growth of women's softball . Retrieved from https://newsok.com/article/5422650/espn-programmers-are-bullish-on-growth-of-womens-softball.

Brown, N. A., Devlin, M. B., & Billings, A. C. (2013). Fan identification gone extreme: Sports communication variables between fans and sport in the Ultimate Fighting Championship. *International Journal of Sport Communication*, **6**(1), 19–32.

Burton, L. J. (2015). Underrepresentation of women in sport leadership: A review of research. *Sport Management Review*, **18**(2), 155–165.

Deitsch, R. (2015). USA–Japan Women's World Cup final shatters American TV ratings record. Retrieved from https://www.si.com/planet-futbol/2015/07/06/usa-japan-womens-world-cup-tv-ratings-record.

Dwyer, B. (2013). The Impact of Game Outcomes on Fantasy Football Participation and National Football League Media Consumption. *Sport Marketing Quarterly*, **22**(1): 33–48.

Funk, D. C. & James, J. (2001). The psychological continuum model: A conceptual framework for understanding an individual's psychological connection to sport. *Sport Management Review*, **4**(2), 119–150.

Funk, D. C. & James, J. D. (2006). Consumer loyalty: The meaning of attachment in the development of sport team allegiance. *Journal of Sport Management*, **20**(2), 189–217.

Geurin-Eagleman, A. N. & Burch, L. M. (2016). Communicating via photographs: A gendered analysis of Olympic athletes' visual self-presentation on Instagram. *Sport Management Review*, **19**(2), 133–145.

Glass, A. (2016). How espnW harnesses the power and importance of a woman's voice. Retrieved from https://www.forbes.com/sites/alanaglass/2016/10/17/how-espnw-harnesses-the-power-and-importance-of-a-womans-voice/#65d1547756c5.

Hobson, J. (2017). 2017 women's final four thrives in Dallas. Retrieved from https://www.ncaa.com/news/basketball-women/article/2017-04-10/2017-womens-final-four-thrives-dallas.

Jones, J. M. (2015). As industry grows, percentage of US sports fans steady. Gallup. Retrieved from www.Gallup.Com/Poll/183689/Industry-Grows-Percentage-Sports-Fans-Steady.Aspx Google Scholar.

Kane, M. J., LaVoi, N. M., & Fink, J. S. (2013). Exploring elite female athletes' interpretations of sport media images: A window into the construction of social identity and "selling sex" in women's sports. *Communication & Sport*, **1**(3), 269–298.

Labrie, C. (2016). Exxon, Soccer United Marketing and sponsorship of women's sports. Retrieved from www.excellesports.com/news/author/christina-labrie.

Lapchick, R. (2016). Gender report Card: 2016 International Sports Report Card on Women in Leadership Roles. The Institute for Diversity and Ethics in Sport, University of Central Florida, USA. Retrieved from https://www.tidesport.org/racial-gender-report-card.

Lim, C. H., Martin, T. G., & Kwak, D. H. (2010). Examining television consumers of mixed martial arts: The relationship among risk taking, emotion, attitude, and actual sport-media-consumption behavior. *International Journal of Sport Communication*, **3**(1), 49–63.

Lough, N. (2018). The case for boosting WNBA player salaries. Retrieved from https://theconversation.com/the-case-for-boosting-wnba-player-salaries-100805.

Maxwell, H. & Lough, N. (2009). Signage vs. no signage: An analysis of sponsorship recognition in women's college basketball. *Sport Marketing Quarterly*, **18**(4): 188–198.

Messner, M. A., Duncan, M. C., & Wachs, F. L. (1996). The gender of audience building: Televised coverage of women's and men's NCAA basketball. *Sociological Inquiry*, **66**(4), 422–440.

Mumcu, C., Lough, N., & Barnes, J. C. (2016). Examination of women's sports fans' attitudes and consumption intentions. *Journal of Applied Sport Management*, **8**(4), 25–47.

Murrell, A. J. & Dietz, B. (1992). Fan support of sport teams: The effect of a common group identity. *Journal of Sport and Exercise Psychology*, **14**(1), 28–39.

Musto, M., Cooky, C., & Messner, M. A. (2017). "From fizzle to sizzle!" Televised sports news and the production of gender-bland sexism. *Gender & Society*, **31**(5), 573–596.

National Federation of State High School Associations (2016). 2016–17 high school athletics participation survey. Retrieved from https://www.nfhs.org/ParticipationStatistics/PDF/2016-17_Participation_Survey_Results.pdf.

Nielsen Sports Women's Sport Research (2018). Global interest in women's sports is on the rise. Retrieved from https://www.nielsen.com/us/en/insights/news/2018/global-interest-in-womens-sports-is-on-the-rise.html.

Nyatawa, J. (2017). College world series draws millions of viewers, best ratings in years. Retrieved from http://columbusnewsteam.com/regional-news/college-world-series-draws-millions-of-viewers-best-ratings-in-years.

Rubin, L. & Lough, N. (2015). Perspectives of Title IX Pioneers: Equity, equality and need. *Journal of Intercollegiate Sport*, **8**(2), 109–130.

Ryan, T. (2016). The fastest growing athletic brands. Retrieved from https://sgbonline.com/the-fastest-growing-active-brands.

Sandomir, R. (2014). WTA announces media deal worth $525 million. Retrieved from https://www.nytimes.com/2014/12/10/sports/tennis/wta-announces-media-deal-worth-525-million.html.

Spencer Stuart (2017). 2017 SpencerStuart Board Index. Retrieved from https://www.spencerstuart.com/~/media/ssbi2017/ssbi_2017_final.pdf?la=en.

Sport & Fitness Industry Association (2014). U.S. Trends in team sports 2014. Retrieved from https://www.sfia.org/reports/sample.php?id=313.

Tulshyan, R. (2015). Racially diverse companies outperform industry norms by 35%. Retrieved from https://www.forbes.com/sites/ruchikatulshyan/2015/01/30/racially-diverse-companies-outperform-industry-norms-by-30/#29e18bc51132.

Wann, D. L. (2006). Understanding the positive social psychological benefits of sport team identification: The team identification-social psychological health model. *Group Dynamics: Theory, Research, and Practice*, **10**, 272–296.

Women's Media Center (2015). The status of women in the U.S. media. Retrieved from www.womensmediacenter.com/reports/the-status-of-women-in-u.s.-media-2015.

Part I
History and evolution of women's sport business

Part I

1

History and evolution of women's sport

Elizabeth A. Gregg and Elizabeth Taylor

Philosophical foundations of women's sport

Numerous variables shaped the involvement of women in sport historically. Arguably, the most significant were medical myths regarding the limited capacity of women to sustain the demands of intense physical activity (Vertinsky, 1987). Victorian ideals defining gender norms also supported the notion that women should not engage in physical activity. Yet these notions hearkened back as far as Aristotle and other ancient philosophers who first positioned women as the weaker sex due to menstruation (Lawlor & Suzuki, 2000; Vertinsky, 1987). Scientists, physicians, and other theorists believed that the "eternal wound" of menstruation was a form of sickness that impaired women from engaging in a variety of activities considered to be taxing (Gregg & Gregg, 2017; Vertinsky, 1987).

The underlying thought process was predicated on the notion that each person was born with a certain level of "vital force" that drained during one's lifetime. Every vigorous physical or mental activity in which one engaged drained the overall lifetime capacity of the individual. Women were believed to be inherently prone to draining their vital force at a more rapid rate than men because of menstruation and, later in life, childbearing (Gregg & Gregg, 2017; Smith-Rosenberg & Rosenberg, 1973). Vertinsky (1987) stated that because medical beliefs were so pervasive, they had "a strong effect upon the medical professional's attitude and consequently the public's attitude toward female exercise and participation in sport" (p. 7). Women in both the United States of America and Europe were impacted by the vital force doctrine.

Any girl or woman who ignored medical advice and participated in intense physical activity was at risk not only of draining her vital force but was also of a range of undesirable physical outcomes. Often referred to as the "female frailty myth," this belief system taught girls and women that they would become masculine, sterile, and their uterus could fall out if they participated in vigorous activity, including but not limited to sport (McCrone, 2014). Because a wide variety of religious doctrines positioned women in the home, appropriate forms of physical activity were often completed in the process of cleaning the house and other domestic chores (Vertinsky, 1987, 1990). This belief system regarding appropriate types of physical activity shaped both late nineteenth- and twentieth-century thought and has even impacted more modern women's sport.

The twentieth century

The twentieth century brought both progress and setbacks for women's sport. In America, one of the most popular forms of physical activity at the turn of the century was basketball, which proved to be a favorite sport for women. Basketball was invented by James Naismith at Springfield College (SC) during the 1891–1892 academic year. Naismith, then a graduate student, was charged by his professor with creating an indoor game that would be complex, exciting, physically demanding, and devoid of the roughness of sports such as football or soccer. The sport, which was an adaptation of rugby, lacrosse, and other established games, proved to be instantaneously successful nationwide (Grasso, 2010; Hult & Trekell, 2010). The game spread nationally once the men left SC, returned to their hometowns, and shared the rules of the game at their local gyms. The rules of the game of basketball were distributed via postal mail as well, which quickly helped the sport become a nationally adopted form of physical activity for both women and men (Hult & Trekell, 1991; Vertinsky, 1994).

The sport of basketball was one of the few team sports that women could participate in on college campuses during the late nineteenth and early twentieth centuries. One notable pioneer in the adoption of basketball for women was Senda Berenson, who introduced an adapted version of the game of basketball at Smith College. Berenson wisely recognized that the one downfall of the men's version of basketball was that it could get rough at times, so she changed the rules to make the sport fit more in line with appropriate Victorian ideals for women. The adapted version was a great success; the game thrived at many institutions of higher education during the early 1900s (Melnick, 2007).

As women gained access to systems of higher education in the late 1870s, new norms regarding socially acceptable behavior for women emerged within American society (Hult & Trekell, 1991). The movement was driven in part by contemporary magazines such as *Godey's Lady's Book*, which outlined appropriate etiquette for women interested in participating in sport and leisure activities. Women's attire was looser, which allowed for freedom of movement and enhanced performance. Often referred to as "bloomers," the new form of acceptable sporting attire allowed women to enjoy sports such as tennis, croquet, and archery, as well as basketball and bicycling (Hogdon, 1973; Hult, 1989).

As the popularity of women's sport continued to grow during the early years of the twentieth century, female physical educators recognized the need to engage in the governance of women's athletics on high school and college campuses across the country. Women who comprised the majority of physical educators believed that the already highly competitive male model was detrimental to the well-being of women. They instead adopted a recreational model of sport. After enjoying a period of social acceptance and progress, organized athletic programs for women sustained a major impediment when the Women's Division of the National Amateur Athletic Federation (NAAF) published the first version of rules for women's sport (Hogdon, 1973). Based largely on aforementioned medical myths that competitive athletics were detrimental to women's health, the official handbook curtailed the growth of intercollegiate athletics for decades (Gregg & Fielding, 2016; Gregg & Gregg, 2017; Hogdon, 1973; Hult, 1989). Non-competitive "play days" replaced competitive sport for women on college campuses across the country.

After the NAAF adopted a highly conservative position on the governance of women's athletics, participation opportunities for women in college were limited to intramurals and non-school activities in the US. The governance structure for women's athletics evolved gradually over the course of several decades. According to Hult (1999), the National Association for Girls and Women in Sport (NAGWS) played a significant role in shaping women's sport during the 1930s and 1940s. Another significant governing body that emerged from the NAAF was the Division for Girls and Women's Sports (DGWS) during the same era. As much of their leadership believed in the medical myths pervasive during the late nineteenth century, competitive women's sport at the amateur and professional levels were limited during this time (Gregg & Fielding, 2016; Gregg & Gregg, 2017).

Women's sport and the law

The need to amend federal laws that restricted women's rights in the United States became apparent as society evolved in the mid-twentieth century. There were several laws passed throughout the 1960s, 1970s, and 1980s that improved the lives of women in society in general, including within the athletic realm. For example, the Civil Rights Act of 1964, which banned discrimination based on national origin, color, race, religion, or gender, enhanced women's opportunities to participate in athletic opportunities. The law also reinforced constitutional voting rights and established the Commission on Equal Employment Opportunity (Hult, 1989). The Civil Rights Act helped women gain access to a wide range of opportunities in both the private and the public sectors. It enhanced the ability of athletic women to participate in competitive sport activities.

The next piece of legislation, and the most significant regarding access to athletic opportunities for women, was Title IX of the Educational Amendments Act of 1972 (Acosta & Carpenter, 2014; Bower & Hums, 2013). Acosta and Carpenter (2014) stated, "Title IX is federal legislation that prohibits discrimination based on sex in educational programs that receive federal money" (p. iii). Title IX applies to programs such as career education, employment, sexual harassment, education of pregnant or parenting students, and athletics (McDowell & Hoffman, 2014). Although Title IX is most frequently associated with sports participation, its original intent was to improve access to and equality of educational opportunities for women. After Title IX was passed, the NCAA and its allies made several attempts to limit the scope of the law, fearing it would compromise college football. In 1974 Senator John Tower from Texas created legislation designed to limit the scope of Title IX to non-revenue sports. The major problem with the Tower Amendment was that any sport could be deemed revenue producing by a given institution. The courts ruled against adopting the Tower Amendment (Carpenter & Acosta, 2005).

About a decade later, another effort was made to limit the scope of Title IX. In the 1984 *Grove City College v Bell* case, two questions were addressed. According to Carpenter and Acosta (2005), the first question asked if "the word 'program' which is found in the one-sentence law called Title IX, refers to the entire institution or only the subunits that receive federal financial assistance?" (p. 119). The second question addressed whether an institution had to receive federal financial assistance from the federal government to adhere to Title IX. The courts determined that only the specific program or unit receiving federal funds had to comply with Title IX. As many athletic departments did not receive direct federal financial assistance, they no longer had to comply with Title IX. The *Grove City* decision crippled the growth of intercollegiate athletics for women. After a decade of adding sports and scholarships, many were almost immediately eliminated (Carpenter & Acosta, 2005; Henderson, 1995). Advocates of women's sport did not have to wait long, however, for progress to be made under Title IX. The Civil Rights Restoration Act of 1987, which was passed over presidential veto in 1988, reversed the *Grove City* decision. The Civil Rights Restoration Act required that any institution that received any federal funds had to comply with Title IX, not just the program or unit receiving monies (Carpenter & Acosta, 2005). After this landmark case, growth of women's college sport resumed.

Within intercollegiate athletic departments, there are three main Title IX categories that departments must comply with: accommodation of interests and abilities (e.g., sport offerings), athletic financial assistance (i.e., athletic-based scholarships), and other program areas (McDowell & Hoffman, 2014). The accommodation of interests and abilities pillar requires that female students be provided with equitable opportunities for participation. Title IX does not require identical offerings (e.g., baseball and softball, men's and women's soccer) but rather an equal opportunity to play. One way in which athletic departments can comply with this category is by sponsoring NCAA-designated emerging sports for women (e.g., triathlon). The athletic financial assistance pillar requires athletic departments to offer athletics scholarship dollars to male and female student athletes proportional to gender enrollment at their institution. Although the number of scholarships provided does not have to be equal by gender, a 50% scholarship given to a female student athlete must equal the amount of a 50% scholarship given to a male student athlete. Finally, the "other program areas" category requires equal treatment of male and female student athletes in the provisions of scheduling of games and practices, travel, and daily, per diem, equipment and supplies, coaching, access to tutoring, publicity and promotions, locker rooms, practice, and competitive facilities, medical and training facilities/services, recruitment of student athletes, housing and dining facilities, and support services.

As women's intercollegiate athletics began to mature, the need to develop a governing body capable of overseeing women's sport became apparent to leaders within the women's athletic governance, primarily the Division for Girls and Women in Sport. The Commission on Intercollegiate Athletics for Women (CIAW), a group appointed by the DGWS, was established in 1966 to fill the void in governance of women's intercollegiate sport. The purpose of the CIAW was to provide an appropriate organizational structure to fit the needs of college women athletes, to develop and publish rules and standards of play, to encourage participation in competitive intercollegiate athletics events, and to sponsor DGWS national championships. Led by intercollegiate athletic pioneers, including Marie Sexton, Lou Magnusson, June McCain, Frances McGill, Frances Schaafsma, Betty McCue, Carol Gordon, Doris Soliday, Lou Jean Moeyer, and Sara Staff Jernigan, the women did their best to provide rules and regulations for a rapidly changing environment. The rules developed by the CIAW shaped the next generation of women's intercollegiate athletic governance (Hult, 1999).

According to Hult (1999), the mission of the CIAW was to develop programs that were consistent with educational goals and objectives of the organization, help with educational enrichment endeavors, develop quality leaders, and encourage outstanding performance among organizational members. By 1967, it became apparent that NCAA President Walter Byers was investigating the feasibility of assuming control of women's intercollegiate athletics – a direct threat to the CIAW. By 1971, it became apparent that the CIAW lacked the organizational framework to successfully govern women's college sport. Accordingly, the Association for Intercollegiate Athletics for Women (AIAW) formed during the 1971–72 academic year. Fran Koeing, Carole Oglesby, Jo Thorpe, Sara Jernigan, and Mary Pavlich Roby were all instrumental leaders in the transition from the CIAW to the AIAW.

The AIAW was founded on the philosophical belief system that women's intercollegiate athletics should be a student-centered educational model. The AIAW sought to avoid the commercial aspects already evident in men's intercollegiate athletics, which they viewed as detrimental to the well-being of the student athlete (Sack & Staurowsky, 1998; Wushanley, 2004). The AIAW model contained significant differences from the model for men's athletics, foremost of which was that the organization did not initially allow women to receive athletic scholarships (Wushanley, 2004). The organization also required women to earn higher grade point averages than men for eligibility, had easier transfer policies, and allowed member organizations to self-police rule violations.

After their attempts to limit the scope of Title IX failed throughout the 1970s, the NCAA began to seriously investigate the feasibility of assuming control of women's intercollegiate athletics, much to the dismay of AIAW leadership. The NCAA was motivated by a range of factors to add women's athletics to their governance structure. One of the most significant variables was the ability to have financial control of women's college sport (Gregg, 2007; Willey, 1996). The NCAA established a variety of incentives to entice AIAW member institutions to join. First, the NCAA offered to reimburse schools that sent women to participate in their championship events – a perk the AIAW could not offer. The NCAA did not require schools to pay an additional membership fee if the university already had an affiliated men's program. Finally, there was a desire among intercollegiate athletic programs collectively to have the same rules (Willey, 1996; Wushanley, 2004). The AIAW filed an anti-trust lawsuit against the NCAA, in the fall of 1981, attempting to block the NCAA from sponsoring national championships for women, but they were unsuccessful. After the NCAA began offering championships for women, AIAW membership declined from 961 schools in the 1980–81 academic year to 730 the following year. As the AIAW relied on membership dues for their operations, this crippled the organization financially. As a result, the AIAW disbanded in 1983 (Willey, 1996).

The demise of the AIAW had a dramatic impact on women serving as coaches or administrators of women's intercollegiate athletics at the time. Under AIAW direction, 90% of women's teams were coached by women. Similarly, 90% of women's teams were administered by women. After the NCAA assumed control of women's intercollegiate athletic governance, percentages of women in both coaching and administrative roles plummeted. In 2017, 39.8% of Division I women's teams were coached by women. Among NCAA Division I schools only 12.9% have a female athletic director (Wushanley, 2004; Lapchick et al., 2018).

Evolution of women's professional sport

Throughout the course of sport history, there have been examples of trailblazers and phenomenal athletes. Babe Didrickson Zaharias is perhaps the best example of an athlete who helped shed light on the physical abilities of women, and open doors for her peers. Born in 1911 in Beaumont, Texas, sport historians credit Zaharias with being the best athlete of the twentieth century, either male or female (Cayleff, 1992). Didrickson Zaharias won two gold medals and one silver medal in the 1932 Olympic Games, which allowed her to gain national prominence. According to Cayleff (1992), "she played semi-professional basketball, softball, enjoyed a short stint as a successful harmonica-playing stage entertainer, and when she turned her will and talent to golf in the thirties, forties, and fifties, she won an unprecedented thirteen consecutive tournaments" (p. 28). Babe recognized the power of promotion, and frequently altered facts such as her age, height, and weight, to enhance the perception of her physical feats. These tactics were not popular with her competitors, who she frequently teased and, in turn, intimidated (Cayleff, 1992, 1996).

Zaharias wore her hair short and dressed in athletic clothing when she was young, which did not win approval with the press. As she aged, she allowed her hair to grow, learned how to wear makeup, and made other attempts at looking more feminine. These efforts, which took place after she got involved with the game of golf, helped Babe to gain favor with the media. In 1934, she became the first woman to compete in a PGA tour event. In 1938, she met her future husband, George Zaharias, who worked as a professional wrestler and later as her promoter. Marriage was the final piece of the personal rebranding campaign that Babe had embarked on.

Although many reports indicate their marriage was primarily one of convenience, Babe kept the details of their relationship private. A founding member of the Ladies Professional Golf Association (LPGA), Zaharias was struck with terminal colon cancer at the pinnacle of her golf career. Although the doctors did not expect she would ever play again, Zaharias returned to tournament play less than a year later to compete in the US Women's Open. She won the event by 12 strokes, which was a record. Babe Didrickson Zaharias died 2 years later at the age of 45.

Although there is evidence that women played professional sport in the late 1800s, the first significant professional sport league for women in America was the All-American Girls Professional Baseball League (AAGPBL), established in 1943. During World War II, minor league teams were forced to disband when men joined the armed services (Fidler, 2006). There was concern that Major League Baseball parks would close, which prompted Philip K. Wrigley to establish the league. Wrigley, who also owned the Chicago Cubs and Wrigley Chewing Gum, sought to provide entertainment for the masses. Originally established as a non-profit organization, the league began with four teams clustered in the Midwest.

Wrigley placed a great deal of emphasis on ensuring that players exuded a feminine image. He contracted with Helena Rubenstein's Beauty Salon to ensure all league players received etiquette training. Women were required to adhere to a league dress code, wear makeup, and appear as attractive as possible (Fidler, 2006). League players also competed in woefully inadequate short skirts. Wrigley quickly lost interest in the league; he sold it to Arthur Meyerhoff in 1944. Meyerhoff focused heavily on advertising and league expansion. He also disbanded the mandatory etiquette training and associated charm school. At its peak, the AAGPBL drew large crowds. On July 4 in 1946, about 10,000 tickets were sold for a game in South Bend, IN. Collectively, the 10-team league sold 910,000 tickets in 1946. After the league decentralized its operations under the leadership of Meyerhoff, revenues declined and teams disbanded. The AAGPBL ceased operation in 1954 (Francis, n.d.). The AAGPBL gained additional notoriety when a film was made about it in 1992, titled "A League of Their Own".

When women began to push back on societal norms that limited their rights in the 1960s, opportunities for women in sport increased (Gregg & Fielding, 2016; Hult, 1989). Leaders in the feminist movement recognized that the high-profile nature of sport would enhance the potential success and notoriety of the women's liberation movement. One notable sporting event that helped improve opportunities for girls and women in sport was the "Battle of the Sexes," a tennis match between the 29-year-old women's professional tennis player, Billie Jean King, and Bobby Riggs, a 55-year-old former professional on the men's tour. Viewed by approximately 48 million people worldwide, the event proved to be a watershed moment in the history of women in sport. As King was victorious, the match not only demonstrated that women were capable of competing with men, but also validated the commercial viability of sport as an entertainment product (Spencer, 2000). The match, which was made into a popular film in 2017, is but one example of how sport became a vehicle through which women were able to advocate for additional societal rights (Brennan, 2017; Hargreaves, 2002).

Billie Jean King is not only a notable figure in professional sport because of her win in the "Battle of the Sexes" match, but also because of her advocacy for women's rights and equal pay. In the years leading up to the iconic competition, King competed on the US Lawn Tennis Association Tour (USLTA). In 1970, King won the women's singles championship in the first Open Era Wimbledon Championship and earned about US$600 in prize money. The men's champion that year was paid US$3,500 for his victory, nearly six times what King earned. In addition to smaller purses, the USLTA also sponsored fewer events for women, making it harder for women to earn a living through their sport participation. Recognizing that the gross inequity was no longer tolerable, a group of nine women, including Billie Jean King, Nancy Richey,

Rosemary Casals, Peaches Bartkowicz, Valerie Ziegenfuss, Kristy Pigeon, Julie Heldman, Kerry Melville Reid, and Judy Tegart Dalton, became known as the "Original Nine" and fought back against the lack of pay equity by forming their own women's tour (Bernstein, 2012; Chan, 2012).

Led by King, the group found a sponsor in cigarette manufacturer Virginia Slims. The tobacco company was but one that capitalized on "feminism in commodity form" (Spencer, 2000, p. 397). Clad in traditionally feminine clothing, the athletic women of the Virginia Slims Tour quickly caught the eye of a wide array of sponsors. In just one year nearly 40 players had registered for the Virginia Slims Circuit, which boasted tournament purses totaling nearly US$310,000 (Chan, 2012). As a result of the success of the tour, King was able to negotiate with the US Tennis Association (USTA; formerly the USLTA) to create a women's division in 1973, which is now known as the Women's Tennis Association (WTA). Today, the WTA is the most profitable professional sport event for women in America. In 2017, 8 of the top 10 highest earning female professional athletes played in the WTA (Badenhausen, 2017).

The year 1973 also marked the first of 80 matches in which American tennis star Chris Evert faced off against Czechoslovakian native Martina Navratilova – a rivalry that helped popularize women's tennis globally (Spencer, 2003). The significance of the rivalry between the two women was fueled not only by the competitive nature of play between Evert and Navratilova, but also by differences in nationality, sexuality, and the ideal feminine physique of the era, which all contributed to the significance of the rivalry. Although Navratilova had a more successful career overall regarding wins, Evert earned more favor from tennis fans and sponsorship dollars than her rival. According to Spencer (2003) "Evert's legacy ultimately resulted from a carefully nurtured image that relied upon displays of traditional femininity" (p. 20). After Navratilova was forced to acknowledge her sexual orientation as lesbian, her image suffered and she lost millions of dollars in endorsements as a result. ESPN created a documentary titled "Unmatched," which highlights Evert and Navratilova's relationship in an ESPN 30 for 30 episodes in 2010. The documentary emphasized the friendship between the two champions years after their rivalry ended (Vecsey, 2010).

Women's tennis continues to be one of the most profitable sports globally. Rivalries and star power have been significant factors in the success of women's tennis. Although a significant pay gap still exists in professional tennis, the range is similar to what is evident for American women in the workforce on average. In 2016, women in professional tennis earned around 63 cents on the dollar compared with their male counterparts. In the American workforce overall, women earn approximately 80 cents on the dollar compared with men in like occupations (Rothenberg, 2016). However, when women's tennis tournaments are held in conjunction with men's, the pay disparity decreases.

The examples above are intended to shed light on the challenges and successes experienced by athletic women throughout the course of modern history. The full scope of the history of women in sport was beyond the scope of this chapter. Although the list is not exhaustive in nature, we carefully selected examples that are not only historically relevant, but also contain issues that are still prevalent today. Each of the aforementioned examples demonstrates that societal gender norms that dictated acceptable behavior for women in the late 1800s and early 1900s still permeate women's sport today.

Future challenges and opportunities

Although the passage of Title IX brought dramatic increases in the number of female athletes, it has had adverse effects on the percentage of women in coaching and administration positions. Pre-Title IX more than 90% of women's teams were coached by women; today however, less than 50% of women's teams are coached by women (Acosta & Carpenter, 2014). Recent years have seen a stagnation in the percentage of women coaching women's teams, and the percentage has not been higher than 50% since 1986. A similar situation presents itself when examining the presence of female athletic directors. Before Title IX, more than 90% of (women's) college athletic departments were led by female athletic directors. Many men's and women's athletic departments combined after the passage of Title IX, presumably to become more economically efficient. As a result, many women lost their leadership positions or were demoted to serve as Senior Women Administrators reporting to their male counterparts. Today 22.3% of athletic departments are run by women across NCAA Divisions I, II, and III (Acosta & Carpenter, 2014). When examining the most prestigious level (Division I), only 12.9% of departments have a female athletic director. Despite efforts from the NCAA to increase representation of women within leadership positions, there are still 11.3% of athletic departments without a single woman in their administrative structure (Acosta & Carpenter, 2014).

This drastic decline, and subsequent leveling off, of coaches and athletic administrators, paired with increases in participation, brings up an interesting question. Are female athletes not interested in pursuing careers in coaching and athletic administration? It is speculated that female college athletes are discouraged by the gendered nature of coaching and athletic administration, or they see the time commitment required for success and subsequent lack of work–life balance as unappealing. Research suggests that women struggle to advance to leadership positions because of limited access to women mentors, gender normalcy (male-centric domain), cultural norms, and homologous reproduction (Kamphoff, 2010; Taylor & Hardin, 2016). In addition, masculine traits have been found to align more with head coaching positions as opposed to assistant coaching roles, suggesting men fit the norm for leadership roles in sport (Burton, Barr, Fink, & Bruening, 2009; Kamphoff, 2010; Madsen, Burton, & Clark, 2017). One study found female assistant coaches had less head coaching self-efficacy and less interest in becoming a head coach, and anticipated fewer positive outcomes associated with being a head coach than their male counterparts (Cunningham, Doherty, & Gregg, 2007).

Several academic outlets have created advocacy campaigns to help spread awareness about the underrepresentation of women in coaching and athletic administration positions. The Tucker Center for Research on Girls and Women in Sport at the University of Minnesota provides an abundance of educational material in the form of infographics, research, and affiliated press releases on the dwindling number of women coaches within the NCAA (e.g., LaVoi, 2017). The Institute for Diversity and Ethics in Sport at the University of Central Florida produces similar work through their Race and Gender Report Cards, which are created for all the major US national sports leagues, including but not limited to Major League Baseball, the National Basketball Association, the National Football League, and the National Collegiate Athletic Association governing college sport. These report cards track changes within the racial and gender composition of employees at all levels within these organizations. Grades are given to organizations based on increases or decreases in racial and gender diversity within positions. The latest grades issued rated the NBA with an overall grade of A− (Lapchick & Balasundaram, 2017), the NFL a B (Lapchick & Marfatia, 2017), the NCAA a C+ (Lapchick et al., 2018), whereas the WNBA earned an overall grade of A. Although these statistics provide historical snapshots of where sport leagues rate in terms of equality, they have done little to enhance the overall level of diversity in male-dominated organizations.

Conclusion

This chapter has outlined some of the significant events, women, belief systems, and laws that have helped shape the history of women's sport. Gender norms, medical myths, and other belief systems helped to prevent women from fully enjoying competitive sport until the twentieth century, long after their male peers. Trailblazing athletes such as Babe Didrickson Zaharias, Billie Jean King, and others helped to prove women were capable of sustaining vigorous competitive activity and helped pave the way for additional participation opportunities and greater wages. Laws such as Title IX and the Civil Rights Restoration Act helped force the hand of reluctant organizations to provide opportunities for women to compete in school-based sport. Although Title IX produced tremendous growth in the area of participation opportunities, it also had unintended consequences. Primarily, it led to the demise of the AIAW, and caused many women employed as either coaches or athletic administrators to lose their position.

Although many gains have been made, there is a long road ahead to realize true equality. Societal norms still influence acceptable forms of physical activity and appearance for women. Hiring practices that favor white males are still prevalent. The glass ceiling still exists in many professional and amateur sport organizations. However, there are certainly signs of hope for equality. The work of the Tucker Center, the Institute for Diversity and Ethics in Sport, and others are steadfast in their mission to enhance the level of diversity in sport. Although their efforts have yet to significantly move the statistical needle in terms of increasing diversity, there are signs that progress is being made. For example, in 2017, the University of Virginia hired the first African–American woman Athletic Director in a Power Five conference (Wang, 2017). Small victories such as this provide hope that additional progress is possible.

Leader profiles

Joan Cronan and Pat Summitt

The University of Tennessee (UT) has been home to several notable leaders in women's intercollegiate athletics. Joan Cronan, the Women's Athletic Director at UT, was integral in building the women's athletic program beginning in the 1970s. Cronan began her career at the College of Charleston where she spent 10 years from 1973 to 1983. She later spent more than two decades at UT, 1983–2012. She is currently a member of the Hall of Fame at both the College of Charleston and UT. Cronan valued relationship building and maintenance as part of her leadership style. The University of Tennessee has a rich history of women's athletics, dating back to 1901 when the athletic department sponsored its first women's varsity sport: basketball (Kloiber, 1994). Department administrators hired Pat Head (later Summitt) in 1974, sparking the beginning of an era for the Volettes as they were then nicknamed. By 1976, UT established a women's athletic department, which operated independently of the men's, was offering athletic scholarships to female student athletes, and had a budget of US$20,000 for seven women's sports. During her early years at UT, Coach Summitt decided the women's athletic department needed its own identity. To Summitt, the Volettes was just a feminized term for Volunteers, the men's athletic department mascot, and sounded like a "chorus of dancing girls." Summitt suggested the Lady Volunteers, and the nickname was quickly adopted by the entire women's athletic department. Cronan's strong work ethic and understanding of the importance of communication allowed her to build a substantial financial base for the Lady Vols. While Cronan oversaw a range of successful coaches and teams, Pat Summitt was the most notable of the coaches.

Summitt attended college at the University of Tennessee-Martin, where she played basketball (Brady, 2016). Summitt completed a Bachelor's degree in 1974, and a Master's degree in 1975, both in physical education. Shortly after completing her first degree, Summitt was named head coach of the University of Tennessee-Knoxville's Women's Basketball team in 1974. Summitt had planned to attend UT as a Master's student, and had secured a graduate assistant position within the School of Health, Physical Education, and Recreation teaching physical activity courses. In addition to her graduate assistant positions she planned to work with the women's basketball team. However, shortly before the school year started the then head coach quit and the assistant coach did not want the position. The athletic director reached out to Pat asking if she would be willing to take the job. With hesitation Summitt accepted the position and started her career as one of the coaches with the most wins in women's intercollegiate basketball history. While coaching, Summitt also earned a spot on the US Olympic Women's Basketball team that won a silver medal at the Summer Olympic Games in 1976. During Summitt's 38 years as the head women's basketball coach at UT, she won 8 national titles, appeared in 18 Final Four's, and captured 16 SEC titles. Summitt's life was cut tragically short in 2016 due to early onset Alzheimer's disease (Brady, 2016).

In late 2014 the University of Tennessee announced they would begin a new branding campaign that included the removal of the Lady Volunteer nickname and logo from all women's teams, except women's basketball. In its place, all UT athletics teams, except women's basketball, would use the *Power T* logo, which had previously symbolized the men's athletic department. This change came shortly after the retirement of both Cronan and Summitt, two of the largest advocates for women's athletics and female student athletes within the department (University of Tennessee Athletics, 2014).

Over the course of their careers, Cronan challenged Summitt to strive to become more successful and, in turn, Summitt helped Cronan to push boundaries in women's intercollegiate athletic administration. Summitt believed that Joan's contributions were integral to the development of the Vols brand. Together, Summitt and Cronan created one of the most successful women's athletic programs in history (Cronan, 2015). In honor of Cronan's significant impact on UT, the university established the Joan Cronan Lady Vol Graduate Fellowship in 2014.

References

Acosta, R. V. & Carpenter, L. J. (2014). Woman in intercollegiate sport: A longitudinal, national study. Thirty-seven-year update, 1977–2014. Retrieved from https://eric.ed.gov/?id=ED570882.

Badenhausen, K. (2017). Serena Williams heads the highest-paid female athletes of 2017. *Forbes*, August 14. Retrieved from https://www.forbes.com/sites/kurtbadenhausen/2017/08/14/the-highest-paid-female-athletes-2017/#138c0e93d0bf.

Bernstein, V. (2012). Rebels who changed a sport reunite. *The New York Times*, April 7. Retrieved from www.nytimes.com/2012/04/08/sports/tennis/rebels-who-changed-womens-tennis-reunite.html.

Bower, G. G. & Hums, M. A. (2013). The impact of Title IX on career opportunities in intercollegiate athletic administration. *Journal of Intercollegiate Sport*, **6**(2), 213–230.

Brady, E. (2016). Legendary Tennessee coach Pat Summitt dies at 64. *USA Today*, June 28. Retrieved from https://www.usatoday.com/story/sports/ncaaw/2016/06/28/pat-summitt-dies-age-64-tennessee-coach-obit-alzheimers/86406296.

Brennan, C. (2017). Billie Jean King, Emma Stone relive history of "Battle of the Sexes." *USA Today*, September 11. Retrieved from https://www.usatoday.com/story/sports/columnist/brennan/2017/09/11/billie-jean-king-emma-stone-battle-sexes/652732001.

Burton, L., Barr, C. A., Fink, J. S., & Bruening, J .E. (2009). "Think athletic director, think masculine?": Examination of the gender typing of managerial roles within athletic administration positions. *Sex Roles*, **61**, 416–426.

Carpenter, L. J. & Acosta, R. V. (2005). *Title IX*. Champaign, IL: Human Kinetics.

Cayleff, S. E. (1992). The "Texas tomboy" the life and legend of Babe Didrikson Zaharias. *OAH Magazine of History*, **7**(1), 28–33.

Cayleff, S. E. (1996). *Babe: The Life and Legend of Babe Didrikson Zaharias*, Vol. 117. Champaign, IL: University of Illinois Press.

Chan, K. (2012). The Original 9. *Women's Sports Foundation*, June 19. Retrieved from https://www.womenssportsfoundation.org/education/the-original-9.

Cronan, J. (2015). *Sport is Life with the Volume Turned up*. Knoxville, TN: The University of Tennessee Press.

Cunningham, G. B., Doherty, A. J., & Gregg, M. J. (2007). Using social cognitive career theory to understand head coaching intentions among assistant women's tennis coaches. *Sex Roles*, **56**, 365–372.

Fidler, M. (2006). *The Origins and History of the All-American Girls Professional Baseball League*. Jefferson, NC: McFarland & Co

Francis, B. (n.d.). League of women ballplayers. Retrieved from https://baseballhall.org/discover/league-of-women-ballplayers.

Grasso, J. (2010). *Historical Dictionary of Basketball*. Lanham, MD: Scarecrow Press.

Hult, J. S. & Trekell, M. (1991). *A Century of Women's Basketball: From frailty to Final Four*. Reston, VA: National Association for Girls and Women in Sport.

Gregg, E. A. (2007). A history of women's intercollegiate athletics at Indiana University-Bloomington: 1965–2001. A historical case study. Doctoral dissertation, Indiana University.

Gregg, E. A. & Fielding, L. W. (2016). The implementation of Title IX at Indiana University: a historical case study. *Journal of Contemporary Athletics*, **10**(4), 241–255.

Gregg, E. A. & Gregg, V. H. (2017). Women in sport: Historical perspectives. *Clinics in Sports Medicine*, **36**(4), 603–610.

Hargreaves, J. (2002). *Sporting Females: Critical issues in the history and sociology of women's sport*. New York: Routledge.

Henderson, J. L. (1995). Gender equity in intercollegiate athletics: A commitment to fairness. *Seton Hall Journal of Sport Law*, **5**, 133.

Hogdon, P. D. (1973). An investigation of the development of interscholastic and intercollegiate athletics for girls and women from 1917 to 1970. Unpublished doctoral dissertation, Springfield College.

Hult, J. S. (1989). Women's struggle for governance in US amateur athletics. *International Review for the Sociology of Sport*, **24**(3), 249–263.

Hult, J. S. (1999). NAGWS and AIAW: The strange and wondrous journey to the athletic summit, 1950–1990. *Journal of Physical Education, Recreation & Dance*, **70**(4), 24–31.

Hult, J. S. & Trekell, M. (1991). *A Century of Women's Basketball. From Frailty to Final Four*. Reston, VA: AAHPERD Publications Sales.

Kamphoff, C. (2010). Bargaining with patriarchy: Former women coaches' experiences and their decision to leave collegiate coaching. *Research Quarterly for Exercise and Sport*, **81**, 367–379.

Kloiber, E. J. (1994). True volunteers: Women's intercollegiate athletics at the University of Tennessee, 1903–1976. Master's thesis, University of Tennessee. Retrieved from http://trace.tennessee.edu/utk_gradthes/2677.

Lapchick, R. & Balasundaram, B. (2017). The 2017 racial and gender report card: the NBA. Retrieved from http://nebula.wsimg.com/74491b38503915f2f148062ff076e698?AccessKeyId=DAC3A56D8FB782449D2A&disposition=0&alloworigin=1.

Lapchick, R. & Marfatia, S. (2017). The 2017 racial and gender report card: NFL. Retrieved from http://nebula.wsimg.com/1a7f83c14af6a516176740244d8afc46?AccessKeyId=DAC3A56D8FB782449D2A&disposition=0&alloworigin=1

Lapchick, R., Feller, A., Boyd, A., Estrella, B., Lee, C., & Bredikhina, N. (2018). The 2017 racial and gender report card: College sport. Retrieved from http://nebula.wsimg.com/5665825afd75728dc0c45b52ae6c412d?AccessKeyId=DAC3A56D8FB782449D2A&disposition=0&alloworigin=1.

LaVoi, N. M. (2017). *Head Coaches of Women's Collegiate Teams: A report on select NCAA Division-I institutions, 2016–17*, February. Minneapolis, MN: The Tucker Center for Research on Girls & Women in Sport.

Lawlor, C. & Suzuki, A. (2000). The disease of the Self: Representing consumption, 1700–1830. *Bulletin of the History of Medicine*, **74**(3), 458–494.

Madsen, R. M., Burton, L. J., & Clark, B. S. (2017). Gender role expectations and the prevalence of women as assistant coaches. *Journal of the Study of Sports and Athletes in Education*, **11**(2), 125–142.

McCrone, K. (2014). *Sport and the Physical Emancipation of English Women (RLE Sports Studies): 1870–1914*. New York: Routledge.

McDowell, J. & Hoffman, J. (2014). Gender issues and controversies in intercollegiate athletics. In G. Sailes (ed.), *Sports in Higher Education: Issues and controversies* (pp. 139–170). San Diego, CA: Cognella, Inc.

Melnick, R. (2007). *Senda Berenson: The unlikely founder of women's basketball*. Amherst, MA: University of Massachusetts Press.

Musto, M., Cooky, C., & Messner, M. (2017). "From fizzle to sizzle!": Televised sports news and the production of gender bland sexism. *Gender & Society*, **31**(5), 573–596.

Rothenberg, B. (2016). Roger Federer, $731,000; Serena Williams, $495,000: The pay gap in tennis. *The New York Times*, April 12. Retrieved from https://www.nytimes.com/2016/04/13/sports/tennis/equal-pay-gender-gap-grand-slam-majors-wta-atp.html.

Sack, A. L. & Staurowsky, E. J. (1998). *College Athletes for Hire: The evolution and legacy of the NCAA's amateur myth*. New York City, NY: Columbia University Press.

Smith-Rosenberg, C. & Rosenberg, C. (1973). The female animal: Medical and biological views of woman and her role in nineteenth-century America. *The Journal of American History*, **60**(2), 332–356.

Spencer, N. E. (2000). Reading between the lines: A discursive analysis of the Billie Jean King vs. Bobby Riggs "Battle of the Sexes." *Sociology of Sport Journal*, **17**(4), 386–402.

Spencer, N. E. (2003). "America's Sweetheart" and "Czech-Mate" A discursive analysis of the Evert–Navratilova rivalry. *Journal of Sport and Social Issues*, **27**(1), 18–37.

Taylor, E. A. & Hardin, R. (2016). Female NCAA Division I athletic directors: Experiences and challenges. *Women in Sport and Physical Activity Journal*, **24**, 14–25.

University of Tennessee Athletics (2014). One Tennessee: Branding restructure, 10 November. Retrieved from www.utsports.com/genrel/111014aab.html.

Vertinsky, P. A. (1987). Exercise, physical capability, and the eternally wounded woman in late nineteenth century North America. *Journal of Sport History*, **14**(1), 7–27.

Vertinsky, P. A. (1990). *The Eternally Wounded Woman: Women, doctors, and exercise in the late nineteenth century*. Manchester: Manchester University Press.

Vertinsky, P. A. (1994). Gender relations, women's history and sport history: A decade of changing enquiry, 1983–1993. *Journal of Sport History*, **21**(1), 1–24.

Vecsey, G. (2010). The best of rivals and best of friends, then and always. *The New York Times*, August 29. Retrieved from www.nytimes.com/2010/08/30/sports/tennis/30vecsey.html.

Wang, G. (2017). 'I'm anxious to get started': Carla Williams introduced as new Virginia athletic director. *The Washington Post*, October 23. Retrieved from https://www.washingtonpost.com/news/sports/wp/2017/10/23/im-anxious-to-get-started-carla-williams-introduced-as-new-virginia-athletic-director/?noredirect=on&utm_term=.1995805337d9.

Willey, S. C. (1996). The governance of women's intercollegiate athletics: Association for Intercollegiate Athletics for Women (AIAW) 1976–1982. Doctoral dissertation, Indiana University.

Wushanley, Y. (2004). *Playing Nice and Losing: The struggle for control of women's intercollegiate athletics, 1960–2000*. Syracuse, NY: Syracuse University Press.

2

The impact of Title IX and other equity laws on the business of women's sport

Ellen J. Staurowsky

The history of the relationship between women and the business of sport is often framed as one that has kept women at the margins. Structurally barred from power hierarchies dominated by men and constrained by limiting societal expectations about women, femininity and athleticism have often been viewed as oppositional rather than complementary, preventing women from full enfranchisement as participants and leaders (Staurowsky, 2016). Given the cultural and financial investment in men's sport and the hold men have had, and continue to have, on the interlocking political, media, financial, and governance organizations and entities that run the sport industry in the United States and internationally, such frameworks can hardly be denied (LaVoi, 2017; Staurowsky, 2016; Wilson, 2017).

That said, the business of sport has always been women's business. Sometimes the involvement of women in the business of sport has required the employment of subversive tactics. At other times, the interests of women have been best served by acts of outright revolution or, the opposite, a studied and quiet dismissal of naysayers. Women have pursued roles as administrators, athletes, coaches, fans, journalists, and executives within different sporting spaces. They have found ways over the centuries to own their sport experiences and to make their presence known regardless of prevailing societal views grounded in "scientific proof" of women as the "weaker sex," who jeopardized their roles as wives and mothers by participating too seriously or zealously in sport (Staurowsky, 2016).

In this chapter, the early roots of women's sport business, as they unfolded in the first half of the twentieth century, will be examined through the case example of Constance Applebee's entrepreneurial influence on the sports of women's field hockey and lacrosse in the US. Attention is then turned to the impact that Title IX and other gender equity laws have had in envisioning expanded opportunities for women in the sport industry.

The early experimentations in sport entrepreneurship of women like Applebee and others in the early twentieth century fostered a sensibility of the possible, and a healthy disregard for messages that discouraged female involvement in sport. If not for their work, Title IX's catalytic effect on the area of athletics, starting in the 1970s, might never have gained traction and/or had the kind of traction that it eventually did. This chapter concludes with thoughts for Title IX's future impact and work that remains for achieving full equality for women in the sport industry.

Constance Applebee's entrepreneurial influence

Within the female sporting space of women's field hockey and lacrosse in the US, entrepreneurialism was the order of the day from the 1900s through the decade of the 1970s when Title IX was passed. An 1899 graduate of the British College of Physical Education, Constance Applebee arrived in the US in 1901 to attend a course at Harvard College. Unimpressed with a curriculum that presented activities such as musical chairs and drop the handkerchief as suitable athletic activities for women, Applebee noted, "We play those games at parties. For exercise we play hockey" (Pendergass, 2016, para. 3). With that, she persuaded her hosts to allow her to give a lecture on the game.

From there, she toured northeastern colleges, fueling enthusiasm for field hockey everywhere she went. By 1904, she was hired as the Director of Physical Education at Bryn Mawr, where she justified sport for women to President M. Carey Thomas, a prominent leader in the suffragist movement seeking to obtain the vote for women, by arguing, "You want all these students to go out and do something in the world, to get the vote. What's the good of their having the vote if they're too ill to use it?" (Pendergass, 2016, para. 10).

Armed with charisma and conviction, "The Apple", as she came to be known, brought considerable community organizing skills to bear in the creation of a movement designed to empower women leaders through sport and to expand the footprint of women's field hockey and lacrosse. She co-founded the American Field Hockey Association (what would become the US Field Hockey Association) in 1901 for the purpose of establishing rules and promoting the sport, effectively serving as the principle architect for the United States to sponsor women's field hockey touring teams abroad, a practice started in 1920 (Gerber, Felshin, Berlin, & Wyrick, 1974).

In that year, a Philadelphia field hockey team's request for the sport to be played in the Olympics was denied, but resulted in an invitation to compete against an English team. As a result, the sport of field hockey would be distinguished from all others, with international competition happening before the creation of a national championship (Gerber et al., 1974). In 1922, Applebee launched a three-week summer camp held in the Poconos that offered intensive skill instruction during the day and lectures on the theory of the game in the evenings, a venture that lasted for more than 70 years (McIntyre & Connolly, 2015). The camp also fostered the growth of women's lacrosse as well, serving as the site for the creation of the US Women's Lacrosse Association (USWLA), the governing body that organized women's collegiate lacrosse championships from 1931 through 1981.

Long before other female sport publications such as *Women's Sports Magazine, Sports Illustrated for Women*, and *espnW* arrived on the scene (Hays, 1997; Courturier, 2010), she founded *The SportsWoman* in 1924. At a time when other magazines devoted to women's issues were an important part of the world of publishing, this was the first to address women's sporting interests, a vehicle owned by a woman with an editorial board comprising women (Couturier, 2010, 2012).

As the sporting space within which Applebee operated was primarily the college and amateur levels, she has historically been viewed as an educator, athletic director, and rules maker, but not as a savvy and visionary business woman whose work actively challenged prevailing ideas that women were not capable either biologically or physically of participating in intensely competitive sport. With each step in the movement she set in motion, more jobs in sport and more diverse jobs in sport became available for women. Some women found stable employment as physical educators, coaches, and program administrators. Some became officials. And others, like Barbara Longstreth in the 1970s, opened up their own sporting goods companies (Crater, 2017).

Although women's sport is typically characterized as being an economic loss leader (Smith, 2012), women's athletic associations often had to fund raise in order to finance their activities and events (Gerber et al., 1974). International tours and the sponsoring of national championships gave rise to women assuming responsibility for the areas of operations, logistics, and event management. Although women physical educators and administrators eschewed the big-business practices employed in men's college sport, they did so out of a desire to run women's programs for women and to avoid commercial forces that they perceived undermined the health and safety of participants (Sack & Staurowsky, 1998).

With the benefit of twenty-first century hindsight, awareness of the lawsuits settled and pending against the National Collegiate Athletic Association (NCAA) and the National Football League (NFL) addressing player health and safety issues and concussions (Sellers, 2017), and disclosures about sexual assaults perpetrated by male coaches and sports medicine personnel against female athletes in the sports of gymnastics and swimming, how prescient the stance of early women physical educators was in their efforts to protect the well-being of female athletes (Connor & Berg, 2018). In effect, female physical educators were not opposed to the business of sport; they were opposed to the wrong kind of business priorities.

This context is important because, even though these early forms of women's college and amateur sport took time to take hold, they were by their very existence offering specific counter-narratives to societal assumptions that women were not suited for and/or not as interested in sport as men. They were also reflective of just how interested some women were in the business of sport and how skilled they were in carving out niches for women sport entrepreneurs to succeed, despite social prohibitions against women competing too seriously in sport.

By the time the convergence of societal forces from the civil rights and women's movements of the 1960s and 1970s resulted in the passage of Title IX, a bill designed to bar sex discrimination in the nation's schools, there was a cadre of women and men sport leaders who understood how to use Title IX's equality mandate to expand the national conversation about women and sport. It was women like Applebee and those who came after her, many of whom became leaders in the movement to achieve equality for women athletes in the 1970s and 1980s, who understood how to leverage Title IX's appeal to Americans' deepest sensibilities about fair treatment and equality that created a tipping point in societal attitudes toward female athletes. In the decades to follow, athleticism in women was no longer viewed as a novelty, aberration, peculiarity of birth, or threat to femininity, but simply the fulfillment of human potential (Staurowsky, 2016). As historian Mary Jo Festle (1996) observed, Title IX has been "the biggest thing to happen to sports since the whistle" (p. 113).

Title IX's impact on the business of sport would manifest in several ways, including the number of female athletes participating in school sports in the US, the number of people working in athletic departments supporting that growth in participation, the number of women working in college and university athletic departments, the attendant competitiveness of women's US teams internationally, and the reverberating impact the growth of women's sport had on other sport industries (e.g., the sporting goods industry, athletic footwear, and apparel companies). Whereas Title IX has had a lasting impact on the business of sport, pathways to equal treatment for women in the sport industry have never been direct and often follow a pattern that some have described as "two steps forward, one step back" (Ford, 2016). Thus, even as women's sport opportunities have grown as a result of Title IX, there have also been notable reversals of fortune for women in certain career avenues within sport. Each of these areas are explored in brief below.

Title IX as a response to sex discrimination

The woman credited as the "godmother" of Title IX for her role in making the case for why sex discrimination was harmful to girls and women in school settings is Bernice (Bunny) Sandler. Blessed with a fervent desire to teach, Sandler taught part-time while earning her doctoral degree in psychology at the University of Maryland in the 1960s. As optimistic as she was about her future, when she started applying for full-time faculty positions she was surprised to be rejected from one academic job after another.

When that rejection occurred in the department from which she had earned her degree, Sandler asked her department chair why she was being passed over and he responded by saying that she "came on too strong for a woman" (Sandler, 2000, para. 3). Sandler understood that to mean that her male colleagues did not like the fact that she had opinions and voiced them. She also learned that women were routinely treated like this in higher education. Despite having credentials and experience, search committees made up mostly of male professors labeled women unqualified or less qualified and ill-suited for faculty life because of their family obligations. Prompted to document what was happening to women in higher education, Sandler became the leading expert on sex discrimination in schools at a time when "the culture had yet to develop a vocabulary to adequately convey that women were being accorded second-class status" (Staurowsky, 2016, p. 21) and where terms like "sexism" and "sexual harassment" were not yet a part of the lexicon (Ware, 2011, p. 46).

Sexism was not reserved for women job seekers, however. It marked the experience of girls and women going to school. As a consequence, female students were often expected to have higher grades and test scores in order to get into college. Schools set up admission quotas to regulate the number of women coming into college. Regardless of qualification, there was a practice of awarding male students more in financial aid resources. In the athletic realm, varsity sport competition for girls and women had not yet received widespread acceptance or recognition.

Sandler shared this record of sex discrimination in the nation's schools with members of the United States Congress. Teaming up with an organization known as the Women's Equity Action League (WEAL), she worked to persuade Representative Edith Green (R-OR) to sponsor a Congressional hearing to consider the barriers women faced in higher education. After seven days of testimony, Green commented "our educational institutions have not proven to be bastions of democracy" (Tolchin, 1976, p. 32). Alongside Representative Patsy Matsu Takemoto Mink (D-HA) and Senator Birch Bayh (D-IN), Title IX became part of the Education Amendments Act of 1972, signed into law by President Richard M. Nixon (Staurowsky, 2016).

Title IX's impact on the business of school sports

Responsibility for the enforcement of Title IX is handled through the US Department of Education's Office for Civil Rights (USDOE-OCR). Like other federal agencies charged with the oversight of federal laws, OCR officials rely on regulations and policies developed through calls for comment and input from school administrators, policy analysts, legislators, and athletic directors from around the country, and clarifications issued through legal opinions. Schools are afforded considerable latitude in responding to the requirements of Title IX. They are not required to offer identical sports but an equitable opportunity to participate. The three major areas reviewed under Title IX as it pertains to athletics include participation opportunities, allocation of athletically related financial aid (aka athletic scholarships), and other benefits (meaning operational areas necessary to support athletic programs).

As a result of the public interest in monitoring gender equity within athletic departments, the US Congress passed the Equity in Athletics Disclosure Act in 1996. As a result, higher education institutions that receive federal financial assistance are required to report annually on the number of participation opportunities provided to athletes, the number of athletes in their programs (athletes may participate in more than one sport, thus the number of participation opportunities can be different from the number of athletes), aggregate expenditures on athletic scholarships, and revenues and expenses associated with programs, broken down by gender, team, and non-gender-specific categories. These reports can be obtained by contacting the Title IX coordinator at individual institutions or by going to the US Department of Education Equity in Athletics Data Analysis Cutting Tool on the web (US Department of Education, 2018). To date, this kind of public reporting is just beginning to occur at the high school level but is happening only at the state level. In Pennsylvania, for example, the Disclosure of Interscholastic Athletic Opportunity Act was passed in 2012 and reports with aggregated data at the state-wide level are now available (Pennsylvania Department of Education, 2018). Few states, however, have entertained such measures. In the absence of national data, much more information is publicly available for college and university athletic programs.

Title IX's three-part test to assess gender equity in athletic participation

A three-part test is used to determine if a school offers athletic participation opportunities to female and male students on an equitable basis. Schools need to satisfy only one of the three parts of the test to demonstrate compliance with Title IX requirements. The three-part test includes substantial proportionality, history and continuing practice of program expansion, and fully accommodating the interests and abilities of athletes. As a practical matter, schools are confronted with three questions:

- Is the percentage of participation opportunities offered to male and female athletes substantially proportional relative to the percentage of male and female students in the undergraduate student body? OR
- Has there been a history and continuing practice of program expansion within the athletic department, meaning teams and/or participation opportunities are added on an ongoing basis to demonstrate program growth and responsiveness to the under-represented sex (who are not exclusively, but often, female)? OR
- Can an athletic department demonstrate that efforts have been exhausted to satisfy the interests and abilities of members of the under-represented sex?

To allow for flexibility in how schools comply, the substantial proportionality standard used to assess athletic participation opportunities is not defined by "strict numerical formulas" (Cantu, 1996). Although in an ideal circumstance the proportions of male to female athletic participation identically match the representation of males to females in the undergraduate population (e.g., 50% female athletic opportunities/50% female undergraduate students), natural fluctuations due to enrollment and/or team participation may alter those proportions, making it unrealistic to require adjustments every year. There is further tolerance for athletic opportunities to be disproportionate to enrollment when "the number of opportunities that would be required to achieve proportionality would not be sufficient to sustain a viable team" (Cantu, 1996).

Satisfaction of the second part of the test requires consideration of factors that demonstrate both a history of program expansion for the underrepresented sex, such as adding teams, upgrading teams to varsity status, increasing participation opportunities, and affirmative responses to requests to add or elevate sports, and mechanisms in place to respond to growing interest over time. The third part of the test, fully accommodating the interests and abilities of the under-represented sex, calls for periodic reviews to determine if there is sufficient unmet need to warrant the addition of athletic teams.

Title IX's oversight of budget allocations

Participation opportunities for athletes to compete on teams are manifestations of budget priorities and allocations. Title IX serves as a tool in monitoring how financial resources are allocated between men's and women's programs. Although Title IX does not require spending to be identical across teams (the gear to outfit a football player costs more than the gear for a cross-country runner), there is an expectation that the spending done ensures that male and female athletes receive an equally good experience when playing. In the area of athletic scholarships, Title IX requires that funding be allocated substantially proportional to the representation of male and female athletes in an athletic department.

Beyond athletic scholarships, there are numerous other program components (referred to in Title IX regulations and policies as "other benefits") that affect the caliber of playing experience athletes have and are subject to Title IX review. These areas include: athletic training facilities and services, equipment and supplies, housing and dining services, locker rooms and facilities, opportunities to receive coaching and academic assistance, publicity, scheduling of games and practices, and equivalent travel and per diem expenses (Staurowsky, 2016).

Title IX's impact on participation at the high school and college levels

As a piece of legislation that affects the development of sport programs within educational settings, Title IX has had a demonstrable impact on the expansion of sport participation opportunities for girls and women. "In broad terms, the influx of girls and women into sport since the passage of Title IX has been remarkable, as reflected in the historic number of female athletes participating in high school and college sport" (Staurowsky, 2016, p. 40). In 1971, the year preceding the passage of Title IX, 7% of the athletes competing on varsity teams at the high school

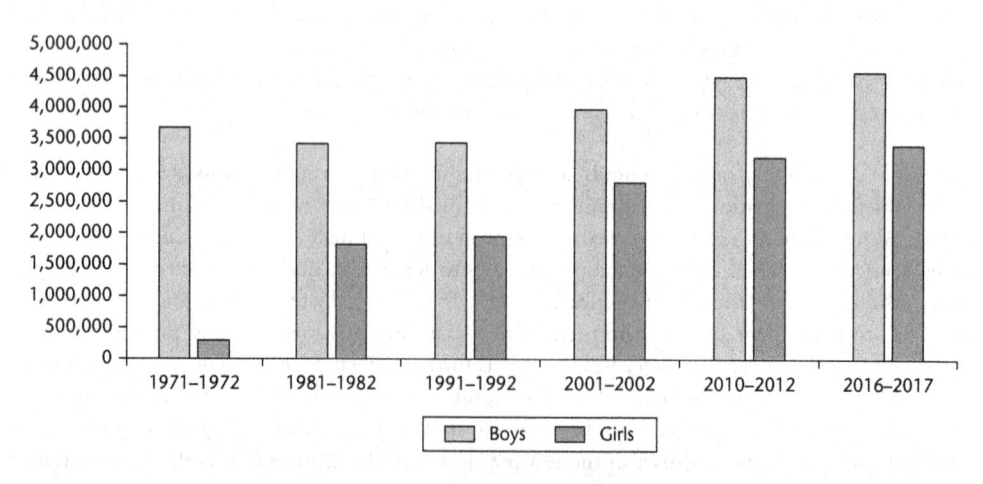

Figure 2.1 Interscholastic varsity sport opportunities by sex 1971–1972 through 2016–2017
Data derived from the National Federation of State High School Association (2017).

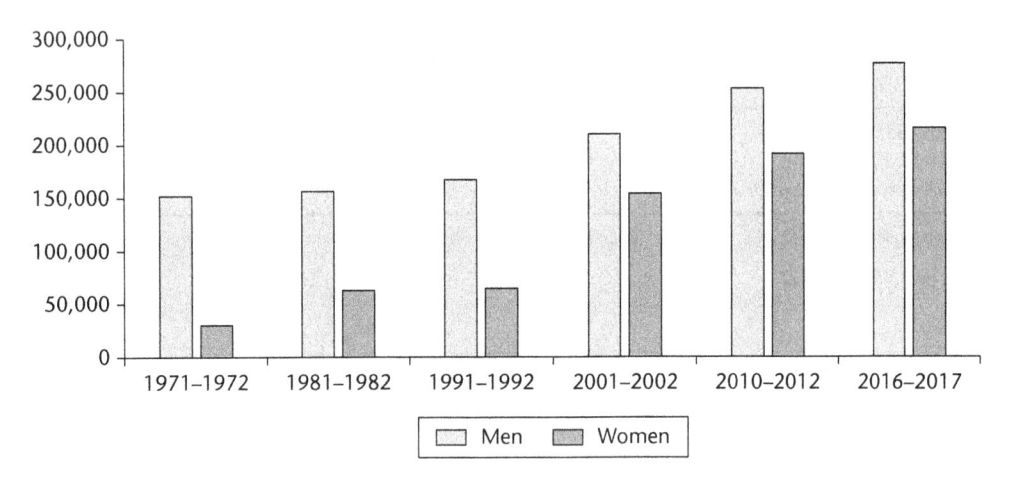

Figure 2.2 Intercollegiate varsity sport opportunities by sex 1971–1972 through 2016–2017
Data derived from the NCAA Sports Sponsorship and Participation Report (Irick, 2017).

level were female (Ware, 2011). At the college level, the average number of teams offered to women was 2.5 with just 16,000 women competing on varsity teams at that time (Acosta & Carpenter, 2014; National Federation of State High School Associations, 2017).

As demonstrated in Figures 2.1 and 2.2, participation numbers for both female and male athletes increased significantly in the decades after Title IX became law. In the four and a half decades since Title IX was enacted, athletic opportunities for girls at the high school level increased more than a thousandfold and nearly 600% for women at the college level. In 2016–2017, there were 3,400,297 female athletes competing on high school varsity teams in the US, comprising 43% of all high school athletes (see Figure 2.1). Of the nearly half a million athletes competing on teams at NCAA institutions, 44% (215,317) were female (see Figure 2.2).

The magnitude of change in the college sport industry post-Title IX

Anecdotal evidence from the immediate years following Title IX's passage reveals large and significant gaps in the allocations of resources to women's athletics at the college level. In 1973–1974, it is reported that, at the University of Washington, the women's program received a modest US$18,000 compared with a US$2.5 million budget for the men's program (Ware, 2011). In 1977, Margaret Roach wrote in the *New York Times* that, at the University of Michigan, women's sports received less than 4% of the athletic budget. Spending on men's athletics at Michigan at the time was a US$5 million a year proposition. Women's athletics, in contrast, received US$180,000. Athletic scholarships were rare for women. In that same year, the women's average share of college and university athletic budgets was 16.4% (Nunez, 1980).

Over time, as greater public scrutiny prompted questions about athletic department budget allocations and as female Title IX plaintiffs won critical decisions in the courts, greater resources in terms of dollars were directed toward women's teams. In 2016–2017, of the nearly US$2.5 billion distributed to NCAA Division I college athletes in the form of athletic scholarships, female athletes received 47% of that allocation, an amount totaling more than US$1.18 billion. In terms of dollars spent on recruiting in NCAA Division I athletic departments, 30% was allocated to women's sports (US$68,032,765) (US Department of Education, 2018).

Table 2.1 Increases in median spending on women's sport at NCAA Division I institutions

	2005 (US$)	2015 (US$)
NCAA FBS institutions	5.5 million	10.5 million
NCAA FCS institutions	2.2 million	4.5 million
NCAA non-football institutions	2.5 million	4.8 million

FBS, Football Bowl Series; FCS, Football Championship Series.

Data from Wilson (2017).

As a measure of recent growth over time during the decade between 2005 and 2015, the median total expenses for women's programs within NCAA Division I nearly doubled across all three subdivisions (NCAA Football Bowl Subdivision, Football Championship Subdivision, and Non-Football) (Table 2.1).

The ongoing process of achieving gender equity

When considered against the results from a report issued by the NCAA Gender Equity Task Force in 1993, continued progress has been made in achieving equity within the college sport sector. In that window of time, which would have marked Title IX's twentieth anniversary, female athletes held 30% of the participation opportunities and women's sport programs received 23% of operating budgets, 30% of athletic scholarship funding, and 17% of recruiting dollars. In 2016–2017, female athletes comprise 43.5% across all three divisions (Wilson, 2017). They receive 43% of athletic scholarship funding and 30% of the dollars spent on recruiting (EADA Report, Division I, 2018).

The quantifiable growth in women's sports since the early 1970s has reverberated through the sport industry overall. Title IX helped to create the US sports nation as we know it today, an industry that is comfortably situated within the leading industries within the US economy (Heitner, 2018). As opportunities for female athletes have expanded, their roles within the sport industry have expanded as well. As discussed elsewhere in this book, women make up significant sectors of sport-viewing audiences and control discretionary spending in the purchase of sporting goods and merchandise. Long gone are the days when sport is monopolized by men and viewed as an exclusive male domain.

The college system provides the infrastructure to support the efforts of US women's Olympic teams and professional women's teams in a variety of sports. At the conclusion of the 2016 Olympic Games, "Had American women competed as their own country, they would have ranked fourth among all nations in the overall medal chart and tied for second in the gold-medal count with 27" (US Olympic Committee, 2016). About the collective accomplishments of the US women's team, world and Olympic champion sprinter several times over, Allyson Felix (who attended and trained at the University of Southern California) commented, "Title IX paved the way and created so many opportunities for women in sport. I feel so proud and so inspired by the strong women on our team" (US Olympic Committee, 2016, para. 15).

On the forty-fifth anniversary of Title IX, the Women's National Basketball Association (WNBA) executives Ruth Riley (General Manager, San Antonio Stars), Swin Cash (Director of Franchise Development, New York Liberty), and Tamika Catchings (Director of Player Programs and Franchise Development for Pacers Sports and Entertainment) marked the occasion by reflecting on the importance of Title IX in fostering their career goals. As

Impact of Title IX and other equity laws

members of the US women's basketball team, they shared the experience of winning gold in the 2004 Olympic Games. Having all been drafted to play in the WNBA in the early 2000s, they believe they were among the first women to enter the college playing ranks knowing that they had the opportunity to play professionally in the US. Talking about Title IX pioneers and the legacy of the WNBA, Catchings said, "I take responsibility for wanting to make sure that the dream and the vision they started for us – that we continue that" (Glass, 2017, p. 2).

At the same time, there remain large gender inequities throughout the system. As women have become more visible as performers and in sporting venues, they have struggled to be seen as executives, head coaches, and sport leaders at all levels. In the college sector, the workplace offers mixed messages for women. There are more women working in college athletic departments and working in more types of jobs than ever before. There has been slow but significant change in the elevation of women into positions within Division I athletic conferences, where 32% of commissioners were women in 2016–2017 (Staurowsky, 2017).

And there have been breakthroughs with women holding over 21% of athletic directorships in NCAA Division I programs (NCAA, 2018), including the appointments of Heather Lyke at the University of Pittsburgh, Sandy Barbour at the Pennsylvania State University (see Leader profile), Jennifer Cohen at the University of Washington (2017), and Debbie Yow (North Carolina State) (Batko, 2017). Irma Garcia, the director of athletics at Division I Football Championship Series (FCS) St. Francis College, was the first Latina to be appointed to such a role in 2011 (NACWAA, 2015). In the fall of 2017, Carla Williams became the first African-American women to be hired as the director of athletics of a Power 5 conference school when she took over the reins at the University of Virginia (Bossip Staff, 2017).

A 10-year analysis of women in the college sport workplace shows that their numbers have grown considerably in positions such as associate and assistant athletic director, marketing/promotions, fund raising, business manager, academic advisor, and compliance director (Figures 2.3 and 2.4). Even as there are more women than ever before in the college workplace, when job growth is considered in relation to the pace at which men are hired in athletic departments, the picture is not as promising. Out of 16 athletic department job categories (excluding coaching) tracked by the NCAA, only 5 are dominated by women, including administrative assistant (94%), life skills (72%), athletic academic advisor (62%), business manager (61%), and

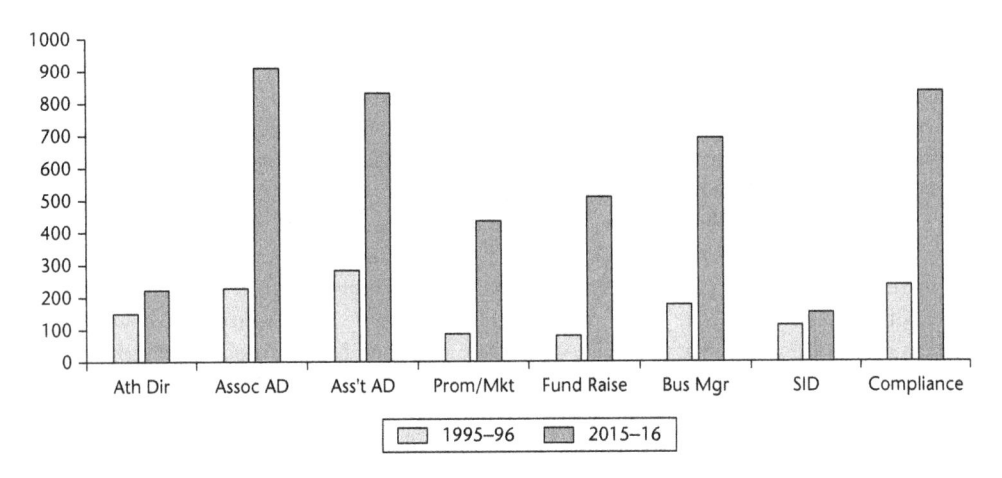

Figure 2.3 Jobs filled by women in NCAA member athletic departments (NCAA, 2016)

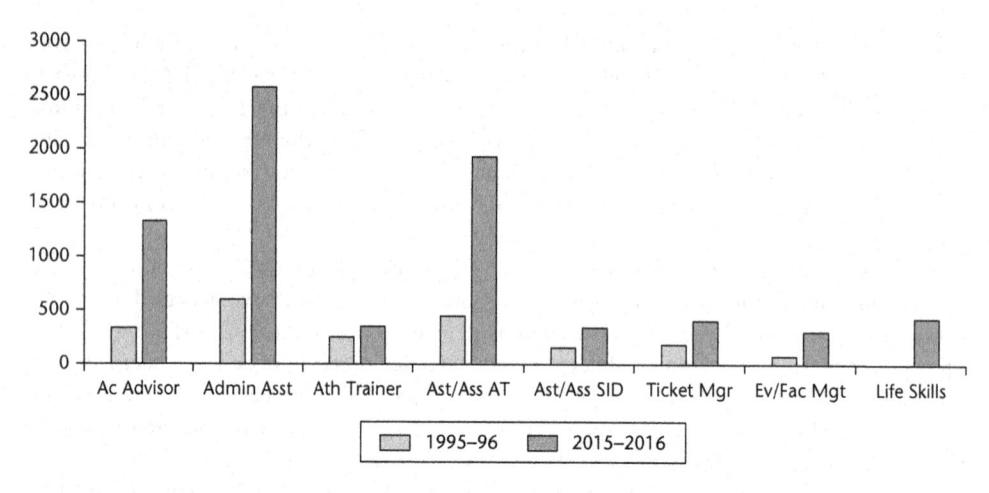

Figure 2.4 Jobs filled by women in NCAA member athletic departments (NCAA, 2016)

compliance (61%) (Staurowsky, 2017). These roles, which are regarded as support roles with little opportunity to contribute to or shape decision-making, are not the kinds of positions that typically lead to athletic director positions (Staurowsky, 2016).

When it comes to college head coaches, just 2 in 10 are women and women comprise less than half of the head coaches of women's teams. Coaches of women's teams at the college level also suffer significant and enduring pay inequities compared with their male counterparts. Wilson (2017) reported that median spending on head coach compensation in NCAA institutions favored men in every division, with the greatest gap occurring at Football Bowl Series (FBS) schools, where head coaches of men's teams received 75% of the money allocated for compensation. Even at Division II and III institutions, head coach compensation is not equitable and gaps in compensation for assistant coaches are nearly as great in Divisions II and III as in Division I.

Conclusion

The impact that Title IX and other gender equity laws have had on the sport landscape has produced progress but the pace of that progress has not always been even and, at times, has taken circuitous routes in forging pathways forward. The sport industry is unusual in the sense that it is organized around a gender binary where attempts at equity and understandings about equality take place within sanctioned sex-segregated environments. There are ongoing negotiations around what constitutes equality and whether separate female sport entities need to look exactly like male sport entities. This ground is constantly shifting.

Title IX offers a double-edged sword in this regard. In 1992, the NCAA Gender Equity Task Force defined a gender equitable athletic department as one where "participants in both the men's and women's sports programs would accept as fair and equitable the overall program of the other gender" (Wilson, 2017, p. 3). As straightforward as that aspirational definition is, there is a question as to what kind of program is being considered. Title IX's liberal feminist mandate, which calls for men and women to be treated the same, leaves little room to contemplate whether sameness is what women want. As legal scholar, Deborah Brake, notes, "It [liberal feminism] does not question the ways in which sport itself is structured to better suit men's interests, nor does it scrutinize any imbalances in the numbers of men and women who benefit from sports" (Brake, 2010, p. 8).

And, so, Title IX's impact on the business of sport is at once inestimable and yet, leaves critical questions left to be examined. In a YouGov national survey ($N = 1,372$), commissioned by the Women's Sports Foundation in 2017, 57% of US adults approved of Title IX, 33% were not sure or didn't know enough to say, and 9% disapproved (Curtis, 2017). The survey also found that 73% of US adults recognized that boys' sports received more support than girls' sports in high school settings and 66% of US adults favored directing new or existing resources to girls sports (Curtis, 2017). This suggests attitudes that predict further change in the future, but the pace of change will continue to fluctuate as forces of resistance exert their influence. As a critical aspect of the women's sport pipeline for jobs and opportunities, inequalities all along the way remain to be remedied. The strength of the women's sector of the sport industry is an indicator and harbinger of the strength of the industry itself.

Leader profile: Sandy Barbour, Director of Athletics, the Pennsylvania State University

As director of athletics at the Pennsylvania State University, Sandy Barbour oversees one of the most expansive and successful athletic programs in the US. Since her appointment in August of 2014, she has emerged as a dynamic leader who has brought vision to a department that supports 800 college athletes competing on 31 varsity teams with a staff of approximately 300. Known for its storied tradition, Barbour oversees a Penn State program that has won 77 national championships and 104 Big-Ten titles all-time, and has an operating budget of approximately US$145 million per year. Her path to becoming a director of athletics started as an undergraduate physical education major at Wake Forest University, Winston-Salem, NC, USA, where she was a four-year letter winner on the field hockey team, a team she captained in her senior year. She played basketball at Wake Forest for two years as well. She also holds a master's degree in sport management from the University of Massachusetts and a master's in business administration (MBA) from Northwestern's Kellogg School of Management. Her trajectory to a Division I athletic directorship began in earnest after coaching field hockey and lacrosse at Northwestern, where she was eventually promoted to recruiting services director and then assistant athletic director (Staff, 2017a). Her reputation grew as she served in numerous capacities at the University of Notre Dame, and eventually served as director of athletics for a three-year period of time at Tulane. Before taking over the program at Penn State, she served as director of athletics at the University of California for a decade. Her stature as a force within the college sport industry is evidenced in her selection in December of 2015 by Forbes as one of the 25 most powerful people in college sports. That year, she was also selected as No. 11 among the most powerful women in sports. For her accomplishments as an executive, she was recognized with the prestigious Under Armour AD of the Year Award given by the National Association of Collegiate Directors of Athletics (NACDA) in 2017. In that same year, she was named to the US Olympic Committee Collegiate Advisory Council (Staff, 2017b).

References

Acosta, V. & Carpenter, L. (2014). Women in intercollegiate sport: A longitudinal, national study, thirty-seven-year update, 1977–2014. Retrieved from www.acostacarpenter.org/2014%20Status%20of%20Women%20in%20Intercollegiate%20Sport%20-37%20Year%20Update%20-%201977-2014%20.pdf.

Batko, B. (2017). Heather Lyke: Pitt AD post "a perfect fit." *Pittsburgh Post-Gazette*, March 20. Retrieved from www.post-gazette.com/sports/Pitt/2017/03/20/pitt-ad-heather-lyke-eastern-michigan-athletic-director/stories/201703200124.

Bossip Staff (2017). Black history: UVA's Carla Williams is the first African–American woman to become athletic director in NCAA Power 5. *Bossip.com*, October 23. Retrieved from https://bossip.com/1595332/black-history-uva-hires-carla-williams-as-first-african-american-athletic-director-in-ncaa-power-five-43081.

Brake, D. (2010). *Getting in the game: Title IX and the women's sports revolution.* New York: New York University Press.

Cantu, N. (1996). *Clarification of Intercollegiate Athletics Policy Guidance: The three-part test.* Washington, DC: Office for Civil Rights. Retrieved from https://www2.ed.gov/about/offices/list/ocr/docs/clarific.html#two.

Connor, T. & Berg, K. (2018). Larry Nassar's victims now focused on MSU, USA gymnastics. *NBC News*, February 8. Retrieved from https://www.nbcnews.com/news/us-news/larry-nassar-s-victims-now-focused-msu-usa-gymnastics-n844871.

Couturier, L. E. (2010). Considering *The Sportswoman* 1924–1936: A content analysis. *Sports History Reviews*, **41**, 111–131.

Couturier, L. E. (2012). Dissenting voices: The discourse of competition in *The Sportswoman*. *Journal of Sports History*, **39**(2), 265–282.

Crater, K. (2017). Longstreth sporting goods and women's professional league announce partnership. *Press release*, September. Retrieved from https://www.longstreth.com/pdfs/news/Longstreth-Womens-Pro-Lacrosse-League-Online-Store-Partnership.pdf.

Curtis, K. (2017). Key findings show majority of U.S. adults support Title IX and believe in the administration's responsibility to uphold the legislation. Press release.

Equity in Athletics Disclosure Report, Division I (2018). Run by author using the US Department of Education Equity in Athletics Data Cutting Tool.

Festle, M. J. (1996). *Playing Nice: Politics and apologies in women's sports.* New York City, NY: Columbia University Press. Retrieved from https://www.womenssportsfoundation.org/media-center/press-releases/june-15-2017-press-release.

Ford, L. E. (2016). Two steps forward, one step back? Strengthening the foundations of women's leadership in higher education. *Journal of Politics, Groups, and Identities*, **4**(3), 499–512.

Gerber, E., Felshin, J., Berlin, P. & Wyrick, W. (1974). *The American Woman in Sport.* Reading, MA: Addison-Wesley Publishing Company.

Glass, A. (2017). How Title IX inspires former WNBA players to pay it forward. *Forbes.com*, June 23. Retrieved from https://www.forbes.com/sites/alanaglass/2017/06/23/how-title-ix-inspires-former-wnba-players-to-pay-it-forward/2/#6a158e1b2d2f.

Hays, C. (1997). The field of sports magazines for and about women is about to get much more crowded. *The New York Times*, April 14. Retrieved from www.nytimes.com/1997/04/14/business/field-sports-magazines-for-about-women-about-get-much-more-crowded.html.

Heitner, D. (2018). This multimillion-dollar men's athleisure startup is coming after Lululemon's market share. *Forbes SportsMoney*, July 27. Retrieved from https://www.forbes.com/sites/darrenheitner/2018/07/27/this-multi-million-dollar-mens-athleisure-startup-is-coming-after-lululemons-market-share/#727ed8157f3b.

Irick, E. (2017). *NCAA Sports Sponsorship and Participation Rates Report: 1981–82 – 2016–17.* Indianapolis, IN: National Collegiate Athletic Association.

LaVoi, N. (2017). Head Coaches of Women's Collegiate Teams: A report on seven select NCAA Division-I conferences 2017–2018. Minneapolis, MN: University of Minnesota. Retrieved from www.cehd.umn.edu/tuckercenter/library/docs/research/WCR_2017-18_Head_Coaches_DI.pdf

McIntyre, A. & Connolly, H. (2015). *An Insider's Guide to Field Hockey.* New York: Rosen Publishing.

National Association of Collegiate Women Athletic Administrators (NACWAA) (2015). Mazza, NACWAA, name administrator of the year honorees. Press release. Retrieved from http://athletics.pittbradford.org/landing/NACWAA.

National Collegiate Athletic Association (2016). Gender Demographics Database. Retrieved from www.ncaa.org/about/resources/research/ncaa-demographics-database.

National Collegiate Athletic Association (2018). NCAA Demographic Database. Retrieved from www.ncaa.org/about/resources/research/ncaa-demographics-database.

National Federation of State High School Associations (2017). *2016–2017 High School Athletics Participation Survey Results.* Indianapolis, IN: National Federation of State High School Associations. Retrieved from https://www.nfhs.org/ParticipationStatistics/ParticipationStatistics.

Nunez, L. (1980). *More Hurdles to Clear: Women and girls in competitive athletics.* Washington, DC: United States Commission on Civil Rights. Retrieved from https://www.law.umaryland.edu/marshall/usccr/documents/cr11063.pdf

Pendergrass, D. C. (2016). Ladies armed with clubs. *Harvard Crimson*, December 1. Retrieved from www.thecrimson.com/article/2016/12/1/constance-applebee-harvard.

Pennsylvania Department of Education (2018). *Disclosure of Interscholastic Athletic Opportunities Act.* Harrisburg, PA: Pennsylvania Department of Education. Retrieved from www.education.pa.gov/Teachers%20-%20Administrators/Interscholastic%20Athletic%20Opportunity/Pages/default.aspx.

Roach, M. (1977). Is Title IX scoring any points in sports? *The New York Times*, September 27. Retrieved from www.nytimes.com/1977/09/27/archives/issue-and-debate-is-title-ix-scoring-many-points-in-field-of-womens.html.

Sack, A. L. & Staurowsky, E. J. (1998). *College Athletes for Hire: The evolution and legacy of the NCAA's amateur myth.* Santa Barbara, CA: Praeger Publishing.

Sandler, B. (2000). Too strong for a woman: The five words that created Title IX. *About Women on Campus* [former newsletter for the National Association for Women in Education].

Sellers, S. M. (2017). NCAA football concussion cases heat up. *Bloomberg News*, October 19. Retrieved from https://www.bna.com/ncaa-football-concussion-n73014471184.

Smith, C. (2012). When it's ok to lose money: The business of women's college basketball. Forbes.com, March 20. Retrieved from https://www.forbes.com/sites/chrissmith/2012/03/29/when-its-okay-to-lose-money-the-business-of-womens-college-basketball/#33c4d52238b5.

Staff (2017a). Sandy Barbour to receive NACDA AD of the year honor on June 13. Press release, June 12. Retrieved from http://news.psu.edu/story/471515/2017/06/12/athletics/sandy-barbour-receive-nacda-ad-year-honor-june-13.

Staff (2017b). Sandy Barbour named to U.S. Olympic Committee Collegiate Advisory Council. Press release, October 20. Retrieved from http://news.psu.edu/story/489309/2017/10/20/athletics/sandy-barbour-named-us-olympic-committee-collegiate-advisory.

Staurowsky, E. J. (2016). *Women and Sport: A continuing journey from liberation to celebration.* Champaign, IL: Human Kinetics Publishers.

Staurowsky, E. J. (2017). Has gender bias come of age in college sport workplaces? Presentation at the North American Society for the Sociology of Sport, November, Windsor, ON, Canada.

Tolchin, S. (1976). *Women in Congress.* Washington, DC: Government Printing Office.

US Department of Education (2018). Equity in Athletics Data Analysis Cutting Tool. Retrieved from https://ope.ed.gov/athletics/#.

US Olympic Committee (2016). Team USA concludes record-breaking Rio 2016 Olympic Games with 121 medals, 46 golds. Press release. Retrieved from https://www.teamusa.org/News/2016/August/21/Team-USA-Concludes-Record-Breaking-Rio-2016-Olympic-Games-With-121-Medals-46-Golds.

Ware, S. (2011). *Title IX: A brief history with documents.* The Bedford Series in History and Culture. New York: Bedford.

Wilson, A. (2017). *45 Years of Title IX: The status of women in intercollegiate athletics.* Indianapolis, IN: National Collegiate Athletic Association.

3
Sociological perspectives of women in sport

Nicole M. LaVoi, Anna Baeth, and Austin Stair Calhoun

Sociological perspectives on women in sport

Sport sociology is a subdiscipline of kinesiology—the study of human movement and its impact on health, society, and quality of life—which focuses on sport as a sociocultural phenomenon. As one of the most powerful, popular, and visible social institutions in the United States, and perhaps around the globe, sport is often viewed as a microcosm within, or reflection of, society. The social institution of sport undoubtedly influences culture and values, and in turn dominant culture and values influence sport. The relationship is inextricably dynamic and bidirectional. Sport sociologists examine how dominant ideologies, values, and beliefs are embedded within the system, structure, policies, and norms of sport to maintain social inequality. In short, sport sociologists study how power is (re)produced. Scholars in this discipline use critical theoretical lenses to expose, deconstruct, and challenge the status quo with the ultimate goal of moving toward social justice within sport contexts, while realizing the distinct and real challenges of unequal power and tangled systems of oppression both in and beyond sport. Still, many sport sociology scholars believe that a dominant "win-at-all-costs" business model often defines the culture of sport, and that model is associated with oppressive ideologies that can be challenged and/or augmented by an alternative paradigm of "justice, citizenship, and equity" acting in turn as a vehicle for social change.

Central to sport sociology—and, specifically, to critical feminist scholars who primarily examine gendered relationships of power to expose systemic inequality, under-representation, exploitation, and marginalization of women in sport—is the documented premise that sport is, and remains, a male domain (e.g., Kane, 1995, 2013). Unarguably, sport is male centered, male dominated, and male led. Sport sociology scholars who employ a critical feminist lens often conduct research within a backdrop of the post-Title IX era. Title IX, passed in 1972 in the United States, was a landmark piece of federal civil rights legislation that made gender discrimination within educational contexts illegal. Unequivocally, Title IX dramatically and irreversibly influenced sport participation opportunities for girls and women. More recently, given that "women" are not a monolithic group, some scholars have applied an intersectional perspective to examine how race, disability, social class, and sexual identity—combined with gender—form multiple and overlapping oppressions for women in sport contexts (LaVoi, 2016).

As of November 2017, sport sociologists within North America have studied women and gender extensively. In the *Sociology of Sport Journal* (*SSJ*)—the seminal academic journal in the field—over the last 20+ years a large majority (397/492 or 80.1%) of all articles published[1] pertained to women, gender, or feminism in some capacity. Gender is a salient variable in sport sociology, and two common areas of scholarly inquiry in *SSJ* include: women in sport media (190/492 or 38.6%) and, to a lesser extent, women in sport leadership/coaching (35/492 or 7.1%). The remainder of this chapter first summarizes key findings within these two areas of sport sociology inquiry as it pertains to women—sport media and leadership positions. Second, it offers theoretically based reasons for the under-representation of women in sport.

Women and sports media

Currently, women play and participate in sports in record numbers and comprise nearly half (~43%) of all athletes at every level of competition; yet, women are disproportionately represented in the sports media. The dramatic and paradoxical under-representation of women occurs in every form of sport media including television (Billings, Angelini, & Duke 2010; Duncan, Messner, Willms, & Wilson, 2005), radio, newspaper, and magazines (Bishop, 2003; Smallwood, Brown, & Billings, 2014; Weber & Carini, 2013), and digital outlets including network-affiliated websites, social media platforms such as Twitter and Facebook, and blogs (LaVoi & Calhoun, 2014). The dearth of coverage for women's sport and female athletes in the US is exemplified by the longitudinal research of Cooky, Messner and colleagues, who have tracked the amount of televised coverage given to women's sports since 1989. Key findings indicate the amount of televised sports coverage devoted to women's sports has hovered around 2% for the last decade. In 2013, that number was at an all-time low (1.6%) (Cooky, Messner, & Hextrum, 2013) and, based on the most recent data, it is currently at 3.2% (Cooky, Messner, & Musto, 2015).

Some scholars hoped that digital media would provide transformative potential for challenging male hegemony and gender ideologies in traditional sport media, but LaVoi and Calhoun argued "based on emerging data, old patterns of media representations that symbolically annihilate female athletes are being reproduced in 'new' media" (LaVoi and Calhoun, 2014, p. 328). Regardless of the medium, based on the data, female athletes receive only ~2–4% of all sport media coverage, a statistic that remains remarkably stable. As Kane, who is featured in the leader profile at the conclusion of this chapter, pointedly observed, "The better sports women get, the more the media ignore them" (Kane, 2013, p. 231).

Kane's comment directly addresses the *quantity* of coverage given to sportswomen, but equally important and implied are the *ways* (i.e., quality of portrayals) in which sportswomen are ignored through framing. When women do receive media coverage, it is in ways that minimize athletic competence and highlight femininity, (hetero)sexuality, and traditional gender stereotypes (LaVoi & Calhoun, 2014). Based on decades of data, female athletes have historically, though not exclusively, through sport media been: *tokenized* and *marginalized* (Messner, Duncan, & Jensen, 1993), *sexualized* (Clavio & Eagleman, 2011; Kane, LaVoi, & Fink, 2013), *feminized* (Jones, Murrell, & Jackson, 1999), *racialized* (Buffington & Fraley, 2008; McKay & Johnson, 2008), *infantilized* (Messner et al., 1993), portrayed as *incompetent* or in a *sarcastic manner* (Cooky et al., 2013), and/or *othered* (LaVoi, Becker, & Maxwell, 2007). How is it possible, within an occupational landscape that boasts a record number of female sport participants, and increasing number of women sport fans, that such disproportionate and disrespectful media coverage occurs? This paradox in sport media is similar to a parallel paradox within the data pertaining to women sport leaders and, for the purpose of this chapter, sport coaches.

Women in sport leadership and coaching

As mentioned above, the number of female sport participants has dramatically multiplied from 1 in 27 (~4%) in 1972 to 2 in 5 (40%) today (Acosta & Carpenter, 2014). Conversely, in the position of head coach—arguably one of the most visible, powerful, lucrative positions in sport—women in the US are under-represented in almost every sport (Acosta & Carpenter, 2014), at every level of competition (LaVoi, 2016), and at every type of institution (LaVoi, 2017). Based on the data, only 23% of all collegiate athletes are coached by women (Acosta & Carpenter, 2014), and less than half (~42%) of female athletes are coached by a woman (LaVoi, 2017). This number is in contrast to the fact that more than 90% of all college female athletes were coached by women before the passage of Title IX in 1972. Acosta and Carpenter's (1974–2014) longitudinal analysis of women in coaching was the forerunner in tracking the initial and drastic decline in the number of women in positions of power in athletics after Title IX. More recently, LaVoi (2016) has argued the decline has terminated; the current trend within the occupational landscape for women coaches in college athletics is *stagnation*.

Therefore, two "unintended consequences" of Title IX resulted in the fact that (1) males currently have access to a legitimate *dual career pathway* into coaching (i.e., the opportunity to coach both males and females), whereas women coach less than half of all females and rarely coach males, and (2) many females grow up never having had a female coach as a same-sex role model, whereas nearly 100% of males enjoy the benefits of having a male coach. Some question why women coaches matter. In *Women in Sports Coaching*, LaVoi (2016) summarized the myriad ways women coaches matter: women coaches offer support and guidance for other women in how to navigate the workplace as a minority; females coached by women are more likely to go into coaching and perceive coaching as a possible career choice; women in positions of power help challenge gender and leadership stereotypes; women bring different perspectives into the workplace and decision-making; women advocate for equality; and finally discrimination, abuse, and harassment are less likely when a gender-balanced workforce is a reality. Women in coaching positions are visible and powerful reminders that help sensitize and expose boys and men to the idea that women can be – and are – competent, successful leaders worthy of respect and admiration.

Others commonly ask why the historic decline and current stagnation occurred. The answer is complicated, multilevel, and dynamic. For a full review of the myriad barriers—including individual, interpersonal, organizational, and societal—that influence women's choices to enter coaching, frame women's perceptions about the field and themselves, keep women marginalized within the coaching profession, impede career advancement, and push women out, see LaVoi (2016) and LaVoi and Dutove (2012). Women now operate within an occupational landscape that boasts a record number of female participants (many of whom have a passion for sport, vast athletic capital, and sport knowledge). How is it then that women in positions of power in sport are still in the minority and that minority status is stagnant?

This perplexing question and many more arise when data illuminates these two paradoxical scenarios. In terms of media, sport sociologists often ask: Who benefits when women are routinely erased or portrayed in ways that minimize their athleticism, precisely at a time in our culture when strong, athletic women are more commonplace and often celebrated? Why are women routinely portrayed in ways that minimize their athletic competence? For women in sport leadership the questions are similar: Why is the percentage of women in positions of power in sport stagnant at a time when the percentage of women in all other occupations is increasing? Who benefits from denying access to, impeding the careers of, and creating an unwelcoming occupational climate for women in sport? To help answer these questions and explain these two paradoxical phenomena, sport sociologists employ theory. Some of the most common theoretical perspectives and constructs utilized by feminist scholars in sport sociology are summarized next.

Theoretical perspectives in sport sociology

Gatekeeping theory

Theoretical frameworks such as gatekeeping theory (Shoemaker & Vos, 2009) have aided sport sociologists in explaining the myriad ways sport media (re)produce power in ways that privilege men. Returning to Kane's assertion that "the media" ignore women in sport, gatekeeping theory also helps us understand *who* comprises "the media" and how those decision-makers and individuals in positions of power shape who and what is covered. According to the most recent data on Associated Press Sports Editors, less than 10% of sports editors or assistant sports editors were women, and women made up a small minority of columnists (12.4%) and reporters (12.6%) (Lapchick, Marfatia, Bloom, & Sylverain, 2016). In sum, a large majority of the sport media "gatekeepers" are men, and, of those men, almost all are white.

Gatekeeping is useful to assess and analyze how and why certain pieces of information pass through "gates." Gatekeeping is a process that occurs at multiple levels, whereby "selecting, producing, transmitting, and shaping information" occur in various networks of people who produce sports media (Creedon, 2014, p. 17). Gatekeeping theory organizes those controls in levels, ranging from macro (societal, systems) to micro (individual). Gatekeeping, after all, is in many ways about power and control and maintaining dominant ideologies, common themes in the discipline of sport sociology. Kim (2007) argued that the "gatekeeping phenomenon exposes the process through which borders and boundaries of social conduct are maintained" (p. 304) and suggested it is intrinsic to conduct, culture, and social regulation.

Examples of gatekeeping in sport media and for women in coaching follow. For sport media, the gatekeeper decides who and what is valued, relevant and interesting enough to be given coverage. When a sports editor claims, "No one is interested in women's sport" (which is, in fact, not true!) it results in not allocating resources to covering women sport—this is gatekeeping. Kane has argued that, when a sport editor claims "no one" is interested, what he really means is *he* is not interested. Similarly a large majority of gatekeeper collegiate athletics directors (ADs) are white males (Lapchick et al., 2016) and researchers have found that male ADs are more likely to hire male coaches for their women's sports programs (Taylor & Hardin, 2016). In addition, the way an issue is framed is saliently related to gatekeepers.

Framing theory

The basis of framing theory (Goffman, 1974) is that individuals (i.e., sports editors or ADs) focus attention on certain events and then place them within a field of meaning. In essence, framing theory suggests that *how* something is presented to the audience (called "the frame" and what sport sociologists often call narratives) influences the choices people make about how to process that information. Frames are powerful communication schemas in which meaning assigned to events, identity, and other culturally significant topics is constructed. As opposed to gatekeeping theory in which the focus is on the process and the act of selection, framing theory is focused on the characteristics or salience of the selection. Framing is the selection, omission, and organization of words, phrases, issues, and events by individuals (i.e., the media, ADs) to explain the news or an event and the ensuing understanding by its audience (Hardin, Lynn, & Walsdorf, 2005). For example, in a 2005 study by Hardin et al., a majority of televised sport commentators (i.e., gatekeepers) of elite women's performances on television framed women's sport coverage with *indifference* including: differentially framing athletes based on gender and sport, considering sexist comments as less offensive than racist comments, and openly disrespecting or disregarding female gatekeepers such as female sport reporters and journalists. Frames matter when generating or sustaining interest. If women's sport is framed indifferently or in uninteresting ways, it is not surprising some fans will find women's sport uninteresting. In turn, gatekeepers won't cover a sport unless fans are interested. This chicken-and-egg scenario with coverage of women's sport is ongoing because the media often do not want to acknowledge their role in creating and/or sustaining interest! In the "second wave" of sport media research, scholars are analyzing how framing of female athletes is interpreted by groups of individuals and how those interpretations impact beliefs and attitudes toward women's sports (Fink, Kane, & LaVoi, 2014; Kane, LaVoi, & Fink, 2013). In sum, sports commentary—whether written or spoken—"frames" the construction of gender and racial hierarchies that privilege white men (Cranmer, Brann, & Bowman, 2014).

Because of the power associated with how stories and individuals are framed, scholars have used framing as a lens for assessing heteronormativity, heterosexism, and homophobia in sport (Calhoun, LaVoi, & Johnson, 2011; Hardin & Whiteside, 2009). Calhoun et al.'s (2011) study is one of the few to merge sport media, gender, and sport coaches. They examined online coaching biographies on intercollegiate athletics websites to determine how and if the inclusion of marital data reinforced or challenged a normative (i.e., heterosexual) culture. Based on the data, they concluded the virtual absence of same-sex partners and the high frequency of heterosexual family narratives perpetuated and encouraged heteronormativity, heterosexism, and homophobia in collegiate athletics. This study, along with others, highlights what sport sociologists often contend—choices of individuals are made within a system. The choice of what goes into an online biography, the ways coaches choose to represent themselves, and the choices of media producers are all made within a broader context where the *ways of seeing*, privilege men and masculine ideals (Cooky & LaVoi, 2012).

Lastly, the problematic and detrimental practices of gatekeeping and framing are particularly deleterious for women of color (Rowe, 2014; Van Sterkenburg & Knoppers, 2004; Whannel, 2013), women who participate in non-traditional sports (Hardin & Greer, 2009; Thorpe, 2005), women who do not fit the heterosexual mold (Griffin, 1998), and women who participate in what Metheny (1965) coined *female-inappropriate sports* like football, rugby, and ice hockey (i.e., sports that require speed, strength, and aggression to perform well—characteristics typically associated with men and masculinity). These aforementioned groups of women with intersectional identities fall outside the dominant group, and lack power within the institution of sport.

Hegemony theory

Correspondingly, it impossible to discuss gatekeeping and framing without discussing power and control; it is also impossible to discuss power and control in sport without discussing hegemony, a scholarly term credited to Antonio Gramsci (Calhoun, 2014). Although Gramsci (1971) did not specifically discuss gender in relationship to hegemonic theory, scholars agree gendered hegemony (frequently called hegemonic masculinity) exists. It is a popular theoretical framework used to explain male dominance, power structures, and gendered inequalities in sport (Connell, 1990; Connell & Messerschmidt, 2005; Fink, 2015; Messner, 1988). Hegemony is understood to be the process by which a dominant social class uses cultural, ideological, and/or economic influences to create consent for its dominance over others. Connell and Messerschmidt (2005, p. 832) provide context for understanding and applying the concept of hegemony to gender:

Hegemonic masculinity was understood as the pattern of practice (i.e., things done, not just a set of role expectations or an identity) that allowed men's dominance over women to continue. Hegemonic masculinity was distinguished from other masculinities, especially subordinated masculinities. Hegemonic masculinity was not assumed to be normal in the statistical sense; only a minority of men might enact it. But it was certainly normative. It embodied the currently most honored way of being a man, it required all other men to position themselves in relation to it, and it ideologically legitimated the global subordination of women to men.

Within hegemonic masculinity, the traits of heterosexuality and aggressive behaviors (e.g., competitiveness, assertiveness) that underlie this dominant form of masculinity, are very often the traits desired and considered the apex of the masculine hierarchy (Connell & Messerschmidt, 2005). As sport is a highly regarded and important social institution in the United States, it can be a mirror for replicating and enforcing idealized masculine traits, like heterosexuality, physicality, and aggressiveness (Birrell, 2000; Messner, 1988). Hegemony therefore becomes a form of gatekeeping because favor is bestowed on certain masculine markers—power and performance—while simultaneously marginalizing females in sport who take on those traits (Griffin, 1992). The same is true in sport coaching. The normative characteristics associated with the praxis of effective coaching (e.g., assertiveness, dominance, confidence, control) are the very characteristics that are associated with men and masculinity, thereby placing women coaches in a lose–lose situation (Burton & LaVoi, 2016). When women conform to normative coaching behaviors, they are perceived to be "acting like a man" and are evaluated less favorably (e.g., they are considered a bitch or a bully) and often sanctioned, reprimanded, or fired. Conversely, when a woman does not conform to normative coaching behaviors, she is perceived as incompetent and irrelevant, and therefore will be less likely to be valued, be compensated fairly, or be the recipient of lucrative sponsorship or endorsement deals. Competence is linked to compensation, and women coaches often fail to benefit from either.

Heteronormativity, heterosexism, and homophobia: the three Hs.

Calhoun et al. (2011, p. 302) wrote a concise summary of these empirical and intertwined concepts:

> Heteronormativity, according to scholars, represents an ideology that denies sexual orientations and behaviors that are not heterosexual. In practice, a heteronormative society confers power to White, heterosexual men. Heteronormativity invokes a societal hierarchy in which heterosexuality is the norm. Stemming from this normatization, heterosexism is evident in the stigmatization and harmful behaviors that arise toward individuals because of (perceived) non-heterosexual practices and behaviors.

Related to the previous two areas of sport sociology, silence (the practice of not framing/including homosexual family narratives in online coaching biographies) and the promotion of heterosexy images of women in sport media are salient markers of the "three Hs" in sport contexts. Researchers in sport have connected heteronormativity and heterosexism to the (re)production of privilege for the dominant group, homophobia among coaches, players, parents, and athletic administrators (Griffin, 1998; Krane, 1997; Krane & Barber, 2005; Norman, 2016), and the marginalization and trivialization of women athletes in the media (Kane & Buysse, 2005; Kane & Lenskyj, 1998). The lesbian stigma attributed to women in sport is well documented (see Griffin, 1998) and remains a powerful process by which women athletes, coaches, and women's sport are marginalized. This means that lesbian athletes have historically been discounted and devalued in the marketplace, and are less likely to receive sponsorships or endorsements compared with heterosexual peers.

Homologous reproduction

Homologous reproduction (Kanter, 1977) is the concept that a dominant group (e.g., men) in power systematically reproduces itself by hiring more men than women. This is true in the context of sport for sport coaching and administrative positions, which historically and currently are dominated by men (Lovett & Lowry, 1994; Sagas, Cunningham, & Pastore, 2006; Stangl & Kane, 1991; Whisenant & Mullane, 2007). Homologous reproduction is the idea that people like to hire people like themselves, which is multiplicatively oppressive for intersecting identities of gender, race, sexual identity, and social class. LaVoi et al. (2007) found that women who were tokens (15% or less of the workforce) within intercollegiate athletics administrative positions reproduced dominant decision-making patterns that "preserved the gender order and hegemonic ideology within men's sport" (LaVoi et al., 2007, p. 38) as it pertained to decisions about portrayal of female versus male athletes on the cover of sport media guides. Women administrators were more likely to portray male athletes in action, in uniform, and on the court than female athletes, which communicates and frames female athletes and women's sport as less athletic and promotes traditional ideals of femininity.

Conclusion

Two lines of sport sociology inquiry were summarized in this chapter, and reasons for the lack of women in the business of sport were illuminated using numerous theoretical lenses. Sport sociologists contend that the disproportionate media coverage of women's sport and current stagnation of women in positions of power despite a strong labor pool are about *power*. These trends are occurring when the proliferation of female athletes and women's sport have helped create a broader cultural context in which female athleticism has become "normalized," and in many cases, celebrated (Cooky & LaVoi, 2012). Over the past four decades, feminist sport scholars have maintained the idea that women are disrupting hegemonic discourses around the meaning and practice of sport, gaining access, popularity, and power, growing in unprecedented numbers, and achieving prestige in a social institution created and dominated by men. As a result, sportswomen are routinely marginalized by the media, denied access to and pushed out of positions of power in sport that matter and are visible (Birrell, 1989; Kane & Lenskyj, 1998; Messner, 1998). In short, the paradoxes and lack of women in sport business can be explained as *gendered relations of power*.

Sport, due to its location as one of the most powerful, popular, and visible social institutions in the United States, and the opportunity through participation in sport to reap a wide array of psychosocial, health, academic, economic, and professional benefits (Wiese-Bjornstal & LaVoi, 2007), serves as fertile ground for the empowerment of women. Sport sociologists using a critical feminist theoretical lens have examined what sorts of counterweights, like those summarized in this chapter, have been harnessed and employed to keep such possibilities at bay (Kane et al., 2013). Sport provides the potential for women to "define themselves in ways that fundamentally alter men's ideological and institutional control of sport" (Kane et. al., 2013, p. 25), which is precisely why post-Title IX paradoxes and power struggles exist and women's presence in sport is, and will likely remain, as Messner argued in 1988, a "contested terrain."

Leader profile: Mary Jo Kane

Mary Jo Kane, Ph.D., is a Professor in the School of Kinesiology, the founding Director of the Tucker Center for Research on Girls and Women in Sport at the University of Minnesota, and a leader in the field of sport sociology. Professor Kane received her Ph.D. from the University

Figure 3.1 Mary Jo Kane
Photo courtesy of the University of Minnesota, Department of Kinesiology

of Illinois Urbana-Champaign in 1985, with an emphasis in sport sociology where she was influenced and mentored by Professor John Loy—one of the founding fathers of sport sociology. Kane learned from Loy to never take shortcuts when engaged in the painstaking quest to conceptualize and design an empirically based study that is methodologically rigorous and grounded within a theoretical framework—a standard of excellence she has passed on to countless numbers of her own graduate students.

Kane is an internationally recognized scholar who has published extensively on the media coverage of women's sports (e.g., the lack thereof) and is also known as an expert on the passage, implementation, and impact of Title IX, including occupational employment trends in women's sports. Her research publications contribute to the body of knowledge on sport, media, and gender (along with a number of other scholars) that documents how women are significantly under-represented in terms of overall media coverage, and are much more likely to be portrayed for their off-court physical attractiveness and femininity than for their on-court athletic accomplishments. In her words, "my scholarly writings are framed within critical feminist theory, which assumes that society is structured around a series of inequitable relationships of power whereby women are systematically devalued and marginalized. Second, and related to the first, is that both lines of inquiry are grounded in the belief—and supported by empirical evidence—that sport is a particularly critical and useful site for the reproduction and maintenance of male power and privilege" (Kane, 2017, p. 88). Her 1995 manuscript, "Resistance/transformation of the oppositional binary: Exposing sport as a continuum," is unarguably known as a seminal and transformational article in sport sociology.

Professor Kane is a pioneering feminist sport scholar. In 1993, Kane founded the Tucker Center for Research on Girls and Women in Sport—the first and only research center of its kind! Housed in the College of Education and Human Development's School of Kinesiology at the University of Minnesota, Kane and Tucker Center scholars have established standards of excellence with respect to scholarly inquiry, graduate education, advocacy, community outreach, and public scholarship related to girls and women in sport. In 1996, Professor Kane was awarded the first Endowed Chair related to women in sport—the Dorothy McNeill and Elbridge Ashcraft Tucker Chair for Women in Sport and Exercise Science. In 2002 she was elected by her peers as a Fellow in the National Academy of Kinesiology, and in 2015 was chosen by her academic peers to receive the North American Society for Sport Sociology (NASSS) Distinguished Service Award. Dr. Kane's legacy as both a scholar and an advocate has made her an instrumental leader in the fight for gender equity for girls and women in sport.

Note

1 This data came from a SCOPUS search or the terms "women", "gender," and "feminism" within the *Sociology of Sport Journal* as of November 2017.

References

Acosta, V. R. & Carpenter, L. J. (2014). Women in intercollegiate sport: A longitudinal national study, thirty-six year update, 1977–2014. Retrieved from www.acostacarpenter.org.

Billings, A. C., Angelini, J. R., & Duke, A. H. (2010). Gendered profiles of Olympic history: Sportscaster dialogue in the 2008 Beijing Olympics. *Journal of Broadcasting & Electronic Media*, **54**(1), 9–23.

Birrell, S. (1989). Racial relations theories and sport: Suggestions for a more critical analysis. *Sociology of Sport Journal*, **6**, 212–227.

Birrell, S. (2000). Feminist theories for sport. *Handbook of Sports Studies* (pp. 61–76). Retrieved from http://dx.doi.org/10.4135/9781848608382.n4.

Bishop, R. (2003). Missing in action: Feature coverage of women's sports in Sports Illustrated. *Journal of Sport & Social Issues*, **27**(2), 184–194.

Buffington, D. & Fraley, T. (2008). Skill in black and white negotiating media images of race in a sporting context. *Journal of Communication Inquiry*, **32**(3), 292–310.

Burton, L. J. & LaVoi, N. M. (2016). An ecological/multisystem approach to understanding and examining women coaches. In N. M. LaVoi (ed.), *Women in Sports Coaching* (pp. 49–62). London: Routledge.

Calhoun, A. S. (2014). Sports information directors and the don't ask, don't tell narrative: Applying gatekeeping theory to the creation and contents of Division I women's basketball online coaching biographies. Doctoral dissertation, University of Minnesota, MN.

Calhoun, A. S., LaVoi, N. M., & Johnson, A. (2011). Framing with family: Examining onlinecoaches' biographies for heteronormative and heterosexist narratives. *International Journal of Sport Communication*, **4**(3), 300–316.

Clavio, G. & Eagleman, A. N. (2011). Gender and sexually suggestive images in sports blogs. *Journal of Sport Management*, **25**(4), 295–304.

Connell, R. W. (1990). An iron man: The body and some contradictions of hegemonic masculinity. In D. Karen & R. E. Washington (eds), *Sociological Perspectives in Sport: The games outside the game* (pp. 141–149). London: Routledge.

Connell, R. W. & Messerschmidt, J. W. (2005). Hegemonic masculinity: Rethinking the concept. *Gender & Society*, **19**(6), 829–859.

Cooky, C. & LaVoi, N. M. (2012). Playing but losing: Women's sports after Title IX. *Contexts*, **11**(1), 42–46.

Cooky, C., Messner, M. A., & Musto, M. (2015). "It's dude time!: A quarter century of excluding women's sports in televised news and highlight shows. *Communication & Sport*, **3**(3), 261–287.

Cooky, C., Messner, M. A., & Hextrum, R. H. (2013). Women play sport, but not on TV: A longitudinal study of televised news media. *Communication & Sport*, **1**(3), 203–230.

Cranmer, G. A., Brann, M., & Bowman, N. D. (2014). Male athletes, female aesthetics: The continued ambivalence toward female athletes in ESPN's The Body Issue. *International Journal of Sport Communication*, **7**(2), 145–165.

Creedon, P. (2014). Women, social media, and sport: global digital communication weaves a web. *Television & New Media*, **15**(8), 711–716.

Duncan, M. C., Messner, M. A., Willms, N., & Wilson, W. (2005). *Gender in Televised Sports: News and highlights shows, 1989–2004*. Los Angeles, CA: Amateur Athletic Foundation of Los Angeles.

Fink, J. S. (2015). Female athletes, women's sport, and the sport media commercial complex: Have we really "come a long way, baby"? *Sport Management Review*, **18**(3), 331–342.

Fink, J. S., Kane, M. J., & LaVoi, N. M. (2014). The freedom to choose: Elite female athletes' preferred representations within endorsement opportunities. *Journal of Sport Management*, **28**(2), 207–219.

Goffman, E. (1974). *Frame Analysis: An essay on the organization of experience*. Harvard, MA: Harvard University Press.

Gramsci, A. (1971). *Selections from the Prison Notebooks of Antonio Gramsci*, ed. and trans. Quintin Hoare and Geoffrey Nowell Smith. New York: International Publishers.

Griffin, P. (1992). Changing the game: Homophobia, sexism, and lesbians in sport. *Quest*, **44**(2), 251–265.

Griffin, P. (1998). *Strong Women, Deep Closets: Lesbians and homophobia in sport*. Champaign, IL: Human Kinetics Publishers.

Hardin, M. & Greer, J. D. (2009). The influence of gender-role socialization, media use and sports participation on perceptions of gender-appropriate sports. *Journal of Sport Behavior*, **32**(2), 207.

Hardin, M. & Whiteside, E. (2009). Token responses to gendered newsrooms: Factors in the career-related decisions of female newspaper sports journalists. *Journalism*, **10**(5), 627–646.

Hardin, M., Lynn, S., & Walsdorf, K. (2005). Challenge and conformity on "contested terrain": Images of women in four women's sport/fitness magazines. *Sex Roles: A Journal of Research*, **53**, 105–117.

Jones, R., Murrell, A. J., & Jackson, J. (1999). Pretty versus powerful in the sports pages print media coverage of US women's Olympic gold medal winning teams. *Journal of Sport &Social Issues*, **23**(2), 183–192.

Kane, M. J. (1995). Resistance/transformation of the oppositional binary: Exposing sport as a continuum. *Journal of Sport and Social Issues*, **19**(2), 191–218.

Kane, M. J. (2013). The better sportswomen get, the more the media ignore them. *Communication & Sport*, **1**(3), 231–236.

Kane, M. J. (2017). Why studying sport matters: One woman's perspective as a sport sociology scholar. In *Reflections on Sociology of Sport: Ten questions, ten scholars, ten perspectives* (pp. 87–100). New York: Emerald Publishing Ltd.

Kane, M. J., LaVoi, N. M., & Fink, J. S. (2013). Exploring elite female athletes' interpretations of sport media images: A window into the construction of social identity and "selling sex" in women's sports. *Communication & Sport*, **1**(3), 269–298.

Kane, M. J. & Buysse, J. A. (2005). Intercollegiate media guides as contested terrain: A longitudinal analysis. *Sociology of Sport Journal*, **22**(2), 214–238.

Kane, M. J. & Lenskyj, H. J. (1998). Media treatment of female athletes: Issues of gender and sexualities. *MediaSport*, 186–201.

Kanter, R. M. (1977). *Men and Women of the Corporation*. New York: Basic.

Kim, S. (2007). Gatekeeping and homophobia: From bouncers in bars to the macro-social, interpersonal, and intrapsychological practices of homophobia. *Integrative Psychological and Behavioral Science*, **41**(3–4), 303–307.

Krane, V. (1997). Homonegativism experienced by lesbian collegiate athletes. *Women in Sport & Physical Activity Journal*, **6**, 141–164.

Krane, V. & Barber, H. (2005). Identity tensions in lesbian intercollegiate coaches. *Research Quarterly for Exercise and Sport*, **76**, 67–81.

Lapchick, R., Marfatia, S., Bloom, A., & Sylverain, S. (2016). The 2016 racial and gender report card: College sport. The Institute for Diversity and Ethics in Sports. Retrieved from http://nebula.wsimg.com/38d2d0480373afd027ca38308220711f?accesskeyid=dac3a56d8fb782449d2a&disposition=0&alloworigin=1.

LaVoi, N. M. (2016). Introduction. In N. M. LaVoi (Ed.), *Women in Sports Coaching* (pp. 1–8). London: Routledge.

LaVoi, N. M. (2017). *Head Coaches of Women's Collegiate Teams: A Report on Select NCAA Division-I Institutions, 2016–2017*. Minneapolis, MN: Tucker Center for Research on Girls & Women in Sport. Retrieved from www.cehd.umn.edu/tuckercenter/library/docs/research/WCR_2016-17_Head_Coaches_FBS_DI.pdf.

LaVoi, N. M., Becker, E., & Maxwell, H. D. (2007). "Coaching girls": A content analysis of best-selling popular press coaching books. *Women in Sport and Physical Activity Journal*, **16**(2), 7–20.

LaVoi, N. M. & Calhoun, A. S. (2014). Digital media and women's sport: An old view on "new" media. In A.C. Billings & M. Hardin (eds), *Routledge Handbook of Sport and New Media* (pp. 320–330). London: Routledge.

LaVoi, N. M. & Dutove, J. K. (2012). Barriers and supports for female coaches: An ecological model. *Sports Coaching Review*, **1**(1), 17–37.

Lovett, D. J. & Lowry, C. D. (1994). "Good old boys" and "good old girls" clubs: Myth or reality? *Journal of Sport Management*, **8**(1), 27–35.

McKay, J. & Johnson, H. (2008). Pornographic eroticism and sexual grotesquerie in representations of African American sportswomen. *Social Identities*, **14**(4), 491–504.

Messner, M. A. (1988). Sports and male domination: The female athlete as contested ideological terrain. *Sociology of Sport Journal*, **5**(3), 197–211.

Messner, M. A., Duncan, M. C., & Jensen, K. (1993). Separating the men from the girls: The gendered language of televised sports. *Gender & Society*, **7**(1), 121–137.

Metheny, E. (1965). Symbolic forms of movement: The feminine image in sports. *Connotations of Movement in Sport and Dance*, 43–56.

Norman, L. (2016). Is there a need for coaches to be more gender responsive? A review of the evidence. *International Sport Coaching Journal*, **3**(2), 192–196.

Rowe, D. (2014). Media studies and sport. *Social Sciences in Sport*, 135–161.

Sagas, M., Cunningham, G. B., & Pastore, D. (2006). Predicting head coaching intentions of male and female assistant coaches: An application of the theory of planned behavior. *Sex Roles*, **54**(9–10), 695–705.

Shoemaker, P. J. & Vos, T. P. (2009). *Gatekeeping Theory*. New York: Routledge.

Smallwood, R., Brown, N., & Billings, A. C. (2014). Female bodies on display: Attitudes regarding female athlete photos in *Sports Illustrated*'s swimsuit issue and *ESPN: The Magazine*'s body issue. *Journal of Sports Media*, **9**(1), 1–22.

Stangl, J. M. & Kane, M. J. (1991). Structural variables that offer explanatory power for the underrepresentation of women coaches since Title IX: The case of homologous reproduction. *Sociology of Sport Journal*, **8**(1), 47–60.

Taylor, E.A. & Hardin, R. (2016). Female NCAA division I athletic directors: Experiences and challenges. *Women in Sport and Physical Activity Journal*, **24**, 14–25.

Thorpe, H. (2005). Jibbing the gender order: Females in the snowboarding culture. *Sport in Society*, **8**(1), 76–100.

Van Sterkenburg, J. & Knoppers, A. (2004). Dominant discourses about race/ethnicity and gender in sport practice and performance. *International Review for the Sociology of Sport*, **39**(3), 301–321.

Weber, J. & Carini, R. (2013). Where are the female athletes in *Sports Illustrated*? A content analysis of covers (2000–2011). *International Review for the Sociology of Sport*, **48**(2), 196–203.

Whannel, G. (2013) Reflections on communication and sport: On mediatization and cultural analysis. *Communication & Sport*, **1**(1): 7–17.

Whisenant, W. A. & Mullane, S. P. (2007). Sport information directors and homologous reproduction. *International Journal of Sport Management and Marketing*, **2**(3), 252–263.

Wiese-Bjornstal, D. & LaVoi, N.M. (2007). Girls' physical activity participation: Recommendations for best practices, programs, policies and future research. In M. J. Kane & N. M. LaVoi (eds), *The Tucker Center Research Report: Developing physically active girls: An evidence-based multidisciplinary approach* (pp. 63–90). Minneapolis, MN: The Tucker Center for Research on Girls and Women in Sport, University of Minnesota.

4
Women trailblazers in sport business

Lynn L. Ridinger and Donna L. Pastore

Working in the business of professional sports is a dream job for many young people, particularly those involved in organized sports. Although females comprise 43% of athletes at the high school level (National Federation of State High School Associations [NFHS], 2018) and 44% at the college level (National Collegiate Athletic Association [NCAA], 2018), their representation in the sport industry workforce, especially at executive levels of management, is not a reflection of this population. Men dominate leadership positions in professional sport organizations whereas opportunities for women have been localized in lower-level jobs with limited access to positions of power and decision-making (Staurowsky & Smith, 2016). Although some progress towards gender equity is evident in front offices at the league level, women are still poorly represented at the team level, holding fewer than 25% of senior leadership positions across US professional sport teams (Lapchick, 2017).

Within the Olympic movement, efforts have been made to achieve gender equity among athletes; however, there is a dearth of women in leadership positions in international sport. In 2000, the International Olympic Committee (IOC) established a 20% minimum threshold for the inclusion of women in administrative structures to address the gender imbalance in sport leadership at the international level (Staurowsky & Smith, 2016). Decades later, the IOC still struggles to meet this minimal standard with women comprising only 24.4% of its members (Lapchick, Davison, Grant, & Quirarte, 2016). Women constitute 31% of members in the United States Olympic Committee; however, most national Olympic committees have far fewer women with a worldwide average of only 9%. Moreover, women represent only 5.7% of International Federation presidents, 12.2% of vice presidents, and 13.1% of executive committee members (Lapchick et al., 2016).

Historically, sport has been the domain of men. Scholars have noted how sport organizations have institutionalized masculinity as an operating principle within sport, identifying male activity as privileged, and reinforcing masculine behavior as the appropriate leadership qualities required in sport (Shaw & Frisby, 2006). Hegemonic masculinity has constrained women's access to leadership positions and gender inequity has prevailed as an institutionalized practice within sport organizations (Cunningham, 2008). Furthermore, women working in the sport industry are more likely than men to be placed in marginalized positions (Whisenant, Pederson, & Obenour, 2002), face obstacles in their career progression (Ingles, Danylchuk, & Pastore, 2000), encounter work–family conflict (Dixon & Bruening, 2005), and lack access to networks, mentoring, and role models (Darvin & Sagas, 2017).

Despite these barriers, there are many success stories of women who have achieved high-ranking management positions and made significant contributions to teams, leagues, and corporations associated with professional and international sport. The stories behind these female pioneers are fascinating and inspirational for the next generation of women who aspire to advance in sport business careers. Rather than attempt to identify and mention all of the women trailblazers, this chapter focuses on just a few of these amazing women, highlighting different individuals within several sectors of the sport industry. This chapter profiles their stories of success and notes the challenges they faced as business leaders working in the male-dominated world of sport.

Baseball

Effa Manley

Effa Manley (March 27, 1897 to April 16, 1981) was the first woman inducted into the National Baseball Hall of Fame. The induction occurred in 2006, 25 years after her death. She and husband Abe were co-owners of Newark Eagles of the Negro National League from 1936 to 1948. Abe provided the money and Effa provided the organization, business expertise, and professionalism, not only for running the team, but also for raising the profile of the Negro Leagues in general (National Baseball Hall of Fame, n.d.). "Few women in baseball have understood how a front office's mosaic of politics, power, money and sport fit together like Effa Manley did" (Ardell, 2005, p. 167). As a result of her business acumen, Manley handled contracts and travel schedules for the Eagles, and she was known for her keen ability to promote the team (National Baseball Hall of Fame, n.d.). As a businesswoman in a man's world and during times of entrenched segregation and racial discrimination, Manley forged ahead in the face of opposition. At an owners' meeting in 1937, another team owner told Abe Manley to "keep your wife at home" after Effa Manley delivered an unfavorable assessment of the league (Luke, 2011). Throughout her ownership, Manley was a leading voice among Negro League owners as she proposed a number of reforms and pushed the envelope to develop a better league. According to Frank "Fay" Young, a sportswriter for the Chicago Defender, "Mrs. Manley knows a few things about baseball and most of the men club owners could take a few tips from her. She is a good business woman" (National Baseball Hall of Fame, n.d., para. 6).

One of Manley's greatest contributions as an owner was fighting for compensation for team owners following Branch Rickey's signing of Jackie Robinson from the Negro Leagues to play Major League Baseball (MLB). Through the efforts of Manley, the Negro Leagues received compensation for Larry Doby, the first African American to play in the MLB American League. This established a precedent for player compensation and provided the Negro Leagues with a new sense of legitimacy and respect from MLB (National Baseball Hall of Fame, n.d.).

Manley was committed not only to baseball and earning respect for the Negro Leagues, but also to civil rights and social activism (National Baseball Hall of Fame, n.d.). Manley worked hard to improve social conditions by marching in picket lines, sponsoring benefit games, and raising money for the National Association for the Advancement of Colored People (NAACP). She was dedicated to empowering Eagles' players both on and off the field by providing discipline, advice, and support through pay raises, loans, job recommendations, and working to get players the best available accommodations when they traveled for away games (Luke, 2011). The Eagles' roster during Manley's tenure included several future Hall of Famers and the team captured the 1946 Negro League World Series by defeating the famed Kansas City Monarchs (National Baseball Hall of Fame, n.d.). Manley was a true trailblazer in the world of baseball.

Kim Ng

A more contemporary trailblazer within MLB is Kim Ng. As Senior Vice President of Baseball Operations since 2011, she oversees all aspects of MLB's international operations and is one of the highest-ranking women in professional baseball (Stanley, 2017). Ng grew up in Queens, New York as a Yankees' fan and earned a Bachelor's degree in public policy from the University of Chicago, where she was a Most Valuable Player (MVP) infielder on the softball team (Caple, 2015). Ng's career in MLB began as an intern for the Chicago White Sox, where she was soon offered a full-time job as Special Projects Analyst in 1991 due to her impressive skills in research and analytics. In 1995, she was promoted to Assistant Director of Baseball Operations for the White Sox and was involved in all facets of daily operations, including contract negotiations, trades and free agent signings, presenting arbitration cases, and tracking player movement (Ardell, 2005).

Ng then spent a year working in the American League front office before being hired by the New York Yankees and becoming the youngest Assistant General Manager in MLB at age 29. By successfully negotiating the contracts of Derek Jeter and Mariano Rivera, among others, she helped Yankees' General Manager Brian Cushman build a team that won three World Series championships in four years (Caple, 2015). In 2001, Ng joined the Los Angeles Dodgers as Vice President and Assistant General Manager. She was the first woman to interview for a General Manager's position when she did so with the Dodgers in 2005. She did not get that job or four other general manager positions that she interviewed for in later years.

According to Joe Torre, MLB's Executive Vice President for Operations, Ng has all of the qualifications needed to be a general manager including broad experience in both the board room and the negotiating room, excellent communications skills, a thorough knowledge of the game, and the drive to handle a demanding schedule. Torre said, "I always talk her up at owners meetings. At some point, somebody just has to ignore the fact that she's a woman and just make a baseball decision" (Caple, 2015, para. 8). In a *SportsBusiness Journal* article, McDonnell (2010) stated, "It saddens me to say that if Ng were a man, she would have become a general manager years ago based solely on her baseball pedigree, vast experience in contract negotiations and her two decades of service to the sport. Unfortunately, it will take an epiphany by one progressive owner to realize that gender should not be a deciding factor in who will run the baseball operations department" (para. 5).

Although Ng has not given up on the prospect of becoming a general manager; she is pragmatic regarding the fact that there are only 30 general manager positions in MLB and is grateful for the opportunities she had to contribute to MLB at both the team and the league levels (Ross, 2011). Ng is comfortable working in the male-dominated industry of MLB, and understands there are unique challenges for women working in the business of sports, as noted in her comment, "As a woman you are sort of a novelty and people will look at you a little bit differently. You just have to work a little bit harder to have people understand that you can do the job" (Ardell, 2005, p. 186).

Basketball

Susan O'Malley

Susan O'Malley, who at age 29 became the first female President of a National Basketball Association (NBA) franchise and President of Washington Sports Entertainment (WSE), is widely respected as a pioneer for women interested in sports business careers. David Stern, former commissioner of the NBA, once said about O'Malley, "She has inspired a generation of women to understand that sports management was a land of opportunity" (Heath, 2007, para. 12). From a young age, O'Malley was clear about her intentions to run a sports franchise and, despite feedback from her teacher that this was an unrealistic goal for a young woman, she went on to have an unprecedented career in the male-dominated sports industry (LAI Speakers, n.d.).

While in college, O'Malley interned with the NBA Washington Bullets (the team name changed to Wizards in 1997) and the National Hockey League (NHL) Washington Capitals. After graduating from Mount St. Mary's College in 1983 with a Bachelor's degree in business and finance, O'Malley worked three years for an advertising firm before joining the Washington Bullets as Director of Advertising in 1986. Five years later, she was named President of both the Bullets and WSE. When she attended her first NBA Board of Governors' meeting, she was the only woman among 26 executives (Heath, 2017).

O'Malley was known for her innovative business ideas and proactive approach to customer service in meeting the needs of ticket holders, sponsors, and the media (LAI Speakers, n.d.). In her first season as President, the Bullets experienced the largest ticket revenue increase in the history of an NBA franchise, and the team achieved its highest season ticket renewal rate to date. By the 2005–2006 season, the Wizards were attracting more than 17,000 fans per game, had 14 sellouts, and earned their second consecutive trip to the NBA playoffs. In 2007, O'Malley graduated from Georgetown University Law School and retired from her role with WSE. In her 20-year tenure with WSE, she helped shape the professional sports landscape in Washington DC. As head of WSE, she also ran the Verizon Center (formerly the MCI Center), the Women's National Basketball League's (WNBA's) Washington Mystics, and Ticketmaster Washington-Baltimore (University of South Carolina, n.d.).

After leaving WSE, O'Malley taught sport business and marketing courses at Georgetown University, St. Joseph's University, and she is currently a faculty member in the College of Hospitality, Retail and Sport Management at the University of South Carolina.

Val Ackerman

Another trailblazer with the NBA and WNBA is Val Ackerman, who has had a long and accomplished career in the sports industry. She is one of the few sports executives who has held leadership positions in both men's and women's sports at the collegiate, professional, national team, and international levels (Big East Conference, n.d.).

After working three years for a New York law firm, Ackerman joined the NBA, starting as a staff attorney in 1988. She then served as a special assistant to league commissioner David Stern before being promoted to Vice President of Business Affairs (Ralph, 2017). Ackerman was also a board member with USA Basketball, where she played a key role in allowing NBA players to represent Team USA, starting with the "Dream Team" at the 1992 Olympics in Barcelona. She also helped establish and showcase the USA women's national basketball team, whose success at the 1996 Olympics in Atlanta led to the launch of the WNBA in 1997 (Ralph, 2017). Ackerman was named the WNBA's first President and she headed the operations of the league for its first eight seasons. According to David Stern, the fact that the WNBA exists is a direct result of Ackerman's efforts and drive behind it (Auerbach, 2013).

After stepping down as WNBA president in 2005, Ackerman became the first female president of USA Basketball, serving a three-year term and leading the organization to gold medal performances by both the US men's and the US women's basketball teams at the 2008 Olympics in Beijing. Ackerman also served as the US representative for men's and women's basketball on the central board of the International Basketball Federation (FIBA) from 2006 to 2014 (Big East Conference, n.d.). In addition, she is a member of the Knight Commission on Intercollegiate Athletics and serves as a board member for both the US Soccer Federation and the Women's Basketball Hall of Fame. Furthermore, Ackerman has done consulting work for the NHL and the NCAA on the status of women's hockey and basketball, she has contributed to espnW.com as a columnist, and she taught sport management classes at Columbia University (Auerbach, 2013). She also serves on the Advisory Board for New York University's Preston Robert Tisch Institute for Global Sport (New York University, n.d.).

In 2013, Ackerman was named commissioner of the newly reformed Big East Conference, a basketball-centric league that does not include any football schools. One of her favorite things about being commissioner of the Big East is being able to further promote women's sports, and she believes that the Big East is at the forefront of empowering female student athletes (Ralph, 2017). However, she has concerns about the lack of women in the business of sports, stating, "Women are grossly under-represented at the management and board level internationally. There needs to be an improvement. We need to have more women in leadership in sports. The people making the hiring decisions have to bring in women. It's then up to women to perform, get themselves into positions to be hired, and move up. Once they get their opportunity, women have to shine" (Ralph, 2017, para. 33).

Football

Amy Trask

The National Football League (NFL) has long been a male-dominated business. The NFL has seen few women break into leadership positions and Amy Trask was the first female to hold the title of Chief Executive Officer (CEO) of a team when she assumed this role with the Oakland Raiders in 1997 (NFL, 2017). Trask received her Bachelor's degree in political science from the University of California at Berkeley and, while working on a law degree at the University of Southern California, she interned with the Los Angeles Raiders legal department (NFL Executive, 2016). After working for a short time with a Los Angeles law firm, Trask was offered a job with the Raiders' legal department in 1987 and she was promoted to CEO 10 years later. As CEO, she oversaw all non-football operations including sponsorships, TV contracts, stadium rights, and representing the Raiders at league meetings (Trask, n.d.).

Trask was considered fearless by owner Al Davis (Silver, 2002) and she did not concern herself with what others thought about her gender. According to Littlefield (2016), Trask said, "If other people wanted to spend their time, their effort, waste their energy worried about my gender – fine. Let them. I wasn't going to waste mine" (para. 35). When Trask was asked if the NFL had to make additional efforts to address the lack of diversity in the league, she replied, "As far as I'm concerned, businesses who do not hire in an inclusive manner deserve to fail. Whatever the business may be, if they're not hiring people because of gender or race, ethnicity or religion, then that business is cutting off its own nose to spite its face . . ." (Bridges, 2017, para. 1). After three decades working in professional football, including sixteen years as CEO of the Oakland Raiders, Trask became an NFL analyst for CBS Sports, and she is also involved with overseeing a new three-on-three startup basketball league, The Big3 (NFL, 2017).

Jacqueline Davidson

A more recent trailblazer who holds a leadership position in professional football is Jacqueline Davidson. She became one of the highest-ranking women in an NFL team front office when she was promoted to Director of Football Administration for the New York Jets in 2015 (Martin, 2015). With regard to her promotion, Jets General Manager Mike Maccagnan said, "She's bright and talented and she has earned this opportunity" (Smith, 2015, para. 4). Davidson started her NFL career in 2004 as a legal intern on the NFL Management Council (Martin, 2015). For the Jets, she is the lead negotiator of player contracts and manages the team's salary cap and player budget. She forecasts NFL salary cap trends and player costs while ensuring the team's compliance with the NFL collective bargaining agreement and league player personnel rules (Game Changers, n.d.). Davidson earned a bachelor's degree in economics from Davidson College and a law degree from Cornell University (Martin, 2015). Breaking into the NFL was the culmination of a lifelong dream for Davidson ("Jackie Davidson defying odds," 2017). Although Davidson may not see herself as a trailblazer (Game Changers, https://gamechangers.davidson.edu/people/jackie-davidson-02), she is very cognizant that, as an African–American female in an executive position in a male-dominated industry, she is a role model for young women.

Hockey

Angela Gorgone

As with the NFL, the National Hockey League (NHL) has seen few women in leadership positions. Angela Gorgone, the NHL's first female Assistant General Manager, grew up in Long Island, New York as an avid Rangers' fan and knew she wanted to work in hockey since the age of six years (Cunningham, 2000). While earning her Bachelor's degree in sport management at Bowling Green State University, she completed an internship with the NHL New Jersey Devils which led to a full-time position as Hockey Staff Assistant. In this role, Gorgone computed statistics, assisted with writing scouting reports and media guides, and helped with community relations (Cunningham, 2000). After four years with the Devils, Gorgone moved to California in 1993 to become the Scouting Coordinator for the newly established Anaheim Mighty Ducks. As one of the few women in hockey operations, she remembers feeling she needed to be perfect all the time, saying, "I never wanted to give them a reason to say, 'Oh well, that's because she's a woman,' " (Commito, 2016, para. 14). Gorgone was well respected for her work ethic and promoted to Assistant General Manager in 1996. She then worked as the Manager of Hockey Operations for the Nashville Predators for two years before retiring from the NHL in 1999.

Heidi Browning

Although relatively new to the sport industry, Heidi Browning is a 25-year marketing veteran who is considered one of the most powerful women in sport as the Executive Vice President and Chief Marketing Officer for the NHL (Stanley, 2017). Since taking on this role in 2016, Browning has been responsible for executing the league's major marketing campaigns, as well as heading up the NHL's environmental and social responsibility initiatives, such as NHL Green and Hockey Fights Cancer (Richards, 2016). Considered a pioneer in digital, mobile, and social media marketing, Browning has spearheaded efforts to grow the NHL by engaging more fans through digital technologies and social media. Her strategy involves modernizing the approach of the NHL to enhance the fan experience and reach out to more casual fans, millennials, and women (Stanley, 2017).

Browning provided sage advice for women who wish to break into sports. In January 2017, the NHL sponsored a panel on Women in Sports Business that covered topics ranging from how women can break into sports to how one can handle the pitfalls (Benjamin, 2017). As one of the panelists, Browning commented, "One thing you notice when you're always working with men is they're fearless. They're fearless in what they say, what they think, how they act, how they behave, and women don't behave that way necessarily. I feel like that's something that we need to embrace" (Benjamin, 2017, para. 10).

Mixed martial arts

Shannon Knapp

Shannon Knapp is President and Owner of Invicta Fighting Championships, the world's largest all-women's mixed martial arts (MMA) organization. Knapp founded Invicta FC in 2012 to provide a major platform for professional female fighters to compete on a consistent basis. Before starting Invicta, Knapp was a longtime veteran in the industry, working as an executive with several top MMA organizations including Ultimate Fighting Championship (UFC), Strikeforce, Affliction, King of the Cage, and International Fight League (IFL) (Kelly, 2015).

Knapp, a graduate of Brown University, grew up in a small Missouri town surrounded by a family of strong women (Kelly, 2015). She always loved combat sports, studied fighting techniques, and became a self-defense instructor, teaching the Israeli discipline Krav Maga (Kendall, 2013). Her MMA career began in 2001 as a broadcaster, conducting backstage interviews where she was able to make strong connections with the athletes. The welfare of the athletes has always been at the heart of Knapp's involvement with MMA. As she said, "My whole entire purpose for getting in the sport was because I thought that I could make a difference. It was all about being an advocate for the sport and the athletes" (Kelly, 2015, para. 7).

As Knapp worked her way up to executive roles with several MMA companies, she encountered gendered stereotyping, which was frustrating, but helped her understand the plight of the female fighters. Several women fighters contacted Knapp in 2011 after UFC's parent company, Zuffa, bought Strikeforce. The women did not feel Zuffa would promote women's fights as Strikeforce had. They were fearful about their futures as fighters and their conversations with Knapp led to the creation of Invicta (Kendall, 2013). Since its inception in 2012, Invicta has been a reliable home for female fighters from around the world, and it continues to be the focal point of women's MMA (Rodriquez, 2018).

Motorsports

Lesa France Kennedy

Lesa France Kennedy's grandfather, Bill France, Sr., founded the National Association for Stock Car Auto Racing (NASCAR) in 1948 and her father, Bill France, Jr. was the CEO of NASCAR from 1972 to 2000. She grew up in the family business and spent many summers selling tickets and concessions at NASCAR events. After earning Bachelor's degrees in economics and psychology at Duke University in 1983, she knew her passion and commitment remained with motorsports and she started her career working for International Speedway Corporation (ISC), a company with the primary business of ownership and operation of NASCAR and IndyCar racetracks (Cain, 2016).

At ISC, Kennedy came up through the ranks serving as Treasurer, Secretary, Executive Vice-President, and President before being named Chief Executive Officer in 2009. She also serves as Vice Chairperson of NASCAR (ISC, n.d.). Kennedy has done much to advance motorsports for the participants and the fans. She spearheaded the Daytona Rising project, a US$400 million makeover of NASCAR's iconic venue, the Daytona International Speedway. She also led efforts to build the nearby complex known as One Daytona, which serves as a shopping, dining, and entertainment destination (Glass, 2016). Kennedy, known for her vision and business acumen, is viewed not only as an influential leader in motorsports, but also as one of the most powerful women in sports. Throughout her career, she has received numerous honors, which include being named the "Most Powerful Woman in Sports" by *Forbes* magazine in 2009 and 2015, "Female Sports Executive of the Year" in 2001 and the "Most Influential Woman in Sports Business" in 2005 by *SportsBusiness Journal*, the "Most Influential Women in Business" by *Volusia Flagler Business Report* in 2006, and one of the "Most Powerful Women in Sports" by *Adweek* in 2016 and 2017 (ISC, 2018).

Kennedy attributes the success of NASCAR not only to her grandfather and father, but also to the women in her life. Kennedy's grandmother, Anne B. France, was the de facto Chief Financial Officer who kept the books, controlled the purse strings, and built the France family fortune (McGee, 2013). Her mother, Betty Jane France, was instrumental in getting more women involved in motorsports by convincing her husband that women should be allowed to work in the garage and pit areas where they had been excluded for decades. She also made her husband aware of the importance of social responsibility and community outreach, and created the NASCAR Foundation (McGee, 2013). Kennedy, inspired by trailblazers in her own family, now serves as the role model for other women who aspire to work in motorsports, an industry dominated by men.

Olympics

Anita DeFrantz

Anita DeFrantz is known around the world for her contributions to the IOC. DeFrantz was the first woman and the first African–American to represent the United States as a member of the IOC when she was elected in 1986. In 1992, she was named a member of the IOC Executive Board and, in 1997, she became the organization's first female Vice President and served in this role until 2001 (see http://anitadefrantz.com/about). She is currently back on the IOC Executive Board after being re-elected in 2013 (see https://www.teamusa.org/About-the-USOC/Inside-the-USOC/Leadership/Board-of-Directors/Anita-L-DeFrantz). She has served on various IOC committees, including the Legal Affairs Commission, the Finance Commission, the Summer Programs Commission, and the Commission on Women in Sports. She is credited with greatly increasing the number of opportunities for women's competition in the Olympic Games. DeFrantz was responsible for spearheading a policy stipulating that by 2000 women must make up at least 10% of the IOC board and 10% of the boards for all 197 National Olympic Committees. She then pushed to raise that to 20% by 2005 (see http://anitadefrantz.com/about).

DeFrantz first became associated with the Olympics through the sport of rowing. She was introduced to the sport as an undergraduate student at Connecticut College, where she earned her Bachelor's degree in philosophy in 1974 before earning a Juris Doctorate degree from the University of Pennsylvania in 1977. DeFrantz was the captain of the US women's eight rowing team that won a bronze medal in the 1976 Montreal Olympics, and she was a member of the 1980 US Olympic team, but did not get to compete because the United States boycotted the Olympic Games being held in Moscow (Penn Biographies, n.d.). DeFrantz was the most outspoken athlete to take a stand against President Jimmy Carter's decision to boycott the Olympics and she brought worldwide attention to the plight of US athletes (Dwyre, 2015).

In addition to her work with the IOC, DeFrantz has been a member of the United States Olympic Committee (USOC) since 1976 and she served as Vice President of the

1984 Los Angeles Olympic Organizing Committee. From 1987 to 2015, DeFrantz served as president of the LA84 Foundation, which was formed to manage the US$93 million surplus that was southern California's share from the Los Angeles Games. Over the years, these funds have grown and the LA84 Foundation has invested more than US$225 million back into the community to support thousands of youth sport organizations (Dwyre, 2015). In 2015, DeFrantz started the Tubman Truth Corporation, an organization dedicated to providing liberty and justice for all people. It was named for Harriet Tubman and Sojourner Truth, two women known for their efforts to abolish slavery and to gain voting rights for women (see https://www.teamusa.org/About-the-USOC/Inside-the-USOC/Leadership/Board-of-Directors/Anita-L-DeFrantz). In addition, DeFrantz serves on the Los Angeles bid committee for the 2028 summer Olympic Games, and she continues to be part of several sport-related commissions and advisory boards (see http://anitadefrantz.com/about).

DeFrantz has received numerous awards and honors throughout her career. These include the 2016 "Olympic Truce Award," being named one of "150 Women Who Shake the World" by *Newsweek* in 2011, one of the "10 Women Who Changed Sport" in the world by French magazine *L'Equipe* in 2010, one of the NCAA's "Most 100 Influential Student Athletes" in 2006, one of the "101 Most Influential Minorities in All of Sports" by *Sports Illustrated* in 2003, and one of the "100 Most Powerful People in Sports" by *The Sporting News* from 1991 to 1999 (see http://anitadefrantz.com/about). DeFrantz has been a trailblazer in Olympic Sports, and, although she was able to help women obtain positions on the IOC board, much work still needs to be done to increase the number of women in leadership roles in international sport (Lapchick et al., 2016).

Soccer

Kathy Carter

Kathy Carter's love of soccer began as a recreational league player at age seven and continued as a high school All-American, followed by serving as the starting goalkeeper for the College of William and Mary from 1987 to 1990. She then started building her career as a successful soccer industry executive, starting with selling corporate sponsorships for the 1994 World Cup Organizing Committee (Kennedy, 2017). When Major League Soccer (MLS) launched in 1996, Carter was hired as Vice President of Corporate Marketing and she served in this role until 1999. She then worked in an executive capacity for several other sport marketing companies, including the Anschutz Entertainment Group before joining the newly created Soccer United Marketing (SUM) in 2003. SUM is responsible for the commercialization of the sport of soccer, which includes sponsorship, licensing, and advertising sales for MLS and other premier soccer properties in North America including US Soccer, the Mexican National Team, Copa America, and CONCACAF properties. Carter held a number of positions with SUM before being promoted to President in 2010. As President, she oversaw more than 100 employees in this multimillion-dollar soccer-centered company (see https://www.teamkathycarter.com/about). After an unsuccessful run to become President of US Soccer, Carter left her position as President of SUM to pursue other opportunities (Carlisle, 2018).

Amanda Duffy

As president of Louisville City FC, Amanda Duffy was the only female President in the United Soccer League's history. She joined the club as Vice President of Operations in 2014 and was quickly promoted to General Manager before taking on the role of President in 2015. Under her leadership, Louisville City FC quickly established a reputation as a winning team with solid fan support, climbing to the top 25 in attendance across all professional soccer leagues in North America (Stanley, 2017). Previously, Duffy worked for seven years at the United Soccer League's (USL's) headquarters and was involved with strategic planning, league management, player registration, and coordinating referee development and assignments. This included overseeing the strategic direction of the W-League, USL's highest level of women's soccer in North America (Duffy, n.d.). Duffy was a former player in the W-League after setting school records in scoring as a player at East Carolina University. In 2017, Duffy moved to the National Women's Soccer League (NWSL) to become the Managing Director of Operations. Duffy helped launch NWSL Media, the marketing, broadcast, and commercial subsidiary of the league (Stanley, 2017).

Sport media

Christine Driessen

Christine Driessen has worked for the Entertainment and Sports Programming Network (ESPN) for over three decades (Christine Driessen, 2015). After graduating from Fordham University in 1977 with a Bachelor's degree in accounting, she worked at a public accounting firm for several years before joining ESPN in 1985. She started as Controller and was named Vice President for Finance and Planning in 1990, before being promoted to Senior Vice President and Chief Financial Officer in 1994. She has held her current position as Executive Vice President and Chief Financial Officer since 1998 (Christine Driessen, 2015). In this role, Driessen oversees 200 employees and all financial operations for ESPN, a company valued at US$40 billion. She serves as financial advisor on strategic planning for all acquisitions, new business ventures and programming initiatives (Glass, 2013). As a key player in negotiating ESPN's major multimedia programming rights, Driessen has been a major influence in ESPN's unprecedented growth over the last few decades. She has been instrumental in driving financial strategy for affiliate distribution deals and launching networks and services such as ESPN2, ESPNEWS, ESPN3, ESPNU, ESPN Deportes, and espnW (Christine Driessen, 2015).

Driessen has been honored with numerous awards including "The Top Ten Female Sports Executives of the Year" by *SportsBusiness Journal* in 1999 and 2000, "50 Most Influential Women in Cable" from 2004 to 2007 by *CableFAX: The Magazine*, "WISE Woman of the Year" by Women in Sports and Events in 2004, "The 20 Most Influential Women in Sport" by *SportsBusiness Journal* in 2005, and "One of the Most Powerful Women in Sports" by *Adweek* in 2017.

Driessen joined ESPN during a time when women's sports were not broadcast regularly on television. However, she has persisted and made great strides to help advance opportunities for women in sports. She helped establish the Global Sports Mentoring Program, a joint ESPN and US Department of State initiative to provide sports opportunities for underserved girls and women worldwide. She also founded ESPN's Executive Women's Forum, an organization dedicated to helping women executives succeed in business and at ESPN by identifying actions to address concerns unique to women, promoting leadership development, and providing networking opportunities for women. She is a member of the diversity council for both ESPN and the Walt Disney Company, and she serves on the board of trustees for the Women's Sports Foundation (Christine Driessen, 2015).

Alison Overholt

As Vice President and Editor-in-Chief of *ESPN The Magazine*, Alison Overholt holds the distinction of being the first female Editor-in-Chief of a national, general-interest sports magazine. She is also the founding and current Editor-in-Chief of espnW, a media platform focusing on women's sports. In her dual role at ESPN, Overholt is responsible for leading a team in the creation of innovative storytelling for *ESPN The Magazine* as well as developing comprehensive, multiplatform content strategies for espnW (Overholt, n.d.).

Sports and fitness have always been part of Overholt's life, as she grew up playing basketball and is still an avid runner (Jung, 2017). After graduating with honors from Harvard University in 1998, Overholt worked as a management consultant for a couple years before beginning her career as a writer for *Fast Company Magazine*, which focuses on technology, business, and design. Looking for opportunities to develop her editorial skills and combine her love of sports, she joined ESPN in 2005 as a general editor of sports business and lifestyle for *ESPN The Magazine*, and, in 2007, she was promoted to senior editor. Overholt was instrumental in the early efforts to develop and launch espnW and she served as its first editor. She left ESPN in 2010 to start a digital media consulting company but returned in 2014 to resume her role as editor-in-chief of espnW and, in 2016, she added the role of editor-in-chief of *ESPN The Magazine* (Overholt, n.d.).

Overholt has received numerous honors for her work, including being named as one of *AdWeek*'s "Most Powerful Women in Sports" and one of *Folio*'s "Top Women in Media" in both 2016 and 2017. She was also recognized as a "Women of Inspiration" in 2016 by the NYC Metro Chapter of Women in Sports and Events (WISE), she was selected as one of the "Top Women in Digital" by *Cynopsis* and she was named a "Game Changer" by *SportsBusiness Journal* in 2015 (Overholt, n.d.).

Overholt has encountered gender stereotyping in her career as a sports writer and editor. She commented, "Almost every interview I've ever done and most speaking appearances where I've taken questions, I inevitably get some version of, 'Don't you think it's harder for you to do your job well because you've never played football?' That sounds like it's about your experience and your skills, but really, that's about being a woman. None of the four men who had this job before me were ever asked if they played football and they're not athletes. I feel confident about my skills and abilities. I've always been able to meet those challenges" (Jung, 2017, para. 26).

Molly Solomon

Molly Solomon is Executive Producer and Senior Vice President of Production and Operations for the Golf Channel. As the first women to serve as executive producer for a national sports network, she is a trailblazer in the world of sport media. Since taking on this role in 2012, she has been overseeing all aspects of production and programming on the Golf Channel, including tournament coverage, news, original productions, and operations (see www.golfchannel.com/about/bio/molly-solomon).

Solomon began her career in sports production at NBC (National Broadcasting Company) in 1990 soon after earning a Bachelor's degree in international politics from Georgetown University. She started as the first female Olympic researcher, compiling biographical and historical information on athletes for the 1992 Olympic Games in Barcelona. During those Olympic Games, she served as a writer and information assistant to NBC sportscaster Bob Costas during primetime coverage (see www.golfchannel.com/about/bio/molly-solomon). Over the next two decades, Solomon served as the coordinating producer for NBC's coverage of the Olympics Games which involved all aspects of operational planning and program development. She received high acclaims for her work during the 2004 Athens Olympics and 2008 Beijing Olympics as the coordinator of hundreds of hours of Olympic programming across a broad array of NBC's family of cable networks, including CNBC, MSNBC, Bravo, USA, and Oxygen. In her final year working with NBC's Olympic division, Solomon was the producer of the Opening Ceremony and primetime coverage at the 2012 London Olympics (see www.golfchannel.com/about/bio/molly-solomon). In between Olympic Games, Solomon was involved with other major events and leagues covered by NBC Sports such as Wimbledon, the US Open, the NBA and WNBA, and numerous golf productions.

Solomon has won ten Sports Emmys during her career at NBC, along with several other prestigious awards including a "Gracie Award" from the American Women in Radio & Television. She was also named "WISE Woman of the Year" by Women in Sports Events in 2008, listed among the "Most Powerful Women in Cable" by *Cablefax: The Magazine* in 2014 (see www.golfchannel.com/about/bio/molly-solomon), and named "One of the Most Powerful Women in Sport" by *Adweek* in 2017 (Stanley, 2017). When asked how she felt about being the first Executive Producer for a national sports network, Solomon replied, "I work in a male-dominated profession, and for a long time I just kept my head down and didn't really want to address the gender issue. As I moved up and this opportunity presented itself, it really made me take stock and realize I could be a role model. I can show women that there is a possibility [for a career] in sports production. I'm extremely proud of it and I hope someday [being a woman] won't be as big of a deal" (Cassell, 2013, para. 5).

Sports agents

Lisa Murray

Lisa Murray serves as Executive Vice President and Global Chief Marketing Officer of Octagon Sports and Entertainment Network (Stanley, 2017). She has been with Octagon for almost three decades and oversees all communications, advertising, and strategic marketing initiatives for the company. Murray helped build Octagon into a world leader in the sports and entertainment market ("Lisa Murray named...," 2017, see www.octagon.com/news/lisa-murray-named-one-adweeks-most-powerful-women-sports). According to Dunn (2016, para. 1), "Her forte, developing and implementing highly-integrated event marketing strategies and activation programs, is highly regarded within the industry." Her event marketing strategies have been successful at the FIFA (Fédération Internationale de Football Association) World Cups, Olympics, and Formula 1 racing. When asked what advice she has for women who would like to enter the sports marketing industry, Murray answered, "Make sure it's your passion and always exceed expectations" (Dunn, 2016, para. 5). In 2017, Murray was named one of the "Most Powerful Women in Sports" by *Adweek* (Stanley, 2017). She was also named to the *Sporting News*' "Power 100" list, and was selected by *SportsBusiness Journal* as a "Game Changer" and as one of the "20 Most Influential Women in the Sport Industry" ("Lisa Murray named," 2017, see www.octagon.com/news/lisa-murray-named-one-adweeks-most-powerful-women-sports). Murray is certainly a trailblazer in the world of sports marketing.

Jill Smoller

Jill Smoller, a former tennis professional, is a pioneer of female sports agents. She began her career in 1996 working in the mailroom of ICM, a Hollywood, California talent firm, but was quickly promoted to agent (Mullen, 2013). Since this time, Smoller has continued to climb the career ladder and today serves as the Senior Vice-President of Sport Marketing at William Morris Endeavor (WME). She is the longtime agent of Serena Williams, and has represented many other top athletes including Allyson Felix, Rick Fox, Kevin Garnett, Florence Griffith Joyner, Dennis Rodman, Pete Sampras, and Tim Tebow. Smoller is noted for her ability to find crossover opportunities in entertainment and the media for her sports clients. She was named by *Adweek* as one of the "Most Powerful Women in Sports" in 2016 and 2017 (Stanley, 2017). Smoller says her biggest challenge is balancing a personal life with a demanding career. "Nobody ever tells you it is harder to stay high up in the game than it is to get there," she said. "You always think the hardest thing is the climb. It's actually much harder to sustain a successful career" (Mullen, 2013, para. 11).

Tennis

Billie Jean King

No discussion of women trailblazers in professional sport would be complete without a tribute to Billie Jean King. King has been a pioneer and leader not only in the sport of tennis, but also in her advocacy work for equal rights regardless of gender, race, or sexual orientation. She has made significant contributions that have transcended sport and she continues to be a social activist for the betterment of all people.

Billie Jean Moffitt was born on November 22, 1943, in Long Beach, California. She started playing tennis at age 11, and made sports headlines at 18 by winning her first Wimbledon women's doubles title. While attending California State University, Los Angeles from 1961 to 1964, she continued to compete in tennis tournaments and married law student Larry King. She went on to claim the world's #1 ranking and turned professional in 1968. As an athlete, she had a legendary career that included winning 39 Grand Slam titles, incorporating a record 20 titles at Wimbledon (Billie Jean King Biography, see https://www.biography.com/people/billie-jean-king-93648).

Although she is known as one of the greatest tennis players of all time, it is her efforts off the court, advocating for equality and social change, that make her a true trailblazer in both sport and society. King jolted the tennis establishment with her views that the sport needed to shed its country-club image and offer equal payouts to both genders (see https://www.biography.com/people/billie-jean-king-936487). In 1970, she and eight other top-ranked players known as the "Original 9" risked their careers by joining forces with *World Tennis* editor Gladys Heldman who secured financial backing from Philip Morris executive Joseph Cullman to start their own professional women's tennis tour, the Virginia Slims Circuit (Spencer, 2000). This led to the establishment of the Women's Tennis Association (WTA), spearheaded by King in 1973. The following year, King and her husband founded World Team Tennis (WTT), a mixed-gender professional tennis league played with a team format. During this time, King also started a women's sports magazine and founded the Women's Sports Foundation (WSF) with the mission to advance the lives of women and girls through sports and physical activity. The WSF is dedicated to creating leaders by ensuring girls have access to sports (WSF, n.d.[a]).

King's most famous push for equality took place on September 20, 1973 at the Houston Astrodome where she faced Bobby Riggs in a tennis match dubbed the "Battle of the Sexes." Riggs, a 55-year-old former Wimbledon champion and self-proclaimed male chauvinist, believed he could still beat any woman tennis player. King finally agreed to take on Riggs after he had defeated Margaret Court in May 1973. King decisively beat Riggs in straight sets (6–4, 6–3, 6–3) before a crowd of over 30,000 spectators and an estimated television audience of 50 million viewers. King acknowledged the pressure she felt that day saying, "I thought it would set us back 50 years if I didn't win that match. It would ruin the women's tour and affect all women's self-esteem" (see https://www.biography.com/people/billie-jean-king-93648, para 13). She knew the match was about much more than just tennis – it was about social change. It has been described as perhaps the most important event in women's tennis history, and was one of the defining moments in the women's movement for equal rights (Spencer, 2000).

King has been the recipient of numerous awards including being named one of the "20th Century's 100 Most Important Americans" by *Life* magazine in 1990. She also received the "Arthur Ashe Courage Award," the NCAA's "Gerald R. Ford Award," and she was the first female athlete to receive the Presidential Medal of Freedom. President Obama, who presented the medal said, "We honor what she calls 'all the off-the-court stuff' – what she did to broaden the reach of the game, to change how women athletes and women everywhere view themselves, and to give everyone, regardless of gender or sexual orientation – including my two daughters – a chance to compete both on the court and in life" (Clarke, 2009, para. 6). The National Tennis Center, home of the US Open, was renamed the USTA Billie Jean King National Tennis Center in 2006, in honor of her contributions to tennis, sports and society, making her the first US woman to have a sports stadium named after her (WSF, n.d.[b]).

Conclusion

The individuals featured in this chapter comprise a small sample of women who have made significant contributions as business leaders in the sport industry. Although their roles varied, these trailblazing women shared some notable characteristics such as having a passion for sports, an astute business sense, a strong work ethic, and a commitment to causes. Several of these women became passionate about sports through their own participation and they attributed the development of their leadership skills to their background as athletes. Ng, Ackerman, and Carter excelled as intercollegiate athletes while King, Smoller, and Duffy competed at the professional level and DeFrantz was an Olympic bronze medal winner. Higher education was another aspect contributing to the success of these women. Many had advanced degrees, including Ackerman, Trask, Davidson, and DeFrantz with Juris Doctorates. They have used their education and training to negotiate contracts, manage salary caps, broker sponsorship deals, implement marketing initiatives, develop policies, and oversee staff.

Keen business acumen is a quality shared by these trailblazers, and their perspectives helped shape the strategic vision for their sport organizations. O'Malley, Kennedy, and Browning have been applauded for their innovative thinking and proactive approaches to customer service and fan engagement. Driessen has been at the forefront of driving financial strategy for ESPN for over 30 years, while Overholt and Solomon adeptly oversee the production of their respective sport media outlets. Hard work and commitment are other attributes shared by these sport pioneers. Ng, Gorgone, Murray, and Carter earned respect through their extraordinary work ethic and ability to exceed expectations. Knapp and Smoller are known for their strong commitment to the welfare of their athletes/clients. Manley, King, and DeFrantz demonstrated dedication not only to their sports, but also to causes of social justice that transcend sport. These amazing women served as beacons in the fight against discrimination based on gender, race, and sexual orientation. Their efforts have paved the way for a more diverse and inclusive workforce in the sport industry; however, there is still work to be done.

Although more women work in the sport industry today than ever before, females are still under-represented in senior and executive levels of management. Gendered processes continue to shape the sport industry and can discourage women from aspiring toward advancement within the field (Burton & Leberman, 2017). In a study on women working in sports and events, Staurowsky, Brown, and Weider (2009) found that women were generally satisfied with their employment experiences; however, they also acknowledged that there were challenges associated with the workforce climate. Most of these women believed there was a double standard that resulted in women having to work twice as hard to receive half the credit. They also indicated that there was a glass ceiling hindering the promotion of women into upper-level management positions. Similar sentiments have been echoed by several women profiled in this chapter, such as Kim Ng, who noted women have to work a little harder to have people understand they can do the job.

Women such as those highlighted in this chapter serve as role models for young women who may be considering a career in sports or other male-dominated industries. It is inspirational to see how these women achieved success despite gendered barriers that are still prevalent in the sports world today. Opportunities for girls and women to participate in sports have improved dramatically since the enactment of Title IX in 1972, and research has revealed consistent findings linking sports participation to women's success in business (see Staurowsky & Smith, 2016). Nevertheless, the increase in playing opportunities for girls and women in sport has not translated into a commensurate growth of women working in sport business, especially in senior management positions. As noted by Val Ackerman, "While the number of women who play sports around the world has grown, the number who influence and lead key sports organizations remains dishearteningly low. This marginalization is short sighted and at odds with the ideals of inclusiveness the sports world increasingly holds dear. Across sports, there is no shortage of areas where more women's voices (and votes) would enrich dialogue, improve decision making and ensure that sports remain in step with the times" (Lapchick et al., 2016, p. 3). As more women move into sport business leadership roles, there is hope that workforce climates can change and more sport organizations will embrace the values of diversity and inclusiveness.

References

Ardell, J. H. (2005). *Breaking into Baseball: Women and the national pastime.* Carbondale, IL: Southern Illinois University Press.

Auerbach, N. (2013). Big East commissioner Val Ackerman embraces critical role. *USA Today*, August 13. Retrieved from https://www.usatoday.com/story/sports/ncaab/bigeast/2013/08/13/basketball-commissioner-val-ackerman/2648761.

Benjamin, A. (2017). Passion key to growth of women in sports business, January 27. Retrieved from https://www.nhl.com/news/passion-key-to-growth-of-women-in-sports-business/c-286191804.

Big East Conference (n.d.). Staff directory – Val Ackerman. Retrieved from www.bigeast.com/staff.aspx?staff=1.

Bridges, F. (2017). Former Raiders CEO Amy Trask reflects on NFL career in her book "You Negotiate Like a Girl." *Forbes*, January 27. Retrieved from https://www.forbes.com/sites/francesbridges/2017/01/27/former-raiders-ceo-amy-trask-reflects-on-nfl-career-in-her-book-you-negotiate-like-a-girl/2/#60044d2374ec.

Burton, L. J. & Leberman, S. (2017). An evaluation of current scholarship in sport leadership: Multilevel perspective. In L. J. Burton & S. Leberman (eds), *Women in Sport: Research and practice for change* (pp. 16–32). New York: Routledge.

Cain, H. (2016). Lesa France Kennedy: Advancing NASCAR with her own vision, March 21. Retrieved from https://www.nascar.com/en_us/news-media/articles/2016/3/21/lesa-france-kennedy-is-another-visionary-in-her-family-daytona-rising.html.

Caple, J. (2015). Will Kim Ng be MLB's first female GM?, September 26. Retrieved from http://abcnews.go.com/Sports/kim-ng-mlbs-female-gm/story?id=34066567.

Carlisle, J. (2018). Kathy Carter leaving position as Soccer United Marketing president, April 9. Retrieved from www.espn.com/soccer/united-states/story/3450180/kathy-carter-leaving-position-as-soccer-united-marketing-president.

Cassell, A. (2013). Golf Channel's Molly Solomon on being a woman in the work of TV sports, October 18. Retrieved from www.fullsailblog.com/golf-channels-molly-solomon-on-being-a-woman-in-the-world-of-tv-sports.

Christine Driessen (2015). Executive Vice President and Chief Financial Officer. Retrieved from http://espnmediazone.com/us/bios/christine-f-driessen.

Clarke, L. (2009). Billie Jean King receives Presidential Medal of Freedom. *The Washington Post*, August 13. Retrieved from www.washingtonpost.com/wp-dyn/content/article/2009/08/12/AR2009081203037.html.

Commito, M. (2016). How Angela Gorgone became the NHL's first female assistant GM. *The Hockey News*, October 30. Retrieved from www.thehockeynews.com/news/article/how-angela-gorgone-became-the-nhl-s-first-female-assistant-gm.

Cunningham, B. (2000). Careers in the NHL: Angela Gorgone, November 6. Retrieved from www.hockeyplayer.com/paid/publish/printer_142.shtml.

Cunningham, G. B. (2008). Creating and sustaining gender diversity in sport organizations. *Sex Roles*, 58, 136–145.

Darvin, L. & Sagas, M. (2017). An examination of homologous reproduction in the representation of assistant coaches of women's teams: A 10-year update. *Gender Issues*, 34(2), 171–185.

Dixon, M. A. & Bruening, J. E. (2005). Perspectives on work–family conflict in sport: An integrated approach. *Sport Management Review*, 8(3), 227–253

Duffy, Amanda (n.d.). Louisville City Futbol Club President. Retrieved from https://www.bizjournals.com/louisville/promo/biophotopage-dup-5/aduffy.

Dunn, L. (2016). Women in business Q&A: Lisa Murray, Chief Marketing Officer and Executive Vice President, Octagon Worldwide, June 9. Retrieved from https://www.huffingtonpost.com/laura-dunn/women-in-business-qa-lisa_b_7541960.html.

Dwyre, B. (2015). Anita DeFrantz to step down as president of LA84 Foundation after 28 years. *Los Angeles Times*, May 30. Retrieved from http://beta.latimes.com/sports/la-sp-0531-anita-defrantz-20150531-story.html.

Game Changers (2011). Jill Smoller. *SportsBusiness Journal*, October 10. Retrieved from https://www.sportsbusinessdaily.com/Journal/Issues/2011/10/10/Game-Changers/Jill-Smoller.aspx.

Glass, A. (2013). CFO Christine Driessen: The financial force behind ESPN. *Forbes*, September 5. Retrieved from https://www.forbes.com/sites/alanaglass/2013/09/05/cfo-christine-driessen-the-financial-force-behind-espn/#36bf649e69bc

Glass, A. (2016). Lesa France Kennedy, International Speedway Corporation debut $400 million Daytona Rising. *Forbes*, February 19. Retrieved from https://www.forbes.com/sites/alanaglass/2016/02/19/lesa-france-kennedy-international-speedway-corporation-debut-400-million-daytona-rising.

Heath, T. (2007). Wizards' O'Malley will step down. *The Washington Post*, June 21. Retrieved from www.washingtonpost.com/wp-dyn/content/article/2007/06/20/AR2007062001514.html.

Ingles, S., Danylchuk, K., & Pastore, D. (2000). Multiple realities of women's work experiences in coaching and athletic management. *Women's Sport and Physical Activity Journal*, 9(2), 1–27.

ISC (2018). Lesa France Kennedy. Retrieved from www.internationalspeedwaycorporation.com/The-Team/Senior-Management/Leaders/Lesa-France-Kennedy.aspx.

International Speedway Corporation (n.d.). Company overview. *Bloomberg*. Retrieved from https://www.bloomberg.com/research/stocks/private/person.asp?personId=355005&privcapId=354995.

Jung, H. (2017). Get that life: How I became the first woman to edit ESPN The Magazine, June 19. Retrieved from: www.cosmopolitan.com/career/a10002145/get-that-life-alison-overholt-espn-magazine.

Kelly, J. (2015). Invicta President Shannon Knapp: The rise of an MMA pioneer, February 27. Retrieved from http://combatpress.com/2015/02/invicta-president-shannon-knapp-the-rise-of-an-mma-pioneer.

Kendall, J. (2013). Shannon Knapp and Invicta move to conquer women's MMA, April 4. Retrieved from https://www.pitch.com/news/article/20568244/shannon-knapp-and-invicta-move-to-conquer-womens-mma.

Kennedy, P. (2017). U.S. Soccer presidential race: Kathy Carter, an MLS original, December 5. Retrieved from https://www.socceramerica.com/publications/article/75957/us-soccer-presidential-race-kathy-carter-an-ml.html.

LAI Speakers (n.d.). Susan O'Malley. Retrieved from https://www.leadingauthorities.com/speakers/susan-omalley.

Lapchick, R. (2017). *The Racial and Gender Report Card*. The Institute for Diversity and Ethics in Sport. Retrieved from www.tidesport.org/reports.html.

Lapchick, R., Davison, E., Grant, C., & Quirarte, R. (2016). *Gender Report Card: 2016 international sports report card on women in leadership roles*. The Institute for Diversity and Ethics in Sport. Retrieved from http://nebula.wsimg.com/0e5c5c3e23367795e9ec9e5ec49fc9b2?AccessKeyId=DAC3A56D8FB782449D2A&disposition=0&alloworigin=1.

Littlefield, B. (2016). No "girlie" here: How Amy Trask became the first female CEO in the NFL, October 14. Retrieved from www.wbur.org/onlyagame/2016/10/14/amy-trask-nfl-ceo.

Luke, B. (2011). *The Most Famous Woman in Baseball: Effa Manley and the Negro Leagues*. Washington DC: Potomac Books, Inc.

Martin, K. A. (2015). Jacqueline Davidson promoted to Jets' director of football administration. *Newsday*, August 1. Retrieved from https://www.newsday.com/sports/football/jets/jacqueline-davidson-promoted-to-jets-director-of-football-administration-1.10698849.

McDonnell, W. G. (2010). Gender barrier weakening in baseball. *SportsBusiness Journal*, April 12. Retrieved from www.sportsbusinessdaily.com/Journal/Issues/2010/04/20100412/Opinion/Gender-Barrier-Weakening-In-Baseball.aspx?hl=Gender%20barrier%20weakening%20in%20baseball&sc=0.

McGee, R. (2013). France Kennedy maintains low but powerful profile. Retrieved from www.espn.com/espnw/news-commentary/article/9301655/espnw-nascar-lesa-france-kennedy-maintains-low-powerful-profile.

Mullen, L. (2013). Making their names. *SportsBusiness Journal*, April 29. Retrieved from https://www.sportsbusinessdaily.com/Journal/Issues/2013/04/29/Labor-and-Agents/Women-In-Representation.aspx.

Stanley, T. L. (2016). Meet the 30 most powerful women in sports. *Adweek*, June 16. Retrieved from www.adweek.com/brand-marketing/meet-30-most-powerful-women-sports-172202.

National Baseball Hall of Fame (n.d.). Effa Manley. Retrieved from https://baseballhall.org/hof/manley-effa.

National Collegiate Athletic Association (NCAA) (2018). Student-athletes 2016–2017 overall figures. Retrieved from http://web1.ncaa.org/rgdSearch/exec/saSearch.

National Federation of State High School Associations (NFHS) (2018). 2016–17 high school athletics participation survey. Retrieved from www.nfhs.org/ParticipationStatistics/PDF/2016-17_Participation_Survey_Results.pdf.

National Football League (NFL) (2017). Influential women in football, June 1. Retrieved from www.nfl.com/photoessays/0ap3000000812590.

New York University (n.d.) *Tisch Institute Advisory Board*. Retrieved from www.scps.nyu.edu/content/scps/academics/departments/tisch-institute/about/advisory-board.html.

NFL Executive (2016). Amy Trask bio, October 7. Retrieved from www.maxwrapup.com/amy-trask-bio.

Overholt, Alison (n.d.). Editor-in-Chief, *ESPN The Magazine* and espnW. Retrieved from https://espnmediazone.com/us/bios/alison-overholt.

Penn Biographies (n.d.). Anita Lucette DeFrantz. Retrieved from www.archives.upenn.edu/people/1900s/defrantz_anita_l.html.

Ralph, P. (2017). Past experiences help Big East Commissioner Val Ackerman enhance conference growth, August 18. Retrieved from www.ncaa.com/news/ncaa/article/2017-08-17/past-experiences-help-big-east-commissioner-val-ackerman-enhance.

Richards, K. (2016). NHL names Pandor's Heidi Browning new Chief Marketing Officer. *Adweek*, September 28. Retrieved from www.adweek.com/brand-marketing/nhl-names-pandoras-heidi-browning-new-chief-marketing-officer-173775.

Rodriquez, V. (2018). Shannon Knapp on female MMA fighters: "I want them to achieve that dream," January 12 Retrieved from https://www.bloodyelbow.com/2018/1/12/16868554/wmma-shannon-knapp-invicta-featherweight-27.

Ross, B. M. (2011). *Playing Ball with the Boys: The rise of women in the world of men's sports*. Cincinnati, OH: Clerisy Press.

Shaw, S. & Frisby, W. (2006). Can gender equity be more equitable? Promoting an alternative frame for sport management research, education, and practice. *Journal of Sport Management*, 20, 483–509.

Silver, M. (2002). Raider family values. *Sports Illustrated*, **97**(15), 52.

Smith, M. D. (2015). Jets promote Jacqueline Davidson to director of football administration, August 1. Retrieved from http://profootballtalk.nbcsports.com/2015/08/01/jets-promote-jacqueline-davidson-to-director-of-football-administration.

Spencer, N. E. (2000). Reading between the lines: A discursive analysis of the Billie Jean King vs. Bobby Riggs "Battle of the Sexes." *Sociology of Sport Journal*, **17**, 386–402.

Stanley, T. L. (2017). The most powerful women in sports: 35 executives and influencers winning over the next generation fans. *Adweek*, June 25. Retrieved from http://www.adweek.com/brand-marketing/the-most-powerful-women-in-sports-35-executives-and-influencers-winning-over-the-next-generation-of-fans/

Staurowsky, E. J., Brown, K., & Weider, N. (2009). Women's reflections on working in the sport industry. Paper presented at the To Remember is to Resist Conference, Toronto, Ontario, Canada.

Staurowsky, E. J. & Smith, M. (2016). Female leaders in corporate sport. In E. J. Staurowsky (ed.), *Women and Sport: Continuing a journey of liberation and celebration* (pp. 195–210). Champaign, IL: Human Kinetics.

Trask, Amy (n.d.). NFL Analyst. Retrieved from https://www.cbspressexpress.com/cbs-sports-network/shows/that-other-pregame-show/bios?id=amy-trask.

University of South Carolina (n.d.). College of Hospitality, Retail and Sport Management – Susan O'Malley. Retrieved from https://www.sc.edu/study/colleges_schools/hrsm/faculty-staff/omalley_susan.php,

Whisenant, W. A., Pederson, P. M., & Obenour, B. L. (2002). Success and gender: Determining the rate of advancement for intercollegiate athletic directors. *Sex Roles*, **47**, 485–491.

Women's Sports Foundation (n.d.[a]). About us – history. Retrieved from https://www.womenssportsfoundation.org/about-us/foundation-history.

Women's Sports Foundation (n.d.[b]). Our athletes – Billie Jean King. Retrieved from https://www.womenssportsfoundation.org/athletes/our-athletes/billie-jean-king.

5

The history of women in sport management academe and the treatment of female faculty members in sport management higher education

Elizabeth Taylor and Elizabeth A. Gregg

Creation and growth of sport management programs

Sport management is a relatively young discipline within the academy. Four scholars, all trained as sport historians, are credited with providing the theoretical foundation for the discipline. Earle Zeigler, Guy Lewis, Stephen Hardy, and Lawrence W. Fielding are considered to be the "founding fathers" of sport management. The four men adopted models, theories, and other business-related ideas from the Harvard School of Business and essentially applied them to sport models. Each academic employed case studies from Harvard as teaching tools. They also wrote textbooks that contained models and information that later served as references for seminal studies (de Wilde, Seifried, & Adelman, 2010).

The founding fathers established academic programs and professional organizations. Zeigler founded the first academic program in sport management at the University of Western Ontario in the early 1950s. James G. Mason established the first sport management program in the United States at Ohio University in 1966. Each program was created to meet the growing need for individuals trained in the business of sport to fill vacancies in a range of organizations. Zeigler went on to be a founding member of the North American Society for Sport Management (NASSM) in September of 1985 (de Wilde et al., 2010; Gregg, Pitts, & Pedersen, 2019). The original purpose of NASSM was to create a forum where scholars could discuss common concerns, interests, and needs. NASSM is currently the largest professional organization within the sport management discipline. The organization holds an annual conference where scholars from around the world come to present research and learn about their colleagues' and peers' research projects. NASSM also is home to two peer-reviewed publications: the *Journal of Sport Management* and the *Sport Management Education Journal* (NASSM, 2018).

Stephen Hardy was a college hockey player at Bowdoin College. Although Hardy intended to be an athletic director, he was convinced by his academic advisor to pursue a Ph.D. Interested in both sport administration and sport history, Hardy advocated for more interdisciplinary work. During the mid-1980s and early 1990s, Stephen Hardy wrote several seminal manuscripts such as "Entrepreneurs, organizations, and the sport marketplace: subjects in search of historians" in 1986 and "Entrepreneurs, structures, strategies: Old tensions in a modern industry" in 1990. Each successfully linked different disciplines into a single publication and helped spur growth within sport management research. Also, in 1985, Hardy was one of the founders of NASSM.

When NASSM was established in 1985, there were approximately 60 undergraduate programs in North America. There are currently about 500 sport management or athletic administration programs in the United States (NASSM, 2018). Growth factors include various technological advancements, the ever-changing nature of the industry, amplified focus on the business and financial aspects of sport, and immense student interest. King (2009) determined about 4,000 students complete a degree in sport management annually (Jones, Brooks, & Mak, 2008; NASSM, 2018). According to Hancock and Hums (2011), sport management students are predominately white males. The researchers estimated that 14% are African–American and about 25% are women. Minten and Forsyth (2014) discovered that, a decade after finishing their degree in sport management, 43% worked in a job related to sports. The graduates not working in sports were employed in a wide range of industries including (but not limited to) the military, social work, civil service, and marketing. The authors attributed the low rate of employment in the sport industry to a myriad variables. Minten and Forsyth (2014) stated "a key finding of the study is that sports students do not necessarily enter higher education with a clear intention to work in sport and are often formulating their career aims as they move through HE into the post-graduation phase" (p. 101).

The demand for sport management programs at both the undergraduate and the graduate level has increased exponentially since the formation of the first academic program. The primary driver of the proliferation of sport management programs was the increased business orientation in the sport industry, which created a need for a transition to education programs for students interested in pursuing a career in sport management. Many physical education and sport science programs evolved into sport management or sport business programs to meet the need for qualified sport-minded business professionals in the industry.

Sport management programs are housed in many different colleges and departments within universities, including kinesiology, sport studies, business, and education. In addition to the 500 sport management programs in the United States, there is also growth in sport management programs globally. There are about 35 programs in the European region, 16 in Canada, 13 in Australia, 4 in New Zealand, 1 in India, one in Africa, and 19 in Asia (NASSM, 2018).

In order to address the curricular needs and guidelines in sport management, the National Association for Sports and Physical Education (NASPE) and NASSM created a proficiency-based minimum level of knowledge needed for Bachelor's, Master's, and doctoral level programs known as *The Standards for Voluntary Accreditation of Sport Management Programs* (NASPE-NASSM, 1993). Core content areas included: management and organizational skills in sports; ethics in sport management; behavioral dimensions in sport; marketing, communication, finance, and economics in sport; legal aspects of sport; governance in sport; and internship or field experience in sport management. The standards were created to provide students with the knowledge and skills necessary to be successful in the sport management industry (Jones et al., 2008).

As the need for a dedicated body to oversee accreditation of sport management programs emerged, NASPE and NASSM leaders established what is known as the Commission on Sport Management Accreditation (COSMA) in 2007. COSMA has accredited over 50 programs in the United States since its inception. COSMA measures program quality based on performance in nearly 20 areas. To earn accreditation, programs must demonstrate that they support a traditional sport management education program as outlined by NASPE. Further,

COSMA expects programs to be able to document competencies, including (but not limited to) the presence of a mission statement and program goals, a strategic plan that aligns with that of its parent institution, support for the holistic development of future sport professionals, the presence of ethical faculty members capable of modeling professionalism, and content within sport management courses that stimulates learning and is delivered appropriately (COSMA, 2017).

History of sport business

The landscape of sport management has grown exponentially over the past several decades. In total, the sport industry is currently estimated to be worth US$496 billion a year in the United States and US$1.3 trillion across the globe (Plunkett, 2014). Since 2006, the estimated worth of the sport industry within the US has grown from US$377 billion to US$496 billion (Plunkett, 2014). Growth within the sport industry is easily illustrated within professional leagues as well. The National Basketball Association (NBA) saw television revenue increases from US$275 million per year in 1995 to US$365 million per year in 2005 (Ourand & Lombardo, 2007). Similarly, the National Football League (NFL) saw broadcasting revenues double from US$1.1 billion annually in the 1994–1997 time period to US$2.2 billion annually from 1998 to 2005 (Rosner & Shropshire, 2004). Within intercollegiate athletics departments, increases in department revenues resulting from high-value network television deals and soaring National College Athletic Association (NCAA) national championship appearance payouts are evident. For the fiscal year 2017, the NCAA generated over US$1 billion in revenue for the first time in history, of which US$817 million came from television and marketing rights (National Collegiate Athletic Association, 2017). In 2010, CBS/Turner and the NCAA entered into a 14-year television and broadcasting deal worth US$10.8 billion and recently agreed to an eight-year extension worth US$8.8 billion (NCAA, 2016).

With these constantly changing trends, athletic administrators are now required to have experience with marketing, compliance, and revenue generation (Hardin, Cooper, & Hoffman, 2013). Research from Hardin et al. (2013) found a slowed career progression for administrators; over 65% held the position of assistant or associate athletic director before securing an athletic director position. Similar shifts can be seen in professional sport as well. Growth in revenue streams have been found through increased attention on ticket and merchandise sales, as well as more lucrative television contracts and the presence of sport-specific networks (Burton & Welty Peachey, 2014; Cheslock & Knight, 2015). The consumption of sport apparel and merchandise is a significant source of revenue for sport organizations. In the US, the licensing of collegiate sports apparel was estimated to be worth about US$4.6 billion in 2014 (Collegiate Licensing Company, 2014). The brand Nike, valued at US$19 billion in 2012, is the most profitable sport apparel and merchandise company in the world. The global corporation employs over 44,000 people. In 2016, Nike Inc. earned US$32.4 billion from annual sales (Giegerich & Kish, 2016).

History and treatment of women in sport management higher education

The field of sport management within higher education institutions is extremely male dominated, similar to that of the broader sport industry, in which men hold most of the head coaching and administrative or management positions within the NCAA, NFL, NBA, and Women's National Basketball Association (WNBA) (Acosta & Carpenter, 2014; Lapchick & Bullock, 2016; Lapchick, Malveaux, Davidson, & Grant, 2016; Lapchick, Nieuwendam, Grant, & Davidson 2016). Research shows female students make up less than 40% of the student populations within undergraduate and graduate sport management programs (Barnhill, Czekanski, & Pfleegor, 2018; Moore & Huberty, 2014; Vianden & Gregg, 2017). Similarly, female faculty members are frequently in the minority. Jones et al. (2008) found most sport management programs (67%) had less than 40% female faculty, with 29% of programs having no female faculty members. Often, male-dominated industries and departments will possess a "gendered culture" that is not only patriarchal and misogynistic, but also resistant to change (Bagilhole, 2014). For example, women working in male-dominated organizations may face increased rates of bullying, incivility, and harassment (Vogt, Bruce, Street, & Strafford, 2007). The lack of a more inclusive culture in sport is at least partly attributable to homologous reproduction, which occurs when leaders within a given organization hire people who tend to act, look, and even think as they do. Homologous reproduction is commonly referred to as the "good old boys network" (Kanter, 1977; Vianden & Gregg, 2017). As the original leaders in the sport industry were primarily former male athletes, homologous reproduction is still a common problem in the sport industry.

Women working in sport management or kinesiology departments report facing many of the same challenges their female peers faced 40 years ago related to incivility and harassment from students, colleagues, and superiors, illustrating the previously described slow-changing culture that can occur within patriarchal male-dominated organizations (Ransdell et al., 2008). This type of culture may increase the prevalence of unethical or unprofessional conduct such as sexual harassment, bullying, and passive–aggressive behavior aimed at women. Without proper repercussions, these types of workplace incivilities may become recognized as acceptable behavior (McCabe & Hardman, 2005; Willness, Steel, & Lee, 2007). In addition, these acts of harassment can lead to a culture where female employees feel devalued or marginalized (Hall & Sandler, 1982; Taylor, Smith, Welch, & Hardin, 2019). Research on women who hold faculty positions within sport management programs suggests the presence of negative cultural issues stems from sexism, sexual harassment, incivility, and gendered barriers from students and colleagues alike (Moore & Huberty, 2014; Sartore & Cunningham, 2014; Sosa & Sagas, 2008; Taylor, Hardin, & Rode, 2017; Taylor, Smith, et al., 2019). These reported harassments reflect the broader culture of many male-dominated industries, including the sport industry, suggesting the need for the academic field of sport management to work to create a more inclusive environment as it educates future sport managers. If sport management education programs are not inclusive, it is likely that students will adopt harassing or discriminatory practices as acceptable and continue to perpetuate them in the field. The following sections provide greater explanation and detail on these issues faced by female sport management faculty members.

Harassment from colleagues and superiors

Experiences of sexism, sexual harassment, incivility, and bullying from colleagues and superiors are common for women working in male-dominated organizations, such as higher education and sport management (Jagsi, Griffith, Jones, Perumalswami, Ubel, & Stewart, 2016; Schuman, 2014; Taylor, Smith, et al., 2019). Sexual harassment has many definitions, but a commonly accepted one is "unwanted sexual advances, requests for sexual favors, and other verbal or physical conduct of a sexual nature" (Rospenda, Richman, & Nawyn, 1998, p. 41). The diverse nature of the definition can make instances of sexual harassment difficult to identify. Within higher education settings, incidents can occur in the following forms: sexual comments made aloud during meetings, inside a classroom, or outside of class or work; ogling, staring, and written notes or emails; or unwanted touching, uncomfortable situations, or invasion of personal space (Benson, 1984; Grauerholz, 1989; Lampman, 2012; Pek & Senn, 2004; Rospenda et al., 1998). Female employees may also have to negotiate instances of sexism in the workplace along with sexual harassment. Sexism is the different treatment, judgment of behavior, and belief that women are unfit to perform certain tasks based on gender (Swim & Cohen, 1997). This includes degrading remarks based on gender and questioning of competency based on gender.

Research on female faculty within the sport management discipline shows they experience sexual harassment, sexism, and incivility from their colleagues and superiors. This harassment manifests itself in a variety of actions including: sexual objectification, heterosexist commentary, questioning of competency, aggressive or hostile mistreatment, and bullying (Taylor, Smith, Welch, & Hardin, 2017, 2019). Surprisingly, these behaviors and harassment are experienced from both male and female colleagues and superiors; Taylor, Smith, et al. (2019) found female faculty members received remarks of a sexual nature about their, and other female faculty's, physical appearance from colleagues. Comments received were often vulgar in nature, including derogatory vocabulary such as "ass" or "boobs" (Taylor, Smith, et al., 2019). In addition, a common occurrence for women in sport management departments is male colleagues or superiors giving "complimentary" commentary about their hairstyle and clothing choice (Taylor, Smith, et al., 2019). Even when not given in a sexual nature, the participants reported feeling very uncomfortable receiving these opinions. When participants would attempt to express their distaste, their male colleagues' responses were often along the lines of, "Well, I'm just complimenting you. You should be flattered." These responses offended the female faculty members involved in the study. Female faculty members also received comments of a hostile and aggressive nature from their superiors; one participant speculated that these individuals may be attempting to "assert their dominance" over female faculty within the department (Taylor, Smith, Welch, et al., 2017). The comments were often made in a disparaging nature and sometimes carried a punishment (e.g., loss of travel funding). These comments often came from department heads or other administrators, as opposed to colleagues of the same tenure. One participant described the hostile encounters she had with her (female) department head as she was going through the tenure and promotion process. She recalled, "she reviewed my tenure papers and wrote in one of the margins, 'you sound pathetic like you are begging for tenure.' " Other female faculty members fell victim to false claims of unprofessional behavior from departmental administrators that left them fighting to keep their job. One faculty in particular had to hire a lawyer to fight claims made against her by her department head (Taylor, Smith, Welch, et al., 2017). Although there was no evidence found to support the claims made, the female faculty member was punished with defunding of travel monies and the ability to make additional money through teaching summer classes. During her time fighting the false claims she was hospitalized for depression and anxiety (Taylor, Smith, Welch, et al., 2017).

Female faculty members also reported receiving heterosexist comments about their life outside of academia (Taylor, Smith, et al., 2019). One participant described a series of "really bizarre and somewhat intrusive comments" surrounding her pregnancies. She recalled, "One colleague said, 'Well, I'm emergency certified so if you end up having the baby here at work, don't worry I'd be glad to deliver it for you.' And I'm thinking, Wow that's really stepping over the line. That's quite an invasion of professional boundaries. No, not interested?" She went on to describe another instance where a colleague asked, "What does your husband think about the fact that you're working so late into your pregnancy? I think you just need to stop working a little sooner." Other female faculty members described instances where their competency and dedication were questioned because they were currently expecting or had children. For instance, several women discussed how their colleagues and department heads questioned their ability to take on additional duties (e.g., summer classes, curricula reconstruction) simply because they had "mom duties." One said, "The assumption was that because I was pregnant at the time I wasn't going to have the time to do my job."

Incivility

Similar to sexual harassment, incivility can occur in a variety of forms (e.g., illustrating a lack of respect for others, rude behaviors or etiquette) and can be seen in all aspects of life (e.g., work and personal: Andersson & Pearson, 1999). Although incivility can occur in all facets of life, researchers have focused on incivility in the workplace because of negative outcomes associated with such behavior. Workplace incivility is often defined as deviant conduct of a low intensity that is not necessarily intended to harm a colleague. Examples of such incivility may include belittling others, showing disdain for someone while they are talking, or engaging in outside tasks during meetings (Andersson & Pearson, 1999; Pearson, Andersson, & Wegner, 2001; Porath & Pearson, 2010). This incivility is often the result of thoughtlessness as opposed to deliberate malice (Porath & Pearson, 2013).

Taylor, Smith, Welch, et al.'s (2017) study revealed that incivility was also prevalent in sport management programs. Female faculty members of all ranks recalled experiences where their colleagues, both male and female, would make unwarranted, and often offensive, comments that questioned their competence, expertise, and position. Female faculty members discussed their experiences of receiving "loud, verbal attacks" from colleagues during departmental or search committee meetings. On the other hand, some faculty members may not receive any interaction from their colleagues. One female faculty member stated, "A friend who is at another school and I had a contest to see who could go the longest without one of their colleagues saying good morning. I won, it was two months." This "chilly climate" that works to make female faculty members feel unwelcome within sport management departments has been found to exist within other industries as well, such as the male-dominated fields of science, technology, engineering, and math (Flam, 1991). In addition, female faculty members described receiving detailed directions on content that should be included in their courses, whereas their male colleagues received no such direction. This incivility toward female faculty members within sport management demonstrates a lack of respect toward female colleagues and a questioning of their competence and content knowledge. This lack of respect and questioning of competence are extremely common for women in male-dominated fields such as corporate America, politics, and the military, especially when women enter into leadership positions (Eagly & Karau, 2002).

These female faculty members also discussed the importance of language when making suggestions to their male colleagues. One faculty member described having to "couch" what she says when making suggestions during departmental meetings. The woman stated:

> For example, instead of being blunt and telling a [male] colleague their idea is flawed I would say, "So that seems like a good idea on this level but on this level, (and this level, and this level,) I don't see how that would work. Here are my concerns . . ."

Research suggests that, in male-dominated organizations, male employees may be the common perpetrator of harassing behaviors, but research specific to sport management found that female faculty members frequently engaged in uncivil behaviors toward their female colleagues (Taylor, Smith, Welch, et al., 2017). One female faculty member stated, "I've been burned by female colleagues far more frequently than I have [by] male and I don't know how to explain that, but that's the truth." Female faculty members discussed experiencing bullying from female faculty members in a public setting (e.g., faculty meeting), only to have the same colleague reach out to them and offer support behind closed doors. When engaging in this bullying behavior, female faculty members may be attempting to gain entry into the "in" crowd network (i.e., network of male faculty), in an attempt to gain organizational status and success. Though a great deal of research has been conducted on incivility in the workplace, and the finding that 98% of employees report having been on the receiving end of incivility (Porath & Pearson, 2013) and 67% of faculty indicate they've experienced generalized workplace abuse (Richman et al., 1999), virtually no research has looked at the female-to-female incivility, bullying, or harassment within the academic world. Increased instances of incivility have been linked to depression, anxiety, increased drinking and drug use, and decreased work satisfaction (Richman et al., 1999; Taylor, Smith, Welch, et al., 2017).

Sexual harassment and incivility are extremely hard to define because of their diverse nature. Research suggests reported rates of sexual harassment and incivility may be lower than actual occurrences because women often do not want to classify their experiences as such. For example, reported rates of sexual harassment are higher when investigators give specific scenarios versus asking participants whether they have been sexually harassed in a dichotomous manner (e.g., yes/no answers: Ilies, Hauserman, Schwochau, & Stibal, 2003). This illustrates that women may not accurately recognize instances of sexual harassment as such behaviors, do not want to classify their experiences as such, or may feel as though harassment comes with the territory of working in a male-dominated department (McLaughlin, Uggen, & Blackstone, 2012). In addition, reported rates of sexual harassment and bullying may be lower than actual occurrences because reporting sexual harassment in the workplace can lead to retaliation, lowered job satisfaction, and greater psychological distress. In certain work environments the most "reasonable" course of action may be to not report these instances (Bergman, Langhout, Palmieri, Cortina, & Fitzgerald, 2002). Taylor, Smith, Welch, et al. (2017) found that the exhausting nature of the process of reporting issues of harassment from colleagues and superiors worked to deter several female sport management faculty members from filing formal complaints.

Contrapower harassment

Although sexual harassment and incivility may be hard to define because of the many different forms and possible scenarios, the typical occurrence involves an individual with greater power harassing or bullying someone of lesser power (e.g., supervisor harassing a subordinate). However, this type of behavior can occur when the roles are reversed, and the subordinate harasses the supervisor, creating an instance of contrapower harassment. Within a higher education setting, contrapower harassment can be defined as "student incivility, bullying, and sexual attention aimed at faculty" (Lampman, Phelps, Bancroft, & Beneke, 2009, p. 331). The faculty member has expert power in the classroom to control course content, grades, and evaluation of the student's performance; however, in the case of a female faculty member and male student, the student may hold coercive power, especially in the male-dominated realm of sport (management), if they behave in a threatening manner (French, 1956). Contrapower harassment can occur in two forms: incivility and sexual harassment.

Contrapower harassment incivility is believed to occur on a continuum and can include written messages, verbal and non-verbal behavior, or physical behavior. Incivility in the academic settings (e.g., classroom, faculty office) can be as simple as a lack of politeness and respect for the instructor or as complex as aggression toward others (Andersson & Pearson, 1999; Cortina, Magley, Williams, & Langhout, 2001; Lampman, 2012). Examples of written messages include confrontational emails and disrespectful or aggressive course evaluations. Verbal incivility includes interrupting the faculty member during class and verbal disrespect such as even asking for a grade change or extra credit. Non-verbal behavior occurs when a student rolls their eyes at a faculty in disdain or falls asleep during class, while physical behavior includes acts of attempted intimidation.

As previously defined, sexual harassment includes unwanted sexual attention such as requests for dates when one party is uninterested, or unwanted sexual touching (Rospenda et al., 1998). In terms of contrapower harassment, sexual harassment may be expressed verbally, non-verbally, or physically. Verbal sexual harassment includes attempting to engage in conversations during or outside of class that are sexual in nature (Benson, 1984; Grauerholz, 1989; Lampman, 2012). The expression of non-verbal sexual harassment includes written notes, e-mails, or comments within course evaluations that are sexist or sexual in nature (Benson, 1984; Pek & Senn, 2004). With recent changes in technology, online course evaluations provide a prime opportunity for students to leave a comment about the appearance of a faculty member with little regard for reprimand due to the anonymity of the evaluation. Physical sexual harassment includes unwanted touching, uncomfortable situations, or invading the personal space of the faculty member (Maihoff & Forrest, 1983; Taylor, Hardin, & Rode, 2017). Research on female sport management faculty members suggests this contrapower harassment is actually very common both in and out of the classroom.

In a sample of 179 female sport management faculty members, more than half reported they had been treated differently because of their gender (e.g., mistreated, slighted, or ignored) or experienced sexual harassment from students, and more than 80% indicated they had faced

Table 5.1 Experiences of incivility

Over the past 12 months how many times has a student(s) done the following?	No.	%
Engaged in distracting, non-class conversations during class		
Never	31	17.3
1–2 times	48	26.8
3–4 times	33	18.4
5 or more times	66	36.9
Showed disdain for disapproval during class (e.g., groaning, rolling eyes, frowning)		
Never	36	20.1
1–2 times	58	32.4
3–4 times	41	22.9
5 or more times	44	24.6
Requested that you make your exams or assignments easier		
Never	43	24.0
1–2 times	65	36.3
3–4 times	28	15.6
5 or more times	43	24.0
Created tension by dominating discussions		
Never	69	38.5
1–2 times	57	31.8
3–4 times	29	16.2
5 or more times	24	13.4
Challenged your authority during class		
Never	87	48.6
1–2 times	54	30.2
3–4 times	22	12.3
5 or more times	16	8.9

Table 5.2 Experiences of sexual harassment from students

Over the past 12 months how many times has a student(s) done the following?	No.	%
Treated you "differently" because of your sex (e.g., mistreated, slighted, or ignored you)		
Never	84	46.9
1–2 times	51	28.5
3–4 times	23	12.8
5 or more times	20	11.2
Put you down or was condescending to you because of your sex		
Never	122	68.2
1–2 times	40	22.3
3–4 times	14	7.8
5 or more times	3	1.7
Made unwelcomed attempts to draw you into a discussion of sexual matters (e.g., attempted to discuss or comment on your sex life)		
Never	168	93.9
1–2 times	10	5.6
3–4 times	28	15.6
5 or more times	1	.6
Stared, leered, or ogled you in a way that made you feel uncomfortable		
Never	142	76.3
1–2 times	28	15.6
3–4 times	6	3.4
5 or more times	3	1.7
Continued to ask you for drinks, dinner, etc., even though you said "No"		
Never	169	94.4
1–2 times	9	5.0
3–4 times	1	.6
5 or more times	0	0.00

incidents of incivility in the classroom (Taylor, Smith, Rode, & Hardin, 2017). Tables 5.1 and 5.2 illustrate more specific instances of incivility and sexual harassment/sexism experienced by female faculty members within sport management departments.

Qualitatively, participants expressed a genuine concern about their experiences with contrapower harassment (see Taylor, Hardin, et al., 2017; Taylor, Smith, Rode, et al., 2017). Participants discussed experiencing opposition from their students based on their gender surrounding topics like professional and academic credentials as well as content area knowledge. One faculty recalled hearing a student whisper, "Oh, we've got a girl teaching this class," as she walked into the classroom. Several other participants discussed how they had students tell them women did not know as much about sport as men did, while others had students report they had "zero content knowledge" on course evaluations despite having a PhD in sport management and relevant industry work experience. Another female faculty member described an instance where a student referred to her using derogatory slang in Spanish, assuming the faculty member would not understand, and illustrating an extremely low level of respect for someone who should receive high levels of respect based on academic credentials and the culture of higher education.

Similarly, several faculty members discussed experiencing sexual harassment and heterosexism from their students. Various female faculty members recalled male students making comments such as, "Ohh, you look hot today," or "Are we going to see you at the bar tonight?" Others reported being told, "Instructors don't look like you!" One participant described an uncomfortable situation where, after disclosing her sexual orientation, her students responded by saying, "You don't look like a lesbian, we actually thought [another female faculty] was the lesbian because of her short haircut."

One participant stated, "In my opinion, something needs to be done about the expression of gender bias in student evaluations." Echoing this, another participant discussed receiving the following comments from a student on her course evaluations: "I was called a 'feminist Nazi bitch.'" Similarly, a participant described receiving course evaluation comments that discussed her "clothes, hair, make-up, looks, sexuality, and fuckability [sic]." Another participant embarrassedly admitted to receiving a tip for making her class better that suggested she "show us her tits [sic]." Many participants mentioned bringing these comments to their male colleagues, who responded by laughing. After receiving numerous course evaluation comments about her appearance such as, "It's so hard to pay attention in class because [female faculty name] is so hot," one faculty member reported a colleague said to her, "You should be flattered; my students never say nice things like that about me." Another faculty had a colleague suggest she, "grow a foot, grow a beard, and become a man," to deal with students when they act disrespectful or disruptive in the classroom (Taylor, Hardin, et al., 2017). This type of response from male colleagues and superiors may shed light on the prevalence of harassing behaviors from students. If students witness male faculty harassing female faculty members or not putting a stop to the harassing of female faculty members, they begin to believe this behavior is acceptable and will begin or continue to engage in it. If an administrator or colleague does not support a female faculty member in these cases, they are assisting in the creation of a hostile work environment, and can be held accountable for it.

These experiences are not surprising, however, given that research suggests students enrolled in kinesiology-related majors (e.g., sport management, therapeutic recreation, kinesiology) report higher levels of perceived hostile and benevolent sexism than previously studied populations of college students and coaches (Taylor, Johnson, Hardin, & Dzikus, 2019). In a sample of over 550 undergraduate and graduate students within a kinesiology and sport studies department, results of the Ambient Sexism Inventory (ASI: Glick & Fiske, 2001) indicated mean scores higher than previous samples of college students (Glick & Fiske, 1996). The ASI measures participants' perceptions of both hostile and benevolent sexism. Students in Taylor, Johnson, et al.'s (2019) sample were found to have an overall mean score of 2.99 (SD = .89; scale range 0–5) and male students scored significantly higher than female students: M = 3.18 versus F = 2.83, respectively. Previous research shows scores for male students range from 2.46 to 2.96 whereas scores from female students range from 1.85 to 2.41 (Glick & Fiske, 1996). Scores of students from Taylor, Johnson, et al.'s (2019) sample were more consistent with research on NCAA Division I coaches; Aicher and Sagas (2009) found male NCAA Division I coaches scored 3.39 on the benevolent sexism scale and 2.90 on the hostile sexism scale, whereas female NCAA Division I coaches scored 2.79 on the benevolent sexism scale and 2.96 on the hostile sexism scale, respectively.

These sexist attitudes could be learned behaviors (see social learning theory literature – Bandura, 1977), stemming from students' cultural background, sport experience, or interactions with male faculty. The presence of these behaviors has negative implications beyond the treatment of female faculty members within the classroom. If male sport management students become sport industry leaders and continue to hold these sexist ideologies, they may be less likely to hire or promote a female employee. Given the prevalence of sexual harassment within the current culture of numerous industries across the United States, and the world, it is important to educate young men and women on what is and is not appropriate behavior in order not to perpetuate the myth that men can "get away with" harassing women. Finally, the level to which female students endorsed the hostile and benevolent sexist beliefs is troubling. High scores on the ASI illustrate a high level of agreement with hostile and benevolent sexist beliefs (e.g., "Many women are actually seeking special favors, such as hiring policies that favor them over men, under the guise of asking for 'equality.' " "A good woman should be set on a pedestal by her man"). High scores within a population of women may indicate female students are attempting to align their beliefs with those of the dominant group (males) in order to be successful in the field and distance themselves from negative gender stereotypes (Aicher & Sagas, 2009; Fernández, Castro, Otero, Foltz, & Lorenzo, 2006). This type of behavior from female students will work to ensure only that the harassing behavior and discriminatory culture of the sport industry and sport management departments do not change. Although many teams and sport organizations are attempting to increase diversity through the creation of chief diversity officers and working groups that focus on diversity initiatives, it is imperative the industry understands the need to create targeted strategies to create a culture that will support and retain a diverse workforce. The time has come for the entire field of sport management to respond to continued calls for diversity within our field and industry, and demonstrate how the culture perpetuated by the history of sport will no longer be tolerated.

Conclusion

Over the past several decades we have seen an increase in the business orientation of sport organizations, creating a need for a greater business emphasis of sport management programs across the world. The growth in the sport industry has increased the number and scope of positions within sport organizations, and allowed the number of sport management academic programs to grow tremendously.

Much like the broader sport industry, sport management programs within higher education institutions are male dominated in terms of both students and faculty. This dynamic can create a hostile environment for female students and faculty members. Research shows that female faculty members still face harassment and discrimination similar to that experienced 40 years ago, suggesting a lack of cultural change. Female sport management faculty members report sexual harassment and incivility from their students, colleagues, and superiors, whereas female sport management students have been found to have higher levels of sexism than the general student body population. To increase diversity within sport management departments and sport organizations, a cultural change reflecting the inclusion of women is necessary. Research suggests that diversity is imperative for the success of an organization, but organizations can attain prolonged diversity only through an inclusive culture. Changes are necessary in order to see continued growth.

Future research should continue to assess the climate within both sport management departments and sport organizations. There is a dearth of research on the experiences of female students within sport management departments and female student interns within sport organizations. These are important populations to engage with because they are the future of sport management and their experiences may shed light on the lack of women within decision-making positions at sport organizations. In addition, a continued investigation of the experiences of female faculty members within sport management programs is needed to understand better how to change the current hostile culture. Research should also explore the experiences of male sport management faculty members, because little is known about their workplace harassment, incivility, institutional supports, job satisfaction, turnover, or well-being.

Leader profile: Dr. Joy DeSensi

Figure 5.1 Joy DeSensi
Photo courtesy of the University of Tennessee

Despite the male-dominated nature of the field of sport management in higher education, the history of a lack of female representation among faculty members and students in this field, and the well-documented challenges that female faculty members face (i.e., incivility and sexual harassment from students, colleagues, and superiors; Taylor, Hardin, et al., 2017; Taylor, Smith, Rode, et al., 2017; Taylor, Smith, Welch, et al., 2017), strong, successful female faculty members who serve as role models and mentors for others in the field do exist. Women trailblazers who helped increase opportunities for women within higher education, and more specifically sport management programs, have made an indelible mark on the field. One notable sport management pioneer was Dr. Joy DeSensi, who lost a long battle with cancer in April 2017.

Dr. DeSensi was a pre-Title IX intercollegiate athlete (rifle) at West Liberty University in West Virginia, and a shooter on the 1968 Olympic rifle team. She received her Master's degree in education from the University of Memphis, Memphis, TN and her doctorate in sport philosophy and administrative theory from the University of North Carolina at Greensboro. During her nearly 40 years spent at the University of Tennessee she served as a professor of kinesiology, recreation, and sport studies in the College of Education, Health, and Human Sciences. She also held roles as department chair and associate dean of the graduate school. Dr. DeSensi played a role in the creation of the North American Society for Sport Management (NASSM), and was honored with the inaugural diversity award for extraordinary contributions to promote diversity and inclusion in 2013. Throughout her career, she was also honored with numerous professional awards including: Scholar Lifetime Achievement Award from the Southern Sport Management Association in 2015; the Rachel Bryant Lecture Award from the National Association for Girls and Women in Sport in 2010; the Distinguished Scholar Award from the National Association for Kinesiology in Higher Education in 2010; and the President's Award from the National Association for Girls and Women in Sport in 2005. In 2015 Dr. DeSensi was named as a fellow of the National Association for Kinesiology in Higher Education. At the university level, Dr. DeSensi was recognized by the University of Tennessee as a Chancellor's Professor in 2008 and she received the Angie Warren Perkins Award for Excellence in Governance and Administration in 2007.

Dr. DeSensi's research interests included sociocultural issues in sport, ethics in sport, and diversity in sport. She was co-author of the widely used *Ethics and Morality in Sport Management*. During her time at the University of Tennessee, Dr. DeSensi mentored many graduate students within the sport management and sociocultural study of sport disciplines, chairing 18 doctoral dissertations, 10 of which were by female PhD students, and she was a member of 33 additional doctoral committees. Advisees of Dr. DeSensi have gone on to be distinguished faculty members at higher education institutions around the country and work in the sport industry.

Notable mentees of Dr. DeSensi include Dr. Sarah Hillyer and Dr. Ashleigh Hoffman, the Director and Assistant Director for the Center for Sport, Peace, and Society housed in the College of Education, Health, and Human Sciences at the University of Tennessee. The Center attempts to create social change, build peace, and empower the underserved populations through sport around the world. Additional mentees of Dr. DeSensi currently work in faculty positions within sport management programs around the country, including Adam Love at the University of Tennessee, Ji-Ho Kim and Dawn Norwood at Wingate University, Lequez Spearman at St. John's University, and Rebecca Russell Buchanan at Emory and Henry College. Finally, Dr. DeSensi mentored PhD students who went on to work in the applied sport setting (e.g., Kendall Rainey, Director of Athletics at the University of Virgina-Wise). She cared greatly for all her students and was passionate about teaching. In addition to her duties in the classroom Dr. DeSensi helped organize the Best Practices in College Teaching, a seminar course for doctoral students and junior faculty at the University of Tennessee. She also served as a member on the Commission for Women, College Mentoring Council, and Women's Studies Advisory Board. In addition, Dr. DeSensi served as a role model for women in sport around the world by illustrating how women can achieve success in a male-dominated industry.

References

Acosta, R. V. & Carpenter, L. J. (2014). Women in intercollegiate sport: A longitudinal, national study, thirty-five year update, 1977–2012. Unpublished manuscript. Retrieved from http://acostacarpenter.org/AcostaCarpenter2012.pdf.

Aicher T. J. & Sagas, M. (2009). Sexist beliefs affect perceived treatment discrimination among college coaches in Division I intercollegiate athletics. *International Journal of Sport Management*, **10**, 243–262.

Andersson, L. M. & Pearson, C. M. (1999). Tit for tat? The spiraling effect of incivility in the workplace. *Academy of Management Review*, **24**, 452–471.

Bagilhole, B. (2014). Challenging gender boundaries: Pressure and constraints on women in non-traditional occupations. In S. Kumra, R. Simpson, and R. J. Burke (eds), *The Oxford Handbook of Gender in Organizations* (pp. 393–416). Oxford: Oxford University Press.

Bandura, A. (1977). Self-efficacy: Toward a unifying theory of behavioral change. *Psychological Review*, **84**, 191–215.

Barnhill, C. R., Czekanski, W. A., & Pfleegor, A. G. (2018). Getting to know our students: A snapshot of Sport Management students' demographics and career expectations in the United States. *Sport Management Education Journal*, **12**, 1–14.

Benson, K. A. (1984). Comment on Crocker's "An analysis of university definitions of sexual harassment." *Signs*, **9**(3), 516–519.

Bergman, M., Langhout, R. D., Palmieri, P., Cortina, L. M., & Fitzgerald, L. F. (2002). The (un)reasonableness of reporting: Antecedents and consequences of reporting sexual harassment. *Journal of Applied Psychology*, **87**, 230–242.

Burton, L. & Welty Peachey, J. (2014). Ethical leadership in intercollegiate sport: Challenges, opportunities, future directions. *Journal of Intercollegiate Sport*, **7**(1), 1–10.

Cheslock, J. J. & Knight, D. B. (2015). Diverging revenues, cascading expenditures, and ensuing subsidies: The unbalanced and growing financial strain of intercollegiate athletics on universities and their students. *Journal of Higher Education*, **86**(3), 417–447.

Collegiate Licensing Company (2014). CLC names top selling universities and manufacturers for 2013–14. Retrieved from www.clc.com/News/Annual-Rankings-2013-14.aspx.

Commission on Sport Management Accreditation (COSMA) (2017). Characteristics of excellence in sport management education. Retrieved from www.cosmaweb.org/academic-quality.html.

Cortina, L.M., Magley, V.J., Williams, J.H., & Langhout, R.D. (2001). Incivility in the workplace: Incidence and Impact. *Journal of Occupational Health Psychology*, **6**(1), 64–80.

de Wilde, A., Seifried, C., & Adelman, M.L. (2010). The culture of history in sport management's foundation: The intellectual influence of Harvard Business School on four founding sport management scholars. *Quest*, **62**(4), 405–422.

Eagly, A. H. & Karau, S. J. (2002). Role congruity theory of prejudice toward female leaders. *Psychological Review*, **109**, 573–598.

Fernández, M. L., Castro, Y. R., Otero, M. C., Foltz, M. L., & Lorenzo, M. G. (2006). Sexism, vocational goals, and motivation as predictors of men's and women's career choice. *Sex Roles*, **55**, 267–272.

Flam, F. (1991). Still a "chilly climate" for women? *Science*, **252**, 1604–1606.

French Jr., J. R. (1956). A formal theory of social power. *Psychological Review*, **63**(3), 181.

Giegerich, A. & Kish, M. (2016). Nike's mixed results: A record $32.4 billion in annual sales, so-so earnings, June 28. Retrieved from https://www.bizjournals.com/portland/blog/threads_and_laces/2016/06/nikes-mixed-results-a-record-32-4-billion-in.html.

Glick, P. & Fisk, S. T. (1996). The Ambient Sexism Inventory: Differentiating hostile and benevolent sexism. *Journal of Personality and Social Psychology*, **70**(3): 491–512.

Glick, P. & Fiske, S. T. (2001). An ambivalent alliance: Hostile and benevolent sexism as complementary justifications for gender inequality. *American Psychologist*, **56**(2), 109–118.

Grauerholz, E. (1989). Sexual harassment of women professors by students: Exploring the dynamics of power, authority, and gender in a university setting. *Sex Roles*, **21**(11–12), 789–801.

Gregg, E. A., Pitts, B., and Pedersen, P. M. (2019). *Contemporary Sport Management*, 6th edn (in press). Champaign, IL: Human Kinetics.

Hall, R. & Sandler, B. (1982). *The Classroom Climate: A chilly one for women*. Project on the status and education of women. Washington, DC: Association of American Colleges.

Hancock, M. G. & Hums, M. A. (2011). If you build it, will they come? *Proceedings of the North American Society for Sport Management Twenty-Sixth Annual Conference*, London, Ontario.

Hardin, R., Cooper, C., & Huffman, L. (2013). Moving on up: Division I athletic directors' career progression and involvement. *Journal of Applied Sport Management*, **5**(3), 55–78.

Ilies R., Hauserman H., Schwochau S., & Stibal J. (2003). Reported incidence rates of work related sexual harassment in the United States using meta-analysis to explain reported rate disparities. *Personnel Psychology*, **56**, 607–631.

Jagsi, R., Griffith, K. A., Jones, R., Perumalswami, C. R., Ubel, P., & Stewart, A. (2016). Sexual harassment and discrimination experiences of academic medical faculty. *Journal of the American Medical Association*, **19**, 2120–2121.

Jones, D. F., Brooks, D. D., & Mak, J. Y. (2008). Examining sport management programs in the United States. *Sport Management Review*, **11**, 77–91.

Kanter, R. M. (1977). Some effects of proportions on group life: Skewed sex ratios and responses to token women. *American Journal of Sociology*, **82**(5), 965–990.

King, B. (2009). New lessons to learn. *Street & Smith's SportsBusiness Journal*, August 24, 4a.

Lampman, C. (2012). Women faculty at risk: U.S. professors report on their experiences with student incivility, bullying, aggression, and sexual attention. *NASPA Journal about Women in Higher Education*, **5**(2), 184–208.

Lampman, C., Phelps, A., Bancroft, S., & Beneke, M. (2009). Contrapower harassment in academia: A survey of faculty experience with student incivility, bullying, and sexual attention. *Sex Roles*, **60**, 331–346.

Lapchick R. & Bullock, T. (2016). The 2016 racial and gender report card: National Basketball Association. Orlando, FL: University of Central Florida, College of Business. Retrieved from http://nebula.wsimg.com/b9943b418cddb15b914afb9d18b62e16?AccessKeyId=DAC3A56D8FB782449D2A&disposition=0&alloworigin=1.

Lapchick, R. Malveaux, C., Davidson, E., & Grant, C. (2016). The 2016 racial and gender report card: National Football League. Orlando, FL: University of Central Florida, College of Business. Retrieved from http://nebula.wsimg.com/1abf21ec51fd8dafbecfc2e0319a6091?AccessKeyId=DAC3A56D8FB782449D2A&disposition=0&alloworigin=1.

Lapchick, R., Nieuwendam, K., Grant, C., & Davidson, E. (2016). The 2016 Women's National Basketball Association racial and gender report card. Orlando, FL: U. of Central Florida, College of Business. Retrieved from http://nebula.wsimg.com/75d5182d7b10f789ad38bc8e9f188ed4?AccessKeyId=DAC3A56D8FB782449D2A&disposition=0&alloworigin=1.

Maihoff, N. & Forrest, L. (1983). Sexual harassment in higher education: An assessment study. *Journal of the National Association for Women Deans, Administrators, and Counselors*, **46**(2), 3–8.

McCabe, M. & Hardman, L. (2005). Attitudes and perceptions of workers to sexual harassment. *Journal of Social Psychology*, **145**, 719–740.

McLaughlin, H., Uggen, C., & Blackstone, A. (2012). Sexual harassment, workplace authority, and the paradox of power. *American Sociology Review*, **77**(4), 625–647.

Minten, S. & Forsyth, J. (2014). The careers of sports graduates: Implications for employability strategies in higher education sports courses. *Journal of Hospitality, Leisure, Sport & Tourism Education*, **15**, 94–102.

Moore, M. E. & Huberty, L. (2014). Gender differences in a growing industry: A case of sport management education. *International Journal of Humanities and Social Science Invention*, **3**(9), 19–25.

NASPE-NASSM Joint Task Force on Sport Management Curriculum and Accreditation (1993). Standards. *Journal of Sport Management*, **7**, 159–170.

National Collegiate Athletic Association (2016). *2004–15 Revenues and Expenses*. Indianapolis, IN: Daniel L. Fulks.

National Collegiate Athletic Association (2017). *National Collegiate Athletic Associate and Subsidiaries: Consolidated financial statements as of and for the year ends August 31 2017 and 2016*. Indianapolis, IN: Deloitte & Touche, LLP.

North American Society for Sport Management (NASSM) (2018). Sport management programs: United States. *North American Society for Sport Management*. Retrieved from http://nassm.com/Programs/AcademicPrograms/United_States.

Ourand, J. & Lombardo, J. (2007). NBA near deal with TV partners. *Street & Smith's SportsBusiness Journal*, June 4. Retrieved from www.sportsbusinessjoumal.com/article/55351.

Pearson, C. M., Andersson, L. M., & Wegner, J. W. (2001). When workers flout convention: A study of workplace incivility. *Human Relations*, **54**, 1387–1419.

Pek, N. K. & Senn, C. Y. (2004). Not wanted in the inbox!: Evaluations of unsolicited and harassing e-mail. *Psychology of Women Quarterly*, **28**(3), 204–214.

Plunkett, J. W. (2014). *Plunkett's Sports Industry Almanac 2017*. Houston, TX: Plunkett Research, Ltd.

Porath, C. L. & Pearson, C. M. (2010). The cost of bad behavior. *Organizational Dynamics*, **39**, 64–71.

Porath, C. L. & Pearson, C. M. (2013). The price of incivility: Lack of respect hurts morale—and the bottom line. *Harvard Business Review*, January–February, 115–121.

Ransdell, L. B., Toevs, S., White, J., Lucas, S., Perry, J. L., Grosshans, O., et al. (2008). Increasing the number of women administrators in kinesiology and beyond: A proposed application of the Transformational Leadership Model. *Women in Sport and Physical Activity Journal*, **17**(1), 3–14.

Richman, J. A., Rospenda, K. M., Nawyn, S. J., Flaherty, J. A., Fendrich, M., Drum, M. L., et al. (1999). Sexual harassment and generalized workplace abuse among university employees: Prevalence and mental health correlates. *Workplace Abuse in Universities*, **89**(3), 358–363.

Rosner, S. & Shropshire, K. L. (2004). *The Business of Sports*. Sudbury, MA: Jones & Bartlett Publishers.

Rospenda, K. M., Richman, J. A., & Nawyn, S. J. (1998). Doing power: The confluence of gender, race, and class in contrapower sexual harassment. *Gender & Society*, **12**(1), 40–60.

Sartore, M. & Cunningham, G. B. (2014). The (gendered) experiences of female faculty members in two health and kinesiology departments. *Women in Sport and Physical Activity*, **22**, 83–91.

Schuman, R. (2014). Nasty and brutish: A scandal in Colorado reveals bullying bros still plague university philosophy departments. *Slate*, February 11. Retrieved from www.slate.com/articles/life/education/2014/02/sexual_harassment_in_philosophy_departments_university_of_colorado_boulder.html.

Sosa, J. & Sagas, M. (2008). Assessing student preconceptions of sport management faculty: Where do women and Latinos stand? *Journal of Hispanic Higher Education*, **7**, 266–280.

Swim, J. K. & Cohen, L. L. (1997). Obvert, covert, and subtle sexism: A comparison toward women and the modern sexism scale. *Psychology of Women Quarterly*, **21**, 103–118.

Taylor, E. A., Johnson, A., Hardin, R., & Dzikus, L. (2019). Kinesiology students' perceptions of ambivalent sexism. *NASPA Journal About Women in Higher Education*, in press.

Taylor, E. A., Hardin, R., & Rode, C. (2017). Contrapower harassment in the sport management classroom. *NASPA Journal about Women in Higher Education*, **11**(1), 17–32.

Taylor, E. A., Smith, A. B., Rode, C. R., & Hardin, R. (2017). Women don't know anything about sports: Female faculty members and contrapower harassment. *Sport Management Education Journal*, **11**, 61–71.

Taylor, E. A., Smith, A. B., Welch, N., & Hardin, R. (2019). "You should be flattered!": Female sport management faculty experiences of sexism and sexual harassment. *Women in Sport & Physical Activity Journal*, in press.

Taylor, E. A., Smith, A. B., Welch, N., & Hardin, R. (2017). Sport management female faculty experiences of harassment from colleagues, Department Heads, and Deans. Paper presented at the meeting of the North American Society for Sport Management, June. Denver, CO.

Vianden, J. & Gregg, E. A. (2017). What's my responsibility? Undergraduate heterosexual white men in sport management discuss increasing diversity in sport. *Sport Management Education Journal*, **11**(2), 88–101.

Vogt, D., Bruce, T., Street, A., & Strafford, J. (2007). Attitudes toward women and tolerance for sexual harassment among reservists. *Violence Against Women*, **13**, 879–900.

Willness, C., Steel, P., & Lee, K. (2007). A meta-analysis of the antecedents and consequences of workplace sexual harassment. *Personal Psychology*, **60**, 127–162.

Part II
Management of women's sport

6

The role of bias in the under-representation of women in leadership positions

George B. Cunningham and Na Young Ahn

Introduction

Across various sport contexts, women are under-represented in leadership roles. Consider, for example, the case of coaching college athletic teams in the United States. According to Acosta and Carpenter (2014), in 1972, women comprised over 90% of the head coaches of all women's teams. Over time, however, this figure shifted downward, such that, as more monies and resources were devoted to women's sports, men filled the coaching roles. According to data from the National Collegiate Athletic Association (NCAA: see www.ncaa.org/about/resources/research/diversity-research), in the 2016–2017 academic year, women held just 40.6% of all head coaching roles. This is the lowest percentage on record. There are even fewer opportunities for women when it comes to serving as a head coach of men's teams, where, of the 9,365 head coaches in 2016–2017, only 465 were women (5.0%). These data show that coaching collegiate athletics in the United States—some of the most lucrative and prestigious coaching roles available—is reserved largely for men.

In seeking explanations for these data, some might suggest that girls and women are simply made differently than boys and men and, as a result, are not interested in sports. Participation rates from youth through high school levels do not support such claims and, instead, have shown steady increases for the past three decades (National Federation of State High School Associations, 2017). Furthermore, gender socialization and differential opportunities to be involved in sport explain many other gender differences in participation rates (Messner & Solomon, 2007). Thus, differences in the number of women and men coaching cannot be explained by an interest in sport.

Others might suggest that the NCAA coaching data are specific to that context, but these arguments also ring hollow. Rather, women are under-represented in national sport organizations, such as the Australian Sports Commission (36%), Sport England (36%), and Coaching Association of Canada (27%; see Cunningham, 2015). Recent analyses of National Olympic Committees show a similar pattern (Ahn & Cunningham, 2017). In these entities, women represented less than 20% of all board members, and 5% of all boards lacked any women. These data show that women are under-represented across many roles—coach, administrator, and board member—in various sport contexts around the world. The data also do much to support Cunningham's (2008) contention that gender inequalities are institutionalized within the sport context.

A number of authors have developed explanations for the under-representation of women in leadership roles, and Burton (2015) offered an integrated summary of the research (see also Cunningham, 2016; Gearity, Mills, & Callary, 2016). In seeking an alternate approach, we adopt a social psychological lens to suggest that bias can largely explain the lack of women in leadership roles. That is, we focus on people and how their interactions with others and their environment help shape their attitudes, beliefs, and actions, specifically with respect to gender. In doing so, we concentrate on the three components of bias—stereotypes, prejudice, and discrimination (Cuddy, Fiske, & Glick, 2008)—and thereby capture the cognitive, affective, and behavioral factors that limit the presence of women in leadership roles. In the following, we first provide the theoretical foundations of bias and then offer research examples to show how bias can shape the opportunities women have to assume leadership positions.

Bias

Stereotypes

Stereotypes represent "the traits that we view as characteristic of social groups, or individual members of those groups, and particularly those that differentiate groups from each other" (Stangor, 2009, p. 2). They represent the attitudes, beliefs, and behaviors people assign to others—that is, those characteristics they believe embody another individual or group of individuals. Importantly, stereotypes are also socially and time bound (Eagley & Karau, 2002). By this, we mean that stereotypes are socially constructed, and what people consider stereotypical for a particular group at one point in time can and frequently does shift.

Cuddy et al.'s (2008) work represents one of the more empirically and theoretically robust conceptualizations of stereotypes. They suggest that people view others along two domains: warmth and competence. Importantly, people can be considered low or high on these dimensions, giving rise to mixed or ambivalent stereotypes. Individuals who are considered warm and competent are generally admired and well regarded. On the other hand, stereotypes associated with high warmth but low competence are commonly associated with pity. People might also be considered cool, or low in warmth, and such beliefs might be matched with high competence—which elicits envy—or low competence—which spurs feelings of contempt. In numerous studies, across various countries, including thousands of participants, Cuddy et al. (2008) have demonstrated the efficacy of the stereotype content model.

Applied to the current discussion of women in leadership, stereotypical perceptions of warmth and competence might disadvantage women in two ways. The first occurs when people adopt paternalistic stereotypes toward women, such that women are considered warm but not competent (Cuddy et al., 2008). As a result, people might take pity on women or try to help them, especially as they are believed to stereotypically lack competence. Within the professional setting, perceived low competence would also severely limit women's upward trajectory. As an illustrative example, Burton, Borland, and Mazerolle (2012), in their interviews with athletic trainers, found that men frequently drew from gender stereotypes to challenge trainers' professional competence. On the other hand, others might view women as competent but not warm—perspectives that are especially salient when women are in male-dominated domains or are seen as a threat (Cuddy et al., 2008; Reuben, Sapienza, & Zingales, 2014). Shaw and Hoeber's (2003) discussion of gendered discourses in sport organizations aptly illustrates these dynamics, because women who were direct were cast as bitches, whereas men who demonstrated similar behaviors were seen as leaders. Interested readers might also consult Chalabaev, Sarrazin, Fontayne, Boiché, and Clément-Guillotin's (2013) and Norman's (2016) work for a discussion of the linkage between ambivalent stereotypes and women's participation in sport and physical activity.

Other scholars have focused on gender stereotypes specifically related to leadership. Schein (1973, 1975) noted that people are likely to develop associations between stereotypes of a manager and stereotypes of a man, in general, but such linkages are weaker when thinking about a woman, in general. Her work, developed over 40 years ago, is still applicable today (Koenig, Eagly, Mitchell, & Ristikari, 2011). Consistent with this perspective, Eagly and Karau (2002)'s role congruity theory suggests that people have different expectations for how women and men will lead. Women are generally stereotyped as communal, meaning they display compassion, helping behaviors, generosity, and courteousness. Men, on the other hand, are expected to display agentic behaviors, including assertiveness, dominance, independence, and confidence. Though both communal and agentic characteristics are seemingly positive in nature, the latter stereotypes are more closely linked with ideas of what makes a successful leader. Though these gender stereotypes have changed over time, especially among men rating women (Duehr & Bono, 2006), they persist (Koenig et al., 2011).

A number of sport management scholars have drawn from these theories to examine the under-representation of women in leadership roles. Burton, Barr, Fink, and Bruening (2009) collected data from students in the United States, who rated masculine managerial subroles as befitting the role of athletic director but feminine managerial subroles as suitable for mid-level management positions. In a study of employees of Turkish sport organizations, Koca and Öztürk (2015) found that employees had a slight preference for men as a manager and that women held less stereotypical views of women as managers. With a focus on coaching, Walker, Bopp, and Sagas (2011) observed that people considered women as capable, but not a good fit when it came to coaching men. Qualitative responses offered additional insights, as one respondent noted, "men respond better to a male authoritative figure" (see Walker et al., 2011p. 168). As a final example, Sartore and Cunningham (2007), in their theoretical paper, argued that communally based attributions toward women—those consistent with Eagly and Karau's (2002) role congruity theory—negatively affect how capable women are viewed and, ultimately, their access to leadership positions in sport organizations.

Collectively, our review shows that stereotypes, as the cognitive component of bias, can shape how people think about women, men, and their suitability for leadership roles. Sport management researchers have consistently demonstrated that gender stereotypes influence how people think about sport leaders and whether women are suitable for these positions. They have also found these effects using varied methodologies and across varied contexts, thereby illustrating the broad salience of stereotypes.

Prejudice

Whereas stereotypes reflect the cognitive dimension of bias, prejudice is in the affective domain. Scientists have traditionally considered prejudice as a negative prejudgment of someone who is different (Allport, 1954), but more recent evidence suggests that this perspective is not necessarily accurate (Brown & Zagefka, 2005). Instead, prejudice represents the differential attitudinal evaluation of people who are different from the self. In this definition, we follow Brown and Zagefka (2005) in suggesting that prejudice involves: (a) the evaluation of people who are similar to the self (in-group members) and those who are different (out-group members); and (b) evaluations and attitudes are more favorable toward in-group members than toward out-group members (see also Brewer, 2007). From this perspective, one may not necessarily hold negative attitudes toward someone who is different—though that is certainly possible; instead, prejudice represents assigning more positive evaluations toward people who are similar than to those who are different.

Prejudice can also be explicit or implicit. Traditional, overt forms of sexism are representative of explicit prejudice. These forms of prejudice are socially constructed, such that people express explicit prejudice against people when it is normative and socially permissible to do so (Crandall, Eshleman, & O'Brien, 2002), and there is some evidence that, within sport, people believe it is appropriate to make derogatory comments about women and their ability (Cunningham, Ferreira, & Fink, 2009). Implicit prejudice, on the other hand, is not deliberately expressed and is, rather, elicited when there is congruence between external stimuli and the association sets people hold that link the stimuli with various attributions (Blair, Dasgupta, & Glaser, 2015). The reactions are automatic, people do not consciously deliberate on them, and they can be activated even if the individual does not believe the attitude is accurate. Importantly, people's implicit attitudes are predictive of their subsequent behavioral responses, just as explicit attitudes are. Thus, though the nature and processes underlying explicit and implicit prejudice are different, the outcomes are frequently similar (Cunningham & Melton, 2014; Reuben et al., 2014).

A number of sport management researchers have examined the role of prejudice in limiting women's upward mobility in sport. Fink (2008, 2016) has argued that sexism is pervasive in sport, negatively affecting women's experiences and opportunities. She also correctly noted that, though many times overt, the nature of sport is such that it simultaneously goes unnoticed and, therefore, "hides in plain sight" (Fink, 2016, p. 2). Cui (2007), for example, examined what were supposedly gender-neutral policies in Chinese national sport organizations. The researcher deconstructed notions of vision, education, and communication ability, showing they were actually ways of expressing prejudice against women and, ultimately, limiting their ability to obtain leadership roles. In a study where the authors explicitly considered the intersection of race and gender, Borland and Bruening (2010) found that black female coaches were very much aware of the barriers they faced in sport, including prejudice based on their race and gender. Walker and Melton (2015) offer another example of how one's various identities intersect to influence experiences and opportunities.

Collectively, the scholarship we reviewed in this section shows that prejudice can negatively affect women and their ability to secure leadership roles in sport. The context is also unique, such that, although sexism is generally looked down on in society, it is tolerated and even expected in sport (Cunningham et al., 2009; Fink, 2008, 2016).

Discrimination

Discrimination is the final form of bias and represents the "inappropriate treatment of individuals due to their group membership" (Dovidio, Brigham, Johnson, & Gaertner, 1996, p. 279). Whereas stereotypes are cognitive in nature, and prejudice is affective, discrimination is the behavioral form of bias. Cunningham (2015) notes that the underlying mechanisms driving discrimination largely depend on the theoretical frame adopted. From a critical perspective, discrimination results from those in power seeking to maintain their privilege and status, subjugating others in the process. Systemic issues also give rise to discrimination, because biases are deeply embedded into schools, legal systems, religious institutions, and other societal systems. From a different perspective, social psychologists might point to intergroup relationships and the grouping of people who are similar or different to the self into in-groups and out-groups, respectively. The in-group favoritism described in the previous section is likely to have behavioral outcomes, such that people might provide more helping, opportunities, and the like to in-group members, relative to their out-group counterparts.

Greenhaus Parasuraman, and Wormley (1990) have further suggested that discrimination can take two forms: access and treatment. Access discrimination occurs when people are denied the opportunity to secure a particular position or enter a given field. It has the potential to affect people who are currently in the field and those who are considering entering it (Bunel, L'Horty, & Petit, 2016; Cunningham & Singer, 2010). Treatment discrimination, on the other hand, occurs when people are on the job. The result is people who are different from the typical majority having differential access to resources and information, negative behaviors directed toward them, and fewer chances for growth and advancement.

Researchers have offered ample evidence of access discrimination in sport. As we discussed in the opening section of the chapter, Acosta and Carpenter's (2014) longitudinal study spanning over 30 years offers the most robust evidence of access discrimination in intercollegiate athletics. Regan and Cunningham (2012) extended on this work to consider the community college setting. Their findings revealed a similar pattern: most athletic directors at this level are men (82.7%), and men are more likely to employ other men as head coaches of women's teams than they are to employ women. Lending support to social psychological perspectives of access discrimination, Regan and Cunningham (2012) also observed that gender influenced the staff composition: women athletic directors were more likely to have all women staff, just as men athletic directors were more likely to have all men staff. A number of authors have offered a similar pattern of findings in their analyses of high school coaches (Lovett & Lowry, 1994; Stangl & Kane, 1991), sports information directors at US colleges and universities (Whisenant & Mullane, 2007), and collegiate head coaches and their staff (Sagas, Cunningham, & Teed, 2006). Of course, access discrimination limits women in other sport activities, too, such as their ability to participate at elite levels (Knijnik, 2015).

In addition, a number of researchers have documented discrimination felt by women in leadership roles. Women working in sport organizations are frequently given fewer opportunities for meaningful work experiences, such as budgeting or overseeing high-profile sports, and, as a result, their work is comparatively limited compared with men's (Hoffman, 2010; Tiell, Dixon, & Lin, 2012). Similarly, in a study of coaches working in South Africa, Kubayi, Coopoo, and Morris-Eyton (2017) found that women reported low salaries, a lack of organizational support, and strained relationships with players' parents, all of which detracted from their coaching experiences. Sagas et al. (2006) have examined returns on human capital investments, such as education and experience, and social capital investment, as well as the type and strength of the connections one has in the sport industry. Their work with coaches (Cunningham & Sagas, 2002) and administrators (Sagas & Cunningham, 2004) shows that women receive fewer benefits for similar investments—a form of treatment discrimination. Reade, Rodgers, and Norman (2009) have offered similar findings in the Canadian context, where women are less likely than men to advance to elite levels of coaching despite having similar human capital investments.

Collectively, the literature reviewed here suggests that women experience multiple forms of discrimination—the behavioral manifestation of bias. As a result, they have limited access to meaningful work and, when they are in administrative or coaching positions, they frequently experience less positive work conditions than men do.

Impact of bias

Thus far, we have reviewed the three forms of bias, all of which, we contend, limit women's ascension to leadership roles in sport. In addition to the direct effects of bias on limited upward mobility, we also suggest that bias might have indirect effects. These occur primarily through self-limiting behaviors and limiting the pool of potential women leaders in the field.

Self-limiting behaviors

Self-limiting behaviors occur when people come to believe or internalize the biased feedback they receive and, as a result, engage in activities that thwart their opportunities or mobility (Ilgen & Youtz, 1986; Sartore & Cunningham, 2007). For example, Sartore (2006) showed that, through the categorization process, people who are different from the majority might receive biased performance appraisals. Over time, the employees might come to internalize the negative feedback, resulting in decreased motivation, confidence, and, ultimately, performance. Note that the root cause was not a deficit on the part of the employee, but, rather, the biased feedback received.

Similar processes might occur for women pursuing leadership positions. Women are aware of the gendered stereotypes and prejudice in the sport industry, because they have experienced such biases or know others who have (Norman, 2010, 2016). Over time, women might internalize this feedback, and women might think that they are not well suited for leadership roles or the sport industry as a whole. In line with this reasoning, Cunningham and colleagues have observed that, when compared with men, women express less interest in being a head coach (Cunningham, Doherty, & Gregg, 2007), are unlikely to apply for a head coaching role (Cunningham & Sagas, 2002; Cunningham, Sagas & Ashley, 2003; Cunningham et al., 2007; Sagas, Cunningham, & Ashley, 2000; Sagas, Cunningham, & Pastore, 2006), and intend to leave the sport industry sooner (Cunningham & Sagas, 2002, 2003, 2007; Cunningham et al., 2003; Sagas et al., 2000; see also Sagas & Batista, 2001). Recent meta-analytic data suggests the influence of gender on occupational turnover from sport reaches beyond the coaching ranks (Cunningham, Dixon, Ahn, & Anderson, 2017). We note again that all available evidence suggests that any gender differences in advancement aspirations or the decision to leave sport are influenced by biases and other social factors experienced by women; they are not the result of inherent or genetic differences between women and men (see also Knoppers, 1987; Norman & Rankin-Wright, 2019).

Limiting the pool

Biases serve to create a limited pool of women who are available to assume leadership roles. This occurs in a number of ways, the first of which is occupational turnover from sport. If women leave sport at an earlier age than men, there are fewer women working in sport who can assume leadership roles. Similarly, when, because of self-limiting behaviors, women do not consider leadership roles as a viable option or apply for such positions, the result is an applicant pool tilted toward men. Both mechanisms serve effectively to limit the pool of potential women in the leadership ranks.

The effects of bias are also observed among people considering sport as a profession. Harris, Grappendorf, Aicher, and Veraldo (2015), in a qualitative study of women enrolled at a US university, found that women anticipated experiencing sexism and discrimination in sport. Interestingly, the students still expressed enthusiasm about entering the sport industry, and Moran-Miller and Flores (2011) have shown that anticipated discrimination does not thwart women's interest in entering sport. These findings run counter to theory and other empirical work demonstrating a different pattern. Specifically, social cognitive career theory predicts that people who anticipate barriers in a career are likely to have less confidence that they will be successful pursuing that path, and, ultimately, they are unlikely to enter the specific field (Lent, Brown, & Hackett, 1994). Cunningham, Bruening, Sartore, Sagas, and Fink (2005) provided empirical support for this theory in their study of sport management students enrolled in programs across the United States. Similarly, women athletes in Kamphoff and Gill's (2008) study, relative to men, were less likely to have an interest in becoming a coach and more likely to point to biases as an impediment. This research shows that women are aware of the gendered barriers women experience in sport and, in many respects, this understanding truncates their enthusiasm to enter the industry.

Conclusions

In this chapter, we adopted a social–psychological approach to understanding the underrepresentation of women in leadership positions in sport. We focused on stereotypes, prejudice, and discrimination as the cognitive, attitudinal, and behavioral components of bias, respectively. The research we reviewed clearly shows that women experience bias in sport and, as a result, have fewer opportunities to assume leadership roles. In the remainder of this section, we highlight three areas for future inquiry and consideration.

First, though there are exceptions, the preponderance of evidence suggests that women experience biases in sport that men do not. The next step is to move beyond documentation of such occurrences and identify ways in which managers and coaches can reduce gender bias. Fink (2016) advocated for similar inquiries. Researchers have shown that leader demographics influence who is hired, but what are other organizational practices, strategies, and structures that influence whether women are in leadership roles? Furthermore, some leagues have instituted hiring guidelines aimed at promoting greater racial diversity, and recent analyses show such mandates have helped create more racial diversity (DuBois, 2015). We are not aware, however, of similar efforts aimed at increasing the pool of women in leadership roles. Why is this the case, and what would such hiring and interview guidelines look like? In short, managers and scholars would benefit from greater attention to systematic approaches that management could use toward reducing bias.

Second, and related to the first point, efforts aimed at creating greater gender equality necessarily must attend to intersectionality, with a focus on how women's multiple identities influence their opportunities and experiences (hooks, 2000). Relatively few scholars have explicitly focused on intersectionality (Borland & Bruening, 2010; McDowell & Cunningham, 2009; Walker & Melton, 2015). However, we see many benefits in scholars considering how women's race, social class, power, sexual orientation, gender identity, and other identities influence the bias they encounter in sport.

Third, much of the scholarship we reviewed was set in the athletics context, whether high school or intercollegiate. Given the large role athletics play in the United States, we certainly understand scholars' draw to that context. That noted, as we have endeavored to illustrate in this chapter, gender bias is pervasive throughout sport, not just athletics. Thus, we see opportunities for future studies in other sport contexts, including eSport (Cunningham, Fairley, Ferkins, Kerwin, Lock, Shaw, & Wicker, 2019; Funk, Pizzo, & Baker, 2019) and men's teams (see also Walker et al., 2011). Our professional profile of Yuen Ting Chan offers more information about women leading men's teams.

Pursuing each of these lines of inquiry will help toward better understanding and ultimately elimination of the bias women face in the sport context. Given the many biases women experience in sport, such advances are sorely needed.

Leader profile: Yuen Ting Chan

Figure 6.1 Yuen Ting Chan

Permission was given by Yuen Ting Chan for the use of personal correspondence and photo.

Yuen Ting Chan is a former head coach of Eastern Sports Club (SC), a professional football team in the Hong Kong Premier League (HKPL), serving from 2015 to 2017. During her tenure, Eastern SC won the national championship and, as a result, her team embarked on the Asian Football Conference (AFC) Champions League 2017 for the first time in their history.

Although the HKPL is not well known compared with other leading professional football leagues in the world, such as the England Premier League (England), Bundesliga (Germany), and La Liga (Spain), it is one of the oldest professional football leagues in Asia (Lee, 2013). Further, football is one of the world's most male-dominated sports when it comes to head coaching. Considering this under-representation of women managers in professional football leagues, Chan's acclaiming performance remains not only groundbreaking, but also sensational.

Not surprisingly, Chan was awarded the AFC Women's Coach of the Year at the 2016 AFC Annual Awards, listed in the BBC's 100 Women of 2016, and placed in the *Guinness Book of World Records* for becoming the first woman manager of a men's professional football team in history. Before becoming a manager in the football world, she was a football player throughout her life and later became a video analyst for Hong Kong Pegasus FC. Then, she worked for Southern District FC as an assistant manager and Hong Kong women's football team.

After extraordinary accomplishments in the football history by leading a men's football team to a top-tier football national league, she resigned from Eastern SC in order to move on to a new journey. She is now completing the AFC Pro License and pursuing a football managerial position outside Hong Kong, China. As a young and passionate football professional, Chan's motto is to have a strong belief, such that she bears social pressures, expectations, and limitations that everyone faces in life. Even though the spotlight and title she received are specific to her and not analogous to the overall sport of football, her achievements are conducive to changing the gendered status quo in sport leadership.

References

Acosta, R. V. & Carpenter, L. J. (2014). Women in intercollegiate sport: A longitudinal study—thirty-seven year update—1977–2014. Unpublished manuscript, Brooklyn College, Brooklyn, NY.

Ahn, N. Y. & Cunningham, G. B. (2017). Cultural values and gender equity on national Olympic committee boards. *International Journal of Exercise Science*, **10**(6), 857–874.

Allport, G. W. (1954). *The Nature of Prejudice*. Cambridge, MA: Preuss.

Blair, I., Dasgupta, B., & Glaser, J. (2015). Implicit attitudes. In M. Mikulincer & P. R. Shaver (eds), *APA Handbook of Personality and Social Psychology*. Vol. 1. *Attitudes and Social Cognition* (pp. 665–691). Washington, DC: American Psychological Association.

Borland, J. F. & Bruening, J. E. (2010). Navigating barriers: A qualitative examination of the under-representation of Black females as head coaches in collegiate basketball. *Sport Management Review*, **13**(4), 407–420.

Brewer, M. B. (2007). The importance of being we: Human nature and intergroup relations. *American Psychologist*, **62**(8), 726–738.

Brown, R. & Zagefka, H. (2005). Ingroup affiliations and prejudice. In J. F. Dovidio, P. Glick, &, L. A. Rudman (eds), *On the Nature of Prejudice: Fifty years after Allport* (pp. 54–70). Malden, MA: Blackwell.

Bunel, M., L'Horty, Y., & Petit, P. (2016). Discrimination based on place of residence and access to employment. *Urban Studies*, **53**(2), 267–286.

Burton, L. J. (2015). Underrepresentation of women in sport leadership: A review of research. *Sport Management Review*, **18**(2), 155–165.

Burton, L. J., Barr, C. A., Fink, J. S., & Bruening, J. E. (2009). "Think athletic director, think masculine?": Examination of the gender typing of managerial subroles within athletic administration positions. *Sex Roles*, **61**(5–6), 416–426.

Burton, L. J., Borland, J., & Mazerolle, S. M. (2012). "They cannot seem to get past the gender issue": Experiences of young female athletic trainers in NCAA Division I intercollegiate athletics. *Sport Management Review*, **15**(3), 304–317.

Chalabaev, A., Sarrazin, P., Fontayne, P., Boiché, J., & Clément-Guillotin, C. (2013). The influence of sex stereotypes and gender roles on participation and performance in sport and exercise: Review and future directions. *Psychology of Sport and Exercise*, **14**(2), 136–144.

Crandall, C. S., Eshleman, A., & O'Brien, L. (2002). Social norms and the expression and suppression of prejudice: the struggle for internalization. *Journal of Personality and Social Psychology*, **82**(3), 359–378.

Cuddy, A. J., Fiske, S. T., & Glick, P. (2008). Warmth and competence as universal dimensions of social perception: The stereotype content model and the BIAS map. *Advances in Experimental Social Psychology*, **40**, 61–149.

Cui, Y. (2007). Striving and thriving: Women in Chinese national sport organizations. *The International Journal of the History of Sport*, **24**(3), 392–410.

Cunningham, G. B. (2008). Creating and sustaining gender diversity in sport organizations. *Sex Roles*, **58**(1–2), 136–145.

Cunningham, G. B. (2015). *Diversity and Inclusion in Sport Organizations*, 3rd edn. New York: Routledge.

Cunningham, G. B. (2016). Women in coaching: Theoretical underpinnings among quantitative researchers. In N. M. LaVoi (ed.), *Women in Sports Coaching* (pp. 223–233). London: Routledge.

Cunningham, G. B., Bruening, J., Sartore, M. L., Sagas, M., & Fink, J. S. (2005). The application of social cognitive career theory to sport and leisure career choices. *Journal of Career Development*, **32**(2), 122–138.

Cunningham, G. B., Dixon, M. A., Ahn, N. Y., & Anderson, A. J. (2017). Gender differences in occupational turnover from sport. Paper presented at the annual conference for the Sport Management Association of Australia and New Zealand, Gold Coast, Australia, November.

Cunningham, G. B., Doherty, A. J., & Gregg, M. J. (2007). Using social cognitive career theory to understand head coaching intentions among assistant coaches of women's teams. *Sex Roles*, **56**, 365–372.

Cunningham, G. B., Fairley, S., Ferkins, L., Kerwin, S., Lock, D., Shaw, S. & Wicker, P. (2019). eSport: Construct specifications and implications for sport management. *Sport Management Review*, in press.

Cunningham, G. B., Ferreira, M., & Fink, J. S. (2009). Reactions to prejudicial statements: The influence of statement content and characteristics of the commenter. *Group Dynamics: Theory, Research, and Practice*, **13**(1), 59–73.

Cunningham, G. B. & Melton, E. N. (2014). Varying degrees of support: Understanding parents' positive attitudes toward LGBT coaches. *Journal of Sport Management*, **28**(4), 387–398.

Cunningham, G. B. & Sagas, M. (2002). The differential effects of human capital for male and female Division I basketball coaches. *Research Quarterly for Exercise and Sport*, **73**(4), 489–495.

Cunningham, G. B. & Sagas, M. (2003). Treatment discrimination among coaches of women's teams. *Research Quarterly for Exercise and Sport*, **74**, 455–466.

Cunningham, G. B. & Sagas, M. (2007). Examining potential differences between men and women in the impact of treatment discrimination. *Journal of Applied Social Psychology*, **37**, 3010–3024.

Cunningham, G. B., Sagas, M., & Ashley, F. B. (2003). Coaching self-efficacy, desire to head coach, and occupational turnover intent: Gender differences between NCAA assistant coaches of women's teams. *International Journal of Sport Psychology*, **34**, 125–137.

Cunningham, G. B. & Singer, J. N. (2010). "You'll face discrimination wherever you go": Student athletes' intentions to enter the coaching profession. *Journal of Applied Social Psychology*, **40**(7), 1708–1727.

Dovidio, J. F., Brigham, J. C., Johnson, B. T., & Gaertner, S. L. (1996). Stereotyping, prejudice, and discrimination: Another look. In C. N. Mcrae, C. Stangor, & M. Hewstone (eds), *Stereotypes and Stereotyping* (pp. 85–102). New York: Springer.

DuBois, C. (2015). The impact of "soft" affirmative action policies on minority hiring in executive leadership: The case of the NFL's Rooney Rule. *American Law and Economics Review*, **18**(1), 208–233.

Duehr, E. E. & Bono, J. E. (2006). Men, women, and managers: are stereotypes finally changing? *Personnel Psychology*, **59**(4), 815–846.

Eagly, A. H. & Karau, S. J. (2002). Role congruity theory of prejudice toward female leaders. *Psychological Review*, **109**, 573–598.

Fink, J. S. (2008). Gender and sex diversity in sport organizations: Concluding comments. *Sex Roles*, **58**(1–2), 146–147.

Fink, J. S. (2016). Hiding in plain sight: The embedded nature of sexism in sport. *Journal of Sport Management*, **30**(1), 1–7.

Funk, D. C., Pizzo, A. D., & Baker, B. J. (2019). eSport management: Embracing eSport education and research opportunities. *Sport Management Review*, in press.

Gearity, B. T., Mills, J. P., & Callary, B. (2016). In N. M. LaVoi (ed.), *Women in Sports Coaching* (pp. 234–254). New York: Routledge.

Greenhaus, J. H., Parasuraman, S., & Wormley, W. M. (1990). Effects of race on organizational experiences, job performance evaluations, and career outcomes. *Academy of management Journal*, **33**(1), 64–86.

Harris, K. F., Grappendorf, H., Aicher, T., & Veraldo, C. (2015). "Discrimination? Low pay? Long hours? I am still excited:" Female sport management students' perceptions of barriers toward a future career in sport. *Advancing Women in Leadership*, **35**, 12–21.

Hoffman, J. (2010). The dilemma of the senior woman administrator role in intercollegiate athletics. *Journal of Issues in Intercollegiate Athletics*, **3**(5), 53–75.

hooks, b. (2000). *Feminist Theory: From margin to center*, 2nd edn. London: Pluto Press.

Ilgen, D. R. & Youtz, M. A. (1986). Factors affecting the evaluation and development of minorities in organizations. In K. Rowland & G. Ferris (eds), *Research in Personnel and Human Resource Management: A research manual* (pp. 307–337). Greenwich, CT: JAI.

Kamphoff, C. & Gill, D. (2008). Collegiate athletes' perceptions of the coaching profession. *International Journal of Sports Science & Coaching*, **3**(1), 55–72.

Knijnik, J. (2015). Femininities and masculinities in Brazilian Women's Football: Resistance and compliance. *Journal of International Women's Studies*, **16**(3), 54–70.

Knoppers, A. (1987). Gender and the coaching profession. *Quest*, **39**(1), 9–22.

Koca, C. & Öztürk, P. (2015). Gendered perceptions about female managers in Turkish sport organizations. *European Sport Management Quarterly*, **15**(3), 381–406.

Koenig, A. M., Eagly, A. H., Mitchell, A. A., & Ristikari, T. (2011). Are leader stereotypes masculine? A meta-analysis of three research paradigms. *Psychological Bulletin*, **137**(4), 616–642.

Kubayi, A., Coopoo, Y., & Morris-Eyton, H. (2017). Perceived hindrances experienced by sport coaches in South Africa. *Journal of Human Kinetics*, **57**(1), 233–238.

Lee, C. W. (2013). From shamateurism to pioneer of Asia's professional football: the introduction of professional football in Hong Kong. *Soccer & Society*, **14**(5), 603–614.

Lent, R. W., Brown, S. D., & Hackett, G. (1994). Toward a unifying social cognitive theory of career and academic interest, choice, and performance. *Journal of vocational behavior*, **45**(1), 79–122.

Lovett, D. J. & Lowry, C. D. (1994). "Good old boys" and "good old girls" clubs: Myth or reality? *Journal of Sport Management*, **8**(1), 27–35.

McDowell, J. & Cunningham, G. B. (2009). Personal, social, and organizational factors that influence black female athletic administrators' identity negotiation. *Quest*, **61**(2), 202–222.

Messner, M. A. & Solomon, N. M. (2007). Social justice and men's interests: The case of Title IX. *Journal of Sport and Social Issues*, **31**(2), 162–178.

Moran-Miller, K. & Flores, L. Y. (2011). Where are the women in women's sports? Predictors of female athletes' interest in a coaching career. *Research Quarterly for Exercise and Sport*, **82**(1), 109–117.

Norman, L. (2010). Feeling second best: Elite women coaches' experiences. *Sociology of Sport Journal*, **27**(1), 89–104.

Norman, L. (2016). Is there a need for coaches to be more gender responsive? A review of the evidence. *International Sport Coaching Journal*, **3**(2), 192–196.

Norman, L. & Rankin-Wright, A. (2019). Surviving rather than thriving: Understanding the experiences of women coaches using a theory of gendered social well-being. *International review for the Sociology of Sport*, in press.

Reade, I., Rodgers, W., & Norman, L. (2009). The under-representation of women in coaching: A comparison of male and female Canadian coaches at low and high levels of coaching. *International Journal of Sports Science & Coaching*, **4**(4), 505–520.

Regan, M. & Cunningham, G. (2012). Analysis of homologous reproduction in community college athletics. *Journal for the Study of Sports and Athletes in Education*, **6**(2), 161–172.

Reuben, E., Sapienza, P., & Zingales, L. (2014). How stereotypes impair women's careers in science. *Proceedings of the National Academy of Sciences*, **111**(12), 4403–4408.

Sagas, M. & Batista, P. J. (2001). The importance of Title IX compliance on job satisfaction and occupational turnover intent of intercollegiate coaches. *Applied Research in Coaching and Athletics Annual*, 15–43.

Sagas, M. & Cunningham, G. B. (2004). Does having "the right stuff" matter? Gender differences in the determinants of career success among intercollegiate athletic administrators. *Sex Roles*, **50**(5), 411–421.

Sagas, M., Cunningham, G. B., & Ashley, F. B. (2000). Examining the women's coaching deficit through the perspective of assistant coaches. *International Journal of Sport Management*, **1**, 267–282.

Sagas, M., Cunningham, G. B., & Pastore, D. L. (2006). Predicting head coaching intentions of male and female assistant coaches: An application of the Theory of Planned Behavior. *Sex Roles*, **54**, 695–705.

Sagas, M., Cunningham, G. B., & Teed, K. (2006). An examination of homologous reproduction in the representation of assistant coaches of women's teams. *Sex Roles*, **55**(7–8), 503–510.

Sartore, M. L. (2006). Categorization, performance appraisals, and self-limiting behavior: The impact on current and future performance. *Journal of Sport Management*, **20**(4), 535–553.

Sartore, M. L. & Cunningham, G. B. (2007). Explaining the under-representation of women in leadership positions of sport organizations: A symbolic interactionist perspective. *Quest*, **59**(2), 244–265.

Schein, V. E. (1973). The relationship between sex role stereotypes and requisite management characteristics. *Journal of Applied Psychology*, **57**(2), 95–100.

Schein, V. E. (1975). Relationships between sex role stereotypes and requisite management characteristics among female managers. *Journal of Applied Psychology*, **60**(3), 340–344.

Shaw, S. & Hoeber, L. (2003). "A strong man is direct and a direct woman is a bitch": Gendered discourses and their influence on employment roles in sport organizations. *Journal of Sport Management*, **17**(4), 347–375.

Stangl, J. M. & Kane, M. J. (1991). Structural variables that offer explanatory power for the underrepresentation of women coaches since Title IX: The case of homologous reproduction. *Sociology of Sport Journal*, **8**(1), 47–60.

Stangor, C. (2009). The study of stereotyping, prejudice, and discrimination within social psychology: A quick history of theory and research. In T. D. Nelson (ed.), *Handbook of Prejudice, Stereotyping, and Discrimination* (pp. 1–23). New York: Psychology Press.

Tiell, B. S., Dixon, M. A., & Lin, Y. (2012). Roles and tasks of the senior woman administrator in role congruity theory perspective: A longitudinal progress report. *Journal of Issues in Intercollegiate Athletics*, **5**, 247–268.

Walker, N. A. & Melton, E. N. (2015). The tipping point: The intersection of race, gender, and sexual orientation in intercollegiate sports. *Journal of Sport Management*, **29**(3), 257–271.

Walker, N., Bopp, T., & Sagas, M. (2011). Gender bias in the perception of women as collegiate men's basketball coaches. *Journal for the Study of Sports and Athletes in Education*, **5**(2), 157–176.

Whisenant, W. A. & Mullane, S. P. (2007). Sport information directors and homologous reproduction. *International Journal of Sport Management and Marketing*, **2**(3), 252–263.

7

The delivery and management of women-only sport events and their future sustainability

Brianna L. Newland

My alarm goes off at 4:30 a.m. and I spring out of bed and grab my pre-packed race bag. I'm already dressed in my triathlon race kit (a "kit" is an outfit designed to be functional for the swim, bike, and run) – I slept in it just in case my three alarms malfunctioned and I didn't have time to dress. The smell of coffee lures me to the kitchen where I fill my travel mug, grab my extra-large bottle of water, and pre-race meal of perfectly proportioned protein–carbohydrate–fat content. Then, I load up my Jeep with my wetsuit, bike, and race essentials and set out for the race! As I set up my gear in transition, I feel an overwhelming sense of strength and calm, which is quite unusual for me on race day. I think that it must be the atmosphere of the event. I look around and observe women of all shapes and sizes – and they are laughing, taking selfies with their gear, hugging one another, and offering last-minute advice. I am attending my first women-only triathlon and I am captivated by the vibe. There is a heightened sense of comradery and community that I had not sensed at gender-mixed events. That is not to say that comradery and community do not exist at these events – they do. But, it is different. At this event, I see all women, whether this event is their first or 50th, looking confident (albeit still nervous) in their skin – or wetsuit, I should say! They are chatting with friends and strangers in eager anticipation of the event start. As we toe the water to begin, I see high-fives, hugs, and words of encouragement. Again, this is not to say this does not happen at gender-mixed events, but the difference is conspicuous. In gender-mixed events, I find that encouragement happens in small groups of friends. At this event, I observed widespread cooperation and support of achievement. As I completed the event, words of encouragement rang out from those who were passing me and from those I passed. I felt supported and encouraged, even as (yet another) person flew past me toward the finish line. After the event, I found myself chatting with complete strangers – and this is quite a large feat given my introverted tendencies. Not only did I find myself rehashing the race, but also my training, work, and other aspects of my life. I felt the community and the support of the other women. The competition was fierce, but the collective support – even by women leaving me in the dust – made it all the more fun. I felt just as challenged as a mixed-gender event, but I found my confidence grew stronger with each pedal stroke and stride toward the finish. It was a unique experience that I look forward to having again.

Author observation of participation in a women-only triathlon

My own participation in running and triathlon events sparked my initial research interests in endurance sport. Mass participation sport events, or active sport events, have steadily grown over the last three decades and I have often wondered what is driving this change. When I ask athletes why they participate in these events, many explain that their love for sport competition and "being an athlete" has led them to running or triathlon or CrossFit. They do it because they still want to compete. A quick review of a sport event calendar, such as those on Active.com or EventBrite.com, illustrates this demand with a cluttered event space filled with an abundance of triathlon, running, cycling, adventure, and, most recently, CrossFit events. Included in this growth is the development of and demand for women-only events and training programs. Events for women are intended to remove barriers by providing a bigger emphasis on community, participation, support, mentorship, and empowerment – beyond the experience of just racing (Giuliani, 2015). But, do women-specific events create a distinct sense of community that supports and empowers women in sport? The following explores how women-only events are shaping the future of adult sport and what this means for future research and practice.

Women's sport participation evolution

USA Triathlon's (USAT) female membership had grown from 27% to over 37% of the total membership by the end of 2014, and continues to grow. USAT, the governing body, claims the growth was due to, "society's acceptance of 'active' women, women feeling more comfortable living an active lifestyle, the growth of women's-only events like the Danskin and Trek Triathlon Series (now Iron Girl), and races focusing on charity involvement and fundraising" (USA Triathlon, 2015, para. 22). To develop women at the collegiate level in the United States, USAT awarded nearly US$1 million to the National Collegiate Athletic Association (NCAA) institutions as part of the Women's Triathlon Emerging Sport Grant. The grant program led to greater participation in the second Women's Collegiate Triathlon season with an at-capacity attendance of 80 women competing for national titles (USA Triathlon, 2015). As noted, the triathlon event marketplace first started offering women-only events in the early 2000s with Iron Girl triathlons and the Danskin and Trek Triathlon Series, organized by Xxtra Mile, LLC, a women's and girls' active lifestyle company (Iron Girl, 2013; Xxtra Mile, LLC, 2010). The Danskin and Trek events merged in 2010 and were bought out by the World Triathlon Corporation in 2013, then rebranded under the Athleta Iron Girl national event series, which offered 12 events across the United States that year (Iron Girl, 2013). Iron Girl now offers 11 international events. Other women-only triathlon events have continued to emerge with DelMo Sports offering its inaugural Philadelphia Women's Tri, duathlon, and aquabike in summer 2018 (DelMo Sports, 2018).

There are a multitude of women-only running events at distances ranging from 5Ks to marathons, many of them partnering with a disease-related cause (Active.com, 2018). According to Running USA's national survey, from 2013 to 2016 women continued to dominate the field for running event finishers at 9.7 million finishers, representing over half (57%) of the field (Running USA, 2017). There are a number of foundations and organizations with the primary goal of supporting women runners. Gazelle Girls hosts 5K, 10K, and half-marathon events for women. The hashtag #wegotsoul exemplifies their energy and community focus, and caters to the interests and needs of women (Gazelle Girls, 2018). The culture and atmosphere created around the events are meant to inspire and support women through running. All of the event proceeds benefit their charity partners, which directly benefit women and girls in their county or region. Another example of an organization supporting females is Girls on the Run (GOTR), a non-profit organization aimed at improving young girls' self-esteem and confidence through running. Although this non-profit is aimed at girls, the participants are teamed with women running mentors who "inspire girls to take charge of their lives and define the future on their terms. It's a place where girls learn that they can" (GOTR, 2018, para. 1). The girls are paired with female certified coaches who teach the importance of life skills and confidence, service, and, of course, running. All participants aim to complete a 5K running event at the end of the program. The GOTR coaches inspire girls to be confident young women who value their fitness and health by running.

It is of interest that recreational cycling among women is very high, but competitive women's cycling is the one endurance sport that struggles to attract women (Bonham & Wilson, 2012: Dixon, Graham, Hartzell, & Forest, 2017) and sponsors (Harris & Maxwell, 2018). Unlike its endurance cousins, triathlon and running, cycling is predominately male and has limited programming and events to attract and retain women. In fact, females account for only 15% of the USA Cycling (USAC) licensed competitive cyclists, which is only a 2% increase since 2009 (Dixon et al., 2017; USA Cycling, 2015). Dixon et al. (2017) observed that sanctioned USAC events often hinder women's progression in the sport because athletes must race against women in higher performance categories due to the lack of women participants at the event. As such, beginners and novice riders must race against advanced athletes who beat them continuously and hinder their ability to move up in category. Unlike triathlon and running, USAC does very little to promote or attract women to the sport, nor do the policies and competitive structures support the advancement of women at cycling events (Dixon et al., 2017; USA Cycling, 2015). To complicate matters even more, the sport struggles to find sponsors willing to commit to supporting events, making it difficult for event organizers to grow the sport (Maxwell & Harris, 2014) Thus, women have very high barriers to entry into cycling and, if they do overcome these, they face even more challenges to develop within it (Dixon et al., 2017).

Meanwhile, CrossFit has exploded onto the sport event scene with a revolutionary approach to fitness as a sport. Not only are they challenging traditional adult competitive sport event delivery, but the women in this sport are also changing the status quo of the female body. These athletes are breaking the mold of past "ideal" body images from being super skinny to one that favors being healthy and fit, with a focus shift from appearance to function (Heywood, 2015; LeBlanc-Bazinet, n.d.). The female athletes in CrossFit are strong, powerful, and well-rounded performers accomplishing feats across a range of athletic tests. These women have rewritten "the beauty idea by replacing it with strength – strong is the new beautiful . . . resulting in women's ability to unlock the potential of their bodies" (Heywood, 2015, p. 22). In a 2013 report, of the 10 million CrossFitters around the world, it was estimated that 60% were women (Markula, 2015). The CrossFit premier event, the CrossFit Games, seeks the fittest women (and men) on earth by challenging them with Olympic power lifts, feats of strength and endurance, combined with the grace and skill of gymnastics. The event series begins with the CrossFit Open, where everyone (novice, amateurs, and pros, alike) competes together at their local CrossFit affiliate in an event that spans the globe. Every CrossFit affiliate across the world hosts the Open at their home location. Athletes registered to compete in the Open complete the workouts released by CrossFit officials and submit their scores through the CrossFit Games app. All athletes are then ranked worldwide, nationally, regionally, and locally through the app. The top 20 males and females in the region move on to regionals, and the very elite (top 5 from regionals) advance to the CrossFit Games, held in Madison, Wisconsin. What is most impressive about the CrossFit events is that men and women compete together in an egalitarian environment that expresses mental and physical toughness, collaboration, camaraderie, and support – no matter your gender, skill level, or ability (Crossfit.com, 2018). CrossFit advocates equal access and opportunity and the egalitarian nature of CrossFit has been acknowledged by other researchers (Heywood, 2015; Knapp, 2014).

Research on women-only events

Despite the growth in demand for women's sport programming and services, there is scant research on women-only events. Much of the work to date has focused on the relationship of sport and women's health (Crofts, Schofield, & Dickson, 2012) and post-event behavior intentions of participants in women-only sport events (Crofts, Dickson, Schofield, & Funk, 2012). In their study of athletes at a women-only triathlon in New Zealand, Crofts, Schofield, and Funk (2012) found that women were motivated to race for the challenge, competition, enjoyment, health, and stress management. This study also examined how event participation affected long-term physical activity, and found that even those who were less active than other athletes before the women-only event continued to rate themselves as active six months post-event. These findings indicate that the event participation could positively influence behavior after the event. Going a step further, Crofts, Schofield, and Dickson (2012) used the psychological continuum model (PCM; Funk & James, 2001) to examine women-only event participants' connections to the sport of triathlon and found that those in the *allegiance stage* of the PCM were more likely to train longer for more sessions per week and were more likely to do other triathlon and non-triathlon sporting events (e.g., a marathon). Those in the *attachment stage* were also more likely to return to the same event, as well as compete in other triathlon and non-triathlon events. Meanwhile, those in the *attracted stage* trained less and were less likely to return to the event or compete in other triathlon or non-triathlon events. Most of the women in Crofts, Schofield, and Dickson's (2012) study classified into the attachment stage.

These findings could have important practical implications for event managers. If managers are interested in finding ways to attract and retain athletes in the event, then it is important to understand how they might be nurtured outside of the event itself. A simple post-event survey with questions that collect data on athletes' current connections to the sport could help identify the specific stages of the participants. Then, programming could be developed based on each category. For example, athletes in the allegiance stage are clearly committed to the sport. Offering discounts to series events, or partner events, could be one way to keep them engaged with the specific event (and series) within the sport. Those in the attachment stage were most likely to return to the event, so offering immediate registration coupons or pre-registration deals would likely entice them to return. For those in the attracted stage, offering programming that helps make them feel more comfortable in the sport would be important. Connecting them to training groups or coaching would help keep them engaged with the sport and the event.

Although the above managerial implications can be helpful, there is more to understand about women participants. In my own exploratory research with women-only running, triathlon, and CrossFit event managers, I discovered four overarching themes in women-only events: intimidation factor, social community, advocacy, and promotion. Below is a review of the findings of interviews with seven event directors of women-only events. The event directors in this study represented CrossFit, running, or triathlon (or both) events in Arizona (AZ), Texas (TX), Michigan (MI), Colorado (CO), Utah (UT), Pennsylvania (PA), and Florida (FL). All names are pseudonyms.

Intimidation factor

All the event directors in the study said they began hosting women-only events because they found women were intimidated by the sport itself (i.e., triathlon, running, or CrossFit) and/or the mixed-gender events. Several noted that the women participating in their events had left sport to have children, build their careers, or both, and were, "petrified of not knowing what to do or how to begin training for the sport, but were really excited to get involved" (Ken, FL). This was confirmed by Barb (CO), who noted that many athletes at her events were trying to rediscover the "athletes they once were, but learning a new sport was frightening." She went on to explain that many of the athletes who train with her club or race her events were "pre-Title IX" and found triathlon later in life. Title IX was recently celebrated by Heather's (MI) event because [the law] "gave women the opportunity to participate in athletics physically and we really support that change." It was important to Heather that her event celebrated the struggle and advancement of women's sport over the last 45 years.

The event directors noted that the intimidation factor can lead to barriers, and women-only events offer a way to reduce that anxiety around training and racing. As John (UT) stated, "our women-only events are entry-level, therefore, the intimidation factor some have, goes away." Heather (MI) explained that her events were more exciting and less intimidating than the mixed gender events and:

> ... for that person who says "someday, someday, someday..." we are breaking down barriers and making [the sport] available so we can turn "someday" into today. For whatever distance, whatever speed, whatever color, whatever shape or size, we try to make our events feel inclusive so women don't feel afraid... we want women to have an exemplary, quality experience. Our goal is to be the premier women's event for the Midwest.

This was echoed by Gwen (TX) who said, "My event attempts to reduce the barriers of entry for triathlon, which include not knowing other triathletes, discomfort undertaking a competitive, male-dominated event, body image insecurities, and concerns of not being 'athletic.'" This was also noted by Jeff (PA) in regard to the CrossFit Open event he hosts:

> ... so, I find that women are more intimidated by the Open than the men in my box [note: a *box* is a term used to describe the gym]. If they [women] are too scared to participate, then I ask them to volunteer to help the judges as a way to ease them in. We also do some of the old workouts from past years so they can see for themselves that they can complete the prescribed workouts. The best part is that we scale everything to the ability of the person so everyone can take part and enjoy a challenge that is best suited for them. At the end of the day, I want *everyone*, not just the women, to feel like they can participate, have fun, and be a part of our community.

Addressing the intimidation factor was a priority for these event directors, who all believed this attracts women to the sport and the culture and community they build at their events maintains their interest in the sport. By building community and removing barriers, women who participated built confidence and self-esteem every time they crossed the finish line or completed the workout for the Open. Jason (AZ) captures this notion for his running events:

> Anytime you add a greater comfort level to an event it increases the amount of participants who come out and allows people to enjoy the sport even more. It also gives women a greater confidence, which increases the likelihood of them continuing to run and passing it on to their own children.

Social community

The event directors all witnessed an increased interest for women-only training groups and programs in their regions and/or their own offerings. And, although they were seeing a demand for these training groups, some noted that it was not translating to events. Given the known intimidation factor discussed above, these pioneers decided it was time to offer events that catered to women in a way that reduced the anxiety, mitigated the barriers, and created safe, fun environments. As

Jason (AZ) observed: "I think they [women] gravitate more toward women-only events because they feel a greater comfort running with other women and it makes for a more even running field (as far as competition goes)." And as Barb (CO) put it, "my event helps women gain the confidence needed to embrace their 'inner athlete' with the support and community of women."

This sense of community and support was also observed by Ken (FL), who said: "I see support and camaraderie at my events, and women feel part of something that makes them feel safe. They are a part of the triathlete community now." Gwen (TX) noted that the women gravitate to the women-only merchandise because wearing it makes them feel part of the "club." She also observed, "much more bonding [compared with mixed-gender events] as the women are waiting in the swim lineup to begin the race." The bonding and socializing were also noted by other event directors:

> My women-only events definitely have a more social aspect to the event. Women tend to stick around longer and arrive earlier to the events, spend time with the vendors, and socialize with each other. The co-ed events tend to be over more quickly and participants show up, run and leave.
>
> *(Jason, AZ)*

And, Barb (CO):

> Women are social animals; we love to chat it up. We love to go for coffee, we love to do Happy Hour together. We love to do "girl weekends." So, women-focused athletic events or trainings give women the chance to do all that WHILE learning how to sweat, manage heart zones, swim, bike, run. They develop a whole new group of friends who enjoy health and fitness and "chatting it up." It becomes a healthy support group.

Each director, in his or her own way, found ways to create community with a culture of collaboration and encouragement, a fun and stress-free atmosphere, through specific vendors that meet women's needs, and opportunities to share the experience together. As Jeff (PA) observed:

> We have women-only events to lessen the intimidation and to make them feel a part of the community. Last year, we had a wine tasting and lululemon day. It was such a big success that the women created an online group to interact and set up social events outside of the box.

Advocacy

The advocacy theme manifested as two subthemes in the data: personal advocacy, and health and wellness advocacy. First, personal advocacy was observed by how women advocated for one another for success in the event and sport. The event directors noted that they witnessed support and encouragement among the women. As Ken (FL) said:

> It's fun for me to be at the start line to see the women giving last minute advice or pep talks. This is different than what I see at my co-ed events. At these events, I see athletes checking their watches, fiddling with their shoes or equipment, and small groups talking. But, at the women-only events, there's more conversation . . . and laughing. And, throughout the race, I hear shouts of encouragement from the other participants. They really care that the woman next to them crosses that finish line. I don't see that kind of support at my co-ed races. No one is pulling for the guy next to him to finish. Well, at least not until their own race is done.

And, Jeff (PA):

> I see the women really encouraging one another to challenge their abilities through events. There is a local women-only weight lifting event that many of our women are afraid to try. A couple athletes gave it a try and their encouragement has led to other women attempting new challenges like these events. What is even better is the support group that goes to the event to cheer the ladies on. That encouragement and support really builds their confidence. It's pretty cool to see.

The second subtheme was to advocate for health and wellness through charity support. As Heather (MI) pointed out, "We, well I, have a serious passion for women's health and wellness. We believe when a woman is healthy, that trickles out into her family, and her community." This concept of health and wellness advocacy was echoed by Gwen (TX):

> Women are far more likely to want to tie in fundraising/philanthropy to bring even more meaning to their experience. Our triathlon partners with [a charity that supports victims of sexual and family violence], and women have the option to donate or become fundraisers for the organization. More women have taken advantage of this option in the all-female event than in the three other co-ed events combined.

And, Barb (CO) noted:

> Cancer survivors are a special part of the team as they support and inspire everyone as they overcome the personal challenges of cancer. But we also give back in other ways. For the past six years we have volunteered to serve meals for the hungry and homeless in our community and since 2013 the team has collected and donated new hoodies to the community youth recovery center at the local hospital for the inpatient chemically dependent teens, among many other programs.

Promotion

The final theme that emerged in the data focused on how women's events should be promoted. All seven of the event directors were clear that the messaging for women-only events should endorse a safe place where women can be introduced to a sport in a welcoming environment that is less intimidating, offers opportunities for social interaction and community, and to advocate for each other and our health and well-being. Many observed that a vast majority of the women participating returned to sport after a very long hiatus from a childbearing and career focus.

Others pointed out that many women had *never* participated in the sport. As Jeff (PA) commented:

> Most of the women, and even the men, have never done an Olympic lift. That's ok – we teach them in progressions. There are a ton of false assumptions about CrossFit out there. I have to ensure my messaging breaks through that crap – sorry – but it is crap. I need to reach those that are afraid to step through that door. It's tough to overcome that, but women need to know the sport is safe and I can help them build strength that will help them here [in the box] and to function in their daily life.

Gwen (TX) made it very clear that event directors need to reconsider the "pink" marketing gimmicks and promotions to attract a broader demographic of women to sport events in the future:

> Women are not a one-size-fits-all, and the changing U.S. demographics demand that a women's event not pander to stereotypes. The "throw some pink/a bow/a tutu on it" model of many large-scale women's events is still attracting a very narrow group of women – usually white, middle to upper class. To appeal to a broader female demographic, the education component is essential because it is far more likely that women of color do not know any other triathletes. I've found that all women benefit from the educational component, but it significantly lowers barriers to entry for underrepresented women.

Conclusion

The results of this exploratory research begin to paint a picture of women-only sport events, specifically from the event managers' perspectives, but there is a great deal of work to be done. The literature on gender differences in sport is growing in general, but it does not focus on women-only events. Based on this literature, we understand that men and women are socialized into sport differently (Messner, 2007; Pritchard et al., 2007) and gendered social expectations have influenced women's participation (Hargreaves, 1990). Knoppers (2003) has noted that antiquated masculine practices have systematically deprived women in sport and have continued to create barriers to entry. Based on the results of this exploratory research, it appears that the women-only events are shaking up the masculine ideals and practices in running, triathlon, and CrossFit by offering events and programming that are intentional in breaking these barriers. To do this, some events have gone the pink or princess route, supplying tiaras and other pink giveaways as a means to attract women and differentiate from mixed-gendered events. However, the participants in this study warned that making the event, equipment, and/or merchandise "pink" is not how women should be attracted to sport. As Gwen noted, the "pink" approach seems to attract a specific demographic, leaving out women of color, creating an exclusive outcome that women-only events claim to avoid. Many event directors in this study stated, in some way, that the "pink" practice was stereotypical, degrading, misogynistic, and discriminatory. In Australian cycling, Giuliani (2015) sees a brand-new approach to races and rides that are focused on attracting more women into the sport, but it's not about running things the "same old way" minus the men – "the marketing is different, the atmosphere altered and the focus is on participation rather than podiums" (Giuliani, 2015, para. 2). This notion was echoed by all event directors in this exploratory study as well.

Ogles and Masters (2003), explored gender differences in marathoners and found the women to fall into the categories of *lifestyle managers* (motivated by health, personal goals, self-esteem, weight concern, and life meaning) and *running enthusiasts* (endorse all nine motives – health, weight, affiliation, recognition, competition, goal achievement, self-esteem, and life meaning). The findings in the current exploratory study support these findings in several ways. The event directors all mentioned improvements in self-esteem, weight concerns, and personal goals as well as a specific focus on health as part of *intimidation* and *advocacy* themes. Furthermore, many athletes specifically seek competition and goal achievement (i.e., crossing that finish line!), and all event directors noted that the women-only events were highly social.

The literature and the results of this exploratory study indicate an increasing demand for active sport event consumption by women. The growth of women-only events illustrates a strong interest in an event offering that caters to the interests and needs of women. For many, women-only events lower the intimidation factor that many women face after a long hiatus from sport due to child rearing and career development. This offers women a lower risk and more supportive entry back into sport. As sport event managers, we must recognize that, in order to attract and retain female athletes, we must better understand the diversity of women as well as their interests and needs. To do so, more research on women-only events is necessary. Adult sport participation can support the health and wellness of both men and women (Newland & Aicher, 2018). However, this exploratory study indicates that women are intimidated by sport participation. It is important to delve into this further in order to find ways to reduce barriers to entry and to ensure continued participation. It is also critical to understand how women are attracted to the sport. This study observed that women seek community and social interaction, but also found it important to advocate for others. A better understanding as to how to incorporate these elements to attract and retain participants is important. In addition, managers should consider how design elements and sponsorship activation could be incorporated into the event to further support social interaction, community, and empowerment. Sponsor product placements or activations that align with the psychographics of the women-specific event can enhance the experience, heighten the sense of community, and reduce the fear by allowing for opportunities to engage with others and learn more about the sport.

Leader profile: Nancy Reinisch, Co-Founder/USAT Certified Coach, Roaring Fork Women's Triathlon Team

Figure 7.1 Nancy Reinisch
Reproduced with permission

Nancy Reinisch was first drawn to women-only sport when she noticed a need for training programs for women on the Western Slope of Colorado, a rural county where there were minimal resources for women athletes. In 1987, at the age of 32, she was self-diagnosed with AOA – *adult-onset athleticism* – and did her first triathlon that same year. As a youngster, she grew up in the years before Title IX gave women equal access to sports. So, as an adult, she found herself training on her own for her first triathlon. There were no books, no videos, no training groups. She realized it was time to connect other women in a supportive and cooperative manner to train for triathlon. Many women who first register for the Roaring Fork Women's Tri Team are terrified of becoming athletes. However, with the encouragement of other members and the mentor coaches, the support quells their fears. Over the past 18 years, Reinisch has watched woman after woman successfully cross the finish line of her first triathlon. As a result, she continues to be committed to the option of woman-only training programs and events.

When Reinisch thinks about what the women-only events and training programs do for women, she thinks social interaction and Oprah. Women are social beings in different ways to men. Women like to chat, process, and celebrate. We call this the "Oprah style of training" because women like to cooperate as well as compete. Women-only events give women a chance to compete while exercising, training, and sweating together. On the Roaring Fork Women's Tri Team, experienced members mentor coach the novice athletes. We utilize a "see one, do one, teach one" philosophy. Each of the members is an "expert of one" and once she crosses that finish line she is invited to share her knowledge with other women. In turn, each woman pays it forward to another member. Reinisch has found that training together creates a strong bond among women that transcends triathlon. This bond provides support through illnesses, deaths, addictions, and other life adversities, and continues with volunteering and philanthropy. Women-only events jump start women's initial participation or return to sport in a safe and fun environment. The confidence they gain allows them not only to move on to more traditional co-ed athletic events, but also to gain self-esteem to meet the rigors of life.

Women-only sport also includes advocacy. Reinisch is a two-time breast cancer survivor who has used triathlon to get her through the rigors of cancer treatment. Her ability to continue to coach and compete, despite the cancer, has inspired others struggling with cancer or illness to use exercise as part of their treatment plan. The lessons learned training for triathlon can help women diagnosed with cancer and other illnesses remain optimistic during their difficult journey. They learn to set goals, use humor, rely on their team, manage injuries, and celebrate crossing finish lines. The same dynamics used to cross the finish line can be used to help meet any major illness milestone. Once again, women like to be supported during times of adversity. In particular, women with cancer often bond as a subgroup of cancer athletes.

Women-only sport is important to women's continued participation in sport. Race directors need to support women-only events as both a gateway to co-ed events and a way to develop women athletes. The benefits to women and to sport in general will be greatly advanced with the continuation of women-only training and sporting events. We must acknowledge that the needs of women athletes are different to those of men and, therefore, we should develop events and programs that support these women into the future.

References

Active.com (2018). Running women only. Retrieved from https://www.active.com/search?keywords=running+women+only&location=Everywhere&category=Activities&daterange=All+future+dates.

Bonham, J. & Wilson, A. (2012). Bicycling and the life course: The start-stop-start experiences of women cycling. *International Journal of Sustainable Transportation*, **6**(4), 195–213.

Crofts, C., Dickson, G., Schofield, G., & Funk, D. (2012). Post-event behavioural intentions of participants in a women-only mass participation sporting event. *International Journal of Sport Management and Marketing*, **12**(3–4), 260–274.

Crofts, C., Schofield, G., & Dickson, G. (2012). Women-only mass participation sporting events: does participation facilitate changes in physical activity? *Annals of Leisure Research*, **15**(2), 148–159.

Crossfit.com (2018). What is CrossFit? Retrieved from https://www.crossfit.com/what-is-crossfit

DelMo Sports (2018). Triathlon events. Retrieved from http://delmosports.com/

Dixon, M. A., Graham, J. A., Hartzell, A. C., & Forrest, K. (2017). Enhancing women's participation and advancement in competitive cycling. *Journal of Applied Sport Management*, **9**(4), 10–21

Funk, D. C. & James, J. (2001). The psychological continuum model: A conceptual framework for understanding an individual's psychological connection to sport. *Sport Management Review*, **4**(2), 119–150.

Gazelle Girl (2018). Why Gazelle Girl? Retrieved from http://gazellegirlhalfmarathon.com/why-run-gazelle-girl.

GOTR (2018). What we do. Retrieved from https://www.girlsontherun.org/what-we-do.

Giuliani, S. (2015). Men not allowed: Women's only events are on the raise, but are they successful? *Ella Cycling Tips*, October. Retrieved from https://cyclingtips.com/2015/10/men-not-allowed-are-womens-only-events-working/

Hargreaves, J. (1990). Gender on the sports agenda. *International Review for the Sociology of Sport*, **25**(4), 287–308.

Harris, J. & Maxwell, S. (2018, June). *The outer line: BMC in crisis – the same old problem.* Retrieved from, https://www.velonews.com/2018/06/news/outer-line-bmc-crisis-old-problem_470061

Heywood, L. (2015). "Strange borrowing": Affective neuroscience, neoliberalism and the "cruelly optimistic" gendered bodies of CrossFit. In C. Nally & A. Smith (eds), *Twenty-first Century Feminism* (pp. 17–40). London: Palgrave Macmillan.

Iron Girl (2013). Iron Girl celebrates 10th anniversary with excited additions to the 2013 event series. Retrieved from https://www.prnewswire.com/news-releases/iron-girl-celebrates-10th-anniversary-with-exciting-additions-to-the-2013-event-series-193322551.html.

Knapp, B.A. (2014). Gender representation in the CrossFit Journal: A content analysis. *Sport in Society*, **18**(6), 688–703.

Knoppers, A. (2003). Women's soccer in the United States and the Netherlands: Differences and similarities in regimes of inequalities. *Sociology of Sport Journal*, **20**, 351–370.

LeBlanc-Bazinet, C. (n.d.). How CrossFit is change female body image. Retrieved from https://www.rehband.co.uk/camille-leblanc-bazinet-how-crossfit-is-changing-female-body-image.

Markula, P. (2015). Is CrossFit a feminist issue? Strong is the new beautiful for CrossFitters. Retrieved from https://www.psychologytoday.com/blog/fit-femininity/201506/is-crossfit-feminist-issue.

Maxwell, S. & Harris, J. (2014). Changing the business model: (2) building the sponsorship base, October. Retrieved from https://www.theouterline.com/changing-the-business-model-2-building-the-sponsorship-base.

Messner M. A. (2007). *Out of Play: Critical essays on gender and sport.* Albany, NY: State University of New York Press.

Newland, B. L & Aicher, T. J. (2018). Aging and sport participation: exploring the influence of addition to sport. Presentation at the conference of the North American Society for Sport Management (NASSM) Conference, Halifax, Canada, June.

Ogles, B. M. & Masters, K. S. (2003). A typology of marathon runners based on cluster analysis of motivations. *Journal of Sport Behavior*, **26**(1), 69–85.

Pritchard A., Morgan N., Ateljevic I., et al. (2007). *Tourism and Gender: Embodiment, Sensuality and Experience.* Wallingford: CABI.

Running USA (2017). U.S road race trends. Retrieved from www.runningusa.org/2017-us-road-race-trends.

USA Cycling (2015). Annual report. Retrieved from https://s3.amazonaws.com/USACWeb/forms/2015%20Annual%20Report.pdf.

USA Triathlon (2015). 2015 USA Triathlon Membership Report. Retrieved from https://www.teamusa.org/usa-triathlon/about/multisport/demographics.

Xxtra Mile, LLC (2010). Danskin triathlon series joins Trek women triathlon series, March. Retrieved from https://www.active.com/triathlon/articles/danskin-triathlon-series-joins-trek-women-triathlon-series.

8

Women in leadership positions within Canadian sport

Guylaine Demers, Lucie Thibault, Sophie Brière, and Diane Culver[1]

Introduction

According to Statistics Canada (2017), Canada's population in 2017 was 36,708,100, dispersed over 10 provinces and 3 territories. Of this population, 50.4% are girls and women. Yet Canadian women are largely under-represented in leadership positions within many industries such as business, law, engineering, and medicine (Barton & Yee, 2017; Belletête & Langelier, 2016; Brière, 2018; Catalyst, 2017; Kay, Alarie, & Adjei, 2016). Sport is another sector where women are under-represented in its many facets – as coaches, officials, administrative and technical staff, leaders of sport organizations, and executive volunteers. The purpose of this chapter is to address policies and strategies that have been undertaken in Canadian sport with regard to women's involvement in leadership.

Canada's sport system has evolved extensively since the early 1990s. These changes have included better programs and services for sport participants and athletes, more formalization and professionalization within non-profit sport organizations, more public policies and funding opportunities to support the activities of sport organizations (compare Thibault & Harvey, 2013). There are now more competitive opportunities for women in more sports, including at the highest levels. Canadian female athletes are increasingly participating in high-performance sport and regularly achieving podium success at Senior World Championships and Olympic and Paralympic Summer and Winter Games. At the 2008 Olympic Games in Beijing, they made up 47% of the team and won 41% of the medals. At the 2010 Vancouver Olympic Winter Games, Canadian women made up 44% of the team and won 56% of the medals. At the 2012 London Olympic Games, Canadian women made up a record 56% of the team and won 50% of the medals. More recently, at the 2016 Rio Olympic Games, women made up 60% of the team and established a new record with an impressive 16 of the 22 Canadian medals awarded to women, constituting 72%.

Beyond these impressive international sport results, a series of significant events have highlighted the extent to which women's sport has recently been featured in Canada:

- 1998: release of the Standing Committee on Canadian Heritage Sub-Committee report entitled *Sport in Canada: Everybody's Business. Leadership, Partnership and Accountability*, including a first set of recommendations to improve the experience of girls and women in sport.

- 2002: Canada hosted the Third World Conference on Women and Sport, held in Montréal, Québec.
- 2009: launch of the second policy on women and sport entitled *Actively Engaged: A Policy on Sport for Women and Girls* (this policy is a revision of the original 1986 Sport Canada Policy on Women in Sport).
- 2010: Vancouver Olympic and Paralympic Winter Games held.
- 2015: The third national conference on women and sport, entitled "The 2015 Conversation," held in Québec City.
- 2015: Canada hosted the FIFA (Fédération Internationale de Football Association) Women's World Cup of Football/Soccer.
- 2016: Creation of a working group on women and sport commissioned by the Federal–Provincial/Territorial Sport Committee (FPTSC) to develop recommendations.
- 2017: release of the Report of the Standing Committee on Canadian Heritage, entitled *Women and Girls in Sport*.
- 2017: Canada wins gold in Australia at the Women's World Rugby Sevens Series tournament in February.
- 2018: release of the government response to the Report of the Standing Committee on Canadian Heritage, entitled *Women and Girls in Sport*.
- 2020: Canada hosts the International Ice Hockey Federation (IIHF) Women's World Championships.

Although these events have contributed to the enhancement of women's access and experiences in sport, there are still several areas that need consideration. One such area is women's involvement in leadership positions within sport organizations. In fact, recent data demonstrate that, within national sport organizations, only 24% of the executive committee members are women, 17% of the chairs/presidents of these executive committees are women, and 32% of the chief executive officers of these sport organizations are women (Adriaanse, 2016). Similar data are reported for multi-sport organizations such as University Sports and the Canadian Collegiate Athletic Association, where women make up only 16% of the top paid positions (Canadian Association for the Advancement of Women and Sport and Physical Activity [CAAWS], 2016) and 19% of the head coach positions (Kidd, 2013). Although Canadian women's competition results in international sport have been impressive, within the context of sport organizations' leadership, a great deal of work is still needed to achieve equity.

This chapter provides an opportunity to describe and analyze in greater detail women's experiences within the context of Canadian sport organizations, as well as the current issues and barriers limiting women's complete involvement and participation in the Canadian sport system. The chapter is divided into four sections: (1) government actions and organizations working toward gender equity; (2) women's involvement in leadership positions; (3) gender-based violence in sport; and (4) future prospects to achieve gender equity in the Canadian sport system.

Government actions and organizations working toward gender equity

Sport Canada, an agency of the federal government, is central to the development of policies and programs that help non-profit sport organizations. Sport Canada "provides leadership and funding to help ensure a strong Canadian sport system which enables Canadians to progress from early sport experiences to high performance excellence" (Sport Canada, 2018, para. 2). In 1986, Sport Canada developed its first Women in Sport Policy. In this policy, leaders of Sport Canada acknowledged that "women [were] underrepresented in executive and senior decision-making positions in sport, both as volunteers and employees" (Canadian Heritage, 20109a, p. 5). These leaders believed that "a clearly articulated policy statement on women in sport [would] help establish a direction that [would] methodically improve the current status of women in sport in coming years" (Canadian Heritage, 2009a, p. 7). The policy considered several key elements such as sport infrastructure, leadership development, high-performance competition, sport participation, resource allocation, education, research, and advocacy, as well as the creation of a Women's Program within Sport Canada. Although the policy and the Women's Program led to some improvements in the status of women in sport, the policy fell short in eliminating the barriers women faced in accessing leadership positions, and failed to address many inequities within Canada's non-profit sport organizations.

The 1986 policy document was revised in 2009. In this most recent document entitled *Actively Engaged: A policy on sport for women and girls*:

> the objective of the policy is to foster sport environments – from playground to podium – where women and girls, particularly as athlete participants, coaches, technical leaders and officials, and as governance leaders are provided with quality experiences; and equitable support by sport organizations.
>
> *(Canadian Heritage, 2009a, p. 6)*

It is important to note that the development of the 2009 policy on sport for women and girls was inherently supported with statements found in both federal government legislation (i.e., Physical Activity and Sport Act 2003) and the overarching Canadian Sport Policy documents (Canadian Heritage, 2012). Specifically, in the 2003 Physical Activity and Sport Act, the objects and mandate of the legislation included a focus to "facilitate the participation of underrepresented groups in the Canadian sport system" (Minister of Justice, 2017, p. 3) whereas the most recent Canadian Sport Policy underscored the importance of inclusion as a policy principle and called for "sport programs [that] are accessible and equitable and reflect the full breadth of interests, motivations, objectives, abilities, and the diversity of Canadian society" (Canadian Heritage, 2012, p. 2). Importantly, leaders of federal as well as all provincial/territorial governments endorsed the Canadian Sport Policy, including its principle of inclusion, accessibility, and equity.

The 2009 policy on sport for women and girls highlighted achievements of women and girls as sport participants, high-performance athletes, coaches, officials, administrative and technical staff, leaders of sport organizations, and executive volunteers of numerous sport organizations operating at the local, provincial/territorial, and national levels, but also identified challenges to equity within Canadian sport. The policy focused on four central areas of intervention:

1. Program improvement: alignment and refinement of programs and activities to enable sport organizations and other sport system stakeholders to deliver innovative quality sport experiences for women and girls;
2. Strategic leadership: proactive promotion of complementary measures within other Canadian and international jurisdictions to strengthen quality sport experiences for women and girls through participation in multilateral and bilateral instruments and fora;
3. Awareness: promoting the benefits for individuals and organizations through meaningful involvement of women and girls; and
4. Knowledge development: expansion, use of sharing of knowledge, practices and innovations concerning the sport experiences of women and girls through research and development (Canadian Heritage, 2009a, p. 7).

The policy also included an action plan that identified specific pathways proposed to achieve gender equity in all aspects of sport along the areas of intervention identified above (Canadian Heritage, 2009b). Although the 2009 policy was well received within the sport community and its action plan provided concrete strategies to achieve the objectives of the policy, gender inequities, particularly with respect to leadership roles, still prevail to this day. As such, the policy and its action plan were criticized for lacking accountability mechanisms to sanction sport organizations that did not comply with the policy. In other words, national sport organizations funded by Sport Canada were not negatively affected by their lack of practices leading to gender equity within their structures, processes, programs, and services (compare Demers, Lay, & Werthner, 2015; Fry, 2017; Safai, 2013). For example, in her review of Sport Canada's policy to enhance girls and women's involvement in Canadian sport, Safai[2] (2013, p. 344) argued that women:

> continue to face obstacles to full participation and representation. Formal mechanisms such as legislation and policy are still needed to push for gender equity in sport; however, such mechanisms cannot succeed without the political will of individuals and groups to adhere, enforce, and be accountable to such interventions.

Along similar lines and in response to a number of criticisms of the 2009 policy, the Report of the Standing Committee on Canadian Heritage investigating women and girls in sport identified several recommendations, including: "measurable objectives and an accountability framework" for the 2009 policy; mechanisms for the federal government to collect data from the sport organizations it funds with regard to "representation of women on boards of directors, programming that serves the unique needs of women and other underrepresented groups and apprenticeship and employment opportunities for women coaches, umpires and officials"; and funding decisions by the federal government "to benefit underrepresented groups in order to ensure that opportunities for girls and women are on par with those for boys and men" (Fry, 2017, p. 43). Fry's report included a total of 16 recommendations for gender equity in sport and providing an inclusive, accessible, and safe sport system for women and girls.

In their response to the Report of the Standing Committee on Canadian Heritage, leaders from the federal government reiterated their support for an inclusive, accessible, and equitable sport system, agreed with the recommendations put forth, and engaged themselves to undertake the necessary strategies to achieve the objectives (Government of Canada, 2018).

In a document reviewing policy and program considerations for sport participation for underrepresented groups in Canada, Cragg, Costas-Bradstreet, Arkell, and Lofstrom (2016, p. 14) noted:

> a lack of female role models both among sport leadership positions – as administrators, executives, coaches, officials, volunteers and board members of sport organizations, where the participation rate of women is about one-third the rate of men – and due to lower levels of media coverage of women's sports, also affect sport participation levels of girls and women.

In addition to government policies to encourage girls' and women's involvement at all levels in sport, there are numerous organizations working toward gender equity. These non-profit organizations are dedicated to promoting girls' and women's involvement in sport, physical activity, and leisure at the national or provincial level. At the national level, we have the Canadian Association for the Advancement of Women and Sport and Physical Activity (CAAWS), founded in 1981 (www.caaws.ca). At the provincial level, we have:

- ProMOTION Plus: British Columbia, founded in 1990 (www.promotionplus.org);
- Égale Action: Québec, founded in 2001 (www.egaleaction.com);
- WomenActive-NS: Nova-Scotia, founded in 2015 (www.womenactive.ca).

These organizations recognize that there is a problem in Canadian sport (including physical activity and leisure) and have undertaken strategies to initiate change. They challenge the long-held beliefs about the system in place, the ways of doing things, and the abiding certainty that all is well in Canadian sport.

These organizations established several programs, activities, and training workshops designed for all members of the sport community, with the goal of shifting the sport system toward inclusion, accessibility, and equity. They also exercise political influence and advocacy, and provide expertise and recommendations to ensure equity in Canadian sport.

CAAWS, ProMOTION Plus, Égale Action, and WomenActive all work with a small staff and budget. Soliciting funds on a yearly basis for programs and services is a constant struggle. In fact, it is impressive to observe how much they achieve with so few resources. It is important to note that they also sometimes face animosity from those who support the status quo. Despite progress that has been made in many sport sectors, current data about women's sport participation have not changed significantly, especially when it comes to leadership roles held in sport organizations. The next section addresses women's leadership and their under-representation within Canadian sport organizations.

Women's involvement in leadership positions

Studies to date show that a considerable amount of work remains to be done for Canadian women to realize all the benefits that participation in sport offers (Adriaanse, 2016; CAAWS, 2016; Donnelly, Banwell, di Carlo, & Kriger, 2016; Kidd, 2013). As stated in the introduction, Canada has accomplished important developments in terms of women's participation as athletes. However, efforts are still required to recruit and retain more women in sport leadership positions as coaches, officials, administrative and technical staff, leaders of sport organizations, and executive volunteers.

Overview of the current situation

Women coaches

In Canada, there are not many coaching jobs held by women. According to current figures, women are under-represented in head and assistant coaching positions. Not only are they under-represented but also their numbers are declining. Within the university level, the results showed that, in 2013, 17% of coaches were female, compared with 19% in 2011 and 20% in 2005 (Donnelly, Norman, & Kidd, 2013). Current data at the national level in Canada show that, out of a total of 54 national teams, there are only 9 women head coaches (16%). At the Olympic level, the situation is no better. Table 8.1 shows the percentage of Canadian women head coaches from 2000 to 2016.

The data are very clear: women have not yet managed to advance in the profession of coaching. With the countless successes of Canadian athletes in international sports, one would think that more women would access coaching positions. It appears that these positions still escape women.

There is a high degree of consistency in the literature about the barriers that women face in sport leadership positions. This is more accurate in the literature about women in coaching

Table 8.1 Percentage of Canadian women head coaches at the Olympic Games

Olympic Games	Women (%)	Men (%)
2000	13	87
2002	21	79
2004	7	93
2006	15	85
2008	9	91
2010	13	87
2012	19	81
2014	10	90
2016	6	94

than in any other sport leadership position. One of the most comprehensive literature reviews on the subject comes from LaVoi and Dutove (2012). Using Brofenbrenner's ecological systems theory, they organized the barriers and supports "from most proximal (individual) to most distal (socio-cultural) to the coach" (LaVoi and Dutove, 2012, p. 17). We explore those barriers in detail in the next section of the chapter. On the research side, LaVoi and Dutove's (2012) analysis identified several gaps: (1) most researchers have studied high-level female coaches (almost no data are available at the youth and interscholastic levels); (2) the research by competitive level is disproportionate; (3) most of the work on female coaches did not employ a framework of intersectionality; and (4) researchers tend to focus more on barriers than on supports. As such, there is an urgent need for more research on women coaches addressing those gaps.

Women officials

Very little information and data are available on officials in Canadian sport. The working conditions of officials vary considerably from one sport to another. Some get paid, but many are volunteers. Some judges and officials benefit from an expense account in addition to remuneration, whereas many are responsible for covering their own expenses. In some sports, the working conditions of officials improve when they climb the ladder, in terms of officiating hierarchy. The requirements to become an official are rigorous for some sports, whereas, in others, it may be relatively easy to access officiating. Based on some sources, the number of females holding officiating/umpiring roles in Canada has remained stable over time and, in some cases, there has been a decline between 1999 and 2008 (Gouvernement du Québec, 2008). Figure 8.1 shows that the numbers of women officials are still very low and women's involvement has historically been less than a third relative to men's involvement (CAAWS, 2016).

Women administrators

The status for women in administrative roles in the sport system is slightly better. In fact, "females are more likely to be involved in administrative and managerial roles in sport [Figure 8.2] than in coaching and officiating roles. At both National Sport Organizations (NSOs) and Multi-Sport Organizations (MSOs), there is a stronger presence of female leaders" (CAAWS, 2016, p. 14) than the numbers of female coaches.

It is worth noting that, in Canada, six major MSOs are led by women who hold positions either as chief executive officers (CEOs) or as presidents. These organizations include the

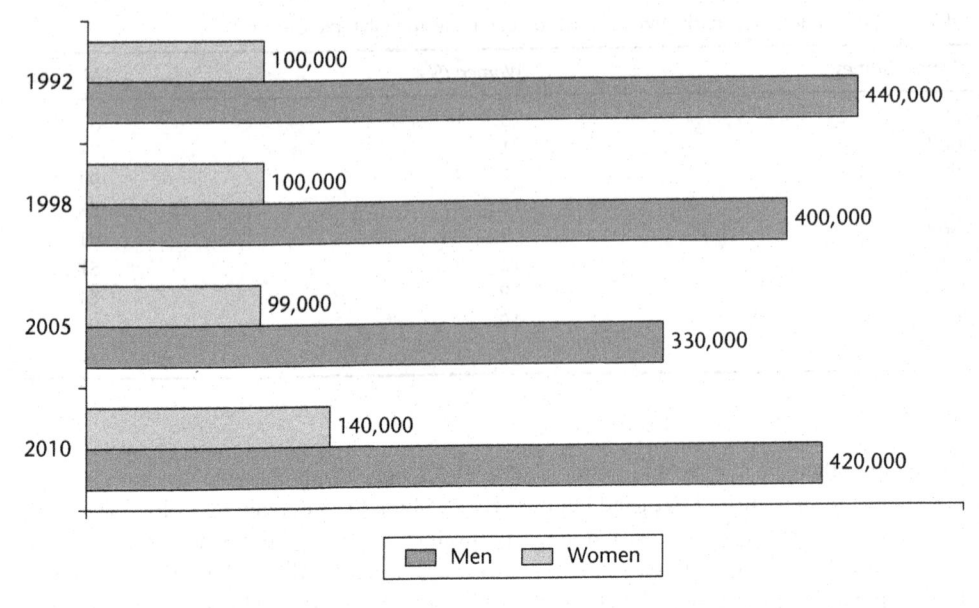

Figure 8.1 Men and women officials in Canada (adapted from CAAWS, 2016)

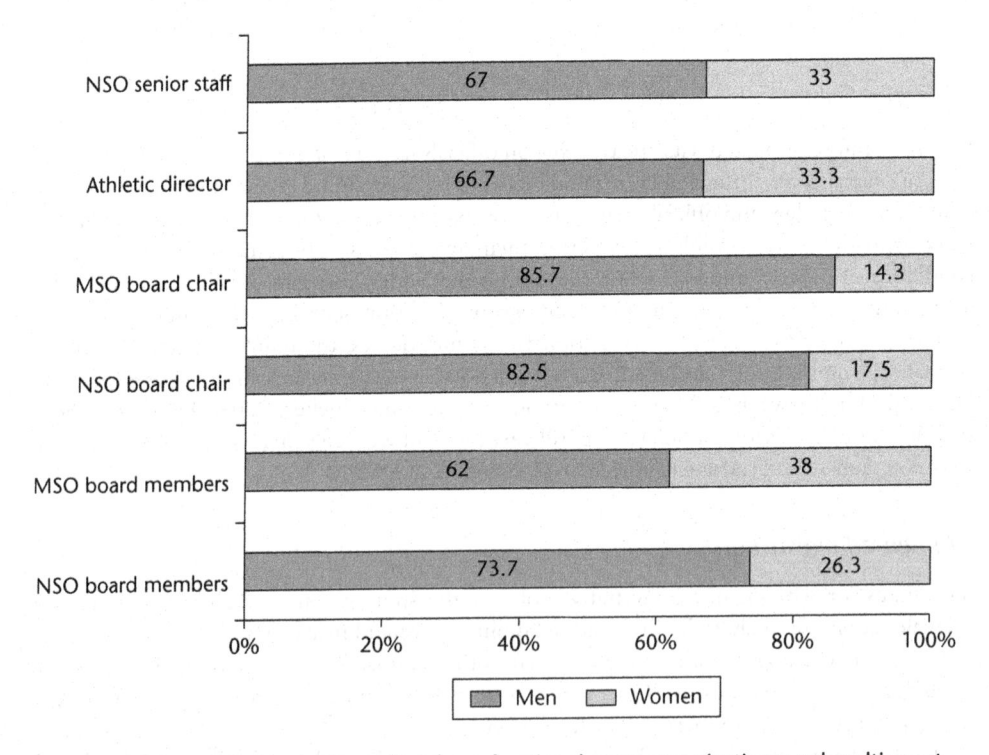

Figure 8.2 Percentage breakdown of leaders of national sport organizations and multi-sport organizations by gender (adapted from CAAWS, 2016)

Coaching Association of Canada, the Canadian Olympic Committee, the Canadian Paralympic Committee, Own the Podium, AthletesCAN, and the Canadian Collegiate Athletic Association. As well, the Canadian Sport Institutes Pacific and the Canadian Sport Institutes Ontario are led by women CEOs. These facts might be an indicator that some important cultural changes are taking place in national sport organizations.

Explaining the under-representation of women in leadership positions

Research from Canada, the United States, Germany, Australia, and Scandinavia has identified numerous persisting barriers to the under-representation of women in leadership positions in sport (compare Adriaanse, 2016; Adriaanse & Schofield, 2013; Allen & Shaw, 2013; Burton, 2015; Hovden, 2006, 2010; Koca & Öztürk, 2015; LaVoi & Dutove, 2012; Ottesen, Skirstad, Pfister, & Habermann, 2010; Pfister & Radtke, 2009; Shaw, 2006). To make sense of these data and to understand the under-representation of women better, several authors suggest a multi-level perspective (Burton, 2015; Donnelly et al., 2016; LaVoi, 2016). Using this perspective, it is possible to classify those barriers at the macro-level (societal), meso-level (organizational), and micro-level (individual) (Table 8.2).

Even with the existence of barriers at the macro (societal) and micro (individual) levels, this review of the literature clearly demonstrates that most barriers identified are located within the meso (organizational) level. As can be seen in Table 8.2, organizational practices and

Table 8.2 Barriers explaining the shortage of women in leadership positions in sport

Level	Main barriers identified in research literature
Macro-societal	• Field marked by sexism (Anderson & Kian, 2012; Pfister & Radtke, 2009) • Racism, homophobia, and marginalization (LaVoi & Dutove, 2012) • Limited impact of legislations and policies on gender and diversity (Adriaanse & Schofield, 2014)
Meso-organizational	• Unfavorable treatment by media (Fink, 2015; Trolan, 2013) • Discretionary rules for nominations (Pfister & Radtke, 2006) • Culture of power and exclusion within decision-making process of the board of directors (Adriaanse & Schofield, 2013) • Rules and procedures and organizational practices (Shaw, 2006, 2007) • Attitudes and stereotypes (Koca & Öztürk, 2015) • Limited involvement originating from problems with "women" (Hovden, 2006, 2010) • Denial of or contesting the problem (Shaw, 2006) • Work conditions of coaches (including challenging professional path, low salary, salary discrepancies with men's salaries, frequent travel, and issues of reconciling workfamily balance) (Allen & Shaw, 2013) • Competition between women coaches (LaVoi & Dutove, 2012) • Intimidation and harassment directed at women coaches (LaVoi & Dutove, 2012)
Micro-individual	• Limited mobility for women coaches (LaVoi & Dutove, 2012) • Lack of self-confidence and feelings of ineffectiveness by women coaches (LaVoi & Dutove, 2012) • Stress and feelings of depression among women coaches (LaVoi & Dutove, 2012) • Lack of knowledge about women's ambitions to hold leadership positions within organizations (Adriaanse & Schofield, 2013)

organizational culture are crucial elements for gender equity within sport organizations. As such, they must be prioritized for organizational change to occur toward gender equity, as well as for ongoing research at the meso-level within the context of sport organizations. Ironically, there appears to be a dearth of research in gender and sport at the meso-level.

In addition to the barriers identified in the research, the actions currently undertaken in Canada highlight the difficult challenges of reaching equity. Equity has not been achieved even though addressing organizational issues (e.g., gender equity) has appeared as a government priority over the last few years (Minister of Justice, 2017; Canadian Heritage, 2009, 2012). To this day, government policies and initiatives have not resulted in progress toward gender equity in sport organizations. It is still difficult to truly capture both qualitative and quantitative data about the presence of women in the various Canadian sport organizations. In addition, it is equally difficult to understand how government and organizational policies and other actions have impacted efforts toward gender equity, and what forces have led to resistance and/or barriers in implementing the Canadian government policy on women and girls in sport. This is an important area of study if we are to truly change attitudes, behaviors, and practices in sport organizations, and create a sport system that is inclusive, accessible, and equitable.

Gender-based violence

There is a steady increase in evidence about sexual harassment and abuse in sport (Kirby & Demers, 2013). Our review of Canadian research on the subject enabled us to identify the following issues: (1) lack of a common definition of violence in sport; (2) lack of data on the prevalence of gender-based violence in sport; (3) lack of education and awareness; (4) lack of dedicated resources to address gender-based violence; and (5) low standards on the provision of safe spaces.

The fact that researchers do not agree on a common definition of sexual violence in sport (sexual abuse and sexual harassment) makes it difficult to compare data between studies and to have a clear picture of the situation. In this respect, Parent, Lavoie, Thibodeau, Hébert, and Blais (2016) pointed out that "it is impossible at this time to know whether the data regarding sexual abuse in sport are a true reflection of what girls and women experience" (p. 2668). In fact, it may reflect an underestimation of the problem because athletes do not always perceive intimate or sexual relationships between athletes and their coaches as sexual abuse (Kirby & Greaves, 1997). Furthermore, Stirling and Kerr (2009) found that many athletes who have experienced sexual abuse do not see themselves as victims because they may consider such behavior to be normal in sport. For their part, Parent et al. (2016) found that 59.4% of male and 40.6% of female athletes perceived sexual contacts with the coach as being consensual. Clearly, athletes lack education about what is consensual contact with someone in a position of authority like the coach.

We do not have substantial Canadian data on the prevalence of the phenomenon. In 1997, Kirby and Greaves reported that 1.9% of 266 adult male and female Canadian elite athletes were sexually abused in the sport environment before the age of 16. More recently, Parent et al. (2016) conducted a survey with 6,450 14- to 17-year-old athletes in Québec (one of the 10 provinces in Canada). Without considering the source of the abuse (relative, coach, etc.) or the type of contact (penetration or not), they found that 8.8% of female athletes had experienced sexual abuse during their lifetime and that they have 4.78 times more risk than male athletes to experience sexual violence in sport.

Sadly, women and girls not only have to be concerned about the barriers preventing their full engagement as sport participants/actors, but must also worry about harassment, discrimination, and sexual abuse. Furthermore, one might assume that it is happening more than we think given the recent cases of sexual abuse and sexual misconduct cases in Canadian sport (compare Banerjee, 2017; Canadian Broadcasting Corporation, 2018a; Canadian Press, 2017; Hall,

2015; Heroux, Seglin, & Houlihan, 2018). The Bertrand Charest case in Alpine ski was one of the cases that received the most media coverage in Canada in 2018 (Canadian Broadcasting Corporation, 2018b). Four former female athletes came out publicly about the sexual abuses they have suffered while training on the national team under Charest's leadership. Following that press conference, the governments (provincial and federal) reacted promptly and put in place different measures to protect and support athletes (e.g., www.sportaide.ca/en/home).

Cragg et al. (2016) underscored the importance for organizations to have harassment and anti-discrimination policies. To this list, we should add the development of codes of conduct within sport organizations. Codes of conduct and policies are not, however, enough. Donnelly et al. (2016) studied 42 provincial sport organizations (PSOs) from Ontario, and 42 national sport organizations (NSOs), and found that 86% of NSOs and 71% of PSOs have anti-harassment policies or procedures, but they noticed that athletes don't know where to find these policies and, most of the time, they don't even know that they exist. Furthermore, only 10% of PSOs and 14% of NSOs have a harassment officer.

We share Stirling and Kerr's (2009) conclusion that it is imperative to create:

> awareness among athletes that performance excellence does not need to come at the cost of personal well-being . . . the most effective way to protect young athletes from abuse is to affect the culture of sport in which the abuse occurs
>
> *(p. 235)*

The good news is that new initiatives have been undertaken in Québec in 2017. A new provincial organization dedicated to support athletes when they experience violence in sport was created: Sport'Aide (www.sportaide.ca). The other initiative is the website (sportbienetre.ca). Their mission is to:

> promote a healthy and safe sport environment for young athletes. Through the dissemination of information and raising awareness, we help members of the sport community (athletes, parents, coaches, administrators, and other stakeholders) to understand, manage and, above all, eliminate violence in sport, in all its forms.
>
> *(translation from Sportbienetre.ca, 2017, para. 1)*

The two websites are now available in both French and English.

Future prospects to achieve gender equity in the Canadian sport system

To initiate change and work toward gender equity in Canadian sport, two approaches are proposed: a theoretical approach (research) and a pragmatic approach (practice).

The theoretical approach or the researcher's perspective

To understand women's under-representation in leadership positions, consideration of a multidisciplinary approach is essential to determine factors related to gender, equality, and organizations. We propose an approach anchored in both *feminist theories* and *institutional theory*.

On the one hand, *feminist theories* allow for a critical analysis of social relationships among women and men within organizational processes and practices (Code, 2000). Specifically, *post-structuralist feminism theories* emphasize the importance of going beyond the study of women's individual paths to understand the systemic factors influencing their path (Calás & Smircich, 2009; Lansky, 2000) and analyze their decisions by contextualizing them locally and globally (Ekinsmyth, 2013; Welter, Brush, & De Bruin, 2014). These theories envision organizational practices as the result of gender-sensitive processes and underscore the importance of considering the contextual and cultural dimensions of organizations (Lee-Gosselin, Brière, & Ann, 2013). These theories interpret organizations as androcentric and heteronormative spaces rather than as open and accessible spaces, where success is based uniquely on competencies, will, and personal achievements (Bhavnani, 2007). The feminist approaches favor an analysis of intersectionality that, in addition to considering the different inequities that exist in women's paths, highlights women's diverse experiences (LaVoi, 2016). Intersectionality (e.g., race and ethnicity, sexual orientation, class, gender, ability) operates at two levels: (1) microsocial: where the effects of inequitable structures on the life of individuals are analyzed; and (2) macrosocial: where power systems involved in the production, organization, and maintenance of inequities are questioned (Bilge, 2010). This perspective offers an alternative that is highly relevant to address the complexity of gender relationships within sport organizations by way of the processes of critique, narrative revision, and experimentation (Shaw & Frisby, 2006).

On the other hand, *institutional theory* stipulates that organizations are socially constituted and subjected to external pressures that influence their structures and practices and allow them to operate legitimately in a domain (Dillard, Rigsby, & Goodman, 2004; Scott, 2014). In this context, institutionalism is the social process by which individuals within organizations come to accept shared interpretations of reality (Palthe, 2014). Institutionalism occurs through regulative (i.e., policies, legislations, work rules), normative (i.e., work norms, expectations, habits), and cognitive (i.e., values, symbols, shared beliefs) processes (Palthe, 2014). Within this perspective, the mutual relationship between the structures and actors is important because it determines the operations of the organization and the basis for institutional change. As noted by Palthe (2014, p. 63):

> institutional theory suggests that social legitimacy, whether regulative (*have to*), normative (*ought to*) or cognitive (*want to*), should be considered as an input to organizational change along with raw materials and other resources upon which the process of change depends.

According to institutional theory, organizational change can occur through stakeholder involvement because these stakeholders can introduce new ways of thinking, alternative ways of doing, and the potential for change, particularly at the cognitive level (Walker & Sartore-Baldwin, 2013).

This overview of the two theoretical approaches allows for a comprehensive set of coherent variables that offer an overarching understanding of the under-representation of women in leadership positions in sport. The combined approaches have never been applied to research in sport. They would allow us to understand better how the culture of sport organizations is contributing to maintaining the status quo, and what strategies need to be developed to have the greatest impact on reaching gender equity.

The pragmatic approach or the perspective of the actors

The most current documentation available to inform practical actions toward gender equity in sport organizations originates from four different sources: (1) the draft recommendations from the working group on women and sport commissioned by the Federal–Provincial/Territorial Sport Committee (unpublished document, 2018); (2) the report on the status of female sport participation in Canada: *Women in Sport: Fuelling a lifetime of participation* (CAAWS, 2016); (3) the Report of the Standing Committee on Canadian Heritage (Government of Canada, 2018) entitled "Women and girls in sport"; and (4) the website www.solutionswomensport.ca based on the outcome of the third national conference on women and sport: *The 2015 Conversation*.

An analysis of the recommendations proposed in these documents made it possible to highlight certain common elements. First, the recommendations seek to inspire actions at every level of the system: macro-societal, meso-organizational, and micro-individual levels. Few recommendations target the system at large; some are linked to sport organizations directly (from sport participation at the community level to high-performance sport) whereas others focus on the individual.

Second, recommendations can be grouped in four thematic areas: participation, leadership, media, and gender-based violence. The recommendations on sport participation aspire to enable more girls and women to benefit from an active lifestyle. The recommendations around leadership focus on solutions to have more women in leadership positions (i.e., coaches, officials, administrative and technical staff, leaders of sport organizations, and executive volunteers) and help those who already occupy these positions. The recommendations' goal for gender-based violence is to help create safe sport environments for all girls and women, regardless of their sexual orientation or gender identity. Finally, the objective of the media recommendations is to make women's sport more visible in the media, and educate the media industry on fair and equitable coverage of women's sport.

Third, the recommendations are all driven by two important principles: accountability and inclusion. Accountability refers to the need for one to be responsible and able to explain actions. Accountability may also include incentives when actions are congruent with policies and strategies, and/or consequences when actions are not. For example, organizations can have policies for harassment but, if they are poorly conceived, outdated, and not practiced, they are meaningless. A monitoring and tracking report is essential and tying the results to incentives and consequences is one of the most effective elements of success. For the inclusive principle, we acknowledge the fact that "no two girls experience sport in the same way. Gendered sport experiences are rich and complex in their diversity and are intertwined with other dimensions of identity" (Government of Canada, 2018, p. 1). Thus, the inclusive principle is linked to intersectionality where one's identities (Figure 8.3) "interact on multiple, interdependent, and often simultaneous levels with racism, sexism, homophobia, and belief-based bigotry, which contributes to 'intersecting' forms of systemic injustice, oppression, and social inequality" (LaVoi, 2016, p. 16).

Below is a summary of the recommendations from the four main sources we used (listed at the start of the pragmatic approach section). These can be seen as critical outcomes to enhance girls' and women's involvement in sport.

1. Policy commitments for women and girls in sport are clear and measurable;
2. Accountability and compliance mechanisms are in place and enforced;
3. Program design and delivery meet the diverse needs of women and girls in sport;
4. Communication and media drive knowledge sharing and behavior change;
5. Female representation in sport leadership positions moves towards parity;
6. All genders work to eradicate gender-based violence in sport;
7. The sport sector systemically uses research and data collection methods to better understand the diverse needs of women and girls in sport;
8. The sport sector intentionally engages in partnerships to reach women and girls for whom intersecting factors create additional barriers to sport participation (e.g. lesbian, gay, bisexual, transgender+ (LBTQ+), indigenous, women with disabilities, etc.);
9. The sport sector conducts sustainability planning, ensuring that medium- and long-term investments are secured for sufficient duration to achieve trend, experience, and system transformation for women and girls in sport.

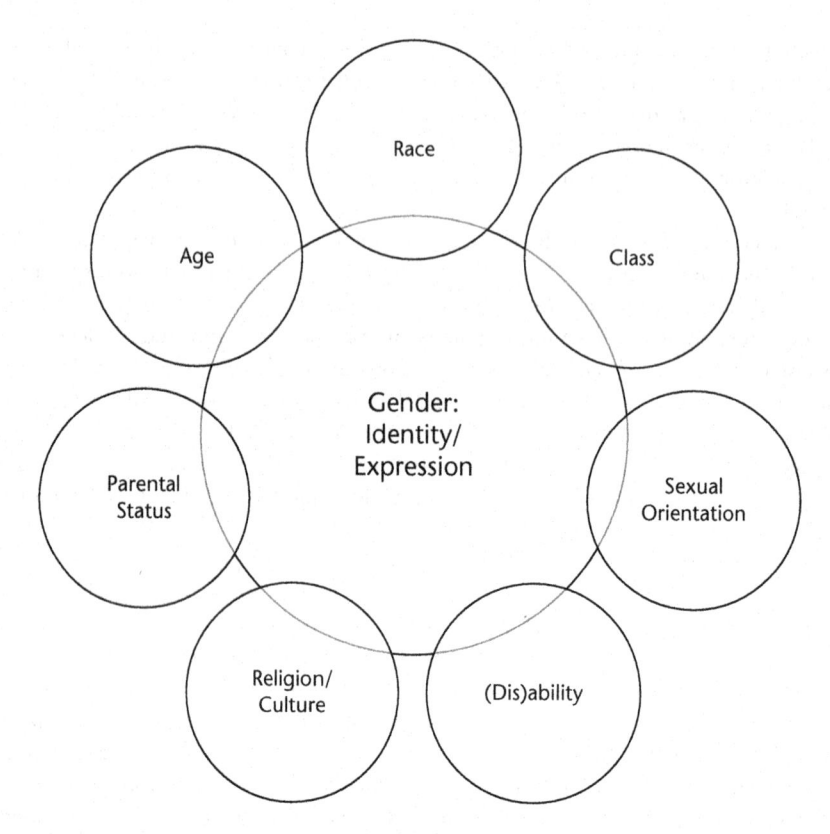

Figure 8.3 Intersectional identities (adapted from LaVoi, 2016, p. 14)

Conclusions

The definition of insanity is doing the same thing over and over again and expecting different results (unknown source). With regard to achieving gender equity in the leadership of Canadian sport, this quotation may be accurate. In the chapter, we have discussed how a women in sport policy has been in place within Canadian sport since 1986, and how calls for a sport system to be inclusive, accessible, and equitable have been featured in several federal government documents over the last 30 years. Although Canadian women's successes as athletes in international competition have exceeded their male counterparts' performances in recent years, women's access to leadership positions in Canadian sport (i.e., coaches, officials, administrative and technical staff, leaders of sport organizations, and executive volunteers) has been limited. As such, gender equity appears to be an elusive concept.

Achieving gender equity in sport is not an easy task given federal, provincial, territorial, and local governments' involvement in Canadian sport and the numerous sport organizations operating at all those levels. Although good intentions and voluntary practices toward gender equity might have been perceived as the least contentious strategies to encourage equity in the leadership of sport organizations, these strategies have been completely ineffective. As Robertson (2016) pointed out "the Canadian approach appears to focus on encouragement as opposed to legislation" (p. 217). So far, the different programs and professional development opportunities offered to women have not had any significant impact on women's representation in leadership positions in sport.

While addressing leaders from the business sector, Barton and Yee (2017, p. 121) noted that it is "time for a new gender-equality playbook. The old one isn't working. We need bolder leadership and more exacting execution." This quotation applies well to Canada's sport system. The solutions to gender equity are beyond requiring "hope and wishful thinking." As Barton and Yee (2017) pointed out, employees need to question strategies, employees and leaders need to show their commitment to gender equity in their actions, bias must be addressed directly, support and help are needed from everyone within the organization, execution of all actions toward gender equity cannot be compromised, "fresh, bold thinking" is needed from leaders and employees, and leaders must have the courage to undertake the necessary changes within the organization (Barton & Yee, 2017, p. 123). Similar actions are required from all sport leaders who must act and change to demonstrate tangible and measurable outcomes with respect to gender equity. Action-oriented recommendations with concrete outcomes and timelines may not be the approach undertaken by government bureaucracies; however, gender equity issues are not being addressed and, as a result, the status of women's leadership within sport is in crisis. We share Marion Lay's understanding of gender equity in sport when she explains that "change has been very slow because we don't have a government that applies the necessary big stick, such as denying funding to non-compliant NSOs. We've set targets, but never quotas" (Robertson, 2013, p. 28). Using specific action-oriented initiatives, based on best practices, and implementing tracking mechanisms to monitor progress and ensure accountability – with incentives and consequences – tied to funding, makes it nearly impossible to ignore the issues. As a collective, researchers and practitioners need to advise governments that a new, action-oriented, measurable outcome-driven process is the only way to ensure real change. Leaders of sport organizations want to know how to achieve gender equity, and it is our collective responsibility to point them in the right direction and help them achieve this objective.

Leader profile: Wendy Pattenden, CEO, Canadian Sport Institute Pacific

Figure 8.4 Wendy Pattenden
Photo courtesy of Canadian Sport Institute Pacific

Wendy Pattenden holds several leadership positions within Canada's sport system. Her primary role is Chief Executive Officer of the Canadian Sport Institute (CSI) Pacific. Wendy has held this role since the inception of the organization in 1999. The CSI Pacific is focused on delivering high-performance sport programs and services to athletes and coaches in British Columbia. CSI Pacific has offices in Victoria, Vancouver, and Whistler, and works in partnership with the national network of Canadian Sport Institutes (Calgary, Ontario, Québec) and a network of regional centers (PacificSport Centers – Columbia Basin, Fraser Valley, Interior BC, Okanagan, Vancouver Island) to assist athletes and coaches achieve sport excellence. Based on collaborative leadership, Wendy has forged relationships with more than 20 national sport organizations and has employed 75 experts to support athletes' and coaches' quest for excellence.

Wendy completed her Master's in Business Administration (MBA) in 2004. In 2005, Wendy authored a report entitled "Performance Priorities in British Columbia." This report launched a new Integrated Performance System (IPS) for sport in British Columbia. Wendy's subsequent report (2008) was the "Integrated Performance System Evaluation Report." These two reports have contributed to better performance results nationally and internationally.

In addition to Wendy's leadership of the CSI Pacific, she is also Chair of the Board of Directors of the Sport for Life (SFL) Society. As a volunteer leader of the SFL Society, Wendy guides and develops the strategic direction of the non-profit agency. The SFL Society is centered on improving the health of Canadians by combining experts from sport, recreation, education, and health sectors to ensure quality programs in sport and physical literacy. The SFL Society strives to deliver the Long-Term Athlete Development model through their partnership with numerous sport organizations.

Wendy is also a voting member of the Canadian Olympic Committee Session, playing a leadership role in the management of the COC and its objectives. She also teaches in the Master in High Performance Coaching and Technical Leadership within the School of Kinesiology at the University of British Columbia. Wendy's foray into sport originated as a world-ranked professional tennis player (top 100 in the world), 12-time Canadian tennis champion and Female Athlete of the Year (City of Greater Victoria). Wendy was inducted to the Greater Victoria Sports Hall of Fame in 2003. Before her role within the CSI Pacific, Wendy served double duty as the Director of Athlete Development and Head of the National Team Coach/Olympic Coach for Tennis Canada.

Notes

1. The authors gratefully acknowledge the financial support of Sport Canada Research Initiative and the Social Sciences and Humanities Research Council of Canada.
2. For an excellent historical overview of Sport Canada's policies for women and girls in sport, please refer to Safai (2013).

References

Adriaanse, J. (2016). Gender diversity in the governance of sport associations: The Sydney Scoreboard Global Index of Participation. *Journal of Business Ethics*, **137**(1), 149–160.

Adriaanse, J. A. & Schofield, T. (2013). Analysing gender dynamics in sport governance: A new regimes-based approach. *Sport Management Review*, **16**(4), 498–513.

Adriaanse, J. & Schofield, T. (2014). The impact of gender quotas on gender equality in sport governance. *Journal of Sport Management*, **28**(5), 485–497.

Allen, J. B. & Shaw, S. (2013). An interdisciplinary approach to examining the working conditions of women coaches. *International Journal of Sports Science and Coaching*, **8**(1), 1–18.

Anderson, E. & Kian, E. M. (2012). Examining media contestation of masculinity and head trauma in the National Football League. *Men and Masculinities*, **15**(2), 152–173.

Banerjee, S. (2017). Ex-ski coach Bertrand Charest found guilty on 37 charges in sex trial. *Toronto Star*, June 22. Retrieved from https://www.thestar.com/sports/amateur/2017/06/22/ex-ski-coach-bertrand-charest-found-guilty-on-37-charges-in-sex-trial.html.
Barton, D. & Yee, L. (2017). Time for a new gender-equality playbook. *McKinsey Quarterly*, **1**, 121–123.
Belletête, V. & Langelier, E. (2016). *Données sur la progression des femmes en sciences et en génie au Québec et au Canada*. Sherbrooke, QC: Université de Sherbrooke. Retrieved from http://compagnie-f.org/wp-content/uploads/2016/06/PresentationStatistiques-28avril-VBelletete.pdf
Bhavnani, K. K. (2007). Interconnections and configurations: Toward a global feminist ethnography. In S. N. Hesse-Biber (ed.), *Handbook of Feminist Research* (pp. 639–649). Thousand Oaks, CA: Sage.
Bilge, S. (2010). Théorisations féministes de l'intersectionnalité. *Diogène*, **225**(1), 70–88.
Brière, S. (2018). *Les femmes dans les métiers et professions traditionnellement masculins; une réalité teintée de stéréotypes de genre nécessitant une analyse critique, systémique, comparative et multidisciplinaire*, rapport final, Québec, Fonds de recherche du Québec-Société et culture (FRQSC).
Burton, L. J. (2015). Underrepresentation of women in sport leadership: A review of research. *Sport Management Review*, **18**(2), 155–165.
Calás, M. B. & Smircich, L. (2009). Feminist perspectives on gender in organizational research: What is and yet to be. In D. Buchanan & A. Bryman (eds), *Handbook of Organizational Research Methods* (pp. 246–269). Thousand Oaks, CA: Sage.
Canadian Association for the Advancement of Women and Sport and Physical Activity (CAAWS) (2016). Women in sport: Fuelling a lifetime of participation. A report on the status of female sport participation in Canada. Retrieved from www.caaws.ca/e/wp-content/uploads/2016/03/FWC_ResearchPublication_EN_7March2016.pdf.
Canadian Broadcasting Corporation (2018a). Gymnastics coach Michel Arsenault under investigation for sex assaults. *CBC News*, January 25. Retrieved from https://www.msn.com/en-ca/sports/news/gymnastics-coach-michel-arsenault-under-investigation-for-sex-assaults/ar-AAv8AXj?ocid=spartandhp.
Canadian Broadcasting Corporation (2018b). Bertrand Charest abuse case spotlights the need for real change. *CBC news.* , June 7 Retrieved from https://www.cbc.ca/sports/olympics/skiing/allison-forsyth-bertrand-charest-1.4694582.
Canadian Heritage (2009a). *Actively Engaged. A policy on sport for women and girls*. Ottawa, ON: Government of Canada. Retrieved from http://publications.gc.ca/collections/collection_2010/pc-ch/CH24-27-2009-eng.pdf.
Canadian Heritage (2009b). *Actively Engaged. A policy on sport for women and girls: Action plan 2009–2012*. Ottawa, ON: Government of Canada. Retrieved from http://publications.gc.ca/collections/collection_2010/pc-ch/CH24-27-1-2009-eng.pdf.
Canadian Heritage (2012). *Canadian Sport Policy 2012*. Ottawa, ON: Government of Canada. Retrieved from http://sirc.ca/csp2012.
Canadian Press (2017). Top Canadian women's gymnastics official charged with multiple sexual offences. *CBC Sports*, December 15. Retrieved from www.cbc.ca/sports/olympics/gymnastics/brubaker-gymnastics-canada-sexual-offences-1.4452217
Catalyst (2017) Women in the workforce: Canada. Retrieved from www.catalyst.org/knowledge/women-workforce-canada.
Code, L. (ed.) (2000). *Encyclopedia of Feminist Theories*. New York: Routledge.
Cragg, S., Costas-Bradstreet, C., Arkell, J., & Lofstrom, K. (2016). *Policy and Program Considerations for Increasing Sport Participation among Members of Under-represented Groups in Canada: A literature review*. Ottawa, ON: Interprovincial Sport and Recreation Council.
Demers, G., Lay, M., & Werthner, P. (2015). The 2015 Conversation on Women and Sport. Conference held in Québec City June 9–12. Retrieved from https://www.solutionswomensport.ca.
Dillard, J. F., Rigsby, J. T., & Goodman, C. (2004). The making and remaking of organization context: Duality and the institutionalization process. *Accounting, Auditing and Accountability Journal*, **17**(4), 506–542.
Donnelly, P., Banwell, J., di Carlo, D., & Kriger, D. (2016). *Women and Girls' Participation, Development and Excellence in Sport*. Centre for Sport Policy Studies Research Report, University of Toronto.
Donnelly, P., Norman, M., & Kidd, B. (2013). *Gender Equity in Canadian Interuniversity Sport: A biennial report* (no. 2). Centre for Sport Policy Studies Research Report, University of Toronto.
Ekinsmyth, C. (2013). Managing the business of everyday life: The roles of space and place in "mumpreneurship". *International Journal of Entrepreneurial Behaviour and Research*, **19**(5), 525–546.

Fink, J. S. (2015). Female athletes, women's sport, and the sport media commercial complex: Have we really "come a long way, baby"? *Sport Management Review*, **18**(3), 331–342.

Fry, H. (Chair) (2017). *Women and Girls in Sport. Report of the Standing Committee on Canadian Heritage*. Ottawa, ON: House of Commons, Government of Canada. Retrieved from www.ourcommons.ca/Content/Committee/421/CHPC/Reports/RP9068268/chpcrp07/chpcrp07-e.pdf.

Government of Canada (2018). Government response to the Report of the Standing Committee on Canadian Heritage entitled *Women and girls in sport*. Ottawa, ON: Government of Canada.

Gouvernement du Québec (2008). La place des femmes dans le sport au Québec. Ministère de l'Éducation, du Loisir et du Sport. Québec. Retrieved from www.education.gouv.qc.ca/fileadmin/site_web/documents/SLS/sport_loisir_act_physique/RapportLandry_PDFS_080528.pdf.

Hall, V. (2015). Marcel Aubut resignation from COC raises spectre of abuse of power in amateur sport. *National Post*, October 7. Retrieved from http://nationalpost.com/sports/olympics/marcel-aubut-resignation-raises-spectre-of-abuse-of-power-in-amateur-sport.

Heroux, D., Seglins, D., & Houlihan, R. (2018). Ex-U.S. athlete tells Speed Skating Canada of head coach's alleged sexual relationships with skaters. *CBC News*, January 19. Retrieved from www.cbc.ca/news/canada/crowe-speed-skating-1.4495942.

Hovden, J. (2006). The gender order as a policy issue in sport: A study of Norwegian sports organizations. *NORA: Nordic Journal of Women's Studies*, **14**(1), 41–53.

Hovden, J. (2010). Female top leaders – prisoners of gender? The gendering of leadership discourses in Norwegian sports organizations. *International Journal of Sport Policy and Politics*, **2**(2), 189–203.

Kay, F. M., Alarie, S. L., & Adjei, J. K. (2016). Undermining gender equality: Female attrition from private law practice. *Law & Society Review*, **50**(3), 766–801.

Kidd, B. (2013). Where are the female coaches? *Canadian Journal for Women in Coaching*, **13**(1). Retrieved from www.coach.ca/files/CJWC_FEB2013_EN.pdf.

Kirby, S. & Demers, G. (2013). Sexual harassment and abuse in sport. In E. Roper (ed.), *Gender Relations in Sport* (pp. 141–161). Boston, MA: Sense.

Kirby, S. L. & Greaves, L. (1997). Foul play: Sexual harassment in sport. *Recherches Féministes*, **10**(1), 5–33.

Koca, C. & Öztürk, P. (2015). Gendered perceptions about female managers in Turkish sport organizations. *European Sport Management Quarterly*, **15**(3), 381–406.

Lansky, M. (2000). Gender, women and all the rest (Part 1). *International Labour Review*, **139**(4), 481–504.

LaVoi, N. M. (2016). A framework to understand experiences of women coaches around the globe. In N. M. LaVoi (ed.), *Women in Sports Coaching* (pp.13–34). New York: Routledge.

LaVoi, N. M. & Dutove, J. K. (2012). Barriers and supports for female coaches: An ecological model. *Sports Coaching Review*, **1**(1), 17–37.

Lee-Gosselin, H., Brière, S., & Ann, H. (2013). Resistances to gender mainstreaming in organizations: Toward a new approach. *Gender in Management: An International Journal*, **28**(8), 468–485.

Minister of Justice (2017). *Physical Activity and Sport Sct S.C. 2003 c.2*. Ottawa, ON: Government of Canada. Retrieved from http://laws-lois.justice.gc.ca/PDF/P-13.4.pdf.

Ottesen, L., Skirstad, B., Pfister, G., & Habermann, U. (2010). Gender relations in Scandinavian sport organizations - a comparison of the situation and the policies in Denmark, Norway and Sweden. *Sport in Society*, **13**(4), 657–675.

Palthe, J. (2014). Regulative, normative, and cognitive elements of organizations: Implications for managing change. *Management and Organizational Studies*, **1**(2), 59–66.

Parent, S., Lavoie, F., Thibodeau, M.-È., Hébert, M., & Blais, M. (2016). Sexual Violence Experienced in the Sport Context by a Representative Sample of Québec Adolescents. *Journal of Interpersonal Violence*, **31**(16), 2666–2686.

Pfister, G. & Radtke, S. (2006). Dropping out: Why male and female leaders in German sports federations break off their careers. *Sport Management Review*, **9**(2), 111–139.

Pfister, G. & Radtke, S. (2009). Sport, women, and leadership: Results of a project on executives in German sports organizations. *European Journal of Sport Science*, **9**(4), 229–243.

Robertson, S. (2013). Opening doors for women: In conversation with Marion Lay. In G. Demers, L. Greaves, S. Kirby, & M. Lay (eds), *Playing it Forward: 50 years of women and sport history in Canada* (pp. 26–39). Toronto, ON: Feminist History Society.

Robertson, S. (2016). Hear their voices: Suggestions for developing and supporting women coaches from around the world. In N. M. LaVoi (ed.), *Women in Sports Coaching* (pp. 177–222). New York: Routledge.

Safai, P. (2013). Women in sport policy. In L. Thibault & J. Harvey (eds), *Sport Policy in Canada* (pp. 317–349). Ottawa, ON: University of Ottawa Press.

Scott, R. (2014). *Institutions and Organizations*, 4th edn. Thousand Oaks, CA: Sage.

Shaw, S. (2006). Gender suppression in New Zealand regional sports trusts. *Women in Management Review*, **21**(7), 554–566.

Shaw, S. (2007). Touching the intangible? An analysis of the Equality Standard: A Framework for Sport. *Equal Opportunities International*, **26**(5), 420–434.

Shaw, S. & Frisby, W. (2006). Can gender equity be more equitable?: Promoting an alternative frame for sport management research, education and practice. *Journal of Sport Management*, **20**(4), 483–509.

Sport Canada (1986). *Sport Canada policy on Women in Sport*. Ottawa, ON: Government of Canada.

Sport Canada (2002). *The Canadian Sport Policy*. Ottawa, ON: Government of Canada.

Sport Canada (2018). *Role of Sport Canada*. Ottawa, ON: Government of Canada. Retrieved from https://www.canada.ca/en/canadian-heritage/services/role-sport-canada.html.

Statistics Canada (2017). *Population by Sex and Age Group*. Ottawa, ON: Government of Canada. Retrieved from www.statcan.gc.ca/tables-tableaux/sum-som/l01/cst01/demo10a-eng.htm.

Stirling, A. E. & Kerr, G. A. (2009). Abused athletes' perceptions of the coach-athlete relationship. *Sport in Society*, **12**(2), 227–239.

Thibault, L. & Harvey, J. (eds) (2013). *Sport Policy in Canada*. Ottawa, ON: University of Ottawa Press.

Trolan, E. J. (2013). The impact of the media on gender inequality within sport. *Procedia – Social and Behavioral Sciences*, **91**, 215–227.

Walker, N. A. & Sartore-Baldwin, M. L. (2013). Hegemonic masculinity and the institutionalized bias toward women in men's collegiate basketball: What do men think. *Journal of Sport Management*, **27**(4), 303–315.

Welter, F., Brush, C., & De Bruin, A. (2014). The gendering of entrepreneurship context. Institut für Mittelstandsforschung Bonn (Hrsg.): Working Paper, 1, 14.

9
Professional women's sport in Australia

Emma Sherry and Chelsey Taylor

Introduction

"For Australian sport, 2017 will go down as a landmark, a milestone, a watershed, the year the dam broke and women flooded into professional sport" (Jeffery, 2017, p. 1). In a year of global attention on gender equality, and the raising of female voices in protest against political and social structures, women's sport in Australia in 2017 became a symbol of the success of female professional athletes achieving success they could have only imagined even five years earlier. This chapter presents the history and evolution of professional women's sport in Australia, with particular attention to current professional leagues and sport codes, and the expansion of professionalization to new and emerging sports across the country.

History of professional women's sport in Australia

Women participating and competing in sport in Australia is not a recent occurrence. Like many countries, women have been playing, competing, and fighting for recognition of their sport achievements for over 100 years, with the first women's cycling race in the world being held in Sydney in 1888. Women have represented Australia at the Olympic Games since 1912, and in international tours for women's sport competition since the 1930s with cricket (1934) and netball (1956) launching their international competition against England. The Australian Open tennis tournament was also the first of the grand slams to provide equal prize money to both the male and female title holders. Since these formative years, the professionalization of women's sport in Australia has been slow; however, we are now witnessing a rapid increase in interest, salaries, and sponsorship for a variety of professional women's leagues – in both traditionally female sports (such as netball), and increasingly growing into new franchises and leagues in the traditionally male football codes and cricket.

According to the Sporting Intelligence website (www.sportingintelligence.com), 4 of Australia's competitions are among the 12 best-paid women's sport leagues in the world – 3 of which are Super Netball League at #2, Women's Big Bash League (cricket) at #8, and W-League (soccer) at #9. The AFL Women's League (AFLW) is not far behind, coming in eleventh place. However, on the rankings of Australia's top 50 sport earners, only 2 women were featured: six-time world surfing champion Stephanie Gilmore (#39 at AUS$1.75m) and World Golf Hall of Famer Karrie Webb (#50 at AUS$1.28m), both falling far behind the top two men: Andrew Bogut (#1 at AUS$16.2m) and Adam Scott (#2 at AUS$15.5m) (www.theline.org.au).

In spite of the success of Australian women's sport on the international stage, women's sport receives less than 10% of televised sport and sport news programming (Sherwood, Osborne, Nicholson, & Sherry, 2017). However, this trend may also be changing, because increased interest in, and availability of, professional women's sport has resulted in increased television coverage – both on traditional media formats and via live streaming. Changes have included the launch of a five-year broadcasting deal for Australian netball for national league games, and the live broadcast of one game per week of the inaugural AFL Women's season on free-to-air television (McIver, 2017; Netball Australia, 2016).

Progress continues to be made, with the 2018 Men's and Women's Cricket Big Bash League finalists receiving equal prize money, new sponsorship opportunities for women's sport, and an increasing number of elite Australian sportswomen competing in international professional leagues such as the US Women's National Basketball Association (WNBA). The following section provides a brief summary of each of the professional women's sport leagues in Australia.

Australian Rules Football

The Australian Rules Football League – Women's (AFLW) was announced in 2016 with the inaugural competition commencing in January 2017. Originally planned for 2020, the AFLW was fast-tracked due to increased commercial and financial attraction, as experienced by other successful female codes (Australian Rules Football League, 2016). The structure of the league currently has eight women's teams under the same club brand as the existing male teams. The AFL, as a national sporting organization, has capped the level of expenditure clubs can dedicate to the women's team to ensure equality across clubs. Player contract agreements between the AFL and the players have a minimum salary of AUS$8,500 in the inaugural season, rising to AUS$9,200 thereafter. The women's wage is a pro-rata equivalent to the male rookies given the current eight-week AFLW home-and-away season and a 24-week contract (Sewell, 2017).

The AFLW have secured a major long-term sponsor in National Australia Bank (NAB) aiming to create a sustainable business model for women's AFL (AFL, 2016). An apparel partnership with Australian clothing retailer, Cotton On, was also struck, ensuring that the match and training clothing has been designed specifically for women, also with the aim of creating a new product for fans (AFL, 2016). Channel 7 and Foxtel both have broadcast rights to the AFLW matches. The two-year broadcast deal saw rights fees waived during the inaugural period (McIver, 2017). The broadcast deal allowed for the profiles of athletes and women's AFL to be raised with minimal risk for the broadcasters. As a result, the inaugural opening round attracted 1.7 million viewers across Australia.

The AFLW has a significant growth strategy to further establish the league. League expansion is in place for 2019, with the addition of two new teams followed by the inclusion of another four teams in 2020 (Gould, 2017). The selected teams provide the AFL with access to "regional hubs," allowing for growth into regional corridors such as Geelong and Tasmania. The AFL anticipates this will grow the fan base and number of individual participants playing Australian rules. The AFL utilize the Women's league as a new era of engagement for fans, particularly with the season commencing before the men's home-and-away season (AFL, 2016). Using suburban, "traditional home" facilities of the clubs is seen by many fans as bringing football back to its community roots, something the men's AFL cannot offer. However, many of these grounds are ill-equipped for the broadcasting of games, which has proven a challenge. The use of suburban grounds has ignited a sense of connection to AFLW clubs, allowing for closer engagement between fans and the AFLW players. The AFLW provides a pathway for girls to engage and participate in Australian rules, a pathway that has not previously occurred; following the inaugural season there was a 76% increase in the number of female teams participating in AFL across Australia (AFL, 2016). The AFLW players are considered role models for the younger female generations, inspiring the development of young talent and higher engagement with the league.

Basketball

The National Basketball Competition originated as a two-round event known as the "Women's Interstate Basketball Conference" in 1981 (Women's National Basketball League [WNBL], 2017a). The league was structured as a home-and-away season comprising three games on one weekend, for financial reasons, with each team contributing AUS$25 per game for the operation of the competition. The following year this expanded to include two extra clubs and the name was changed to the Women's National Basketball League (WNBL, 2017a). In 1983, a second division was added, forming a women's conference with 20 competing teams across 2 divisions. In 1989, the WNBL received its first sponsorship deal worth AUS$258,000 from apparel company Pony, as well as a broadcast deal with the Australian Broadcasting Corporation (ABC) for finals coverage. In 1993, the WNBL teams agreed to invest in the ABC broadcasting, allowing for weekly broadcasting of the WNBL (WNBL, 2017a).

The ABC has maintained coverage of the WNBL, although lobbying was required in 2001 to maintain the broadcast. In 2006, WNBL coverage was increased to two games per weekend. The league grew from eight teams in 2007 to ten teams, including one New Zealand team. In 2008, a second Queensland team was introduced. The teams' ownership structure has varied throughout the history of the WNBL. Today there are three clear ownership structures comprising private ownership and controlled state sporting organizations, and state government (WNBL, 2017a). Currently the league has been shortened to a 3-month season, in which teams compete in 21 games across 13 rounds, followed by playoffs and the grand finale. In 2017 FOX Sports signed a broadcast deal, broadcasting one game per week as well as assisting the WNBL in the commercial development of the league (WNBL, 2017b).

The WNBL is taking measures to ensure Olympic and international basketballers return to the WNBL courts. The league focus remains on community engagement, positioning the league as having a unique community orientation while remaining a professional league (WNBL, 2017b). Strong community orientation sees the elite athletes having a higher availability and global access to fans when compared with other professional sports. The WNBL is seen as playing an important role in providing "real role models" (WNBL, 2017b, p. 3). An aspect of community development and role modelling includes an Australian Sports Commission (ASC)-funded program for coaching education of WNBL players, allowing the athletes to deliver grass roots coaching programs, specifically focusing on schools (Anderson, 2017). Demand from players and the need to remain competitive in the growing professional environment led to a new pay deal in 2017, resulting in a minimum wage at AUS$7,500 with an average salary of AUS$33,600 (Lulham, 2017a). This is a significant rise from previous seasons, with some players only having expenses covered with an average salary of AUS$16,000 (Nicholson, 2016). Future plans for the WNBL to remain competitive involve strengthening commercial value, including sponsorship packaging, marketing, and new community engagement initiatives to drive attendance and viewership (WNBL, 2017b).

Cricket

Female cricket at an international and national level has existed for some time; however, not in the format of a professional commercial league. After the success of the men's commercial Twenty–20 Cricket League – Big Bash League (BBL), in 2015 Cricket Australia announced the launch of the Women's Big Bash League (WBBL). The professional women's Twenty–20 cricket league commenced the inaugural season in December 2015. The purpose behind the launch of WBBL was to inspire more females to engage in the sport of cricket (Cricket Australia, 2015). The structure of the WBBL sees all eight teams aligned with the male BBL teams under one brand. This assists the clubs and league in creating commercial efficiencies and appealing to a broader range of fans, spectators, and sponsors.

Channel Ten has a broadcast deal hosting 12 WBBL matches per season, with the remaining matches streamed on the Cricket Live App and via cricket.com.au. WBBL matches are played in various locations around Australia, including regional and rural areas to increase the reach of elite cricket (Kanoniuk, 2017). Cricket Australia has plans of global recognition surrounding WBBL; the focus is about creating sustainable pathways for women and girls in elite cricket (Cricket Australia, 2017). Player payments have increased throughout the WBBL lifecycle so far; in 2016, the minimum retainer was AUS$7,000, and the current season minimum retainer is over AUS$10,000. By 2020 the minimum wage for a WBBL athlete will be over AUS$11,500 (ABC, 2017a). Cricket is attempting to position the WBBL as the top female sport league globally, focusing on entertainment and digital interactions as well as inspiring young girls and women into grass roots cricket (Cricket Australia, 2017).

Netball

In 1985, the Australian Institute of Sport created the Esso Netball Super League, the first national netball competition; 1986 marked the Players Trust Fund policy, which entitled elite netball players to receive compensation (Netball Australia, 2017b). Commercially driven netball leagues have been in existence since 1996, when the National Netball League (NNL) incorporated as a company (Netball Australia, 2017a). In 1997, the sponsored "Commonwealth Bank Trophy Competition" had its inaugural year. After four years of existence as a separate entity the NNL Company was deregistered, and the Commonwealth Bank Trophy competition then formed part of the national sport organization governance, Netball Australia. In 2007, the Commonwealth Bank Trophy Competition ceased operation to make way for a league restructure in 2008 with Netball Australia launching the semi-professional ANZ Championship (Netball Australia, 2017b). The ANZ Championship was partnered with Netball New Zealand, comprising five Australian and five New Zealand teams (Hand, 2009). The ANZ Championship existed in its current structure until 2016, and limited growth in the structure of the ANZ Championship was attributed to the desire to move the athletes from semi-professional to professional status requiring consolidation as opposed to growth of the league (Hand, 2009). The league restructure in 2016 eliminated the New Zealand teams from the competition and rebranded the league to become the Suncorp Super Netball League (SSN). The SNN comprised eight teams, with five existing teams from the ANZ Championship supported by the state sporting organization. Three new teams based in Queensland, New South Wales, and Victoria were added. These new teams are strategically partnered with existing male code club brands including Melbourne Storm (NRL), GWS Giants, and Collingwood Magpies (AFL) (Super Netball, 2017a).

The SNN season extends across 14 weeks and a three-week finals series ending in August (Super Netball, 2017b). The Super Netball League includes a five-year naming right sponsorship deal for the league with Suncorp Bank, and the inclusion of clubs with less reliance on Netball Australia. A five-year broadcast deal with Nine Networks multichannel 9GEM and Telstra TV was struck. As a result of increased income for Netball through broadcasting and sponsor deals, a collective playing agreement was reached in late 2016 to take place in the inaugural season of the SNN. Player contracts saw players becoming full-time professionals with the average salary extending to AUS$67,500 (Netball Australia, 2016). The Netball Live App provided fans with more engagement and involvement opportunities, encouraging more exposure and therefore more lucrative sponsorship deals to support the league. The current focus of the league surrounds the growth of innovative engagement. Innovative engagement includes the use of the Netball Live App for live score, statistics, and player updates, as well as Live Pass and Telstra TV, offering higher levels of on-demand engagement and alternative options to consume SSN, considered to be the essential element in growing the SNN (Super Netball, 2017b).

Soccer

The Women's National Soccer League was first established in 1996, lasting eight years, discontinuing in 2004. Due to the growing popularity of soccer and the entrance of the Socceroos, Australia's national representative men's soccer team, into the World Cup, the W-League was established in 2007 with the inaugural season commencing in 2008. The W-League comprises 9 teams competing across 14 rounds, 12 games, and 2 bye-rounds, in a home-and-away season. All clubs within the W-League are aligned with the existing male A-League team's business model aside from Canberra United, which operates independently to the A-League Franchise (Canberra United, 2017). This structure is utilized as a commercial tool in influencing female football fans and enabling more opportunities for fans in general to consume more high-quality football, particularly through double headers (Football Federation Australia [FFA], 2015).

The W-League intends to use digital growth to further connect with fans, using positive brand image to encourage participation in women's football. The league has plans to expand to 20–30 rounds, including full commercialization and professionalization of women's football (FFA, 2015). The purpose of expanding the league from 14 to 20 or more rounds is to develop players to an international standard, mimicking those of rival international leagues (FFA, 2015). FOX Sports and Special Broadcasting Service (SBS) currently broadcast all W-League matches throughout the season (SBS, 2017). A major partner in Westfield was secured across a range of FFA initiatives, including the naming rights of the W-League (2017). Westfield is a major retail brand, controlling a large portion of retail centres throughout Australia. Several smaller sponsorship deals have been secured pertaining to the W-League; however, the business structure is largely dependent on broadcast deals and sponsorship packaging, including the A-League and other product offers of FFA. A new collective bargaining agreement arose throughout 2017 in order for the W-League to remain competitive with its players compared with other leagues, which saw the average athlete salary increase from AUS$7,000 to AUS$15,500, with an extra AUS$2,000 added for the following season (Lulham, 2017b).

Individual professional sports

In addition to the established women's professional sport competitions outlined above, it is important also to acknowledge the individual female athletes who excel in their field of endeavour. This section focuses primarily on Australian athletes in tennis, golf, and surfing. As noted earlier, the top earning (prize-money) female athletes in Australia are Stephanie Gilmore (surfing) and Karrie Web (golf).

Surfing in Australia has a long and proud history of excellence, with Layne Beachley leading the charge. The earnings from the World Surf League (WSL) Championship Tour are often supplemented or even surpassed by endorsements and ambassador fees, with Gilmore reportedly earning approximately AUS$1.5 million through her partnerships with Sanitarium, Nikon, and Ford (Townsend, 2015). Surfing is one of the more lucrative women's professional sports, with the number of events and prize money offered similar to the men's tour. Lifestyle surf brands and endorsements are particularly lucrative for female athletes, and Australian athletes have consistently been well represented on the international circuit.

Although tennis may be the most lucrative individual sport for women, Australia has found varied success on the tour and rankings, which is reflected in our tennis players not appearing in the top earners' lists. In addition, a study by the International Tennis Federation found that, although there was substantial prize money offered in the sport of tennis, very few could make a profit, due to the large expenses required to participate on the international circuit (ABC, 2015). When reviewing the World Tennis Association (WTA) lifetime earnings rankings, the first Australian athlete appears at #19 – Samantha Stosur. We do not find another until #79 with Rennae Stubbs, who retired from the game in 2011 (WTA, 2017).

A similar story can be found in the sport of golf, with a history of exceptional female golfers in Australia, most famously Karrie Webb. Webb appears in the Australian top 20 athlete earners overall, and second on the Ladies Professional Golf Association (LPGA) career money list (LPGA, 2018). Currently, Australia has only one female golfer in the top 20 rankings, and only 4 in the top 100 earners of all time.

Australia has a long history of success in individual professional women's sports, particularly in tennis, golf, and surfing. The impact of the incredible growth in professional women's leagues on the ability of individual sports to develop and retain elite athletes remains to be seen. This growth continues into the current day, and the following section outlines the future of professional women's sport in Australia.

New leagues in 2018 and beyond

With the exceptional growth in opportunities for women's professional sport in Australia since 2015, the increased competition between sport codes for both talented athletes and fans has resulted in many traditionally men's sport codes announcing the imminent launch of their own women's leagues. With the success of the AFLW in its inaugural season, the other two football codes – rugby union and rugby league – saw the opportunity to announce the formation of new professional competitions in 2016 for a 2017 launch. As a relatively small professional sport market, for both fan engagement and talent, these announcements can be largely viewed as each sporting code ensuring that they are not left behind in the wave of focus on women's professional sport. With a short history of talent development and high-level competition, many athletes playing in the inaugural AFLW season were those who transferred from another sport, such as field hockey, athletics, netball, or basketball. Ash Barty, currently ranked as Australia's highest female tennis player, famously took a year off tennis to play a season in the WBBL. For the sports of rugby union and rugby league, it has been a case of jump now or be left behind.

Women's rugby union has had a strong history of success, particularly with the national team taking the gold medal in the Rugby 7s competition at the 2016 Rio Olympic Games. In December 2017, Rugby Australia announced the launch of a national women's league, the Super W 15-a-side competition. The announcement was not without its controversy, because its original plan was to launch a professional competition, without paying any of its athletes. This announcement resulted in a strong public backlash, and left many questioning why a female athlete would choose to play in a league without pay, when there are an increasing number of options with better pay and conditions for female athletes such as AFL, soccer, and netball. However, after a new deal negotiated between Rugby Australia and the Rugby Union Players' Association, professional female rugby union players have since been awarded increased pay and conditions for representation on the national team (ABC, 2017b).

December 2017 was a busy month of announcements for the two rugby codes, with the National Rugby League (NRL) also confirming that it would launch its national elite women's rugby league competition in 2018, with up to six teams aligned with established NRL clubs (ABC, 2017c). The competition will not be established as a stand-alone league in its inaugural year, but instead matches will be played as double headers during the men's NRL finals series, with the NRL women's championship title played before the men's NRL grand finale. This league will also be supported by a stand-alone State of Origin match between traditional rivals New South Wales and Queensland, and a variety of state league competitions, to build depth of talent.

The increased focus on women's professional sport bodes well for those who wish to play, watch, or support women's leagues in future. The next challenge for each and every one of these leagues will be to maintain the momentum, grow the depth of talent, and work towards equity in wages, profile, and conditions for athletes. Currently the professional women's sport landscape is experiencing a turf war. As the market continues to be saturated with the growth of professional women's leagues, talent development across the breadth of sports will become a focus. Several athletes have participated in multiple different codes at the elite level, with new collective bargaining agreements the ability of women to code hop will decrease. This is evident with athletes such as Olympian and AFLW player Kim Mickle, and basketballer and AFLW player, Erin Phillips, among the code jumping names (Colasimone, 2016).

Securing ongoing broadcast deals and sponsorship packages will ensure the future of collective bargaining agreements. For many codes only short-term deals are in play (i.e. two-year AFLW broadcast deal). Concerns are paramount surrounding the divide between the male and female codes, in particular the wage gap. It will be crucial to ensure the ongoing development of coverage and sponsorship dollars to boost the growth across the female codes.

Currently elite access to facilities and resources for many of the female codes is sub-par, although throughout Australia several government grants have recently been made available to ensure equality in the conditions of training facilities for women's sport in general, including elite women's sport.

Conclusion

Since 2015, Australia has seen an explosion in growth in professional women's sport, particularly in the expansion and launch of a variety of national leagues and competitions. The largest growth in professional women's sport has been the expansion of women's teams into established, traditionally male sports, the four football codes (soccer, AFL, rugby league, and rugby union) and cricket. The ability of these traditionally male sport codes to control the Australian sport media news cycle has benefits for these emerging female competitions, but it is not yet possible to gauge the impact of this growth on the traditionally female sports of netball and basketball, and the poaching of athletic talent from one sport to the next.

The ability to earn a living from playing professional sport in Australia for women remains limited to a few, with the new women's football codes still providing very minimal salaries and conditions for their athletes. As such, there remains much progress to be done, but the future of women's professional sport in Australia looks bright.

Leader profile: Stephanie Beltrame

Figure 9.1 Stephanie Beltrame
Photo courtesy of Getty Images, with kind permission from Stephanie Beltrame

Women's cricket in Australia has a long and proud history; the profile of the national team and league and their strategic importance have never been more prominent. Much of this increased focus has been the result of the work of Stephanie Beltrame.

Beltrame is the Head of Media Rights at Cricket Australia, starting her career with cricket in 2003 as the media manager for the women's national team. Beltrame has been instrumental in securing the biggest ever broadcast deal for Cricket Australia. In 2013, she led negotiations that resulted in AUS$450 million from Channel Nine for international cricket, and an additional AUS$100 million from Channel 10 for the rights to the domestic Twenty–20 competition – the Big Bash League (Saltau, 2013).

This negotiation resulted in securing greater increased television coverage for both the national women's team and the Women's BBL. As a result of these successful negotiations, ESPN noted Beltrame in their top 10 most influential women in Australian sport in 2016. The significance of this change can be illustrated by the increase in television coverage. In 2006 women's cricket coverage consisted of a 30-minute highlight show each week. In 2017, the Women's Ashes was played against England, with all games broadcast on free-to-air or streamed live, as was the Women's BBL, resulting in over 100 hours of coverage on free-to-air television.

In our discussion about her role at Cricket Australia, and influence in women's sport, Beltrame noted:

the work was done, there were many who had been pushing for recognition and increased focus for women's sport, what we are seeing now is the groundswell of support across the sporting codes for women's competition, and this has reached a tipping point.

Beltrame is a formidable negotiator and, since starting her career with Cricket Australia, has completed her MBA. She notes that the key to her success has been preparation, and being prepared to call the bluff of those in the room. In an interview with Saltau (2013), she noted that, "if I know my material, I don't care who's in the meeting." When asked about the future of women's cricket and its ongoing success, Beltrame stated that:

> for the sport to grow, we need to make every effort in every area that means focusing on the schedule of play, the media opportunities, talent development, high performance, sponsors and coaching. It is like a garden, for our sport to grow, we need to truly take care of it.

Beltrame outlines her passion and support for women's sport most clearly in her LinkedIn profile statement:

> I believe that a strong industry/economy/team/country/society/workplace is built on diversity, in particular gender equity. I am passionate about advancing the position of females and understand that I have a role to play in contributing to this evolution.

Stephanie Beltrame is a woman with an aim and a strategy for growing women's sport in Australia and beyond, and her place as one of the most influential women in Australian sport is well deserved.

In addition to her role with Cricket Australia, Beltrame also sits as a Director on the Board of Vicsport, a not-for-profit advocacy organization for Victorian sport organisations.

References

ABC (2015). Less than two per cent of men, three per cent of women can make living on ATP and WTA tours, according to report. Retrieved from www.abc.net.au/news/2015-01-19/most-tennis-players-cannot-make-a-living-on-tour-review-finds/6024914.

ABC (2017a). Cricket pay deal huge for women as Australia's female cricketers get massive windfall. Retrieved from www.abc.net.au/news/2017-08-03/cricket-pay-deal-lauded-womens-pay/8772186.

ABC (2017b). NRL to launch national women's rugby league competition with "up to six" teams. Retrieved from www.abc.net.au/news/2017-12-06/nrl-to-launch-national-womens-rugby-league-competition/9231548.

Australian Rules Football League (AFL) (2016). 2016 Annual Report. Retrieved from http://s.afl.com.au/staticfile/AFL%20Tenant/AFL/Files/Images/compressed_2016-AFL-Annual-Report%20(1).pdf.

Anderson, D. (2017). WNBL players to engage with schools through coaching grants. Retrieved from http://basketball.net.au/wnbl-players-to-engage-with-schools-through-coaching-grants.

Canberra United (2017). History. Retrieved from https://www.canberraunited.com.au/history

Colasimone, D. (2016). Women's AFL competition could spark turf war with netball, cricket, W-League and rugby. Retrieved from www.abc.net.au/news/2016-09-15/turf-war-in-womens-sport-would-be-great-for-female-athletes/7844516.

Cricket Australia (2015). Schedule, broadcast, first players announced for Women's Big Bash League. Retrieved from www.cricketaustralia.com.au/media/media-releases/schedule-broadcast-first-players-announced-for-womens-big-bash-league/2015-07-10.

Cricket Australia (2017). Australian cricket strategy: 2017–2020. Retrieved from www.cricketaustralia.com.au/about/our-strategy.

Football Federation Australia (FFA) (2015). Whole of Football Plan. Retrieved from www.wholeoffoot ballplan.com.au/pdfs/Whole_of_Football_Plan.pdf.

Gould, R. (2017). North Melbourne and Geelong set to join AFL Women's in 2019 further expansion in 2020. Retrieved from www.heraldsun.com.au/sport/afl/aflw/north-melbourne-and-geelong-set-to-join-afl-womens-in-2019-further-expansion-in-2020/news-story/642c7266077324b9049cb8fa4cb 680bc.

Hand, G. (2009). Netball resists expansion despite boom. *Sydney Morning Herald*, July 23. Retrieved from www.smh.com.au//breaking-news-sport/netball-resists-expansion-despite-boom-20090723-duqx.html.

Jeffery, A. (2017). The landmark year women flooded into professional sport. *The Australian*, December 30. Retrieved from https://www.theaustralian.com.au/sport/more-sports/the-landmark-year-women-flooded-into-professional-sport/news-story/c7b533c63311dd59d585e9cf89b87319.

Kanoniuk, C. (2017). WBBL03 fixtures confirmed. Retrieved from https://www.bigbash.com.au/news/wbbl03-womens-big-bash-league-fixtures-schedule-draw-tickets-tv-ten-2017-18/2017-07-31#.

Ladies Professional Golf Association (LPGA) (2018). Career money. Retrieved from http://www.lpga.com/statistics/money/career-money?year=2018.

Lulham, A. (2017a). Minimum wage for WNBL players now in place under new deal. *Daily Telegraph*, November 25. Retrieved from https://www.dailytelegraph.com.au/sport/swoop/minimum-wage-for-wnbl-players-now-in-place-under-new-deal/news-story/8bae46f28b90285fe17f39313788ae37.

Lulham, A. (2017b). W-League players kick goal with landmark deal struck. *Daily Telegraph*, September 11. Retrieved from https://www.dailytelegraph.com.au/sport/swoop/wleague-players-kick-goal-with-landmark-deal-struck/news-story/84aa2191c160e8defad5717b2a440eb7.

McIver, D. (2017). AFLW: Media coverage of women's competition "almost inconceivable." *ABC News*. Retrieved from www.abc.net.au/news/2017-02-06/aflw-almost-inconceivable-coverage-breaking-new-ground/8245672.

Netball Australia (2016). New national netball league – what you need to know. Retrieved from http://netball.com.au/new-national-netball-league-need-know.

Netball Australia (2017a). About Netball Australia. Retrieved from http://netball.com.au/about-netball-australia.

Netball Australia (2017b). Through the years. Retrieved from http://netball.com.au/history-and-traditions/through-the-years.

Nicholson, L. (2016). Basketballers Demand Minimum Wage as Competition for Female Talent Heats Up. *Sydney Morning Herald*, October 4. Retrieved from www.smh.com.au/sport/basketball/basketballers-demand-minimum-wage-as-competition-for-female-talent-heats-up-20161004-gruikk.html.

Saltau, C. (2013). Ms Cricket. *Sydney Morning Herald*, June 5. Retrieved from www.smh.com.au/sport/cricket/ms-cricket-20130607-2nvr5.html.

Sewell, E. (2017). AFL agrees to new deal that will see every AFLW player earn more in season two of competition. *Herald Sun*, November 2. Retrieved from www.heraldsun.com.au/sport/afl/aflw/afl-agrees-to-new-deal-that-will-see-every-aflw-player-earn-more-in-season-two-of-competition/news-story/b919a9cc29d0fa24f43a9f99dd7a2be4.

Sherwood, M., Osborne, A., Nicholson, M., & Sherry, E. (2017). Newswork, news values, and audience considerations: Factors that facilitate media coverage of women's sports. *Communication & Sport*, **5**(6), 647–668.

Special Broadcasting Service (SBS) (2017). SBS Broadcast W-League and Matildas Matches. Retrieved from https://theworldgame.sbs.com.au/article/2017/10/23/sbs-broadcast-w-league-and-matildas-matches.

Super Netball (2017a). About. Retrieved from https://supernetball.com.au/about.

Super Netball (2017b). Season 2018 revealed. Retrieved from https://supernetball.com.au/2017/10/11/season-2018-revealed.

Townsend, L. (2015). Steph Gilmore is the highest paid woman in Australian sport, February 23. *Stab*. Retrieved from https://stabmag.com/news/steph-gilmore-is-the-highest-paid-woman-in-australian-sport.

W-League (2017). W-League partners. Retrieved from https://www.w-league.com.au/partners.

Women's National Basketball League (WNBL) (2017a). *History of the WNBL*. Retrieved from http://wnbl.com.au/league/history-of-the-wnbl.

Women's National Basketball League (WNBL) (2017b). WNBL media guide 2017/18. Retrieved from http://wnbl.com.au/assets/14766_baskaus_wnbl-media-guide_2017-18_final_high-res.pdf.

World Tennis Association (WTA) (2017). Career prize money leaders. Retrieved from www.wtatennis.com/sites/default/files/basic_page_files/all_career_prize_money_08may2017.pdf.

10

From the battlefield to the board room

The place of gender in sex-integrated sport

Donna de Haan and Lucy Dumbell

For the first time in Olympic history, every participating nation sent at least one female athlete to the 2012 Olympic Games in London. At the Rio Olympics in 2016, 47% of the medal opportunities were open to women, 45% of all athletes were female, and some nations, such as the United States, sent more female than male athletes. In April 2017 the International Olympic Committee (IOC) approved the program for the 2020 Tokyo Olympics, which included a net increase of 15 events (many of which were supported because of their female participation rates), and there will be twice as many mixed events as Rio (an increase from 9 mixed events to 18). These changes may result in the highest representation of female athletes in Olympic history (Figure 10.1). There is the potential for Tokyo to see 48% of participants being female, a 10% increase since the 2000 Olympics in Sydney.

The policy changes implemented by the IOC to increase female participation are examples of a liberal feminist approach to equality. Indeed, most of the advancements in women's sports over the last 40 years can be characterized as liberal feminism. Fundamentally liberal feminism advocates women's greater involvement in sport by enhancing their opportunities to join existing institutions and structures – such as the Olympic Movement. For example the passage of Title IX legislation in the United States in 1972 offered women, among many other rights and protections, equal opportunity to participate in athletics (Yiamouyiannis & Osborne, 2012). Since 1972, female participation in US high school sports has increased by more than 900%. The emphasis for equality in sport appears to be focused on participation, with an anecdotal belief that, if there are enough women on the playing field, there will naturally be enough women willing and able to take up leadership roles such as coaching or positions within governance. However, there is a lack of evidence to show a causational link between participation and representation. For example, although 45% of athletes at the Rio Olympics were female, less than 10% of the coaches were female and only one International Federation (IF) was led by a woman.

As Hovden (2012) explains, liberal feminist discourses have shaped women's fight for equality and helped increase the number of female participants in sport. The practice of redistributive feminism may increase numbers in certain aspects of sport, but does little to challenge or radicalize the gendered culture of sport as an institution. Indeed, critics of liberal feminism point to a lack of critique of basic gender relationships, a focus on state action that links women's interests

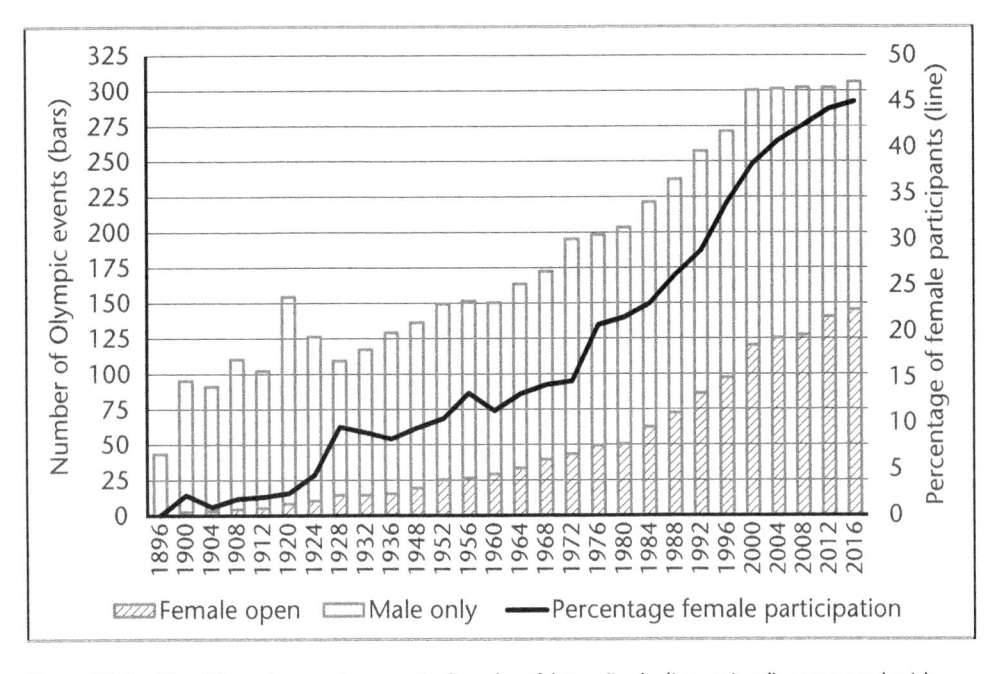

Figure 10.1 The Olympic events open to female athletes (including mixed) compared with the total number of events (bars) and the percentage of female participants in the Olympiad (line)

to those of the powerful, a disregard for the intersection of class or race, and a lack of analysis of ways in which women are different from men. As Burke (2010, p. 21) argues:

> This acceptance of the maleness of notions of excellence in sport, has resulted in difficulties in females accessing opportunities as coaches to produce different methods of play, as female-run administrative bodies to produce different philosophies of sport and create new sports, and as female players to speak with authority about their experiences in supposedly male sports.

As a consequence of concerns about the shortcomings of liberal feminism as a conceptual frame for research and policy development, scholars and practitioners have looked to other frameworks to provide a lens through which to discuss and understand gender and sport (Shaw & Frisby, 2006). Socialist feminism, for example, has responded by looking more closely at the interrelationships of gender, race, and class located within capitalism, patriarchy, and neocolonialism (e.g. Burke, 2001; Hargreaves, 1990; Scraton & Flintoff, 2013). Meanwhile, poststructuralist feminists provide conceptual challenges to the macro-analysis of the structural approaches of liberal and socialist feminism (e.g., Markula, 2018; Roth & Basow, 2004; Scraton & Flintoff, 2013). In this chapter we aim to contribute further to this discourse by exploring the place of gender in a sex-integrated sport via three different feminist theories: liberal feminism, socialist feminism, and poststructuralist feminism. The research question driving this inquiry is whether sex-integrated competition in sport can provide a conducive environment for gender equality on the field (participation) and in the boardroom (decision-making)? To answer this question, we begin by presenting the sociocultural context of equestrian sport and the Eurocentric military-influenced development of the sport within the Olympic context. We then review the place of gender in this unique sporting context, paying attention to not only participation but also power and representation. Finally, we share the experience of Amanda Bond, the Chair of the Para-Equestrian Committee of the Fédération Equestre Internationale (FEI), the international governing body of equestrian sport. In the conclusion, we return to the conflicting discourses of (in)equality in equestrian sport and discuss if this unique sex-integrated sport offers any unique gender-related management insights.

The evolution of equestrian sport: military, men, and medals

Much research concerning sport focuses on its place in social life (what it is, where it comes from, what form it takes), and the meaning that sport has for individuals, the community, and culture in general (Birrell, 1981; Blanchard, 1988; Bromberger, 1995). The evolution of equestrian sport primarily centers on the need to practice and develop equestrian (riding) skills for the purpose of transportation, hunting, warfare, or animal husbandry (cattle herding, for example) (de Haan, 2015). It is important to acknowledge that "equestrian sport'" is not therefore a homogeneous entity with global formulaic characteristics. There are some obvious, as well as often subtle, sociocultural nuances about the place of equestrian sport in different contexts around the world, which should be considered when discussing the place of gender in equestrian sport. For example, in the American West, women readily rode astride for work and transportation; however, in keeping with European modernity, it was deemed at the time inappropriate for women to ride astride because feminine attire was not conducive to this style of riding (Adelman & Knijnik, 2013). The place of gender in the context of equestrian sport cannot therefore simply be explained by class relations and the sexual division of labor (Marxist feminism) or by men's power over women (radical feminism).

Equestrian sport made its debut at the Summer Olympics in 1900, although it failed to appear in the next two Summer Olympics. The evolution of the new equestrian sports in the modern Olympic program could be seen as symbolic of the classical formulations of Olympic ideology, which were founded in the worldview of modernism (de Haan, 2015). Real (1996) reviews the Olympic ideals of the first decades of the modern games with reference to aristocratic privilege and Eurocentric ideals. During the twentieth century equestrian sport mirrored the aristocratic, upperclass, Eurocentric, male-dominated zeitgeist of the Olympic Games (de Haan, 2015). Indeed, while discussing capital and gender relations in sport, Hargreaves (1990, p. 295) argues that:

> modern sport is a repository for dominant ideology in its celebration of ruthless competition, aggression and violence and in its embodiment of elitism, nationalism, racism, militarism, imperialism and sexism and . . . the machismo ethos in sport, by bonding men together, becomes a fundamental expression of male power and domination over women.

The genesis of equestrian sport in the modern Olympics began in 1900 and was predominantly shaped by military influence until 1948. The historical relationship between man and horse in warfare echoes Hargreaves' (1990) description of modern sport. The equestrian events chosen for inclusion in the modern Games reflected the European military influence seen elsewhere in the Olympic movement. The disciplines had roots in European riding, classical horsemanship, and foxhunting, and ultimately tested the cavalry skills required at that time (de Haan & Dumbell, 2016). By applying a social feminist lens to the evolution of the equestrian disciplines, it is possible to identify dominant cultural discourses. By looking more closely at the interrelationship of gender, race, and class located within capitalism, patriarchy, and neocolonialism, it is possible to identify Eurocentric cultural bias as the dominant framework. For example, although western styles of riding are represented alongside European styles of riding in elite competition such as the World Equestrian Games, it is only the European style that is present in the Olympic Games (de Haan, 2015).

The second period of development of equestrian sport began in 1952 and was characterized by the inclusion of non-military and female riders (de Haan & Dumbell, 2016). In 1952, women were allowed to compete only in dressage; in 1956, showjumping was opened to female competitors and, in 1964, women were finally allowed to compete in the eventing competition (Hedenborg, 2009). Allowing women access to the ubiquitous symbolic system of the gendered hierarchy of equestrian sport could be seen as an opportunity to challenge the dominant discourse of male hegemonic power and masculinity. Indeed Scraton and Flintoff (2013) explain that, as a result of exploring the complex interrelationship between capitalism and patriarchal power relations, socialist feminism shifted the emphasis from solely looking at women's experience to looking more critically at gender. In turn this led to the exploration of male power through the concept of hegemonic masculinity (Connell, 1987, 1995, 2008). This body of work then developed into a large area of study (men and masculinities), which created a space for men to engage with feminist theorizing (e.g. Messner, 1992; Sabo, 1985; Sabo & Runfola, 1980). More recently, the amount of scholarship in the field of gender relations in equestrian sports during the second half of the twentieth century has grown and shed valuable light on the gendered distribution patterns both within and outside Olympic Equestrian competition (de Haan & Dumbell, 2016; Dumbell, Johnson & de Haan, 2010; Dumbell, Douglas, & Rowe, 2017). There is also a developing body of scholarship that explores how men as a group enjoy privileges through the construction of unequal gender relations within this sex-integrated sport (Dashper, 2012b; Hedenborg, 2015; Hedenborg & White, 2012). In addition, there is a small but growing body of literature that uses equestrian sport as a site in which to discuss constructs of gender and identity and sexuality (Dashper, 2012a, 2013).

Participation is not the same as presence and power

Hargreaves (2002) explains that the historical justification for sex-segregating sport was built around the ideas of sexual difference and the belief in the unsuitability of sport and physical activity for girls and women. Discussions on sport and gender are often focused on the physicality or the performance aspect of sport, which highlights the differences between the sexes based on the biological and socially constructed gender order in society. The biological bases for sex segregation in sport are often contested. Liberal feminists argue that differences in female sport participation are the result of socialization practices carried out by institutions (Scraton & Flintoff, 2013). As Dashper (2012b) explains, in the context of equestrian sport, there are no sex-based biological advantages for either males or females, "masculine sporting abilities such as speed and strength are less significant . . . strength of a rider plays a role, but this is limited as within the equestrian partnership the horse will always be the stronger partner" (p. 215). Indeed, to truly compare the gendered physicality of equestrian sport with other sports, we must define the physicality to which we refer. For example, within the Olympic discipline of Dressage, the first of the disciplines to allow female competitors, scoring and hence placing are based on the quality of the horse's individual required movements. Therefore, correct training is rewarded within the scoring system and the gender of the rider is negligible, because it is the physical performance of the horse, rather than the human athlete, that is judged (de Haan, 2015).

Since 1964 all three disciplines have been open to female athletes. There are individual and team medals available across the three equestrian disciplines. Countries are free to choose the best riders for individual and team selection, irrespective of gender. For the purpose of this discussion, we therefore describe equestrian sport as sex integrated. Within the context of Olympic sport we differentiate: (a) sex-integrated sport – participation opportunities open to male and female athletes to directly compete against each other; (b) sex-segregated sport – participation opportunities restricted to one sex; and (c) mixed-sex team sports – where there has to be representation from both sexes in a team, usually one male and one female, as in sailing, table tennis, and tennis in Rio 2016.

McDonagh and Pappano (2008) adopt a radical feminist position by suggesting the removal of sex segregation as a way to redress the marginalization and "othering" of female athletes. They explore the ways that sex segregation in sport operates as a powerful tool in the ideological and material subordination of women. In their review of how athlete "identity" is constructed and framed within a sex-integrated sporting experience, de Haan, Sotiriadou, and Henry (2015) noted an absence of "othering." They found that there was an absence of gender as a construct of identity in the way riders saw themselves and how support staff such as coaches saw the athletes. However, they concluded that this did not mean participants were gender blind. Indeed, a wider review of discourses associated with equestrian sport highlights that sex integration does not necessarily equate to participatory parity or gender-neutral discourse. As Anderson (2009) explains, sex desegregation is "a politically charged proposition" (p. 11) and one that many feminist scholars have shied away from considering fully. This chapter attempts to engage in that conversation. In this section we discuss specifically female participation in the sex-integrated sport of equestrian, in the context of the Olympic program of sports that remains predominantly sex segregated. Having set the scene from a participation perspective, we then discuss the proportional representation of women in decision-making positions on boards of governance.

Participation

The IOC has taken a predominantly liberal feminist approach to gender equality in the context of participation. For example, in 1992 they stated that any new sports included in the Olympic program must be open to male and female participants. Currently all international federations (IFs) offer Olympic events (medal opportunities) to both male and female athletes (Table 10.1). Although there were more events available for male athletes in Rio 2016 than for female ones (Table 10.1), there were no male-only sports. However, there were two Olympic sports that were open only to female athletes: synchronized swimming and rhythmic gymnastics. At Rio 2016 there was one sex-integrated Olympic sport, Equestrian, with six medal opportunities, three mixed-sex team medal opportunities within three separate sports, and the other 295 medals (97%) were for sex-segregated events. IFs demonstrate variation in the participation of the sexes in their Olympic events, from boxing, where an athlete is nearly seven times more likely to be male than female, to gymnastics (which includes both artistic and rhythmic gymnastics), where there are nearly two female athletes for every male athlete due to rhythmic gymnastics' status as a female-only discipline. As a sex-integrated sport, equestrianism has the potential to show huge bias because there are no inbuilt constraints such as gender quotas; however, as seen in Table 10.1, at Rio 2016 gender representation in equestrian was comparable to other sports.

Building on Dumbell and de Haan's (2012) comparison of athlete profiles over 50 years of Olympic equestrian events, Table 10.2 presents an analysis of participation at 10 Olympic Games. Reflecting the wider representation of women in the Olympics, the number of female athletes competing in equestrian disciplines has increased over the years, but has not yet reached 50%. Analysis of the gender patterns among Olympic competitors shows that on average only 6% of equestrian competitors were female in the early years, compared with twenty-first-century

Table 10.1 Participation and medal opportunities in recognized sports in Rio 2016

International federation	Male medal opportunities	Male participants	Female medal opportunities	Female participants	Participation M:F odds ratio
AIBA: Boxing	10	250	3	36	6.94
ICF: Canoe	11	243	5	114	2.13
UWW: Wrestling	12	236	6	112	2.11
UCI: Cycling	9	323	9	196	1.65
FEI: Equestrian	6[c]	123	6[b]	76	1.62
FISA: Rowing	8	330	6	209	1.58
ISSF: Shooting	9	240	6	154	1.56
IJF: Judo	7	238	7	153	1.56
IWF: Weightlifting	8	156	7	104	1.50
FIFA: Football	1	288	1	216	1.33
WS: Sailing	6[c]	217	5[c]	163	1.33
ITF: Tennis	3[c]	105	3[c]	94	1.12
IAAF: Athletics[a]	24	1,267	23	1,198	1.06
BWF: Badminton	3[c]	88	3[c]	86	1.02
FIH: Hockey	1	207	1	205	1.01
WR: Rugby	1	149	1	148	1.01
IGF: Golf	1	60	1	60	1.00
UIPM: Modern Pentathlon	1	36	1	36	1.00
ITTF: Table Tennis	2	86	2	86	1.00
WT: Taekwondo	4	64	4	64	1.00
FIBA: Basketball	1	144	1	144	1.00
IHF: Handball	1	142	1	142	1.00
FIVB: Volleyball	1	192	1	192	1.00
WA: Archery	2	64	2	64	1.00
FIE: Fencing	5	106	5	106	1.00
ITU: Triathlon	1	55	1	55	1.00
FINA: Aquatics[a]	22	1,057	24	1,072	0.99
FIG: Gymnastics	9	114	9	210	0.54
Total	169	6,800	144	5,679	1.20

a These figures are the sum of athletes competing in each event and therefore an individual athlete may have competed for more than one medal and been counted more than once if they entered more than one event.
b Including one medal for mixed-sex event.
c As a sex-integrated sport the sexes directly compete for the same medals.

Games where this figure has increased to 36%. At the 2016 Rio Olympics, women made up 45% of the 11,237 athletes who competed in the Games and 47% of the events were open to women (either sex segregated or mixed). This figure was closely mirrored in the 38% of female athletes competing in the Equestrian events.

De Haan (2015) noted that the equestrian disciplines could not been seen as a homogeneous group, but that each had their own subculture. Showjumping, for example, remains dominated by male competitors, seeing only a slight increase from 5% female participation in the early Games to 18% in recent Games. This disproportionate representation cannot simply be explained by competition results. Before women's inclusion in showjumping in the 1956 Olympics, women have been successfully competing in the sport. In order to strengthen the

Table 10.2 Gender distribution of competitors (developed from Dumbell & de Haan, 2012)

	Dressage			Showjumping			Eventing			Total		
	M	F	Sum	M	F	Sum	M	F	Sum	M	F	Sum
1952	20	4	24	51	0	51	59	0	59	130	4	134
1956	28	9	37	68	5	70	56	1	57	152	12	164
1960	12	5	17	68	3	71	73	0	73	153	8	161
1964	15	7	22	43	4	46	47	1	48	103	13	116
1968[a]	≤20	≥6	26	≤44	≥7	51	≤48	≥1	49	104	22	126
Total	75	25	100	230	12	238	235	2	237	538	37	575
Odds ratio	75%	25%	3.00	97%	5%	19.17	99%	1%	117.50	94%	6%	14.54
2000	23	25	48	62	12	74	59	23	82	134	70	204
2004	24	28	52	66	11	77	52	23	75	142	62	204
2008	19	28	47	61	16	77	42	28	70	122	72	194
2012	16	34	50	59	15	74	48	26	74	123	75	198
2016	21	39	60	60	14	74	42	23	65	123	76	199
Total	103	154	257	308	68	376	243	123	366	644	355	999
Odds ratio	40%	60%	0.67	82%	18%	4.53	66%	34%	1.98	64%	36%	1.81

a The Olympic report does not list all competitors so some data are not exact.

male-only national teams, successful female riders at the time were asked to lend the "team" their horses for male riders to compete. Pat Symthe first joined the British Showjumping Team in 1947, the same year she won her first open category. Before competing in the 1956 Olympics, where she won a bronze medal and was made an Officer of the Most Excellent Order of the British Empire (OBE: a British order of chivalry rewarding contributions to the public outside the civil service) in the same year, Smythe had been asked to loan her best horse, Prince Hal, to the male-only team (Smythe, 1954). Success in riding comes from the right partnership between horse and rider; Prince Hal simply did not perform for the male riders. Although the combination of Symthe and Prince Hal had been immensely successful on the international circuit, when she was finally selected for the Olympic team, the male coach had blacklisted the horse and Smythe had to compete on her less talented and less experienced second horse. This example from showjumping in the 1950s highlights that, even though women gained access to the sport, their sporting experience was significantly influenced by patriarchy and capitalism. Today, outside of Olympic competition, on the professional global showjumping circuit, patriarchy and capitalism remain dominant discourses. Big money competitions such as the Longines Global Champions Tour offer prize money for a class of €400,000 (equivalent to over US$470,000) – far more than is offered in the other disciplines.

Reflecting the patriarchal control discussed in showjumping, before their inclusion in the Olympic competition, successful female eventers were also asked to hand over their carefully trained and valuable horses for use within all male teams. Although the sport has always relied heavily on the cooperation of independent owners, women riders were expected to hand over their horses without question or reward. In 1956, British rider Sheila Willox, who placed second at Badminton (considered the best and toughest eventing course in the world – even more challenging than any Olympic course) – was asked to loan her horse. "They came to me in the collecting ring at Badminton before Showjumping (the final part of the competition) and said they wanted me to make my horse available for the male Olympic riders. I said no. I told them that 'High and Mighty' was my only horse and I had no money to replace him" (Burke, 1997, p.108). The selectors persisted and put immense pressure on the 20 year old, who finally agreed to sell rather than lend her horse. Of the three disciplines, Eventing has the closest affiliation with the military, and it was the last of the disciplines to allow female competitors. However, it has seen the largest growth from 1% female competitors in the early years, to 34% of the competing athletes now being female.

Women were most likely to be competing in Dressage both then and now, although they now form a much greater proportion, with 60% of competitors at twenty-first-century Olympic Games being female, compared with 25% in earlier Games. Hedenborg and White (2012) suggest that a likely explanation for the higher number of women in Dressage compared with the other Olympic disciplines is due to the fact that Dressage riding was (and arguably still is) more compatible with an accepted femininity. Of all the disciplines, the subtleties of dressage require empathy and consideration as to how to coax the best performance from the horse, allowing the horse's natural paces to show. Dressage was the subculture in which Dashper (2012a) conducted an ethnographic study using inclusive masculinity as the framework to explore the changing nature of masculinities in sport. She noted that an increasing acceptance of openly gay men in equestrian sport resulted in a decreased level of homophobia, but that this did not necessarily result in a reduction in the polarization between masculinity and femininity. Through a post-structuralist lens we can note dressage competitors demonstrate more inclusive forms of masculinity but that they are still constructed in opposition to a devalued femininity.

Participation is only one aspect of sport at an elite level; performance remains the dominant measure of success. With regard to medals won, four nations have dominated Olympic equestrianism in the twenty-first century: Germany, Great Britain, the United States, and the Netherlands. Despite the fact that to date there are no longer any explicit, formal barriers to participation for females at any level of equestrian sport (within the context of culturally specific, gendered sporting access), Travers (2008) notes that this does not simply translate to equality of opportunity. Dressage has more female Olympic athletes in this century in all four of these nations, whereas showjumping sees great variability in female representation across the four dominant nations in Olympic equestrian sport in the twenty-first century (Table 10.3). Indeed, as a result of a three-year ethnographic study of gender relations in equestrian sport, Dashper (2012b) refers to "subtle discrimination and hidden barriers [which] combine to produce a glass ceiling effect at the top levels of the sport, denying many women participatory parity in relation to their male peers" (p. 217). Specifically Dashper (2012b) refers to three distinct barriers: (a) a combination of gender and class, (b) financial pressures, and (c) the barrier of "family." What can be seen from Table 10.3 is that these successful equestrian nations overall demonstrate more equitable representation than the average for the sport. Although there is individual variation, it would appear that, in selecting the athletes most likely to achieve medal success, they are selecting from both sexes and both sexes are enabling success within equestrian sport.

Table 10.3 Participation of the sexes in Olympic equestrian sport in dominant nations of the twenty-first century compared with all equestrian athletes (OR = odds ratio)

	Dressage			Show Jumping			Eventing			Total		
	M	F	M:F OR	M	F	M:F OR	M	F	M:F OR	M	F	M:F OR
GER	3	16	0.19	16	4	4.00	14	9	1.56	33	29	1.14
GBR	10	19	0.53	17	0	Undefined	5	18	0.28	31	28	1.11
USA	7	12	0.58	10	10	1.00	11	12	0.92	28	34	0.82
NED	6	13	0.46	19	1	19.00	4	3	1.33	29	17	1.71
ALL	103	154	0.67	308	68	4.53	243	123	1.98	644	355	1.81

Horse ownership

We cannot discuss participation and power in equestrian sport without highlighting the unique aspect of horse ownership. At the Olympic level, horse ownership is governed by the Fédération Equestre Internationale (FEI (International Equestrian Federation). In Olympic competition the rider and horse must share the same nationality and a horse's nationality is determined by that of its owner. According to Chapter V Article 139, of the FEI regulations for 2017 (FEI, 2017a), the following rules apply:

> 4. Horses entered for the Olympic Games must be the property of Owners of the same nationality as the Athlete by 15th January of the year of the Games (see Olympic Regulations).

The imposed date of registration creates a "transfer window" of ownership bringing in issues of national, political, and economic pressures. As nations secure qualification at an Olympic Games, the pressure to acquire or keep appropriate horse power until the registration date can alter the combination of horse and rider who ultimately compete. At this level of the sport, horses are commodities, and in a similar fashion to stock options their value fluctuates based on performance, with basic economic principles of supply and demand affecting the market value. Horses are also unfortunately highly susceptible to injury, resulting in a potential loss of all value. From a sport development perspective, emerging markets such as the Middle Eastern countries of Saudi Arabia and Qatar are becoming very involved in the top end of ShowJumping and bring with them substantial economic buying power. Rob Hoekstra, Performance Manager for Britain's Showjumping team, explains that the buying power of these countries has "definitely moved the whole sport and business up a level . . . they've got a big budget, and horses at that level are of course expensive, probably between £500,000 and £2.5m each" (Williams, 2012). The cost or value of horses at the Olympic level of the sport is not generally public knowledge. However, it was reported in the press that three of the British horses, Valegro, Uthopia, and Alf, which were part of the gold medal winning Dressage team at the 2012 Olympics, were expected to be auctioned off post-Games for about £20 million (Harper, 2012).

Dumbell et al. (2017) identified that most British Olympic athletes in the twenty-first century do not own any part of their horse. This trend continues beyond Britain (Table 10.4), because 65% of athletes from the dominant nations did not own their horse. There was no clear trend witnessed as to whether this is affected by gender, and it has been suggested that commercial factors and national funding systems have a greater effect on athlete horse ownership. That said, Coutler (2013) reports increased business skills and focus within male equestrian athletes compared with female athletes, and the advantage that taking a more instrumental approach to the

Table 10.4 The pattern of horse ownership (part or whole) of Rio 2016 competitors (OR = odds ratio)

Proportion with stake	Dressage		ShowJumping		Eventing		Overall
	Male	Female	Male	Female	Male	Female	M:F OR
GER	0	0	0.67	1	1	0.67	1.40
GBR	0.5	0.5	0.24	–	0	0	1.45
USA	0	0.33	0	0	0	0	0.00
NED	0.33	1	0.5	–	1	0.5	0.84
Sum (%)	29	33	38	33	43	33	35

horse can have in protecting an equestrian athlete if a horse is sold or removed from their care (Dashper, 2014). This may provide male athletes with an advantage (Dashper, 2012b); however, this advantage would not seem translate into over-representation. As we have highlighted in this chapter, however, showjumping is the most commercialized equestrian discipline and has by far the greatest proportion of male athletes (see Table 10.3) within the Olympic equestrian events.

Decision-making

Mirroring the push for parity on the playing field, the IOC is also highlighting the need to increase women's representation in decision-making positions at all levels within sport, from the IOC to national governing bodies (NGBs). In line with the liberal feminist approach, the IOC has recommended that 30% of the board members of IFs, national Olympic committees (NOCs), and NGBs should be female (Henry & Robinson, 2010). Several studies have reviewed the use of targets and quotas (e.g., Adriaanse & Schofield, 2014, in Australia, and Claringbould & Knoppers, 2007, 2008, in the Netherlands). Henry, Radzi, Rich, Shelton, Theodoraki, and White (2004) concluded that this approach had been successful to the point of raising awareness of gender inequalities and had unlocked a source of skilled, educated, and committed individuals who contributed to improving Olympic governance. However, the researchers also highlighted several limitations to this approach. Some organizations viewed the targets as a ceiling to be attained rather than a base from which to build, and, even when minimum targets were achieved, they did not necessarily lead to the adoption of policy initiatives that fostered women's participation in executive decision-making. Critiques of this liberal feminist approach highlight the fact that simply adding women to a male culture does little to facilitate equity (e.g., Henry et al., 2004; Knoppers & Anthonissen, 2005; Sotiriadou, de Haan, & Knoppers, 2017). As Betzer-Tayar, Zach, Galily, and Henry (2017, p. 11) explain:

> as long as women continue to be merely a significant minority at the top of the leadership ladder, their voices may be marginalized and their sociocultural status may be discursively constructed as the "other", in relation to the norm for the male-dominated boards of executives.

Indeed, even though many NOCs found the IOC's earlier target of 20%, set in 1996, a challenge, Henry and Robinson (2010) contended that a target of 30% by 2017 was required to build on previous momentum. IOC President Thomas Bach has significantly increased the number of women appointed to a commission since his election in 2013, with 38% of places now taken by women, a historic high for the IOC (International Olympic Committee, 2017). Despite these promising figures, men continue to dominate key decision-making positions across all aspects of sport, and the percentage of women in governing and administrative bodies in the Olympic movement remains low. Of the 28 IFs representing sports at the Rio 2016 Olympics, no IF currently has a board with more female members than male, one IF has no female board members at all, and just one sport has a female president. Only 21% of the IFs meet the requirement of 30% female board members (see the dark line in Table 10.5). On average, a board member is nearly five times more likely to be male. The International Hockey Federation seems to be most successfully taking their participation level (almost equal) into their board (also equal). Despite the increase in female participation within the Olympic Program, the majority of the sports remain sex segregated and, despite IFs being responsible for the governance of sport participation among both men and women, decision-making powers remain with men.

Table 10.5 Board membership of International Federations of recognized sports in Rio 2016 (dark line shows where IOC-recommended 30% female would be) (OR = odds ratio)

International federation	Participation M:F odds ratio	Gender of IF first	Gender of IF second	Total	Male	Female	M:F OR
ISSF: Shooting	1.56	Male	Male	13	13	0	∞
IJF: Judo	1.56	Male	Male	22	21	1	21
AIBA: Boxing	6.94	Male	Male	21	20	1	20
UCI: Cycling	1.65	Male	Male	16	15	1	15
IGF: Golf	1.00	Male	Male	13	12	1	12
UIPM: Modern Pentathlon	1.00	Male	Female	13	12	1	12
WR: Rugby	1.01	Male	Male	10	9	1	9
FIFA: Football	1.33	Male	Female	36	32	4	8
ITTF: Table Tennis	1.00	Male	Male	8	7	1	7
FINA: Aquatics	0.99	Male	Male	23	20	3	6.67
WT: Taekwondo	1.00	Male	Male	29	25	4	6.25
FIBA: Basketball	1.00	Male	Male	7	6	1	6
ICF: Canoe	2.13	Male	Male	14	12	2	6
IWF: Weightlifting	1.50	Male	Male	14	12	2	6
UWW: Wrestling	2.11	Male	Male	7	6	1	6
FEI: Equestrian	1.62	Male	Female	18	15	3	5
IHF: Handball	1.00	Male	Male	17	14	3	4.67
FIVB: Volleyball	1.00	Male	Male	17	14	3	4.67
ITF: Tennis	1.12	Male	Female	15	12	3	4
IAAF: Athletics	1.06	Male	Male	27	21	6	3.50
WA: Archery	1.00	Male	Male	13	10	3	3.33
BWF: Badminton	1.02	Male	Male	25	18	7	2.57
FIE: Fencing	1.00	Male	Male	20	14	6	2.33
FISA: Rowing	1.58	Male	Male	6	4	2	2
ITU: Triathlon	1.00	Female	Male	8	5	3	1.67
WS: Sailing	1.33	Male	Male	8	5	3	1.67
FIG: Gymnastics	0.54	Male	Male	7	5		1.40
FIH: Hockey	1.01	Male	Male	14	7	7	1
Totals	1.20	97%	82%	430		88	4.89

It is evident that participation numbers are far more equitable than leadership positions in governing organizations. Federations have been part of the Olympic movement for different lengths of time. However, it is not possible to simply relate male dominance in governance to a history of male-dominated sport, as Table 10.6 shows. The FEI was formed in 1921. Despite this lengthy history and its military roots the FEI has a similar make-up to many IFs, and has more women members than the majority of boards. That said, the International Triathlon Union (ITU) is a more modern organization, founded in 1989, and its governance includes more than 30% women. Interestingly, triathlon includes a mixed event in its World Championships consisting of a four-person team, two men and two women. This format was on the program of the 2010 Singapore Youth Olympic Games and is due to be included in Tokyo 2020 (ITU, 2017). The ITU is also the only IF currently to have a female president.

At the most senior level, however, females serve in the top two positions of the FEI, whereas the British Equestrian Federation (BEF) does not state who is their second in

Table 10.6 Participation and representation

International federation	Present on the Olympic program since	Participation			Representation		
		Number of male athletes at the 2016 Rio Olympics	Number of female athletes at the 2016 Rio Olympics	Male:female odds ratio	Male board directors	Women board directors	Male:female odds ratio
ISSF: International Shooting Sport Federation	1896	341	214	1.59	13	0	∞
WR: World Rugby	2016	149	148	1.01	9	1	9
FEI: International Equestrian Federation	1900	123	76	1.62	15	3	5
ITU: International Triathlon Union	2000	55	55	1	5	3	1.67

command, and the other three national federations have all-male leadership. The overpopulation of males in the top two positions of IFs is also evident (see Table 10.5). Just five IFs (18%) have a female in one of these positions, with the ITU being the only IF to have a female president, and just four other IFs have females in their second position: FEI, FIFA (Fédération Internationale de Football Association – football), UIPM (Union Internationale de Pentathlon Moderne – modern pentathlon), and ITF (International Tennis Federation – tennis). The four most successful national federations in equestrian sports at the Olympics would all meet the guidance of 30% female representation as a minimum (Table 10.7). Interestingly two of them have more female than male members, although none of them is below 30% male representation (United States Equestrian Federation [USEF] with 37% being the lowest proportion of males and Deutsche Reiterliche Vereinigung [FN – German Equestrian Federation] with the lowest proportion of females at 31%). It is therefore surprising that their IF, the FEI, has just 17% of their members who are females, with a member being five times more likely to be male.

There have been 14 different presidents of the FEI (Table 10.8). The first 10 were all male and of notable title, apart from Magnus Rydman from Finland who held the presidency from 1939 to 1946. The first female president in 1986 (five years after the appointment of the first female member of the IOC) was HRH The Princess Royal; she has since been followed by two more female presidents, both of whom are of royal descent. Princess Anne was also elected as an IOC member in 1988, becoming only the fifth woman to join that body. In this context we highlight the interrelationship of gender, class, elitism, and access to the higher echelons of sport governance, whereby it would appear that gender combined with significant social status (royal or noble decent) facilitates access to an otherwise patriarchal institution.

Table 10.7 Number of current male and female board members per country NF + FEI (equestrian IF) board membership

Federation	First (second)	Number of directors	Male members	Female members	M:F odds ratio
FEI: International Federation of Equestrian Sports Fédération Equestre Internationale	Male (female)	18	15	3	5
British Equestrian Federation (BEF)	Male (none)	12	5	7	0.71
United States Equestrian Federation (USEF)	Male (male)	19	7	12	0.58
Koninklijke Nederlandse Hippische Sportfederatie (KNHS – the Netherlands)	Male (male)	17	11	6	1.83
Deutsche Reiterliche Vereinigung (FN – Germany)	Male (male)	13	9	4	2.25

Table 10.8 The two most senior members of the FEI board

Years in office	FEI President	Sex	Years in office	FEI Secretary Generals	Sex
1921–1927	Baron du Teil	Male	1921–1951	Major Georges Hector	Male
1927–1929	Colonel G. J. Maris	Male			
1929–1931	Major J. K. Quarles van Ufford	Male			
1931–1935	General Guy V. Henry	Male			
1935–1936	General Baron Max Frh. Von Holzing-Bertstett	Male			
1936–1939	Lt. Col. J. K. Quarles van Ufford	Male			
1939–1946	M. Magnus Rydman	Male			
1946–1954	General Baron Gaston de Trannoy	Male	1951–1956	Major Roger Moermans d'Emaus	Male
1954–1964	HRH Bernard, Prince of the Netherlands	Male	1956–1976	Chevalier Henry de Menten de Horne	Male
1964–1986	HRH Prince Philip, Duke of Edinburgh	Male	1976–1988	Mr. Fritz O. Widmer	Male
1986–1994	HRH Princess Anne, The Princess Royal	Female	1989–1995	Mr. Etienne Allard	Male
1994–2006	HRH The Infanta Doña Pilar de Borbòn	Female	1996–2005	Dr. Bo Helander	Male
			2005–2006	Mr. Jean-Claude Falciola	Male
2006–2014	HRH Princess Haya Al Hussein	Female	2006–2007	Mr. Michael Stone	Male
			2008–2011	Mr. Alex McLin	Male
			2011–2014	Mr. Ingmar De Vos	Male
2014–	Ingmar De Vos	Male	2014 –	Mrs. Sabrina Ibáñez	Female

The current president of the FEI is Mr. Ingmar De Vos from Belgium, who has held the position since 2014 (FEI, 2017b). The current Secretary General of the FEI is the first woman to hold that office since its introduction in 1921 (Table 10.8). Previously FEI Director, Governance and Affairs (since 2011) and interim Secretary General from 2014, Mrs. Ibáñez was appointed in January 2015 with unanimous support (FEI, 2015).

It is interesting that the FEI have continuously had one male and one female in the top two positions since 1986, when the first female president was appointed (HRH Princess Anne, The Princess Royal of England) (see Table 10.8). This gender equality within the leadership of equestrian sport does provide a model that may offer valuable insights to other sports in ensuring that female representation is meaningful and high profile in support of future development.

Conclusion

Here, we return to the conflicting discourses of (in)equality in equestrian sport and consider whether this unique sex-integrated sport offers any unique gender-related management insights. The research question driving this inquiry is whether sex-integrated competition in sport can provide a conducive environment for gender equality on the field (participation) and in the boardroom (decision-making)?

In a sex-integrated sport the initiatives advocated by liberal feminism of quotas and active promotion of female sport can have only limited impact. That equestrian sport has achieved comparable female participation in many IFs, despite no quotas being used, suggests the barriers to participation (socialist feminism) are not insurmountable in a sex-integrated sport. This does not mean that equestrian sport has no barriers to participation, and in fact there is variability between the events, where showjumping is still male dominated, and in dressage we are nearing a point that we could soon be concerned about male under-representation. A sex-integrated sport poses fewer challenges to a postcultural feminist approach because the competitors' sex is not an issue, and there are role models representing a range of gender and sexualities within equestrian sport. There remain event-/discipline-specific challenges to overcome, and these may interact with socialist feminist ideas of how commercialism and male-dominated media representations are influential in elite sport. Overall Olympic equestrian sport is an example of how sex-integrated competition can facilitate participation from both sexes, although it also demonstrates how the individual event's social and competition context affects participation by the genders.

The gender balance seen in Olympic competitors in many sports does not translate to a similar gender balance in the governing bodies. The governing bodies of IFs remain a male-dominated domain. The IF for equestrian sport (the FEI) has a greater proportion of female board members than most other Olympic IFs, but does not demonstrate the 30% female membership advocated by the IOC. The FEI has, however, demonstrated gender equality in the top two posts for over 30 years. In this way, it is unusual among IFs, and equestrian sport could contribute valuable insights to support transferring the relative success of the agenda to increase the female participation in the Olympics and increasing the gender equality within the governing bodies of international sporting federations.

Leader profile: Amanda Bond

British born, Amanda Bond is a key player in the world of equestrian sport. Her career started in the UK at Hartpury College, where, as a graduating student, she took up her first role working for the college. Over the course of 14 years, Bond's career at Hartpury developed from one of lecturer to Deputy Principal. During this time, it was her role as Event Director for the FEI World Para Dressage Championships, as well as several international dressage and Eventing championships, that led to her first posting outside of the UK. Due to quarantine restrictions, the equestrian competitions of the 2008 Beijing Olympic and Paralympic Games took place in Hong Kong. Bond worked for the organizing committee of the Beijing 2008 Games, based at the equestrian venue in the co-host city of Hong Kong. On returning to the UK she was appointed CEO of British Dressage. During that time, she was seconded to work as discipline manager at the London 2012 Olympic and Paralympic Games.

Recently Bond returned to Hong Kong. In her current role as an Executive Manager of the Hong Kong Jockey Club, she is responsible for overseeing equestrian matters outside of racing, with the aim of developing equestrian sport in the region. With over 25,000 employees, the Jockey Club is the largest employer in Hong Kong, and it is also one of the largest charitable donors in the world. Bond is responsible for leading a team of 250 staff. She also manages four equestrian centers and helps key stakeholders with the strategic delivery of equestrian events in Hong Kong. Her role encompasses all aspects of the sport from the grassroots level through to the elite teams who represent Hong Kong on the world stage. She also sits on the Board of the Hong Kong Equestrian Federation and the Riding for the Disabled Association.

Bond explains that, in her "spare" time, she is the chair of the FEI Para Equestrian Technical Committee and was the Foreign Technical Delegate for the 2015 European Championships and the 2016 Rio Paralympic Games. She is one of only two female chairs from 14 FEI standing and technical committees.

References

Adelman, M. & Knijnik, J. (eds) (2013). *Gender and Equestrian Sport: Riding around the world*. Dordrecht, the Netherlands: Springer.

Adriaanse, J. & Schofield, T. (2014). The impact of gender quotas on gender equity in sport governance. *Journal of Sport Management*, **28**, 485–497.

Anderson, E. (2009). The maintenance of masculinity among the stakeholders of sport. *Sport Management Review*, **12**, 3–14.

Betzer-Tayar, M., Zach, S., Galily, Y., & Henry, I. (2017). Barriers to women's access to decision-making positions in sport organizations: The case of establishing a girls' volleyball academy in Israel. *Journal of Gender Studies*, **26**(4), 418–431.

Birrell, S. (1981). Sport as ritual: Interpretations from Durkheim to Goffman. *Social Forces*, **60**, 354–376.

Blanchard, K. (1988). Sport and ritual: A conceptual dilemma. *Journal of Physical Education, Recreation & Dance*, **59**, 48–52.

Bromberger, C. (1995). Football as world-view and as ritual. *French Cultural Studies*, **6**, 293–311.

Burke, J. C. (1997) *Equal to the Challenge: Pioneering women of horse sports*. New York: Howell Book House.

Burke, M. (2001). Sport and traditions of feminist theory, Doctoral dissertation, Victoria University. Retrieved from http://vuir.vu.edu.au/259/1/02whole.pdf.

Burke, M. (2010). Radicalising liberal feminism by playing the games that men play. *Australian Feminist Studies*, **19**(44), 169–184.

Claringbould, I. E. C. & Knoppers, A. E. (2007) Finding a "normal" woman: Selection processes for board membership. *Sex Roles*, **56**, 495–507.

Claringbould, I. & Knoppers, A. (2008). Doing and undoing gender in sport governance. *Sex Roles*, **57**, 81–92.

Connell, R. (1987). *Gender and Power*. Stanford, CA: Stanford University Press.

Connell, R. (1995). *Masculinities*. Sydney, Australia: Allen & Unwin.

Connell, R. (2008). Masculinity construction and sports in boys' education: A framework for thinking about the issue. *Sport Education and Society*, **13**(2), 131–145.

Coutler, K. (2013). Horse power: Gender work and wealth in Canadian show jumping. In: M. Adelman, and J. Knijnik (eds), *Gender and Equestrian Sport: Riding around the world* (pp. 165–181). Dordrecht, the Netherlands: Springer.

Dashper, K. (2012a) "Dressage is full of queens!": Masculinity, sexuality and equestrian sport. *Sociology*, **46**, 1109–1124.
Dashper, K. (2012b) Together, yet still not equal? Sex integration in equestrian sport. *Asia-Pacific Journal of Health, Sport and Physical Education*, **3**, 213–225.
Dashper, K. (2013). Beyond the binary: Gender integration in British equestrian sport. In: M. Adelman and J. Knijnik (eds), *Gender and Equestrian Sport: Riding around the world* (pp. 37–53). Dordrecht, the Netherlands: Springer.
Dashper, K. (2014). Tools of the trade or part of the family? Horses in competitive equestrian sport. *Society and Animals*, **22**(4), 352–371.
De Haan, D. (2015). Evaluating the experience of the Olympic and Paralympic Games in the career histories of elite equestrian athletes, Doctoral dissertation, Loughborough University. Retrieved from https://dspace.lboro.ac.uk/dspace-jspui/handle/2134/17384.
De Haan, D. and Dumbell, L. (2016). Equestrian sport at the Olympic Games from 1900 to 1948. *The International Journal of the History of Sport*, **33**(6–7), 648–665.
De Haan, D., Sotiriadou, P., & Henry, I. (2015). The lived experience of sex integrated sport and the construction of athlete identity within the Olympic and Paralympic Equestrian disciplines. *Sport in Society*, **18**, 1–18.
Dumbell, L. & De Haan, D. (2012). Has the Barrier been Jumped? A comparison of athlete profiles over 50 years of Olympic equestrian events. Paper presented at ICSEMIS 2012 Convention, Glasgow, July.
Dumbell, L. C., Douglas, J., and Rowe, L. (2017). Demographic profiling of British Olympic equestrian athletes in the twenty-first century. *Sport in Society*, 1–14, http://dx.doi.org/10.1080/17430437.2017.1388786.
Dumbell, L., Johnson, J-L., & de Haan, D. (2010). Demographic profiling of elite dressage riders. *The International Journal of Sport and Society*, **1**(3), 15–24.
Fédération Equestre Internationale (FEI) (2015). The FEI Secretary Generals. Retrieved from http://inside.fei.org/system/files/FEI%20Secretary%20Generals%20since%201921.pdf.
Fédération Equestre Internationale (FEI) (2017a). FEI General Regulations, 23rd edn. Retrieved from http://inside.fei.org/sites/default/files/GENERAL_REGULATIONS-Eff.1January2017_Clean-Final%2022_Dec_2016.pdf
Fédération Equestre Internationale (FEI) (2017b). The FEI Presidents. Retrieved from https://inside.fei.org/fei/about-fei/history/fei-presidents-since-1921.
Hargreaves, J. (1990). Gender on the sport agenda. *International Review for Sociology of Sport*, **25**(4), 287–307.
Hargreaves, J. (2002). *Sporting Females: Critical issues in the history and sociology of women's sport*. London: Taylor & Francis.
Harper, T. (2012). London 2012 Olympics: Golden horses of Team GB to go up for sale. *London Evening Standard*, August 8. Retrieved from https://www.standard.co.uk/news/london/london-2012-olympics-golden-horses-of-team-gb-to-go-up-for-sale-8022068.html.
Hedenborg, S. (2009). Unknown soldiers and very pretty ladies: Challenges to the social order of sports in post-war Sweden. *Sport in History*, **29**, 601–622.
Hedenborg, S. (2015). Gender and sports within the equine sector: A comparative perspective. *International Journal of the History of Sport*, **32**(4), 551–564
Hedenborg, S. & White, M. H. (2012). Changes and variations in patterns of gender relations in equestrian sports during the second half of the twentieth century. *Sport in Society*, **15**, 302–319.
Henry, I. P. & Robinson, L. (2010). *Gender Equity and Leadership in Olympic Bodies*. Lausanne: International Olympic Committee.
Henry, I.P., Radzi, W., Rich, E., Shelton, C., Theodoraki, E., & White, A. (2004). *Women, Leadership and the Olympic Movement*. Loughborough: Institute of Sport and Leisure Policy, Loughborough University and the International Olympic Committee.
Hovden, J. (2012). Discourses and strategies for the inclusion of women in sport – the case of Norway. *Sport in Society*, **15**(3), 287–301.
International Olympic Committee (2017). IOC announces composition of its commissions – 38 per cent of members now women. *IOC*, April 25. Retrieved from https://www.olympic.org/news/ioc-announces-composition-of-its-commissions-38-per-cent-of-members-now-women.
International Triathlon Union (2017). Triathlon Mixed Relay. Retrieved from https://www.triathlon.org/multisports/triathlon_mixed_relay.
Knoppers, A. E. & Anthonissen, A. F. (2005). Male athletic and managerial masculinities: Congruencies in discursive practices? *Journal of Gender Studies*, **14**, 123–135.

McDonagh, E. & Pappano, L. (2008). *Playing with the Boys: Why separate is not equal in sports*. New York: Oxford University Press.

Markula P. (2018). Poststructuralist feminism in sport and leisure studies. In: L. Mansfield, J. Caudwell, B. Wheaton, & B. Watson (eds), *The Palgrave Handbook of Feminism and Sport, Leisure and Physical Education* (pp. 393–408). London, England: Palgrave Macmillan.

Messner, M. (1992). *Power at Play: Sports and the problem of masculinity*. Boston, MA: Beacon Press.

Real, M. R. (1996). The postmodern Olympics: Technology and the commodification of the Olympic Movement. *Quest*, **48**, 9–24.

Roth, A. & Basow, S. A. (2004). Femininity, sports, and feminism: Developing a theory of physical liberation. *Journal of Sport and Social Issues*, **28**(3), 245–265.

Sabo, D. (1985). Sport, patriarchy and the male identity: New questions about men and sport. *Arena Review*, **9**, 1–30.

Sabo, D. & Runfola, R. (eds) (1980) *Jock: Sports and male identity*. Englewood Cliffs, NJ: Prentice Hall.

Scraton, S. & Flintoff, A. (2013). Gender, feminist theory, and sport. In: D. L. Andrews & B. Darrington (eds), *A Companion to Sport* (pp. 96–110). Oxford: Wiley-Blackwell.

Shaw, S. & Frisby, W. (2006). Can gender equity be more equitable?: Promoting an alternative frame for sport management research, education, and practice. *Journal of Sport Management*, **20**, 483–509.

Sotiriadou, P., de Haan, D., & Knoppers, A. (2017). Understanding and redefining the role of men in achieving gender equity in sport leadership. Retrieved from https://library.olympic.org/Default/doc/SYRACUSE/171304/understanding-and-redefining-the-role-of-men-in-achieving-gender-equity-in-sport-leadership-popi-sot

Smythe, P. (1954). *Jump for Joy*. London. England: Cassell & Co. Ltd.

Travers, A. (2008). The sport nexus and gender injustice. *Studies in Social Justice*, **2**, 79–101.

Williams, O. (2012). London 2012: Are GB victims of the horse transfer window? *BBC*, January 10. Retrieved from http://news.bbc.co.uk/sport1/hi/equestrian/16442105.stm

Yiamouyiannis, A. & Osborne, B. (2012). Addressing gender inequities in collegiate sport: Examining female leadership representation within NCAA sport governance. *SAGE Open*, **2**(2), 1–13. Retrieved from https://doi.org/10.1177/2158244012449340.

11
Migratory process of Brazilian Olympic women

Katia Rubio, Neilton Ferreira Junior, and Gislane Ferreira de Melo

Introduction

The Olympic Games of the Modern Age have survived throughout the twentieth century's two World Wars and two declared and two veiled boycotts (Grix, 2012; Kellett, Hede, & Chalip, 2008; Riordan, 2006). Nevertheless, a new commercial order was established with the arrival of the televised Olympic Games. The visibility athletes received via televised coverage caused commercial businesses to want to associate themselves with high-achieving athletes, but, without a formal association with the Olympic Games, athletes had to be creative to publicize their corporate partners. For example, at the 1972 Munich Games, swimmer Mark Spitz got on the medal podium and put his shoes around his neck to display the corporate logo. Although it was expressly prohibited, this showed the world who was sponsoring him, because the sponsor had little space on the athlete uniform, a single piece of clothing, which gave little visibility to the brand (Papanikolaou, 2012; Oeiras & Preuss, 2004).

This situation highlighted the necessity to revisit the future of the Olympic movement in relation to its amateurism and professionalism. The participation of big companies in the funding of the Games was inevitable, especially considering the necessities imposed by the host city. The professionalization movement in which some athletes were engaging was understandable, because their lives were dedicated to training and competing, and therefore having another occupation to earn money that would sustain themselves and their families was nearly impossible (Rubio, 2006).

According to Ferrando (1996) amateur athletes are those who do not have either a trainer or the specific training for their area of expertise. This concept emphasizes the sports practice of European bourgeoisie in the late nineteenth and twentieth centuries which was maintained by most of the leaders of the contemporary Olympic movement. Almost all of those members came from privileged groups, be it socially, economically, and/or politically. However, high-performance sport became so technically qualified that its most prominent and dedicated practitioners were brought closer by their social extraction from the working class, which the ruling bourgeoisie intended to keep out of sport. For this reason, the author refers to the high-performance athletes as "sports workers," as a counterpart to their professional practice, generous advertising contracts, professional, medical, and social safety requirements, and a distancing from the so-called Olympic ideal. The athletes with this profile, despite their varied social extraction, were almost always from middle to low social classes, and point out that sports are an impediment to the pursuit of another occupation, which causes these athletes to seek professionalization in their sport.

The migratory process related to the profession of being a soccer player is widely studied not only in Brazil, but also in most of the world by specialists from several areas of knowledge (Elliott, 2014; Frick, 2009; Giulianotti & Robertson, 2007; Lanfranchi, 1994; Magee & Sugden, 2002). These same factors do not occur in Olympic sport, where rules of being amateur persisted until the 1980s, and in less than three decades points to an exhaustion already observed by international Olympic leaders (Agergaard & Ryba, 2014; Engh & Agergaard, 2015; Maguire, 2011; Rubio, 2006, 2016).

The amateur athlete was, by definition, one who had neither coaches nor training in his or her sport. The emphasis given to the unpaid sports practice of the European bourgeoisie of the late nineteenth and early twentieth centuries was maintained by most of the leaders of the contemporary Olympic movement, almost all of them members of privileged social, economic, and/or political groups (Rubio, 2001).

If, during the amateur phase (from the start of the Olympic competitions in 1896 until the end of the 1980s), the athlete's role was restricted only in executing her skills perfectly, this role suffered radical transformations when she moved to a more professional stance. In addition to being a performer, the athlete was now required to also serve as the representative of brands and commercial interests in a globalized world. Starting in adolescence, the athlete undergoes a migratory process in search of the best opportunities to develop her skills; she is transformed into a migrant laborer in search of a market to sell her skilled labor. During this process, the athlete suffers intense losses of familial, social, cultural, and emotional order, and also acquires new values that reorganize her subjectivity.

The process of continuing professionalization in Olympic sport since the 1980s radically changed the position of the athlete within the Olympic movement. Since the start of contemporary Olympic history, the athlete was only the accomplisher of sport prowess without actually occupying the same prominence and importance as people in political positions, who interfered in the direction of Olympic ideals in general.

Throughout the twentieth century until the 2016 Olympic Games in Rio de Janeiro, successive Olympic leaders denied the relationship between politics and sports. Since 1920, however, international political issues interfered in Olympic competitions, sometimes in the form of individual boycotts (e.g., the revoked invitation to Germany as a result of World War I), sometimes in the use of the Games as publicity for a political regime (e.g., Berlin in 1936), or as a bloc demonstration during the Cold War with boycotts of the Moscow and Los Angeles Olympic Games by the United States and the Soviet Union, respectively. Latent political interests came to be integrated with the then-explicit economic needs, both in the maintenance of the overall sport system, and in the delivery of the Olympic Games in particular. As such, the boundaries between the public and the private, and between national and international interests, were transformed into fluid and fragile objects.

Thrown in the middle of this process is the athlete, protagonist of the sport spectacle, bystander of the macrostructure of the Olympic system, and exiled from power structures historically constituted to be occupied by nobles, aristocrats, and bureaucrats from all over the world. Since the creation of the International Olympic Committee in 1894, until the present, the Olympic movement has dictated the norms and directions for international sport. Through the international federations, rules for the competitive practice of sports modalities around the world were created, which applied to those who wished to demonstrate their physical abilities in the execution of the specific technical gestures required by their specific Olympic modalities. This autocratic and centralized system determined not only institutional directions of the sport, but interfered directly in the lives of the protagonists of the Olympic Games.

With these changes, professional athletes began to cross several borders, not only internal, but also now external. These constant changes brought about by the incessant search for technical improvement and income led researchers to take an interest in the concept of transnationalism. Transnationalism was initially studied by Stead and Maguire in 2000 with male soccer players. Ten years later, Agergaard and Botelho (2010) began to conduct their research with women in soccer (Tiesler, 2016).

In transnationalism, people live their lives across various political boundaries. Transnational migrants are confronted with deeply rooted hegemonic categories, such as race and ethnicity, which may appear identical, but are very different positions in different regions. The use of the transnational concept is, therefore, focused on cultural and political power projections by various forms of governance, each claiming jurisdiction over a population in a particular space. Transnationalism, in Smith's (2001) description, departs from units of limited analysis in the sense of a theoretically more problematic conceptualization of space and place.

The relevance of this study comes from the increasingly common incidence of geographic displacement of athletes due to the dynamics of the organization of sports teams and the professionalization process. During the migratory process, athletes live intense phases of adaptation and loss, in addition to the acquisition of new values that reorganize their subjectivity. Therefore, the purpose of this research is to describe the number of national and international migrations performed by our women Olympic athletes, as well as comparing this migration during the amateur and professional eras.

Methods

Initially, we conducted a qualitative study through the life stories of women Olympic athletes. The interviews were open-ended and departed from an essential issue, which aims to take into account memory, its dynamism, and the need for subjective treatment to emerge from the constructed narrative. Second, quantitative data for descriptive research was taken from the interviews to address the research objectives. A spreadsheet was created to catalogue the data in variables of interest for subsequent analysis.

Our sample included 444 women Olympic athletes who participated in the Olympic Games from 1932 to 2012. The interviews were completed in a reserved place (face to face or virtual) in order to preserve the integrity of the subject, as well as that of the interviewer and the quality of the interview, without disregarding the specific conditions and needs of the interviewees. The time of the interview was also determined by the subject, according her availability. For the descriptive analysis of the data, means, deviations, and frequencies were used for the analysis.

Results

According to the map of Brazil it is possible to identify Olympic athletes by states and regions. The definition of the human development index (HDI) by region, a condition to understanding for regional discrepancies, is also highlighted in Figure 11.1.

Figure 11.1 Number of Olympic athletes and their federative states of birth

Green – North (Rondônia, Acre, Amazonas, Roraima, Amapá, Tocantins)
Orange – Northeast (Bahia, Sergipe, Alagoas, Pernambuco, Paraíba, Rio Grande do Norte, Ceará, Piauí, Maranhão)
Yellow – Midwest (Mato Grosso do Sul, Mato Grosso, Goiás, Distrito Federal)
Red – Southeast (Minas Gerais, São Paulo, Rio de Janeiro e Espírito Santo)
Blue – South (Rio Grande do Sul, Santa Catarina e Paraná)

It can be observed that the vast majority of Brazilian female Olympic athletes are from the Southeast region, followed by the South, Northeast, Midwest, and finally the North region.

Tables 11.1–11.3 show the migrations performed by Brazilian Olympic athletes, at both the national and the international levels.

From these images, we see that women who remained in their home state during their sports career (28.4%) were mostly born in SP (37%), RJ (33%), and PR (10%). Of those who migrated within the country, the main destination states are those that have sports clubs with a larger structure such as São Paulo, Rio de Janeiro, Minas Gerais, Paraná, and Rio Grande do Sul. Finally, those who went abroad opted for European countries and the United States of America, totaling a percentage of 33% of athletes.

Our analysis based on Table 11.2 shows that, since the 1980s, when the process of professionalization of Olympic athletes began, the work opportunities abroad led the international migration to grow at a completely different pace from the previous decades.

National migrations occur more frequently among swimming, athletics, soccer, volleyball, triathlon, judo, and rhythmic gymnastic athletes, these being modalities that have benchmark training centers and sports clubs indicated to athletes by the respective federations themselves. As for international migrations, athletes from team sports such as basketball, volleyball, handball, and soccer left Brazil more often in search of better salaries and professional opportunities.

Table 11.1 Federative state that started the sport and migrations carried out

Original state that started the sport[a]	Remained in the state	National migration	International migration	National and international migration	Total
AC	0	1	0	0	1
AL	0	2	0	1	3
AM	0	1	0	0	1
ASIA	0	0	0	1	1
BA	2	8	1	3	14
CE	0	4	0	0	4
DF	1	13	0	5	19
ES	1	1	1	1	4
EUA	0	0	1	0	1
GO	0	1	0	0	1
MA	0	1	0	3	4
MG	4	15	4	10	33
M,	0	2	0	1	3
MT	3	1	0	0	4
PA	1	2	1	0	4
PB	0	5	1	0	6
PE	3	5	0	3	11
PI	1	0	0	0	1
PR	13	10	3	6	32
RJ	42	33	14	14	103
RN	1	3	0	1	5
RS	3	13	3	7	26
SC	4	5	2	2	13
SP	47	47	39	17	150
Total	126	173	70	75	444

a For names of states in full please see https://en.wikipedia.org/wiki/States_of_Brazil.

For these Olympians, Europe and the United States appear to be top choices in terms of providing the most desired conditions.

In the 1980s and 1990s the overseas migratory movement began with volleyball athletes who went to Italy, Portugal, and Spain, and also with basketball athletes who went to Europe. Starting in 2000, volleyball athletes began to return to Brazil, when lucrative sponsorships and clubs started investing in the sport, a strong national championship was set up with well-organized teams in the main states of the Federation, and payments to athletes became more compatible with what they had experienced abroad.

As for the basketball athletes, the data indicate that they sought the European continent, more specifically countries such as Spain, Italy, Portugal, and Hungary, as well as the United States, after the launch of the Women's National Basketball Association (WNBA). However, only a few of these athletes were invited to play in the WNBA, so most international athletes migrating still went to Europe. Handball players have set sail for that same continent, to countries such as Hungary, Austria, Turkey, Denmark, Poland, Russia, and Romania. It is also noteworthy that most of these athletes are no longer in Brazil, and almost all of them are competing on teams representing Hungary and Austria.

Table 11.2 Migration over the decades

Participation over the decades	Remained in their states	National migration	International migration	National and international migration	Total
Until 1959	11	8	0	1	20
1960–1979	4	6	2	3	15
1980–1989	21	19	7	11	58
1990–1999	20	30	18	14	82
Since 2000	70	110	43	46	269
Total	**126**	**173**	**70**	**75**	**444**

Table 11.3 National and international migrations by Olympic modality

Modality	Remained in their state	National migration	International migration	National and international migration	Total
Athletics	18	39	9	2	68
Basketball	2	12	16	12	42
Boxing	3	0	0	0	3
Canoeing	0	2	0	0	2
Cycling	4	2	0	0	6
Fencing	3	0	0	0	3
Soccer	7	17	10	12	46
Artistic gymnastics	4	9	1	1	15
Rhythmic gymnastics	9	8	0	1	18
Handball	10	5	9	10	34
Equestrianism	2	0	3	2	7
Judo	11	10	4	2	27
Weightlifting	2	0	0	0	2
Wrestling	1	1	0	0	2
Synchronized swimming	6	2	2	1	11
Swimming	12	18	3	4	37
Modern Pentathlon	0	1	1	0	2
Rowing	2	3	0	0	5
Diving	4	0	0	0	4
Taekwondo	0	2	1	0	3
Tennis	4	0	3	0	7
Table tennis	2	3	0	1	6
Archery	0	1	0	0	1
Shooting sports	3	1	0	0	4
Triathlon	0	3	1	0	4
Sailing	6	3	3	0	12
Beach volleyball	6	5	0	1	12
Volleyball	5	26	4	26	61
Total	**126**	**173**	**70**	**75**	**444**

Migration outcomes for Brazilian women athletes

Olympic-level athletes have a personal profile that involves a high degree of dedication to a life of workouts and competitions, often starting in late childhood. Considering the dedication required to build a career with a goal to reach the Olympic Games and years of investment, which often involves numerous life changes, the decision to travel to a club, city, state, or country can also represent the beginning of a new phase where achievements that have remained latent have space and nourishment to manifest themselves.

The professionalization process of Olympic sport occurred unevenly around the globe. Countries with a tradition in sport management quickly adapted to the Olympic rules that allowed athletes to enter into professional contracts with clubs and companies. These countries not only facilitated access to the professionalization of their athletes, but also became important labor markets for foreign athletes where this process was slow to take place or simply did not happen.

A similar process can be observed within Brazil, where regional differences have led athletes from states lacking policies for sport development to specific places for specialized sport practice in search of better training conditions, mainly in the south and south-east regions of the country. The displacement caused by the urgency for better training and financial conditions to advance the development of the athlete's career triggers a process of adaptation, socialization, and acculturation within different patterns. For athletes, it is not always easy to assimilate to a new region. The food, the climate, and the characteristic linguistic codes often lead the migrant athlete to feel like a foreigner within their own country, making adaptation difficult and sometimes compromising their overall athletic performance.

When this displacement occurs outside their home country, there is often additional, aggravating factors, such as lack of mastery of the local language and other cultural codes, which also involves experiences with discrimination and prejudice, either based on the pigmentation of their skin or the fact that they are "the other", the "outsider," the "foreigner."

Brazilian athletes who participated in the Olympic Games before 1980 hardly ever left the country, except for official competitions. Those who had the opportunity for internships and international experiences took advantage of the contacts made by relatives or friends, especially when they had foreign ancestry. The goal of amateurism was to achieve an outstanding level of athletic excellence in a country where women had little or no access to advanced training (Rubio, 2017). Discriminated against, with no opportunities to evolve in their athletic careers, and without financial support to carry them through the stages of development toward Olympic level, few athletes could live this experience because they were required to depend directly on the resources provided by their families.

As seen in Table 11.2, after the 1980s when the athletes became more professionalized, there were several migrations to Europe and the United States. The most outstanding athletes in the international competitions started to look for work opportunities in these countries with good results. These changes were necessary for Brazilian sponsors and clubs to value the Brazilian athletes, as well as to mobilize the confederations to hold international events and create wider visibility for the athletes.

After the 1980s, basketball and volleyball athletes were the first to seek out opportunities in the European job market, with their well-structured championships and an established professional system in each sport, respectively. In the 1990s this was also the case with handball athletes, a process that coincided with the first Olympic participation of the Brazilian team.

In the specific case of soccer, Brazilian women athletes have greater prestige and opportunities abroad, contrasting with the lack of opportunities and amount of disrespect the athletes experience within Brazil. Unlike Europe, the United States, and now Asia, in Brazil there is no incentive for women's soccer development. No well-organized regional or national championships exist. Even so, Brazilian athlete Marta was voted the best player in the world five times, an achievement resulting from her active participation as an athlete in Sweden.

In individual sports, few Brazilian women athletes preferred to leave the country. In swimming, for example, athletes first migrated to the United States, not for the purpose of financial gain, but for the necessity for technical improvement and education in the form of university scholarships. Very few artistic and rhythmic gymnasts, rowers, judokas, or boxers left the country. The migratory process in these sports occurred internally, part of them caused by the displacement of the training centers where these athletes worked.

Citing the last migration, that is, the one realized after the end of their career, it can be observed that the athletes who were from the interior of São Paulo, Rio de Janeiro, Paraná, Santa Catarina, Rio Grande do Sul, and Minas Gerais return to their cities of origin. Some go to work in their own schools, training centers, or on social projects that aim to serve children who need special attention. This return to their hometown comes after the completion of a college or specialization course.

Conclusion

The contemporary athlete inhabits a world dominated by communication generated by large media conglomerates and also by social networks. Their professional achievements are multiplied by generating around themselves a heroic image uncommon to most human beings (Rubio, 2001). This public portion of the athlete's life is intertwined with and diluted by the private sphere, from which emerge emotions that are rarely revealed such as fear, loneliness, and depression – feelings associated with social isolation and distance from family and from friends (Carter, 2007, 2011). The temporal dimension of athletic life contributes to this scenario, given that sport competition seasons last for a few months, depending on the state or country in question, and it does not follow the calendar of normal professions.

The migration of Brazilian women Olympic athletes occurred and still occurs within the country, moving from hometowns because of little or no sport-oriented structure to locations with benchmark training centers. These migratory processes provoke a transformation of social and cultural patterns, which in some cases leads to the need for new changes for the athlete due to the lack of adaptation to the new training site. Considering the many displacements experienced during an athlete's career, there are cases where they lose their point of origin, their "home base," which causes a difficulty in deciding where to settle down at the end of a career.

Another migratory process is the one that takes the athlete abroad, a fact that occurred mainly after the professionalization of the Olympic sport and continues to be true today. This process is often promoted with two main purposes. The first was the search for technical improvement without the purpose of a salary increase, and also the possibility of studying at a renowned university, as is the case of athletes in swimming, track and field, and tennis. The second purpose is to play professionally, targeting salaries and premiums paid above the average in Brazil. This type of migration occurs in greater numbers in team sports such as basketball, volleyball, handball, and soccer.

This study can contribute to the expansion of analyses on the psychosocial, labor, and geopolitical implications of the migratory process of athletes. It invites sport institutions and governments to reflect on the need to adopt career transition policies and programs that meet the specifications of each sporting modality, and especially the needs of women athletes.

Leader profile: Katia Rubio, Ph.D.

Figure 11.2 Katia Rubio

Katia Rubio is an outstanding researcher of the Olympic movement in Brazil. Over 20 years she has studied the memory of Brazilian sport through the biographical narratives of the Olympic athletes. She is the author of important works on the role and protagonism of women in sports, such as *As mulheres e o esporte olímpico brasileiro* (Rubio, 2011) and *Toque de gênio: a história e os exemplos de Fofão* (Rubio & Grilo, 2018).

References

Agergaard, S. & Botelho, V. (2010). Female football migration: Motivational factors for early migratory processes. In J. Maguire and M. Falcous (eds), *Sport and Migration: Borders, boundaries and crossings* (pp. 157–172). London: Routledge.

Agergaard, S. & Ryba, T. V. (2014). Migration and career Transitions in professional sports: Transnational athletic careers in a psychological and sociological perspective. *Sociology of Sport Journal*, **31**, 228–247.

Carter, T. F. (2007). Family networks, state interventions and the experience of Cuban transnational sport migration. *International Review for the Sociology of Sport*, **42**(4) 371–389.

Carter, T. F. (2011). Re-placing sport migrants: Moving beyond the institutional structures informing international sport migration. *International Review for the Sociology of Sport*, **48**(1) 66–82.

Elliott, R. (2014). Brits abroad: A case study analysis of three British footballers migrating to the Hungarian Soproni Liga. *Soccer & Society*, **15**(4), 517–534.

Engh, M. H. & Agergaard, S. (2015). Producing mobility through locality and visibility: Developing a transnational perspective on sports labour migration. *International Review for the Sociology of Sport*, **50**(8), 974–992

Ferrando, M. G . (1996). *Los deportistas olímpicos españoles: un perfil sociológico*. Madrid: Consejo Superior de Deportes.

Frick, B. (2009). Globalization and factor mobility: The impact of the "Bosman-Ruling" on player migration in professional soccer. *Journal of Sports Economics*, **10**(1), 88–106.

Giulianotti, R. & Robertson, R. (2007). Forms of glocalization: globalization and the migration strategies of Scottish football fans in North America. *Sociology*, **41**(1), 133–152.

Grix, J. (2012). The politics of sports mega-events, *Political Insight*, **3**(1), 4–7.

Kellett, P., Hede, A. M., & Chalip, L. (2008). Social policy for sport events: Leveraging (relationships with) teams from other nations for community benefit. *European Sport Management Quarterly*, **8**, 101–121. https://doi.org/10.1080/16184740802024344

Lanfranchi, P. (1994). The migration of footballers: The case of France, 1932–1982. In J. Bale and J. Maguire (eds), *The Global Sport Arena: Athletic Talent Migration in an Independent World*. (pp. 63–77). London: Frank Cass.

Magee, J. & Sugden, J. (2002). "The world at their feet": Professional football and international labor migration. *Journal of Sport & Social Issues*, **26**(4), 421–437.

Maguire, J. (2011). *Sport and Migration*. London: Blackwell Publishing Ltd.

Papanikolau, P. (2012). The spirit of the Olympics vs. commercial success: A critical examination of the strategic position of the Olympic Movement. *International Journal of Humanities and Social Science*, **2**(23), 1–5.

Oeiras, C. & Preuss, H. (2004). *Economics of Staging the Olympics: A Comparison of the Games 1972–2008*. Northampton: Edward Elgar Publishing.

Riordan, J. (2006). Amateurism, sport and the left: Amateurism for all versus amateur elitism. *Sport in History*, **26**(3), 468–483.

Rubio, K. (2001). *O atleta e o mito do herói*. São Paulo: Casa do Psicólogo.

Rubio, K. (2006). *Medalhistas olímpicos brasileiros: memórias, história e imaginário*. São Paulo: Casa do Psicólogo.

Rubio, K. (2011). *As Mulheres e o Esporte Olímpico Brasileiro*. Sao Paulo: Casa do Psicólogo.

Rubio, K. (2016). Memória, esquecimento e meta-história: entre Mnemosine e Letho. In K. Rubio (ed.), *Narrativas biográficas: da busca à construção de um método*. São Paulo: Laços.

Rubio, K. (2017). Processos migratórios e deslocamentos: caminhos que levaram atletas de modalidades coletivas aos jogos olímpicos de Barcelona em 1992. *Olimpianos – Journal of Olympic Studies*, **1**(1), 53–65.

Rubio, K. & Grilo, R. (2018). *Toque de gênio: a história e os exemplos de Fofao*. Sao Paulo: Editora Laços.

Smith, M. P. (2001). *Transnational Urbanism: Locating Globalization*. Oxford: Blackwell.

Stead, D. & Maguire, J. (2000). "Rite de passage" or passage to riches? The motivation and objectives of Nordic/Scandinavian players in English League Soccer. *Journal of Sport and Social Issues*, **24**(1), 36–60.

Tiesler, N. C. (2016). Three types of transnational players: differing women's football mobility projects in core and developing countries. *Revista Brasileira de Ciências do Esporte*, **38**(2): 201–210.

12

Management of professional women's golf in the United States

Melissa Davies and Eric Hungenberg

In 1950, 13 women wanting to play professional golf founded the Ladies Professional Golf Association (LPGA) in the state of New York. Today, the association has served as one of the longest running and most successful women's professional sport associations in the world. This chapter highlights the history of the LPGA, the elements that have supported its growth, current challenges within the LPGA, and directions for future growth. LPGA's Chief Commercial Officer, Jon Podany, also offers insight on the status of the league today (see boxed content throughout the text). Last, an industry profile on Sandi Higgs, Vice President, Creative Group and Brand Management for the LPGA is provided.

History of women's golf

Origins of women in golf

The specious phrase, "Gentleman Only, Ladies Forbidden" is often uttered to describe golf's origins. Although unfounded, the perpetuation of this fabrication can certainly be linked to a game, which at its inception was exclusionary and intended for the male gender. Despite golf's persistently male-dominated directorate, women maintained a prominent role in changing and developing the game. No better example of this was the case of Mary Queen of Scots, who reigned over Scotland from 1542 to 1567 and demonstrated a great passion for golf. In the 1550s, Mary commissioned the first golf course to be built at St. Andrews and was even credited as being the first lady to swing a golf club (Cook & MacDonald, 2016). A number of historians, in fact, attribute golf's influence across Scotland and the United Kingdom to Mary, the Queen.

However, her enthusiasm for golf would manifest itself in scandal after being condemned by her political enemies for playing golf just days after the death of her royal husband, Lord Darnley, in 1567 (Campbell & Satterley, 1999). Prosecutors of the Queen of Scotland suggested that, by playing golf, she was exhibiting disrespectful, if not suspicious, behavior following the mysterious death of Darnley. Notable Scottish historian, George Buchanan, even went so far as to write that the queen was engaged in "sports that were clearly unsuitable to women"

(Flannery & Leech, 2004, p. 261). The chauvinistic culture at the time would ultimately lead to the Queen's imprisonment, and one is left to wonder whether the same rules would have applied had Lord Darnley played a few holes following the death of the Queen.

In the centuries succeeding the Queen, women's role in golf went largely unchronicled. This was in part the result of continuous male elitist tactics, withholding the game from those not engaged in business and private club social gatherings. One particular individual who worked incredibly hard at preventing women from playing golf was Scottish judge Lord Moncrieff, who in the late nineteenth century proclaimed that women should abstain from hitting the ball any farther than 60 yards. As cited in Concannon (1996, p. 185), he believed "the posture and gestures required for a full swing are not particularly graceful when the player is clad in female dress," insinuating that women's attention should be directed to fashion, rather than sport. Thus, in keeping with this recommendation, The Royal and Ancient Golf Club of St. Andrews' (R&A) members built the wives a putting green next to the Old Course in St. Andrews called "The Himalayas." The putting green was built with the intent to provide women with a leisure activity while the men played golf. However, a venue designed specifically for women would have unintended consequences. By providing a practice area located on one of golf's most sacred grounds, St. Andrews sparked the interests of female enthusiasts and triggered a steady rise in women's golf participation, culminating in the first women's golf association in 1867, The Ladies Club. By 1898, roughly 20 golf clubs throughout Scotland and England were accommodating women (Scottish Golf History, 2017).

Rise in organized women's golf

Greater inclusivity during the late nineteenth century incited a number of key events in women's golf history. The formation of the Ladies Golf Union (LGU) in Great Britain in 1893 was a pivotal mark in the growth of women's competitive golf. The LGU became a governing body for organized tournaments, beginning with the first British Women's championship at St. Anne's Golf Club in Lancashire, the same year as its inauguration. In addition, the creation of the handicap system by Londoner Issette Miller came as a result of the creation of the Wimbledon Ladies Club in 1887. Conceived in 1893, her handicap system was one of the first ideas intended to level the playing field between competitors of different abilities, and continues to contribute to a more appealing game, whereby players of all genders and skill levels can compete.

Despite ongoing protests from the patriarch suffragists, women's golf was thriving in the United Kingdom and the ripple effect would eventually be felt in America as well. In an 1891 article, *The New York Times* reported that "an outdoor pastime which appears to be gaining favor in this country, and especially in the vicinity of New York, is the Scottish national game of golf" (Anonymous, 1891, p. 20). Similarly, the *Chicago Tribune* the following year suggested that "golf is the coming game" (Anonymous, 1892, p. 35). Yet, unlike golf's originators, many American institutions, such as Baltimore College, did not exclude female participation, but rather encouraged it, believing the game was an appropriate means of female physical activity and education. This made golf uniquely welcoming to women when other sports were not. This would have a tremendous impact on its popularity in America. In fact, in 1894 it was written in *The New York Times*: "Golf is not limited to any particular class of individuals. Ladies and children can play the game as well as men, and in nearly all the golf clubs which have been recently organized, the women show as keen an interest as the men themselves" (Anonymous, 1894, p. 16). The immediate enthusiasm felt in the United States led to the first women's amateur championship in 1895.

Formation of the Ladies Professional Golf Association

As more opportunities for competitive golf in America and abroad became realized, women began to take full advantage of the platform to showcase their talents, affirming the reports described in the quote above in *The New York Times*. Among players, arguably the most notable was Babe Didrickson-Zaharias, who had already established herself as one of the world's greatest female athletes because she won two gold medals at the 1932 Olympic Games in hurdles and long jump. However, that would only be the start of her athletic prowess because she became the first women to compete in a men's tournament, the Los Angeles Open. Although she missed the cut in her first event, she went on to make three consecutive PGA Tour cuts in 1945 (McGowan, 2014). After more women followed suit, the demand for a women's specific circuit became evident. In 1950, Babe Didrickson-Zaharias became a co-founder of the LPGA (McInerny, 2015). The official Articles of Incorporation as a nonprofit entity were reviewed at a tournament in Wichita, Kansas, and then formally signed on October 9, 1950, in New York by players Patty Berg, Helen Dettweiler, Sally Sessions, Betty Jameson, and Helen Hicks. Also credited as charter members were Alice Bauer, Marlene Bauer Hagge, Bettye Mims Danoff, Opal Hill, Marilynn Smith, Shirley Spark, and Louise Suggs.

After a long-lasting, arduous battle to garner respect and acceptance in golf, it came as no surprise that the LPGA emphasized inclusivity in its competitive membership. The organization's nondiscriminatory stance opened participation to women of all races and origins. Early members' courage, skill, and tenacity were instrumental in shaping a tour that got its start with only 13 members to a tour that is currently made up of 460 players representing 27 countries (McInerny, 2015).

League challenges and their implications on growth

How would you describe the current state of the LPGA?

LPGA: The LPGA is in a very healthy state right now, arguably the healthiest it has been in its history. There are a variety of data points that support this, including: (1) prize money is at an all-time high ($65 million); (2) the number of hours of TV (430+) and worldwide distribution (500+ million households) are at all-time highs; and (3) more young girls are being introduced to the game than ever before (junior girls are the fastest growing segment in the game).

However, securing sponsorship investment in U.S. based tournaments continues to be a challenge we at the LPGA face when growing the game. The interest and demand is stronger in other regions of the world, particularly Asia, than the U.S. but we want to maintain a balanced schedule with a strong North American base and manageable travel schedule for players.

(LPGA Chief Commercial Officer, Jon Podany)

History of growth

LPGA Tour commissioner Michael Whan has led the LPGA Tour through growth over the last eight years, with the strategic mission to see more events played, with higher prize money, in more countries, and with competitive fields of players representing nations from all over the globe. When Whan started as commissioner in 2010, he set out with the goal of reaching US$100 million in prize money. At the time, the goal was lofty, because the LPGA faced its lowest number of official events since 1972, with just 23 events and a total prize money pool of US$40.5 million. By comparison, the PGA, in 2010, produced 45 events and presented roughly US$285 million for its competitors (Ferguson, 2010). However, the LPGA experienced progress, as evidenced by strengthening their schedule to 34 tournaments in 2016 with prize money totaling US$63.1 million. In 2017, the total prize money grew to US$67 million, which provides reason for optimism despite falling short of Whan's original US$100 million goal.

Vice President for Television and Emerging Media for the LPGA, Brian Carroll, attributes the growth to organizational strategies centered on the following: (a) growing women's golf by teaching the game to youth, (b) working on fan following and engagement via TV, social, mobile, digital, and onsite (Gregg, 2014), and (c) maximizing coverage of the LPGA events, particularly on the weekends (Sirac, 2015).

> **How have these initiatives shaped the LPGA Tour's current market potential?**
>
> LPGA: The LPGA has built a global footprint, creating television distribution opportunities around the world. It has also made our players more accessible, allowing fans a chance to get to interact with our players on a more personal level. LPGA players go out of their way to provide a great experience for fans and sponsors and have become role models to many young fans as a result. Lastly, we have committed to meeting our partner needs by listening and understanding their corporate objectives. This has made us more flexible, innovative, and willing to go the extra mile to satisfy all of our key stakeholders.
>
> *(LPGA Chief Commercial Officer, Jon Podany)*

LPGA objectives have also been aided in recent years by greater collaborative efforts between the LPGA and PGA Tours through increased cross-marketing efforts (Lombardo, 2017). For instance, in March of 2016, the two leagues announced their strategic alliance, which was aimed at collaborative marketing, and included initiatives such as the possibility of hosting a joint event between the men's and women's leagues. In addition, the PGA Tour now includes LPGA updates during television coverage on CBS and the Golf Channel, while also linking LPGA news through PGA Tour. com and other digital platforms (Lombardo, 2017). This alliance also called for the PGA Tour to represent the LPGA in its television negotiations. Despite progress in partnering with the bargaining power of the PGA Tour, it is important to note that the LPGA's single largest source of revenue today is not US broadcast rights, but rather the Korean television contracts (Newport, 2008).

> **Describe the partnership that exists between the LPGA and the PGA Tour?**
>
> LPGA: The LPGA and PGA Tour formed a "strategic alliance" in 2016 which focuses on 4 key areas: (1) co-promotion and co-marketing opportunities; (2) developing a tournament that features both men and women professionals in the same tournament; (3) the PGA Tour representing the LPGA in the next round of TV rights negotiations; and (4) growth of the game initiatives such as better integration between The First Tee program and LPGA-USGA Girls Golf. Honestly, before this alliance, while there was some cooperation on industry initiatives, there really wasn't much active dialogue and activities.
>
> *(LPGA Chief Commercial Officer, Jon Podany)*

Management of US professional women's golf

LPGA viewership

LPGA fans align well with other prominent sport leagues when it comes to key demographic variables. For example, according to Nielsen Sports and US Census Data, the median household income of LPGA fans ranks third behind the English Premier League (EPL) and the National Hockey League (NHL) at US$72,500, which is just ahead of the PGA Tour, with fans earning it an average of US$71,800 (Lombardo, 2017). Similar to the PGA Tour, the median age for an LPGA fan is 63 years, though the PGA does skew slightly older at 64 years, with 43% of fans falling in the baby boomer age group from 45 years to 64 years (Fans of PGA, Anonymous, 2011; Lombardo & Broughton, 2017). This data indicates favorable market conditions for the LPGA, but, according to Statista's Nielsen Scarborough data, the number of Americans who say they are very interested in the LPGA has slowly declined from 2008 to 2017, whereas the number of people who have attended an LPGA events in the United States from 2008 to 2017 have remained relatively stable (NBCUniversal, 2017). Viewership of the LPGA on TV has also remained relatively consistent from 2011 to 2017, with 11.73 million people watching the LPGA on TV in 2016–2017 (NBCUniversal, 2017).

Although the LPGA has continued to grow internationally, this focus on foreign players and events may be contributing to the stagnant growth in domestic viewership. During the 2018 season, for example, there were 20 tournaments played in North America (one in Canada), whereas there were 14 events played overseas in Europe, Asia, the Caribbean, and Australia. Furthermore, the schedule has the final eight events leading up to the Tour Championship played across Asia, before returning for the final event of the year in Florida. When events are overseas, they present fewer primetime broadcast opportunities for fans to tune into to watch live, much less provide fans with the opportunities to attend events in person. Together, there may be less excitement developed by playing so many events abroad leading up to the culminating event of the season.

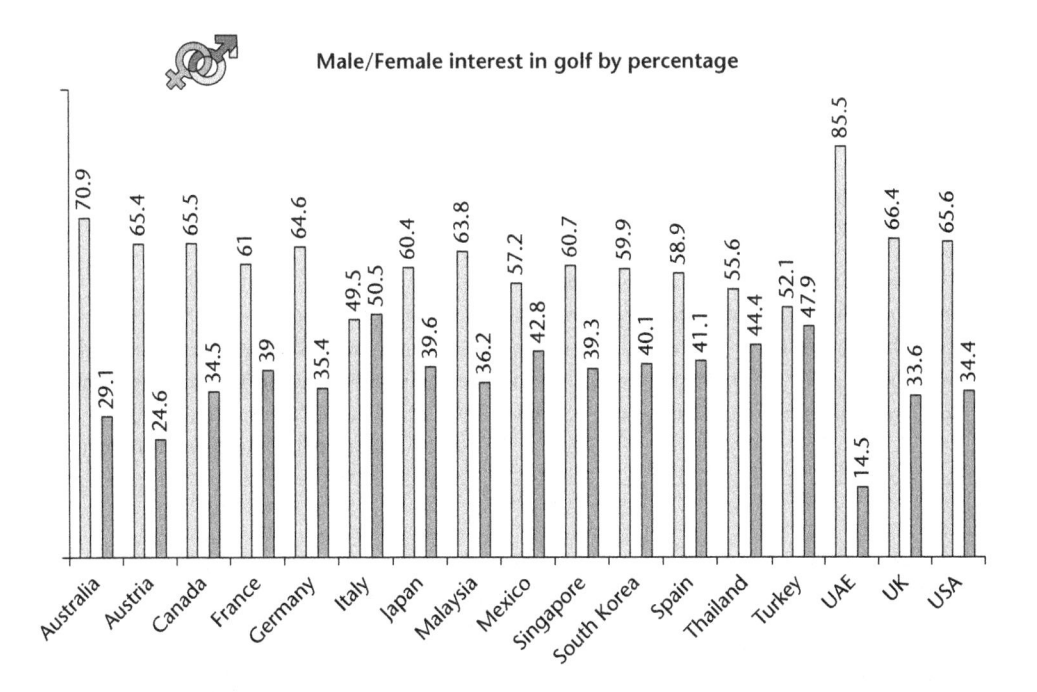

Figure 12.1 Interest in golf around the world

Another opportunity for the LPGA to drive intrigue throughout the season is through their CME Race to the Globe point system. Similar to the FedEx Cup on the PGA Tour, the LPGA has a point system called the Race to the CME Globe, in which players earn points throughout the season and a winner is crowned after the results from the final Tour Championship. Unlike the PGA Tour, which has four consecutive playoff events leading up to their Tour Championship, where each event is worth more points than the last, the LPGA's playoff system includes only season long point totals, before a modified reset at the Tour Championship. The LPGA might consider moving some of the schedule around to allow for more playoff events to occur domestically or, better yet, bridging the global and North American intrigue, by scheduling the first two playoff events in Asia, but returning to build some of the intrigue back in North America before the Tour Championship. Strengthening fan bases internationally has certainly become a fundamental strategy for sport leagues of all kinds, but, according to Richard Broughton, Director at Ampere Analysis, securing and retaining domestic audiences are the key to long-term security (Connelly, 2016). Figure 12.1 compares male and female interest in golf across a variety of countries.

Media coverage

It has been well documented that female athletes and women's sports receive diminutive media coverage in relation to male athletes and men's sports (Fink, 2015). As is the case across women's sport, the LPGA receives considerably less media attention than its PGA Tour male counterparts. Available tax records from 2013 revealed that the PGA Tour Inc. brought in US$1.075 billion in total revenue with US$364.8 million coming from TV rights and an additional US$290 million from sponsors. By comparison, in the same year the LPGA earned US$102.8 million in total revenue, with US$14.6 million coming from TV and US$5.8 million from sponsors (Saffer, 2016). Such imbalances have not gone unnoticed by those who have a stake in the LPGA's well-being. In a confidential survey disseminated to LPGA players by ESPN in 2017, the two biggest issues facing the LPGA Tour related to pay and overall media coverage disparities between the men's and women's tours (Clemmons, 2017).

Is the pay gap between LPGA and PGA Tour discussed at the LPGA level?

LPGA: With respect to the pay gap, it is certainly something we are well aware of, but all we can do is keep building the organization, growing purses, attracting investment, etc. so that we can close the gap over time. Prize money is up nearly +70% over the past 7–8 years, so we are making some progress. We are finding more and more sponsors and partners who want to positively make a difference in the women's game – companies like KPMG, CME Group, Rolex, ANA, Evian, etc.

(LPGA Chief Commercial Officer, Jon Podany)

Recent evidence of the LPGA's struggle to secure sustainable broadcasting revenue appeared in May 2017, when the Ochoa Match Play event held in Mexico became the first Tour event since 2012 to be produced without television coverage. This occurred despite a long list of prominent LPGA golfers on site. Ochoa's event started as a showcase stroke play event limited to just 36 golfers, from 2008 to 2016, before the new match play format opened the field to 64 golfers. The

Mexico City-based event saw younger stars like Michelle Wie and Brooke Henderson, alongside LPGA legends like Annika Sorenstam, Juli Inkster, and Lorena Ochoa, in an exciting match play format. LPGA tournament organizers all said that they wished the event could have been broadcast, but that the Mexican event would have cost US$1 million to produce. Meanwhile, domestic events generally only cost around US$750,000 to cover, and sponsors of the event (Citibanamex, AeroMexico, and Delta) were unable to cover the broadcast costs (Nichols, 2017).

Canadian golfer Brooke Henderson said: "the fans want to be able to watch it. On Twitter, I've received a lot of fans watching the two of us [her sister Brittany is her caddie], and it's the same with a lot of the girls, wishing it was [televised]" (Washchyshyn, 2017, para. 12). Michelle Wie expressed the lack of TV coverage being a shame, and that it was especially noticeable when compared with the last time the players played match play, which was at the Solheim Cup, where there were thousands of people watching on the grounds and "it was televised, every second of it" (Washchyshyn, 2017, para. 10). Although this event had so much potential, and was really designed to showcase golf in Mexico, the lack of coverage in 2017 resulted in the tournament being left off the LPGA schedule in 2018, and it is not clear whether it will continue.

Critics of female sport would suggest that inequitable media coverage is purely a product of what is and what is not popular. In other words, if audiences were captivated by Lexi Thompson as equally as they are by Phil Mickelson, then the media would be more inclined to allocate comparable coverage. But this thinking triggers the ancient chicken or egg paradox. For instance, Perdue professor Chery Cooky suggests that much of our perceptions of women's sport are attributable to media (Bodenner, 2015). To paraphrase the highly regarded scholar, men's sports are naturally going to be viewed as sensational when compared with women's sport because they receive greater production budgets, higher-quality coverage, more talented commentary, and significantly greater analysis before and after events. Thus, sport that contains poorer television angles, less experienced commentating, and fewer backstories are likely to be perceived as less exciting. As a consequence of this theory, one may argue that increased media attention paid to women's sport will logically ensure a more knowledgeable, engaged, and enthusiastic audience – an audience that could be leveraged into securing improved sponsorship revenue.

> **How would you describe the current coverage of LPGA events and where it may be headed**
>
> LPGA: All women's sports struggle for their share of media coverage and the LPGA is no different. Further, traditional media has cut back on their staff and travel to sporting events. Thus, the emphasis is to create our own content, and to continue to build our digital and social platforms and engagement.
>
> *(LPGA Chief Commercial Officer, Jon Podany)*

That being said, the LPGA does receive higher media attention than many other women's sport leagues. In fact, the LPGA owned 4 of the top 10 viewed women's sporting events in 2017. The 2017 Solheim Cup event received a 0.7 rating on NBC, which was the tournament's highest rating in more than a decade. The Women's British Open earned the highest ratings in 2017 on NBC with 1.1 million viewers (Paulsen, 2017a). Table 12.1 compares these ratings with other women's sport broadcast coverage in 2017.

Table 12.1 Top-rated women's sport events in 2017

Sport	Event	Viewers
WCBB	South Carolina vs. Miss. State	3,830,000
WCBB	Miss State vs. UCONN	2,760,000
W TENNIS	US Open semifinals Sloane Stephens vs. Venus Williams	2,000,000
WCWS	Oklahoma vs. Florida	1,740,000
W Golf	British Open	1,100,000
W Golf	Solheim Cup	968,000
W TENNIS	Australian Open Serena Williams vs. Venus Williams	926,000
W Golf	PGA Championship	840,000
W Golf	US Open	790,000

WCBB: Women's college basketball; WCWS: Women's College World Series.
Data retrieved from Paulsen (2017b).

Although traditional media coverage has been controlled and limited in the past, today the LPGA and its athletes can promote themselves more purposefully thanks to the popularity of new media platforms (Clavio & Kian, 2010). Social media, in particular, provides an excellent outlet for golfers to promote their brand and control their messaging, both related to performance on the course and to sustain interest off the course. According to the LPGA's director of social media marketing, Tina Barnes-Budd, "It's just about giving the fans access and a behind the scenes look at what they might not get to see otherwise" (Lenzi, 2015, para. 4). Social media also lend themselves well to the LPGA, which has such an international presence in both the events they play and the athletes who represent the Tour. Furthermore, 24 events in 2017 were won by players aged 24 years or younger, reinforcing the LPGA's belief that media platforms designed to reach a younger audience align well with its prominent stars.

In early 2018, the LPGA partnered with the athlete-marketing platform, Opendorse, to help provide Tour players with access to LPGA content to create new social revenue stream opportunities (Holmes, 2018). The LPGA's Senior Director of Social Media/Marketing said "Our athletes are some of the most social savvy and brand active on the planet, so tying them to the great work Opendorse is doing is a natural fit" (Holmes, 2018, para. 4). This approach allows the LPGA to maximize the marketability of their individual athletes by helping their players engage with fans around the world in a professional and technologically driven way.

In what ways has the LPGA altered its marketing strategies under its new leadership? New target markets? Use of technology?

LPGA: Our marketing efforts have placed a greater emphasis on creating our own content through digital and social channels. In particular, we have put a lot more emphasis on video, such as player interviews, tournament previews and recaps, "insider" stories, live "look-ins," walking the range, etc. Our followers on Facebook, Twitter, Instagram, etc. have all increased dramatically, and we harness the collective reach of not only the LPGA handles but also those of our players, tournaments and other constituents.

(LPGA Chief Commercial Officer, Jon Podany)

Arai, Ko, and Ross (2014) suggested that an athlete's brand image comprises three brand-association dimensions: athletic performance, attractive appearance, and marketable lifestyle. Natalie Gulbis, a widely known LPGA golfer, uses Instagram very much in line with Arai et al.'s (2014) brand model by posting about her athletic expertise, her community outreach, and references to travel, or in line with what could be described as a marketable lifestyle (Davies & Mudrick, 2017). For the LPGA, social media are a tool to strengthen brand messaging. In an interview with the then Vice President for Television and Emerging Media for the LPGA, Brian Carroll explained that social media have helped make players approachable and fun to interact with, which aligns with the LPGA slogan, "see why it's different out here" (Gregg, 2014). Overall, the user-generated content provided by social media sites creates a new opportunity to increase the awareness of LPGA golf and its golfers, provides value to sponsors, and sustains engagement with fans.

Diversity on tour

Women have been the fastest-growing segment of golfers in the United States, according to statistics from the National Golf Foundation (2017). According to multiple market research organizations, females make up around 20–25% of the US golfing population (National Golf Foundation, 2017; Statistic Brain Research Institute [SBRI], 2018), up from the 19% experienced from 2008 to 2012. This has come as a result of signature programs such as *Get Golf Ready*, an initiative designed to educate first comers to golf's basic elements. The program, which started in 2009, has been built around three themes: friendly, affordable, and socially engaging. The industry-wide program is available at courses throughout the country and welcomes both men and women participants. In 2015, however, over 66% of participants in the program were women (PGA, 2016). Sandy Cross, director of diversity and inclusion for the PGA Tour, noted that the program's social aspect has possibly resonated with women more than with men, and that women are staying in the game, and spending in the game, long after the program reaches its six-week conclusion (Brennan, 2013).

But both a success and a challenge that face women's professional golf is the racial diversity among the athletes on Tour. When Tiger Woods rose to dominance in the early and mid-2000s, many people thought this would open the door to other black golfers, but in many ways this wasn't the case. The LPGA, in conjunction with the USGA, has tried to increase the diversity among golfers in the United States with a nonprofit Girls Golf program. For the last 25 years, more than 300,000 girls have been able to join the program for as little as US$10 for equipment, facility access, and instruction. Despite these efforts to keep costs low and to be inclusive, only 14% of participants were Native American, 9% were African–American, and 9% were Hispanic (National Golf Foundation, 2017).

Before Se Ri Pak joined the LPGA in 1998, there were no Koreans in the LPGA and roughly 75% of players on the Tour's money list were American. This make-up has completely reversed itself today, where, in 2018, there are over 40 Korean players in the top 100 world rankings (Mell, 2017). In 2017, Koreans had won more than half of the LPGA events staged that year (Mell, 2017). Trends have similarly also reversed when looking at the LPGA money list. Before 1994, only one non-American topped the money list, but, since 1994, only one American (i.e., Stacy Lewis in 2014) has led the money list in earnings (Sirac, 2015).

Although the dominance of PGA Tour legend Tiger Woods did not have the level of influence on the number of black golfers emerging in the sport, Woods' niece, Cheyenne Woods, has now been joined by two other African–American golfers on the LPGA Tour. This is the first time in league history that three African–American golfers have participated on the Tour.

Furthermore, the 2016 Qualifying School (Q-School) was the most diverse class, yet, with 13 countries represented in the top 20 golfers competing for Tour status (Alvarez, 2017). This includes the first time an Icelandic, Ecuadorian, and Israeli competed, and only the second time an Indian golfer played on Tour.

In 2016, Whan noted that the two themes that accounted for the LPGA's continued growth were globalness and youthfulness. The growing diversity, as noted above, has covered the first theme, but the Tour has also seen a very young leaderboard in recent years, as described earlier. Ten years ago, the average age of a winner on the LPGA Tour was 28.2 years; in 2010 it was 26.1, and in 2015, it was 24.3 years (DiMeglio, 2016). In 2016, the oldest champion on the LPGA was the US Open winner, Brittany Lang, who was just 30 years old. This dominance among the younger players presents the LPGA with tremendous affirmation that the developmental strategies adopted in the last decade are coming to fruition.

With regard to sexual orientation, the largely conservative golf world has not fully embraced the LGTBQ community. Although the LPGA has not yet formally promoted their inclusive stance on LGTBQ players and fans, there have been several athletes on Tour who have come out and been included in the World Golf Hall of Fame or received other prominent honors, e.g., Karrie Webb (Australia).

What role does the LPGA believe it has in contributing to the growth of women's golf?

LPGA: Actually, women/girls have been one of the bright spots of golf participation over the past few years. Girls are the fastest growing segment in golf right now. In 1995, only 17% of junior golfers were girls, now 34% of junior golfers are girls. The LPGA-USGA Girls Golf program was only reaching 5,000 girls per year in 2010. It now is reaching more than 70,000 girls per year. The golf industry has collectively come to realize the importance of women to the overall health of the game. Further, the LPGA Teaching and Club Professional division has grown from 1,200 teachers to nearly 1,700 teachers so they are increasing their reach and influence on the game.

(LPGA Chief Commercial Officer, Jon Podany)

LPGA leadership

Today, the LPGA is led by its eighth commissioner, Michael Whan, who has been in the role since 2010. Whan, with a strong marketing background, was hired to "enhance business relationships, increasing exposure for the players, and maximize the LPGA experience for fans" (LPGA.com, 2018, para. 1). As noted above, Whan has overseen growth to both the number of LPGA events, including growth in international events, and the prize money allocated to LPGA events.

Before Whan, the LPGA saw some interesting operational and marketing strategies, which many suggest played a role in the LPGA's decline. Ty Votaw was the man behind one of the more interesting marketing approaches for the league while he served as commissioner of the LPGA from 1995 to 2005. In 2002, Votaw introduced a marketing plan called the Five Points of Celebrity, which was designed to align with the sport as an entertainment marketplace. Essentially, Votaw tried to develop a plan that elevated the LPGA players into celebrities using the five points in the plan: performance, approachability, passion and joy, appearance, and relevance. The implementation of the plan relied on a player to assess how their individual strengths embodied particular points, and then the LPGA would promote them to fulfill specific market segment interests. However, some accused Votaw of focusing too heavily on appearance, and marketing only sex appeal, which many felt compromised the athletes' status as professional athletes and women just to promote the organization (Wolter, 2010). Votaw insisted that this was not the case; he emphasized that the Five Points of Celebrity was an overall package intended to bring more fans (i.e., heterosexual male fans) to LPGA events (Sherman, 2002).

Votaw served as commissioner for six years, until passing the baton to the LPGA's first female commissioner, Carolyn Bivens. Bivens served from 2005 to 2009 with strong intentions to grow the LPGA's prominence, in line with the PGA Tour. Through what was called "Vision 2010," Bivens pushed for higher purses, better healthcare, and pension packages for the athletes. Bivens also helped to acquire the Futures Tour (now the Symetra Tour) and made strong broadcast deals with Golf Channel and J Golf (Wei, 2009). Despite these successes, however, Bivens rubbed golfers and sponsors up the wrong way, in large part due to her notorious attempt to implement an "English Rule," where golfers on Tour were required to speak basic English or risk suspension from the Tour.

> **How has Michael Whan's leadership strengthened the PGA Tour?**
>
> LPGA: Mike Whan is a tremendous leader. He has built a strong culture, centered around putting the customer first, trust, transparency and "can do" attitude. One of our key values is to "Act Like a Founder" which means we should embody the values of our original 13 founders who did whatever it took to make the organization successful and to leave the organization better than we found it.
>
> *(LPGA Chief Commercial Officer, Jon Podany)*

Language controversy

In 2008, the LPGA faced harsh criticism when it tried to propose a harsh penalty for members who couldn't demonstrate a basic level of communication in English. The proposal was to have golfers who had been members on Tour for more than two years suspended from playing privileges until their English improved. New Tour members were allowed a two-year grace period to adjust to this new rule. The idea to have LPGA members work toward communicating better in English was not widely contested, but rather it was the harsh penalty of suspension associated with failure to communicate that caused a stir. This controversy came at a time when there was a growing field of South Koreans coming to play in American events. In 2017, South Koreans held six of the top 10 spots on the LPGA Top 100 money list (PGA, 2017). In 2008, when this controversial policy was enacted, there were just four American golfers in the top 20 on the official money list (LPGA.com)

The LPGA Commissioner at the time, Carolyn Bivens, defended this policy by highlighting differences faced by the LPGA compared with athletes in other sports. Bivens noted, for example, that, to earn money for tournament purses, LPGA players must engage with sponsors and fans on a weekly basis. In addition to media interviews and acceptance speeches, the direct language interaction comes when LPGA players are paired with amateur golfers (e.g., sponsors, fans) in the pro-am events that precede every tournament. In these events, on average, non-LPGA participants pay between US$15,000 and US$25,000 per foursome to get the chance to play with an LPGA professional. Bivens contended that, to earn these funds, LPGA players should be expected to be able to converse and entertain their playing partners.

Maximizing sponsorships, which account for nearly 100% of the Tour's funding, have also been touted as a reason for encouraging golfers who play in American events to speak English. Golf has been proven to offer diverse ranges of sponsorship options and properties ranging from individual events, to tours, to the athletes showcasing their skills. With respect to the last, athletes have high expertise in athletics, and this credibility transcends sport brands, wielding increased trust, perceptions of quality, and status from various consumer demographics (Koernig & Boyd, 2009). Furthermore, athletes present a special marketing platform as consumers' attitudes toward the sponsor are often aligned with fans' positive or negative perceptions of the athlete on and off the playing field. However, consumers want to know that sponsorship decisions are authentic, and athletes who were incapable of speaking to their target audiences and failed to embody US cultural norms were believed to be a concern among prospective sponsors. This reservation likely emanated from a growing appreciation of the sponsorship deals to become integrated in the consumer's life and go beyond brand association to a more in-depth brand fit (Belzer, 2013).

In addition to the controversy surrounding Bivens' language policy, the LPGA was losing its most prominent stars to early retirement, which didn't help the LPGA's ability to attract US-based sponsors. Both Annika Sorenstam and Lorena Ochoa, well known LPGA stars, chose early retirement during the mid-2000s, leaving many to wonder who would replace two of the Tour's greatest figureheads and revenue-generating athletes. Fortunately for the LPGA, the void was quickly filled by a growing number of Asian players, which forced the Tour to bend and stretch its global direction (O'Neill, 2011). By embracing new markets and accepting a more diversified look, the LPGA created new, lucrative sponsorship agreements from Asian-based companies, making it less necessary to conform to American-based sponsor needs. This may reflect a clash between the American business model and accommodating growth that comes with an international tour. However, the LPGA does not have the financial ability to hold out for the most lucrative sponsor. The league does not have the PGA's luxury of being pursued by multiple television networks; on many occasions, in fact, they are often forced to purchase access if they want their brand showcased on television. That being said, the LPGA does offer language training centers onsite at each event for athletes who do want to work on developing their English (Gregg, 2014).

Language controversy (started in 2008 with the language competency rule). Where is this today?

LPGA: This really is no longer an issue in the LPGA. Virtually all of our players speak at least some English. There are only a few players per year who come to the LPGA who don't speak English, but players are taking it upon themselves to learn English as they recognize the value to themselves and the organization for them to be able to communicate.

(LPGA Chief Commercial Officer, Jon Podany)

Conclusion

At its inception in 1950, the LPGA's 13 founders embarked on a business venture that was riddled with challenges. In its early years, LPGA tournaments lacked professional organization and were often described as amateurish affairs. This was likely due to (1) events being deficient in marshals and volunteers, (2) tournament fields commonly rounded out with undeserving amateur players, and (3) tournament prize money that rarely exceeded player costs for participating (Kirsch, 2009). Further host golf courses were presented to players in rough condition, and often required the players to set their own hole and tee placements. Despite these hardships, however, the entrepreneurs who trail blazed a future for existing stars would exhibit unyielding courage, resolution, and resourcefulness. The product of this ingenuity and perseverance is a tour that is 67 years young, and arguably coming off its best years in history (Pepper, 2016).

Although the LPGA Tour's progressive mentality has positioned the property favorably, it still faces challenges inherent to most women's sport organizations. Certainly, they are no longer forced to recruit participants to their events or require their athletes to establish their own rules. There are numerous challenges, however, that the Tour continues to tackle, including pay inequalities, media coverage, sponsorship acquisition, and the handling of a global tour. To transform these obstacles into opportunities, the executive leadership team within the LPGA remains committed to key stakeholders, ensuring its sponsors, players, and digital partners who distribute its content all have their needs met. These stakeholders are the key cogs in the LPGA's engine that make it successful and lead to its future stability.

As illustrated in this chapter, thanks to improved marketing strategy, leadership, and consumer trends, the LPGA is primed for future success. For instance, its social marketing campaigns intended to grow participation and interest in young female golfers are paying dividends, evidenced by expansion in girl's golf programs and instruction. Recent partnerships with organizations capable of lifting the LGPA's profile, such as the strategic alliance with the PGA Tour, collaborations with the PGA of America to elevate the KPMG Women's PGA Championship, and improved relations with the United State Golf Association (USGA) have all contributed to the reshaping and expansion of women's golf. Its diverse field of players has opened new markets, as well as existing and prospective corporate partners. This international flare has enabled the LPGA to introduce new domestic events, as well as international events, such as the Ladies Scottish Open, added as a co-sanctioned event with the Ladies European Tour, and the New Zealand Open in 2017. The trends, in addition to improved technological features aimed at augmenting the viewer's experience, make the future of women's professional golf a bright one.

Describe the LPGA Tour 10 years from now. How do you envision the business model evolving?

LPGA: I think the LPGA will be even more global, have even more strategic partnerships, and have new lines of business that drive revenue and growth. On the global front, this could include ownership or alliances with other tours around the world and increased office/staff presence around the world. Partnerships could expand to other sporting entities and entertainment organizations. New lines of business could include LPGA stores/retail, which has been launched in Korea, and LPGA golf courses around the world.

(LPGA Chief Commercial Officer, Jon Podany)

Leader profile: Sandi Higgs, LPGA Vice President – Creative Group and Brand Management

Figure 12.2 Sandi Higgs

Sandi Higgs has played an integral role in the LPGA tour's digital growth from the time she joined the organization in 1986. As one of just two media coordinators in the late 1980s and into the early 1990s, Higgs recognized the need to expand the tour's marketing reach if they were to keep pace with the progressing interest in the Tour. When Higgs started, much of the TV footage was being filmed and set away on a shelf. Higgs pushed to purchase the software necessary to start the LPGA's own archive and to ultimately license Tour footage. Higgs was also forward thinking in 1995 when she convinced her superiors to invest in creating a website, which led to the purchase of the www.lpga.com domain name. Higgs would spend the next 20 years overseeing the growth of the LPGA.com site, as well as managing the video archive and footage licensing sales.

Higgs was originally interested in playing golf professionally. She played in both high school and college, for the University of Florida, before pursuing the LPGA Tour Qualifying School and playing on mini-tours. When Higgs failed to earn a spot on Tour in her first couple of attempts, she decided to return to the University of Florida to work in their Sports Information Department. It was from here that she applied for and secured her position with the LPGA, nearly 32 years ago.

Sandi Higgs currently serves as the Vice President for the LPGA Creative Group. When asked about the role that the LPGA plays in advancing women's sport, Higgs noted that one of the main tenets of the LPGA is empowering young girls and women. The Girls Golf program has introduced thousands of girls to the game since it started in 1989. Meanwhile, the Tour also sponsors leadership academies for teenage girls that help develop leadership skills. Higgs shared that many of the LPGA tournaments now host Women in Business Summits and that the LPGA Women's Network was recently launched to help women in golf learn, connect, and grow.

Higgs offers advice to aspiring sport business professionals by saying that working in sports requires passion. "It's long hours – it's weekends and nights. There's a lot of unsexy, behind-the-scenes work in sports, but if you love it, it won't matter." For Higgs, she particularly finds fulfillment by working in women's sport because she feels an added sense of appreciation for the work she's doing from the women on Tour, which helps make her efforts worthwhile.

References

Alvarez, A. (2017). The new face of golf: The LPGA is more diverse than ever, but is that enough to grow the game? *Excellesports.com*, Jan 20. Retrieved from www.excellesports.com/news/lpga-tour-diversity-growth.

Anonymous (1891). Golf is growing in New York. *The New York Times*, October 4, p. 15.

Anonymous (1892). Golf is the coming game. *Chicago Tribune*, August 7, p. 35.

Anonymous (1894). Society's latest pastime. *The New York Times*, June 10, p. 16.

Anonymous (2011). Fans of PGA, LPGA Tours continue to skew older, have higher incomes. *Street & Smith's SportsBusiness Journal*, July 28. Retrieved from www.sportsbusinessdaily.com/Daily/Issues/2011/07/28/Research-and-Ratings/Golf-demos.aspx.

Arai, A., Ko, Y. J., & Ross, S. (2014). Branding athletes: Exploration and conceptualization of athlete brand image. *Sport Management Review*, **17**(2), 97–106.

Belzer, J. (2013). The (r)evolution of sports sponsorships, April 22. Retrieved from www.forbes.com/sites/jasonbelzer/2013/04/22/the-revolution-of-sport-sponsorship.

Bodenner, C. (2015). Why aren't women's sports as big as men's? Your thoughts. *The Atlantic*, June 9. Retrieved from https://www.theatlantic.com/entertainment/archive/2015/06/women-and-sports-world-cup-soccer/395231.

Brennan, B. (2013). PGA looks to women to grow golf. *Forbes*, February 7. Retrieved from https://www.forbes.com/sites/bridgetbrennan/2013/02/07/pga-looks-to-women-to-grow-golf/#26996cad52bb.

Campbell, M. & Satterley, G. (1999). *The Scottish Golf Book*. Champaign, IL: Sports Publishing.

Clavio, G. & Kian, T. M. (2010). Uses and gratifications of a retired female athlete's Twitter followers. *International Journal of Sport Communication*, **3**(4), 485–500.

Clemmons, A. K. (2017). LPGA confidential survey: Players speak up about inequality. *ESPN*, July 10. Retrieved from http://abcnews.go.com/Sports/lpga-confidential-survey-players-speak-inequality/story?id=48558528.

Concannon, D. (1996). *From Tee to Green: An illustrated anthology of classic golf writing*. London: Headline.

Connelly, T. (2016). The problem for sports broadcasters' declining viewing figures goes beyond just live streaming. *The Drum*, November 10. Retrieved from www.thedrum.com/news/2016/11/10/the-problem-sports-broadcasters-declining-viewing-figures-goes-beyond-just-live.

Cook, S. & MacDonald, R. (2016). *How to Speak Golf*. New York: Flatiron Books.

Davies, M. & Mudrick, M. (2017). Brand management in a niche sport: An LPGA golfer's use of Instagram. *Global Sport Business Journal*, **5**(1), 1–22.

DiMeglio, S. (2016). Youth movement in full swing on LPGA Tour. *USA Today*, June 9. Retrieved from https://www.usatoday.com/story/sports/golf/lpga/2016/06/08/lydia-ko-ariya-jutanugarn-lpga-tour/85620040.

Fink, J. (2015). Female athletes, women's sport, and the sport media commercial complex: Have we really "come a long way, baby"? *Sport Management Review*, **18**(3), 331–342.

Ferguson, D. (2010). PGA Tour unveils 2011 schedule with 45 events, few changes from 2010. *Professional Golf Association*, December 2. Retrieved from www.pga.com/pga-tour-unveils-2011-schedule-45-events-few-changes-2010.

Flannery, M. & Leech, R. (2004). *Golf Through the Ages, Six Hundred Years of Golfing Art*, Limited Edition. Fairfield, IA: Golf Links Press

Gregg, E. (2014). Interview with Brian Carroll, Vice President for Television and Emerging Media, LPGA. *International Journal of Sport Communication*, **7**, 52–55.

Holmes, E. (2018). Opendorse partners with LPGA to grow players' social media presence. SportsPro, February 14. Retrieved from www.sportspromedia.com/news/opendorse-lpga-grow-players-social-media-presence.

Kirsch, G. B. (2009). *Golf in America*. Champaign, IL: University of Illinois Press,

Koernig, S. K. & Boyd, T. C. (2009). To catch a tiger or let him go: The match-up effect and athlete endorsers for sport and non-sport brands. *Sport Marketing Quarterly*, **18**(1), 15–37.

Ladies Professional Golf Association (LPGA) (2017). Official money. Retrieved from www.lpga.com/statistics/money/official-money.

Lenzi, R. (2015). LPGA embraces social media. *Professional Golf Association*, July 13. Retrieved from www.pga.com/news/lpga-tour/lpga-embraces-social-media.

Lombardo, J. (2017). Joint PGA Tour, LPGA tourney still in the works. *Street & Smith's SportsBusiness Journal*, April 3, p. 19.

Lombardo, J. & Broughton, D. (2017). Going gray: Sports TV viewers skew older. *Street & Smith's SportsBusiness Journal*, June 5, p. 1.

McGowan, T. (2014). From Mary Queen of Scots to Rio 2016: The history of women's golf. *CNN*, September 15. Retrieved from http://edition.cnn.com/2014/09/15/sport/golf/history-of-womens-golf/index.html.

McInerny, P. M. (2015). Ladies Professional Golf Association. In M. Dodds, J. T. Reese, & S. Barbara (eds), *Sports Leadership: A reference guide* (pp. 97–98). Santa Barbara, CA: Mission Bell Media.

Mell, R. (2017). Koreans dominating LPGA like never before. *The Golf Channel*, October 25. Retrieved from https://www.golfchannel.com/article/golf-central-blog/south-koreans-dominating-lpga-never.

National Golf Foundation (2017). *Golf Industry Overview: 2017 Edition*. Retrieved from www.ngf.org.

NBCUniversal (2017). Number of TV viewers of the LPGA Tour (women's golf) within the last 12 months in the United States from autumn 2011 to spring 2017 (in million). *Statista*. Retrieved from https://www.statista.com/statistics/480139/cable-or-broadcast-tv-networks-lpga-tour-women-s-golf-watched-within-the-last-12-months-usa.

Newport, J. (2008). How the LPGA bungled on English. *Wall Street Journal*, September 13. Retrieved from https://www.wsj.com/articles/SB122125269803829639.

Nichols, B. A. (2017). LPGA misses big opportunity with Lorena Ochoa Match Play not on TV. *GolfWeek*, May 5. Retrieved from http://golfweek.com/2017/05/05/lpga-misses-big-opportunity-with-lorena-ochoa-match-play-not-on-tv.

O'Neill, D. (2011). Future is murky for the LPGA event. *St. Louis Post Dispatch*, June 8. Retrieved from www.stltoday.com/sports/golf/future-is-murky-for-lpga-event/article_0ab6acf0-e29a-5f87-9fb4-169ad21a86b0.html.

Paulsen (2017a). Solheim Cup viewership best in years in NBC return. *Sports Media Watch*, August 22. Retrieved from www.sportsmediawatch.com/2017/08/solheim-cup-ratings-nbc-most-watched-years/#prettyPhoto.

Paulsen (2017b). Halftime most watched sporting events in 2017. *Sports Media Watch*. Retrieved from www.sportsmediawatch.com/2017/07/halftime-most-watched-sporting-events-nfl-nba-cfb-playoff-ncaa-tournament.

Pepper, D. (2016). The good, the bad, and the ugly of the LPGA Tour's 2016 season. *ESPN*, November 21. Retrieved from www.espn.com/golf/story/_/id/18098616/the-good-bad-ugly-lpga-tour-2016-season.

PGA (2016). Get Golf Ready thrives as affordable, fun introduction to golf. PGA of America, April 14. Retrieved from https://www.pga.com/play-golf-america/get-golf-ready/get-golf-ready-thrives-affordable-fun-introduction-golf.

Saffer, M. (2016). Dollars but no sense: Golf's long history of shortchanging women. *ESPN*, April 8. Retrieved from www.espn.com/espnw/sports/article/15160220/big-gap-earnings-men-women-professional-golfers.

Scottish Golf History (2017). Retrieved from www.scottishgolfhistory.org/early-womens-golf/ii-early-womens-golf-clubs.

Sherman, E. (2002). Commissioner Ty Votaw says tour isn't trying to sell sex appeal, but appearance is important. *Chicago Tribune*, May 30. Retrieved from http://articles.chicagotribune.com/2002-05-30/

sports/0205300216_1_increase-television-viewership-lpga-commissioner-ty-votaw-ladies-profes sional-golf-association.

Sirac, R. (2015). LPGA continues its growth, announces 34 tournaments, $63.1 million in purses for 2016. *Golf Digest.*, November 20 Retrieved from https://www.golfdigest.com/story/lpga-continues-its-growth-announces-34-tournaments-dollar631-million-in-purses-for-2016.

Statistic Brain Research Institute (SBRI) (2018). Golf player demographic statistics. Retrieved from https://www.statisticbrain.com/golf-player-demographic-statistics/.

Wei, S. (2009). The undoing of LPGA commissioner Carolyn Bivens. *The Huffington Post*, August 13. Retrieved from https://www.huffingtonpost.com/stephanie-wei/the-undoing-of-lpga-commi_b_230837.html.

Wolter, S. (2010). The Ladies Professional Golf Association's five points of celebrity: "Driving" the organization "fore-ward" or a snap-hook into the next fairway? *International Journal of Sport Communication*, **3**, 31–48.

Washchyshyn, M. (2017). New LPGA Match Play is a smash hit. The only thing missing is the audience. Golf.com, May 5. Retrieved from www.golf.com/tour-news/2017/05/05/new-lpga-match-play-smash-hit-only-thing-missing-tv-audience.

13
Socio-historical development of Korean women's golf

Hyun-Duck Kim, Hongyoung Kim, and Colleen McGlone

Korean professional golf, especially women's golf, has shown notable development and success over the last four decades. In fact, over these 40 year, Korean women's golf has nurtured numerous golf professionals such as Se Ri Pak, Grace Park, Mi-Hyun Kim, Jiyai Shin, Inbee Park, and So Yeon Ryu. Global success of Korean women's golf has made an impact on the Korean society and its success has aroused curiosity regarding the basis and reason of this success. In this chapter, the authors bring women's golf in South Korea to light identifying the socio-historical development of Korean women's golf. In order to identify the elements contributing to this development the authors describe the organizational movement from its initial establishment to the current status and compare women's professional golf and men's professional golf. Furthermore, the authors also describe the educational development of golf among the populace in South Korea for a better understanding of the positioning of women's golf and its development.

At the 2016 Rio Olympic Games in Brazil, Inbee Park made history by winning an Olympic gold medal. She was the first woman to do so since golf had been removed from the Olympic Games after the 1904 Olympics, 106 years earlier. This noteworthy achievement is just one of the many that Park has amassed over her career, including other monumental moments in golf history such as achieving a Grand Slam and becoming the youngest player to become eligible for the Ladies Professional Golf Association (LPGA) Hall of Fame. Park has been at the center of the most memorable moments in the 650 years of recorded golf history in the minds of most Koreans with her miraculous wins at the KPMG Women's Professional Golf Association (PGA) Championship (2015), her wins at the United States Women's Open (2008, 2013), British Open (2015), and completing the proverbial "Grand Slam" of golf by 2016. Completing a career "Grand Slam" includes winning all the "major" golf tournaments during a career. In the history of women's golf, only seven women have completed a career "Grand Slam". The Women's "Grand Slam" is defined by time periods also known as eras, including the Western Open Era, which included the Women's Western Open, LPGA Championship, US Women's Open, and the Titleholders Championship. Two women accomplished the feat of winning all four of these tournaments during their careers. Mickey Wright and Louise Suggs completed career "Grand Slams" during this era. The Du Maurier Classic era was the next era. This era included four majors: Kraft Nabisco Championship, LPGA Championship, US Women's Open, and Du Maurier Classic. Again, two women were able to complete career "Grand Slams" during this era: Juli Inkster and Pat Bradley. Most of the eras included four major tournaments. The next era that defined the "Grand Slam" history was the Women's British Open era. This era included the Kraft Nabisco Championship, LPGA Championship, US Women's Open, and the Women's British Open. Only one woman completed the career "Grand Slam" during this period and that was Annika Sorenstam. The current era is called "The Evian Championship Era." The tournaments included in this era include: the ANA Inspiration, LPGA Championship, US Women's Open, and the Women's British Open. South Korean golfer Inbee Park is the only woman who has accomplished a career "Grand Slam" during this era.

Although Inbee Park is one of the most visible representatives of Korean women's golf, there are many great Korean golfers on the world stage, both male and female. For example, both Kyoungju (K. J.) Choi and Yang Young-eun are recognized globally. K. J. Choi accumulated 20 wins as a professional golfer, which made him one of Asia's best golfers. Yang Young-Eun, nicknamed "Tank," dramatically defeated Tiger Woods in the 2009 PGA Championship. These accomplishments were significant achievements because many of them came during or after the Asian financial crisis. The financial crisis, which occurred in 1997, made a considerable impact on Korean society and significantly depressed the national economy. During this period, Ms. Se Ri Pak's success on the LPGA Tour stimulated increased interest in golf for Koreans. Since then, the leaderboard of the LPGA has been filled with Korean women. Korea is also well known as the country that sponsors most of the LPGA tour events. These events bring in participants and viewers from around the world, including members of several professional alliance organizations, many of which are from the United States.

The game of golf in Korea carries a somewhat distinguished social status. This status has helped many Korean women in the effort to achieve both equality and equity for women in society because these concepts relate to women's sport participation and education. For example, the social role and status of women have significantly changed due to the Korean modern sports era. As part of South Koreas tradition and history, Confucianism and patriarchal social culture dominated general societal norms of Korea, which meant that social roles between men and women were divided. In this regard, women were exposed to comparatively limited social activities, often omitting sports and other leisure activities because they required physical strength. These activities were widely available and enjoyed by men during the era. As women had limitations in social participation and activities, women's participation in sports, such as golf, was even more passive (Lee & Lim, 1998). As such, the purpose of this chapter is to discuss the socio-historical development of women's golf including the evolution of associated women's sport organizations. Moreover, emerging issues of commercialization and education relating to women's golf in Korea are also presented.

The beginning era of golf in Korea

The very first golf course on the Korean peninsula was founded in 1900 by the British. This first course was the Wonsan Golf Course, which is located in the north-eastern part of North Korea. It is of interest that Wonsan Golf Course was used only by the British, excluding Korean or any other non-British golfers. In 1921, the Hyo Chang Won Golf Course, designed by H. E. Daunt, was the first course built for public access (Korea Golf Association, 2001). In the early 1900s, due to Japanese colonization from 1910 to 1945, most of the golfers in Korea consisted of foreigners including Japanese. Not many Koreans had the opportunity to experience the game of golf during their visits overseas. As a result most Koreans had a less than favorable opinion of golf based on the lack of opportunity to play, combined with the fact that this new public access course was being built on sacred ground where the royal tombs of the Chosun dynasty were located (Cho, 2017a).

After additional golf courses had been built, more golf tournaments and rounds of golf began to be played in Korea. The increased number of golf courses exposed the need for higher levels of organization and management in the emerging golf industry. Ultimately, this led to the establishment of the Korea Golf Association in 1966. After the establishment of the national golf association, the Korea Professional Golfers' Association was created in 1968, and was the first professional sport organization founded in Korea. In 1978, the Korea Professional Golfers' Association established a department for ladies and the Korea Ladies Professional Golf Association was officially founded in December 1991 (Korea Golf Association, 2001).

Korea Golf Association

The golf courses that were built before 1953 were almost entirely destroyed during, and as a result of, both World War II and the Korean War. After the truce agreement with North Korea in July 1953, the Korean War came to a temporary halt. Although the war was not active, the United States' armed forces remained stationed in the southern part of the Korean peninsula. The end of the war created an opportunity for American soldiers and civilians working for the US government to fly to Japan for golf trips, which occurred mostly on the weekends and during holidays. At this time, it became evident that there was an increased need for more golf courses to be developed in South Korea. From this time, golf became a means for not only expanding pastime and leisure activities for residents but also for increasing tourism for foreigners (Min, 2009).

The first golf course built after the Korean War was named "Seoul Country Club." However, the name was changed in 2009 to Seoul Children's Grand Park under the Seoul Metropolitan Facilities Management (2015). Before the foundation of the Korea Golf Association, Seoul Country Club took on the role as the national golf organization. This responsibility was due to the absence of such an organization in Korea at the time. This meant that all international inquiries about the business and management of golf in the region, which were sent to Korea's national golf organization, had to be directed to the Seoul Country Club. This new role required Seoul Country Club to send two Korean golf professionals, at its own expense, to the 1956 Canada Cup, which is also known as the fourth World Cup of Golf. This new role meant that the Seoul Country Club had to take an interim role from 1945 until the advent of the Korea Golf Association in 1965. As the game continued to expand, Korea was invited to join the Asia Pacific Golf Federation as a member in 1965. As a result of the expansion, Seoul Country Club realized the imminent need for the formation of a national golf organization, and, in 1965, the board president arranged a preparation committee to establish a national golf organization in Korea. The next year (1966), the Korea Golf Association was founded to develop and promote the game of golf in Korea, which included working toward goals such as vitalizing golf tournaments, developing a pool of talented young golfers, and developing international competitiveness. After its foundation, the first Golf Championship held by the president of the Korean Golf Association was presented in 1968. As one might expect, other domestic golf tournaments made up of professional and amateur level games soon followed. As the game and the industry expanded and evolved, the Korea Golf Association soon sent golf professionals and amateurs to international events and invited world famous golf professionals from different countries to participate. Despite the Korea Golf Association's devotion and commitment to promoting golf in Korea, the general public perceived golf as a sport for politicians and the upper class. Women's golf was relatively non-existent due to cultural limitations up until 1997, when 26 girls were given the opportunity to participate in a Korean youth golf program sponsored by the Korean Golf Association (Achenbach, 2004).

In November 1979, the Korea Golf Association planned to recruit a national golf team with skilled amateur golfers. Golf had been selected as one of the sports played in the 1982 Asian Games held in New Delhi, India. The first Korea national golf team was recruited with the cooperation and support of Kyunghee University's physical education college. The team consisted of three male golfers and one female golfer, all of whom were student athletes. This first national team trained for six months, using three different levels of strength and conditioning techniques and skill proficiency drills. Professor Seungil Kim, the founding member and fifth president of the Korean Collegiate Golf Federation, mentioned:

> In order to participate in the first Asian Games golf event in 1982, we voluntarily selected students who could play golf among the students of the college of physical education rather than those who had been systematically trained. Nowadays more than 20 universities have golf related departments and programs, but in the late 1960s, only one university (Kyunghee University) had a small golf driving range at that time.
>
> *(Olympic Council of Asia, 2006)*

After its first year, the Korea Golf Association launched the national team program with five qualifying evaluation tryouts and winter training. In 1983, the Korea Golf Association started developing juniors from K-12 through college. With the passionate work of the Korea Golf Association, the Korea national golf team won the silver medal in men's golf during the 1982 Asian Games, and their first gold medal in the 1986 Asian Games in the men's golf team competition and the silver medal in the men's golf individual competition. Girls' and women's participation was increasing during this time as result of the advent of the junior golf program. However, this growth was limited for cultural and economic reasons.

Junior and college golf organization

As participation rates increased and economic conditions improved it became an important step to structure golf participation in Korea. The Korean Golf Association has three affiliated federations: (1) the Korean Collegiate Golf Federation, (2) the Korea Junior Golf Association, and (3) the Korea Elementary School Golf Association.

Korean College Golf Federation

As the interest in golf increased over time, many college students began to participate, and the Korean College Golf Federation was founded in 1984 to establish golf as a collegiate sport, and to support the development of Korea's golf industries further. The Korean College Golf Federation held it inaugural amateur tournament that same year. Currently, the Korean College Golf Federation hosts 19 tournaments each year and has 32 participating universities. Before the Korean College Golf Federation was founded, a few college golf enthusiasts formed student organizations at universities including Kyunghee University, Yonsei University, Korea University, and Dongkuk University. These organizations agreed to gather for golf outings twice a year (Korea Golf Association, 2001). During this period, colleges in Seoul and other regional universities such as Kyunghee University, Yonsei University, and Korea University offered golf practice facilities, and added golf classes as a regular course offered to college students. The collegiate programs had limited participation opportunities for women during the 1980s; however, these opportunities have expanded because women's golf has seen much success in Korea as well as with changing sociocultural factors.

Korea Junior Golf Association

In January of 1985, golf was selected as a category within the student-athlete sport category (Kyunghyang Shinmun, 1985) and, with the effort of Korea's golf-related organizations which assisted in developing junior golf classes, interest in junior golf increased. With increased interest and the growing needs of junior golf organizations, teachers in middle school and high school gathered and established the Korean Junior Golf Association in 1989. Not many students registered in the early years. However, in the late 1990s the Korean Junior Golf Association's member institutions increased significantly and, in 2018, there were 1,334 members registered. In 2000, the Korean Junior Golf Association began to hold 12 golf tournaments annually (Korean Junior Golf Association, 2017). The Korean Junior Golf Association not only executes golf tournaments but also implements golf rule classes for its members. Girls' participation in golf has experienced growth since the first youth program was created in 1979. This growth rapidly expanded after Se Ri Pak's success during the late 1990s. Opportunities for participation in youth programs expanded to include elementary aged girls. These organized youth programs that have emerged in Korea may account for the high number of female Korean golfers who are experiencing success today.

Korea Elementary School Golf Association

Before the foundation of the Korean Elementary School Golf Association, elementary student golfers, from first through sixth grades, had to play in the Korean Junior Golf Association tournament at a bonus or exhibition level of competition. However, as interest in the game at the elementary level increased following Se Ri Pak's US Women's Open win in 1998, the Korean Elementary School Golf Association was established in 2003. This Association was founded to discover and promote young talented golfers and increase the popularity of golf at the elementary school level. Currently, out of 6,000 elementary schools in Korea, 1,355 schools are associated with the Korean Elementary School Golf Association (2017). The number of affiliated schools is critical evidence of the popularity of golf for young children and adolescents.

Korea Ladies Professional Golf Association

During the 1970s, the interest in amateur golf increased not only among men but also among women (Table 13.1). However, there was no pathway for women to become golf professionals at that time. Therefore, the Korean Professional Golfers' Association started women's golf activation projects in the 1970s. On May 28, 1978 the first women's golf professional membership was presented to four women (Korea Professional Golfers' Association, 2017). At the time, there was no women's golf organization in Korea, and thus the women's golf professional qualification test was conducted at the same time and as the men's. As a result, four more women golfers achieved and earned professional memberships in August 1978.

In 1978, a total of eight women held professional golf memberships. In addition to the initial women's golf professionals, these eight women participated in the men's professional golf championship held in 1978 at Hanyang Country Club. The women's game was categorized as a subdivision of the men's game, and the prize money was minuscule compared with the men's. Before the advent of the Korean Ladies Professional Golf Association, the evaluation criteria for the women's professional golf-qualifying test were equivalent to the men's. However, one of the first female professionals, Ok-Hee Koo, went overseas to Japan and the United States and played at the professional level to develop her professional career. Therefore, there was a strong case for establishing a women's golf organization in order to develop and support women's golf in Korea.

Table 13.1 Comparison between KPGA and KLPGA

	KPGA (men)	KLPGA (women)
Year established	1968	1978 (under KPGA), est. 1988
No. of events (current)	20	32
Total prize money (US$)	13 million	19 million
The highest prize money per event (US$)	1.3 million	1.2 million
No. of events with < US$0.9 million prize money	8	5
No. of professional members	6,190	2,366

Information retrieved from official Korea Ladies Professional Golf Association (2017) and Korea Professional Golfers' Association (2017).

In February 1988, the Korean Ladies Professional Golf Association was established. In the early years after the foundation of the professional association, the performance level for the women's professional and amateur levels was similar. This level of performance, combined with the association's weak administration of the organization concerning securing tournament sponsors and creating international events, meant that there was little to no exposure of the women's game and women's golf, in general, was kept out of the spotlight. A significant turning point for success with regard to the Korean Ladies Professional Golf Association came after Se Ri Pak won two majors in 1998. She won the 1998 US Women's Open and McDonald's LPGA Championship. In addition, in the late 1990s several competitive women golfers emerged from Korea, including Grace Park, Mi-Hyun Kim, Jiyai Shin, Inbee Park, So Yeon Ryu, and others. The increased level of performance combined with the increasing popularity of golf led the Korean Ladies Professional Golf Association to reclassify its professional membership into three categories: tour professional, semi-professional, and teaching professional. As a result, the prize money in women's professional golf also grew. During the late 2000s, several Korean women's golf professionals earned a living playing golf (H. K. Kim, 2011). Currently, the Korean Ladies Professional Golf Association presents 32 professional competitions, and the entire prize money purse is up to US$19 million which exceeds the amount available to men. Within the 32 professional tournaments, five events include prize money over US$900,000. The highest prize money for a single Korean women's tour event was offered in 2018 at the KEB Hana Bank Championship (Korea Ladies Professional Golf Association, 2017).

Commercialization of golf in Korea

Corporate entities realized that tour professionals could become used in advertising as endorsers to promote a product or brand. These corporate sponsors learned to utilize every space on a golfer from head to toe as a way to increase brand awareness. As social awareness and interest in golf grew, the media began to take note. All three major television broadcasting systems in Korea created golf-related content for their viewership and, in 1999 a golf-centered cable channel, "SBS Golf 44" was established (Yang, 2010). With the general public's consistent interest in golf more and more media channels aired golf and golf-related content. In 2005, "J Golf," a cable channel that specialized in golf, was founded followed by "KBS Sports" and "MBC ESPN." These media channels broadcast most of the major golf tournaments played all around the world, including the Korean Tour, KLPGA Tour, PGA Tour, LPGA Tour, PGA of Europe, and European Tour events (Yang, 2010). Through these golf broadcasts, viewers can be persuaded to purchase the same product that they see tour professionals wearing. As women golf professionals demonstrate outstanding performances and show commendable attitudes during tournament play, golf sponsorship, especially women's golf sponsorship, has increased along with the development of golf broadcasting in Korea (Park, 2015).

After Se Ri Pak's win in the 1998 US Women's Open, many junior golfers were motivated to become successful players on the LPGA Tour. The effect of Se Ri Pak on Korean girl's golf is equivalent to Tiger Wood's influence on US junior golf (H. K. Kim, 2011). During the 2000s, both men's and women's golf succeeded internationally. In the early 2000s, K. J. Choi and Y. E. Yang had great performances while participating in the PGA Tour, and Sang-Moon Bae and Kyung-Tae Kim dominated the Korean Tour. In the case of women's golf, Grace Park and Mi-Hyun Kim were internationally successful, including success on the LPGA Tour. However, among Korean golfers, only the women succeeded throughout the years in dominating the golf scene internationally. Most of these women golfers started their professional careers participating on the KLPGA Tour, continuously developing public interest and popularity not only domestically but also internationally (Lee, 2016).

As a result of Se Ri Pak's success in the LPGA Tour, many junior golfers admired her. Within the junior golf scene, prodigious young golfers were called "Se Ri Kids." Jiyai Shin, Inbee Park, N. Y. Choi, and So Yeon Ryu are paragons for Se RiKids (Yojin Construction, 2017). After the late 1990s, many young female golfers decided to turn professional in their early 20s. These young professional women golfers dreamed of becoming successful both domestically and abroad, and many of them succeeded, making both domestic and international women's golf tours popular among the Korean public. Se Ri Pak earned the first large sponsorship contract in Korean golf history in 1996 with Samsung, which offered a total of US$2.75 million for 10 years of sponsorship including a signing bonus payment of US$700,000, an annual salary of US$90,000, coach and manager fee of US$45,000, housing fee of US$36,000, and training fee of US$55,000 (Joo, 2009). This unprecedented contract was displayed to full effect after Se Ri Pak's two LPGA Tour wins in 1998. Pak's clothing included embroidered Samsung logos, which exposed the Samsung brand throughout the world. This sponsorship has been estimated as creating the equivalent of about US$200 million of advertising for Samsung, which is an exponential value considering what Se Ri Pak was paid by her sponsor. Through Samsung and Pak's sponsorship example, Korean corporations expanded their brand awareness through sport marketing, specifically via sponsorship of women's professional golfers and women's tournaments (Jung, 2016).

Based on the early success of golf sponsorship, Korean companies boldly expanded their sponsorship by creating a professional golf team. This is a not a unique sponsorship activity; however, in terms of sponsorship investment potential compared with other professional sports such as baseball, soccer, or basketball, golf requires relatively less capital and is typically more effective in leveraging the brand due to numerous exposure opportunities and the established luxury brand image that exists within the golf sponsorship environment. As women's golf broadcast ratings exceeded men's golf ratings, corporations believed that women's golf was more effective than men's and, as such, it was a better sponsorship investment rather than sponsoring one or two individual male golfers (Park, 2012).

The first women's professional golf team that was sponsored was the Hi-Mart Women's Golf Team. This team was founded in the spring of 2002 and consisted of top players from KLPGA (Hi-Mart, 2017). The Hi-Mart Women's Golf Team was the only women's professional golf team from 2002 to 2008, a total of seven years. In 2009, Hoban Construction created the Hoban construction women's golf team (Kang, 2017). In 2010, Yojin Construction created the Yojin women's golf team and in 2011 the Hanhwa Women's Golf Team was established. Later on, the Hanhwa Women's Golf Team recruited golfers from both the KLPGA and the LPGA. The Hanhwa Women's Golf Team was the first women's golf team to recruit not only Korean golfers but also foreign golfers (Song, 2011). In 2016, two more corporations created women's golf teams: SG Golf and Munyoung Group (Yojin Construction, 2017).

Along with the golf boom, KLPGA Tour events developed in terms of size and sponsorships. In the late 1990s, the KLPGA tour conducted only seven events per season, and all seven were three-round events (54 holes). In addition, the average prize money payout was approximately US$90,000. In 2007, the number of events tripled bringing the total number of events to 32 and average prize money was US$670,000 (Yojin Construction, 2017).

Evolving social issues of golf

Negative stereotype as luxury sport

Golf culture in Korea is typically perceived as a luxury sport and a tool used for political corruption, involving a high level of "gaming" or "betting" during golf rounds. The culture also has a history of female caddies being sexually harassed (C. R. Kim, 2004). Compared with other sports, golf has a relatively large real estate share, and the process of building a golf course includes noises of explosion, waves of explosions, and construction dust which makes it inconvenient for people who work or live in proximity to the construction. Moreover, building a golf course can destroy agricultural estates and historic sites. These factors contributed to a negative perception of the game, at times historically. When these factors were minimized or alleviated, the perception of the golf culture rebounded in a positive manner creating a more favorable image of the game.

With successful women golfers, the image of golf has been elevated, which has helped to expand public perception is a positive way. As a result, there has been an increase in public interest and participation in golf. This, in turn, has led the government to revise policies involving golf course construction and, thus, has alleviated the construction problems previously described. Currently, golf courses are providing not only golf rounds and dining services but have also created various tour packages to promote golf in Korea (Yang, 2008). As most of the population begins to have access to golf, the golf industry can change its image from a luxury sport enjoyed by few to a leisurely pastime enjoyed by many (S. Y. Kim, 2012). According to a recent Gallup Korea survey, 43.1% of survey participants perceived golf as a "luxurious sport." This survey result implies there is still a somewhat negative attitude toward golf (Cho, 2017b).

Golf education in Korea

As discussed earlier, the success of women's golf has created several positive effects. However, there have been some negative consequences as well. One example of an adverse effect of the early success is that many adolescents and young adults wanted to become golf professionals. Some of these young girls and women were talented golfers, and they were regarded as elite sport athletes. As a result, their education program differed from other students. Korea's elite sports system starts from student-athlete programs, which recruit students who possess an outstanding athletic talent, and their academic records are waived when entering higher education. Most of these student athletes receive scholarships from the school. Therefore, student athletes can solely focus on their own sport. Elite sport systems can help athletes by increasing performance levels and focusing on participating in many competitions. On the other hand, for competition and tournament preparation, student athletes could not regularly participate in classes, which led to a decline in their scholastic ability and maladjustment after graduation (S. Y. Kim, 2012). To become a tour professional junior golfers spend approximately US$1,000–1,500 for their monthly golf lessons and US$2,000–3,000 for their monthly golf rounds. Use of the above estimate of costs suggests that, to learn and practice golf to become a tour professional, approximately US$5,000 is spent on a monthly basis. In the winter vacation season, junior golfers participate in training camps held in warm south-east Asia, which costs US$10,000–15,000 for the entire period. In a year, junior golfers who are striving to become a tour professional spend at least US$60,000–100,000 on average (Lee, 2014). The cost of training for golfers in Korea is much higher than that of other sports because golf has a variety of costs such as green fees, lessons, cart/caddy fees, and special taxes charged by golf facilities. Female golfers can decrease or avoid these fees as a result of sponsorship deals through their affiliated organizations.

Conclusion

The significance of golf as a sport and how it affects the overall welfare of Koreans has changed throughout modern Korean history. Since 2014, the budget allocation for the sports divisions under the Ministry of Culture, Sports, and Tourism exceeded the allocations of the tourism and culture divisions. This fact indicates that there has been, and probably will continue to be, an ever-increasing number of sports-related events that support essential public interests for various groups of people. As a result of the government's effort to improve welfare through sports, South Korea's sports culture has experienced growth evidenced by the rate of sports participation and opportunity. However, the diversity of sporting activities still demands attention.

Golf is still considered a means to enter college and may be seen as a promising endeavor for economic success when choosing future career paths for young girls. The game of golf enjoys a strong consumer and corporate following which makes the industry and sport itself attractive to a large number of media channels and sponsors. That is, many companies are investing heavily in commercial marketing activities utilizing women professional golfers. This sponsorship and media coverage helps raise the prize pool (purse) for the women's professional golf tour/league and the salary level of those players on teams, which are now ahead of any other professional league in Korea. It seems that the early history of women's golf in Korea has produced a culture of enduring public interest in both the sport and women who play it.

References

Achenbach, J. (2004). Korea has hottest golf market in the world. Retrieved from https://golfweek.com/2004/05/15/korea-has-hottest-golf-market-world.

Cho, S. W. (2017a). A relationship between Royal Tombs of Chosun Dynasty and golf courses. *Golf Digest Korea*, August 18. Retrieved from http://sports.news.naver.com/golf/news/read.nhn?oid=435&aid=0000001576.

Cho, S. W. (2017b). A development plan according to the golf popularization trend, Master's thesis. Retrieved from www.riss.kr/search/detail/DetailView.do?p_mat_type=be54d9b8bc7cdb09&controlno=39dcabb74474419dffe0bdc3ef48d419.

Hi-Mart (2017). Hi-Mart Public Relations Center. Retrieved from https://www.himart.co.kr/pr/golf.jsp#TAB1.

Joo, M. H. (2009). Famous golf professional's dad, arrears $300,000 tax payment. *Newsen*, April 21. Retrieved from www.newsen.com/news_view.php?uid=201704211111323035

Jung, D. H. (2016). Analytic research on the management of KLPGA, Master's thesis. Retrieved from www.riss.kr/search/detail/DetailView.do?p_mat_type=be54d9b8bc7cdb09&control_no=63ab08fa55b6a188ffe0bdc3ef48d419.

Kang, Y. M. (2017). Hoban Construction makes women's golf team. *Sports World*, March 10. Retrieved from http://sportsworldi.segye.com/content/html/2009/03/10/20090310005158.html.

Kim, C. R. (2004). An analysis of fraternal golfer's subcultural characteristics in the perspective of symbolic interaction by George H. Mead, Doctoral dissertation. Retrieved from www.riss.kr/search/detail/DetailView.do?p_mat_type=be54d9b8bc7cdb09&control_no=e6c77fc8d3aae884ffe0bdc3ef48d419#redirect.

Kim, H. K. (2011). A study on the history of Korea women's golf, Doctoral dissertation. Retrieved from www.riss.kr/search/detail/DetailView.do?p_mat_type=be54d9b8bc7cdb09&control_no=fc7c4824c98cbdedffe0bdc3ef48d419.

Kim, S. Y. (2012). A study on cultivation of elite golf players through the revitalization of school physical education, Master's thesis. Retrieved from www.riss.kr/search/detail/DetailView.do?p_mat_type=be54d9b8bc7cdb09&control_no=152c731dc79b4f37ffe0bdc3ef48d419.

Korea Elementary School Golf Association (2017). Registered School Status. Korea Elementary School Golf Association. Retrieved from www.kesga.or.kr/doum/index.jsp.

Korea Golf Association (2001). *Korea Golf 100 Years*. Seoul, Korea: Korea Golf Association.

Korea Ladies Professional Golf Association (2017). KLPGA Tour Schedule. Retrieved from https://www.klpga.co.kr/web/tour/tourList.do?dcode=RE&flag=3.

Korea Professional Golfers' Association (2017). *Korea Professional Golfers' Association History*. Retrieved from www.kpga.co.kr/about/history/openHistory01.kpga.

Kyunghyang Shinmun (1985). University student-athlete freshmen counted 925. *The Kyunghyang Shinmun*, January 15, pp.8

Lee, C. S. (2016). Analysis on the factors in success of KLPGA, Master's thesis. Retrieved from www.riss.kr/search/detail/DetailView.do?p_mat_type=be54d9b8bc7cdb09&control_no=b15fbd72f25512d5ffe0bdc3ef48d419.

Lee, S. J. (2014). Comparative analysis of golf education systems in Korea and USA, Master's thesis. Retrieved from www.riss.kr/search/detail/DetailView.do?p_mat_type=be54d9b8bc7cdb09&control_no=6456115534619742ffe0bdc3ef48d419.

Lee, Y. H. & Lim, M. S. (1998). Prospect and development of Korea women's elite sports. *Korean Alliance for Health, Physical Education, Recreation, and Dance*, **12**, 46–50.

Min, H. S. (2009). [Republic of Korea's The 1st] "Golf Powerhouse" Korea's golf starting point Gunjari Golf Course. *The Chosun Media*, November 7. Retrieved from news.chosun.com/site/data/html_dir/2009/10/06/2009100601765.html.

Olympic Council of Asia (2006). Games. Retrieved from www.ocasia.org, December 3, 2017.

Park, H. J. (2015). Influence of professional golfers' social contribution on golfer image and sponsor brand loyalty, Master's thesis. Retrieved from www.riss.kr/search/detail/DetailView.do?p_mat_type=be54d9b8bc7cdb09&control_no=4e7b81817ff39830ffe0bdc3ef48d419.

Park, J. S. (2012). A study on brand image strategy through sports marketing – primary focus on golf marketing, Master's thesis. Retrieved from www.riss.kr/search/detail/DetailView.do?p_mat_type=be54d9b8bc7cdb09&control_no=4f9c2993f566e608ffe0bdc3ef48d419.

Seoul Metropolitan Facilities Management (2015). "Children's Grand Park." Retrieved from http://new.sisul.or.kr/global/main/en/sub/park.jsp.

Song, H. G. (2011). Hanhwa Group creates women's golf team, January 10. Retrieved from www.nocutnews.co.kr/news/791655

Yang, G. M. (2008). A strategic measure for popularization of golf, Master's thesis. Retrieved from www.riss.kr/search/detail/DetailView.do?p_mat_type=be54d9b8bc7cdb09&control_no=10750b6ce19a544affe0bdc3ef48d419#redirect.

Yang, J. M. (2010). A study on directions for developing TV sports relay broadcasting: With a focus on golf relay broadcasting on TV, Master's thesis. Retrieved from www.riss.kr/search/detail/DetailView.do?p_mat_type=be54d9b8bc7cdb09&control_no=1691400f42b78acfffe0bdc3ef48d419.

Yojin Construction (2017). Yojin Construction women's golf team introduction. Retrieved from www.yojingolf.co.kr/introduction.htm.

Part III
Economics and financial aspects of women's sport

Part III

14
The relative success story of the WNBA

David Berri

Introduction

Professional team sports have historically been a male-dominated venture. Leagues featuring women have been both relatively uncommon and typically did not last very long. In recent years, however, a variety of leagues has been launched. These include the Women's National Basketball Association (WNBA), National Pro Fastpitch (NPF), the National Women's Soccer League (NWSL), and the National Women's Hockey League (NWHL). Of these, the WNBA has been the most successful. This is true whether we look at attendance, revenues, or longevity. Despite this success, critics of the WNBA are not impressed. After all, when it comes to attendance and pay the WNBA doesn't come close to what we see in the National Basketball Association (NBA). In 2016–17, the average NBA team attracted 17,884 fans per contest (ESPN, 2017). In addition, the average player was paid US$6.1 million during the 2017–18 season (Basketball Reference, 2018a). In contrast, in 2017 the average WNBA team only attracted 7,716 fans and average salary was reported to be only US$75,000 (Berri, 2017a).

So, these basic numbers seem to say clearly the WNBA is not nearly as successful as the NBA. But the story is more involved than just looking at a few numbers. This chapter puts the WNBA story into the context of professional team sports history and offers an exploration into player pay in women's basketball. This discussion illustrates how the WNBA has been – in a relative sense – quite successful with respect to attendance, but with respect to salaries, more work needs to be done from the player's perspective.

WNBA history in perspective

According to WNBA.com (2018a), the WNBA was essentially born on April 24, 1996. On that day, the NBA Board of Governors gave their approval to launch the WNBA in June of 1997. Initially this league consisted of eight teams. As Table 14.1 indicates, four of those franchises (Las Vegas Aces, Los Angeles Sparks, New York Liberty, and Phoenix Mercury) survive today. The other four (the Charlotte Sting, Cleveland Rockers, Houston Comets, and Sacramento Monarchs) eventually failed.

Table 14.1 The franchises of the WNBA from 1997 to 2018

WNBA franchises	First year	Last year
Las Vegas Aces*	1997	Current team
Los Angeles Sparks	1997	Current team
New York Liberty	1997	Current team
Phoenix Mercury	1997	Current team
Chicago Sky	1998	Current team
Washington Mystics	1998	Current team
Dallas Wings†	1999	Current team
Minnesota Lynx	1999	Current team
Indiana Fever	2000	Current team
Seattle Storm	2000	Current team
Connecticut Sun	2003	Current team
Atlanta Dream	2008	Current team
Sacramento Monarchs	1997	2009
Houston Comets	1997	2008
Charlotte Sting	1997	2006
Cleveland Rockers	1997	2003
Orlando Miracle	1999	2002
Miami Sol	2000	2002
Portland Fire	2000	2002

* The Las Vegas Aces were originally the Utah Starzz. In 2003, the Starzz moved to San Antonio and became known as the Silver Stars. In 2014, the name was shortened to just Stars. And then after the 2017 team the franchise moved to Las Vegas and became knows as the Aces.

† The Dallas Wings were originally the Detroit Shock. After the 2009 season, the Shock moved to Tulsa. And then after the 2015 season the franchise moved to Dallas and became known as the Wings.

But other teams joined the WNBA after 1997. Two of these – the Miami Sol and Portland Fire – ceased to exist in 2002. Another franchise – the Dallas Wings – began as the Detroit Shock in 1999, but still continues to exist today. In all, 18 teams have been part of the WNBA. As of 2018, 12 teams continue to play. All of the current teams have existed since 2008 and none has departed the WNBA since 2009. So, it appears that after a rocky start the WNBA has stabilized. Unfortunately, there is a similar story when we look at average game attendance. As Figure 14.1 illustrates, WNBA average attendance rose above 10,000 per game in the league's second and third years. Across the next few years, however, average attendance generally declined. But then, after reaching a low of 7,318 in 2015, league average attendance rebounded in both 2016 and 2017.

Although average game attendance in 2017 reached 7,716, the highest mark since 2011, this mark is still far off the attendance record set in 1999. Caution is warranted when comparing today's numbers with what was seen in the first few years. Initially each WNBA team was affiliated with an NBA franchise and the WNBA was very much a subsidized league. In addition, tickets were often given away. Today, teams like the Chicago Sky, Connecticut Sun, Dallas Wings, Las Vegas Aces, and Seattle Storm are independent franchises. In addition, league sources indicate that teams appear to be less likely to give tickets away. Therefore, today's attendance figures reflect a league that is more independent and more clearly in the business of selling tickets. Not surprisingly, attendance figures are not as high as they were when the league received substantial funds from the NBA and were often setting the price of a ticket equal to zero.

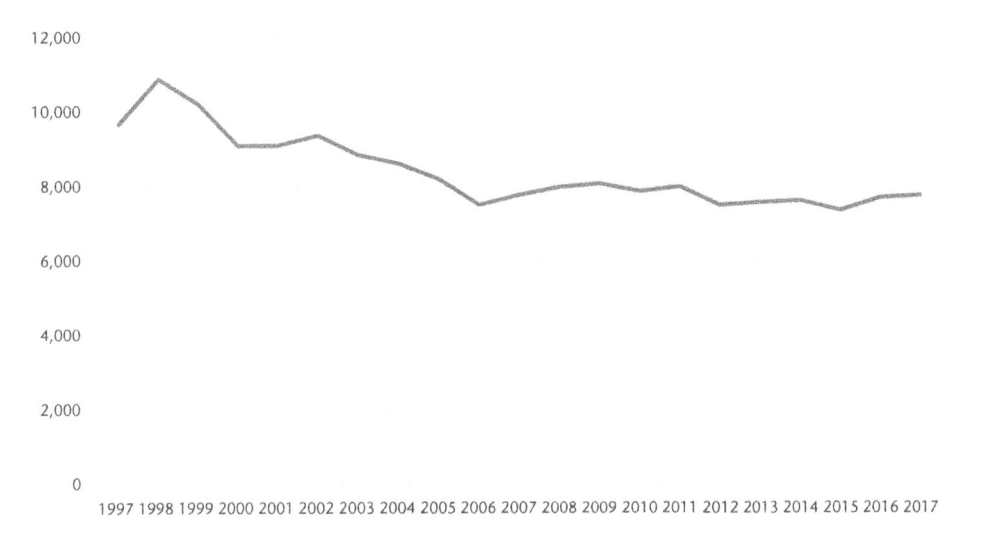

Figure 14.1 WNBA average per-game attendance

Source: The attendance data from 1997 to 2016 can be found at: www.sportsbusinessdaily.com/Daily/Issues/2016/09/20/Research-and-Ratings/WNBA-attendance.aspx

For 2017, see the following: www.wnba.com/news/wnba-scores-highest-attendance-six-years-record-breaking-season

Nevertheless, observers of the WNBA are skeptical about the league's progress. In September of 2015, Adam Silver, the commissioner of the NBA, said, "It's (the WNBA) not where we hoped it would be. We thought it would have broken through by now" (Payne, 2015). Silver's disappointment with the league was echoed by Maya Moore, the All-Star forward with the Minnesota Lynx and former college star at the University of Connecticut. In May of 2015, Moore wrote the following for *The Players' Tribune* (Moore, 2015):

> After four years and two national championships, I went No. 1 in the 2011 WNBA Draft. That's when I felt the drop. There's this unnatural break in exposure for the highest level of women's basketball in the world. Wait, what happened here? That's a question we as WNBA players ask ourselves. We go from amazing AAU experiences to high school All-American games to the excitement and significant platform of the collegiate level to . . . this. All of that visibility to . . . this. Less coverage. Empty seats. Fewer eyeballs. In college, your coaches tell you to stay focused on your team and the game – not the media attention. But you know you're on national television. You know people are following you. You can feel the excitement. And then as a professional, all of that momentum, all of that passion, all of that support – the ball of momentum is deflating before my eyes.
>
> "Gone."

Both Silver and Moore focused on the same issue. The WNBA simply does not draw as much attention as they hoped. These views, however, seem to lack historical perspective. Consider the early history of the NBA. The NBA began as the Basketball Association of America in 1947.

In 1949, the league was re-branded as the NBA. In 1949–50, the NBA consisted of 17 teams. Of these, six did not return for the 1950–51 season. Three more were gone by the end of the 1954–55 season. The eight remaining teams still survive in 2017–18. But only two of these, the New York Knicks and Boston Celtics, are still playing in the same market with the same name. In the NBA's 21st season, it looked remarkably similar to the WNBA today. In 1969–70 the NBA consisted of 14 teams. All of these teams continue to exist today, although five of these are now playing in a different city from where they were in 1970. The league also had a number of star players familiar to NBA fans. The Rookie of the Year was Kareem Abdul-Jabbar. The NBA All-Star game featured such players as Walt Frazier, John Havlicek, Willis Reed, Oscar Robertson, Elgin Baylor, Elvin Hayes, and Jerry West. Although Bill Russell had just retired the year before, the finals featured an amazing seven game series between the New York Knicks and Los Angeles Lakers (featuring the legendary Wilt Chamberlain).

Although these teams and players are legends in NBA history, very few people actually saw these players play. In 1969–70 the average team drew 310,073 fans across the entire season. That works out to just 7,563 fans per game.[1] Yes, that is less than an average WNBA team after 21 seasons. It was not until the 1975–76 season that average per-game NBA attendance passed the 10,000 mark. And it wasn't until the 1988–89 season that this average pushed past the 15,000 mark. Again, attendance today is 17,884 per game, but 47 years ago it was only 42.3% of this mark.

This is also not an isolated story. Consider the history of Major League Baseball (MLB). The National League (NL) came into existence in 1876. In 1901, the American League (AL) was also founded and together the NL and AL comprised Major League Baseball. The early history of each league was fraught with turmoil. Of the eight teams that comprised the National League in 1876, only two survived past 1880.[2] The eight teams in the American League in 1901 fared a bit better. Only the Baltimore Orioles failed.[3] But three teams (the Washington Senators, Philadelphia Athletics, and the Milwaukee Brewers) eventually departed their 1901 location. The Cleveland Blues and Boston Americans eventually changed their names. Only two teams, the Chicago White Sox and Detroit Tigers, have remained in the same place with the same name since 1901.

Once again, the WNBA has existed for over two decades and there is hope that the league has stabilized. The history of baseball, however, suggests that it will not be surprising if that is not the case. In 1921 (the 21st season of the American League), MLB consisted of 16 teams. All of these franchises continue to exist today, but six are now playing in a different city in 2018. The World Series in 1921 featured the New York Giants and the New York Yankees. The Yankees, led by Babe Ruth, ultimately lost to the Giants. Although Ruth, with 59 home runs,[4] was clearly the biggest star in baseball, future Hall-of-Famers like Roger Hornsby, Ty Cobb, Tris Speaker, George Sisler, and Walter Johnson were also playing in 1921. Once again, with all this talent one would expect interest in MLB to be very high. But it wasn't. Even after 21 years of MLB history, average league attendance in 1921 was only 7,391 per game. Six teams drew fewer than 5,000 fans per contest and only 2 teams out of 16 drew more than 10,000 (Baseball Reference, 2018b). In sum, Major League Baseball after 21 years looked a lot like the WNBA today.

But 47 years later[5] in 1968, average per game attendance in MLB was 14,217 (Baseball Reference, 2018c). In other words, MLB after 21 seasons drew 49.3% of the fans it was drawing per game 47 years later. Attendance for MLB continued to grow after that. In 2017, the average team drew 30,042 fans (Baseball Reference, 2018d). A similar story would be told by the National Football League (NFL). The first official season of the NFL was in 1922.[6] The NFL in 1922 had 18 teams. Only three teams, the Chicago Bears, Green Bay Packers, and Chicago

Cardinals, survived the 1920s. So, 15 teams of the original 18 failed within the first few years of the NFL being formed.

Once again, the WNBA has existed for more than two decades so it is useful to think about how well the NFL was doing at this age. The NFL reached its 21st season in 1942. Given that this was in the midst of World War II it is not surprising attendance was very low. By 1947, World War II was over. That year an average NFL team attracted 183,744 fans.[7] With each team playing six games, the average NFL team saw 30,624 fans per game. Flash forward 47 years to the 1994 season and the average NFL game attendance reported was 62,636. In other words, attendance in 1947 was 48.9% of what it was 47 years later.

Table 14.2 captures the basic pattern we see in the NBA, MLB, and the NFL. In each of these sports, attendance came close to doubling in the 47 years after the league reached its 21st season. Of course, that means that it took decades for this to happen. But what this data suggests is that the stories we hear about the WNBA today would be the same stories someone might say about the NBA, MLB, and the NFL after 21 seasons. All of these leagues struggled to find an audience. All of these leagues saw teams come and go and move from market to market, trying to find a viable home. In sum, what we see in the WNBA today is not unusual.

So, why are people like Silver and Moore so disappointed? The issue is perspective. College teams and national teams tend to do better than teams in the early years of a professional league's existence. The primary issue is familiarity. In 2009, Maya Moore and the University of Connecticut faced Angel McCoughtry and the University of Louisville in the National Collegiate Athletics Association (NCAA) women's basketball championship game. Attendance for that game was 18,478 fans (NCAA, 2009a). That season, the University of Connecticut also averaged more than 10,000 fans per game (NCAA, 2009b). A similar story is evident when Maya Moore plays for the US national team. Those games tend to draw larger audiences than those seen in the WNBA.

With respect to both college and national games, the audience knows something about the teams they are watching. A citizen of the United States doesn't have to know any of the players to know that they are rooting for Team USA in an international game. Likewise, alumni and fans of the University of Connecticut will root for the Huskies whenever one of the school's teams plays. But now imagine you take the same player on the Huskies or on Team USA and put them on the Seattle Storm or Minnesota Lynx? The casual fan is presented with a problem. Both teams are not very familiar and both lack much history.

This was the same problem facing observers of the NBA in 1970. The Lakers and Celtics didn't have much history. But, as time went by, history happened. Eventually Julius (Dr. J) Erving came along and people were reminded of Elgin Baylor. Then Erving was followed by players like Michael Jordan, Kobe Bryant, and LeBron James. The play of all these players had more meaning because a history had happened before them, which gave fans perspective. The same story is also

Table 14.2 Attendance snapshots in major professional team sports

League	Attendance after 21 seasons	Attendance 47 years later	Percentage of second and third columns
National Basketball Association	7,563 (1969–70)	17,884 (2016–17)	42.3
Major League Baseball	7,391 (1921)	14,217 (1968)	49.3
National Football League	30,624 (1947)	62,636 (1994)	48.9

true for teams. A game between the Lakers and Celtics in 2018 has more meaning because these two franchises have contended for so many NBA titles.

In the future, this will probably be true for the WNBA. Players will come along who remind people of Maya Moore and other WNBA stars today. In the future, games between the Minnesota Lynx and Los Angeles Sparks will have more meaning because these teams faced each other in the 2016 and 2017 WNBA finals. Both series were quite competitive (each series took five games to decide) and it is likely both of these series will be remembered each time these teams face each other in future years. The dramatic competitions we recently saw between the Lynx and Sparks are necessary to create the history a league needs to thrive. However, as the history of the NBA, MLB, and NFL indicates, the history of a league takes decades to be written. So, none of this benefits Moore today. But future players will appreciate, or at least should appreciate, all that Moore is doing today!

The gender-wage gap in professional basketball

What is Moore getting out of playing for the WNBA now? According to Megdal (2017), Moore will be paid US$113,000 to play in the WNBA in 2018. The highest paid player in 2018 according to Megdal (2017) will be Chiney Ogwumike, who will be paid US$117,500 by the Connecticut Sun. In contrast, basketball-reference.com says the highest paid player in the NBA in 2017–18 is Stephen Curry. His salary is reported to be US$34,682,550 (Basketball Reference, 2018a). Therefore, the highest paid player in the NBA is paid 295.2 times more than the highest paid player in the WNBA. This suggests that there is a substantial gender-wage gap in professional basketball. Of course, there are substantial differences in revenue between the two leagues. This was essentially the point Adam Silver made in 2015, in the same press conference where he noted the WNBA was "not where we hoped it would be" (Payne, 2015). In that same press conference, Silver added at that time that the WNBA was not profitable enough to increase the pay of WNBA players (Payne, 2015).

But is all that true? To address this issue, we need to think about both revenue and wages in the two sports leagues. According to Badenhausen (2018), the NBA earned US$7.368 billion in revenue in 2016–17. The NBA shares about 50% of its revenue with its players, so the players split of the revenue in 2016–17 was about US$3.7 billion.[8] As Berri (2017a) details, a similar analysis is a bit more involved for the WNBA. Total attendance for the WNBA in 2017 was 1,574,078. The average minimum ticket price for eight WNBA teams that season was reported to be US$16.88. Therefore, gate revenue was at least US$26.56 million for the league. In addition, the WNBA receives US$25 million per year from the broadcasting deal it signed with ESPN. Therefore, we know WNBA revenue in 2017 was at least US$51.56 million. The WNBA also earns revenue from a Twitter deal, sponsorships, and merchandise sales. This means that the US$51.56 million figure is clearly an understatement.

Megdal (2017) reported salary data for 102 of the 157 players who appeared in games in 2017. The average salary across this sample was US$71,635. Two years before this report, however, a story reported the average WNBA salary was US$75,000 (Sefko, 2015). If we accept the slightly higher figure, then total salaries in the WNBA were only US$11.775 million, which means that the WNBA paid, at most, 22.8% of its revenue to its players in 2017. Not only does the WNBA share a smaller percentage of its revenue with its players, but it also has a much smaller gap between the pay of the best players and the pay of the average player. Again, the top player in the WNBA in 2017 was paid only US$117,500, or 57% more than the average player.

Let us imagine, as Berri (2017b) originally did, that the NBA paid its players like the WNBA. First, the NBA and it players split revenue evenly, resulting in an average NBA player being paid US$6,110,639. But, in the WNBA, players only receive 22.8% of revenue. If this were the case in the NBA the average salary would be only US$2,790,892. In addition, the highest wage in the WNBA is only 57% higher than the average. Therefore, the highest wage in the NBA if pay were structured as it is in the WNBA would be only US$4,372,397. Once again, Stephen Curry was the highest paid player in 2017–18 with a salary of US$34,682,550. If he were paid like a WNBA player, however, he would be paid more than US$30 million less. Even if the NBA had the same revenues, Stephen Curry and other top NBA stars would get much less if the NBA paid players like the WNBA did. This naturally leads to the question of what WNBA players would be paid if the WNBA, with the same revenues it has now, paid like the NBA?

Measuring economic exploitation in the WNBA

Now let us imagine a world in which the WNBA pays its players like the NBA. Again, the NBA splits its revenues equally with its players. With US$51.56 million in revenue in 2017 (again, that estimate is a minimum), the WNBA players (if it were the NBA) would be receiving US$25,782,283. With 157 players, the average salary would then be US$164,212. Stephen Curry was paid 5.68 times more than the average NBA player in 2017–18. If the WNBA followed that pattern, the top player in the WNBA would be paid US$932,029. Currently the NBA, like the WNBA, does limit the pay of its top players. What if the WNBA followed the lead of other leagues (such as MLB) and did not limit the pay of the very best players?

To answer this question, we need to determine who is "best." Given that the objective of each team is to win, it makes sense to determine best by measuring how many wins each player produces. To do this, Berri (2008) estimates the following model with team box score statistics:[9]

$$\text{Wins} = a_0 + a_1 \times \text{PTS/PE} - a_2 \times \text{Opp.PTS/PA} + e_i \tag{1}$$

where

> Wins = team winning percentage (i.e., wins per game)
> PTS = points scored per game
> PE = possession employed[10] = FGA + x × FTA + TOV − OREB
> PA = possession acquired = Opp.FGM + x × Opp.FTM + Opp.TOV + DREB + TMREB
>
> Opp. = opponent
>
> FGA = field goal attempts per game
>
> FTA = free throw attempts per game
>
> TOV = turnovers per game
>
> OREB = offensive rebounds per game
>
> FGM = field goals made per game
>
> FTM = free throws made per game
>
> DREB = defensive rebounds per game
>
> TMREB = team rebounds per game (that change possession)

Equation (1) was estimated with data from both the WNBA and the NBA. The results reported in Table 14.3 indicate that essentially the process by which wins are determined in each league is quite similar. For example, an additional point scored per game increases winning percentage by 0.033 in both sports. Other box score statistics also have a similar impact on wins in both leagues.

Given the definitions of possessions employed and possessions acquired, we can also derive the impact on wins for most of the box score statistics tracked for players and teams.[11] Again, the results reported in Table 14.4 indicate that these factors generally have the same impact on wins in both the WNBA and NBA.

In sum, the link between the statistics tracked and wins in both leagues is essentially the same.[12] The story told by this link is quite similar to understand. Wins in basketball, whether the game is played by women or men, are primarily about a team acquiring the ball without their opponent scoring (i.e., grabbing defensive rebounds and forcing turnovers), keeping the ball away from their opponent (avoiding turnovers and grab offensive rebounds), and turning possessions into points (shooting efficiently from the field and getting to the free throw line). These are the factors that primarily determine how many wins a player produces.[13] To determine the value of each win, let us return to the idea that, in a league where revenues are evenly split, all WNBA players would receive US$25,782,283. If players were paid only for wins, then each of the 204 regular season wins in the WNBA in 2017 would be worth US$126,379.

Table 14.3 Estimating Equation (1) for the WNBA and the NBA

Years	Marginal value WNBA	Marginal value NBA
	1997–2017	1986–87 to 2016–17
Points	0.033	0.033
Possessions employed	−0.031	(0.034)
Points surrendered	−0.033	(0.032)
Possessions acquired	0.032	0.033

Table 14.4 The impact on wins of various box score statistics in the WNBA and NBA

Player factors	WNBA marginal value	NBA marginal value
Points	0.033	0.033
Field goal attempts	−0.031	−0.034
Free throw attempts	−0.014	−0.015
Offensive rebounds	0.031	0.034
Turnovers	−0.031	−0.034
Defensive rebounds	0.032	0.033
Steals	0.032	0.033
Team factors	WNBA marginal value	NBA marginal value
Opponent's points	−0.033	−0.032
Opponent's field goals made	0.032	0.033
Opponent's free throws made	0.014	0.015
Opponent's turnovers	0.032	0.033
Team rebounds*	0.032	0.033

* Team rebounds are defined as rebounds that are not assigned to individual players who change possession. The method for estimating these was reported in Berri (2008).

Table 14.5 The top 10 WNBA players in 2017

Top 10 WNBA players in 2017	Team	Wins produced	Value of wins (US$)	2017 salary (US$)*	Difference (US$)
Sylvia Fowles	Minnesota Lynx	9.7	1,222,827	109,000	1,113,827
Jonquel Jones	Connecticut Sun	9.4	1,193,532	47,774	1,145,758
Nneka Ogwumike	Los Angeles Sparks	7.9	992,787	111,000	881,787
Candace Parker	Los Angeles Sparks	7.6	954,559	113,500	841,059
Chelsea Gray	Los Angeles Sparks	6.7	852,263	45,994	806,269
Skylar Diggins-Smith	Dallas Wings	6.6	829,864	113,500	716,364
Courtney Vandersloot	Chicago Sky	6.5	825,293	111,000	714,293
Maya Moore	Minnesota Lynx	6.4	809,006	111,000	698,006
Alyssa Thomas	Connecticut Sun	6.2	782,670	62,055	720,615
Elena Delle Donne	Washington Mystics	5.4	680,525	113,000	567,525

* Salary data comes from summithoops.com. The site does not report Elena Delle Donne's salary for 2017. The figure cited is what summithoops.com reports for her in 2018.

As Table 14.5 indicates, Sylvia Fowles, the 2017 WNBA Most Valuable Player, led the league with 9.7 wins produced. Given the value of a win she was worth US$1.22 million. This mean that Fowles was worth US$1.11 million more than she was paid. Although Fowles was the most productive, she was not the most underpaid. That "honor" went to Jonquel Jones who was worth US$1.19 million but only paid US$47,774. If the WNBA paid like the NBA, the top players in the WNBA would make much more than they are currently being paid. In fact, the top WNBA players would be paid salaries quite similar to what top women basketball players are paid to play in other countries. The majority of WNBA players will continue to play professional basketball when each WNBA season ends. According to WNBA.com (2018b), 89 women were playing outside the United States after the 2017 WNBA season concluded. The primary reason for this is the money non-WNBA teams are willing to pay.

As Lindsey Harding noted in 2017 (Caple, 2017):

> It used to be that the money was in Italy, Spain, Russia – it used to be everywhere. But now Russia and Turkey and China are the three places that have a lot of money for women's basketball. Korea is pretty decent, but Russia and Turkey is where a lot of the money is. A lot of Americans, a lot of WNBA players especially, are in Turkey. Not just first division but also in second division, where they have a lot of money.

It was reported in 2014 that star WNBA players Sylvia Fowles, Maya Moore, and Brittney Griner were all paid US$600,000 to play in China (Gaines, 2014). Diana Taurasi was paid US$1.5 million in 2015 by UMMC Ekaterinburg, a women's basketball team in Russia. In addition, this team paid Taurasi her WNBA salary to *not* play in the WNBA in 2015 (Draper, 2015). The analysis of the WNBA data suggests that the top players could be paid similar wages in the WNBA, but the league's rules prevent this from happening. As a consequence, we have a case of a star player being paid not to play in the league.

The case of Taurasi is also not a one-time event. As Berri (2018c) notes, Emma Meesserman produced 17.6 wins for the Washington Mystics from 2013 to 2017. Despite this production, however, Meesserman announced she would not play in 2018 in an effort to rest her body from the year-round schedule as a professional player in women's basketball. Obviously, having top talent avoid playing in a specific league is not helpful. But it appears to be a direct consequence of how the WNBA has structured its labor market.

Looking forward to the future

We have learned the WNBA is doing at least as well as can be expected given the age of the league, with respect to league attendance and franchise stability. The league is not doing as well from the player's perspective with respect to salaries. But, overall, it seems likely the WNBA is a league that will survive and, if its future plays out in a fashion similar to the history of the NBA, we can expect the future of the WNBA to be much brighter than its present. All of this means that there will be many more stories told about the WNBA as it continues to progress. We should note, however, that other stories have already been told. Harris and Berri (2016) explored how efficiently minutes were allocated in the WNBA whereas Harris and Berri (2015) looked at the efficiency of the WNBA draft selection process. Both studies uncovered results similar to what had been previously reported in the NBA.

In addition, Darvin, Pegoraro, and Berri (2017) looked at gender and coaching in the WNBA. About half of the head coaches in the WNBA are men, and men also hold all the head coaching jobs in the NBA. In sum, there is a preference for organizations to hire men to lead professional basketball teams. The data from the WNBA, however, revealed that the gender of the coach did not impact player performance, which suggests that bias toward men is not supported by the data. Going forward we can expect more stories to be told. Essentially any story that can be told with NBA data can be told with WNBA data. The exception is that the WNBA allows us also to explore gender issues. Therefore, going forward, even better stories will be told with data from the WNBA. And these stories will have even more meaning as the history of the league continues to be written.

Leader profile: Terri Jackson, Director of Operations for the WNBPA

1   **What is your role with the player association?**

I am the director of operations for the powerful, the strong, the amazing, the intelligent, the diverse, the beautiful, and the beautifully diverse women who play basketball at the highest, most elite level in the world. The players form the membership of the Women's National Basketball Players Association, the very first sports union for women. I work for them. As the title would suggest, the WNBPA Director of Operations plays a critical leadership role that not only reports to player leadership – an executive body and a board of player representatives – but to the entire membership. I am called to serve as their voice and primary advocate.

I have found that the role requires me to be at all times a collaborator and effective communicator. Given my professional experience and training as an attorney in sports and higher education, I am fundamentally grounded in a lead-serve approach. In areas of governance and board relations, group licensing and marketing, as well as labor and collective bargaining, I am expected to make tough decisions and remain committed to implementing those decisions in the best interest of the WNBPA. And while there is no typical day, I work hard to gain their trust, protect their interests while looking to raise their profiles as professional athletes and raise the visibility of the game.

2 What are the challenges facing the WNBA player's association going forward?

Though we are one of the more under-resourced unions in professional sports, I do not see challenges. Instead, I see opportunity. We have many, many opportunities to:

- Build consensus: communication between the PA staff and the leadership is the starting point and we reemphasize the importance of real-time communication between the leadership and the entire membership on a monthly basis. This is especially important when preparing for collective bargaining negotiations.
- Demonstrate the value of professional women athletes. When the league determines that there is value in being more supportive of working women, working mothers, with actions and policies, and looks to promote what it means to be a working mom who plays at such a high level, then I am certain that we will have a league that is not only well defined with players who are invested but also a league that is well respected.
- Show the force and the strength of unions. The ability to understand how our history gives us strength for our future. This union was started because the NBPA staff, its membership – NBA players – and their agents reached out to the players of the WNBA in its early days and showed them the value of organizing. Building upon the lessons of the past, I have come to recognize and this next age of player leadership has come to recognize that continuing to build relationships in the labor movement will be key.

Notes

1. The history of NBA attendance can be found at APBR.org (2018).
2. The story of the early history of attendance in baseball was told by Berri (2018a).
3. The original Orioles only played in 1901 and 1902. The Baltimore Orioles we know today were known as the Milwaukee Brewers in 1901. In 1902 this team moved to St. Louis and became known as the Browns. In 1954 the team moved to Baltimore and became the Orioles. See Baseball Reference (2018a).
4. Ken Williams and Bob Meusel tied for second in Major League Baseball with 24 home runs.
5. This is the same time period between the NBA after 21 seasons and the NBA today.
6. The American Pro Football Association (APFA) was founded in 1920. After two seasons, that league changed its name to the NFL (History.com, 2018).
7. The data for NFL attendance was noted by Berri, Schmidt, and Brook (2006) and originally appeared in the Sporting News' *Pro Football Guide* (Carter, 2000).
8. Technically the NBA shares basketball-related income (BRI) with its players. BRI is not the same as total revenue so the split with players is not quite US$3.7 billion.
9. Berri (2008) details the wins produced model, a model originally noted in Berri et al. (2006). This model built off of what was reported by Berri (1999) and Berri and Krautmann (2006). Wins produced have also been reviewed in Berri and Schmidt (2010) and Berri (2012). It was applied to the WNBA in Berri and Krautmann (2013) and also to college men's basketball in Berri (2016). Darvin et al. (2017) also applied wins produced to college women's basketball and the WNBA. Berri (2018) reviewed all of this research.
10. Possession employed and possession acquired were originally derived in Berri (2008). The value of x is derived from a model that determines how many team rebounds change possession. For details, see Berri (2008).
11. As Berri (2008) details, the value of each statistic is determined by taking the derivative of wins with respect to each box score statistic at the point of means.
12. Berri (2018b) reports the same results for NCAA Women's Basketball and NCAA Men's Basketball.
13. Berri (2008) also detail the impact of assists, blocked shots, and personal fouls on wins. Berri and Schmidt (2010) adds to the model by incorporating the diminishing returns effect of defensive rebounds.

References

APBR.org (2018). NBA/ABA Home attendance totals, February 27. Retrieved from www.apbr.org/attendance.html.

Badenhausen, K. (2018). NBA team values 2018: Every club now worth at least $1 billion. Forbes.com, . Retrieved from https://www.forbes.com/sites/kurtbadenhausen/2018/02/07/nba-team-values-2018-every-club-now-worth-at-least-1-billion/#67f603657155 (accessed February 7, 2018).

Basketball Reference (2018a). 2017–18 NBA player contracts. Retrieved from https://www.basketball-reference.com/contracts/players.html.

Baseball Reference (2018b). 1921 MLB attendance & team age. Retrieved from https://www.baseball-reference.com/leagues/MLB/1921-misc.shtml (accessed February 27, 2018).

Baseball Reference (2018c). 1968 MLB attendance & team age. Retrieved from https://www.baseball-reference.com/leagues/MLB/1968-misc.shtml (accessed February 27, 2018).

Baseball Reference (2018d). 2017 MLB attendance & team age. Retrieved from https://www.baseball-reference.com/leagues/MLB/2017-misc.shtml (accessed February 27, 2018).

Berri, D. (1999). Who is most valuable? Measuring the player's production of wins in the National Basketball Association. *Managerial and Decision Economics*, **20**(8), 411–427.

Berri, D. (2008). A simple measure of worker productivity in the National Basketball Association. In B. Humphreys and D. Howard (eds), *The Business of Sport* (pp. 1–40), 3 volumes. Westport, CT: Praeger.

Berri, D. (2012). Measuring performance in the National Basketball Association. In S. Shmanske and L. Kahane (eds), *The Handbook of Sports Economics* (pp. 94–117). Oxford: Oxford University Press.

Berri, D. (2016). Paying NCAA athletes. *Marquette Sports Law Review*, **26**(2), 479–491.

Berri, D. (2017a). Basketball's growing gender wage gap: The evidence The WNBA is underpaying players. *Forbes.com*. September 20. Retrieved from https://www.forbes.com/sites/davidberri/2017/09/20/there-is-a-growing-gender-wage-gap-in-professional-basketball/#379ad74536e0.

Berri, D. (2017b). Stephen Curry would hate to be paid like women in professional basketball, December 30. Retrieved from https://www.forbes.com/sites/davidberri/2017/12/30/stephen-curry-would-hate-to-be-paid-like-women-in-professional-basketball/#5360e233492c.

Berri, D. (2018a). *Sports Economics*, New York: Worth Publishers/Macmillan Education.

Berri, D. (2018b). The future of the National Pro Fastpitch League looks difficult – and that is not surprising. *Forbes.com*, February 6. Retrieved from https://www.forbes.com/sites/davidberri/2018/02/06/the-future-of-the-national-pro-fastpitch-league-looks-difficult-and-that-is-not-surprising/#606a9ed23410

Berri, D. (2018c). The WNBA's labor market leads Emma Meesseman to skip the 2018 WNBA season, *110 Percent Spots Blog*, February 15. Retrieved from https://www.110percentblog.com/single-post/2018/02/15/The-WNBA%E2%80%99s-Labor-Market-Leads-Emma-Meesseman-to-Skip-the-2018-WNBA-Season.

Berri, D. & Krautmann A. (2006). Shirking on the court: Testing for the dis-incentive effects of guaranteed pay. *Economic Inquiry*, **44**(3). 536–546.

Berri, D. & Krautmann A. (2013). Understanding the WNBA on and off the court. In E. M. Leeds & M. Leeds (eds), *Handbook on the Economics of Women in Sports* (pp. 132–155). Northampton, MA: Edward Elgar Press.

Berri, D. & Schmidt M. B. (2010). *Stumbling on Wins: Two Economists Explore the Pitfalls on the Road to Victory in Professional Sports*. Princeton, NJ: Financial Times Press.

Berri, D. J., Schmidt M. B., & Brook, S. L. (2006). *The Wages of Wins: Taking Measure of the Many Myths in Modern Sport*. Redwood City, CA: Stanford University Press.

Caple, J. (2017). For WNBA stars who play overseas, positives outweigh negatives. *ABC News*, January 25. Retrieved from http://abcnews.go.com/Sports/wnba-stars-play-overseas-positives-outweigh-negatives/story?id=45034501.

Carter, C. (ed.) (2000). *Pro Football Guide*. Sporting News.

Darvin, L., Pegoraro, A., & Berri, D. (2017). Are men better leaders? An investigation of head coaches' gender and individual players' performance in amateur and professional women's basketball. *Sex Roles*, **78**(7–8), 455–466.

Draper, K. (2015). Diana Taurasi's Russian team is paying her to skip the WNBA season, February 3. Retrieved from https://deadspin.com/diana-taurasis-russian-team-is-paying-her-to-skip-the-w-1683643165.

ESPN (2017). NBA Attendance Report– 2017. Retrieved from www.espn.com/nba/attendance/_/year/2017.

Gaines, C. (2014). Brittney Griner makes 12 times as much money playing basketball in China. *Business Insider*, April 21. Retrieved from www.businessinsider.com/brittney-griner-basketball-china-2014-4.

Harris, J. & Berri D. (2015). Predicting the WNBA draft: What matters most from college performance. *International Journal of Sport Finance*, **10**(4), 299–309.

Harris, J. & Berri, D. (2016). If you can't pay them, play them: Fan preference and own-race bias in the WNBA. *International Journal of Sport Finance*, **11**(3), 163–180.

History.com (2018). This day in history: 1920 professional football is born, February 27. Retrieved from www.history.com/this-day-in-history/professional-football-is-born.

Megdal, H. (2017). Updated: The high post hoops WNBA salaries database. *High Post Hoops*, August 28. Retrieved from https://highposthoops.com/2018/08/15/wnba-salary-database.

Moore, M. (2015). (In)Visibility *The Players' Tribune*, April 30. Retrieved from https://www.theplayerstribune.com/maya-moore-wnba-visibility/?xrs=RebelMouse_tw.

National Collegiate Athletics Association (2009a). Box score (final) Louisville vs. Connecticut, July 4). Retrieved from http://fs.ncaa.org/Docs/stats/w_basketball_champs_records/2009/d1/html/champ09.htm.

National Collegiate Athletics Association (2009b). 2009 NCAA women's basketball attendance. Retrieved from http://fs.ncaa.org/Docs/stats/w_basketball_RB/reports/Attend/09att.pdf.

Payne, M. (2015). NBA Commissioner Adam Silver on the WNBA. "It's not where we hoped it would be." *Washington Post*, September 17. Retrieved from https://www.washingtonpost.com/news/early-lead/wp/2015/09/17/nba-commissioner-adam-silver-on-the-wnba-its-not-where-we-hoped-it-would-be.

Sefko (2015). Why WNBA has never been stronger as league enters Dallas market, July 26. Retrieved from https://sportsday.dallasnews.com/dallas-mavericks/mavericksheadlines/2015/07/26/sefko-why-wnba-has-never-been-stronger-as-league-enters-dallas-market.

WNBA.com (2018a). History, February 27. Retrieved from www.wnba.com/history.

WNBA.com (2018b). WNBA players playing overseas, February 27. Retrieved from www.wnba.com/wnba-players-playing-overseas.

15
Public expenditure on women's sport and gender equality among recipients of public expenditure in European sport

Pamela Wicker

Introduction

In many European countries, public expenditure is directed towards elite sport and institutions within the organized sport system (Hallmann & Petry, 2013). For example, in Germany, the Federal Ministry of the Interior allocates funding to the German Olympic Sports Confederation, which, in turn, funds national sport organizations (Petry & Hallmann, 2013). In Finland, the Ministry of Education and Culture finances the Finnish Sports Federation (Vehmas & Ilmanen, 2013). In France, the Ministry of Sports provides subsidies to national sport organizations (Fischer, 2013). In the Netherlands, the Ministry of Health, Welfare, and Sports subsidizes the National Olympic Committee and the National Sport Federation (Hoekman & Breedveld, 2013). These examples show that governmental institutions fund elite sports by providing subsidies to sport organizations, with the type of government institution and recipient varying by country.

However, providing financial support does not imply that governments can affect decision-making in sport organizations. Sport systems in many European countries are couched in a three-sector economy, meaning that there is a distinction across public sector (state), private sector (market), and third sector (voluntary sector) (Downward, Dawson, & Dejonghe, 2009). Institutions of the organized sport system (e.g., national sport organizations, National Olympic Committees) belong to the voluntary sector given their non-profit status. This status implies independence of the state and autonomy in decision-making (Horch, 1994), limiting government influence on the use of funding and decision-making processes.

Within European sport systems, the influence of other sectors on voluntary sport organizations varies because of differences in the organizational arrangements of sport. The VOCASPORT (Vocational Education and Training related to Sports in Europe) typology was established by the VOCASPORT Research Group (2004) and aimed at conceptualizing differences and similarities in sport policy systems between European countries. This typology distinguishes four types of policy systems (Henry, 2009): the missionary configuration is closest to the ideal-type distinction across the three sectors because the voluntary sector acts with delegated powers and has great decision-making autonomy (e.g., Germany, Austria, Denmark, Sweden). The bureaucratic configuration is characterized by an active government that regulates and monitors the sport system (e.g., Belgium, Finland, France, Spain). For example, one way of regulation is to build subsidies into conditions related to employee qualifications and organizational goals (Vos, Breesch, Késenne, Van Hoecke, Vanreusel, & Scheerder, 2011). The entrepreneurial configuration exhibits a high degree of market involvement (e.g., the United Kingdom, Ireland), whereas sport is produced through collaboration of all three sectors in the social configuration (e.g., the Netherlands). Hence, the influence of the public and/or private sector differs across policy systems.

One area outside sport in which governments across Europe exhibited influence on organizations is the issue of gender equality in executive boards. Governments in many European countries, such as Norway and Germany, have introduced some form of gender quota for listed or public companies (e.g., Bozhinov, 2017; Sisjord, Fasting, & Sand, 2017). These gender policies recognize the fact that the share of females in leading positions does not materially increase when organizations are simply encouraged to appoint more women. A similar situation can be observed in sport, where gender differences are particularly pronounced (Cunningham & Sagas, 2008) given its competitive nature and historically male domination. In fact, gender differences on the field translated into gender differences off the field, such as into boardrooms and executive committees. Sport organizations across Europe disclose a female share in leading positions below the *gender balance zone* of 40–60% (European Commission, 2014; Ottesen, Skirstad, Pfister, & Habermann, 2010; Sisjord et al., 2017; Skirstad, 2009). The question then is how can gender equality be improved, and what role do public expenditures play in this regard?

Against this societal and political background, the purpose of this chapter is to discuss gender equality in elite sport in Europe through the lens of public expenditure. This expenditure can be targeted directly at sport organizations, elite sport events, or personnel, with the last two being less likely. The indirect path is that national sport organizations pass on public money to elite sport coaches and athletes, for example. For both paths, the question of how recipients of public expenditure are concerned with gender equality is discussed. The discussion focuses on elite sports in general and Olympic sports in particular, because the role of public expenditure is particularly pronounced for the latter and professional sport leagues can generate more revenues from private entities. This chapter takes a broader European perspective with a focus on western European countries. Depending on the reflected topic and the availability of data and academic research, specific countries are selected for the discussion.

Public expenditure on women's sport

The discussion of public expenditure on women's sport is constrained by the intermediary role of national sport organizations, combined with the scarcity of data on public expenditure that is targeted directly at elite sport events or personnel. Austria is an exception because information about the allocation of government funding to several areas of elite sport is publicly available. The detailed listing of public expenditure allows a gender-specific analysis, which gives indications about gender equality.

The Austrian Ministry for Sport (2012) identified the 10 most important major sport events that received public funding between 2007 and 2011. These included five sport events where both genders competed, such as the 2013 World Championships in Alpine Skiing, the 2012 Youth Olympic Games, and the 2010 European Championships in Judo, and another five events that included only male competitions, such as the 2008 European Championships in Football, the 2010 European Championships in Handball, and the 2011 European Championships in Volleyball. Several female-only events were also subsidized by the government in 2007, such as the European Championships in Fistball and two World Cups in Fencing, but they did not make it to the top 10 list based on funding (Austrian Ministry for Sport, 2012). This overview suggests that both genders did not equally benefit from public expenditure.

Table 15.1 summarizes public expenditure on different areas in Austria by year (Austrian Ministry for Sport, 2011). Public expenditure on female-only events supports the above conclusion: between 2007 and 2011, the government spent between €15,560 and €75,760 on female-only sport events. Government spending on female-only events is equivalent to between 0.5% and 6.3% of total public expenditure on sport events. Mixed events (including both genders) represent the largest share of public expenditure, making up between 35.9% (2010) and 81.5% (2011) of total spending on sport events. Public expenditure on elite sport coaches shows a similar picture. Both total expenditure and share of total spending signal that female coaches are rarely recipients of government funding. This spending pattern is probably rooted in female under-representation in elite sport coaching positions as observed in other European countries (see section "Elite sport coaches and gender equality").

Public expenditure on gender mainstreaming, based on gender-specific criteria, indicates that the Austrian government is concerned about gender equality in national sport associations and has taken financial measures to promote women in sport. Table 15.1 shows that approximately a quarter of total public funding for national sport associations is provided based on gender-specific criteria. Moreover, the Austrian government allocated an increasing six-digit Euro figure on gender mainstreaming and women's sport between 2007 and 2011. This money was also distributed among national sport associations.

Recipients of public funding and gender equality

European elite sport systems receive financial support from their governments, with the way in which the money is distributed and the size of funds varying by country (Hallmann & Petry, 2013). The use of funding is at the discretion of sport organizations. In the absence of information about the gender-specific use of government subsidies in most European countries, other indicators are advanced that give information about gender equality in elite sport.

The first indicator is the share of women in leading positions. Existing research has agreed that a share of females between 40% and 60% represents the *gender balance zone* and indicates gender equality (e.g., Ottesen et al., 2010). Gender equality in leading positions is important because executive boards decide on the use of money. Existing research from political sciences has found that male and female leaders differ in their use of funding (Chen, 2013), suggesting that gender distribution in executive boards of sport organizations might also affect the allocation of money. The second indicator is gender equality among elite sport coaches, which gives information about the extent to which sport organizations are concerned with gender equality in their elite sport personnel. The third indicator is at the athlete level, where the discussion focuses on equal pay. The next sections discuss these aspects of gender equality among recipients of government funding.

Sport governing bodies and gender equality

Share of women in leading positions

Gender equality in sport is on the agenda of the European Commission (2014) and the European Institute for Gender Equality (EIGE, 2015). Both institutions have compiled reports that indicate low levels of gender equality in decision-making positions at all levels of sport. On the

Table 15.1 Public expenditure on women's sport in Austria, 2007–2011

Public expenditure for	2007	2008	2009	2010	2011
Sport events – female only (€)	33,860	75,760	15,560	70,260	20,000
Sport events – female only (% of total expenditure on events)	4.5	6.3	1.2	5.7	0.5
Sport events – mixed events (€)	434,780	478,395	790,700	446,280	3,451,820
Sport events – mixed events (% of total expenditure on events)	58.3	61.8	59.0	35.9	81.5
Female coaches (€)	39,762	0	14,500	n.a.	n.a.
Female coaches (% of total expenditure on coaches)	3.2	0	1.8	n.a.	n.a.
Gender mainstreaming – women's sport (€)	165,400	289,900	300,000	273,170.98	329,856.29
National sport associations by gender-specific criteria (mean) (€)	13,811,237.96	13,866,297.55	13,067,251.15	12,814,325.20	17,688,783.89
National sport associations by gender-specific criteria (% as share of total expenditure; mean value)	25.5	25.1	24.9	25.2	27.8

Own calculations based on Austrian Ministry for Sport (2011). n.a. = data not available

international level, 38% of the 52 European sport federations did not have a woman on their board and 88% had a share of women below 25%. Out of the 52 federations, only 2 had a female president (European Commission, 2014). These were Marijke Fleuren at the European Hockey Federation and Lis Nielsen at the European Ramblers' Association.

On the national level, the average share of women is only 14% in all decision-making positions of continental confederations of Olympic sports in Europe in 2015 (EIGE, 2015). Specifically, the proportion of women is 4% among presidents or chairpersons, 9% among vice-presidents or vice-chairpersons, 15% among board members for the highest decision-making body, and 22% among general directors or general secretaries (EIGE, 2015). Traditionally, Scandinavian countries, and in particular Sweden and Norway, report higher shares than other European countries (Ottesen et al., 2010).

The share of women in decision-making positions in national sport associations across European Union (EU) member states in 2015 supports the above notions: only Sweden has entered the gender balance zone with a share of 43%. All other countries have shares below 40%, with 3% in Poland representing the lowest share of all EU countries (EIGE, 2015). Previous studies have shown that the share of women among executives in national sport associations amounts to 33% in Sweden, 37% in Norway, 27% in Finland, 15% in Germany (European Commission, 2014), and 25% in Denmark (Ottesen et al., 2010). Earlier research for Norway has reported a female share of 17% for leading positions in sport organizations (Hovden, 2010), indicating that the representation of women has increased over the years. However, the numbers also reveal that achieving gender equality in the boardroom of sport organizations represents a challenge, even for countries leading in gender equality. For example, Norway was ranked third in the 2016 Global Gender Gap Report (World Economic Forum, 2016).

Table 15.2 summarizes the share of women in sport organizations in Germany in 2016. It shows that women are under-represented in leading positions, whereas the average share of women is higher in administrative (non-leading) positions. Sport governing bodies with special tasks (e.g., university sport, company sport, police sport, Special Olympics Germany) tend to have higher female representation than national sport associations and state sports confederations. The overview indicates large differences among sport organizations, with female shares ranging between both extremes of 0% and 100%. These figures indicate that women are not represented in the same manner in leading positions of national and state sport organizations as they are in community sport. Approximately 40% of members in local community sports clubs are women (German Olympic Sports Confederation [DOSB], 2016a), similar to Norway (Hovden, 2010). Likewise, female athletes are important to elite sporting success in Germany. Since the 2000 Games, the share of female medalists has been between 36.0% and 46.7% in the summer Olympic Games (Table 15.3). In the winter Games, this proportion was between 52.9% and 62.1%. Given that female athletes have fewer opportunities to win medals, women have contributed over-proportionately to the final medal count. The importance of women in both amateur and elite sports raises the question, why are women still under-represented on the boards of sport governing bodies?

Table 15.2 Share of women in publicly funded sport organizations in Germany in 2016

Organization	Share of women (%)		
	Mean	Minimum	Maximum
Executive board			
National sport associations	17.5	0	40.0
State sports confederations	25.2	11.1	44.4
Sport governing bodies with special tasks	32.4	0	55.6
Administrative office (full-time employment)			
National sport associations	52.3	0.0	100
State sports confederations	56.9	44.4	69.2
Sport governing bodies with special tasks	63.8	33.3	100
1. Administrative office (leading positions)			
National sport associations	19.2	0	60.0
State sports confederations	13.5	0	100
Sport governing bodies with special tasks	50.0	0	100
Delegates of member meetings			
National sport associations	17.7	0	39.4
State sports confederations	17.2	8.5	25.1
Sport governing bodies with special tasks	33.0	0	44.7

Own presentation based on DOSB (2016b).

Table 15.3 Female competitions and German female medalists in the summer and winter Olympic Games, 2000–2016

Olympic Games	Share of female competitions (%)	Share of female medalists in Germany (%)
Summer Games		
Sydney 2000	41.7	36.0
Athens 2004	43.0	46.7
Beijing 2008	43.5	42.9
London 2012	45.2	32.5
Rio de Janeiro 2016	45.8	41.7
Winter Games		
Salt Lake City 2002	44.7	58.3
Turin 2006	45.1	55.2
Vancouver 2010	45.2	62.1
Sochi 2014	46.2	52.9

Own calculations.

Explanations for female under-representation

Several explanations for female under-representation in boardrooms of sport organizations have been advanced (for overviews, see Burton, 2015; Cunningham, 2008; Cunningham & Sagas, 2008). For example, Adriaanse and Schofield (2014) have explained gender inequality with structures of social practice that are subsumed under a four-dimensional *gender regime* (Connell, 2009). The first dimension is production relationships reflecting traditionally gendered divisions of labor. The second is power relationships including exercise of authority, patriarchy, and males dominating females (Adriaanse & Schofield, 2014). Existing research has shown that masculine hegemony is a constraint to gender equality (Adriaanse & Schofield, 2013), and that hegemonic masculinity restricts access for women to boards and leadership positions (Burton, 2015).

Emotional relationships represent the third dimension and include patterns of attachment and hostility between males and females, which can be seen in the ways they support or undermine each other's work (Adriaanse & Schofield, 2014). Previous research has found that gender-equal governance is facilitated through influential men supporting women on the board (Adriaanse & Schofield, 2013), as opposed to undermining their way to the upper echelons of decision-making. The fourth dimension, symbolic relations, captures beliefs about gender equality (Adriaanse & Schofield, 2014). Board directors and chief executive officers must be committed to gender equality in governance so that it can be achieved (Adriaanse & Schofield, 2013). In particular, the selection process is critical. However, males often frame and impact this process in a way that insures that the male-dominated culture on boards is reproduced and female entrance is made difficult (Claringbould & Knoppers, 2007).

Importantly, changes in the above relationships cannot be prescribed by external institutions, meaning that beliefs and attachment can be changed only by the individuals themselves. Connell (2009) has stressed that gender is a social process that must be learned and experienced. Therefore, achieving gender equality is complicated and challenging, and males must be willing to change their behavior and mindset.

Strategies to increase gender equality

Different strategies can be pursued to increase the share of women in leadership positions, such as the implementation of gender quotas, self-imposed regulations, and using gender policies as funding tools. An often-discussed strategy is the implementation of a gender quota. As sport organizations in western European countries are voluntary (non-profit) organizations, they are not subject to government legislation. For example, in Denmark, equal opportunity legislation did not impact sport organizations (Ottesen et al., 2010). Nevertheless, as sport is also a mirror of society, broader societal and political developments are reflected in sport organizations. Accordingly, public debates on gender equality and the implementation of gender quotas for private or public companies have affected sport organizations in several European countries, such as Norway and Sweden (Ottesen et al., 2010). These Scandinavian countries can be considered Europe's pioneers because their sport organizations became concerned with gender equality in the 1980s.

For example, the Norwegian Olympic and Paralympic Committee and Confederation of Sports (NIF) chose to follow societal changes and incorporated gender equality in its own statutes (Ottesen et al., 2010). In Norway, the process of gender quota legislation started in 1979, with several amendments and extensions being made before sanctions had to be introduced in 2005 for companies unwilling to comply (Sisjord et al., 2017). Within sport, the process started in 1987 when the General Assembly of the NIF passed a gender quota system for boards within the NIF, as well as national and regional federations. This gender quota was refined in 1990 and in 2007, and the NIF decided on its application to all sport organizations (Skirstad, 2009). Exceptions were accepted only under extraordinary conditions and not meeting the quota led to new elections (Sisjord et al., 2017). The quota was effective. The NIF, most national federations, and all regional federations composed their executive boards in line with the gender quota (Sisjord et al., 2017). Similar to Norway, the official public equal opportunities strategy affected sport organizations in Sweden (despite being autonomous) and they decided to be proactive (Ottesen et al., 2010). The results included the development of an equal opportunities plan and Swedish men expressing favorable attitude toward equal opportunities and a desire to change the situation.

The German Olympic Sports Confederation (DOSB) is an example of a self-imposed regulation that is not binding for national or regional sport organizations. To improve gender equality, it included regulations concerning elected members and executive board members in its statutes. Of the 15 elected members, at least five had to be female, ensuring a female share of at least 33%. On the executive board, at least 30% of members must be female (DOSB, 2015).

In the absence of gender quotas and self-regulating efforts, governments might consider putting pressure on sport organizations by requesting achievements in gender equality in exchange for government funding. In England, the implementation of gender equality policies has been discussed for a while, including the role of such policies as funding tools (Shaw & Penney, 2003). More than a decade later, the government published its Sporting Future strategy (HM Government, 2015), including several measures for improving diversity in leadership positions. Accordingly, the publicly funded governing bodies Sport England and UK Sport have established a list of governance criteria that national sport associations must meet in order to receive public funding. As part of this new *Code for Sports Governance*, national sport associations are expected to have at least 30% gender diversity on their executive boards to reflect the public they represent more adequately. In addition to reductions in public funding, the government also considers further punitive measures, such as withdrawing public support when national governing bodies bid to host major sport events (BBC, 2016). In the case of the English Football

Association, which enjoys billions of dollars in revenue from the sale of broadcasting rights, such a measure may even be more effective than reducing public funding.

Effects of increasing gender equality

This section discusses how increasing gender equality might affect sport organizations and elite sport systems. In terms of organizational outcomes, previous research has found that sport organizations with a higher share of women on the board experience fewer organizational problems (Wicker, Breuer, & von Hanau, 2012). Specifically, organizations with at least 40% women on the board reported significantly smaller problems with regard to the recruitment and retention of members, volunteers, and coaches, the financial situation, and dealing with bureaucracy and demographic changes in the region. These positive organizational outcomes can be explained by differences in leadership styles between women and men (e.g., Cunningham & Sagas, 2008). They suggest that reporting a higher share of women in leading positions is not only good in itself, but can also be beneficial for sport organizations.

Gender equality can also be beneficial to elite sport systems. Existing research has documented a positive effect of gender equality in a country on the number of Olympic medals won by men and women (Berdahl, Uhlmann, & Bai, 2015). This result also holds when controlling for population size and gross domestic product, which are well-established predictors of Olympic medal success (Forrest, McHale, Sanz, & Tena, 2017). Likewise, a country's level of gender equality was found to be positively associated with the women's national football teams' international sporting performance in terms of FIFA ranking points (Jacobs, 2014). These findings suggest that increasing gender equality facilitates a release of the performance potential of both women and men.

Elite sport coaches and gender equality

In many western European countries, elite sport coaches are directly or indirectly funded by the government. The discussion about gender equality among elite sport coaches focuses on employment and coach characteristics, including qualifications and pay.

Starting with employment, elite sport coaching across Europe is characterized by a low share of women. For example, the share of women among national coaches was estimated at 10% in Germany, 11% in Sweden (European Commission, 2014), 10% in the UK (HM Government, 2015), and 14% in Norway (Fasting, Sisjord, & Sand, 2017). Even though Norway can be considered a leader in Europe in terms of promoting and reinforcing gender equality in and outside of sport (Fasting et al., 2017), female representation among elite sport coaches is still far away from the gender balance zone. Altogether, it seems still to be difficult for women to obtain leading coaching positions. This scarcity of women in visible coaching positions should not be underestimated because same-gender role models are important for recruiting coaches at lower levels of sport (Greenhill, Auld, Cuskelly, & Hooper, 2009).

Once hired, female and male coaches were found to be similar, but not equal (e.g., Fasting et al., 2017; Wicker, Orlowski, & Breuer, 2016). For instance, in Norway, female coaches were younger and had less coaching experience than their male counterparts, but the share of coaches with their own athletic career at the international level and with coach education was higher among women (Fasting et al., 2017). In Germany, female coaches have similar coaching experience and tenure despite being significantly younger (Table 15.4). The monthly net income of female coaches is lower, but the gender difference is not statistically significant, indicating that there is no empirical evidence for a *gender wage gap* in elite sport coaching (Wicker et al., 2016).

It is interesting that female coaches are less likely to be married and have children, suggesting that elite sport coaching is associated with family constraints for women, but not for men. Research in the UK indicating that work–life balance poses a challenge to female elite sport coaches supports this finding (HM Government, 2015).

Concerning formal coaching qualifications, Table 15.4 shows that female coaches in Germany are significantly less likely to possess an A- or B-license, the highest coaching licenses in the German sport system, and to have a DOSB-Diploma, a coaching degree from the Coaching Academy of the German Olympic Sports Confederation. These findings are supported by official statistics showing that the share of women decreases with increasing coaching qualifications, whereas 50% of coaches with a C-license for high-performance sport are women. The share of women among coaches with an A-license is below 15% (DOSB, 2016b). Table 15.4 further reveals that female coaches are significantly less likely to coach athletes who are among the top five in their sport worldwide. Altogether, these numbers indicate that acquiring high-level coaching qualifications may pose a barrier unique for female coaches, making it difficult to reach the upper echelons of elite sport coaching.

Elite athletes and gender equality

This section discusses gender equality among elite athletes through the lens of government funding, and centers on pay of national team players in football. Even though direct public funds

Table 15.4 Characteristics of publicly funded female and male elite sport coaches employed in Germany in 2015 (mean values or share of respondents as a percentage)

Variable	Women (n = 39)	Men (n = 147)	Student's t-test	P
Age (years)	39.9	43.8	−2.076	0.039*
Years of experience as a coach	15.7	17.7	−1.122	0.264
Years in current coach position	8.4	7.9	0.354	0.724
Migration (%)	10.3	13.6	−0.552	0.581
Coach is married (%)	69.2	87.1	−2.696	0.008**
Coach has at least one child (%)	33.3	62.6	−3.356	0.001***
Monthly net income (€)	2485.15	2866.32	−0.827	0.409
Weekly working hours	41.2	50.9	−3.862	<0.001***
Top5 (%)	25.6	65.3	−4.680	<0.001***
Top10 (%)	33.3	21.1	1.602	0.111
Top15 (%)	41.0	13.6	3.995	<0.001***
A-License (%)	64.1	79.6	−2.035	0.043*
B-License (%)	38.5	21.1	2.254	0.025*
C-License (%)	20.5	11.6	1.457	0.147
DOSB-Diploma (%)	12.8	35.4	−2.757	0.006**
DOSB-License (%)	5.1	4.8	0.094	0.925
University degree in sports sciences (%)	38.5	42.9	−0.492	0.623

Own calculations based on data from Wicker et al. (2016); *$P<0.05$; **$P<0.01$; ***$P<0.001$.

are relatively small in commercialized sports such as football, sport governing bodies tend to pay reduced taxes as a result of their legal form – an indirect form of public funding. Hence, player payments are related to indirect government support.

The public debate started with five top players of the US national team appealing for workplace discrimination in 2016. They argued that, with several World Cup titles and Olympic gold medals, they were far more successful than their male counterparts, but received lower payments by the US Soccer Federation for appearances on the national team and advancing in deeper rounds in international tournaments (Das, 2016). From an economic viewpoint, gender differences in pay are typically explained by differences in commercial revenues (e.g., broadcasting rights, game revenues) (Conerly, 2016), which may, however, not hold in this specific case (Das, 2016).

Potentially inspired by the discussion in North America, the Norwegian Football Association was the first governing body to determine equal pay for female and male players on national teams. Equal pay was achieved because the male national team was willing to forgo a specific proportion of their revenues generated through commercial activities. Although the resulting pay differences tend to be minimal for males, payments for females increased significantly. Female players consider it an important sign of recognition that could be a signal for other parts of society (Sportschau, 2017b). Having a similar goal in mind, the Danish female national team put pressure on their national governing body by going on strike. The team did not compete in a World Cup qualifier game and a friendly match. Discussions between the female national team and the sport governing body were still ongoing at the time of this writing (Sportschau, 2017a).

Conclusion

This chapter discussed gender equality in sport in Europe through the lens of public expenditure. Independent of whether government funding is targeted directly at recipients or indirectly via sport governing bodies, gender equality in leading positions of sport governing bodies, in elite sport coaching, and in terms of equal pay for athletes has not yet been achieved – with a few exceptions in Norway and Sweden. Excluding women from executive boards and coaching positions leaves a large gap in unexploited potential because talent is not drawn from the widest pool available. Several strategies to increase gender equality have been discussed, including the opportunity to use gender policies as a funding tool. The current academic debate focuses on identifying barriers for women and developing strategies to improve gender equality. Future research should examine the effectiveness of strategies to increase gender equality, for example by studying the relationship between gender composition of executive boards and performance of sport governing bodies.

Leader profile: Bibiana Steinhaus

In football, a male-dominated sport,[1] not only female players fight for gender equality, but also female referees. Bibiana Steinhaus, born in March 1979, is a referee in German professional football (Figure 15.1). She is the first female referee ever who refereed a match of the male Football Bundesliga, the top tier of professional football in Germany. This match on September 10, 2017 received considerable media attention. With her excellent performance, Steinhaus demonstrated that females have the ability to referee male games, despite all objections that have been put forth in the past.

Her achievement can be considered outstanding because opposite-sex referees are the exception in professional football. Accordingly, Steinhaus's career started in women's football

Figure 15.1 Bibiana Steinhaus refereeing her first game in the first division of German male soccer (Football Bundesliga) in September 2017, together with Vedad Ibisevic from Hertha BSC Berlin (Source: picture alliance/Thomas Eisenhuth/dpa-Zentralbild/ZB)

where she regularly refereed games in the Women's Bundesliga, the German Cup, and in international women's football tournaments, including European Championships, World Championships, and the Olympic Games. She is the first female referee who has refereed a World Cup final, an Olympic final, and a Champions League final in women's football. Given this track record, she has already been considered one of the best referees (if not the best referee) in women's football.

The road to her breakthrough in men's football has been long and not without obstacles. Generally speaking, referees start in amateur leagues. When they receive favorable evaluations and perform better than other referees of the same status group, they can get promoted to a higher status, such as a second division Bundesliga referee and a first division Bundesliga referee. Promotions are separate for male and female leagues. Hence, Steinhaus had to outperform several male referees throughout her career to achieve the status of a first Bundesliga referee in male football.

The promotion from second to first division took 10 years because she had refereed a game of the second Bundesliga in the 2007–2008 season. During this period, she had to demonstrate her refereeing ability by serving as fourth referee in first division games (e.g., overseeing the coaching zone, announcing substitutions and extra time). Hence, she was patient, persistent, and willing to showcase that she can earn respect in this male-dominated business. She is a role model in terms of perseverance, dedication, and the fight against discrimination of females. Therefore, Bibiana Steinhaus can be considered a female leader who made significant contributions to the way women are perceived in a male-dominated sport like football.

Note

1 With one out 17 executive board members being female (5.9%), the German Football Association is below the German average of national sport associations (see Table 15.2).

References

Adriaanse, J. A. & Schofield, T. (2013). Analysing gender dynamics in sport governance: A new regimes-based approach. *Sport Management Review*, **16**, 498–513.
Adriaanse, J. A. & Schofield, T. (2014). The impact of gender quotas on gender equality in sport governance. *Journal of Sport Management*, **28**, 485–497.
Austrian Ministry for Sport (2011). Sportförderbericht 2007–2011. Retrieved from https://www.sportministerium.at/de/themen/sportbericht (accessed November 16, 2017).
Austrian Ministry for Sport (2012). *Sportförderbericht Sportgroßevents*. Retrieved, from https://www.sportministerium.at/de/themen/sportbericht (accessed October 26, 2017).
BBC (2016). Funding warning for sports governing bodies under new gender diversity code. Retrieved from www.bbc.com/sport/37823821 (accessed October 9, 2017).
Berdahl, J. L., Uhlmann, E. L., & Bai, F. (2015). Win–win: Female and male athletes from more gender equal nations perform better in international sports competitions. *Journal of Experimental Social Psychology*, **56**, 1–3.
Bozhinov, V. (2017). Shareholder wealth effects of policies promoting women on boards: Evidence from Germany. SSRN Working Paper. Retrieved from https://papers.ssrn.com/sol3/papers.cfm?abstract_id=3006020 (accessed November 16, 2017).
Burton, L. (2015). Underrepresentation of women in sport leadership: A review of research. *Sport Management Review*, **18**, 155–165.
Chen, L. (2013). Do female politicians influence public spending? Evidence from Taiwan. *International Journal of Applied Economics*, **10**(2), 32–51.
Claringbould, I. & Knoppers, A. (2007). Finding a "normal" woman: Selection processes for board membership. *Sex Roles*, **56**, 495–507.
Conerly, B. (2016). U.S. women's soccer salaries: The economic justification for paying the men more. Retrieved from https://www.forbes.com/sites/billconerly/2016/04/12/womens-soccer-salaries-the-economic-justification/#670852971ad8 (accessed October 19, 2017).
Connell, R. (2009). *Gender*. Cambridge: Polity Press.
Cunningham, G. (2008). Creating and sustaining gender diversity in sport organizations. *Sex Roles*, **58**, 136–145.
Cunningham, G. & Sagas, M. (2008). Gender and diversity in sport organizations: Introduction to a special issue. *Sex Roles*, **58**, 3–9.
Das, A. (2016). Pay disparity in U.S. soccer? It's complicated. Retrieved from https://www.nytimes.com/2016/04/22/sports/soccer/usmnt-uswnt-soccer-equal-pay.html (accessed October 19, 2017).
DOSB (2015). Satzung des DOSB. Retrieved from https://www.dosb.de/de/organisation/wir-ueber-uns/satzung-und-ordnungen (accessed October 26, 2017).
DOSB (2016a). Bestandserhebung 2016. Retrieved from https://www.dosb.de/medien-service/statistiken (accessed October 26, 2017).
DOSB (2016b). Gleichstellungsbericht. Retrieved from https://www.dosb.de/de/gleichstellung-im-sport/service/downloads/gleichstellungsbericht (accessed October 26, 2017).
Downward, P., Dawson, A., & Dejonghe, T. (2009). *Sports Economics. Theory, evidence and policy*. Oxford: Butterworth-Heinemann.
European Commission (2014). *Gender Equality in Sport*. Retrieved from http://ec.europa.eu/sport/events/2013/documents/20131203-gender/final-proposal-1802_en.pdf (accessed October 20, 2017).
European Institute for Gender Equality (EIGE) (2015). Gender equality in sport. Retrieved from https://www.eige.europa.eu/sites/default/files/documents/mh0215937enn.pdf (accessed October 20, 2017).
Fasting, K., Sisjord, M. K., & Sand, T. S. (2017). Norwegian elite-level coaches: Who are they? *Scandinavian Sport Studies Forum*, **8**, 29–47.
Fischer, C. (2013). France. In K. Hallmann & K. Petry (eds), *Comparative Sport Development: Systems, participation and public policy* (pp. 61–74). Heidelberg: Springer.
Forrest, D., McHale, I. G., Sanz, I., & Tena, J. D. (2017). An analysis of country medal shares in individual sports at the Olympics. *European Sport Management Quarterly*, **17**(2), 117–131.

Greenhill, J., Auld, C., Cuskelly, G., & Hooper, S. (2009). The impact of organisational factors on career pathways for female coaches. *Sport Management Review*, **12**, 229–240.

Hallmann, K. & Petry, K. (eds) (2013). *Comparative Sport Development: Systems, participation and public policy*. Heidelberg: Springer.

Henry, I. (2009). European models of sport: Governance, organisational change and sports policy in the EU. *Hitotsubashi Journal of Arts and Sciences*, **50**, 41–52.

HM Government (2015). Sporting future: A new strategy for an active nation. Retrieved from https://www.gov.uk/government/uploads/system/uploads/attachment_data/file/486622/Sporting_Future_ACCESSIBLE.pdf (accessed March 13, 2017).

Hoekman, R. & Breedveld, K. (2013). The Netherlands. In K. Hallmann & K. Petry (eds), *Comparative Sport Development: Systems, participation and public policy* (pp. 119–134). Heidelberg: Springer.

Horch, H. (1994). On the socio-economics of voluntary organisations. *Voluntas*, **5**(2), 219–230.

Hovden, J. (2010). Female top leaders – prisoners of gender? The gendering of leadership discourses in Norwegian sports organizations. *International Journal of Sport Policy and Politics*, **2**(2), 189–203.

Jacobs, C. (2014). Programme-level determinants of women's international football performance. *European Sport Management Quarterly*, **14**(5), 521–537.

Ottesen, L., Skirstad, B., Pfister, G., & Habermann, U. (2010). Gender relations in Scandinavian sport organizations – a comparison of the situation and the policies in Denmark, Norway and Sweden. *Sport in Society*, **13**(4), 657–675.

Petry, K. & Hallmann, K. (2013). Germany. In K. Hallmann & K. Petry (eds), *Comparative Sport Development: Systems, participation and public policy* (pp. 75–86). Heidelberg: Springer.

Shaw, S. & Penney, D. (2003). Gender equity policies in national governing bodies: An oxymoron or a vehicle for change? *European Sport Management Quarterly*, **3**(2), 78–102.

Sisjord, M. K., Fasting, K., & Sand, T. S. (2017). The impact of gender quotas in leadership in Norwegian organised sport. *International Journal of Sport Policy and Politics*, **9**(3), 505–519.

Skirstad, B. (2009). Gender policy and organizational change: A contextual approach. *Sport Management Review*, **12**, 202–216.

Sportschau (2017a). Dänemarks Fußballerinnen sagen WM-Qualifikationsspiel ab. Retrieved from www.sportschau.de/fussball/frauenfussball/frauenfussball-daenemark-wm-qualifikation-absage-100.html (accessed October 19, 2017).

Sportschau (2017b). Nationalspielerinnen bekommen mehr Geld. Retrieved from www.sportschau.de/fussball/international/norwegen-fussball-equalpay-100.html (accessed October 10, 2017).

Vehmas, H. & Ilmanen, K. (2013). Finland. In K. Hallmann & K. Petry (eds), *Comparative Sport Development: Systems, participation and public policy* (pp. 47–60). Heidelberg: Springer.

VOCASPORT Research Group (2004). Vocational education and training in the field of sport in the European Union: situation, trends and outlook. Retrieved from eose.org/wp-content/uploads/2014/03/vocasport-Final-Report-English-Version.pdf (accessed June 1, 2018).

Vos, S., Breesch, D, Késenne, S., Van Hoecke, J., Vanreusel, B., & Scheerder, J. (2011). Governmental subsidies and coercive isomorphism. Evidence from sports clubs and their resource dependencies. *European Journal for Sport and Society*, **8**(4), 257–280.

Wicker, P., Breuer, C., & von Hanau, T. (2012). Gender effects on organizational problems – evidence from non-profit sports clubs in Germany. *Sex Roles: A Journal of Research*, **66**(1), 105–116.

Wicker, P., Orlowski, J., & Breuer, C. (2016). Human capital, formal qualifications and income of elite sport coaches. *International Journal of Sport Finance*, **11**(3), 204–220.

World Economic Forum (2016). *The Global Gender Gap Report 2016*. Retrieved from http://reports.weforum.org/global-gender-gap-report-2016 (accessed October 20, 2017).

16
The new gender equity in elite women's sports

Dionne Koller

Gender equity in sports is an issue that many believe has been resolved. It is no longer abnormal or even outright prohibited for women and girls to participate, and they do so in record numbers. Women in my classes often are not familiar with Title IX—the groundbreaking federal law that prohibits gender discrimination in education programs that receive federal funding—and its application to sports. Many do not understand why it was necessary to legally require gender equity in education-based sports programs. Others believe that Title IX largely has achieved its purpose, and that women and girls have the same opportunities to participate in sports as men.

Measured by participation statistics, it is clear that women and girls who choose to participate in sports have come a long way. In 1971, 1 in 27 girls participated in high school sports. By 2008, that number grew to 1 in 2.4 (Women's Sports Foundation, 2009). The National Federation of State High School Associations (NFHS) participation data show that, in 1971, just before Title IX was enacted, there were 3,666,917 boys and 294,015 girls participating in high school athletics (Acosta & Carpenter, 2012). Today, more than 3.4 million girls participate in high school sports, compared with a little over 4.5 million boys (NFHS, 2017).

Similarly, at the intercollegiate level, there has been substantial growth in the number of female athletes. In 1970, before the enactment of Title IX, there were only 2.5 women's teams per school and only about 16,000 total female intercollegiate athletes (Acosta & Carpenter, 2012). By 2012, the average number of women's teams per school was 8.73. Today, there are over 200,000 female intercollegiate athletes (National Collegiate Athletic Association [NCAA], 2016).

Social norms around women's and girls' participation in sports have also changed dramatically. Before the passage of Title IX, the message to females, taken as a seemingly natural understanding and reinforced by the law, was that sports were an activity for males only. Sport programs played a role in reinforcing these gender stereotypes by signaling that sport participation by women was not normal (Koller, 2012). Since Title IX, the law and court decisions enforcing it have sent the message that women and girls are entitled to participate in athletics, and on terms equal to men and boys. The law helped to erode the stigma that formerly attached to women's participation in sports and shifted the dynamic, so that an ever-greater stigma now attaches to institutions and individuals who discriminate against women athletes (Koller, 2012).

Measured then by the change in numbers of participants and social norms in the years since Title IX was enacted, some might suggest that gender equity in sports is a reality. However, decades of increased sport participation by women and changing social norms, although significant, do not signal the end of the struggle. First, there is still important work to do to ensure that all women and girls benefit from Title IX's mandate, especially girls and women of color and those from disadvantaged socioeconomic backgrounds. And, in addition to ensuring even wider participation, there is a new focus in the battle for gender equity in sports. Beyond simply getting women in the game, the fight now frequently focuses on equal pay and benefits—especially at the elite level.

Recent actions taken by elite women's soccer and hockey players have shed light on striking disparities in pay and benefits between the men's and the women's programs. Such examples make clear that, although women and girls today have much greater access to sports than ever before, and have enjoyed remarkable success, it is also apparent that greater access has not necessarily translated to equitable treatment, especially in the form of pay and other benefits for elite women athletes. This chapter explores the legal contours of this issue and argues that the next step in the fight for gender equity in sport is ensuring that our elite women athletes are provided equitable treatment and compensation.

Title IX and elite women's athletics

At the outset, it is important to consider the role of Title IX in shaping our understanding of gender equity in sports and increasing the number of female athletes. Congress enacted Title IX in 1972 to prohibit discrimination on the basis of gender in all education programs receiving federal financial assistance. Title IX is not targeted to and makes no mention of athletics programs (Title IX, 20 U.S.C. § 1681(a)).

Congress subsequently directed what was then the Department of Health Education and Welfare to prepare regulations that would implement Title IX in the area of intercollegiate and interscholastic sports (Education Amendments of 1974). Title IX's application to sports was frequently challenged, first by the NCAA and later by groups representing men's sports interests. Courts have uniformly held that the statute and its implementing regulations are constitutional (Koller, 2010), and, despite the backlash, the law has shaped the way educational institutions structure their athletics programs for more than 45 years.

Title IX's goals are said to be twofold. First, the statute and regulations seek to guarantee equal athletic opportunity for women and girls currently participating in education-based sports programs. The second goal is to send a message through equal athletic opportunity to prospective female athletes, on the theory that providing gender equity in athletics will develop women's interest in participation. This has been called the "trickle down" theory (Olson, 1991) and it is assumed that Title IX will not simply guarantee formal equality, but also shape norms for sports participation in a way that inspires women and girls to participate (Brake, 2001).

Scholars have explained that Title IX, as applied to sports, takes an approach to equality that differs from the approach reflected in other sex discrimination laws (Brake, 2001). Title IX does this by going beyond a formal equality approach to achieve a kind of substantive equality as well (Cohen, 2005). This is because, as courts and scholars have long recognized, a purely formal equality interpretation of Title IX would achieve little, because differences between men's and women's interest in athletics are the result of discriminatory social relationships and institutional practices that "construct" such differences (Brake, 2001). Historically, only men had the opportunity to develop the interest and ability to participate in sports. Women were conditioned not to seek athletic opportunities or participate in sports, and opportunities for them to do so were severely limited (Buzuvis, 2006).

As a result of this, the law had to account for the fact that women naturally would not have the same interest and ability to engage in sports because of significant past discrimination. Title IX's substantive equality approach is referred to as "structural equality," and it is based on the notion that women's expressed interest in athletics cannot be weighted equally against men's because such "interest" might instead be the result of social factors that discourage women's athletic participation, rather than the result of authentic choices (Brake, 2001). Instead, the theory is that changing the structure of athletics by creating opportunities for women to participate and removing stigmas against such participation are what is needed to develop women's interest in sports (Koller, 2010).

Title IX incorporates this substantive, structural approach to equality primarily through the so-called "three-part test" for compliance. Through this test, schools are required to create opportunities for girls and women to participate in sports to stimulate females' interest in participating (Brake, 2007). Title IX does not require gender-neutral assessments of athletic ability, but instead allows institutions to offer separate male and female teams (Brake, 2010). More than that, Title IX has a substantive equality element in that it does not require institutions to offer the same sports for men and women. Title IX grants women greater rights to try out for a men's team (and is much more restrictive in allowing men to try out for a women's team) because of the history of discrimination against women in sports (Brake, 2010). It is clear, then, that the theory and practical impact of Title IX, and the discourse around it, has focused most heavily on opportunities for women and girls to *participate*.

In addition to its success in expanding overall participation opportunities for women, Title IX's narrative has often focused on the number and success of elite female athletes. For example, the court in *Cohen v. Brown University* 1996 stated that:

> One need look no further than the impressive performances of our country's women athletes in the 1996 Olympic Summer Games to see that Title IX has had a dramatic and positive impact on the capabilities of our women athletes, particularly in team sports. These Olympians represent the first full generation of women to grow up under the aegis of Title IX. The unprecedented success of these athletes is due, in no small measure, to Title IX's beneficent effects on women's sports ... what stimulated this remarkable change in the quality of women's athletic competition was not a sudden, anomalous upsurge in women's interest in sports, but the enforcement of Title IX ...
>
> *(Cohen, 101 F.3d 155)*

Similarly, in upholding Title IX, the court in *Neal v. Bd. Of Trustees of Cal. State Univs.* 1999 explained that:

> [T]his past summer, 90,185 enthusiastic fans crowded into Pasadena's historic Rose Bowl for the finals of the Women's World Cup Soccer match ... the victory sparked a national celebration and a realization by many that women's sports could be just as exciting, competitive, and lucrative as men's sports ...
>
> *(Neal, 198 F.3d 763)*

Government officials also often cite the development and success of elite female athletes as a reason to support Title IX. For example, the Department of Education's Office of Civil Rights (OCR) has highlighted women's basketball as an example of Title IX's success. The OCR stated that:

In 1972, 132,299 young girls played high school basketball. In 1994–95 the number had increased to 412,576, an increase of over 300 percent. In the last two years, women's basketball has come of age with the gold-medal victory of the American women's basketball team at the 1996 Olympics, the increased media attention to the NCAA women's basketball tournament, and the development of two professional women's basketball leagues.

(Department of Education, 1997, para. 2)

The OCR also touted women's success in soccer, stating that "in one sport that is more and more a favorite for young girls—soccer—the results have led to a World Cup Championship. In 1996, the U.S. National soccer team captured the first-ever women's Olympic medal in this sport before a crowd of 76,481, and in doing so, established its position as the world's premier women's soccer program" (Department of Education, 1997, para. 4).

Policymakers have also explicitly linked Title IX to the success of the United States Olympic program. Indeed, many members of Congress hoped the law would increase our pipeline of female Olympians. As stated by one Department of Education official:

Senator Hatch has perhaps captured the essence of the meaning and promise of Title IX. In 1984, on the Senate floor, he observed that there were few, if any, Senators who did not want Title IX implemented so as to continue to encourage women throughout America to develop into Olympic athletes . . .

(Amateur Sports Act: Hearing 1995)

Gender equity and the Amateur Sports Act

Although Title IX provided the legal framework for gender equity in education-based sport programs, the law's reach has been felt far beyond sports in schools. Most prominently, Congress incorporated Title IX's goal of encouraging more girls and women to participate in sports into the Amateur Sports Act. Congress enacted the Amateur Sports Act in 1978 for the purpose of improving our nation's overall performance in Olympic and elite international competition (Koller, 2016). Although Title IX applies to educational programs that receive federal funding, it does not apply to the United States Olympic Committee (USOC), a private corporation, or US Olympic movement sports, all of which are regulated by private national governing bodies (NGBs) (Ted Stevens Olympic and Amateur Sports Act 2012).

Nevertheless, Congress incorporated in the Amateur Sports Act Title IX's intent to promote gender equity in sports. Congress did so by providing that one of the purposes of the USOC was to "encourage and provide assistance to amateur athletic activities for women" (Ted Stevens Olympic and Amateur Sports Act, 36 U.S.C. § 220503(12)). The statute also requires sport NGBs to "provide equitable support and encouragement for participation by women where separate programs for male and female athletes are conducted on a national basis" (Ted Stevens Olympic and Amateur Sports Act, 36 U.S.C. § 220524(6)). Consistent with the early 1970s' drive to create more athletic opportunities for women, these general provisions are aimed at supporting and encouraging "participation," and are not focused on other measures of equality, such as equal pay or benefits.

From this perspective, Title IX's principles have provided an important payoff through the American Olympic movement in that a greater number of female athletes and greater support for female athletics have meant, predictably, more and better elite women athletes (Rubin, 2016). The USOC has harnessed this increase in women's sport participation and translated it into substantial representation for women in the American Olympic program. For instance, in the 2016 Rio Olympic Games, Team USA comprised 291 women and 263 men (USOC, 2016). In the 2018 Winter Games, there were 109 women and 135 men (Team USA, 2018). From the perspective of *participation opportunities*, the US Olympic movement is living up to the ideals expressed through Title IX.

Moreover, in addition to citing participation statistics, the USOC touts its effectiveness in providing support to women athletes by referencing the *success* of the women in the Olympic program. The USOC stated in its most recent report to Congress that "[e]quality was once again at the forefront, with American women winning more than half of Team USA's medals at the Olympic and Paralympic Games" (USOC, 2016, p. 3). Indeed, women's success in the Olympic Games is the reason why the United States is frequently at the top of the overall medal counts (Rubin, 2016). This trend is evident across winter and summer sports, with women winning more medals than men in the recent 2018 winter Olympics (Gajanan, 2018). Yet, although participation statistics and winning can be a measure of how robust the support for women's athletics is, the examples of the women's national soccer and hockey teams, explained below, demonstrate that these measures alone do not necessarily correlate with equitable treatment and are therefore an incomplete measure of equality.

The gender pay gap

Participation opportunities and athletic success are, however, only part of the story. For elite female athletes, the ability to participate is not the issue. Instead, the issue is in many cases equitable support and compensation. The pay gap in elite athletics reflects the unequal pay that is evident throughout the US workforce. In 2016, women working full time in the United States typically were paid just 80 percent of what men were paid (Miller, 2017). The pay gap has narrowed since the 1960s, due to women's progress in education and greater workforce participation. At this rate, women are expected to reach pay equity with men in 2059. Data from recent years, however, suggest that pay equity might not be achieved until 2119. The pay gap affects women from all backgrounds, at all ages, and at all levels of educational achievement (Miller, 2017).

Like women's participation and interest in athletics, the pay gap is a complicated issue influenced by many factors. Thus, the pay gap can reflect women's and men's choices. Similar to interest in athletics, these choices are influenced by social norms and gender stereotypes. Women and men often choose different college majors and career paths. Pay gaps between men and women are, however, evident at every education level and in nearly all occupations. Researchers have therefore asserted that not all of the gender pay gap can be accounted for by different choices such as college major, occupation, work hours, or time out of the workforce for childcare. Research suggests that discrimination and bias against women in the workplace are also a factor (Miller, 2017).

The law has not always been effective at closing the gender pay gap. Congress enacted the Equal Pay Act (EPA)—the first law prohibiting gender discrimination—in 1963. The EPA provides that male and female employees in the same workplace be paid equally for equal work (Eisenberg, 2010). The legal concept of equal pay for equal work therefore came long before Title IX and the movement to increase women's participation in sports. At the time the EPA was passed, women represented only one-third of the workforce and employers openly discriminated on the basis of sex in determining pay. Under the EPA, a female employee can legally establish a claim for discrimination by showing that she was paid differently, compared with her male peers, for equal work that requires "equal skill, effort, and responsibility," and that is performed under the same or similar working conditions (Eisenberg, 2010).

As with athletics since Congress enacted Title IX, in the decades since the EPA was passed, substantial numbers of women have entered the workforce, including in areas that were once dominated by men. This is especially true for professional and executive-level positions in fields such as law and medicine. Increasing numbers of women are also attaining higher levels of education, with young women more likely than men to enroll in college and earn Bachelor's and Master's degrees. About 50 percent of all professional and doctoral degrees are awarded to women (Eisenberg, 2010).

Yet, despite gains in education, professional women and those with more experience do not earn compensation on a par with their male peers. Research shows that the gender pay gap actually increases with the level of educational attainment and years of work experience. For instance, women university professors are on average paid 81 percent of the amount paid to their male peers (Eisenberg, 2010). In law, research shows that male lawyers routinely out-earn women, with female lawyers earning 77% of what their male peers did (Weiss, 2016). Similarly, women physicians and surgeons earn just under 60% of the incomes earned by their male peers, and women in management occupations earn only 72% of the earnings of comparable men. Wage gaps also exist for top women executives. In 2017, of the 15 highest paid executives in the United States, two were women. Although the highest paid male made almost US$244 million, the top woman made less than US$41 million (Carpenter, 2017). It is clear across a range of occupations that, as women achieve higher professional status, they experience a significant gender wage gap that is even greater than that for women in blue-collar employment (Eisenberg, 2010).

The pay gap in women's sports reflects this phenomenon. The equal pay issue in elite athletics was famously raised in 1973, when tennis great Billie Jean King formed the Women's Tennis Association and lobbied for equal prize money at the US Open. Since then, the pay gap in women's elite sports has remained a persistent issue. In the 1990s, women professional athletes were still earning far less than their male peers, and the trend has continued into the twenty-first century (Campbell, 2017). The pay disparity is present in both individual and team sports. The Professional Golf Association tour, for example, awards millions more in prize money than the Ladies Professional Golf Association tour. Similarly, the National Basketball Association pays its players hundreds of thousands of dollars more in average annual salary than the Women's National Basketball Association (Campbell, 2017).

As with other occupations, the difference in pay between male and female athletes has been justified by factors other than discrimination. Thus, sports organizers and commentators cite the perceived differences between male and female athletes' skills and abilities, and the fact that female athletes and teams generate less revenue than men (Campbell, 2017). In addition, in the professional sport realm, efforts to close the pay gap have not been successful due to limited legal options. In most cases, women's professional sports leagues or tours are operated separately from those for males. As they do not share a common employer, women are unable to claim that gender discrimination resulted in lower pay (Campbell, 2017).

Gender equity in sports: The next frontier

In 2016, the gender equity conversation around sports, at least for elite athletes, moved from emphasizing participation and success to demanding equal pay and benefits. This shift was the result of the unique circumstances presented by the US Women's National Soccer team. Five members of the team brought a claim against the NGB for soccer in the United States, the United States Soccer Federation (USSF), alleging that they were discriminated against on the basis of gender in violation of the Equal Pay Act and Title VII of the Civil Rights Act (Das, 2016).

In their complaint, the women detailed the ways in which their pay and benefits were less generous than those provided to their male peers. The players also asserted that the lower pay and unequal treatment occurred despite the fact that the women's team has been far more successful than the men's. The women stated that their team "has enjoyed unparalleled success in international soccer, winning three World Cup titles and four Olympic gold medals—an accomplishment that no other country on the men's or women's side has reached in Olympic competition." The women also noted that their team has been ranked number one on the world "for the last 7 years" (Perez, 2016, para. 2).

The women asserted that, after their World Cup victory in 2015, the USSF earned a projected US$17 million profit, with a net profit of US$5 million for the women's team and a net loss of nearly US$1 million for the men's national team. Despite this, the women claimed that they were paid "substantially less" than men's national team players, including receiving between 38 and 72 percent of the compensation that men receive for participating in international matches. The women also asserted that, in 2015, the men's national team earned US$9 million for losing in the World Cup Round of 16, whereas the women earned only US$2 million for winning the World Cup. The women claimed that the disparity affected other elements of their compensation, including their per diem while traveling (for example, men received US$62.50 for domestic travel and US$75 for international, compared with US$50 and US$60 for women) (Das, 2016).

What was unique about the claims made by the US Women's Soccer team compared with claims made by women athletes in the past is that the women were employed by the same employer as the men, the USSF. With a single employer, the women were able to use anti-discrimination law to attempt to advance their claim. In addition, the women's team also was in the unique position of generating, at least in the short term, far more revenue, viewership, and fan interest than the men. Finally, the women had achieved greater athletic success than the men, with their many World Cup and Olympic wins. Although the women received strong public support, very few men's national team players publicly supported their efforts.

Similarly, the US Women's National Hockey team, in 2017, announced that they would boycott the upcoming world championships if USA Hockey did not agree to increase their pay and benefits to be more consistent with what the men were provided (Berkman, 2017). The women sought a livable wage so they could focus on their training. At the time of the boycott, they earned US$6,000 every four years in connection with the Olympics. Although the men were not paid by USA Hockey because the men's national team comprised National Hockey League professionals, both teams were given other types of support (Bach, 2018). The women also argued that they did not get equal equipment, staff, and per diem and travel benefits (Bach, 2018). For example, the women had to share rooms when traveling, whereas the men were provided their own accommodations and paid transportation for their guests. The women also noted that they had to fly to games in economy class, whereas the men traveled in business class (Perez, 2017).

Similar to the Women's National Soccer team, the women's hockey players have been very successful, winning numerous Olympic medals and seven out of the last eight world championships. Most recently, the team won the gold medal at the 2018 winter Olympic Games. USA Hockey ultimately came to an agreement with the team, pledging to provide increased compensation and benefits similar to the men's program. Among other things, the women will earn a "livable wage" of US$70,000 per year (Berkman, 2017).

Significantly, after the women's team announced that it would not play without equitable pay, the men's program supported them, and potential substitute players, such as those playing intercollegiate hockey, voiced solidarity with the team and turned down USA Hockey's offers to replace the team. This unity meant that USA Hockey would not have been able to field a team for the world championships, and public opinion strongly favored the women. The unity was at least partially made possible by the fact that the men's players could easily support the women because, on the men's side, the players come from the National Hockey League, where they earn far more than the women, who do not have professional league employment.

Although both the women's soccer and the women's hockey teams ultimately came to new agreements that provide greater compensation and benefits (though the women's soccer team's claim is still pending with the Equal Employment Opportunity Commission), the outcome of any legal claim of discrimination is far from clear. For example, a court ruled in favor of US Soccer that the parties had a collective bargaining agreement, the terms of which would prohibit the players from going on strike (*U.S. Soccer Fed'n v. U.S. Women's Nat'l Soccer Team Players Ass'n* 2016). In addition, in the Equal Pay case, US Soccer asserted a variety of defenses, including that the pay differential was due to, in the language of the Equal Pay Act, "any factor other than sex." The analysis might also have been complicated by the fact that, unlike most jobs, elite athletics is deliberately sex segregated. Measuring equality when an employer operates essentially separate workplaces for its male and female employees might have been an issue, as well as questions of the role of the collective bargaining agreement in establishing the women's compensation.

Yet, while the ultimate legal resolution of pay equity claims is uncertain, the cultural, normative victories have been far clearer. Both women's teams enjoyed strong public support that was undoubtedly fueled, at least in part, by their respective teams' competitive success. For instance, in addition to media and public support, the United States Senate unanimously voted in favor of a resolution calling on USSF to provide the women's soccer team with equal wages (Cauterucci, 2017). Moreover, changing cultural norms around female sport participation in the decades since Title IX meant that the women no longer needed to justify an equal right to participate, but could instead make a strong claim for equal treatment. Importantly, the efforts of the women's national soccer team also quite likely had international implications, as Norway announced in 2017 that it would pay its male and female players equally. In that case, the men's team agreed to slightly lower pay to achieve equality, something that has not happened in the United States (Payne, 2017).

Implications for the future

The impact of the women's national soccer and hockey teams' success will likely be seen in other Olympic movement sports. Although both teams received strong public support, this was at least partly due to the fact that they are both highly successful teams that generate a great deal of prestige for the United States in international competition. Such success arguably should not be a factor in pay determinations, because the standard is equal pay for equal work, and the outcome of the athletic "work" should not matter. In addition, because these pay disputes occurred in the context of the Olympic movement, and not purely professional sports, there was a common national governing body that could be held accountable for the women's treatment. This is in contrast to professional women's sports leagues, which operate as separate entities from their male counterparts.

The Olympic movement context therefore provides an opening for equitable athlete pay to be tackled in an even more meaningful way. As it did in 1978 when it passed the Amateur Sports Act and required the USOC and NGBs to encourage women's participation in athletics, Congress could add a provision to the statute now that required a stronger commitment to gender equity, including in the area of pay. In this way, Olympic movement sports can lead the way for pay equity across all sports.

Figure 16.1 Angela Ruggiero

Leader profile: Angela Ruggiero

Angela Ruggiero is one of the greatest athletes in US Olympic history and is breaking gender barriers in the regulation of Olympic movement sports. Ruggiero is a member of the United States Olympic Committee Board of Directors and, since 2016, represents the United States on the International Olympic Committee (IOC) Executive Board. In 2010, she was elected to represent all Olympic athletes on the IOC Athletes' Commission, and in 2014 she was elected vice chair and later became chair of the Commission. Ruggiero also participated in IOC commissions to inspect cities that were competing to host the 2018 Olympic Games, and participated on the Coordination Commission for the 2018 Games. Ruggiero's status within the Olympic movement is noteworthy given the dearth of women in such leadership positions. Only 4 out of 15 IOC Executive Board members are women, and only seven out of 26 IOC commissions are chaired by women. In addition, only 20 percent of national Olympic committee executive board members are women.

Ruggiero was an Olympian in the sport of women's ice hockey, and participated in four Olympic Games from 1998 to 2010, winning with her team gold (1998), silver (2002 and 2010), and bronze (2006) medals. While competing as a member of the US Women's National Hockey Team, Ruggiero competed in more games than any man or woman in USA Hockey history. She participated in 10 world championships, with her teams winning the gold four times. Ms. Ruggiero played hockey for Harvard University, where she won a national collegiate championship and was a four-time All-American and an Academic All-American.

Ruggiero earned a Master of Education in Sports Management from the University of Minnesota and a Master of Business Administration from Harvard Business School. Her career included a stint on Donald Trump's reality show *The Apprentice* and at the hedge fund firm

Bridgewater Associates. Ruggiero is also active in numerous organizations, including serving on the executive board for the Women's Sports Foundation. She recently made history by pledging her brain to the Concussion Legacy Foundation, an organization studying chronic traumatic encephalopathy and concussions. Ruggiero reportedly made the pledge so that the project would have more female athlete brains to study to better understand the impact of sport concussions on both genders.

References

Acosta, R. V. & Carpenter, L. (2014). *Women in Intercollegiate Sport. A Longitudinal, National Study, Thirty Five Year Update, 1977–2012.* Retrieved from www.acostacarpenter.org.

Bach, N. (2018). Before the USA women's hockey team clinched gold, they fought for equal pay. *Fortune*, February. Retrieved from http://fortune.com/2018/02/22/usa-womens-hockey-gold-equal-pay.

Berkman, S. (2017). U.S. Women's team strikes deal with USA hockey. *The New York Times*, March 28. Retrieved from https://www.nytimes.com/2017/03/28/sports/hockey/usa-hockey-uswnt-boycott.html.

Brake, D. (2001). The struggle for sex equality in sport and the theory behind Title IX. *University of Michigan Journal of Law Reform*, **34**(1–2), 13.

Brake, D. (2007). Symposium: Celebrating thirty-five years of sport and Title IX: Title IX as pragmatic feminism. *Cleveland State University Law Review*, **55**(4), 513.

Brake, D. (2010). *Getting in the Game: Title IX and the Women's Sport Revolution.* New York: New York University Press.

Buzuvis, E. (2006). Survey says . . . a critical analysis of the new Title IX policy and proposal for reform. *Iowa Law Review*, **91**(3), 821.

Campbell, H. (2017). Superior play, unequal pay: U.S. women's soccer and the pursuit for pay equity. *University of San Francisco Law Review*, **51**(3), 545.

Carpenter, J. (2017). The gender pay gap doesn't close, even at the very, very top. *CNN Money*, December 13. Retrieved from https://money.cnn.com/2017/12/13/news/companies/women-executive-pay/index.html.

Cauterucci, C. (2017). The Senate passed a unanimous resolution supporting equal pay for U.S. women's soccer, May 27. Retrieved from https://slate.com/human-interest/2016/05/the-senate-passed-a-unanimous-resolution-supporting-equal-pay-for-u-s-womens-soccer.html.

Cohen, D. S. (2005). Title IX: Beyond equal protection. *Harvard Journal of Law and Gender*, **28**(2), 217.

Das, A. (2016). Top female players accuse U.S. Soccer of wage discrimination, *The New York Times*, March 31. Retrieved from https://www.nytimes.com/2016/04/01/sports/soccer/uswnt-us-women-carli-lloyd-alex-morgan-hope-solo-complain.html.

Department of Education (1997). Title IX: 25 years of progress, June. Retrieved from https://www2.ed.gov/pubs/TitleIX/index.html.

Eisenberg, D. (2010). Shattering the Equal Pay Act's glass ceiling. *Southern Methodist University Law Review*, **63**(1), 17.

Gajanan, M. (2018). Team USA's women are beating the men in the Olympics medal count. *Time Magazine*, February 23. Retrieved from http://time.com/5172622/winter-olympics-american-women-medals.

Koller, D. L. (2010). Not just one of the boys: A post-feminist critique of Title IX's vision for gender equity in sports. *Connecticut Law Review*, **43**(2), 401.

Koller, D. L. (2012). How the expressive power of Title IX dilutes its promise. *Harvard Journal of Sport and Entertainment Law*, **3**(1), 103.

Koller, D. L. (2016). Putting public law into "private" sport, *Pepperdine Law Review*, **43**(3), 681.

Miller, K. (2017). The simple truth about the gender pay gap, Fall. Retrieved from https://www.aauw.org/resource/the-simple-truth-about-the-gender-pay-gap.

National Collegiate Athletic Association (2016). Sports sponsorship and participation rates report (2015–2016). Retrieved from www.ncaa.org/about/resources/research/sports-sponsorship-and-participation-research.

National Federation of State High School Associations (2017). 2016–2017 high school athletics participation survey. Retrieved from https://www.nfhs.org/ParticipationStatistics/ParticipationStatistics.

Olson, W. (1991). Beyond Title IX: Toward an agenda for women and sports in the 1990s. *Yale Journal of Law and Feminism*, **3**(1), 105–116.

Payne, M. (2017). Norway to pay men's and women's soccer teams equally after men agree to slight pay cut. *The Washington Post*, October 8. Retrieved from https://www.washingtonpost.com/news/

early-lead/wp/2017/10/08/norway-to-pay-mens-and-womens-soccer-teams-equally-after-men-agree-to-slight-pay-cut/?utm_term=.46cc9e7b597c.

Perez, A. J. (2016). Five women's players file a wage discrimination complaint against U.S. soccer, complaint Attachment A, March 31. Retrieved from https://www.usatoday.com/story/sports/soccer/2016/03/31/us-women-soccer-wage-discrimination-carli-lloyd-alex-morgan/82460844.

Perez, A. J. (2017). Five things to know in U.S. women's hockey team showdown with USA hockey. *USA Today*, March 27. Retrieved from https://www.usatoday.com/story/sports/nhl/2017/03/27/us-women-hockey-team-boycott/99683488.

Rubin, J. (2016). U.S. women's Olympic dominance is not a fluke. *The Washington Post*, August 22. Retrieved from https://www.washingtonpost.com/blogs/right-turn/wp/2016/08/22/u-s-womens-olympic-dominance-is-not-a-fluke/?utm_term=.23e83e8fd4a1.

Team USA (2018). Pyeonchang 2018 Meet Team USA. Retrieved from https://www.teamusa.org/PyeongChang-2018-Olympic-Winter-Games/Team-USA/Athletes.

United States Olympic Committee (USOC) (2016). Quad Report 2013–2016. Retrieved from file:///C:/Users/fines/AppData/Local/Packages/Microsoft.MicrosoftEdge_8wekyb3d8bbwe/TempState/Downloads/2013-16%20USOC%20Quad%20Report%20(1).pdf.

Weiss, D.C. (2016). Full-time female lawyers earn 77 percent of male lawyer pay, *ABA Journal*, March 17. Retrieved from www.abajournal.com.

Women's Sports Foundation (2009). Women's sports & fitness facts & statistics. Retrieved from file:///C:/Users/fines/AppData/Local/Packages/Microsoft.MicrosoftEdge_8wekyb3d8bbwe/TempState/Downloads/wsf-facts-march-2009.pdf.

Statutes and court decisions

Amateur Sports Act: Hearing Before the Subcomm. on Consumer Affairs, Foreign Commerce, & Tourism of the S. Comm. on Commerce, Sci. & Transp., 104th Cong. 12 (1995) (statement of Norma Cantu, Assistant Secretary, Office for Civil Rights, Department of Education).

Cohen v. Brown Univ., 101 F.3d 155 (1st Cir. 1996).

Education Amendments of 1972, Pub. L. No. 92-318, § 901, 86 Stat. 235 (codified at 20 U.S.C. § 1681(a) (2012)).

Education Amendments of 1974, Pub. L. No. 93-380, § 844, 88 Stat. 484, 612 (codified at 20 U.S.C. § 1681 (2012)).

Neal v. Bd. of Trs. of Cal. State Univs., 198 F.3d 763 (9th Cir. 1999).

Ted Stevens Olympic and Amateur Sports Act, Pub. L. No. 105-225, 112 Stat. 1253, 1466-78 (1998) (codified as amended at 36 U.S.C. §§ 220501-29 (2012)).

U.S. Soccer Fed'n v. U.S. Women's Nat'l Soccer Team Players Ass'n, 190 F.Supp.3d 777 (N.D. Ill. 2016).

17
Social entrepreneurship

Carrie W. LeCrom and Allison B. Smith

In 2006 Liz Wolfson was working a job she liked but didn't love. Searching for a job that would inspire her passions, she was gifted two books: *Learning Like a Girl* (Meehan, 2007) and *Odd Girl Out* (Simmons, 2002) Peripherally engaged in the feminist world, these books gave Wolfson the direction for which she'd been yearning, taking her back to childhood memories of the learning and growing she personally experienced on the basketball court her parents built in the backyard and at an all-girls summer camp. Wolfson said, "Something about those two books just sparked my internal and external personalities thinking, if I can guarantee young girls an elongated life of energy and love and action and movement, which is what always made me and still makes me feel alive, I want to do that" (L. Wolfson, personal communication, December 8, 2017).

Thus, began a journey to give every young girl a place and space to fully become themselves. Wolfson spent months researching sport in school, physical education, obesity, health education, and legislation, and the politics of the US education system. Finding that physical activity not only brings joy, energy, and confidence to young people, but also improves memory, attention, and cognition left her wondering why it was not more central to core academics. Meanwhile, she met Nina Safane, a student athlete at Brown University, where Wolfson had also competed, who was similarly passionate about education, girls' empowerment, and sport. The duo set out to create an educational model based on movement and optimal wellness for all girls. In 2010, Girls Athletic Leadership Schools Inc. (GALS) opened their flagship middle school in Denver, Colorado, welcoming girls of all backgrounds. Since that time, GALS Inc. has expanded to four schools in two cities (Denver and Los Angeles), with two more locations set to open in 2019. Approximately 900 young people are learning every day through this innovative educational model that embraces movement and sport like few other schools do.

What is social entrepreneurship?

Although to date there is no clear definition of the term "social entrepreneurship," the above example outlines what social entrepreneurs may look like. Social entrepreneurs are individuals or organizations that exhibit entrepreneurial behaviors to address social problems or issues. They are mission driven, utilizing their business skills to address social, cultural, and environmental issues aimed at the greater good. According to Leadbeater (1997, p. 2):

Social entrepreneurs will be one of the most important sources of innovation. Social entrepreneurs identify under-utilised resources – people, buildings, equipment – and find ways of putting them to use to satisfy unmet social needs. They innovate new welfare services and new ways of delivering existing services.

Social entrepreneurs are altruistic, and their success is therefore measured not by profit generated, but by social impact. As a result, most social entrepreneurship takes the form of non-profit organizations where, even if they do turn a profit, they invest that money back into the community or social change initiatives. However, social entrepreneurs can be found at the intersection of the non-profit, volunteer, and for-profit sector, cutting across many sizes and types of organizations.

Characteristics of social entrepreneurs

Social entrepreneurs tend to be driven, determined, charismatic individuals who are creative at identifying unmet needs and finding untapped resources to fill those needs (Dees, 1998; Nigam & Ghai, 2016). They deeply care about doing social good, but they are not just do-gooders. They approach their work innovatively and creatively by first understanding the larger social context in which they will operate, then finding ways to fill that space. Similarly, they are not just philanthropists, activists, company foundations, or socially responsible organizations. Rather, social entrepreneurs strategically work to determine root causes of social issues, and use their business acumen to address these creatively, often challenging the status quo (Seelos & Mair, 2005).

According to Nigam and Ghai (2016, p. 110): "An important feature of social entrepreneurs is that they have an unwavering belief in everyone's innate capacity to contribute meaningfully to economic and social development." This belief in everyone contributing and helping is particularly well paired with a deep desire for social change, which has emerged as a defining characteristic of the millennial generation (Emeagwali, 2011; Girl Scouts Research Institute, 2008). Millennials are defined as the generation born between 1981 and 1997 and, as of 2015, they became the largest generation in the current workforce (Fry, 2015). Millennials are a unique generation who grew up with technology at their fingertips and have displayed a strong desire to do work that is meaningful to them. Their understanding of technology works to their advantage, because many social entrepreneurs have found that the utilization of social networking, crowd sourcing, and other alternative, creative ways of utilizing technology have helped them achieve their goals (Elkington & Hartigan, 2008; Malecki, 1997). Given these traits and characteristics, we may see a rise in social entrepreneurs in the coming decades.

Challenges of social entrepreneurs

As a result of some of the above listed characteristics, social entrepreneurs can be labeled as dreamers or idealists, but in reality, their success is contingent on their practicality and realism (Nigam & Ghai, 2016). Still, there are challenges in social entrepreneurship that should not be discounted. Funding is an issue for social entrepreneurs because much of their work tends to cost money rather than make money. Unlike traditional entrepreneurs, who bring products and services to the marketplace to make a profit, social entrepreneurs invest their business acumen in addressing social issues. They often offer programming that helps those who have the least ability to pay for the services (Elkington & Hartigan, 2008; Mair & Marti, 2006), so finding sources of funding is challenging and critical.

Social entrepreneurs, at least initially, often rely on grants and investors to fund their work. This can be especially difficult without a product to demonstrate or measurable results to depict. Yet when working to impact social issues, measuring change can be a challenge:

> The real problem may not be the measurement per se, but how the measures may be used to "quantify" the performance and impact of social entrepreneurship. Many consider it very difficult, if not impossible, to quantify socio-economic, environmental and social effects.
>
> *(Mair & Marti, 2006, p. 42)*

This can present challenges not only in securing and sustaining funding, but also in communicating the impact of the work being done overall.

In addition, sustainability of programs can prove difficult for social entrepreneurs (Elkington & Hartigan, 2008). This is due to the arduous task of funding programs, which is also a result of how quickly society is changing. It is hard to predict the future of social needs and be responsive to those, but this is critical to the success of social entrepreneurs. For this reason, leadership is paramount. Social entrepreneurial leaders need to be flexible, creative, and constantly in tune with societal changes.

Social issues

Social entrepreneurs who can successfully navigate the waters of an ever-changing environment have the ability to impact many. Social issues are broad reaching and multifaceted, and social entrepreneurs can be found in all areas of social change. Some of the issues addressed in this realm include poverty, marginalization, environmental sustainability, human health, reconciliation, and gender equity, among others.

Sport has been introduced into the world of social entrepreneurship, given its ability to connect so many people through a common interest. However, the use of sport in social entrepreneurship has not been carefully studied (Schulenkorf, 2017), although it has been applied to social change initiatives addressing numerous issues, utilizing numerous sports, and in numerous countries across the globe (Svensson & Woods, 2017). Although not a magic bullet, sport can cut across differences such as language, religion, race, and gender (Trunkos & Heere, 2017; Wolff, 2011). If properly organized, clearly focused, and grounded in the local community, its impact can be great (Schulenkorf, 2010; Sherry, 2010). These unique characteristics that sport can bring to social change initiatives make it a unique and creative approach to social entrepreneurship.

Gender-specific sport programming

Many social entrepreneurs operating in the sport sector have created programming specifically focused on women and girls. This has come as a result of research indicating there are advantages to this approach. Single-sex education and programming has grown in popularity since 2006 when the US Department of Education loosened its Title IX regulations on single sex education (Novotney, 2011). In the 2011–2012 school year, 506 schools across the United States offered single-sex education opportunities, with 116 of these being specific single-sex schools (National Association for Single Sex Public Education, 2017). Research has found that there are advantages to single-sex education or programming, especially for girls (Kessels & Hannover, 2008; Sax, 2011). This has trickled down into sport programming through social entrepreneurs, both inside and outside the school setting.

All-girls or all-women physical activity and sport programming has physical, emotional, and social benefits for the participants. Girl-centered sport and physical activity programming has been shown to have a positive effect on teaching girls life skills that transfer to other domains and foster healthy development (Perkins & Noam, 2007; Weiss, 2008, 2011; Weiss, Kipp, & Bolter, 2012; Weiss, Stuntz, Bhalla, Bolter, & Price, 2012). Cooky (2009) insists that programs that reflect cultural norms, girls' interest, and co-construction of the program with both girls and organizers can be seen as an empowerment tool for the female participants. Women who reflected on attending an all-girls camp in their youth indicated that the camp allowed them to challenge gender norms, learn skills in career development, resilience, self-esteem, confidence, and independence – factors that influenced their development and value as women (Whittington, Garst, Gagnon, & Baughman, 2017). Due to these results, issues including obesity, health, and gender empowerment have emerged as clear fits and well-utilized connections to sport in the social entrepreneurship realm, all of which are often of paramount importance to women and girls specifically.

Issues impacting women and girls

Obesity and health

Obesity and health disparities are areas in which social entrepreneurs and their programs are working to create an impact in the lives of young people, to be carried into adulthood. The percentage of children facing obesity in the United States has more than tripled since the 1970s; currently, about one in five school-aged children is obese (Fryar, Carroll, & Ogden, 2014; Ogden et al., 2016). Although obesity research has focused on children in general, the largest increases in obesity have been observed in African–American girls (Troiano, Flegal, Kuczmarski, Campbell, & Johnson, 1995; White & Russell, 2012). One-quarter of African–American girls and adolescents are obese, compared with 14% of white girls (Ogden, Carroll, Kit, & Flegal, 2012). African–American girls are at a higher risk of becoming obese than their white counterparts, increasing their likelihood of obesity and weight-related chronic diseases in adulthood (Braunschweig et al., 2005; Field, Cook, & Gillman, 2005; Pi-Sunyer, 2002; Pratt et al., 2013).

Many social entrepreneurs are looking to tackle the childhood obesity epidemic through the use of sport and physical activity. For example, *Power-Up*, a Chicago-based after-school program, used a 14-week nutritional and physical activity course to tackle issues of obesity in youth (Choudhry et al., 2011). Choudhry et al. (2011) found that the girls in the program decreased their obesity levels from 52% to 46%, healthy attitudes revolving around making better nutritional choices rose from 77% to 90%, and plans to try new sports rose from 80% to 88%. Another example is GENYOUth, an organization that partners with the National Dairy Council and the NFL to form the *Fuel Up to Play 60* program, an initiative aiming for good nutrition and at least 60 minutes of physical activity daily (Fuel Up to Play 60, 2017). Since *Fuel Up to Play 60* launched in 2007, it now reaches more than 73,000 schools and 38 million students; 18 million students have access to healthier foods at school, 17 million have access to more physical activity, and 16 million students are more physically active (National Dairy Council, 2015).

Sport- and activity-based social entrepreneurship solely directed at young girls has begun to flourish in the past two decades. Girls on the Run, a non-profit organization with the mission to inspire young girls to "be joyful, healthy and confident using a fun, experience-based curriculum which creatively integrates running" offers a 10-week, twice a week after-school program to girls in the third through fifth grades. This program combines talking about social, emotional, and mental challenges, along with the importance of fitness and physical activity through stretching, conditioning, and running activities (Girls on the Run, 2017, para. 1). Girls on the Run has been evaluated by a number of scholars and findings have indicated that the girls perceived the program to help with social and physical self-concept, as well as their attitudes toward healthy living (DeBate, Pettee, Zwald, Huberty, & Zhang, 2009; Martin, Waldron, McCabe, & Choi, 2009; Waldron, 2007). This programming is important and influential because it can lead to lifelong wellness and health practices into adulthood, creating strong, healthy, confident women.

Another example is the Girls Just Wanna Have Fun (GJWHF) program, which was designed and developed in response to the gap in physical activity between boys and girls in Canada (Bean, Forneris, & Halsall, 2014). In eastern Ontario, Canada, only 243 young girls compared with 1,012 young boys participated in sport and physical activity programs across several boys and girls clubs in 2008–2009 (Boys and Girls Clubs of America, 2013). GJWHF focuses on at-risk, low-income girls learning life skills through an awareness of talk and physical activity (i.e., cooperative games, dance, volleyball, basketball, kickboxing, yoga, lacrosse, skating, and swimming (Bean et al., 2014). Researchers found that the program was successful in the development of connections between the girls, the opportunity for participant-driven leadership, communication, and support with program leaders, and the exposure and engagement in a variety of physical activities (Bean et al., 2014). Finally, shifting to whole body health (mental, physical, emotional), Goals for Girls was created in 2007 to build confidence and self-esteem in girls in the United States and abroad (goalsforgirls.com). Several times a year, Goals for Girls takes an American-based girls soccer team to countries around the world (e.g., India and South Africa) to conduct soccer clinics, tournaments, and exhibition games, while simultaneously teaching life skills through soccer, classroom, and cultural exchange leadership activities. The focus on each trip provides the girls with their own leadership development as well as a social change project that the girls take back to their home communities.

Sport dropout

Sport dropout is another social issue that has been related to health and physical activity levels in women, which is being addressed by social entrepreneurs. It is estimated that over 38 million children are involved in youth sports each year, and that 75% of American households with school-aged children have at least one child participating in youth sport (Safe Kids USA Fact Sheet, 2011). However, 70% of children drop out of organized sports by the age of 13 (O'Sullivan, 2015) and, by the age of 14, girls are dropping out of sport at two times the rate of boys (Sabo & Veliz, 2008).

Girls drop out of sport for a multitude of reasons, including less access to facilities and coaches, lack of options, lack of role models, and social stigmas (Sabo, Veliz, & Staurowsky, 2016; Women's Sport and Fitness Foundation, 2015). Perhaps the most cited reason for girls dropping out of sport is due to body image, self-confidence, and self-esteem issues, which they carry into adulthood. Young girls (and women) struggle with feelings of incompetence when it comes to sport skills or are self-conscious about their bodies (Eccles, Barber, Jozefowicz, Malenchuk, & Vide, 1999; Eccles & Harold, 1991; Women's Sport and Fitness Foundation, 2015). By middle adolescence, girls are twice as likely as boys to experience issues with major depression (Cyranowski, Frank, Young, & Shear, 2000; Hyde, Mezulis, & Abramson, 2008; Staurowsky et al., 2009). This depression is heightened by their biological and hormonal changes through puberty. Dealing with these intense changes along with depression can cause other lifelong issues such as parental conflicts and unrealistic standards with beauty and social expectations (Mental Health America, 2016; National Institute of Mental Health, 2008).

Many of the issues mentioned above could be remedied or alleviated through continued participation in sport. For girls who grow up and develop into working women, sport participation can assist with their physical, emotional, and even psychological health. Girls who are active in their adolescence and early adulthood are 20% less likely to develop breast cancer later in life, or become smokers or illicit drug users (Lagerros, Hsieh, & Hsieh, 2004; Melnick, Miller, Sabo, Farrell, & Barnes, 2001; Staurowsky et al., 2009; Yusko, Buckman, White, & Pandina, 2008). Through sport participation young girls learn important skills that translate into adulthood and the workforce such as teamwork, leadership, and confidence (Women's Sport Foundation, 2017a). Girls and women who play sports have a more positive body image, higher psychological well-being, self-confidence, and self-worth, and have lower levels of depression than girls and women who do not play sports (Women's Sport Foundation, 2017b). In their study of 400 female executives, espnW and EY found that there was a correlation between athletic participation and business success. Specifically, more than half (52%) of the women executives played sports at the collegiate level and 80% reported they had played sports at one point in their lives (Zarya, 2017).

Given the physical, mental, and emotional benefits women reap from participation in sport as youths, many social entrepreneurs are focusing on the benefits to young girls and looking to address the sport dropout issue. For example, Ho et al. (2017) used a positive youth development-based sports mentorship program with students from 12 secondary schools in Hong Kong, China. The results of the program indicated that students felt empowered, and their mental well-being, self-efficacy, resilience, physical fitness, lower limb muscle strength, dynamic balance, and overall physical activity levels improved with the intervention (Ho et al., 2017). Similarly, SMART Girls, created by the Boys and Girls Club of America, uses small-group health and fitness prevention/education courses for girls aged 8–18 to assist in self-esteem enhancement (SMART Girls, 2017). SMART Girls utilizes women mentors to assist the girls in being active, exploring societal attitudes and values, building lifelong healthy eating and physical fitness skills, and learning the importance of developing a healthy relationship with themselves and others (SMART Girls, 2017). Lastly, Black Girls Smile seeks to empower young African–American girls to take ownership of their mental health through promoting a sense of worth, positive decision-making, and fighting the stigmas associated with mental health in the African–American community (Black Girls Smile, 2017).

Critiquing sport social entrepreneurship

Although there is clearly a space for social entrepreneurs in the sport sector, and many of those programs are impacting social change positively, there are criticisms to be addressed. The challenges of social entrepreneurs generally mirror those who operate through a sport platform. Funding programs is difficult, because their outcomes are tough to measure and are generally under-evaluated (Coalter, 2007). In addition, they are not always given a critical eye when it comes to evaluation. As social entrepreneurial organizations are seen to be doing good in the community and/or world, they can come across as evangelical about the good work they are doing and lack critical assessment and reflection. This can become an issue because sport begins to be seen as a magic bullet that creates change automatically. Yet scholars have suggested that this is not the case and that there are keys to success, including items such as strong strategic direction, local knowledge and participation, and focused and effective goals and objectives (Schulenkorf, 2010; Sherry, 2010).

In addition, sports-based social programming tends to be led and directed by privileged individuals, whereas the interventions are for those at risk. This has the ability to create power and inequality differences, while also failing to fully address systemic issues (Darnell, 2012; Levermore & Beacom, 2012; Spaaij, Schulenkorf, Jeanes, & Oxford, 2017). If not thoughtfully created and implemented, these issues run the risk of being more harmful than helpful, because they continue to perpetuate the cycle of privilege and power.

Finally, social entrepreneurship focused specifically on issues impacting girls and women also faces challenges. There is the thought that participation in all-girl programming can mask or give the illusion that inequality and privilege do not exist, when in actuality these concepts are alive and real (Rauscher & Cooky, 2016). All-girl programming that uses physical activity to assist with health epidemics such as obesity can have backlash and contribute to a "harmful fat phobic message for girls" (Rauscher & Cooky, 2016, p. 288). In addition, all-girl programming can be very exclusive in its targeting. Minority groups such as African–Americans and Latinas are often left out of programs when they tend to be most at risk for social issues. For women who live in poverty and deal with issues such as malnutrition and disease, sport is not present in their daily lives (Hancock, Lyras, & Ha, 2013). Finally, there are very few sport social entrepreneurial programs that target women specifically. Most programming is specifically targeted to girls, with the hope that they carry the skills learned into adulthood, so there tends to be a programming void for women specifically.

Leader profile: Patti Phillips, CEO, Women Leaders in College Sports

Figure 17.1 Patti Phillips

Patti Phillips is a dynamic woman leader who has committed her life's work to creating opportunities for and supporting other women leaders in the sport industry. As the CEO of Women Leaders in College Sports (formerly NACWAA), Phillips has opportunities every day to work with female collegiate athletic directors, commissioners, and aspiring sport professionals, focusing on leadership, teamwork, and culture, while providing guidance on ascending the ranks within the collegiate athletics world. Her background prepared her well for this role, beginning her career as a collegiate basketball and volleyball coach, then moving on to positions within the National Collegiate Athletics Association (NCAA) and Win for KC (a female-focused program within the Kansas City Sports Commission and Foundation), and finally landing at Women Leaders in College Sports in 2010. In discussing her current job, Phillips clearly sees how each former job developed her leadership skills in different ways, culminating in what she calls the "perfect" job for her. "I like to tell people to work in your zone of genius. This job in every facet is mine," says Phillips.

As a woman whose primary job is to support, advocate for, and educate other women on the business of collegiate sports, Phillips spends a lot of time considering issues facing women in the industry. She mentions numerous challenges (sexual harassment, unconscious bias, the arms race, work–life balance), many of which come back to a common solution. If we can get more women into leadership roles in the industry, some of the issues will remedy themselves. As college athletics is still primarily run by white men (presidents, athletic directors, coaches), there is a lack of diversity, which exacerbates the problems. Therefore, Phillips sees one of her primary responsibilities as helping educate women on the path to the top and advocating for them in athletic director and commissioner searches. Phillips notes: "we follow the trends in the industry. We're teaching women, at a very young age now, in all of our institutes, the importance of being strategic about your career within this industry." If we can get more women in leadership positions, there will be less bias, less loneliness, and a climate more focused around inclusion and diversity. Building up women leaders is the goal of Women Leaders in College Sports, and not just for the women. It's really a win for everyone – the student athletes, the staff, the coaches, and society as a whole.

References

Bean, C. N., Forneris, T., & Halsall, T. (2014). Girls just wanna have fun: A process evaluation of a female youth-driven physical activity-based life skills program. *SpringerPlus*, **3**(1), 1–15.

Black Girls Smile (2017). In need of help? Programs & much . . . much more . . . Retrieved from: www.blackgirlssmile.org/programs

Boys and Girls Club of America (2013). *Smart Girls*. Retrieved from: www.bgca.org/whatwedo/HealthLifeSkills/Pages/SMARTGirls.aspx.

Braunschweig, C. L., Gomez, S., Liang, H., Tomey, K., Doerfler, B., Wang, Y., & Lipton, R. (2005). Obesity and risk factors for the metabolic syndrome among low-income, urban, African American schoolchildren: The rule rather than the exception? *American Journal of Clinical Nutrition*, **81**, 970–975.

Choudhry S., McClinton-Powell, L., Solomon, M., Dawnavan, D., Lipton, R., Darukhanavala, A., & Burnet, D. L. (2011). Power-Up: A collaborative after-school program to prevent obesity in African American children. *Progress in Community Health Partnerships: Research, Education, and Action*, **5**(4), 363–373.

Coalter, F. (2007). *A Wider Social Role for Sport: Who's keeping the score?* Abingdon: Routledge.

Cooky, C. (2009). "Girls just aren't interested": The social construction of interest in girls' sport. *Sociological Perspectives*, **52**, 259–283.

Cyranowski, J. M., Frank, E., Young, E., & Shear, M. K. (2000). Adolescent onset of the gender difference in lifetime rates of major depression: A theoretical model. *Archives of General Psychiatry*, **57**(1), 21–27.

Darnell, S. (2012). *Sport for Development and Peace: A critical sociology*. London: Bloomsbury Academic.

DeBate R. D., Pettee G. K., Zwald, M., Huberty, J., & Zhang Y. (2009). Changes in psychosocial factors and physical activity frequency among third- to eighth-grade girls who participated in a developmentally focused youth sport program: a preliminary study. *Journal of School Health*, **79**(10), 474–484.

Dees, G. (1998). The meaning of social entrepreneurship. Retrieved from https://entrepreneurship.duke.edu/news-item/the-meaning-of-social-entrepreneurship.

Eccles, J. S., Barber, B., Jozefowicz, D., Malenchuk, O., & Vide, M. (1999). Self-evaluations of competence, task values, and self-esteem. In N. G. Johnson, M. C. Roberts, & J. Worrell (eds), *Beyond Appearance: A new look at adolescent girls*, (pp. 53–84). Washington, DC: American Psychological Association.

Eccles, J. S. & Harold, R. D. (1991). Gender differences in sport involvement: Applying the eccles–expectancy–value model. *Journal of Applied Sport Psychology*, **3**, 7–35.

Elkington, J. & Hartigan, P. (2008). *The Power of Unreasonable People*. Boston, MA: Harvard Business School Publishing.

Emeagwali, N. S. (2011). Millennials: Leading the charge for change. *Techniques: Connecting Education and Careers*, **86**(5), 22–26.

Field, A. E., Cook, N. R., & Gillman, M. W. (2005). Weight status in childhood as a predictor of becoming overweight or hypertensive in early adulthood. *Obesity Research*, **13**, 163–169.

Fry, R. (2015). Millennials surpass Gen Xers as the largest generation in U.S. labor force. *Pew Research Center*, May 11. Retrieved from www.pewresearch.org/fact-tank/2015/05/11/millennials-surpass-gen-xers-as-the-largest-generation-in-u-s-labor-force.

Fryar, C. D., Carroll, M. D., & Ogden, C. L. (2014). *Prevalence of Overweight and Obesity among Children and Adolescents: United States, 1963–1965 through 2011–2012*. Atlanta, GA: National Center for Health Statistics.

Fuel Up to Play 60 (2017). Fuel up to play 60. Retrieved from: https://www.genyouthnow.org/programs/fuel-up-to-play-60.

Girls on the Run (2017). What we do: 3rd–5th grade program. Retrieved from: https://www.girlsontherun.org/What-We-Do/3rd-5th-Grade-Program.

Girl Scouts Research Institute (2008). Change it up: What girls say about redefining leadership. Retrieved from www.girlscouts.org/content/dam/girlscouts-gsusa/forms-and-documents/about-girl-scouts/research/change_it_up_executive_summary_english.pdf.

Hancock, M., Lyras, A., & Ha, J. P. (2013). Sport for development programmes for girls and women: A global assessment. *Journal of Sport for Development*, **1**(1), 15–24.

Ho, F. K. W., Louie, L. H. T., Wong, W. H., Chan, K. L., Tiwari, A., Chow, C. B., et al. (2017). A sports-based youth development program, teen mental health, and physical fitness: An RCT. *Pediatrics*, **140**(4), e1543.

Hyde, J. S., Mezulis, A. H., & Abramson, L. Y. (2008). The ABCs of depression: Integrating affective, biological, and cognitive models to explain the emergence of the gender difference in depression. *Psychological Review*, **40**, 818–826.

Kessels, U. & Hannover, B. (2008). When being a girl matters less: Accessibility of gender-related self-knowledge in single-sex and coeducational classes and its impact on students' physics-related self-concept of ability. *British Journal of Educational Psychology*, **78**(2), 273–289.

Lagerros, Y. T., Hsieh, S. F., & Hsieh, C. C. (2004). Physical activity in adolescence and young adulthood and breast cancer risk: a quantitative review. *European Journal of Cancer Prevention*, **13**, 5–12.

Leadbeater, C. (1997). *The Rise of the Social Entrepreneur*. London: Demos.

Levermore, R. & Beacom, A. (2012). *Sport and International Development*. London: Palgrave Macmillan.

Mair, J. & Marti, I. (2006). Social entrepreneurship research: A source of explanation, prediction, and delight. *Journal of World Business*, **41**, 36–44.

Malecki, E. J. (1997). *Technology and Economic Development: The dynamics of local, regional, and national change*. University of Illinois at Urbana-Champaign's Academy for Entrepreneurial Leadership Historical Research Reference in Entrepreneurship. Retrieved from https://ssrn.com/abstract=1496226.

Martin, J. J., Waldron, J. J., McCabe, A., & Choi, Y. S. (2009). The impact of "Girls on the Run" on self-concept and fat attitudes. *Journal of Clinical Sport Psychology*, **3**(2), 127–138.

Meehan, D. (2007). *Learning Like a Girl: Educating our daughters in schools of their own*. New York: Public Affairs.

Melnick, M. J., Miller, K. E., Sabo, D., Farrell, M. P., & Barnes, G. M. (2001). Tobacco use among high school athletes and nonathletes: Results of the 1997 youth risk behavior survey. *Adolescence*, **36**, 727–747.

Mental Health America (2016). Annual report 2016. Retrieved from: www.mentalhealthamerica.net/sites/default/files/Annual%20Report%202016%20FINAL.pdf.

National Association for Single Sex Public Education (2017). Single-sex schools/schools with single-sex classrooms. What's the difference. Retrieved from www.singlesexschools.org/schools-schools.htm.

National Dairy Council (2015). Fuel up to play 60 snapshot. Retrieved from: https://www.genyouthnow.org/reports/fuel-up-to-play-60-snapshot

National Institute of Mental Health (2008). *Women and Depression: Discovering hope.* Bethesda, MD: National Institute of Mental Health, National Institutes of Health, US Department of Health and Human Services.

Nigam, A. & Ghai, R. K. (2016). Social entrepreneurship: An overview. *Splint International Journal of Professionals*, **3**(3), 107–111.

Novotney, A. (2011). Coed versus single-sex ed. Does separating boys and girls improve their education? Experts on both sides of the issue weigh in. *APA*, **42**(2), 58.

Ogden, C. L., Carroll, M. D., Kit, B. K., & Flegal, K. M. (2012). Prevalence of obesity and trends in body mass index among U.S. children and adolescents, 1999–2010. *Journal of the American Medical Association*, **301**, 483–490.

Ogden, C. L., Carroll, M.D., Lawman, H. G., Fryar, C. D., Kruszon-Moran, D., Kit, B. K., & Flegal, K. M. (2016). Trends in obesity prevalence among children and adolescents in the United States, 1988–1994 through 2013–214. *Journal of the American Medical Association*, **315**(21), 2292–2299.

O'Sullivan, J. (2015). Why kids quit sports. Changing the Game Project. Retrieved from: http://changingthegameproject.com/why-kids-quit-sports.

Perkins, D. F. & Noam, C. G. (2007). Characteristics of sports-based youth development programs. *New Directions for Youth Development*, **115**, 75–84.

Pi-Sunyer, F. X. (2002). Medical complications of obesity in adults. In C. G. Fairburn & K. D. Brownell (eds), *Eating Disorders and Obesity*, 2nd edn (pp. 467–472). New York: Guilford Press.

Pratt, C. A, Boyington, J., Esposito, L., Pemberton, V. L., Bonds, D., Kelley, M., et al. (2013). Childhood Obesity Prevention and Treatment Research (COPTR): Interventions addressing multiple influences in childhood and adolescent obesity. *Contemporary Clinical Trials*, **36**(2), 406–413.

Rauscher, L. & Cooky, C. (2016). Ready for anything the world gives her?: A critical look at sports-based positive youth development for girls. *Sex Roles*, **74**, 288–298.

Sabo, D. & Veliz, P. (2008). *Go Out and Play: Youth sports in America.* East Meadow, NY: Women's Sports Foundation.

Sabo, D., Veliz, P., & Staurowsky, E. J. (2016). *Beyond x's & o's: Gender bias and coaches of women's college sports.* East Meadow, NY: Women's Sports Foundation.

Safe Kids USA Fact Sheet (2011). A national survey of parents' knowledge, attitudes, and self-reported behaviors concerning sports safety. Retrieved from: https://www.safekids.org/research-report/national-survey-parents-attitudes-and-self-reported-behaviors-concerning-sports.

Sax, L. (2011). *Girls on the Edge: The four factors driving the new crisis for girls-sexual identity, the cyberbubble, obsessions, environmental toxins.* New York: Basic Books.

Schulenkorf, N. (2010). Sport events and ethnic reconciliation: Attempting to create social change between Sinhalese, Tamil and Muslim sportspeople in war-torn Sri Lanka. *International Review for the Sociology of Sport*, **45**(3), 273–294.

Schulenkorf, N. (2017). Managing sport-for-development: Reflections and outlook. *Sport Management Review*, **20**, 243–251.

Seelos, C. & Mair, J. (2005). Social entrepreneurship: Creating new business models to serve the poor. *Business Horizons*, **48**, 241–246.

Sherry, E. (2010). (Re)engaging marginalized groups through sport: The homeless world cup. *International Review for the Sociology of Sport*, **41**(1), 59–71.

Simmons, R. (2002). *Odd Girl Out: The hidden culture of aggression in girls.* Boston, MA: Houghton Mifflin Harcourt.

SMART Girls (2017). SMART Girls helps girls develop toward healthy attitudes. Retrieved from https://www.bgca.org/programs/health-wellness/smart-girls.

Spaaij, R., Schulenkorf, N., Jeanes, R., & Oxford, S. (2017). Participatory research in sport-for-development: Complexities, experiences and (missed) opportunities. *Sport Management Review*.

Staurowsky, E. J., DeSousa, M. J., Ducher, G., Gentner, N., Miller, K. E., Shakib, S., et al. (2009). *Her Life Depends on It II: Sport, physical activity, and the health and well-being of American girls and women.* East Meadow, NY: Women's Sports Foundation.

Svensson, P. G. & Woods, H. (2017). A systematic overview of sport for development and peace organisations. *Journal of Sport for Development*, **5**(9), 36–48.

Troiano, R. P., Flegal, K. M., Kuczmarski, R. J., Campbell, S. M., & Johnson, C. L. (1995). Overweight prevalence and trends for children and adolescents: The national health and nutrition examination surveys, 1963 to 1991. *Archives of Pediatrics and Adolescent Medicine*, **149**(10), 1085–1091.

Trunkos, J. & Heere, B. (2017). Sport diplomacy: A review of how sports can be used to improve international relationships. In C. Esherick, R. E. Baker, S. Jackson, & M. Sam (eds), *Case studies in sport diplomacy* (pp. 1–18). Morgantown, WV: FIT Publishing.

Waldron, J. J. (2007). Influence of involvement in the girls on track program on early adolescent girls' self-perceptions. *Research Quarterly for Exercise and Sport*, **78**(5), 520–533.

Weiss, M. R. (2008). Field of dreams: Sport as a context for youth development. *Research Quarterly for Exercise and Sport*, **79**, 434–449.

Weiss, M. R. (2011). Teach the children well: A holistic approach to developing psychosocial and behavioral competencies through physical education. *Quest*, **63**, 55–65.

Weiss, M. R., Kipp, L. E., & Bolter, N. D. (2012). Training for life: Optimizing positive youth development through sport and physical activity. In S. M. Murphy (ed.), *The Oxford Handbook of Sport and Performance Psychology* (pp. 448–475). New York: Oxford University Press.

Weiss, M. R., Stuntz, C. P., Bhalla, J. A., Bolter, N. D., & Price, M. S. (2012). "More than a game": Impact of The First Tee life skills programme on positive youth development: Project introduction and year 1 findings. *Qualitative Research in Sport, Exercise, and Health*, **5**, 1–31.

White, J. & Russell, J. (2012). Prospective associations between physical activity and obesity among adolescent girls: Racial differences and implications for prevention. *Archives Pediatrics and Adolescent Medicine*, **166**(6), 522–527.

Whittington, A., Garst, B. A., Gagnon, R. J., & Baughman, S. (2017). Living without boys: A retrospective analysis of the benefits and skills gained at all-female camps. *Journal of Experiential Education*, **40**(2), 97–113.

Wolff, A. (2011). Sport saves the world. *Sports Illustrated*, **115**(12), 62–74.

Women's Sport and Fitness Foundation (2015). Changing the game for girls. Retrieved from: https://www.womeninsport.org/wp-content/uploads/2015/04/Changing-the-Game-for-Girls-NGB-Factsheet.pdf?x99836.

Women's Sport Foundation (2017a). Do you know the factors influencing girls' participation in sports? Retrieved from: https://www.womenssportsfoundation.org/support-us/do-you-know-the-factors-influencing-girls-participation-in-sports.

Women's Sport Foundation (2017b). Benefits – Why sports participation for girls and women. Retrieved from: https://www.womenssportsfoundation.org/advocate/foundation-positions/mental-physical-health/benefits-sports-participation-girls-women.

Yusko, D. A., Buckman, J. F., White, H.R., & Pandina, R. J. (2008). Alcohol, tobacco, illicit drugs, and performance enhancers: A comparison of use by college student athletes and nonathletes. *Journal of American College Health*, **57**(3), 281–289.

Zarya, V. (2017). What do 65% of the most powerful women have in common? *Sports*, September 22. Retrieved from: http://fortune.com/2017/09/22/powerful-women-business-sports.

18
Business analytics in women's professional sports

Ceyda Mumcu

This chapter discusses the use of analytics in professional women's sports. The chapter starts with the growth and progression of analytics in the sport industry. This section introduces the history of the use of analytics in the industry, its progression over time, and the diversified utilization of analytics. The second section of the chapter presents the state of women's professional sports in the United States with regard to their use of analytics. The final section focuses on the use of business analytics in mainstream sports to draw attention to the progress needed in women's professional sports.

Growth of analytics in sport

Analytics have been used in the sport industry both on and off the field. The early practices in sport were focused on the on-field applications. Initially player performance and game strategy were analyzed to field the best combination of players, improve performance of teams, and increase the likelihood of winning. With the success of the Oakland As in the early 2000s, Major League Baseball (MLB) teams and teams from other professional sport leagues started to utilize sport analytics. In 2019, teams use analytics for a myriad of purposes including fielding a team, developing a game plan, building rosters, informing draft and trade decisions, distributing the salary cap, and measuring athletes' contributions to the team brand and brand awareness.

With the popularity of Michael Lewis' book *Moneyball*, published in 2003, sport analytics started to attract attention from more than just general managers and coaches. Sport fans demonstrated interest by seeking out more complex statistics beyond the historical box scores. Today, the use of analytics has expanded far beyond player personnel departments in professional sports, providing insight to multiple audiences. To address this appetite, sport media are increasingly providing complex statistics for sport fans who are consuming more analytical content than ever (Steinberg, 2015). There are even websites dedicated exclusively to analyses of sport statistics (e.g., FiveThirtyEight.com). The availability of extensive statistics and analytics has also influenced the growth of fantasy sports and sports betting.

In addition to the on-the-field applications, analytics is increasingly used for off-field aspects of sports. Sport leagues and their franchises/teams, as well as sport associations and their tours, act as businesses and perform various tasks to operate their leagues, teams, and events successfully. In this process, they make many data-driven decisions in all functional areas (marketing, finance, operations, human resources, etc.). The term "business analytics" is used for the off-the-field applications of sport analytics, and it is the process of transforming data into insights to advance decision-making within a business. According to Min (2016, p. 1), business analytics refers to:

> a broad use of various quantitative techniques such as statistics, data mining, optimization tools, and simulation supported by the query and reporting mechanism to assist decision makers in making more informed decisions within a closed-loop framework seeking continuous process improvement through monitoring and learning.

Business analytics are also used to predict the future based on historical data on past business activities (Min, 2016).

Within the sport industry, business analytics has been used in ticketing, marketing, digital and social media, sponsorship valuation, and so on. However, women's professional sports are lagging behind men's professional sports in utilizing business analytics in their operations. The next section focuses on the state of women's professional sport with regard to the use of business analytics, and the application of business analytics in sport is detailed later in the chapter.

State of business analytics in US women's professional sport

This section focuses on the Ladies Professional Golf Association (LPGA), Women's Tennis Association (WTA), Women's National Basketball Association (WNBA), and National Women's Soccer League (NWSL). Although there are other women's professional sports in the United States (i.e., National Pro Fast pitch, Women's Hockey League), the focus in the following sections is limited to these four professional sports leagues/associations.

The LPGA is the oldest professional women's sport organization in the United States. It was established in 1950 and has continued operation since its inception. In 2017, the LPGA organized 34 events in 15 countries, and the association had 220 active golfers, 57% of whom were non-US-born players representing 32 countries (see LPGA.com). Although the association's website does not report any positions devoted to business and data analytics, there is one full-time position focused on business analytics and marketing research within the association, and the position is supported by several interns (Curtin, 2017).

The WTA is the second oldest professional women's sport organization, founded in 1973. In 2017, the WTA organized 55 events, four grand slams in 31 countries, and had 2,500 players from nearly 100 nations. Based on the list of executives and their titles, as published on the association's website, the WTA does not have a department or an individual focused on business and data analytics. However, further online research on LinkedIn identified three individuals with the titles of Senior Director, Data Analyst, and Digital Marketing Analyst.

The WNBA and the NWSL are younger leagues when compared with the LPGA and the WTA. The WNBA was established in 1996 and started its first season with eight teams in 1997. Over the years, several franchises have been disbanded and some others relocated. In 2017, the league had 12 teams with a total of 144 players on team rosters. Of these 12 teams, 7 teams (Minnesota Lynx, San Antonio Stars, Indiana Fever, New York Liberty, Los Angeles Sparks, Phoenix Mercury, and Washington Mystics) are associated with their National Basketball Association (NBA) counterpart. According to the front office personnel records on the teams' websites, only three WNBA teams (Lynx, Seattle Storm, and Phoenix Mercury) have business analytics/intelligence departments, and the size of the departments vary from a single staff member for Seattle Storm to six employees for Minnesota Lynx. However, it is important to stress that Seattle Storm is owned individually, whereas the other two teams are owned and operated by the corresponding NBA team in the market. Thus, although the size of business analytics departments is larger for the Minnesota Lynx and the Phoenix Mercury, the staff is tasked with generating insights for both the NBA and the WNBA teams under their umbrella.

Further online research was conducted on all of the WNBA teams to identify any other employee tasked with business analytics and intelligence, yet not listed on the teams' official websites. This research identified Monumental Sports and Entertainment as the owner and operator of the Washington Mystics, in addition to Washington Capitals (NHL), Washington Wizards (NBA), Washington Valor (AFL), Baltimore Brigade (AFL), Capital One Arena, Eagle Bank Arena, and Kettler Capitals Iceplex. The focus of the business analytics team within Monumental Sports and Entertainment is revenue generation. Thus, analytical approaches are utilized for ticketing, food and beverage, merchandizing, and corporate partnership. However, when it comes to the Washington Mystics, use of analytics is focused on ticket renewal, account retention, and repricing of tickets (Falkson, 2017).

The NWSL was formed in 2012, and started play in 2013 with eight teams. In 2017, the league had 10 teams with a total of 218 players. Four of the ten teams (Houston Dash, Orlando Pride, Portland Thorns, and North Carolina Courage) are owned and operated by Major League Soccer (MLS) or North American Soccer League (NASL) teams. By successfully completing its fifth season in 2017, the NWSL has become the most consistent women's professional soccer league in the United States. Two previous women's professional soccer leagues were Women's United Soccer Association (WUSA) and Women's Professional Soccer (WPS), both of which lasted only three years due to declining fan support and media coverage, and limited corporate support (Michaelis, 2003; Pethchesky, 2012; Rovell, 2003). Currently, NWSL is in its 6th season and successfully continues operation. However, the NWSL and its franchises are behind the industry trend with regard to use of business analytics. Based on the front office directories on the franchise websites, there is not a single position focused on business analytics within the NWSL and its teams. However, the four teams operated by their male counterpart are likely to have some use of business analytics through the sharing of front office resources with their male counterpart. For example, David Tagliarino – Senior Vice President of Houston Dynamo and Dash – stated that there are two full-time employees who manage and oversee customer relationship management (CRM), ticket, and retention analytics, and five full-time members who are focused on sponsorship and commercial revenue, and they use data in lead generation and assessment of sponsorship market (Tagliarino, 2017).

The extent of business analytics application varies among sport leagues and franchises in the United States. For example, major sport leagues, such as MLB, NBA, NFL, and NHL, utilize business analytics more heavily than women's professional sports and, as a result, these leagues are advancing the sport industry in use of business analytics. In 2014, 97% of MLB teams, 80% of NBA teams, 56% of NFL teams, and 23% of NHL teams had data analysts (Drayer & Maxcy, 2014). In contrast, in 2007 MLS started use of business analytics at the league level instead of the franchise level and, during the mid-2010s, MLS teams started to invest in CRM systems, hiring their own data analysts. In 2017, it was estimated that all MLS teams had business analytics staff in their front office (Tagliarino, 2017). Clearly, women's professional sport leagues and associations are behind this industry trend, and this is most probably due to the WNBA and NWSL being in the early phase of the product life cycle compared with the NBA and MLS. Similarly, the WTA and the LPGA appear to have limited resources to invest in the area of analytics, which seems to be common for all women's sport leagues and associations.

Table 18.1 State of business analytics in women's professional sports

LPGA	WTA
Current state: • It was established in 1950 • In 2017, the LPGA and its tours organized 34 events in 15 countries • In 2017, there are 220 active golfers **Business analytics:** • In 2017, there is one full-time position for business analytics within the LPGA • This position is supported with part-time, seasonal interns	**Current state:** • It was founded in 1973 • In 2017, the WTA and its tours organized 55 events, 4 grand slams in 31 countries • In 2017, there are 2500 active tennis players **Business analytics:** • In 2017, there are three full-time positions for business analytics within the WTA • Larger tours might have their own business analytics staff

WNBA	NWSL
Current state: • It was established in 1996 • In 2017, there are 12 teams with a total of 144 players on team rosters • In 2017, seven teams are associated with a NBA team **Business analytics:** • In 2017, four teams have full-time business analytics positions • Size of the business analytics department ranges from 1 to 12	**Current state:** • It was formed in 2012 • In 2017, there are 10 teams with a total of 218 players • In 2017, four teams are associated with a MLS or a NASL team **Business analytics:** • In 2017, there are no business analytics positions within the NWSL teams • Houston Dash has support of Houston Dynamo business analytics staff

During the introduction stage of the product life cycle, the market for the product is small and sales are low, yet they increase in time. Thus, the overall revenue generated is limited, whereas the cost of research and development, testing, and marketing are high, especially in competitive industries such as sports and entertainment. The narrow fan base for women's sports and lower attendance numbers than for men's sports are indicative of the smaller market and the earlier life cycle of the women's sport products. However, rather than evaluating women's sports as unworthy and hopeless businesses, a realistic, objective comparison should be drawn by relying on the current metrics of women's sport leagues and the metrics of men's sports from earlier years. In 2016, the WNBA completed its 20th season with an average attendance of 7,318 (Berri, 2016) and better than ever ratings and online engagement (Associated Press, 2016). In its 20th season, the NBA barely averaged 6,000 fans per game (Berri, 2016). In addition, although only half of the WNBA teams are profitable in the early stage, some NBA teams are still losing money in the league's 70th season. Based on this comparison, the WNBA is a more successful business than the NBA in its introductory life cycle. Thus, women's professional team sports are in the introductory stage of their product life cycle, but they experience growth and indicate promise for the future.

On the other hand, the LPGA and the WTA are further on in their product life cycle, because they were established in 1950 and 1973, respectively. However, these two women's sports are inherently different from the WNBA and NWSL. Athletes are not employees of the tournaments or the league, and the tournaments are owned and operated separately without any revenue sharing or seeking of parity within the association. Thus, the business model of women's golf and tennis is different, and their need for business analytics differs from teams that are looking to fill their seats regularly throughout the season.

These are not to dismiss the reality of low-ticket prices, lack of women's sports programming in media, and lower broadcasting rights and sponsorship revenues for the women's leagues and associations. Thus, women's professional sports lack the financial resources that men's professional sports have today. When the lack of resources is coupled with the price point of CRM and analytics systems and services, it is clear that the women's professional sports cannot justify or afford the investment in the technology and, therefore, they lag behind the trend in the industry.

Type of analytics used in women's professional sports

As the previous section demonstrated, use of business analytics is limited in women's professional sports. None the less, the LPGA and WTA, and some of the teams within the WNBA and NWSL, utilize business analytics to a degree in their operation. The LPGA and WTA focus more on consumer insights and marketing, content and media performance, branding, and sponsorship sales and evaluations. On the other hand, WNBA and NWSL teams focus more on ticket sales and pricing, customer retention and account renewals, fan profiling, sponsorship lead generation, and sales.

Both the LPGA and the WTA generate consumer insights to provide meaningful products and services at their events, increase attendance and merchandise sales, identify target audience, and utilize in sponsorship sales and services. These insights rely on audience profiles, including demographic characteristics, behavioral tendencies at these organizations' events, and media consumption habits. In addition to consumer insights, content and media performance are measured. Reports are compiled with the information derived from the organizations' website and social media platforms, the tournaments' resources, and the syndicated data purchased from third-party entities. Content and media performance focus on where, what, how, and when audiences consume content, along with identifying the public relations value of these efforts. Both consumer insights and media performance are valuable tools in sponsorship valuation and sales. Potential sponsors evaluate the value of sport properties based on the size and characteristics of their consumers, and the media performance. Thus, consumer insights and media metrics such as ratings, impressions, and media equivalencies are extremely important in prospecting sponsors and sales of sponsorships. Finally, the LPGA and WTA conduct marketing research for brand awareness and market position of their organizations within the competitive sport industry, and measure the economic impact of their events on the respective geographic areas (Curtin, 2017; Frame, n.d.; Tan, n.d.).

Sport teams from the WNBA and NWSL perform similar analyses to the LPGA and WTA, but also conduct different business analytics due to the different business needs. The primary focus of business analytics for the women's professional basketball and soccer teams is ticket sales and pricing (Falkson, 2017; Kolehmain, 2017; Tagliarino, 2017). These leagues analyze historical and real-time data on ticket prices and sales to assess the impact of scheduling, identify revenue generated and capacity sold per game and season, predict sales for upcoming games, and adjust ticket and package pricing. Another practice pertaining to ticket pricing is tracking changes in real time in the secondary market, which is then used to adjust prices in the primary market to increase direct sales through the teams.

These teams also use CRM systems to store information on their current fans and prospects. This information is particularly useful in creating customer profiles, lead generation, and prospecting. With the information stored on current customers, teams can predict accounts' likelihood of renewal, improve customer services and offerings, and increase customer retention. The information gathered on prospects helps sales staff to offer meaningful packages and prices, and increase the likelihood of closing sales successfully. Similar to the LPGA and WTA, customer profiles and insights are used in sponsorship sales.

Finally, women's professional team and individual sports rely on analytics in sponsorship development and account assessment. Data on industry trends, in terms of corporations' interest in sport properties, prior sponsorship deals, assets purchased for these deals, cost of sponsorships, and key contacts for sponsorship sales, allows teams to pursue potential sponsors successfully and communicate more effectively.

Business analytics in men's professional sports

This section summarizes the use of business analytics in men's professional sports to present how analytics could improve the efficiency of women's professional sports. In addition to the summary of the general use of business analytics, most current improvements in men's professional sports are detailed to provide direction for the future in the sport industry.

Analytics in ticketing

Undeniably, ticket sales and pricing receive a great deal of attention from sport franchises, because ticket sales are one of the main revenue sources for these organizations. In the early 2000s, sport teams realized that they were not utilizing pricing to its full potential because sport fans were paying more for tickets in the secondary ticket market. Longitudinal analyses of ticket sales and pricing revealed the opportunity to price tickets variably, based on the quality of the opponent and the timing of the game. Forecasting and trend analyses predict expected demand for the games and the value perceived by the sport fans, which result in better pricing tactics and higher number of tickets sold. In recent years, although teams continue to price their tickets variably at the start of the season, based on the expected demand and the price–value proposition, they also utilize dynamic pricing, which is adjusting ticket prices upward or downward based on real-time market conditions including demand, scarcity, and so on. The ultimate goal of analytics on ticket pricing is to set optimal prices to maximize revenue. For more information about ticket pricing and analytics, please refer to Fried and Mumcu (2017).

In addition to pricing of tickets, sales of tickets are important for sport organizations for obvious reasons. From a ticket sales perspective, analytics are used for two main purposes: retention and upsell of current fans, and acquisition of new consumers for both business-to-customer (B2C) and business-to-business (B2B) accounts. As known in the industry, servicing current fans is less costly than acquiring new fans (Mullin, Sutton, & Hardy, 2014), and increasing the frequency of sales to existing fans is more likely than acquiring new fans (Mumcu, 2017a). With this knowledge, it is no surprise to see the great deal of attention current ticket purchasers and season ticket holders receive from an analytics perspective. In order to identify the likelihood of ticket package renewal and continued attendance, retention and propensity models are utilized in the sport industry. With these models, sport organizations identify current accounts that are likely to renew their ticket packages, those that are undecided (also known as fence sitters), and the ones likely to churn. As a result of these models, sales teams can reach out to fence sitters in a timely manner and retain them, upsell frequent attendees by offering meaningful packages, and increase sales and revenue efficiently.

Demographics and psychographics of current ticket purchasers provide useful insights in acquiring new fans and customers. Sport properties develop look-a-like models to create a profile for existing customers, which are used in the acquisition of new fans and customers. Knowledge of who an organization's current fans are and how they behave allows sport properties to chase after new consumers who are similar to the current, devoted, valuable fans. Furthermore, lead-scoring models are used to identify prospects who are more likely to become paying customers. Thus, insights from the current fan base result in increased effectiveness of marketing and sales campaigns and tactics, and build a sales pipeline.

A remaining issue in ticket sales was that, once primary ticket buyers sold their tickets in the secondary market, sport properties lost the information on who the consumer in their facilities enjoying the experience really was. This has been an important hurdle to overcome due to missing the resale and upsell opportunities as a result of not having the information of the attendees, and potential mismatch between promotional offerings and services available at the venues, and the attendees' wants and needs. Ticketmaster's new digital ticketing system, called Presence, can track the life cycle of a ticket through the secondary market and identify the purchasers. The new technology allows teams to track the number of times a ticket changes hands in the market. For example, the report for the Orlando Pride-Atlanta United FC game indicated that approximately half of the tickets were resold at least once, more than a third of the tickets were resold twice, and some others resold at least three times (Fisher, 2017). In addition, the data allows teams to observe the patterns and trends in ticket sales and exchanges. Data provided new prospects for the Orlando Pride's 2018 season ticket holder list, and increased the number of fans identified in their CRM by 20% (Fisher, 2017). Knowledge of who is actually in the building and how tickets were exchanged provides a much deeper understanding of the market. The system provides valuable insights in identifying prospects, pricing tickets, and scheduling games.

Although data provides valuable insights on who to sell, how to sell, what to offer, and so on, it is important not to get lost in analyzing ticket sales and pricing, and stay focused on providing a good experience for the fans. Without the experience, fans will not return to the events just for the price.

Analytics in fan engagement

To fill stadiums and arenas, sport teams and organizations need to have a deep understanding of who their fans are, and what their wants and needs are, and provide engaging, fun, exciting experiences to their patrons. This is where customer intelligence comes into play. In addition to the core sport product, the game day experience is impacted by a variety of things. Traffic to the venue, parking, entry to and exit from the venue, and lines at concession stands and restrooms are just a few such considerations for sport fans. Sport organizations can track these with technology, find solutions to the issues, and improve attendees' experience in real time. For example, the Allianz Arena of the Bayern Munich Football Club of Bundesliga has extensive technology that allows for enhancement of the live arena experience for their visitors during matches. On an ordinary game day, the team welcomes 75,000 attendees to their arena and aims to enhance visitors' experience with digital technology provided by SAP, a multinational software corporation. Their visitors are provided information on alternate travel methods, current time traffic data, and alternate routes to the arena via their app. As cars arrive at the stadium, the team can observe the movement of the masses via heat maps and direct them to different entrances to improve visitors' experience with parking and ease their entrance to the arena. By using weather sensors, the temperature in the arena and offerings in the concession stands are adjusted, which results in a comfortable experience with higher concession sales. In addition, during the game, sentiment analysis of fans' social media comments and current match data are analyzed to identify popular players of the match, which leads into real-time adjustments in merchandise stores (i.e., inventory, pricing, promotions) for higher sales. Finally, at the end of the game, as all attendees want to exit the arena and go home, it is common to experience delay and congestion. In these times, they provide additional services such as vouchers in restaurants, and tickets to public relations conferences via an app to delay some of the fans' departure from the arena and improve attendees' experience (Ereth, 2016).

Analytics in marketing and digital media

The goal of marketing is to place the brand in the minds of the customer, increase awareness, and entice them to spend their limited discretionary income on the products and services marketed. In this endeavor, marketing campaigns and tactics are implemented, and their outcome and effectiveness are measured. In order to optimize marketing budgets, sport organizations analyze the return on investment (ROI) of their marketing campaigns and tactics, and pursue the ones with the most positive return. The ROI is measured by comparing the revenue generated against the cost of the marketing activity (Lauren, 2011). Cost per lead, number of wins, cost of customer acquisition, customer life-time value, and incremental sales are some of the most frequently utilized metrics (Mumcu, 2017a). Insights derived from data analyses allow organizations to engage with their customers effectively, by sending the right message to the right person at the right time via the right platform (Green, 2015).

In addition to traditional marketing methods, digital marketing is heavily used in the sport industry. More and more people rely on websites and mobile applications for information search and purchases. In 2014, 87 million individuals consumed sport content by visiting websites on a computer and 62 million by using their smartphones (Ourand, 2014). Individuals spent an average of 105 minutes during a visit to websites via computer and 92 minutes via smartphone, and time spent on sport websites increased by 22% in 2015 (Nielsen Report, 2016). Thus, websites have become the face of sport organizations, because they are the main information source where the organization controls the messaging and content. For example, Arsenal Football Club of the English Premier League developed a digital membership, which allows members to access all team videos and content free of charge. As a result, approximately 70% of their 1.3 million digital members worldwide are based outside the United Kingdom (Metral, 2016). This allows the team to control the content their fans consume, and gain insights about their fans from a 360-degree view, which could then be used in monetizing the fans by offering additional services. With search engine optimization, ad words, pixel tracking, and heat maps, sport organizations can track the traffic to their website, and determine how their audience arrived at their website. In addition, they can assess the effectiveness of their website through various metrics such as number of page views, number of unique visitors, entry page, landing page, visit duration, click-through, and conversion rate. Finally, by using A/B testing, sport websites can measure the effectiveness of their design and content (Mumcu, 2017b).

In 2017, 81% of the US population was using social media (Statista.com, 2017) and 86% of Americans were identified as sport fans (Barr, 2017). Thus, social media is one of the main outlets where people spend most of their time, and it is a primary source of sport information. Sport organizations rely on social media to engage with fans, increase brand awareness, communicate with their fans, control damage to their reputation, provide customer service, and support their bottom line. Social media allows sport organizations to interact with their fans outside their geographic location, and grow their fan base. Some metrics used in measuring the effectiveness of social media are reach, engagement, traffic, sentiment analysis, cost per action and click, click-through rate, cost per new follower, and cost per impression (Mumcu, 2017b). Mobile applications are also a part of digital media used to communicate directly with sport fans. In 2017, the Jacksonville Jaguars unveiled a new mobile app to enhance fans' socialization and engagement. In addition to the traditional app features of sending updates, statistics, scores, and so on, the app features a live chat room, private messaging, a game day chat room for fans at the game, and a marketplace map of tailgates at the venue and neighborhood bars and restaurants (Retting, 2017). Although the app has just become available and more features are to be added in the future, it will clearly provide an enormous amount of data about Jaguars fans' socialization and consumption rates.

In addition to the web, social media, and applications, email marketing has proven its worth in this era. Sport fans opt in to receive emails from their favorite teams, leagues, and events. Email marketing provides several advantages over the traditional communication mix. It is cheaper, easier to personalize, and easier to measure its performance. Some of the metrics used in analyzing the performance of email marketing are open rate, click-through rate, and churn metrics such as unsubscribe, hard bounce rate, and complaint/spam rate (Mumcu, 2017b). In addition, A/B testing of emails reveals the best way to design the emails and present content. By using these metrics, sport organizations gain insight into what is most successful in reaching fans, getting their attention, and prompting them to act. Examples from the sport industry revealed that personalized emails have been more successful in reaching sport fans. Major League Soccer (MLS) experienced a 39% increase in unique click rate when personalized emails were used as opposed to static email (Metral, 2016).

Digital marketing, as a whole, provides advantages over traditional marketing, especially from an analytics and measurement perspective. Traditional marketing campaigns and their effectiveness are measured after the campaign due to the time needed to compile data. However, digital marketing allows real-time measurement and, as a result, instant modifications. Sport organizations then adjust their marketing activities based on the insights derived from these analyses. Due to women's sports being the focus of this chapter, information on analytical methods, definitions, and calculations of metrics used by women's teams and leagues is limited. For more detailed information on marketing and digital marketing analytics, definitions of metrics, and their calculation, please refer to Mumcu (2017a, 2017b). For more examples on the use of business analytics in mainstream sports, please visit the websites of SAS, SAP, Nielsen, Umbel, Hootsuite, Marketo, and similar companies.

Analytics in sport sponsorship

Sponsorships are one of the largest revenue sources in the sport industry. In 2016, global sport sponsorship spending in fees was US$60.1 billion, and was predicted to rise to US$62.8 billion in 2017 (IEG.com, 2017). Corporate partners sign sponsorship deals with sport properties for various reasons such as increasing public awareness, enhancing brand image, increasing sales and market share, and generating media benefits. To retain corporate interest, sport properties have to provide a meaningful return and direct benefits to the corporation. Sponsorship analytics aim to measure the ROI of the sponsorship. Traditionally, consumers' awareness of the sponsor, perception of the sponsor's brand, and consumers' likelihood of purchasing the corporate partner's products and services over their competitors in the marketplace were assessed. In addition, media equivalencies and public relations impressions have been measured to present the media benefits of the sponsorships. Teams and sponsors have also used third party companies such as Nielsen Sports, which acquired Repucom in 2016, to become the global leader in sport intelligence. Nielsen Sports has a media evaluation tool called Sport 24, which tracks and evaluates exposure of all brands detected in global sports and events, and provides a neutral standardized measure to compare against (Nielsensports.com, n.d.), making them the current gold standard in the industry.

With the changing media landscape (e.g., cord-cutting, over-the-top sport programming) and omni-channel marketing approaches used by sport organizations (traditional, social, digital), corporate partners now have alternate assets available through sponsorship packages and access to additional measurement techniques. Across all major league sports, corporate partners are interested in the digital and social media benefits offered through their sponsorship package (Scott, 2017). With the use of social and digital media, new approaches to the measurement of sponsorship ROI have become available. The National Association for Stock Car Auto Racing (NASCAR) utilized Wasserman Group's Social Media Scoreboard to measure the ROI of sponsorships, and found that 18% of NASCAR fans made purchases from a sponsor as a result of a social media post. In addition, Nielsen Social found that consumers who tweet about NASCAR are four times more likely to tweet about its sponsors than other US brands on average (Scott, 2017). Thus, the use of social and digital media in this sponsorship example provided additional measurement for the examination of sponsorship outcomes.

Conclusion

Men's professional sport organizations have been increasingly utilizing business analytics and taking advantage of the developments in this field. However, women's professional sports are behind this industry trend, because a limited number of women's professional sport organizations have the opportunity to use business analytics. Women's sports are lagging behind this industry trend due to financial instability, lack of available resources, and being in an earlier product life-cycle stage than most professional men's leagues. In order to use business analytics competitively, women's sport organizations need to invest in technology, infrastructure, and personnel. With the current state of affairs, women's professional sport organizations are unable to justify the investment needed for business analytics, because the outcome of analytics might not offset the cost of the investment. However, as technology advances and more data becomes available, and additional services and measurement techniques arise, the impact of business analytics in the sport industry will become increasingly prevalent.

Leader profile: Laura Meyer, VP of Business Intelligence, Minnesota Timberwolves & Lynx

Laura Meyer is in her 12th season with the Minnesota Timberwolves & Lynx, and in her second season as the Vice President of Business Intelligence. In her current role, Meyer is responsible for driving the organization's business objectives and strategic initiatives through data acquisition, analysis, and visualization. Before her current role, she served as Sr. Director of Business

Figure 18.1 Laura Meyer

Intelligence, Director of Revenue Strategy and Operations, Sr. Manager of Sales Strategy and Integration, and Ticket and Premium Seating Supervisor. A native of Cincinnati, Ohio, Meyer graduated magna cum laude from the University Scholars honors program at Xavier University, with a degree in Sports Management and a double minor in Business and Psychology.

Some of her achievements at the Minnesota Lynx, as they relate to business analytics, are as follows:

- First WNBA team to institute dynamic pricing across all inventory types.
- Leader in WNBA in utilizing the team's full tech stack, including CRM and data warehouse, to maximize sales representatives' efficiency and continually growing MN Lynx fan base.
- Purposefully applying vetted sales operations processes, best practices, and technologies that contributed to the MN Lynx reaching profitability in 2012 and growing revenues each year since.
- Leading the Lynx's conversion to 100% digital ticketing in 2015, which made the team the first professional franchise, men's or women's, to be completely digital.
- Overseeing the seat relocation, pricing, inventory, lead strategy, and logistics for the relocation to Xcel Energy Center and Williams Arena in 2017, and then back to the Target Center in 2018.
- Despite temporary relocations into different venues, MN Lynx leads the WNBA in attendance and revenue.

With regard to her role as a woman leader, Meyer stated:

> I found out quickly it wasn't enough just to lead by example. It's a challenge to keep strong-talented women in our industry, when the environment naturally poses obstacles and reasons to choose something different. We founded the Women in Sports Leadership Council in our organization as a way to provide opportunities to be a leader, develop skill sets for working in a male-dominated industry, and grow professionally while building stronger relationships with your peers. Over its years of existence we've seen the evolution from an all-male executive group to a balanced leadership team in both gender and diversity with four female Vice Presidents out of 11 all whom grew from within the company.

References

Associated Press (2016). WNBA's 20th season produces strong numbers and ratings, August 1. Retrieved from www.espn.com/wnba/story/_/id/17195190/wnba-20th-season-produces-strong-numbers-ratings.
Barr, A. (2017). Sports fans and social: Some statistics, May 10. Retrieved from https://www.crowdynews.com/blog/sports-fans-social.
Berri, D. (2016). Think the WNBA is in trouble? Let's talk some NBA history, June 3. Retrieved from www.huffingtonpost.com/david-berri/think-the-wnba-is-in-trouble-lets-talk-nba-history_b_10279354.html.
Curtin, K. (2017). An unpublished interview with Kerrilyn Curtin: Director of Market Research and Planning at LPGA/Interviewer: Ceyda Mumcu. New Haven, CT.
Drayer, J. & Maxcy, J. (2014). Sport analytics: Advancing decision making through technology and data. Retrieved from www.fox.temple.edu/cms/wp-content/uploads/2014/04/final-MaxcyDrayerIBITReport.pdf.
Ereth, J. (2016). Sports intelligence – the role of technology in professional sports, June 22. Retrieved from https://www.eckerson.com/articles/sports-intelligence-the-role-of-technology-in-professional-sports.
Falkson, A. (2017). An unpublished interview with Adam Falkson: Director of Business Intelligence at Monumental Sports and Entertainment/Interviewer: Ceyda Mumcu. New Haven, CT.
Fisher, E. (2017). How teams benefit from tracking ticket's life cycle. *Sport Business Journal*, **20**(16). Retrieved from https://www.sportsbusinessdaily.com/Journal/Issues/2017/08/07/In-Depth/Tracking-tickets.aspx.
Frame, N. (n.d.). LinkedIn page. Retrieved from https://www.linkedin.com/in/nicholas-frame-04941542.
Fried, G. & Mumcu, C. (2017). *Sport Analytics: A data-driven approach to sport business and management*. New York: Routledge.
Green, F. (2015). Social CRM: Debunking the myth. Fan engagement 2015: data-driven marketing best practices. Paper presented at Europe Conference in November 2015. Retrieved from www.sportsanalyticseurope.com/presentations-fan-engagement.
IEG.com (2017). Sponsorship spending forecast: continued growth around the world, January 4. Retrieved from www.sponsorship.com/IEGSR/2017/01/04/Sponsorship-Spending-Forecast--Continued-Growth-Ar.aspx.
Kolehmain, K. (2017). An unpublished interview with Kris Kolehmain: Director of Business Intelligence at Seattle Storm/Interviewer: Ceyda Mumcu. New Haven, CT.
Lauren, G. H. (2011). *Business Analytics for Sales and Marketing Manager: How to compete in the information age*. Hoboken, NJ: John Wiley & Sons, Inc.
Metral, M. (2016). How business analytics is disrupting the sports industry, April 13. Retrieved from http://impakter.com/how-business-analytics-is-disrupting-the-sports-industry.
Michaelis, V. (2003). WUSA ceases operations after three years. *USA Today*, September 15. Retrieved from www.usatoday.com/sports/soccer/wusa/2003-09-15-wusa-folds_x.htm.
Min, H. (2016). *Global Business Analytics Models: Concepts and applications in predictive, healthcare, supply chain, and finance analytics*. Indianapolis, IN: Pearson FT Press.
Mullin, B. J., Hardy, S., & Sutton, W. A. (2014). *Sport Marketing*, 4th edn. Campaign, IL: Human Kinetics.
Mumcu, C. (2017a). Analytics in sport marketing. In G. Fried and C. Mumcu (eds), *Sport Analytics: A data-driven approach to sport business and management* (pp. 91–114). New York: Routledge.
Mumcu, C. (2017b). Analytics in digital marketing. In G. Fried and C. Mumcu (eds), *Sport Analytics: A data-driven approach to sport business and management* (pp. 115–129). New York: Routledge.
Nielsen Report (2016). The year in sports media report, February 3. Retrieved from www.nielsen.com/content/dam/corporate/us/en/reports-downloads/2016-reports/nielsen-year-in-sports-report-feb-2016.pdf.
Nielsensports.com (n.d.). Media evaluation. Retrieved from http://nielsensports.com/connected-solutions/media-evaluation.
Ourand, L. (2014). Sports media. *Sport Business Journal*, **17**(4), 16–19.
Pethchesky, B. (2012). Women's professional soccer is officially dead. Retrieved from http://deadspin.com/5911436/womens-professional-soccer-is-officially-dead (accessed January 16, 2013).
Retting, M. (2017). Jacksonville Jaguars app enables fans from around the world to chat, September 23. Retrieved from https://www.sporttechie.com/app-jacksonville-jaguars-fans-chat/?utm_source=SportTechie+Updates&utm_campaign=14a27f20e2-SportTechie_Weekly_News&utm_medium=email&utm_term=0_5d2e0c085b-14a27f20e2-294437401.

Rovell, D. (2003). Still a business, not a cause. Retrieved from http://espn.go.com/sportsbusiness/s/2003/0915/1616775.html.

Scott, N. (2017). Maximizing sponsorship ROI in an omni-channel world. *Journal of Digital and Social Media Marketing*, **4**(4), 318–328.

Statista.com (2017). Percentage of US population with a social media profile from 2008–2017. Retrieved from https://www.statista.com/statistics/273476/percentage-of-us-population-with-a-social-network-profile.

Steinberg, L. (2015). Changing the game: The rise of sports analytics. Retrieved from https://www.forbes.com/sites/leighsteinberg/2015/08/18/changing-the-game-the-rise-of-sports-analytics/#554984bb4c1f.

Tagliarino, D. (2017). An unpublished interview with David Tagliarino: SVP and COO at Houston Dynamo, Houston Dash, and BBVA Compass Stadium/Interviewer: Ceyda Mumcu. New Haven, CT.

Tan, X. [Xiyu] (n.d.). LinkedIn page. Retrieved from https://www.linkedin.com/in/xiyu-yolanda-tan/?lipi=urn%3Ali%3Apage%3Ad_flagship3_search_srp_top%3BveOAx%2BCMQ7SxdZ6%2BhA9%2Ftg%3D%3D&licu=urn%3Ali%3Acontrol%3Ad_flagship3_search_srp_top-search_srp_result&lici=%2BoDPAtekS9CT6RU55VV7YA%3D%3D.

Part IV
Leadership and governance

19
Under-representation of women in leadership roles in women's sport

Laura J. Burton

We continue to celebrate women reaching top leadership positions in sport in the United States, including the selection of former Women's National Basketball Association (WNBA) player Jamila Wideman as Vice President of Player Development for the National Basketball Association (NBA), and the first Latina (Desiree Reed-Francois) and first black woman (Carla Williams) to lead major college athletic programs, along with seven other women hired to lead Division I college athletic departments in 2018. However, we continue to observe "glacially slow progress towards the advancement of women into sport leadership" (Burton & Leberman, 2017, p. 16). Girls and women make up almost half of all sport participants, yet they are not being equally represented and led by women at any level of participation within the United States or internationally (Acosta & Carpenter, 2014; Lapchick et al., 2017). As a result, the aspirations, experiences, challenges, and expectations of girls and women in sport are not voiced, given that women have not yet attained a "seat at the table" of leadership in sport organizations (Burton & Leberman, 2017). This chapter examines factors that contribute to the "glacially slow progress" toward equitable representation in leadership positions within US sport organizations. Before examining those myriad factors, the chapter is framed using the concept of the Leadership Labyrinth put forward by Alice Eagly and Linda Carli (2007).

Leadership labyrinth

Scholars with an interest in women's experiences in sport leadership continue to push against the notion of "fixing the women" and call attention to the structural and societal constraints that must be revealed, challenged, and changed if individual women are to reach and retain positions in leadership, including leadership in sport (see Shaw & Frisby, 2006).

The Leadership Labyrinth (Eagly & Carli, 2007) has been used to describe the challenges that women face when attempting to reach leadership positions in business and has also been explored as a framework to understand the under-representation of women in sport coaching (Burton & LaVoi, 2016). Eagly and Carli (2007) utilize the metaphor of a labyrinth to describe the barriers to women's advancement in leadership, noting that it is "not the glass ceiling, but the sum of many obstacles along the way" (p. 2) that impede women's progress toward leadership.

As detailed below, there are myths associated with the glass ceiling that need to be "debunked" to help describe women's experiences on the path toward attaining sport leadership positions.

A glass ceiling for women in sport leadership?

Using the metaphor of the glass ceiling implies that no women can reach the highest level of leadership in sport organizations. However, there are many women who have reached the highest levels of leadership, including, for example, Lisa Borders (President, WNBA), Michele Roberts (Executive Director, NBA Players' Association), Katrina Adams (President and CEO, United States Tennis Association, Val Ackerman (Commissioner, Big East Conference), and Dawn Hudson (Chief Marketing Officer, National Football League). As noted earlier, women also lead major athletic departments in Division I Football Bowl Subdivision universities, including Carla Williams (University of Virginia) and Desiree Reed-Francois (University of Nevada, Las Vegas).

The "glass ceiling" metaphor also implies that there is a transparent obstacle that is difficult for women to see from a distance. Unfortunately, the obstacles women face are often very real, visible, and not at all subtle. Women are well aware of the many constraints they face in sport leadership, including the lack of opportunity to lead major men's professional sport organizations, because no women presently hold the position of CEO or President of a men's professional sport organization. However, men do hold the most senior leadership positions in women's sport organizations, including Steve Simon (CEO, Women's Tennis Association) and Michael Wann (CEO, Ladies Professional Golf Association).

Finally, the "glass ceiling" metaphor implies that there is a single barrier to women's advancement to leadership positions; however, the barriers that women face are numerous and complex, and impact them at multiple points along their career paths. Furthermore, women are not impacted at the penultimate point in their career, but instead the barriers and challenges women face cause many to leave at multiple points along their career paths. This loss of women along their career paths in sport leads to a smaller pool of qualified candidates from which to draw for senior level positions (Eagly & Carli, 2007; Hancock & Hums, 2016).

The experience of the labyrinth for women in sport leadership

All women are not failing to reach top leadership positions in sport organizations, but many are facing obstacles and challenges along their sport career paths. The labyrinth metaphor can help to better understand and address this vexing problem of why, given the incredible increase in the number of girls and women participating in sport in the United States, we continue to document "glacially slow progress" for women in sport leadership. After the passage in 1972 of landmark civil rights legislation, Title IX of the Education Amendments Act, which included language requiring federally funded institutions (e.g., K-12 schools, universities) to provide equal opportunities in academic and extracurricular activities for the under-represented sex, girls' participation in high school sports jumped from 294,015 to 3,324,326 in 2016. Title IX also impacted college sport participation because only 64,390 participated in 1972, but by 2013 211,886 participated in college sports (NCAA report Title IX – Wilson, 2017). Clearly, when provided opportunities to participate in sports, girls and women take full advantage.

The metaphor of a leadership labyrinth is compelling because women have and continue to hold leadership positions in sport organizations, which supports the notion that as "labyrinths have routes to the center, it is understood that goals are attainable" (Eagly & Carli, 2007, p. 3). Furthermore, as has been described in work examining the opportunities available to and barriers faced by women in sport leadership (Burton, 2015; Burton & Leberman, 2017), the labyrinth metaphor recognizes that there are obstacles, but that some of those obstacles are not completely discouraging, because there is a path to success (Eagly & Carli, 2007).

As described in the labyrinth, women experience general bias at all levels of their careers. Research over the past 20 years has demonstrated that individuals associate men and women with different traits and men, compared with women, are expected to demonstrate traits more broadly associated with leadership (Eagly & Karau, 2002). Furthermore, this bias against women in leadership is perpetuated because leadership is viewed as more closely aligned to men and male traits and behaviors, so women are viewed as not capable of being successful leaders. When women demonstrate those leadership traits necessary to be successful leaders, they face the double bind of acting outside expectations and not being liked for doing so (Heilman, 2012). As women face a double bind in leadership, they often develop a leadership style that includes characteristics women are expected to demonstrate (communal) along with the characteristics expected of a successful leader (agentic).

In addition, the leadership labyrinth describes the challenges women face as resulting from increased expectations with regard to familial responsibilities. As women continue to take on most of the family responsibilities, they face more significant career interruptions and have fewer hours of employment per year. These interruptions decrease opportunities for advancement and earnings for women (Eagly & Carli, 2007). As a result of those family responsibilities and expectations, women often lack the time or capacity to engage in the networking and socializing necessary to build social capital in a work environment. Social capital is an important component of leadership development (McCallum & O'Connell, 2009), and having less access to opportunities to build social capital can negatively impact women's leadership development (Katz, Walker, & Hindman, 2018).

A multi-level approach

The next sections detail the most current scholarship conducted to date that has examined why there continue to be so few women leading sport organizations in the United States. This review applies a multilevel perspective to examine the under-representation of women in sport leadership (Burton, 2015; Burton & LaVoi, 2016; Burton & Leberman, 2017; Dixon & Cunningham, 2006), because gender issues in sport are "situated in multi-level, sometimes subtle, and usually taken-for-granted structures, policies, and behaviors embedded in sport organizations" (Fink, 2008, p. 147). Before detailing the multi-level factors, two important frameworks, gender and power, impacting women's experiences in sport leadership must be discussed.

Sport leadership as masculine

Any discussion of leadership in sport organizations must first include an understanding that sport is a gendered space. Unfortunately, women are often situated as "other" in the social institution of sport, and the presence of women in sport, as athlete, coach, manager, or leader, is under constant scrutiny (Fink, 2016; Kane, 1995). Recent examples include sexist discussions of female athletes at the Rio 2016 Olympic Games (e.g., Guest, 2016), as announcers attributed Hungarian Olympian Katinka Hosszú's 400-meter individual medley gold medal and world record-breaking performance to her now former husband who served as her coach during the Olympics. Furthermore, in 2017 when ESPN announced long-time sports analyst, Beth Mowins, as the first woman to call a Monday night National Football League (NFL) game (Dicaro, 2017), viewers took to Twitter to describe Mowin's voice as "shrill" and "annoying."

As described by Anderson (2009), sport is a space used to "actively construct boys and men to exhibit, value and reproduce traditional notions of masculinity" (p. 4).

Women's experiences in sport leadership must be framed by understanding gender as fundamental to both organizational and social processes (Connell, 2009). Gender can have an influence on organizational practices, as cultures, interactions, and gender-appropriate behaviors are linked to socially constructed masculine or feminine ideals in the operations of sport organizations (Britton & Logan, 2008). Furthermore, recognition of gender as a social process provides a framework to examine how and why gender is such a powerful factor in the social and organizational processes that define sport organizations (Kihl, Shaw, & Schull, 2013).

Influence of power

Power is "the influence over a group or individual and provides the ability to change another person's behavior, actions, or attitude" (Kane, 2015, p. 5). Power must be addressed within the context of sport leadership because it highlights the influence of gender in interactions, structures, and processes of sport organizations (Shaw & Frisby, 2006). Thus, gender not only shapes identities, but also operates as an axis of power. There are typically six sources of power ascribed to leaders within sport organizations. First is reward power, which is the ability to provide rewards to subordinates. Second, coercive power carries aspects of punishment if subordinates do not meet expectations. Leaders hold legitimate power based on formal positions or titles, whereas leaders holding referent power command "such a presence of personality that group members are compelled to follow" (Kane, 2015, p. 6). Expert power refers to holding particular skills, knowledge, or expertise, and informational power is a situation-specific form of power that provides leaders with knowledge to support subordinates in meeting specific tasks (Kane, 2015).

A newly developed conceptual model that examines how power is manifest in the promotion and selection of women to top-level positions in organizations (Auster & Prasad, 2016) can be applied to how women are selected and promoted to senior leadership positions in sport organizations (Burton & Leberman, 2017). First, as an antecedent component of this model, a dominant ideology of leadership (i.e., what leadership "should be") is created by those in positions of power and is applied to perpetuate role incumbent schema used to assess candidates for leadership positions (Auster & Prasad, 2016). As power is held by similar "in-group" members (predominantly white, heterosexual men), individuals from out-groups experience increased bias when seeking promotion to higher-level positions (Auster & Prasad, 2016).

Committee practices, including evaluation of candidates, decision-making protocols, committee selection, and meetings, are impacted by social dominance processes because power held by those on hiring committees can negatively impact those who do not reflect "in-group" membership. These processes can influence promotion bias and promotion outcomes (Auster & Prasad, 2016). Work by Schull, Shaw, and Kihl (2013) demonstrated that stakeholders used power to reinforce the gendered norms of an intercollegiate athletic department. They described how stakeholders with an interest in maintaining power in a women's athletic program actively supported the hiring of a male athletic director for a newly merged athletic department that would control both the men's and the women's programs. As described by Schull et al. (2013), the stakeholders' support for a male athletic director was based on the perception that, if a female athletic director was to be selected, she would be "eaten up alive" (p. 71) by members affiliated with the men's athletic programs. Therefore, stakeholders associated with the women's athletic program actively campaigned for a specific type of male candidate over campaigning for a female candidate. Furthermore, stakeholders aligned with the men's athletic department, as a result of their power and political influence, had access to key decision-makers and financial support of the university, as well as critical constituents in the media. Finally, the stakeholders established criteria to support the hiring of the new athletic director that appeared to be gender neutral, but actually "privileged a certain type of masculinity in the sport context—a man who values gender equity" (Schull et al., 2013, p. 76).

The links to power and gender can also be understood through the structure of sport organizations and where women are positioned (legitimate power) within them. As detailed in the Race and Gender Report cards produced by the Institute for Diversity and Ethics in Sport, women are under-represented in positions of power or influence at senior leadership levels across all sports. Furthermore, power also influences gendered relations in sport organizations in at least three different ways. First, as men are over-represented in higher status jobs, power connects to gender in the structure of organizations, with men receiving higher pay and more status within organizations. Also, power is demonstrated through social practices that portray men as powerful and women as compliant, and therefore positions and tasks are constructed to favor men. Finally, power can be used in the process of gender identity formation within the organization such that external forces of power "endorse particular meanings of gender, and internal pressures dictate the degree of one's compliance" (Ely & Padavic, 2007, p. 1131).

Sociocultural (macro) perspective on women in sport leadership

Sport operates within a wider context of societal norms and practices operating at the level of individual nations and also globally. The focus of this chapter is on a US-based sport leadership, so the focus at the macro level will be US based. To examine the under-representation of women at the sociocultural (macro) level in the United States requires situating sport as a gendered institution, where all processes in sport operate within a shared understanding of sport as masculine. Most individuals working in the sport sector share an assumption that work and organizational practices are gender neutral, which serves to reinforce male dominance in sport leadership (Burton, 2015). Sport organizations have institutionalized masculinity as a way of operating, where male activity is privileged, and masculinity and masculine behavior are regarded as leadership qualities necessary in sport (Cunningham, 2010; Fink, 2016; Shaw & Frisby, 2006). For those who do not embody this type of masculine behavior, perceptions of their skills as leaders and the individual's recognition of leadership ability are called into question (Heilman, 2012).

Organizational demography, those individuals (based on race/ethnicity, religion, gender, sexual identity) who hold certain positions, influences perceptions about who is appropriate for particular positions, and therefore appropriate to perform particular work, within an organization (Ely & Padavic, 2007). As described previously, men have and continue to dominate leadership positions in all sport organization in the United States (Acosta & Carpenter, 2014; Lapchick et al., 2017). As noted in the previous section, men hold most of the leadership positions in intercollegiate sport, whereas women hold a limited number of leaderships positions, including leadership at the athletic director level at Division I (7%), Division II (23%), and Division III levels (30%). In the NFL, women do hold positions of leadership within league offices (34% in 2017), yet no women currently hold the CEO or president position for an NFL team. Only one woman, Amy Trask, former CEO of the Oakland Raiders, has ever held that position. In Major League Baseball (MLB) women hold only 20% of senior level positions in the league office and 27% of senior administration positions at the team level. The NBA does comparatively better than the NFL and MLB, because 39% of women hold senior level positions in league offices and six women have served as CEO or in team president positions. In the

WNBA 39% of senior level positions are held by women, six women serve in CEO positions, five hold the position of General Manager and notably 11 women are team owners (Lapchick et al., 2017). Based on these data, the demography of leadership positions in sport organizations is highly skewed to male leaders, with the noted exception of the WNBA, one of the only women's professional sport organizations. This skewed gender ratio serves to reinforce the notion of masculinity and masculine leadership as the norm in sport.

Women may perceive limited opportunities for advancement when exposed to the inequities in organizational demography that disproportionately favor men (Hancock & Hums, 2016). As a result of the assumption that a certain type of masculinity (heterosexual and physically dominant) is required to lead sport organizations, men maintain control of the most senior levels of leadership in US sport (see information above) and have higher rates of organizational success (e.g., rates of career advancement) (Whisenant, Pedersen, & Obenour, 2002).

Organizational (meso) level perspectives on women in sport leadership

Next, it is important to understand that the practice of gender within organizations contributes to gender inequity and disparity (Martin, 2003). Organizational level factors include governance, policies, and various other organizational operations.

Operational and functional practices

The operations and functional practices within sport organizations serve to disadvantage women in leadership. Within intercollegiate athletic administration in the United States, women athletic administrator duties follow a more stereotypical feminine approach toward work focused on caring for student athletes (Inglis, Danylchuk, & Pastore, 2000). In a US women's professional sport organization, men marginalized women in the organization by minimizing the women's strategic influence in marketing strategies and undermining the women's authority by requiring women to conduct menial tasks below their level of authority (e.g., vacuum the office, take out the mail) (Allison, 2016). Female athletic directors noted higher expectations to engage in "service"-based work, including committee work, when compared with their male counterparts (Taylor & Wells, 2017).

Organizational policies and procedures

Organizational policies and procedures can influence access for women to leadership positions in the sport sector. In 2016, in an effort to increase diversity (both gender and racial diversity) in leadership within intercollegiate athletics, the National Collegiate Athletic Association (NCAA) asked presidents and chancellors representing all member institutions (i.e., colleges and universities participating in NCAA-sanctioned intercollegiate sports) to sign a pledge to "identify, recruit and interview individuals from diverse backgrounds in an effort to increase their representation and retention as commissioners, athletics directors, coaches and other leaders in athletics" (NCAA, 2016, para. 2). However, in 2017, select members of Congress sent a letter to NCAA president Mark Emmert requesting progress on that pledge. Emmert noted that the NCAA has no influence on university hiring practices, but that there will be continued efforts to provide strategies that will support the development of cultures that value diversity (Johnson, 2017). Although these efforts by the NCAA are noteworthy, a pledge of support to increase diversity lacks the necessary influence to make meaningful change from a policy perspective.

Work–family and family–work interface scholars have also examined how the organizational practices of sport organizations can be gendered. Work by Machida-Kosuga, Schaubroeck, and Feltz (2016) explored the impact of work and family conflict on leader self-efficacy for women in intercollegiate athletic administration, and revealed a negative relationship between perceived work–family conflict and their leadership self-efficacy. Women working in intercollegiate athletic leadership may struggle to maintain "a high level of self-efficacy about their leadership when their home lives interfere with their work" (Machida-Kosuga et al., 2016, p. 172).

Organizational culture

The organizational culture, "the set of shared, taken-for-granted implicit assumptions" (Schein, 1996, p. 236), of most sport organizations supports and perpetuates norms, values, and behaviors that reinforce hegemonic masculinity. Though scholars note that an organizational culture "that values diversity and capitalizes on the benefits such differences can bring to the workplace" contributes to success (Cunningham, 2008, p. 137), there are few sport organizations that demonstrate a diverse culture (Cunningham & Fink, 2006).

Sport organizations led by those who value gender equity and foster a diverse organizational culture had more positive organizational outcomes for women and men. These positive outcomes included stronger organizational commitment and intentions to stay in the organization (Spoor & Hoye, 2013). Importantly, organizational practices that supported women had a similar impact on the men working in that organization, including higher commitment and greater intention to stay, indicating that providing support for women can have a more significant impact on the entire organization (Spoor & Hoye, 2013) and is therefore beneficial to the organization as a whole.

Most intercollegiate athletic departments operate in organizational cultures that value similarity, and most people in athletic departments support the norms, values, and beliefs of white, Christian, able body, heterosexual men (Fink, Pastore, & Riemer, 2001). As a result, women and other minority groups exist as "other" within intercollegiate athletic department cultures (Walker & Melton, 2015). In addition, intercollegiate athletic departments foster and support organizational cultures that valorize heavy workloads and time in the office (Dixon & Bruening, 2007), which place significant time demands on individuals in the organization and have differing impacts on the ability of men and women to address demands of work and family. Many intercollegiate athletic administrators noted only modest support for work–life supportive cultures in their athletic departments (Dixon, Tiell, Lough, Sweeney, Osborne, & Bruening, 2008), yet others have noted improvements under a new generation of athletic directors (Taylor & Wells, 2017). Of note, women holding positions of leadership as intercollegiate athletic conference commissioners described the constant requirement of negotiating work and family responsibilities in order to hold their positions. Further, these leaders expected and accepted this as a "normal" requirement for women hoping to succeed in intercollegiate athletics leadership positions (Taylor, Siegele, Smith, & Hardin, 2018).

Social processes

Social processes, as a component to organizational culture, can also be analyzed to understand the informal, everyday practices taking place within an organization (Acker, 1992). Informal networks within sport organizations were important social process within these organizations, with both an old boys' network and old girls' network having an influence (Shaw & Frisby, 2006).

Informal social networks have significant impacts on opportunities for and promotion to leadership positions (Katz et al., 2018). Women working as athletic directors noted the continued challenge for donors and other influential stakeholders to include them in informal practices such as golf outings (Taylor & Wells, 2017). Furthermore, examination of the informal networks of male athletic directors, when compared with the networks of senior woman administrators (SWAs), revealed "a highly cohesive network of predominantly male leaders and largely noncohesive network of female leaders" (Katz et al., 2018, p. 114). Katz et al. noted that cohesive informal networks advantage male athletic directors because those networks provide access to information and other important interpersonal communication that help men to obtain and retain leadership positions.

Stereotypes

Stereotypes about perceptions of appropriate leaders, although created external to sport organizations, influence women's experiences of leadership within these organizations. The prototypical leader of a sport organization is expected to demonstrate more masculine managerial behavior than feminine managerial behavior (Burton, Barr, Fink, & Bruening, 2009), whereas women are less likely to be considered for or deemed appropriate in positions of leadership in sport (Hancock & Hums, 2016). When women are in leadership positions, they are unfavorably evaluated because they demonstrate attributes and behaviors perceived as incongruent with their appropriate gender roles (Eagly & Karau, 2002). Leadership stereotypes in intercollegiate sport have negative impacts on women, because women were perceived as capable of success in leadership positions yet considered unlikely to be hired for such positions over equally comparable men (Burton, Grappendorf, & Henderson, 2011). African–American women working as intercollegiate athletic directors described the impact of intersecting gender and racial stereotypes in their work, noting they perceived their leadership abilities were under scrutiny and faced unwarranted criticism for their decisions when compared with their male colleagues (McDowell & Carter-Francique, 2017).

However, although leadership in sport is perceived to require more stereotypical masculine attributes or is more closely linked with more stereotypical male gender roles, findings in intercollegiate athletic administration do not support a preference for male leaders. Athletic administrators perceived that both male and female leaders would provide positive organizational outcomes when leading athletic departments (Burton & Welty Peachey, 2009; Welty Peachey & Burton, 2011).

Access and treatment discrimination

Other factors to consider at the organizational level are access and treatment discrimination. Access discrimination excludes members of certain groups from entering the organization, whereas treatment discrimination occurs when individuals from certain groups receive fewer organizational resources than they would legitimately deserve (Greenhaus, Parasuraman, & Wormley, 1990). One form of access discrimination, homologous reproduction, occurs when individuals in power in the organization maintain influence by allowing only those with similar characteristics to them the ability to access positions of power and influence within the organization (Kanter, 1977). Women have been excluded from the hiring process in sport by being denied access as a result of the "old boys' network" and homologous reproduction (Aicher & Sagas, 2009; Hoffman, 2011; Regan & Cunningham, 2012; Whisenant & Mullane, 2007). The influence of the "old boys' network" is perceived to be waning by some female athletic directors (Taylor & Wells, 2017), a noted improvement for women working in intercollegiate athletics. Yet, Wells and Kerwin (2017) noted that women and racial minority men and women perceived barriers to career advancement in intercollegiate athletic administration based on their gender and race.

There is also evidence in sport organizations that women are impacted by treatment discrimination because they are denied access to resources, rewards, or on-the-job opportunities that they legitimately deserved (Aicher & Sagas, 2009; Cunningham & Sagas, 2007). In intercollegiate athletics, women in the senior woman administrator position were denied opportunities to engage in important oversight roles in budgeting and leading men's sports programs, which negatively impacted their abilities to build skill sets toward positions of athletic director (Claussen & Lehr, 2002; Grappendorf, Pent, Burton, & Henderson, 2008; Pent, Grappendorf, & Henderson, 2007; Tiell, Dixon, & Lin, 2012).

Individual (micro) level research on women in leadership

At the individual (micro) level of analysis, researchers examine how individuals understand and make meaning of their expectations, experiences, and understanding of power, policies, and procedures operating at the organizational level. In addition, researchers examine the self-limiting behaviors in which individuals engage within their work environment and the assumptions made about how they interact within an organization.

Human and social capital

Human capital is developed through education, job training, on-the-job experiences, and the like, and accrues social capital resources through a network of relationships with peers, supervisors, and subordinates (Sagas & Cunningham, 2004). The experiences of women in intercollegiate athletic administration revealed that social capital was more influential for men advancing in sport organizations than it was for women (Sagas & Cunningham, 2004). Other research about intercollegiate athletic administrators noted differences on the impacts of social capital for men's and women's careers can negatively impact women's career aspirations and intentions to advance in sport organizations (Cunningham & Sagas, 2002). Yet mentoring can prove critical to advancement in sport organizations. It can provide women with professional development opportunities, including access to networks, new job responsibilities, and opportunities to develop new skill sets (Hancock, Grappendorf, Wells, & Burton, 2017).

Self-limiting behaviors

Work by Sartore and Cunningham (2007) utilized symbolic interactionism to examine the lack of women in leadership of sport organizations. Their framework described how "ideological gender beliefs may serve to inhibit women within sport organizations through internal identity comparison processes that may subsequently result in the unconscious manifestation of self-limiting behaviors" (p. 259). Work using the theory of planned behavior revealed that women holding positive intentions toward pursuing athletic director positions demonstrated confidence in their ability to pursue the position, based on strong mentoring and support to develop their skill sets, confidence in their ability to acquire the necessary skills to be successful, and support from spouses/family. In comparison, those with lower intentions to pursue the athletic director position noted perceived difficulty of balancing demands of the position and family responsibilities, race and/or gender discrimination, and role incongruence (e.g., fundraising/external efforts vs. supporting student athletes) (Veraldo & Ruihley, 2017). Hancock and Hums (2016) also noted value incongruence as a factor dissuading women from pursuing the athletic director position.

Conclusion

As detailed by the depth and breadth of research explored in this chapter, understanding the continued under-representation of women in sport leadership is a complex issue. However, newly emerging research indicates that women are reporting more favorable experiences leading sport organizations. Key takeaways from this emerging research include fostering informal networks for women in sport leadership. Men in sport leadership must work with their female colleagues to help create more closely linked connections because informal networks provide both men and women important access to career development opportunities. In addition, those in leadership must recognize that leadership is not 'gender neutral' and that gender bias (along with race/ethnicity bias and sexual orientation bias) influences who has access to, and how individuals are evaluated in, leadership. Furthermore, leaders must scrutinize organizational policies and procedures that appear to be "gender neutral," and recognize that those policies/procedures may negatively impact women and impede their career advancement. Leaders of sport organizations must carefully scrutinize recruitment and hiring practices, professional development training, work assignments, and other work place policies (e.g., flextime, family leave policies) to be sure these practices are not inadvertently benefiting men over women (Bohnet, 2016).

Work by Nicole LaVoi and her colleagues at the Tucker Center for Research on Girls and Women in Sport provided a practitioner-focused report that was designed to showcase best practices for the recruitment, hiring, and retention of women in college coaching (LaVoi & Wasend, 2018). Similarly, scholars, including many referenced in this chapter, can work with sport leaders to provide practitioner-focused reports to help connect research to practice to increase the number of, and provide better support for, women in sport leadership. With scholars and advocates continuing to call for greater gender equity in leadership in sport organizations (e.g., NCAA Office of Diversity and Inclusion, NFL Diversity Initiative) we can be hopeful that scholars and practitioners can work together to provide actionable steps to ensure that more women have access to a "seat at the table" of sport leadership.

Leader profile: Amy Huchthausen, Commissioner, America East Conference

Amy Huchthausen has been the commissioner of the America East Conference since 2011. She is the fourth conference commissioner and is the first woman to lead the 9-member conference sponsoring 13 intercollegiate sports at the NCAA Division I level. Huchthausen is a progressive leader who has elevated the conference to national prominence by establishing the conference as a leader in diversity and inclusion through both a partnership with the "You Can Play" Project in 2012 and by becoming the first conference to be included as a member of the LGBT SportSafe Founders Club in September of 2016. She has also increased the visibility of the conference by launching the creation of a co-branded network, "The AE on ESPN3," on which content from all member schools is available via ESPN's digital platform. Huchthausen began her career working in compliance at the Big East Conference and then as director of compliance for the Missouri Valley Conference and assistant director of compliance and governance at the Atlantic Coast Conference. She then moved to the NCAA national office as the Director of Academic and Membership Affairs. She has also served as a member of the NCAA Division I Academics/

Figure 19.1 Amy Huchthausen

Eligibility/Compliance Cabinet and Legislative Review & Interpretations Committee. When discussing the opportunities and challenges for women in intercollegiate athletic leadership, Huchthausen commented that there are still decision-makers in more senior positions who are not comfortable working with individuals who look different from them, but she sees progress in a new generation of female leaders who are gaining the experience needed to move into the ranks of leadership. She believes that, as women continue gaining experiences to help build their leadership skill set, there will be more progress toward an increase of women into senior leadership in both intercollegiate and professional sport organizations. Huchthausen highlighted the importance of both recruitment of women into the field of sport and then the retention of women as ways to continue to build a new pipeline of experienced women in sport leadership.

References

Acker, J. (1992). Gendering organizational theory. *Classics of Organizational Theory*, **6**, 450–459.
Acosta, R. V. & Carpenter, L. J. (2014). Women in intercollegiate sport. A longitudinal, national study, thirty-seven year update 1977–2014. Retrieved from www.acostacarpenter.org.
Aicher, T. J. & Sagas, M. (2009). An examination of homologous reproduction and the effects of sexism. *Journal for the Study of Sports and Athletes in Education*, **3**(3), 375–386.
Allison, R. (2016). From oversight to autonomy: Gendered organizational change in women's soccer. *Social Currents*, **4**(1), 71.
Anderson, E. D. (2009). The maintenance of masculinity among the stakeholders of sport. *Sport Management Review*, **12**(1), 3–14.

Auster, E. R. & Prasad, A. (2016). Why do women still not make it to the top? Dominant organizational ideologies and biases by promotion committees limit opportunities to destination positions. *Sex Roles*, **75**, 177–196.

Britton, D. M. & Logan, L. (2008). Gendered organizations: Progress and prospects. *Sociology Compass*, **2**(1), 107–121.

Bohnet, I. (2016). *What Works: Gender equality by design*. Cambridge, MA: Belknap Press of Harvard University Press.

Burton, L. J. (2015). Underrepresentation of women in sport leadership: A review of research. *Sport Management Review*, **18**, 155–165.

Burton, L. J., Barr, C. A., Fink, J. S., & Bruening, J. E. (2009). "Think athletic director, think masculine?": Examination of the gender typing of managerial subroles within athletic administration positions. *Sex Roles*, **61**, 416–426.

Burton, L. J., Grappendorf, H., & Henderson, A. (2011). Perceptions of gender in athletic administration: Utilizing role congruity to examine (potential) prejudice against women. *Journal of Sport Management*, **25**, 36–45.

Burton, L. J. & LaVoi, N. M. (2016). An ecological/multisystem approach to understanding and examining women coaches. In N. M. LaVoi (ed.), *Women in Sports Coaching* (pp. 49–62). Oxford: Routledge.

Burton, L. J. & Leberman, S. (2017). An evaluation of current scholarship in sport leadership: multilevel perspective. In L. J. Burton & S. Leberman (eds), *Women in Sport Leadership: Research and practice for change* (pp. 16–32). Oxford: Routledge.

Burton, L. & Welty Peachey, J. (2009). Transactional or transformational? Leadership preferences of division III athletic administrators. *Journal of Intercollegiate Sport*, **2**(2), 245–259.

Claussen, C. L. & Lehr, C. (2002). Decision-making authority of senior woman administrators. *International Journal of Sport Management*, **3**, 215–228

Connell, R. (2009). *Gender*. Cambridge: Polity.

Cunningham, G. B. (2008). Creating and sustaining gender diversity in sport organizations. *Sex Roles*, **58**, 136–145.

Cunningham, G. B. (2010). Understanding the under-representation of African American coaches: A multilevel perspective. *Sport Management Review*, **13**(4), 395–406.

Cunningham, G. B. & Fink, J. S. (2006). Diversity issues in sport and leisure: Introduction to a special issue. *Journal of Sport Management*, **20**, 455–465.

Cunningham, G. B. & Sagas, M. (2002). The differential effects of human capital for male and female division I basketball coaches. *Research Quarterly for Exercise and Sport*, **73**(4), 489–495.

Dicaro, J. (2017). Safest bet in sports: Men complaining about a female announcer's voice, September 18. Retrieved from https://www.nytimes.com/2017/09/18/sports/nfl-beth-mowins-julie-dicaro.html.

Dixon, M. A. & Bruening, J. E. (2007). Work-family conflict in coaching I: A top-down perspective. *Journal of Sport Management*, **21**(3), 377.

Dixon, M. A. & Cunningham, G. B. (2006). Data aggregation in multilevel analysis: a review of conceptual and statistical issues. *Measurement in Physical Education and Exercise Science*, **10**(2), 85–107

Dixon, M., Tiell, B., Lough, N., Sweeney, K., Osborne, B., & Bruening, J. (2008). The work/life interface in intercollegiate athletics: An examination of policies, programs, and institutional climate. *Journal for the Study of Sports and Athletes in Education*, **2**(2), 137–159.

Eagly, A. H. & Carli, L. L. (2007). Women and the labyrinth of leadership. *Harvard Business Review*, 63–71.

Eagly, A. H. & Karau, S. J. (2002). Role congruity theory of prejudice toward female leaders. *Psychological Review*, **109**(3), 573–598.

Ely, R. & Padavic, I. (2007). A feminist analysis of organizational research on sex differences. *Academy of Management Review*, **32**(4), 1121–1143.

Fink, J. S. (2008). Gender and sex diversity in sport organizations: Concluding comments. *Sex Roles*, **58**, 146–147.

Fink, J. S. (2016). Hiding in plain sight: The embedded nature of sexism in sport. *Journal of Sport Management*, **30**(1), 1–7.

Fink, J. S., Pastore, D. L., & Riemer, H. (2001). Do differences make a difference? Managing diversity in division IA intercollegiate athletics. *Journal of Sport Management*, 15(1), 10–50.

Guest, K. (2016). While women triumph at Rio 2016, the media is competing to see who can demean them the most, August 9. Retrieved from: www.independent.co.uk/voices/rio-2016-women-sexism-female-gold-medal-athletes-treatment-by-media-bbc-nbc-a7180476.html.

Grappendorf, H., Pent, A., Burton, L., & Henderson, A. (2008). Gender role stereotyping: A qualitative analysis of senior woman administrators' perceptions regarding financial decision making. *Journal of Issues in Intercollegiate Athletics*, **1**, 26–45.

Greenhaus, J. H., Parasuraman, S., & Wormley, W. M. (1990). Effects of race on organizational experience, job performance evaluations, and career outcomes. *Academy of Management Journal*, **33**(1), 64–86.

Hancock, M. G., Grappendorf, H., Wells, J. E., & Burton, L. J. (2017). Career breakthroughs of women in intercollegiate athletic administration: What is the role of mentoring? *Journal of Intercollegiate Sport*, **10**(2), 184–206.

Hancock, M. G. & Hums, M. (2016). A "leaky pipeline"?: Factors affecting the career development of senior-level female administrators in NCAA Division I athletic departments. *Sport Management Review*, **19**, 198–210.

Heilman, M. E. (2012). Gender stereotypes and workplace bias. *Research in Organizational Behavior*, **32**, 113–135

Hoffman, J. L. (2011). The old boys' network. *Journal for the Study of Sports and Athletes in Education*, **5**(1), 9–28.

Inglis, S., Danylchuk, K., & Pastore, D. (2000). Multiple realities of women's work experiences in coaching and athletic management. *Women's Sport and Physical Activity Journal*, **9**(2), 1–27.

Johnson, R. (2017). NCAA president Mark Emmert responds to congressional call for answers on hiring diversity, November 10. Retrieved from https://www.sbnation.com/college-football/2017/11/10/16626104/ncaa-president-mark-emmert-hiring-diversity.

Kane, M. J. (1995). Resistance/transformation of the oppositional binary: Exposing sport as a continuum. *Journal of Sport and Social Issues*, **19**(2), 191–218.

Kane, G. (2015). Leadership theories. In J. F. Borland, G. M. Kane, & L. J. Burton (eds), *Sport Leadership in the 21st Century*. London: Jones & Bartlett Publishers.

Kanter, R. M. (1977). *Men and Women of the Corporation*. New York: Basic Books.

Katz, M., Walker, N. A., & Hindman, L. C. (2018). Gendered leadership networks in the NCAA: Analyzing affiliation networks of senior woman administrators and athletic directors. *Journal of Sport Management*, **32**(2), 135–149.

Kihl, L. A., Shaw, S., & Schull, V. (2013). Fear, anxiety, and loss of control: Analyzing an athletic department merger as a gendered political process. *Journal of Sport Management*, **27**(2), 146–157.

Lapchick, R., et al. (2017). The racial and gender report card. Retrieved from www.tidesport.org/racialgenderreportcard.html.

LaVoi, N. M. & Wasend, M. K. (2018). *Athletic Administration Best Practices of Recruitment, Hiring and Retention of Female Collegiate Coaches*. Minneapolis, MN: Tucker Center for Research on Girls & Women in Sport.

McCallum, S. & O'Connell, D. (2009). Social capital and leadership development: Building stronger leadership through enhanced relational skills. *Leadership & Organization Development Journal*, **30**(2), 152–166.

McDowell, J. & Carter-Francique, A. (2017). An intersectional analysis of the workplace experiences of African American female athletic directors. *Sex Roles*, **77**(5–6), 393–408.

Machida-Kosuga, M., Schaubroeck, J., & Feltz, D. (2016). Leader self-efficacy of women intercollegiate athletic administrators: A look at barriers and developmental antecedents. *Journal of Intercollegiate Sport*, **9**(2), 157–178.

Martin, P. Y. (2003). "Said and done" versus "Saying and doing" gendering practices, practicing gender at work. *Gender & Society*, **17**(3), 342–366.

National Collegiate Athletic Association (NCAA) (2016). The pledge and commitment to promoting diversity and gender equity in intercollegiate athletics. Retrieved from www.ncaa.org/about/resources/inclusion/ncaa-presidential-pledge.

Pent, A., Grappendorf, H., & Henderson, A. (2007). Do they want more?: An analysis of NCAA senior woman administrators' participation in financial decision making. *Journal for the Study of Sports and Athletes in Education*, **1**(2), 157–174.

Regan, M. & Cunningham, G. (2012). Analysis of homologous reproduction in community college athletics. *Journal for the Study of Sports and Athletes in Education*, **6**(2), 161–172

Sagas, M. & Cunningham, G. B. (2004). Does having "the right stuff" matter? Gender differences in the determinants of career success among intercollegiate athletic administrators. *Sex Roles*, **50**(5), 411–421.

Sartore, M. L. & Cunningham, G. B. (2007). Explaining the under-representation of women in leadership positions of sport organizations: A symbolic interactionist perspective. *Quest*, **59**(2), 244–265.

Schein, E. H. (1996). Culture: The missing concept in organization studies. *Administrative Science Quarterly*, **41**, 229–240.

Schull, V., Shaw, S., & Kihl, L. A. (2013). " If a woman came in . . . she would have been eaten up alive": Analyzing gendered political processes in the search for an athletic director. *Gender & Society*, **27**, 56–81.

Shaw, S. & Frisby, W. (2006). Can gender equity be more equitable?: Promoting an alternative frame for sport management research, education, and practice. *Journal of Sport Management*, **20**, 483–509.

Spoor, J. R. & Hoye, R. (2013). Perceived support and women's intentions to stay at a sport organization. *British Journal of Management*, DOI: 10.1111/1467-8551.12018.

Stangl, J. M. & Kane, M. J. (1991). Structural variables that offer explanatory power for the underrepresentation of women coaches since title IX: The case of homologous reproduction. *Sociology of Sport Journal*, **8**(1), 47–60.

Taylor, E. A., Siegele, J. L., Smith, A. B., & Hardin, R. (2018). Applying career construction theory to female National Collegiate Athletic Association Division I conference commissioners. Journal of Sport Management, 20(18), 321–333

Taylor, E. A. & Wells, J. E. (2017). Institutionalized barriers and supports of female athletic directors: A. *Journal of Intercollegiate Sport*, **10**(2), 157–183.

Tiell, B. S., Dixon, M. A., & Lin, Y. (2012). Roles and tasks of the senior woman administrator in role congruity theory perspective: A longitudinal progress report. *Journal of Issues in Intercollegiate Athletics*, **5**, 247–268.

Veraldo, C. M. & Ruihley, B. J. (2017). Theory multilevel perspective of planned behavior and women in senior-level athletic administration. *Sport, Business and Management: An International Journal*, **7**(1), 21–37.

Walker, N. A. & Melton, E. N. (2015). The tipping point: The intersection of race, gender, and sexual orientation in intercollegiate sports. *Journal of Sport Management*, **29**(3), 257–271.

Wells, J. E. & Kerwin, S. (2017). Intentions to be an athletic director: Racial and gender perspectives. *Journal of Career Development*, **44**(2), 127–143.

Welty Peachey, J. & Burton, L. J. (2011). Male or female athletic director? exploring perceptions of leader effectiveness and a (potential) female leadership advantage with intercollegiate athletic directors. *Sex Roles*, **64**(5), 416–425.

Whisenant, W. A. & Mullane, S. P. (2007). Sport information directors and homologous reproduction. *International Journal of Sport Management and Marketing*, **2**(3), 252–263.

Whisenant, W. A., Pedersen, P. M., & Obenour, B. L. (2002). Success and gender: Determining the rate of advancement for intercollegiate athletic directors. *Sex Roles*, **47**, 485–491.

Wilson, A. (2017). *45 Years of Title IX: The Status of Women in Intercollegiate Athletics*. Retrieved from www.ncaa.org/about/resources/inclusion/title-ix-45-years.

20
Women's roles and positions in European sport organizations
Historical developments and current tendencies

Gertrud Pfister

Introduction: Background and questions

Currently, sport plays a large role in many countries, in particular in industrialized nation states, but people, mostly boys and men, living in the global south use sport, often football, as a way of identifying with their countries. Sport seems to be a "global" inheritance, but the focus on this game impedes insights into the large variety of "movement cultures" that still influence the sport habits and tastes of the populations (in the sense of Bourdieu). Sports have various histories and traditions but they have – at least in part – the same roots.

At the turn of the nineteenth century three different forms of physical culture developed in Europe: gymnastics in Sweden, *Turnen* in Germany, and sport in England. In different combinations and mixtures these three forms spread first throughout Europe and then through the whole world. Common to all three forms is their political and military orientation as well as their exclusion of girls and women. Per Henrik Ling, the founder of Swedish gymnastics, had not only a strong focus on "military exercises," but also on health; German *Turnen*, developed by Friedrich Ludwig Jahn in Berlin, aimed at bringing forth "real men who were able and willing to fight for liberation of Germany from French occupation. At the grounds used since 1811 for exercising (*Turnplätze*) women were only spectators" (Pfister, 2003, p. 67). Since the end of the nineteenth century the Anglo-American model of modern sport – invented by men for men – spread worldwide; sport activities, exercises and performance, as well as aims, norms, and values (above all competition and records), corresponded to the needs and the ideals of men.

In western countries, women began to participate in *Turnen* and some recreational sports in the last third of the nineteenth century, but they played only marginal roles (Pfister, 1980, 1998). At competitions, they were banished to the spectators' rows, from where they could admire the victors from a distance. Leadership roles were reserved for men, and only very few and audacious women dared to fight for women's rights in sport as well as in society as a whole.

In western countries and beyond, girls and women were expected to satisfy their need for movement by performing elegant and graceful exercises aimed above all at improving health and beauty.

Johann Adolf Ludwig Werner (1794–1866), one of the founders of girls' gymnastics, described the positive effects of gymnastic exercises in the following terms: "Strengthening [a girl's] muscles will have the effect that the roses and lilies of health will blossom on her cheeks and that the goddesses of beauty and grace will adorn her limbs" (quoted in Blümcke, 1928, p. 81). In the second half of the century, various concepts of women's gymnastics and sports developed in western countries, for example, in Denmark, Germany, and France, but also in the United States of America. However, propriety and decorum, along with women's roles and the myth of the "weaker sex" formed great barriers, preventing the large majority of women from taking part in sport competitions and even in recreational physical activities, including gymnastics, *Turnen*.

The participation of female athletes in the Olympic Games mirrors the situation of women in the sport movement. A brief look at the history of the Games reveals that women initially were outsiders at the Olympics, and that the integration into the Olympic Movement took decades. In 1896 women were not allowed to take part in the Games at all. In 1900, there were "officially" only two sports, tennis and golf, organized for women, but they participated in several other events, among them ballooning and dressage, which the IOC did not consider "Olympic"; in 1928 only four sports were open to female participants.

Since the nineteenth century, the exclusion of women from numerous disciplines, ranging from rowing and cycling to football and long-distance running, was considered "natural" and "taken for granted" and so it was scarcely discussed, let alone criticized. For years, exertion, strength, and endurance, but especially bodily contacts and fights, were looked on as male preserves (see the overview in Pfister, 2013).

The first team sport that women were allowed to compete in at the Olympic Games was volleyball in 1964; this was followed in 1976 by handball and basketball, in 1980 by hockey, and in 1996 by football (soccer). Endurance sports became women's Olympic events only in 1984, when cycling and marathon running debuted (Pfister, 2000). As late as 1996 only 40% of the competitions were reserved or accessible for women (Wilson, 1996, p. 187). Currently, female athletes compete in all sports, even in boxing or ski jumping, which seemed previously to be too dangerous for the "weak sex".[1]

However, it must be borne in mind that "men's sports" seem to appeal to only a small minority of mainly young women and that the rise of women's sports is largely confined to western industrialized countries. This is shown, for example, in the contributions published in *Sport and Women: Social issues an international perspective* (Hartmann & Pfister, 2003). The contributions reveal not only how differently sport is structured in the various countries, but also how the chances of women being able to participate in sport as well as the labeling of sports as male or female differ from country to country. There was, however, one feature common to all the 16 countries covered: women in positions of leadership formed only a small minority.

In the following text people in leading positions are considered to be those in the top bodies of sport federations and institutions, irrespective of their individual activities, resources, or competencies. They are generally concerned with the planning and coordination of tasks and activities, with the development and deployment of personnel as well as with evaluation and control. Their roles and the qualities required them to differ significantly according to their actual positions or the tasks they are entrusted with, which may range from the chairman or chairwoman as a figurehead to the treasurer or the public relations officer.[2] It must be taken into account that, depending on the sports system prevailing (which differs decisively, for example, between Europe and the USA), management tasks in sport may be carried out in a voluntary capacity or by full-time employees. This text provides an analysis of the presence of women in decision-making bodies of sport, taking into consideration various international and national organizations.

Female leaders in international sport organizations including the Olympic movement

Throughout his life, Baron de Coubertin, the founder of the Olympic Games of the modern era, was convinced that women's principal task in the Olympic family was to crown the victors. In spite of the opposition of Coubertin and many of his supporters, women have officially participated in the Games since 1900 – not only in growing numbers of competitors but also in an increasing number of disciplines (Pfister, 2000). However, women's participation in Olympic competitions has not led to an increase of influence and power. For a long time the International Olympic Committee (IOC) was a "men's club" which denied access to women. It was not until 1981 that the first two women, Pirjo Haggmann (Finland) and Flor Isava-Fonseca (Venezuela), were co-opted into the IOC. In 1995, 7 of the 107 IOC members were women. Finally, since the middle of the 1990s, the IOC has taken up initiatives to increase the number of women leaders in executive bodies of sports organizations. Members were asked to increase the proportion of women in decision-making bodies, in particular in the Olympic Movement, to 20% by 2010. The rationale for the advancement of women is anchored in the Olympic Charter:

> The IOC strongly encourages, by appropriate means, the promotion of women in sport at all levels and in all structures, particularly in the executive bodies of national and international sports organisations with a view to the strict application of the principle of the equality of men and women
>
> *(Article 2, Paragraph 5 of the Olympic Charter)*[3]

But, in spite of all the IOC's good intentions and efforts, the situation did not fundamentally change: in 2001, when, according to the IOC resolution 10% of the positions of leadership should have been filled by women, there were only 11 women among the 126 members of the IOC (i.e., 8.7%).

However, information in the "Key Dates in the History of Women in the Olympic Movement" and in the current directory of the IOC Commissions (revised in 2017) demonstrates that there has been a continuous increase in the number of women on important boards and committees since the 1980s as well as an increasing attention on women's issues (Key Dates, 2018). Various measures of the IOC and the more than 200 NOCs (National Olympic Committees) include publications, conferences, and awards in the context of women's issues.

In the spring of 2017, the IOC emphasized that 38% of its members were women. The organization also released data on the current composition of its various committees; however, in most of them women are still a small minority. The Executive Board of the IOC is made

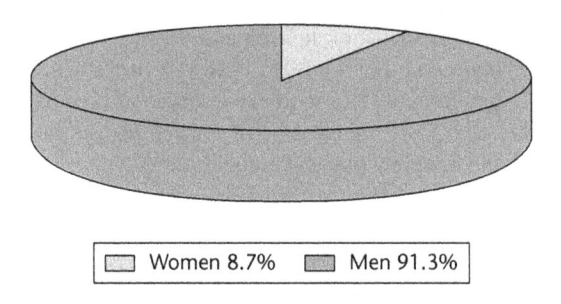

Figure 20.1 Gender representation in the IOC in 2001

up of 15 members, 11 men (including the male president as well as 3 male co-presidents) and 4 women (including one co-president).

Men also dominate in the 30 committees that are responsible for various tasks, reaching from the program of the Olympic Games to Olympic Education – 26% of the members of these committees are women. Some examples of this include seven men and one woman active in the Ethics Commission. The Marketing Commission is dominated by men: 17 of the 18 members, whereas the Commission for Culture and Olympic Education consists of 23 men and 4 women. Not a single woman works in the Committee on Olympic Solidarity, consisting of 15 members. The large commission "Sport and Active Society" has a male president and 41 members – 26 are men and 14 are women. The honorary members include 3 women and 38 men (see IOC Commissions, Revised in 2017 – see https://www.olympic.org/news/ioc-announces-composition-of-its-commissions-38-per-cent-of-members-now-women).

It must be borne in mind, however, that most of the members of these commissions are IOC members, meaning – until quite recently – there have been few women to choose from. Nevertheless, a number of external experts are also appointed to these commissions, but it does not seem that this practice increases the chances of women reaching a fair representation on the boards and committees of the organization.[4] In addition, it has to be taken into consideration, that 77% of the heads of the 31 committees are men. Clearly, influence and power do not depend only on formal positions and the sex of a leader does not necessarily determine his or her politics, but gender justice should be an aim of the Olympic Movement – especially with regard to the distribution of power.

There are several ways to promote women and to increase their numbers, visibility and, influence. The IOC Women and Sport Trophy is one of numerous opportunities to increase recognition and empowerment for women. Each year, the IOC Women and Sport Awards are given to women, men, or organizations that have made remarkable contributions to the development, encouragement, and reinforcement of women's participation in sport. Introduced in 2000, the award highlights role models and change agents in the pursuit of gender equality. Six trophies are distributed each year, one for each of the five continents and one at the world level. The winners work to promote gender equality through different projects and are also supported with a grant to help them continue and extend their work.

Not only in the IOC but also in the NOCs the decision-makers have almost always been, and often still are, men. In the year 2000 only 3 of the 199 NOCs had women presidents and less than 25% had women holding an executive post as vice president or secretary general. Nevertheless, 42% or the organizations had women on their executive committees (Ferris, 2000) and, in 2002, 113 of the 200 NOCs had achieved the IOC's target of a 10% share of women in their executive bodies (Ruloß, Hartmann-Tews, Combrink, Nicolai-Meier, & Luetkens-Hovemann, 2003, p. 25).

But sheer numbers do not say anything about influence and power. Women, for example, are still largely excluded from participation in international meetings, as Gunilla Lindberg, the only woman on the Executive Board of the IOC, observed critically in a speech at the conference "Play the Game." She illustrated this with the example of the annual congress of NOCs in Rio de Janeiro in the year 2000, attended by 400 delegates from 192 NOCs: of the 400 delegates, 392 were men and 8 were women (Lindberg, 2003).

Since 1996, the IOC's advocacy activities have been supported by the organization of quadrennial World Conferences on Women and Sport. The objectives of the five quadrennial World Conferences on Women and Sport have been to: create awareness about women's role in sport; assess the progress made in the area of gender equality in sport; and define future priority actions to promote women in sport.

Each of the Women and Sport Conferences has resulted in a series of recommendations for the Olympic movement, and has guided the work of the IOC and its Women in Sport Commission. Uneven gender relations can also be found in the international sports federations, with men dominating the decision-making committees and women playing, if at all, a marginal role or a role as "token" women.

Women are also marginalized in individual sports federations: in the year 2000, roughly one-third of the 61 international federations of Olympic sports disciplines, e.g., swimming, athletics, fencing, and so on, had elected women to their executive committees. Five federations had elected a female president, while three federations had a woman secretary general (Ferris, 2000).

Gender arrangements in sports organizations: Women in leading positions in various federations and countries

The situation in various organizations and countries

A survey carried out by the Amateur Athletic Foundation in Los Angeles at the beginning of the 1990s showed that only 5% of the approximately 13,000 positions in decision-making bodies in international sports organizations were filled by women (DeFrantz, 1991).

In the following overview of the composition of executive bodies in selected European countries, it must be borne in mind that the term "sport" has different meanings in different languages and different cultures. Here, sport is regarded as a comprehensive term for "physical exercise," which includes gymnastics and fitness and ranges from top-level competitive sports to recreational sports and "sport for all." The ways in which sport is structured, organized, and financed also differs significantly from country to country, along with the traditions and ideologies, the hopes and expectations, as well as the aims and values that are bound up with sport. The popularity of the various sports, the extent to which populations take part in sporting activities, and the proportion of women who take up sport likewise show enormous variations. It is thus quite astonishing that despite all these differences there is one noticeable similarity: the gender hierarchy and the imbalance of power in sports organizations, and institutions appear to be a universal phenomenon.

Based on a research project in several European countries, colleagues and I found that the executive boards of sport organizations on all levels and in all sports are still a male domain: the presidential seats seem to have even attached a sign – men only.

To be able to identify the significance of sports structures for the gender arrangements in leading positions, countries were selected that had similar social and gender orders but different sports structures. Moreover, the choice of countries was based on practical considerations, i.e., the language in which the information was available. A worldwide overview of gender, sports structures and positions of leadership would indeed be a highly interesting and important project.

We focused on 66 national sports federations (in 11 countries representing 6 "gender-neutral" sports such as swimming and tennis) and found only 3 female presidents (Austria: gymnastics; Germany: swimming; and the Netherlands: tennis). The majority, 95%, of the federations had less than 50% of executive committees made up of women. However, to address this problem some federations demand the representation of both genders in decision-making committees (e.g., the International Basketball Federation [FIBA] and the International Football Association [FIFA]).

Denmark: An example

An analysis of gender ratios in Danish sports federations is especially interesting because Denmark is a welfare state with a high rate of women's employment and an excellent childcare system, and also a country in which there is general consensus that equality has been achieved between the sexes.

As in Germany, the sports system in Denmark is based on clubs and federations, which follow the principles of democracy, voluntary work, and reciprocity. As in Germany, too, sports clubs receive support from the state because of their work in the community, meaning that membership fees — and thus barriers preventing access to sport — can be kept low. In contrast to Germany, Denmark has three umbrella organizations for sport: the association for company sports (DFIF), the Danish Gymnastic Association (DGI), which is responsible for numerous sports at the "sport for all" level, and the Danish Sport Federation (DIF), which is made up of the individual sports federations and is responsible for top-level sports as well as recreational and leisure sports. The DIF is at the same time the NOC and represents Denmark in the Olympic Movement. Elite sport is coordinated by "Team Denmark," a state-funded body (Ibsen & Ottesen, 2004).

In 2002, 36% of the male and 32% of the female Danish population were members of a sports club. However, the relatively high percentage of female members is not reflected in the number of women in decision-making bodies (Ottesen, 2004).

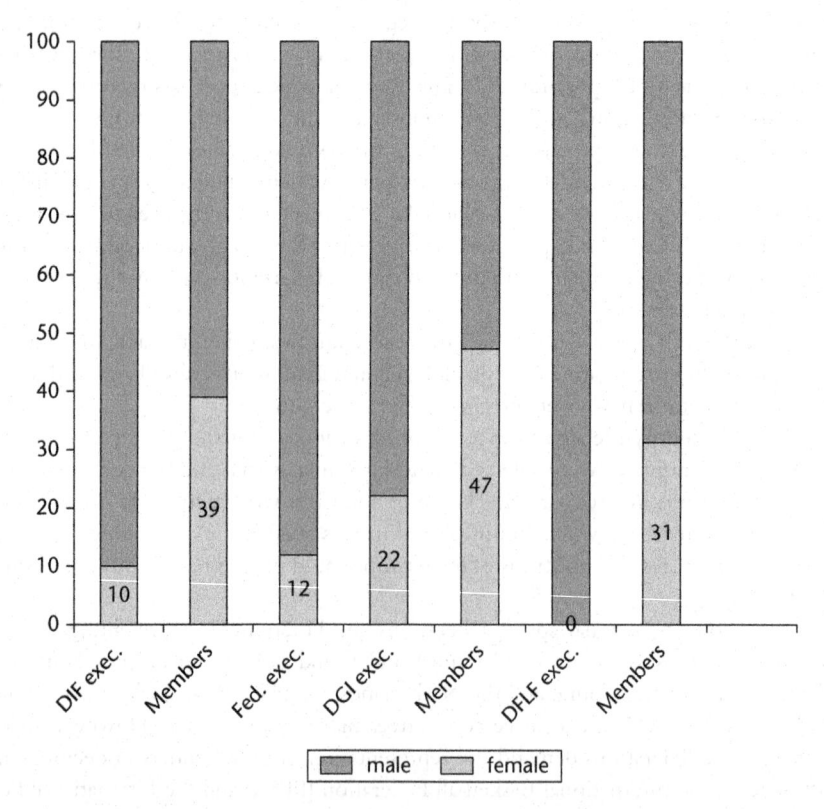

Figure 20.2 Women leaders in Danish sports organizations (in percentages)

In the year 2000, the percentage of women in the DIF's executive committee was 10%, in the DGI 22%, and in the DFIF (the company sports association) 0%. In the highest bodies of the 56 individual sports federations, the percentage of women amounted to 12%. Some of the federations, such as the handball or the volleyball federations, had not a single woman on their executive committees (Pfister, Habermann, & Ottesen, 2003).

The United States of America

The sports structures as well as the organization of sport in the USA differ fundamentally from the sports systems existing in Germany and Scandinavia, where clubs are the basic units of sport, based on the principles of voluntary work and subsidization with state support.

In the USA, there are no umbrella organizations covering all types and areas of sport; instead there are various sports structures running parallel to each other. Sport, on the one hand, is closely linked with the education system and is organized by schools, colleges, and universities. At the same time, there are professional sports with their own organizations and leagues, and these are the focus of media attention resulting in public interest. In addition, there is the YMCA (Young Men's Christian Association), a nationwide organization that provides all kinds of sports, particularly in the area of health and fitness. In some sports such as soccer, volleyball, basketball, and swimming there are clubs that organize sport, including leagues and tournaments, at local or regional levels.

The most important amateur sports organizations in the USA are the AAU (Amateur Athletic Union), an umbrella organization for the 58 individual sports federations, and the NCAA (National Collegiate Athletic Association), a member-driven association with representatives from 1,200 colleges and universities, which governs intercollegiate athletics, and organizes national championship competitions in different sports and for all three competitive levels (Hums & MacLean, 2004).

In the AAU power lies predominantly in men's hands, with all five leading positions (those of president, two vice presidents, the secretary general, and treasurer) being filled by men. Only five national sports federations have a woman as their leading executive – and most of these are federations responsible for women-dominated sports, i.e., trampoline and tumbling, soccer, field hockey, dancing, and cheerleading.[5]

Sports organizations as a male preserve: A global phenomenon

Today, decision-making bodies in sports organizations and institutions are still dominated by men, and not only is this true of the countries discussed here but also seems to be a worldwide phenomenon, as shown, for example, in the contributions published in Hartmann and Pfister (2003). Further examples can be taken from their study: in France, for instance, 95% of the presidents of sports federations are men (Dechavanne & Hartmann-Tews, 2003) and in Spain only one single sports federation has elected a woman as its president (Puig & Soler, 2003). Gender ratios are somewhat better balanced in Norway, not least because of the introduction of a quota regime in 1987. In 1998, 30% of executive committee members in Norwegian sports federations, and 38% of the executive board of the umbrella organization for Norwegian sports, were women (Fasting, 2003).[6] An overview of gender distribution in the positions of leadership in the sports systems of various countries is also given in *The Challenge of Change*, edited by Ilse Hartmann-Tews and her staff, and published by the Ministerium für Städtebau [Ministry of Urban Planning] (see note 6). The volume contains a wealth of data and facts documenting the trend, described above, towards gender hierarchies in the world of sport.

With regard to gender hierarchies, sports organizations merely reflect the gender arrangements existing in a particular society, which allocate power, status, and prestige to men and women in unequal proportions. Just as in the world of sport, vertical as well as horizontal gender segregation is a distinctive feature of not only the labor market but also industry and business, politics, and the sciences (Wirth, 2001).

Despite the similarities in the findings presented, they must be interpreted and evaluated with great caution. For one thing, it must be taken into account that any comparison of the situation of women in different countries in the field of sport, as well as outside it, is immensely difficult because of the differences in the prevailing cultures, structures, and sports systems. Furthermore, for a number of reasons great care must be taken in comparing the statistical data available. As mentioned above, the term "sport" means different things in different languages; likewise, the tasks assigned to leading employees as well as the resources at their disposal differ from country to country. Thus, it must be asked whether in positions that have the same designation, for example the president of a sports federation, the holders of the title play similar roles in the various sports systems. For this reason, intercultural comparisons can only, on the basis of the data available, point to more or less rough trends that are observable.

In spite of the clearly proven and apparently universal gender hierarchies in the world of sport, there are noticeable differences in the extent of gender discrimination between one country and another. Although at the end of the 1990s, for example, 13% of all Australian sports federations were headed by a woman president, there was not a single woman president, as mentioned above, in Spanish sports federations. We also should not forget that, in some countries, especially in Norway but also in Australia, considerable progress has been made in the past 20 years with regard to the inclusion and integration of women in positions of leadership in the world of sport.

A key question concerns the debate on women and power in the different countries as well as in international organizations. Is the fact that women are under-represented in decision-making bodies noticed at all? Or is it discussed? Or identified as a problem? Are debates taking place, is research being conducted, are initiatives and strategies being developed aimed at changing the status quo? In several countries such as Norway, Canada, Australia, and Germany, measures and schemes have been developed to increase the numbers of women in positions of leadership and/or to implement gender mainstreaming in sport.[7] In other countries such as Denmark and also Norway equality of opportunity was an issue that was taken up in the 1980s, but is now considered accomplished and has been "crossed off the list" (Fasting, 2003). It may be assumed, moreover, that in a great many countries and organizations no one cares about gender hierarchies in sport, in spite of the great interest shown in the Brighton Declaration of 1994, which had the aim of ensuring that women had access to all areas and all levels of sport.[8]

Nevertheless, at the international level not only the IOC but also a number of organizations and working groups have taken up the cause of promoting women in sport. One might mention in this respect the European and the International Working Groups on Women and Sport, the International Association of Physical Education and Sport for Girls and Women (IAPESGW), and Women Sport International.[9] In addition, several research projects have been conducted which identified at least some of the reasons for the gender hierarchy in sport organizations. The results of these projects show that there is no simple explanation but that numerous interrelated facts and processes, decisions of individuals, and structures of the organizations, as well as gendered discourses and practices in the various countries, contribute to the marginalization of women in the decision-making boards and committees of sport organizations (Doll-Tepper, Pfister, Scoretz, & Bilan, 2005).

Leader profile: Professor Gudrun Doll-Tepper

Professor Dr. Gudrun Doll-Tepper is a professor in the Department of Education and Psychology at Freie Universitaet Berlin. She received her Master's degree and Doctorate at Freie Universitaet Berlin and her postdoctorate degree ("Habilitation") at Johann Wolfgang Goethe Universitaet, Frankfurt/Main. Her research interests include the inclusion of persons with disabilities in physical education and sport, the role of physical activity as part of a healthy lifestyle, equal opportunity and participation of girls and women in physical education and sport, and different approaches to talent identification and development in sport. She has written numerous articles on adapted physical activity and sport for persons with disabilities, physical education, and sport pedagogy, as well as on issues related to women in leadership positions. Dr. Doll-Tepper and her team organized several world congresses in Berlin, Germany, for example the International Symposium on Adapted Physical Activity in 1989, the AIESEP World Congress in 1994, the World Summit on Physical Education in 1999, and the International Congress on "Women, Sport & Leadership" in 2004.

Dr. Doll-Tepper was President of the International Council of Sport Science and Physical Education (ICSSPE) from 1997 to 2008. Since 2009 she has been an honorary member and special adviser for the ICSSPE, and in 2016 she was elected Honorary President of the ICSSPE. In 2006, she was elected Vice-President for Education/Olympic Education of the German

Figure 20.3 Professor Gudrun Doll-Tepper

Olympic Sports Confederation, and since 2007 she has been Chairperson of the German Olympic Academy. In 2005, she received a Doctor of Laws (h.c.) from the Memorial University of Newfoundland (Canada) and in 2008 a Doctor (h.c.) from KU Leuven (Belgium). For many years she has been active in the Olympic movement, for example as an academic contributing to the Culture and Education Programme of the Youth Olympic Games and as a member of the commissions on "Olympic Education" and "Women in Sport." She has been awarded several prestigious international and national awards, including the FIEP (Fédération Internationale d'éducation Physique) Gold Cross of Honor of Physical Education, the Jürgen Palm Award of TAFISA (The Association for International Sport for All), the Paralympic Order of the IPC (International Paralympic Committee), the Paralympic Scientific Award of the IPC, the European Laurel Award, the Flambeau d'Or of Panathlon International, and the Cross of Merit, First Class, of the Federal Republic of Germany.

Notes

1 https://www.sports-reference.com/olympics/sports/RGY/.
2 On managers, their tasks and activities there is a plethora of literature, academic studies, as well as help and guidance books; see, for example, Steinmann and Schreyögg (2000); for the field of sport, see Wadsack (1996), among others.
3 Compare Mascagni Stivachtis (2000, p. 33). See also the IOC's homepage at: www.olympic.org/uk/organisation/commissions/women/index_uk.asp.
4 Compare the IOC's homepage at: www.olympic.org/uk/organisation/index_uk.asp; for the current commissions, see https://stillmed.olympic.org/media/Document%20Library/OlympicOrg/IOC/Who-We-Are/Commissions/All-Commissions/Commissions-of-the-IOC-2017.pdf.
5 See www.aausports.org/exec/aau/national_chairs.cfm?publicationID=12.
6 *The Challenge of Change* (2003), published by the Ministerium für Städtebau contains a comprehensive bibliography on the subject of "Women in positions of leadership in sport."
7 On Norway, see Fasting (2003). On Canada, see www.caaws.ca (accessed 18 December 2003). On Australia see www.ausport.gov.au/womenu.htm.
8 Compare www.iwg-gti.org/e/brighton.
9 An excellent website with links to relevant groups and organizations is that of the Canadian Association for the Advancement of Women and Sport and Physical Activity, to be found at www.caaws.ca.

References

Becker-Schmidt, R. (1994). Geschlechterverhältnis, Technologieentwicklung und androzentrische Ideologieproduktion. In N. Beckenbach & W. van Treeck (eds), *Umbrüche gesellschaftlicher Arbeit* (pp. 527–538). Göttingen: Schwartz.
Blümcke, A. (1928). *Die Körperschule der deutschen Frau im Wandel der Jahrhunderte*. Dresden: Limpert.
Dechavanne, N. & Hartmann-Tews, I. (2003). Sport development and inclusion of women in France. In I. Hartmann & G. Pfister (eds), *Sport and Women. Social issues in international perspective* (pp. 70–83). London: Routledge.
DeFrantz, A. (1991). Progress made, pitfalls and conditions for further advancement of women in the Olympic movement. In F. Landry, M. Landry, & M. Yerlès (eds), *Sport: The third millennium*, Proceedings of the International Symposium, Quebec City, Canada, May 21–25, 1990 (pp. 413–417). Sainte Foy: Les Presses de l'Université Laval.
Doll-Tepper, G., Pfister, G., Scoretz, D., & Bilan, C. (eds) (2005). *Sport, Women & Leadership*. Congress Proceedings. Köln: Sport und Buch Strauß.
Fasting, K. (2003). Women and sport in Norway. In I. Hartmann & G. Pfister (eds), *Sport and Women. Social Issues in International Perspective* (pp. 15–35). London: Routledge.
Ferris, E. (2000). Promoting women sports leaders. *Olympic Review*, February–March, 29–32.
Hartmann, I. & Pfister, G. (eds) (2003). *Sport and Women. Social Issues in International Perspective*. London: Routledge.

Hums, M. A. & MacLean, J. C. (2004). *Governance and Policy in Sport Organizations*. Scottsdale, AZ: H. Hathaway Publishers.

Ibsen, B. & Ottesen, L. (2004). Sport and welfare policy in Denmark: The development of sport between state, market and community. In K. Heinemann (ed.), *Transformation of the Welfare State and New Orientations of Sport*. Schorndorf: Hofmann.

Key Dates (2018). Key dates in the history of women in the Olympic movement. Retrieved from https://www.olympic.org/women-in-sport/background/key-dates

Lindberg, G. (2003). IOC missing the gender target. In J.S. Andersen (ed.), *Play the Game* (p. 17). Copenhagen: DGI.

Mascagni Stivachtis, K. (2000). Women's participation in the Olympic movement. *Olympic Review*, XXVI-21, February–March, 29–32.

Ottesen, L. (2004). Sports participation, gender and the welfare state. *Sportwissenschaft*, **34**(3), 311–326.

Pfister, G. (1980). *Frau und Sport*. Frankfurt am Main: Fischer.

Pfister, G. (1990). The medical discourse on female physical culture in Germany in the 19th and early 20th centuries. *Journal of Sport History*, **17**, 183–199.

Pfister, G. (1998). Mehrheit ohne Macht? Frauen in der Turn- und Sportbewegung. In M. Krüger (ed.), *Innovation aus Tradition* (pp. 42–50). Schorndorf: Hofmann.

Pfister, G. (2000). Women and the Olympic Games. In B. Drinkwater (ed.), *Women in Sport* (pp. 3–19). Oxford: Blackwell.

Pfister, G. (2003). Cultural confrontations: German Turnen, Swedish gymnastics and English sport – European diversity in physical activities from a historical perspective. *Culture, Sport, Society*, **6**(1), 61–91.

Pfister, G. U. (2013) Women at the Olympic Games. In Qatar Olympic & Sports Museum, Qatar Museums Authority, A. Amendt, C. Wacker, & S. Wassong (eds), *Olympics: Past & present*. Prestel, München, Publications of the Qatar Olympic & Sports Museum (QOSM), bind 2, pp. 227–235.

Pfister, G., Habermann, U., & Ottesen, L. (2003). *Geschlechterverteilung in Führungspositionen des dänischen Sports*. Kopenhagen: Unveröffentlichter Projektbericht.

Puig, N. & Soler, S. (2003). Women and sport in Spain. In I. Hartmann & G. Pfister (eds), *Sport and Women. Social Issues in International Perspective* (pp. 83–102). London, New York: Routledge.

Rulofs, B., Hartmann-Tews, I., Combrink, C., Nicolai-Meier, Y., & Luetkens-Hovemann, S. (2003). *The Challenge of Change: Frauen in Führungspositionen des Sports*. Düsseldorf: Ministerium für Städtebau und Wohnen (Ministry for Urban Planning), Kultur und Sport des Landes Nordrhein-Westfalen.

Steinmann, H. & Schreyögg, G. (2000). *Management. Grundlagen der Unternehmensführung*. Wiesbaden: Gabler.

Wadsack, R. (1996). *Ehrenamtliche Arbeit im Verein*. Niedernhausen: Falken.

Wilson, W. (1996). The IOC and the status of women in the Olympic Movement: 1972–1996. *Research Quarterly for Exercise and Sport*, **67**(2), 183–192.

Wirth, L. (2001). *Breaking through the Glass Ceiling. Women in management*. Genf: ILO.

21
Socio-political context in which the business of women's sport takes place in Latin America

Rosa López de D'Amico

It is a challenge to write about Latin America, particularly due to the extension and differences that embrace the countries coexisting in the region. One of the first challenges is that there is not even one unique definition of Latin America. For example, one definition is linguistic, referring to those countries that have as their mother tongue Spanish, Portuguese, or French, all Romance languages that have Latin as the common root. Another definition refers to the geographical distribution that starts in the south of North America, which is precisely Mexico, and ends in Argentina/Chile; nevertheless, in this definition a country such as Guyana, just to name one, is included, and they speak English. Some organizations, such as the United Nations Development Programme (UNDP), refer to Latin America and the Caribbean, and it includes all countries from Mexico down with their various linguistic families (UNDP, 2018). The geographical division identifies four areas of Latin America: North America, Central America, South America, and the Caribbean. This chapter views Latin America more through the linguistic definition lens, and focuses more on Spanish-speaking countries, because Chapter 11 deals with Brazil. Notably, it is impossible to speak about them all: Argentina, Bolivia, Brazil, Chile, Colombia, Costa Rica, Cuba, Dominican Republic, Ecuador, El Salvador, Guatemala, Haiti, Honduras, Mexico, Nicaragua, Panama, Paraguay, Peru, Puerto Rico, Uruguay, and Venezuela. To provide readers with a general view, references are made to only some of these countries within the chapter.

One similarity among Latin American countries is a common history of being colonies of various masters (López de D'Amico & Benn, 2016), a land of grace that was invaded by the colonizers over a vast area in which many indigenous groups lived with a high level of social organizational structures, such as the Mayas, Aztecs, and Incas, to mention but a few. But their downfall was their wealth, and for that reason they were massacred and became slaves in their own lands (Galeano, 1995). Latin America is a region in which the inhabitants have had to struggle to defend their lands and culture, but not always successfully. The first battle was between the indigenous people and the colonizers. Next, they experienced long independence battles, for example, the Spanish-speaking countries battled against Spain and later experienced many civil wars to try to establish their socio-structural way of life. When countries were settled and determining their governance structures, many regions suffered dictatorial periods, particularly in the twentieth century. It is important to highlight that women were instrumental in those socio-structural creation processes; however, they were ignored and it is only in recent years that their contributions toward independence have been acknowledged (Vargas, 2010).

Latin America is a region of contrast. For example, there are high levels of inequality in terms of economic income distribution (Comisión Económica para América Latina y el Caribe [CEPAL], 2014), fewer women in the labor market and differences in salaries (CEPAL, 2016), and high levels of femicide (Yagoub, 2016); yet also diversity exists among ethnic groups and multiracial peoples, a great biodiversity rich in mineral resources as well as natural beauties. The region has also had more women as president, and still today a higher number of women in parliaments than in other parts of the world. In this last aspect, there is no doubt that the Millennium Development Goals (MDGs), and since 2016 the Sustainable Development Goals (SDGs) or Agenda 2030, have moved countries to try to respond to the goals; governments have compromised to fulfill those goals, particularly because, in the MDG, the third objective was specifically to "promote gender equality and empower women"; as it was not achieved, it is present in the SDG in the fifth objective as "gender equality." The gender equality and empowerment of women and girls are one area on which there has been a big emphasis, and the aforementioned agendas incorporate gender in various areas.

It is estimated that in Latin America there is a population of 654,514,845. The largest age group is between 15 and 19, and more broadly between 19 and 64 years of age (the Latin American and Caribbean Demographic Centre CELADE, 2017). Girls and teenagers in Latin America and the Caribbean represent nearly one-fifth of the population, which is mostly urban and represents almost half of the female population. Women represent 17% of the total population in the region; boys in the same age group represent 18% of the total population (Céspedes & Robles, 2016). The highest number of girls and teenagers are concentrated in Brazil, Mexico, and Colombia; in the Caribbean, Jamaica has the highest number of girls and teenagers. Girls and teenagers represent over 40% in countries such as Guatemala, Bolivia, Honduras, Paraguay, and Haiti, whereas in Uruguay Chile and Cuba they represent less than 30%. In countries such as Honduras, Nicaragua, El Salvador, and Panama, the number of girls and women living in rural areas represent more than 40%, whereas in Argentina and Uruguay it is less than 10%.

According to Bidegain (2017) Latin America and the Caribbean are the only regions in the world where, for more than 40 years, states have gathered with the objective of establishing political compromises to eradicate gender inequalities and discrimination against women in order to move toward accomplishing human rights principles. The agreements have been settled since the celebration of the first regional conference focused on the integration of women into the economic and social development of Latin America, which took place in Havana, Cuba in 1977. The gender regional agenda was possible due to the articulated work of government, feminist and women's organizations, and the support of the United Nations. Thus far, 13 conferences have been celebrated.

Women in Latin American society

Latin American women have had an important role in the history of their homelands; they were instrumental in the independence battles that these regions went through. Since the arrival of the colonizers, women have played an important role in maintaining the independence of their lands. With the arrival of the colonizers, indigenous women fought next to their male counterparts to free themselves from the invaders, and there are many stories of famous indigenous women who were leaders in battles and resistance. During colonial time, women again fought for independence in many different roles; it was a brutal period and the women who were caught in battle suffered worse treatments than men, and in the twentieth century many women again played different roles to fight against criminal dictatorial regimes (Carosio, 2010; López de D'Amico, 2016).

Scull (2016) theorized that women in Latin America have had more chances to be in the public political discussion than women elsewhere, because they were allowed to participate in the guerrilla process in many countries in Latin America. For example, Dilma Rousseff participated during the dictatorial period in Brazil, and many years later arrived at the presidency of Brazil. Another example is in Nicaragua, where:

> the first guerrilla force that managed to liberate a major city during the 1979 insurrection was composed entirely of women. We women joined revolts and became experienced in grassroots organising, political activism, diplomacy, and combat. When it came time to build democratic societies, we claimed a place in governments and power structures.
>
> *(Belli, 2016, p. 3)*

Nowadays, the region represents a challenge; it is the region that has had the most women as head of state; so far 11 women have served as presidents in Latin American countries. The first woman president of a country was the Argentinian Isabel Perón in 1974, and so far there have been several who were re-elected and more women candidates are running for presidency. Women's participation in the public political sphere has increased meaningfully, being present at the parliamentary level, and they are also take more ministerial responsibilities. The process has not been easy, and many complexities have arisen.

Women have had to face difficult campaigns and even in government there are still sectors of the population that react against women, as indicated by the feminist Valdés when speaking about Bachelet: "Our patriarchs resented [Bachelet's win] and the fact that she followed through with her campaign promise to appoint a Cabinet with gender parity." Valdés continued, "She also appointed women [to the Cabinet] that the political parties didn't want. They resented it, and they made us pay for that" (Viñas, 2014, p. 1).

Now, going back in history, matriarchal communities existed in the new world and, in general, in all the structural developments of the various indigenous groups there was a balanced gender relationship in terms of labor responsibilities. There were women leaders (*cacicas*) who had a hereditary right from either their mother or their father. Another characteristic of the pre-Colombian civilization was a warrior character that women had, and some women had political leadership that later was destroyed and ignored by the invaders (Ramos, 2014). With the arrival of the colonizers, native women lost all their rights and privileges, and moreover the cultural structural order that existed in their communities. They became objects that were used, abused, abandoned, and sold. After the destruction of the moral and economic structure of the millenarian civilization of the indigenous communities, the colonial period was imposed under the most brutal regime that legitimized the violation of all sorts of human rights to the indigenous people, not to mention indigenous women becoming third-class citizens, enduring the same treatment received by African–American women. Some indigenous women who participated in the resistance against the colonizers included Anacaona (Domincan Republic), Gaitana (Colombia), Yanequeo (Chile), Juliana (Paraguay), and Ana Soto (Venezuela). In Nicaragua, indigenous women did *huelga de amores* ("love riots") in which they refused to have sexual intercourse so as not to have slave children (Mazzei, 2011; Ramos, 2014). In spite of years of exploitation and mistreatment, there are still indigenous women who present with new ways of resistance, such as Rigoberta Menchú Tum (Guatemala), Martha Sanchez Nestor (Mexico), Verónica Huilipan (Mapuche – Argentina), Tarcila Rivera Zea (Peru), María del Carmen Cruz Ramírez (México), and la Comandanta Ramona (Mexico).

In terms of female representation and women's rights to participate in the political decisions that affected them, it is interesting to highlight what Francisco de Miranda[1] indicated in 1792:

> For my part I recommend just one thing, wise legislator: the women. Why within a democratic government half of the individuals, women, are not directly or indirectly represented, while they are subject to the same severity of laws that men do to their liking? Why at least they are not consulted about the laws that concern them more particularly, such as those related to marriage, divorce, education of girls, etc.? I confess that all these things seem to me as unheard usurpations and very worthy of consideration on the part of our wise legislators.[2]
>
> *(Miranda, 1982, p. 124)*

In spite of that interesting quotation, there were no big changes in the political participation of women in the society's development in the twentieth century, but indeed they participated quietly. Güezmes and Aguirrezabal (2015) summarized the periods of women's participation in Latin American public political life in the twentieth century. The time period between 1929 and 1961 can be called the "suffragist period," because this is the time in which women's right to vote was obtained in the whole region. From 1962 to 1990 is the "stagnation period" – the sporadic presence of women in the politics of their countries. The period of "sustained progress" is between 1991 and 2011, because there were implementations of specific policies, quotas, and other mechanisms. Since 2012 there has been a period of "sustained equality," because it has promoted democratic parity.

The Inter-Parliamentary Union (IPU) and the UNDP (2017, p. 20) acknowledge that:

> Gender parity in parliament is still far from being realized – 23.3 per cent of the world's parliamentarians were women in June 2017 . . . . Women's political participation is a tool through which gender equality in both the political process and society can be increased in general.

According to data from the IPU, as of January 2018, Bolivia, Cuba, Nicaragua, and Mexico are among the first 10 countries that have higher numbers of women in parliament (IPU, 2018). In the Global Gender Gap index, Nicaragua appears in the 6th position and, interestingly, Latin America and the Caribbean region have 70% of gender parity compared with the global weighted average of 68%. Numerous studies suggest that a higher equality in gender drives toward better economic development. (World Economic Forum, 2018). It is interesting that, in the early nineteenth century, the Frenchman Charles Fourier pointed out a phrase that indicated "Social progress . . . occurs by virtue of the progress of women toward liberty, and social decline by virtue of decreases in the liberty of women" (Goldstein, 1982, p.100).

By 2012 the number of women elected to municipal legislative bodies was increasing and, according to the research, particularly in those countries in which there were women's quotas for elections (Rodríguez, 2012). Currently, in 60% of the Latin American countries, there is a female organizational body who has ministerial rank. Women's presence in the courts of justice in Latin America have increased, and in 13 countries of the Latin American and Caribbean region more than 50% of their magistrates in the higher Court of Justice are women. Including the parliament elections in 2015–2016, Latin America is the region that has the most women in legislative bodies. Bolivia has 53.1% and Cuba, Ecuador, Nicaragua, and Mexico have an average of 40% of representation from women (CEPAL – Naciones Unidas, 2018).

Table 21.1 Latin American female Ministers of Defense

Name	Country	Period
Michelle Bachelet	Chile	January 2002 to September 2004
Viviane Blanlot Soza		2006–2007
Marta Lucía Ramírez	Colombia	August 7, 2002 to November 10, 2003
Azucena Berrutti.	Uruguay	March 1, 2005 to March 3, 2008
Nilda Garré	Argentina	December 2005 to December 2010.
Guadalupe Larriva González	Ecuador	January 15, 2007 to January 25, 2007
Lorena Escudero Durán		February 2, 2007 to August 30, 2007
María Fernanda Espinoza		November 29, 2012 to September 26, 2014
María Cecilia Chacón	Bolivia	April 6 to September 26, 2011
María Liz García	Paraguay	Since June 6, 2012
María Fernanda Espinoza	Ecuador	Since November 28, 2012
Martha Ruiz Sevilla	Nicaragua	February 2014
Carmen Meléndez	Venezuela	July 2013 to October 2014

Another aspect in which there have been changes is the participation of women at a ministerial rank, not considered the traditional social areas, because we can observe in Table 21.1 that there are some women who had been Minister of Defense:

There are more female heads of state in Latin America than in any other continent, but progress to curb sexism and discrimination in all spheres of society is still low. Yet, despite the culture of machismo that is the traditional stereotype by which Latin America has been identified, women have emerged as political leaders at a remarkable and unexpected rate. There is no doubt that the Millennium Development Goal was responsible for the big move that some countries made in order to work for the empowerment of women, so ministerial offices were created and/or more women state offices were opened, government started to implement quotas of women participating in political elections, and other important recognitions were implemented to make women more visible. For example, at the start of Bolivian president Evo Morales' second term appointment, his cabinet consisted of the same number of men and women (Viñas, 2014).

In spite of the fact that, by 2016, the region was at the top of female representation in parliaments, which represents 27.5%, it is still far from obtaining parity (Unión Interparlamentaria [ONU], 2016). Besides, in the labor market there are still gaps in salaries between men and women (CEPAL, 2014, 2016), although it is less evident in groups of women who have less education; women who have 13 or more years of academic education are 25.6% less than men (Rico & Trucco, 2014).

Nowadays the region has more policies and institutions for facing discrimination in a more direct way and they are in better condition than in the past. It has been a long historical process that has produced important progress; nevertheless there are still gaps of inequalities that have not allowed achievement of the complete celebration of women's autonomy and rights.

Women and sport

As happens in the world of sport worldwide, Latin America is no exception in terms of the lack of parity in the presence of women in sport, in general (see López de D'Amico, 2016; López de

D'Amico, Benn, & Pfister, 2016). Lapchick, Davison, Grant, and Quirarte (2016) indicated that the leadership in sport is an exclusive club of men. In the report, they indicated that there is an under-representation of women in top positions across international sport. From the top down, female representation among the 90 members (at the time of data collection) of the International Olympic Committee (IOC), of which 22 are women, is 24.4%; women make up only 5.7% of international federation (IF) presidents, 12.2% of vice presidents, and 13.1% of executive committee members. In Latin America there is one female president of a national Olympic committee, Puerto Rican Sara Rosario Vélez.

Women's various roles in sport are under-represented in the world as well (Fasting, Sand, Pike, & Matthews, 2014). In Europe, a region in which several policies relating to women's rights in sport have been generated, Wickstrøm (2017) highlights that ethnic minorities are clearly under-represented in governance and coaching structures in European football clubs and, in particular, women are similarly under-represented.

However, the topic of women in sport is receiving more and more attention (e.g., EY, 2017) and in Latin America this is also taking place. It is important to highlight that, in some countries, such as Cuba, women's participation is sport has been promoted for more than five decades, whereas in others in the region it is a process that has been more evident in the last 15 years (e.g., Ferreira Rocha, 2016; López de D'Amico, 2016; López de D'Amico et al., 2016). This section of the chapter highlights the participation of some women in elite sports that are not considered the traditional "feminine sports" and have not been mentioned in the publications indicated above. The chosen ones are from the last 20 years; nevertheless, there is once exception in "Queta" from Mexico.

Enriqueta "Queta" Basilio (Mexico) was the first woman ever to ignite the Olympic flame in the Olympic Games; it took place in Mexico in 1968, where she was a track-and-field athlete. She was elected to the federal parliament (2000–2003) and is a permanent member of the Mexican Olympic Committee. She is one of the leading people responsible for organizing an annual celebration that commemorates the Mexico 1968 Olympic Games, called the symbolic flame for peace and sport (*Fuego Simbólico por la Paz y el Deporte*).

Football (soccer) is a big sport in the region, and in many countries it is the number one sport. As in other regions, it has been dominated by men in Latin America. In spite of the fact that there is an increase in women's participation in football, they do not receive the same media coverage and/or financial support that men's football does (see Elsey & Nadel, 2016). Brazil, Argentina, and Uruguay are the only nations that have held women's football championships for more than 20 years, although the positive side is that more countries have begun implementing women's football teams and championships (see Sandoval, 2017), for example, Venezuela, Costa Rica, Chile, Colombia, El Salvador, and Panamá, to mention some of them. Speaking about younger generations, it is interesting to mention that the first woman nominated to the Puská award, in the first three places, is Latin American:

> A living proof of how well the female football has improved, and specially the Venezuelan team, is the talented Daniuska Rodríguez. With only 18 years of age, this Latin American player was nominated for the Puskás 2016 price for Best Goal of the Year. She was nominated due to her majestic goal against Colombia in the final group stage at Women's U-17 Sudamericano Championship. The votes were not enough to give the award to Rodríguez but she is the first woman to be ever nominated. Thanks to that special performance, Venezuela won said tournament in 2016 reaffirming the great moment that the region is still currently enjoying.
>
> *(Sandoval, 2017, para. 3)*

It is interesting that the second woman to be nominated to this award was another Venezuelan, Deyna Castellanos, in 2017 (BBC Mundo, 2017).

When speaking about women's football, it is compulsory to mention Marta Vieira da Silva (Brazil), who won the prestigious FIFA (Fédération Internationale de Football Association) Women's World Player of the Year award five years in a row (2006–2010), the most times any player (male or female) has won it. She has received many other awards and international recognition as a four-time member of the Brazilian Olympic team (2004, 2008, 2012, 2016) winning the silver medal in two of those Games. In the last two years, two Latin Americans placed in the top three of the Best FIFA Women's Players (as it was called after 2015) were: Marta Vieira da Silva (2016) and Deyna Castellanos (2017).

In judo there are two athletes who have been mentioned for their achievements. Idalys Ortiz from Cuba, who competes in the over 78kg, has participated in three Olympic Games (2008, 2012, 2016) placing her in the top three in the category, in addition to six world championships with medals in all of them. In 2008, she became the youngest Olympic medalist in the heavyweight category, winning a bronze medal. Another important athlete, Paula Pareto (nickname *La peque*), who won the gold medal in 2016 Olympic Games, also won the bronze medal in 2008 and is the first Argentinian woman to win more than one medal in individual sport.

In BMX/Bicicross, without question, Mariana Pajón, the two times Olympic gold medalist and World Champion is an icon in her country of Colombia. She is the first Latin American woman to win two consecutive Olympic gold medals; in 2013 she created her own foundation to support children to practice BMX. There are two other Latin Americans who have achieved important places in competition: Doménica Azuero from Ecuador (World Junior Champion) and Stefany Hernandez from Venezuela (World Champion and bronze medal in the 2016 Rio Olympics).

In track and field's triple jump, Caterine Ibargüen from Colombia became an example, because she has won all the titles in this discipline, earning the gold medal in Rio 2016. She has been in the top of this discipline for more than 15 years; as well as dedicating herself just to the triple jump in the last 10 years, in the past she also participated internationally in high jump and long jump. Curiously, another Latin American, Yulimar Rojas, from Venezuela, has become a rising star because in the last three years her name has been highly touted in this world of sport; she also won the World Championships and the silver medal in the Rio 2016 Olympic Games.

In field hockey, the Argentinian Luciana Aymar is extremely notable, as she was distinguished as the best hockey player of the world on eight occasions; she is considered the best female hockey player of all time, and in 2008 she was declared a legend of hockey by the International Hockey Federation. She participated in four consecutive Olympic Games (2000, 2004, 2008, 2012) and has since signed contracts with numerous important brands in Argentina (e.g., Rexona, Gatorade, ICBC, Midea, and Nike). She is considered one of the most beloved athletes by the media. After her retirement, Florencia Habif, another Argentinian, was also distinguished as a best player in hockey.

In Peru, the achievements of female volleyball players (e.g., Seoul Olympics 1988; Cecilia Tait – inducted, in 2005, into the Volleyball Hall of Fame), surfers (e.g., Sofía Mulánovich – first Latin American to be inducted into the Surfers' Hall of Fame) and boxers (e.g., Kina Malpartida – World Champion in the women's World Boxing Association [WBA] super-featherweight category – nowadays a business woman) have played an important part in breaking down barriers that are not just about gender, but also about ethnicity (e.g., Analí Gómez). Several of the outstanding volleyball athletes have also become politicians and been elected to the national congress (Wood, 2012). It is of interest that another important athlete, Paloma Noceda, who is a watercross World Champion, is nowadays a member of the national congress.

There are other athletes who have had great achievements, such as tennis player Mónica Puig, the first Olympic Gold medalist from Puerto Rico and the first Latin American woman to win a Gold medal in this sport. Paola Longoria (Mexico), the most awarded racquetball player of all time; in 2013, *Forbes Magazine*'s Mexico edition named Longoria as one of the 50 most influential women in Mexico. Regla Torres (Cuba) was distinguished as the Best Volleyball Player of the Century by the Fédération Internationale de Volleyball (FIVB). There are several Latin American World Champions in the sport of boxing, such as Carolina Rodríguez (nickname *Krespita*) from Chile, Hanna Gabriels (Costa Rica), and Oxandia Castillo (Dominican Republic).

These women athletes have also had to struggle against the stereotypes that affect the society surrounding them. For example, Fabiana Claudino, the captain of the Brazilian volleyball team in the Olympic Games 2016, and three-time Olympic Gold medalist (2008, 2012, 2016), was the subject of racial discrimination in her own country (see Panato, 2015; Simon, 2015). There are others who have experienced mistreatment due to their political views.

In the referee area it is important to highlight Silvia Regina, who was the first woman FIFA referee in Brazil and the first Latin American to participate in an international male soccer championship of Conmebol. Claudia Umpiérrez (Uruguay) was the first woman FIFA referee in Uruguay who participated in the first division of the male championship. There are many others, but still much more is needed to make the society in general accept them without any discriminatory comments because these still happen (e.g., Sports Life, 2016).

Latin American women participate in all sports and are present in all the different roles played. The women mentioned in this chapter have all become stars in their home countries and have become role models. They have become public images and participate in various areas of society; many participate in politics and are active political leaders with responsibilities at the government level. So, the business of women in sport in Latin America is very diverse and varies from one country to another, but women are breaking stereotypes.

Conclusion

In Latin America, as in other places in the world, women in sport have struggled to position themselves in the various roles of sport. As athletes, women have been participating, now as referees/judges, coaches, and officers, but they are still struggling hard to be there. The important thing is that they know it and they speak out about it. For example, Elsey and Nadel (2016, p. 10) indicate:

> It is easier for women to become a nation's president than to be president of a football federation. At the federation level, the directors of national associations are entirely men. Women need to be represented on executive committees. They should have their own representatives, with full voting rights, because otherwise women's soccer is completely ignored. So, too, should federations work with the sports media to promote women's soccer and to televise women's national team games.

This quote refers particularly to soccer, but it is also a reality in many other sports. There are winds of change and the media are crucial in that respect (e.g., Campbell, 2017, Siang, 2017). Women in sport are becoming more popular and this has happened in other spheres, because their visibility and serving as role models have inspired more women, particularly young women, to get involved: "as women's sport begins to be taken more seriously, and women athletes gain respect and attention, the popularity of sport among younger women is also starting to increase – levelling the playing field later in their lives and careers" (EY, 2017, p. 2). As an example, last year in Venezuela marked the first time ever that a woman (María Soto) won the presidency of the Venezuelan Softball Federation, after a male president who was in office since 1987; she is a professional, former Olympian and captain of the women's team. Her image was familiar to society because softball had been in the media for a long period of time.

In the framework of SDPs, it is important to take into account that, to achieve gender equity and equality in sport, it is necessary to consider it as part of the agenda. Gender policies are not just limited to social policies; they are broader than that, involving environment, economics, technology, infrastructure, and climate change, and sport is part of all that. In sport, all women have a place, and they can all be included, so cultural patterns need to be transformed, and education and democratic participation are important to promote inclusion.

Leader profile: María José Soto Gil

María Soto is an athlete, sport leader, and business administrator. She was a member of the Venezuelan Olympic Softball team in Beijing 2008. She started practicing baseball together with her brother José in 1982, and continued until 1992 when she turned to softball. At first not much convinced her to practice softball, but she started as part of the Carabobo (state) team, and they won, on four consecutive occasions, the National Junior Games. Immediately, from

Figure 21.1 María José Soto Gil

1994, she was asked to be part of the Venezuelan Softball National Team and has been there ever since; she was the captain of the team for 18 years. That same year she participated at the Softball Pan American Championship in Guatemala, and she was the youngest player. In 1997, she was offered a scholarship to study at the University of Mobile in Alabama (USA) where she graduated in Business Administration with a major in management. She also supported her university team to be in the highest rank of the National Athletic Intercollegiate Association (NAIA). Later, she was hired by the university to serve as a coach from 2004 through 2006. In 2006, the team won the NAIA national championship. She achieved the greatest dream of most athletes in 2007: to compete in the Olympic Games. At the 2008 Olympics, Soto said, "It was an honor to walk in front of the Venezuelan Olympic Delegation with the flag of my country on behalf of my fellow players as the softball team was chosen to be the flag bearer." At the 2010 World Championships in Venezuela, the International Softball Federation announced that an athlete was going to be elected to be part of the board by the first time ever, and Soto won with 16 votes; four years later she was re-elected. In 2014, the International Softball Federation and the Baseball Federation decided to join forces and the World Baseball Softball Confederation (WBSC) was developed; Soto was named as the athlete representative until 2021. Soto was elected as the first woman president of the Venezuelan Softball Federation in 2017, a major achievement. In that same year, at the First Congress of the WBSC she was elected as member at large of the board for the Softball Division during the period of 2017–2021. She is a member of the commission that has been in the quest to re-incorporate softball and baseball to the Olympic Games programme; she participated in various meetings with the IOC and the Tokyo 2020 Organizing Committee. They achieved their goal, because softball and baseball are back in the Olympic Games, starting in 2020. Now her dream is for the Venezuelan softball team to qualify for Tokyo 2020 and to make baseball and softball stay in the Olympic program for Paris 2024 and Los Angeles 2028.

Notes

1 Francisco de Miranda (1750–1816) Venezuelan politician, military, diplomatic, writer, humanist, and visionary. He is known as "The First Universal Venezuelan" and "The Great Universal American."
2 "Por mi parte os recomiendo una cosa sabio legislador: las mujeres. ¿Por qué dentro de un gobierno democrático la mitad de los individuos, las mujeres, no están directa o indirectamente representadas, mientras que sí están sujetas a la misma severidad de las leyes que los hombres hacen a su gusto? ¿Por qué al menos no se les consulta acerca de las leyes que conciernen a ellas más particularmente como son las relacionadas con matrimonio, divorcio, educación de las niñas, etc.? Le confieso que todas estas cosas me parecen usurpaciones inauditas y muy dignas de consideración por parte de nuestros sabios legisladores" (Miranda, 1982, p. 124)

References

BBC Mundo (2017). Deyna Castellanos, la sensación venezolana de 18 años cuya nominación a los premios The Best puso a la FIFA en el ojo del huracán. Retrieved from www.bbc.com/mundo/deportes-41696386.
Belli, G. (2016). Why has "macho" Latin America elected more female leaders than the US? *The Guardian*. Retrieved from https://www.theguardian.com/global-development-professionals-network/2016/nov/07/macho-latin-america-elected-more-female-leaders-than-us.
Bidegain, N. (2017). *La Agenda 2030 y la Agenda Regional de Género Sinergias para la igualdad en América Latina y el Caribe*. Serie Asuntos de Género. Santiago, Chile: CEPAL.
Campbell, R. (2017). Career opportunities for women in sports business on the rise. Retrieved from https://www.thebalance.com/career-opportunities-for-women-in-sports-business-3113255.

Carosio, A. (2010). Las mujeres en el proceso independentista. *Centro de Estudios de la Mujer (CEM-UCV)*. Retrieved from www.rebelion.org/noticia.php?id=109320.

CELADE (2017). America Latina: Estimaciones y proyecciones de población a largo plazo. 1950–2100. UN CELADE. Retrieved from https://www.cepal.org/es/temas/proyecciones-demograficas/estimaciones-proyecciones-poblacion-total-urbana-rural-economicamente-activa.

Céspedes, C. & Robles, C. (2016). *Niñas y adolescentes en América Latina y el Caribe. Deudas de igualdad*. Santiago de Chile: Publicación de las Naciones Unidas.

Comisión Económica para América Latina y el Caribe (CEPAL) (2014). *Panorama Social de América Latina 2014* (LC/G.2635-P). Santiago de Chile: Publicación de las Naciones Unidas.

Comisión Económica para América Latina y el Caribe (CEPAL) (2016). *Panorama Social de América Latina 2015, Documento Informativo*. Santiago de Chile: Publicación de las Naciones Unidas.

Comisión Económica para América Latina y el Caribe (CEPAL) – Naciones Unidas (2018). Observatorio de Igualdad de Género de América Latina – Poder legislativo: porcentaje de mujeres en el órgano legislativo nacional: Cámara baja o única y el Caribe. Retrieved from https://oig.cepal.org/es/indicadores/poder-legislativo-porcentaje-mujeres-organo-legislativo-nacional-camara-baja-o-unica.

Elsey, B. & Nadel, J. (2016). South American soccer is ignoring its women. *Vice Sports*. Retrieved from https://sports.vice.com/en_ca/article/pgnazz/south-american-soccer-is-ignoring-its-women.

EY (2017). Good sports: why business needs more sportswomen. Women's sports are getting more and more attention. Here's why that's good for business. Retrieved from https://consulting.ey.com/good-sports-why-business-needs-more-sportswomen.

Fasting, K., Sand, T., Pike E. & Matthews, J. (2014). *From Brighton to Helsinki. Women and sport progress report 1994–2014*. Finland: Finish Sports Confederation Valo.

Ferreira Rocha, B. (ed.) (2016) *Inspirational Women in America: Making a difference in physical education, sport and dance*. Brazil: Universidade Federal de Juiz de Fora & IAPESGW.

Galeano, E. (1995). *Las venas abiertas de América Latina*, 64th edn. Bogotá, Colombia: Tercer Mundo Editores.

Goldstein, L. (1982). Early feminist themes in French utopian socialism: The St.-Simonians and Fourier. *Journal of the History of Ideas*, **43**(1), 91–108

Güezmes, A. & Aguirrezabal, I. (2015). *La hora de la igualdad sustantiva Participación política de las mujeres en América Latina y el Caribe Hispano*. México: ONU Mujeres.

Inter-Parliamentary Union (IPU) (2018). Women in national parliaments. Retrieved from http://archive.ipu.org/wmn-e/classif.htm.

Inter-Parliamentary Union & United Nations Development Programme (2017). *Global Parliamentary Report 2017*. Paris: Inter-Parliamentary Union & UNDP.

Lapchick, R. Davison, E., Grant, C., & Quirarte, R. (2016). *Gender Report Card: 2016 International Sports Report Card on Women in Leadership Roles*. The Institute for Diversity and Ethics in Sport. Retrieved from http://nebula.wsimg.com/0e5c5c3e23367795e9ec9e5ec49fc9b2?AccessKeyId=DAC3A56D8FB782449D2A&disposition=0&alloworigin=1.

López de D'Amico, R. (2016). Latin American women and leadership in sport. In. G. Bravo, R. Lopez de D'Amico, & C. Parrish (eds), *Sport in Latin America Policy, Organization, Management* (pp. 46–61). London: Routledge.

López de D'Amico, R. & Benn, T. (2016). Latin America. An introduction. In R. López de D'Amico, T. Benn, & G. Pfister (eds), *Women and Sport in Latin America* (pp. 3–17). London: Routledge.

López de D'Amico, R., Benn, T., & Pfister, G. (2016). *Women and Sport in Latin America*. London: Routledge

Mazzei, M. (2011). Felipe Pigna: "En América latina se da una rebelión temprana que no sucede en otras partes del mundo." Retrieved from https://www.clarin.com/historia/entrevista_felipe_pigna-mujeres_tenian_que_ser_0_SkDM7uK3vXe.html.

Miranda, F. de (1982). *América espera*. Caracas: Fundación Biblioteca Ayacucho.

ONU Unión Interparlamentaria (2016). Las mujeres en el parlamento en 2015. Retrieved from http://archive.ipu.org/pdf/publications/WIP2015-s.pdf.

Panato, D. (2015). Bicampeã olímpica, Fabiana diz ter sofrido insultos racistas em jogo de vôlei. *JCNET*. Available at: https://www.jcnet.com.br/Esportes/2015/01/bicampea-olimpica-fabiana-diz-ter-sofrido-insultos-racistas-em-jogo-de-volei.html (accessed March 1, 2018).

Ramos, D. (2014). Heroínas Americanas. Historias que no se cuentan. *Mito Revista Cultural*, **44**. Available at: http://revistamito.com/heroinas-americanas (accessed September 10, 2017).

Rico, M. & Trucco, D. (2014). *Adolescentes: Derecho a la educación y al bienestar*. Santiago de Chile: CEPAL/UNICEF.

Rodríguez, A. (2012). La participación política de las mujeres en América Latina y el Caribe, una mirada a lo local. Available at: https://oig.cepal.org/sites/default/files/gobernabilidad_local_y_genero.pdf (accessed March 14, 2018).

Sandoval, M. (2017). Women's football in Latin America. *LatinAmerican Post*. Living Sports. Available at: https://www.latinamericanpost.com/index.php/sports/15431-women-s-football-in-latin-america (accessed March 2, 2018).

Scull, J. (2016). Mujeres Guerrilleras de Latino America – Cuba, México, Nicaragua, Colombia, El Salvador. Retrieved from https://medium.com/@jules000120/mujeres-guerrilleras-de-latino-america-cuba-mexico-nicaragua-colombia-el-salvador-38579e5a0e32.

Siang, S. (2017). Change is happening for women in the sport industry. Retrieved from https://www.huffingtonpost.com/sanyin-siang/change-is-happening-for-w_b_3949493.html.

Simon, Y. (2015). The 10 best Latina athletes. Retrieved from www.latina.com/entertainment/buzz/best-latina-athletes-women-sports.

Sports Life (2016). The dangers of being a female referee in Latin America. Retrieved from www.news.com.au/sport/sports-life/the-dangers-of-being-a-female-referee-in-latin-america/news-story/4d9f6e31f4247ac325a14e6956bbe7f5.

United Nations Development Programme (UNDP) (218). *UNDP in Latin America and the Caribbean*. Retrieved from www.latinamerica.undp.org/content/rblac/en/home/operations/about_undp.html (accessed July 28, 2018).

Vargas, I. (2010). *Mujeres en tiempos de cambio*. Caracas: Colección Bicentenario.

Viñas, S. (2014). Latin women take the helm. *World Policy Journal*. Retrieved from https://worldpolicy.org/2014/03/18/latin-women-take-the-helm.

Wickstrøm, M. (2017). Representation on and off the pitch. Play the game. Retrieved from www.playthegame.org/news/news-articles/2017/0409_representation-on-and-off-the-pitch.

Woods, D. (2012). Women and sports in Peru. *Revista Harvard Review of Latin America Sport*. Retrieved from http://revista.drclas.harvard.edu/files/revista/files/sports.pdf?m=1410443392.

World Economic Forum (2018). ¿Cuál es la brecha de género en 2017 (y por qué se está ampliando)? Retrieved from https://www.weforum.org/es/agenda/2017/11/cual-es-la-brecha-de-genero-en-2017-y-por-que-se-esta-ampliando.

Yagoub, M. (2016). Why does Latin America have the world's highest female murder rates? Retrieved from https://www.opendemocracy.net/democraciaabierta/mimi-yagoub/why-does-latin-america-have-worlds-highest-female-murder-rates.

22
National sporting organizations and women's sport participation
An Australian focus

Katie Rowe

Background

Sport has traditionally been considered an activity participated and engaged in more often by males than by females. In the Australian context, participation statistics tell a consistent story where boys and men are more likely than girls and women to participate in sport, particularly organized club-based sport and team sport (Commonwealth of Australia, 2016a, 2017). Research suggests this gender divide in participation widens during adolescence as boys continue to play sport, while girls begin to drop out (Commonwealth of Australia, 2017; Eime, Harvey, Sawyer, Craike, Symons, & Payne, 2016). This sees women being far less likely than men to participate in organized sport. Such a gender divide in organized sport participation has prompted the Australian Government to focus on this issue, introducing initiatives such as the Girls Make your Move campaign launched in 2016 (Commonwealth of Australia, 2016b). Moreover, national sporting organizations (NSOs) are increasingly conscious of the need to address the gender divide in sport participation in their specific sports.

Sport in Australia is delivered through a club-based system. A network of community sport clubs operates throughout Australia, providing people, particularly children and adolescents, with opportunities to participate in sport. Each club typically focuses on delivering one particular sport (e.g., a basketball club or a soccer club), and is affiliated with a national, and often state, governing body for that particular sport (Shilbury, Phillips, Karg, & Rowe, 2017). This structure provides strategic and governance oversight to community sport clubs and ensures that participants can access sport participation opportunities locally. In Australian sport, particularly within community sport clubs, men typically have remained in positions of decision-making power over many decades, taking on roles as coaches, committee members, board members, and paid staff (Richards, 2016; Shilbury et al., 2017). Such male-dominated environments have been shown to present barriers for community clubs in efforts to attract and retain female participants, despite the best of intentions of male committee members, coaches, and volunteers (Rowe, Sherry & Osborne, 2018). To further exacerbate the issue, many Australian sporting facilities lack fundamental attributes, such as female changing rooms and toilets, required to make them appropriate for, and supportive of, female participants (State Government of Victoria, 2017). These sport facilities were often built in times when so few girls and women participated in, and watched, sport that only male facilities were deemed necessary. This is an issue governments across Australia are currently working to address.

The elite women's sport landscape has also suffered from a lack of exposure and investment to date. Commercialization of sport changed the sporting landscape substantially for male athletes (Shilbury et al., 2017), who progressively experienced improved conditions, particularly access to full-time wages, to support their sporting pursuits. Professional sport then became a realistic career aspiration for young men and boys. Despite these improved conditions for male athletes, women's sport across the globe has remained underfunded. largely in response to limited commercial investment in women's sport (Farrell, Fink, & Fields, 2011). Female athletes have therefore continued to struggle to balance work and training requirements in their pursuit of sporting excellence. Moreover, the limited media coverage of women's sport has meant that children, particularly young girls, have not been exposed to elite female sport role models to the same extent as male sporting role models. Research has shown that exposure to sporting role models can encourage girls to participate in sport and physical activity (Young, Symons, & Pain, 2015), further compounding a complex set of issues facing women's sport and female participation.

The range of issues and challenges highlighted to this point only scratch the surface of those facing Australian NSOs and governments in their efforts to increase sport participation among women and girls. Not only are girls and women facing male-dominated traditions and cultures, but at times they must also contend with infrastructure that sends a clear message that girls are an afterthought in the club context. They see male athletes in the media, whereas female athletes continue to work hard to realize their dreams behind the scenes. However, the wheels of change continue to turn in Australia and other parts of the world.

Action is currently being taken by government and other stakeholders to address the issue of women's leadership and involvement in sport, through the introduction of mandatory governance principles, board diversity quotas, and female coach and leadership programs (Richards, 2016). This has seen NSOs work toward increasing the number of women on their boards, with government funding increasingly being contingent on NSOs reaching a target of 40% women on their boards. NSOs can also nominate women from within their sport to take part in leadership workshops offered by Sport Australia (former the Australian Sports Commission, Australia's national sport agency). Or NSOs can apply for grants, through Sport Australia, to run development initiatives for women leaders within their sport. This highlights several changes occurring in Australian sport, with a focus on women's leadership.

From a commercial perspective, NSOs and national leagues are increasingly recognizing the market potential of women and girls with respect to their participation in, and spectatorship of, sport. In particular, NSOs of traditionally male-dominated sports such as Australian Rules football, soccer, and cricket have begun focusing their attention on establishing professional women's leagues, and encouraging more women and girls to participate in these sports. NSOs are taking steps to improve conditions and pay deals for women athletes and to find ways to bring women's sport into mainstream media through broadcast deals and media coverage.

One might ask what these leadership, commercial, and professional developments mean from a participation perspective. And what role NSOs play in supporting and leveraging this increased focus on women's sport at the elite level into growing grassroots participation among women and girls. This chapter presents two examples of Australian NSOs, which govern traditionally male-dominated sports. These include the sports of cricket and Australian Rules football. In recent years, the NSO for each of these sports has taken steps to engage women, with participation being one piece of a much larger agenda around women's engagement. Before presenting these examples, it is useful to consider what we know about sport development and the processes in which NSOs engage as they seek to attract, and retain, participants. The next section provides a basic summary to help readers make sense of the practical examples provided later in the chapter.

Sport development

In understanding how and why NSOs take action to encourage women to participate in their particular sport, it is useful to examine the literature in relation to the concept of sport development. Sport development systems are typically designed to achieve two fundamental objectives: (1) to increase the number of participants engaged in a sport; and (2) to maximize athlete performance output in a sport (Green, 2005). In the Australian context, NSOs, and their respective state governing bodies (SSOs) receive funding with exactly these two sets of objectives in mind. As NSOs have become increasingly strategic in their approaches to sport development, sophisticated systems have been established that aim to bring children into a sport at a young age and retain them, using a series of strategies that form player development pathways (Sotiriadou, Shilbury, & Quick, 2008). To develop this understanding, Sotiriadou et al. (2008) examined the sport development processes engaged in by 35 Australian NSOs over a period of 4 years. Building on earlier conceptual understanding of sport development provided by Green (2005), with regard to the recruitment, retention, and transition of athletes, Sotiriadou et al. (2008) proposed a model that detailed a series of actions taken by NSOs with respect to sport development. The proposed framework highlighted the range of sport development stakeholders, strategies, processes, and pathways that collectively form the sport development systems of NSOs.

Key sport development strategies used by NSOs in developing an effective sport development system include: player development programs at three key levels, including mass participation, talent identification, and talent development; the provision of facilities, competitions, and events; development and provision of coaches, umpires, and administrators; and specific promotional activities to leverage elite completions and athletes, and promote participation opportunities. These strategies collectively form a sport development system that drives three key development processes, including attraction, retention/transition, and nurturing of participants and athletes. These strategies, with support from appropriate stakeholders, provide a structured way for NSOs to work in delivering sport participation and development opportunities.

In recent years, Australia's national sport agency, Sport Australia, has encouraged NSOs to align their sport development strategies with an athlete development framework built from research conducted in the Australian elite sport context (Gulbin, Croser, Morley, & Weissensteiner, 2013), titled the Foundation, Talent, Elite, Mastery (FTEM) framework. The FTEM emphasizes the importance of children developing key movement skills in fun environments throughout childhood. Those participants who are interested in progressing further in a particular sport, and have the talent to support this desire, may move into talent pathways, which seek to enhance their sporting capability and performance potential. This framework aligns with many key principles of long-term athlete development (LTAD) (Balyi, Way, & Higgs, 2013), commonly applied in settings such as the United States and Canada. This review of sport development concepts demonstrates that the role of an NSO is to build a system and pathway that encourages participants to enter the sport and remain involved in the sport for as long as possible, realizing their potential along the way.

NSOs focus on providing participation programs (including modified junior sport programs, talent identification programs, and talent development programs), trained coaches, access to facilities and competitions, and promoting the sport more broadly, drawing on the profile of professional leagues and athletes. However, one challenge many Australian sports and NSOs have faced, even within highly structured systems, is how to encourage more women and girls to participate in their sports. Clearly, the absence of professional women's competitions and poor coverage of women's sport in Australia (Paterson & Matzelle, 2014) means that young girls have not been exposed to successful female athletes in the same way that young boys have with male athletes. However, when examining the issue further, one can identify problems in relation to other fundamental sport development requirements such as coaches, facilities, competitions, and the absence of pathways for girls. The following sport examples seek to highlight how two Australian NSOs have worked toward encouraging women and girls to participate in male-dominated sports, by strengthening their sport development systems and leveraging from elite women's sport success.

Cricket Australia

Cricket is a popular game in Australia, which has traditionally been dominated by males (Hickey, Harrison, Ollis, & Mooney, 2016). However, Cricket Australia, the national governing body for cricket, has signaled its intention to change this. In its current strategic plan (2017–2022), Cricket Australia states that it intends to become the "leading sport for women and girls" in Australia (Cricket Australia, 2017a, p. 13), a mantle held currently by the sport of netball, when considering team sport participation (Commonwealth of Australia, 2016a, 2017). To ensure cricket becomes the leading sport for women and girls, Cricket Australia intends to focus its efforts on the following goals and actions:

- Achieve gender equity across Australian Cricket;
- Accelerate opportunities for women in all areas and levels of our game;
- Grow female participation sustainably, and make sure women and girls find cricket clubs welcoming and enjoyable places to be;
- Provide a viable professional career path for female talented athletes, who will be supported by an expansive and structured pathway;
- Grow women's elite cricket, with the World T20 the largest women's sports event seen in Australia, while remaining number one in all formats; and,
- Deepen cricket's fan base by entertaining women and girls, including through the BBL and international men's cricket.

(Cricket Australia, 2017a, p. 13)

This multi-dimensional approach seeks to embed women in all aspects of the game of cricket and to ensure that women are considered equals on and off the field, in cricket contexts. This can be contrasted with the experiences of girls who played cricket in years gone by, who were given no choice but to play on boys' teams if they decided to participate in cricket, due to low participation numbers, and systemic biases towards boys' participation (Hickey et al., 2016). To support its focus on women and girls, Cricket Australia launched the "Growing Cricket for Girls Fund," investing an initial AU$1.5 million, in 2016 (Cricket Australia, 2017b). Subsequent investment from commercial partner, the Commonwealth Bank, has seen the fund prepare to invest a total of AU$6 million over four years into girls' cricket. Cricket Australia's CEO, James Sutherland, has proudly proclaimed this to be the "largest investment by an Australian national sporting organization into teenage girls' sport" (Cricket Australia, 2017b, para. 7). To date, this fund has supported the establishment of 363 new teams and 46 new all-girl competitions around the country.

Women and girls have responded to this strategic investment and action taken by the governing body for cricket. Female cricket participation is on the rise in Australia, with progressive growth having been recorded over the past five years (Cricket Australia, 2014, 2015, 2016, 2017a, 2017b, 2017c). The 2016–17 participation figures indicate that girls' cricket participation grew by 25% in that year, with female participants now making up 27.5% of the total cricket participants (Cricket Australia, 2017b). This has increased from 19% in 2012. The introduction of the Women's Big Bash League (in the 2015–16 season), a professional league, and the success and increased profile of the Australian Women's Cricket team (across multiple forms of the game) have clearly played an important role in encouraging more females to participate in the game. But, importantly, CEO James Sutherland recognizes that the profile benefit provided by elite women's cricket does not in and of itself ensure a sustainable future for female cricket participation. He highlights the importance of women feeling welcome and included in the cricket community and having a positive experience participating in the sport:

> The interest in the elite level of our game has now translated to our grassroots. That simply means, though, that we need to meet this demand, tackling the needs of clubs and schools, providing kids and particularly girls with a welcoming and suitable environment, and supporting our volunteers.
>
> *(Cricket Australia, 2017b, para. 4)*

The additional strategic action required, as highlighted by the CEO of Cricket Australia, focuses on the retention process (Sotiriadou et al., 2008). Elite cricket, particularly the men's and women's Big Bash Leagues, which involve a shorter version of cricket in which games last approximately three hours, has played a key role in raising the profile of the game and reinvigorating the interest of junior participants. However, with this growth, particularly the strong female numbers, club and facility constraints emerge that require strategic action. Cricket Australia recognizes the importance of ensuring that suitable infrastructure is available for female participants. The organization has stated its intention to see AU$1 billion, invested in facility development and upgrades, by 2022, to ensure female participants have access to appropriate facilities (Cricket Australia, 2017b).

In operationalizing objectives to grow the game for women and girls, particularly with respect to the participation component of this objective, Cricket Australia relies on substantial support from its state member associations across the six Australian states. These SSOs work to support club level cricket participation and take action to deliver programs at the grassroots level. In recent years, SSOs have worked in different ways to grow the game of cricket for women and girls, introducing different programs and pathway opportunities. As examples, most SSO websites now include pages dedicated to female participation opportunities and/or pathways into cricket (e.g., Cricket New South Wales, Cricket Queensland, and Cricket Victoria). Girls are now featured in marketing materials and messaging, which would not have been the case a decade or more ago. A whole of sport strategy has been proposed, which theoretically runs from the top level, through to the grassroots. In 2017, Cricket Australia committed to paying elite, female Australian cricketers a record high wage, the highest of any sport in the country (ABC News, 2017). In its pursuit of gender equity in cricket, Cricket Australia announced in 2017 that the two elite, national cricket teams (male and female) would no longer be referred to as the Australian Cricket Team (in reference to the men's team) and the Southern Stars (in reference to the women's team). The two teams were formally to be referred to as the Australian Women's Cricket Team and the Australian Men's Cricket Team, giving equal titles to each team (Cricket Australia, 2017c). This was symbolic of a broader intention to value women's cricket to the same extent as men's cricket. And, although the intentions are strong, and the strategy is in place, community club culture, traditions, and norms can be difficult to shift and the sport has its challenges ahead in ensuring that community cricket clubs are prepared to welcome and support women and girls into the sport.

Reflecting on the information presented above, Cricket Australia has committed to building a cricket culture that provides inclusive environments for women and girls, improving facilities, and providing programs and pathways to ensure that female participation experiences are positive. Given the longstanding male dominance in Australian cricket, which still sees 73% of participants being male (Cricket Australia, 2017b), Cricket Australia and its respective SSOs would certainly not claim to have all the answers or have achieved all there is to achieve in the sport, with respect to female participation and gender equity; much work still remains. However, through establishing a clear vision for women in the sport of cricket, investing in a range of key strategic areas and working towards reshaping the culture of the sport, the cricket landscape is changing and the national governing body for cricket has used the recent elite, commercial success of the game, particularly the male and female Big Bash Leagues, to build a sustainable future for the game, with a strategic focus on women and girls, and their involvement and participation in the sport.

Australian Rules football: The Australian Football League

A similar story is told in the sport of Australian Rules football, commercially Australia's largest football code/league, which has traditionally been a male-dominated sport. Despite such male dominance, and the existence of systemic barriers and inequalities, women's interest in the game has remained and women have sought opportunities to participate for generations (Hess, 2017). To support and formalize women's participation in the sport, a series of women's football leagues were established through the 1980s and 1990s (Victoria 1981, Western Australia 1987, South Australia 1990). Yet, a supporting system for the attraction and retention (Sotiriadou et al., 2008) of female participants was lacking, and participation opportunities and pathways for women and girls remained limited and difficult to access. Those who wanted to participate in the sport were required to play with boys at the junior level, and experienced gaps in their participation pathway, in their mid to late teenage years.

Over the past decade, pathways have begun to form and the depth of competition has continued to grow. This push has largely come from women and girls wanting access to participation opportunities. Similar to the sport of cricket, grassroots football delivery is largely supported and managed by SSOs across Australian states, with a club system providing the main participation setting. The push for women's involvement in the Australian Football League (AFL) was supported by the appointment of staff to drive and support women's football at the state level (Mitchell, 2016), developing a pathway and relevant opportunities for women and girls. In 2010, recognizing the growth and growing interest in women's football, the AFL commissioned a report into women's football. This report provided a series of recommendations in relation to junior football development and the prospect of a national league for women. The AFL subsequently engaged in a pilot testing and development process where it staged a series of women's football exhibition matches that were played from 2013 to 2016 in different formats. The success of these matches in terms of attendance and broadcast interest (commercial success) led the AFL to announce the establishment of a national women's competition, to be launched in 2017. To ensure that this competition would be viable and sustainable over time, the AFL needed to address the existing gaps in pathways for girls around the country at the grassroots level in all Australian states.

Much work has since been undertaken to advance the pathways that exist for girls in the sport. The AFL now promotes a pathway for girls (AFL, 2018) that commences with a modified sport program, AFL Auskick, which introduces girls (and boys) to a modified version of the game, with a smaller-sized ball, smaller-sized field, and a range of activities designed to build skills and enjoyment of the game. This program was in place and available to girls long before the establishment of the women's league. What has changed are the options that exist beyond this point. Beyond the entry level, girls have the option to progress into a junior girls' league and then a youth girls' league, essentially filling the gaps that existed between the age of 12 and senior level competition. Although not all clubs across the country have established girls' teams, many leagues exist, providing opportunities for girls to follow this path if they choose, with the support of their families. Some clubs also offer specific Auskick sessions for girls, where there is a demand. From the youth girls' level, the pathway moves to senior level women's competitions around the country, playing in a division that suits the level of development and interest of individual participants. To support those with elite aspirations and those wanting to refine and develop their skills, academies have been established to identify and develop talented young athletes in the sport. Moreover, talent transfer programs have been put in place to recruit girls into the sport from other sports.

In order to support clubs wanting to establish girls' teams, the AFL has developed a 'Female Football Club Guide' (AFL, 2017a), designed to assist clubs in establishing inclusive environments, with a focus on female participants. The guide provides advice to clubs in the following areas:

- First impressions of the club;
- Fun – 10 things parents and coaches need to know;
- Recruiting new junior and youth girls players;
- Coaching female footballers;
- Facilities;
- Showcasing the social aspects of your club; and,
- Including everyone.

(AFL, 2017a, p. 4)

Many of these recommendations focus on principles of inclusion more broadly; however, the objective is to focus on providing clubs with strategies to make the sport and club culture better suited to the needs and preferences of women and girls. As was noted with respect to female engagement in cricket, the sport has a long way to go in terms of changing a deeply entrenched culture of male dominance, which saw a lack of participation and development opportunities in football for women and girls, for decades. However, national level commitment, demonstrated by the NSO in putting in place strategies to attract, retain, and develop female footballers, and women's engagement in the game more broadly, is an important step in harnessing the interest of young women and girls in the sport of Australian Rules football.

A substantial increase in girls' participation was seen in 2015 and 2016, after the women's exhibition matches played from 2013 to 2016 and particularly after the announcement of the national women's league to be launched in 2017. In 2015, rates of female participation increased by 46%, seeing 163 new female teams introduced and females making up 22% of all participants (AFL, 2015). By 2016, women and girls accounted for 27% of all AFL football participants, with a 56% increase in the number of female community clubs, a further 19% growth in total rates of female participation, and a 21% growth in the number of 5–12 year olds participating in the entry level program, AFL Auskick. By the end of the inaugural year of the women's AFL (2017b), Australian Rules football had experienced a further 76% growth in the number of female teams participating in competitions, with female players making up a total of 30% of all AFL football participants. These results suggest that the establishment of an elite, women's presence in the sport, and the provision of competitions and pathways for women and girls, are actions that have been well received in the community and are leading to increased interest and participation among females.

Unfortunately, in the background of this story of success, the AFL's level of commitment to the elite women's league (AFLW) and women's football more broadly, have been criticized by individuals within the media and by the women's football community. As the AFL looks to grow and expand the league by including additional teams in season three (2019), a conference-style season structure has been proposed, with further revisions to rules having been discussed, in attempts to increase the visual appeal, and commercial viability, of the game. This has not been well received, particularly by women footballers looking to forge a career as serious athletes playing the sport they love. The proposed duration of the 2019 season (seven matches, two finals) arguably places a lower value on the women's game when compared with the men's game (season of 23 weeks and 4 rounds of finals). Moreover, the AFL chose not to charge for entry fees into AFLW matches in seasons one and two and players' wages have remained low. The growth in community football participation among women and girls is a clear positive outcome that has occurred in response to the AFL's strategies and actions to establish community and elite pathways for women and girls to participate and excel in the sport. However, the AFL's commitment to the elite women's competition also seems crucial. Many chapters in the story of AFLW remain unwritten. Early signs have been positive for the game. But time will tell as to how the league will evolve over the coming years and how women and girls, and the broader football community, will respond.

Conclusion

What we see in each of the examples presented and the leader profile story below is both the value of having an elite women's competition in place to raise the profile of the sport among women and girls, and the importance of establishing a sound sport development system that provides development opportunities for women and girls. Clearly structured pathways need to be in place, with female-only opportunities, and sporting role models in the form of elite female athletes to raise the profile of the sport and attract female participants. When reflecting on the framework proposed by Sotiriadou et al. (2008), attraction and retention processes necessitate the use of sport development strategies that focus on the provision of player development programs, facilities, competitions, events, coaches, umpires, and managers, to ensure that women and girls have positive experiences participating in sport. This is critically supported by promotion of sporting opportunities, with a focus on elite competition and role models, among other strategies.

The sporting examples of cricket and Australian Rules football can be contrasted with the sport of netball and the work done by its NSO, Netball Australia, to encourage girls to participate in sport in Australia over the past 80 years. While females are an emerging market for sports such as cricket and AFL football in Australia, netball has provided a strong sport participation outlet for Australian girls and women since its inception. Netball Australia and its SSO network have established participation programs, pathways and competitions with women and girls in mind. The Australian Netball Team, the Diamonds, and the national league for the sport (Suncorp Super Netball League and its former iterations) certainly do not receive anywhere near the same degree of media coverage that professional male athletes and men's leagues do. However, these athletes have provided elite role models for girls for decades and the success of the Australian Diamonds has provided elite female role models for junior netballers. When girls enter a netball pathway, either through the modified sport program for netball, NetSetGo, or through a school, club, or social pathway, women and girls are in the majority; opportunities exist to participate, and the norms of female participation that exist in the sport of netball help to reinforce girls' involvement in the sport.

Knowledge exists about how an NSO can build a sport development system that attracts and retains participants and nurtures talent though established pathways (Gulbin et al., 2013; Sotiriadou et al., 2008). Each of the sports discussed to this point, including cricket, football, and netball, have been successful in building strong participant bases over many decades. However, none of these sports has yet established a system that collectively attracts and retains an equal proportion of male and female participants. Each has traditionally been limited by cultural norms around sport participation, but also systemic biases toward one gender over another. Time will tell as to how successful Cricket Australia and the AFL will be in their endeavors to attract and retain women and girls. However, each organization is working toward building a sport development system that achieves this outcome and using systematic sport development approaches in doing so.

Leader profile: Chyloe Kurdas

At five-years-old Chyloe Kurdas knew she would never get to play professional football; she knew that door was closed to her. But she has worked, instead, to make sure that door will never be closed for any other five-year-old girl, and her dedicated efforts will reap their rewards . . . with the opening bounce of the new national women's AFL competition.

(Mitchell, 2016, para. 1)

Figure 22.1 Chyloe Kurdas

Chyloe Kurdas is a pioneer of women's Australian Rules football. As a player, Kurdas faced many barriers in her participation pathway. She set about changing the AFL landscape to ensure that no other young girl with an interest in the sport would face the same obstacles she had encountered as a child. She served on her football club board for eight years, in addition to serving four years on the board for the women's football league in the state of Victoria. She also worked with Victorian SSO for Australian Rules football, AFL Victoria, for 10 years, growing women's football from the grassroots and developing a female high performance pathway and system (Mitchell, 2016). This role involved establishing and supporting female leagues, competitions, events and development academies across the state. The system needed to be sustainable to ensure the growth would continue for years to come. In her playing days, Kurdas recalls some of the challenges she and other female footballers faced: "we had issues trying to access training facilities and playing grounds, accessing change rooms that were appropriate for women and girls . . . and had to fight tooth and nail to even borrow a football to train with" (Mitchell, 2016, para. 11). These were the issues the system needed to address for female sport participants in the state of Victoria and, ultimately, the nation.

Through her actions in establishing a system to support female football participation and development in Victoria, Kurdas sees a bright and sustainable future for women and girls in Australian Rules football. She is confident that the group of participants and athletes currently moving through development pathways will reinvest back into the sport as coaches, leaders, and role models to see the next generation of female participants and players grow, develop, and continue to evolve the game towards a sustainable future for women's football in Australia:

> when you invest in their understanding of the game these women don't only want to play it; they want to lead it, coach it, facilitate it and lead the organisation and the industry, and not just only in female football. We have some terrific women and we have amazing leaders and future leaders who could really play a strong role in male football and other parts of life, in business and government and so on.
>
> *(Mitchell, 2016, para. 23)*

References

ABC News (2017). Australian female cricketers reaping benefits of new pay deal. Retrieved from www.abc.net.au/news/2017-08-03/cricket-pay-deal-lauded-womens-pay/8772186.
Australian Football League (2015). Women's participation soars in 2015. Retrieved from www.afl.com.au/news/2015-10-13/womens-participation-in-afl-soars-in-2015.
Australian Football League (2017a). Female football club guide. Retrieved from www.aflcommunityclub.com.au/fileadmin/user_upload/Play_AFL/Female_Footy/AM_3987_Womens_Football_Club_Guide_D5_lores.pdf.
Australian Football League (2017b). Women's growth helps it record numbers. Retrieved www.afl.com.au/news/2017-11-30/football-participation-hits-record-numbers.mobileapp.
Australian Football League (2018). Female football. Retrieved from www.aflcommunityclub.com.au/index.php?id=495.
Balyi, I., Way, R., & Higgs, C. (2013). *Long-term Athlete Development*. Champaign, IL: Human Kinetics.
Commonwealth of Australia (2016a). AusPlay: Participation data for the sport sector. Summary of key national findings. Retrieved from https://www.ausport.gov.au/__data/assets/pdf_file/0007/653875/34648_AusPlay_summary_report_accessible_FINAL_updated_211216.pdf/
Commonwealth of Australia (2016b). Girls make your move. Retrieved from www.health.gov.au/internet/girlsmove/publishing.nsf/Content/home.
Commonwealth of Australia (2017). AusPlay: Women and girls participation. Retrieved from https://www.ausport.gov.au/__data/assets/pdf_file/0011/665921/34953_Ausplay_factsheet_SODA_access2.pdf.

Cricket Australia (2014). National participation hits one million. https://www.cricket.com.au/news/media-release-national-cricket-participation-hits-one-million/2014-08-11.

Cricket Australia (2015). Census results reveal cricket's changing face. Retrieved from https://www.cricket.com.au/news/james-sutherland-cricket-australia-census-results-female-participation-9-percent-cultural-diversity/2015-08-04.

Cricket Australia (2016). Cricket becomes Australia's No. 1 participation sport. Retrieved from https://www.cricket.com.au/news/cricket-australia-census-participation-numbers-women-men-children-james-sutherland/2016-08-23.

Cricket Australia (2017a). Cricket Australia strategy 2017–2022. Retrieved from www.cricketaustralia.com.au/about/our-strategy.

Cricket Australia (2017b). Record numbers playing cricket. Retrieved from https://www.cricket.com.au/news/national-cricket-census-play-cricket-facilities-audit-james-sutherland-2016-17/2017-08-11.

Cricket Australia (2017c). New official name for Australian women. Retrieved from https://www.cricket.com.au/news/australia-womens-cricket-team-southern-stars-name-change-world-cup-united-kingdom/2017-06-07.

Eime, R. M., Harvey, J. T., Sawyer, N. A., Craike, M. J., Symons, C. M., & Payne, W. R. (2016). Changes in sport and physical activity participation for adolescent females: A longitudinal study. *BMC Health*, **16**, 533–541.

Farrell, A., Fink, J. S., Fields, S. (2011). Women's sport spectatorship: An exploration of men's influence. *Journal of Sport Management*, **25**(3), 190–201.

Gulbin, J. P., Croser, M. J., Morley, E. J., & Weissensteiner, J. R. (2013). An integrated framework for the optimisation of sport and athlete development: A practitioner approach. *Journal of Sport Sciences*, **13**, 1319–1331.

Green, B. C. (2005). Building sport programs to optimize athlete recruitment, retention and transition: Toward a normative theory of sport development. *Journal of Sport Management*, **19**, 233–253.

Hess, R. (2017). Growth of women's football has been a 100-year revolution. It did not happen overnight. Retrieved from http://theconversation.com/growth-of-womens-football-has-been-a-100-year-revolution-it-didnt-happen-overnight-71989.

Hickey, C., Harrison, L., Ollis, D. & Mooney, A. (2016). The professionalization of Australian women's cricket: New times and new opportunities. Retrieved from http://dro.deakin.edu.au/view/DU:30084751.

Mitchell, B. (2016). Chyloe Kurdas: Terrific women can really play a strong role in football. *ESPN*. Retrieved from www.espn.com.au/afl/story/_/id/17436838/chyloe-kurdas-pioneer-women-football.

Paterson, J. & Matzelle, R. (2014). *Women in Sport Broadcasting Analysis*. Commonwealth of Australia, Canberra: Australian Sports Commission.

Richards, R. (2016). Women's sport. Retrieved from https://www.clearinghouseforsport.gov.au/knowledge_base/organised_sport/sport_and_government_policy_objectives/womens_sport.

Rowe, K., Sherry, E. & Osborne, A. (2018). Recruiting and retaining girls in table tennis: Participant and club perspectives. *Sport Management Review*. Advanced online publication. Retrieved from https://doi:10.1016/j.smr.2017.11.003.

Shilbury, D., Phillips, P., Karg, A., & Rowe, K. (2017). *Sport Management in Australia: An organisational overview*, 5th edn. Crows Nest, NSW: Allen & Unwin.

Sotiriadou, K., Shilbury, D., & Quick, S. (2008). The attraction, retention/transition, and nurturing process of sport development: Some Australian evidence. *Journal of Sport Management*, **22**, 247–272.

State Government of Victoria (2017). Female friendly infrastructure guidelines. Retrieved from http://sport.vic.gov.au/publications-and-resources/female-friendly-sport-infrastructure-guidelines.

Young, J. A., Symons, C. M., & Pain, M. D. (2015). Role models of Australian female adolescents: A longitudinal study to inform programmes designed to inform physical activity and sport participation. *European Physical Education Review*, **21**, 451–466.

23
Governance of women's sport in China

Hanhan Xue and Joshua I. Newman

Perhaps no other nation has experienced a rapid transformation in the sport industry like that taking place in contemporary China. Sport has historically played various ludic, ideological, and instrumental functions in the People's Republic of China—from the foundational *cuju* games played by soldiers and social elites in Qi during the Warring States Period (c. 450–340 BC) to the labor-rendering physical culture programs of the mid-twentieth-century socialist China (Xu, 2009). Although once a primary apparatus for state-based health promotion and geopolitical symbolism, today sport in China is big business. It is widely cited in government documents and media discourses as a driving force for urban development, economic growth, and the kind of economic globalization that might further fuel China's emergence as a world superpower (Xinhua News Agency, 2015; Ye, 2017). In this chapter, we look at how this burgeoning sport industry articulates to new political machinations (i.e. "socialism with Chinese characteristics"), new commercial networks and market relationships (i.e. "post-Socialist" state capitalism), and new expressions of national identity (post-Sinocentric nationalism). More specific to our interests here, we are interested in how all of these changes have been constituted by, and constitute, a large-scale re-ordering of gender roles and gender identities within the sector and beyond.

More specifically, we are concerned with how, and to what effect, the concurrent transformations of the political economy and gender politics intersect within the industrial and administrative practice of Chinese sport. We aim to provide a brief sketch of the historical base framing the gendered structures, ideals, and practices of women's sport in contemporary China. First, we outline the role that girls and women have played in traditional and emerging Chinese sport cultures. We then provide an analysis of women's role in and governance practices of (women's) sport in contemporary China, along with how the Chinese sport administrative body approaches the role of women, as well as how women athletes and managers respond to ever-changing organizational structure and policy development. We conclude the chapter with a discussion of how these gendered and gendering practices might affect future women sport managers and industrial actors more generally in China.

Girls and women in the history of Chinese sport

Much like in other national contexts, women's role in Chinese society has a long and complicated history. For centuries, the Confucian patriarchal doctrine of obedience to the father before marriage, to the husband during marriage, and to the son(s) after the death of the husband defined women's roles in and outside of the family (Leung, 2003). Before the revolution in 1911, women were widely relegated to orders of subservience and social control—perhaps best exemplified by the bodily practice of foot-binding (Adams, 2009).

Gender roles and gender inequalities are, of course, not unique to China. By most accounts, however, compared with most western societies China witnessed significant progress toward gender equity under the Communist government of Mao Zedong (c. 1949–1976) (Brownell, 2005). From the outset, Mao made it clear that women would play an equal role in the establishment of the Chinese communist state. Where for centuries women were often seen as ornamental beauties or domestic servants, for the Chinese Communist Party (CCP) under Mao, women and their bodies were viewed as instrumental in advancing the labor power and productive (and reproductive) capacities of the state. For women, as for men, Mao promoted the ideas of *yundong* (movement and exercise), whereby activity and movement would be actively promoted to eradicate the "passivity and weakness that ailed China" (Brownell, 2005, p. 1179). These *bodies of work* were encouraged to partake in various exercise and physical cultural activities as a way of maximizing fertility and productivity. Under such an instrumentalist approach, women took up work in the fields and in the factories during the day, participated in state-sanctioned physical culture programs in the evenings, and became state-incentivized "Glorious Moms" who would play a critical role in boosting the population of the world's largest country (Fan, 1997). As one state dispatch illustrates, this synergy of women's bodies, productive labor, and reproductivity became a central concern for the CCP:

> Women of the New China not only require immense patriotic enthusiasm, scientific knowledge and work skill, but also healthy bodies. Only when they have healthy bodies can women be able to participate in economic, cultural and military work and be able to produce and nurture a new and healthy generation.
>
> *(Fan, 2003, p. 225)*

In this way, women were seen to serve an equal role to men in developing a healthy, productive, and powerful China, because, in Communist China, Mao famously proclaimed, "women hold up half the sky" (Leung, 2003).

Mao, however, believed that organized sport was a distraction to the more important tasks of Chinese citizens—to advance the State's economy through labor. As Fan (2003, p. 227) noted:

> At the beginning of the PRC the focus of Communist sports culture was to provide a basis for rationalizing physical exercise and improving productivity in response to a state eager to use all possible means to build the new country rapidly. Competitive sport was not the immediate concern of the Party. Mass sport was the concern.

In 1952, the State Council established the State Physical Education and Sports Commission (later the General Administration of Sport of China) to promote exercise and mass sport participation. The Council was responsible for administering widespread participation in various physical culture programs—with equal representation from men and women.

During the period immediately before and during the Cultural Revolution (c. 1966–1976), the CCP invested considerable state resources into developing training programs for elite female athletes. This shift toward an emphasis on competitive sport—and specifically on women's competitive sport—became the hallmark of Chinese sport culture in the second half of the twentieth century (Fan, 2003, 2004). Millions of young girls between the age of five and ten were selected by Party administrators and placed in intensive training centers[1] with the expressed two-pronged purpose of: (1) raising the overall standard of girls' and women's athletics in the country and (2) demonstrating to both domestic and international audiences, through sport, the primacy of gender equality in "New China" (Fan, 2003). In these training centers, elite women athletes underwent "hard, disciplined military-type training [which] include[d] qualities of hardship, difficulty and injury, and toughness of spirit, body, skill, training and competition" (Fan, 2003, p. 229).

As a result, Chinese women excelled in elite level international sport competition throughout the second half of the twentieth century. "Internationally," Dong and Mangan (2008, p. 783) write, these Chinese female athletes "were increasingly a force to be reckoned with." These women became representative embodiments of a developing nation, in some ways not only usurping or challenging traditional gender roles but also inverting them: elite female athletes were celebrated as "superwomen," put on display for the Chinese masses and for the world as the ultimate expressions of communist egalitarianism and pro-national excellence. Although, during the second half of the twentieth century "the men's national team won nothing and came nowhere close to winning anything" (Dong & Mangan, 2008, p. 786), women's teams and women athletes were surfacing as central characters in the national story.

By the early 1980s, the notion of "competition" emerged a foundational principal for organizing girls' and women's sport in China. Competition was believed to "promote activism"—a double entendre that pronounced both the centrality of physical activity in women's lives and the purposefulness of elite sport participation (to activate the State and its interests through bodily practice, to actively produce social and ideological perspectives through sporting endeavors, etc.). In short, sport participation "could stimulate the nation's enthusiasm and motivate people to strive for excellence" (Fan, 2003, p. 232). In this way, women athletes such as fencer Luan Jujie and volleyball player Lang Ping were—as their predecessors had been—agents for advancement of state ideology. However, different from Mao's Cultural Revolution, the ideology had shifted. Much like in Chinese society more generally, ideas of openness, pro-market growth (*kai fang*), and competition came to dominate the planning and administration of women's sport.

The gender structure in China's national sport organizations

As China has transited towards a socialist market economy, the country's sport governance system has undergone significant yet slow reforms with regard to organizational structure and sport policy development. Chinese women—who have achieved unprecedented athletic success on the playing fields—have played an active role in participating in this reform process. However, they are still substantially under-represented in management and professional positions, in particular in the decision-making bodies of China's national sport organizations (NSOs) (Cui, 2007).

Organizational restructuring and women's role in sport administration

Before the 1980s, the Chinese central government controlled and regulated all sport-related activities and funding under a centrally planned system (Jones, 1999). The economic reform—which started in 1978 and introduced market principles into the national economy through privatization, market pricing, and devolution of political–economic power to the regions and the localities (Harvey, 2007)—has led to gradual transformation of Chinese sport governance system. A major step was to restructure existing sport government agencies toward distancing central government oversight from everyday operations and management (*guanban fenli*) of sport activities to improve efficiency and efficacy. The Sports State Commission (*guojia tiwei*), originally established in 1952, was restructured to be the General Administration of Sport of China (GASC, *guojia tiyu zongju*) in 1998. The GASC—which consists of 12 administrative departments, 21 competition management centers, and 21 relevant service, research, and supportive institutions—plays an important role in directing and overseeing different levels of sport activities (State Council, 2014b). The GASC also administers the two largest Chinese NSOs—All-China Sports Federation (ACSF)[2] and the Chinese Olympic Committee (COC) (Figure 23.1).

Although the government still exerts substantial influence over the operation of NSOs, sport organizations in China are increasingly encouraged to demonstrate commercial solvency and operate as quasi-autonomous organizations (Theodoraki, 2004). Since 2015, some sport organizations and associations such as the Chinese Football Association have been further reformed to function and operate completely independently from the government through the establishment of their own financial and management systems.

The ongoing structural reforms in the organization of sport in China have significantly increased professional opportunities for both men and women in what are now more specialized, professionalized, and market-oriented organizations. However, the GASC and most NSOs possess a distinctive gender structure, with men dominating leadership positions whereas women typically are assigned to less powerful assisting positions or given symbolic positions as "window dressing" (Fan, 2003, p. 233). For example, as of 2002, there were 117 female middle-level administrators (accounting for 20%) out of 585 middle-level cadres in the GASC. Furthermore, there were only 3 female department directors (out of 54 department directors) and 19 female vice department directors (each department usually has only 1 department director and 1–5 vice department directors) (Cui, 2007). It has worsened to the extent that currently not a single one of the GASC departments is directed by a woman (see Figure 23.1). Moreover, female sport leaders, not surprisingly, are often assigned to be in charge of non-core sport activities (such as amateur sport and youth sport) or peripheral business functions (such as accounting and office support). These positions tend to offer fewer opportunities for promotion on the organizational ladder (Cui, 2007).

These discriminatory practices (i.e., women assigned to less powerful deputy positions and held responsible for peripheral sport and relevant activities) exclude women from central decision-making roles in NSOs, and limit female sport administrators' influence over policy development and organizational practices. Women find it difficult to "break the glass ceiling" in the administrative structure in the sport environment in China for several reasons. One important reason is that men control boards and promotion committees in NSOs and tend to exclude female candidates in the hiring and promotion procedures (Cui, 2007). Moreover, a widespread view is that social prejudice and patriarchal dispositions against women have persisted in the reform era China (Bowen, Wu, Hwang, & Scherer, 2007). As noted earlier, many in Chinese society hold a traditional view that women should stay at home and take care of families despite the CCP's commitment to gender equality and Mao Zedong's proclamation that "women hold up half of the sky" (Fan, 2003).

As such, according to a national survey in 2010, more than 72% of Chinese women stated that they didn't get hired or promoted due to gender discrimination. In particular, over 75%

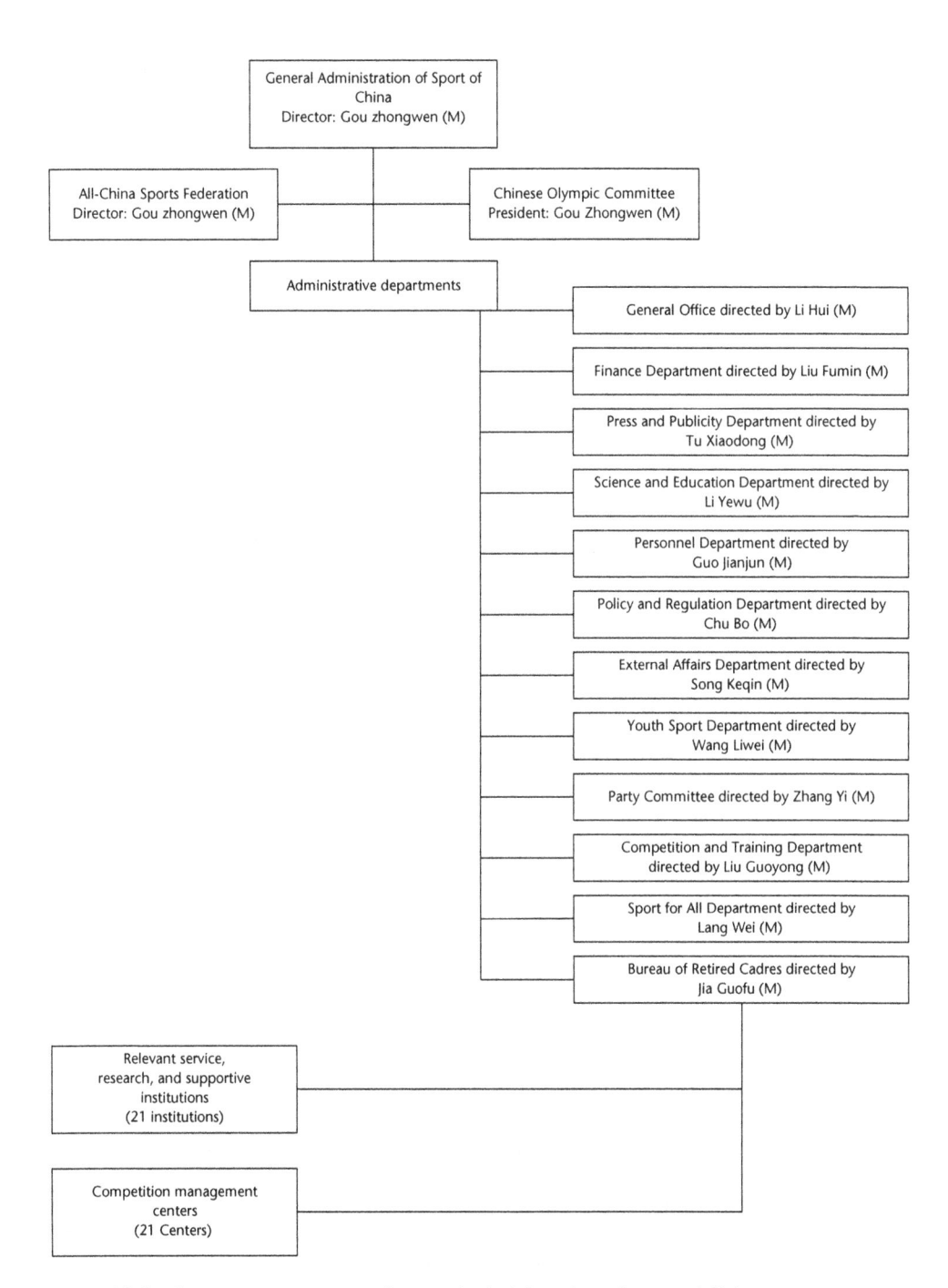

```
┌─────────────────────────────────┐
│ General Administration of Sport │
│           of China              │
│  Director: Gou zhongwen (M)     │
└─────────────────────────────────┘
         │
   ┌─────┴──────────────────────────┐
┌──────────────────────┐   ┌──────────────────────────┐
│ All-China Sports     │   │ Chinese Olympic Committee│
│ Federation           │   │ President: Gou Zhongwen(M)│
│ Director: Gou        │   └──────────────────────────┘
│ zhongwen (M)         │
└──────────────────────┘

    ┌──────────────────────────┐
    │ Administrative departments│
    └──────────────────────────┘
         ├── General Office directed by Li Hui (M)
         ├── Finance Department directed by Liu Fumin (M)
         ├── Press and Publicity Department directed by Tu Xiaodong (M)
         ├── Science and Education Department directed by Li Yewu (M)
         ├── Personnel Department directed by Guo Jianjun (M)
         ├── Policy and Regulation Department directed by Chu Bo (M)
         ├── External Affairs Department directed by Song Keqin (M)
         ├── Youth Sport Department directed by Wang Liwei (M)
         ├── Party Committee directed by Zhang Yi (M)
         ├── Competition and Training Department directed by Liu Guoyong (M)
         ├── Sport for All Department directed by Lang Wei (M)
         └── Bureau of Retired Cadres directed by Jia Guofu (M)

┌──────────────────────────┐
│ Relevant service,        │
│ research, and supportive │
│ institutions             │
│ (21 institutions)        │
└──────────────────────────┘

┌──────────────────────────┐
│ Competition management   │
│ centers                  │
│ (21 Centers)             │
└──────────────────────────┘
```

Figure 23.1 Governance structure of general administration of sport of China

Source: General Administration of Sport of China Official website: www.sport.gov.cn

Note: (M) refers to male

believed they were "being dismissed" due to marriage or childbirth (Yang, 2012). In addition, although market-oriented reform has boosted the overall economy, it has also increased the rate of unemployment, and thus raised financial and economic uncertainty for families. Moreover, there has been a growing sentiment within the public sphere that women should leave the job market and take the responsibility for family care in order to create domestic stability and play a more active role in addressing the ongoing decline in national birthrate (Liu, Li, & Yang, 2015; Phillips, 2017; Anonymous, 2001). Other factors that exacerbate women's under-representation in the power structure in China include stereotyped perceptions from organizational peers on female inferiority, concerning inadequate capabilities and lack of knowledge or skills to handle professional work (Cui, 2007). For example, women in sport management were stereotypically portrayed as "gossips, being emotional and too concerned about trivial things," according to interviews with sport administrators in Chinese NSOs (Cui, 2007, p. 397).

Gender discrimination therein, at both societal and organizational levels, has consequently significantly deteriorated female sport administrators' authoritative status. Women sport leaders' decisions and behaviors easily become the subject of rumor and gossip, and result in public accusation. A prominent example is the Chinese public controversy and opposition over the team manager of China's national diving team and Deputy Director of the National Swimming Management Center, Zhou Jihong's rigorous administration of the Chinese diving team. Despite the fact that China's diving dominates the world and generates numerous Gold medals, Zhou is negatively portrayed in the public sphere as an extremely aggressive (*yi chang qiang shi*), stern (*bu gou yan xiao*), and ruthless (*qiang ying*) woman. Most notably, she was derided for her decision to dismiss Tian Liang, a medal-winning diver, from the national diving team for the diver's frequent involvement in commercial activities in 2005 (Anonymous, 2017; NetEase, 2009). In this case and others, woman sport administrators are often framed in dichotomous ways: as either "too soft, weak, or lacking ability" (Cui, 2007) or "too harsh, abrasive, or competitive" (NetEase, 2013).

Despite women still facing inequality, discrimination, and other significant challenges in leadership positions in Chinese sport organizations, the State has made certain efforts to improve women's status. In the face of increased concerns in the western media (and domestic society) that calls into question Chinese women's human rights and well-being, the Chinese government has paid more attention to women sport administrators' employment, career development, and personal well-being since the 2008 Beijing Olympic Games. Since 2009, the GASC has specifically developed a series of training seminars and programs covering topics ranging from sport administration skills development and women administrators' psychological health, to relationships and family (GASC, 2014).

As scholars and public commentators have made clear, the commercialization of sport has not necessarily brought about gender equality in sport organizations. There continues to be a wealth of opportunities for girls and women to play sports, with a high level of funding for elite women athletes, but there is still plenty of work to be done in the hiring and promotion practices of most NSOs (Fan, 2003). Although female administrators continue to face many obstacles within China's ever-changing sport organization and gender structures, female athletes have, in fact, played a major role in China's Olympic strategy and the promotion of China's socialist modernization and restructuration (Fan, 2003).

Olympic strategy and women

In 1995, the Chinese government explicitly established an Olympic strategy (*Aoyun Zhengguang Jihua*) to channel nationwide resources for elite athletes to compete for Olympic Gold medals

(*Juguo Tizhi*)—in order to promote China's economic and political power and create a new image for the country through sports on the international stage (Ren, 2010). To maximize the number of Olympic Gold medals won by Chinese athletes, Chinese sport officials focused particularly on "small (*xiao*)," "skillful (*qiao*)," "difficult (*nan*)," "female (*nv*)," and "a few (*shao*)" sports (Xu, 2013).[3] Under these guiding principles, female athletes have gained substantial financial and administrative resources and achieved tremendous athletic success. For example, among the 407 athletes who competed at Athens in 2004, 269 were women and only 138 were men (Hays, 2011). Female athletes contributed more than half of the Gold medals for China in the 2008 Olympic Games. Chinese women have never lost a single Gold medal in table tennis since the 1988 Seoul Olympic Games. Women athletes' success is referred to as "the blossoming of the Yin (female) and the withering of the Yang (male)" in China (Riordan & Dong, 1999, p. 160). Chinese women athletes have consequently been regarded as inspirational role models for all Chinese and are proudly called "iron women soldiers (*niang zi jun*)" by the public (Fan, 1997, 2003; Tencent, 2016). Brownell (1995, p. 228) contended that the success of Chinese women can also be attributed to the forced work ethic of women and their willingness and ability to "eat bitterness."

With extensive state and institutional support, as well as individual efforts, a few top Chinese female elite athletes have quickly become celebrities or leaders in business, politics, entertainment, or other fields. For example, Deng Yaping, Yang Yang, and Guo Jingjing[4] have each successfully traversed their career paths by obtaining higher education in top Chinese universities and acquiring professional jobs, or being involved in community and charitable activities after retiring from elite sports. After her career as a short track speed skater, Yang Yang enrolled in Tsinghua University's Business Administration Major program and eventually became an International Olympic Committee member and Vice President of Chinese Olympic Committee after retirement. In 2013, she started her own business by establishing and operating a winter sports center and skating schools in the cities of Shanghai and Harbin (Xinhua News Agency, 2016). Similarly, Deng Yaping, a legendary Chinese table tennis player, served as a member of the IOC Ethics Commission and Sport and Environment Commission after retirement in 1997. Meanwhile, she became a member of the Chinese People's Political Consultative Conference. She gained her Bachelor's degree in English at Tsinghua University in 2001, followed by a Master's degree from the University of Nottingham in 2006, and she completed her PhD degree program in Jesus College (a constituent college of the University of Cambridge) in 2008. In 2010, Deng took a further step in her political career by being appointed as the President of Goso.cn, a news search engine launched by *People's Daily* (the CCP's mouthpiece newspaper) (Liang, 2010). In 2016, she was invited to serve as a mentor in Schwarzman College at Tsinghua University.

Although a few top Chinese female elite athletes have achieved professional success and gained incredible media exposure and public visibility, many women athletes—those who are at the bottom of the Chinese elite sport system—have actually struggled to find work and some even live in poverty after retirement. For example, *Shanghai Daily*, a local Chinese newspaper, reported a story about a 35-year-old retired female acrobat champion, Liu Fei. Liu was unable to find a stable job after retirement due to lack of education and work experience. She was temporarily hired by an acrobatic training school as a coach, earning less than 600 yuan (about US$90) a month. But she was laid off soon due to the school's inferior financial performance (Liu, 2014). *China Sports Daily*, a newspaper run by China's Physical Education and Sport Committee, estimated that, of the country's 300,000 retired athletes, 80% are jobless, injured, or impoverished. Although there are no official statistics on how many of these athletes are women, given overall trends where only 63% of eligible women are in the workforce (compared with 78% of eligible men), and that the number of women athletes is equivalent to the number of men, it is safe to assume that most of these jobless retired athletes are women (Lim, 2008; World Bank Databank, 2017a, 2017b). Low education level, physical injuries due to harsh training, and insufficient non-sport-related capabilities and skills leave retired elite athletes—in particular female athletes—unprepared and ill-equipped to deal with the pressure from an increasingly competitive job market and to manage relationships with their families and marriages (Ting, 2008). However, Deng Yaping, as a successful female role model, asserted that female athletes have advantages to become successful outside of sports and encouraged retired female athletes to create their own business to solve career struggles. Deng said, "they are more persistent, they can endure hardship, and that's the key point for them to make achievements in business" (Dong, 2017, para. 11). She also suggested the government create relevant policies to support female athlete entrepreneurship, such as the development of sport funds and grants, as well as offering tax incentives and preferential loan programs (Dong, 2017).

The rise of sports consumption in China: The changing role of women

As is often the case in China, recent reforms in the Chinese sporting system since the 2010s have extended to state policies that emphasize and promote the commercial and market-based aspects of the Chinese sport industry (State Council, 2014a). According to a 2014 policy, named *Opinions on Accelerating the Development of Sports Industry and Promoting Sports Consumption* (No. 46 document), the Chinese government plans to grow the sport sector into a 5-trillion-yuan (US$813 billion) industry by 2025 in order to find a new engine to boost employment and drive domestic consumption (State Council, 2014a). This new reform plan represents the Chinese government's focus shifting from the traditional elite sports-based Olympic strategy toward a national strategy that will capitalize on all sporting activities, ranging from fitness, grassroots sports, sport goods, and services, to elite sports.

Under the reform plan, there has been increasing involvement of women in commercial and entrepreneurial activities in the sport field. The technological development, the desire to expand knowledge, the paradigm of lifelong learning—associated with policy-oriented sport industry development—led to new changes in the role women athletes and entrepreneurs perform across various aspects of the Chinese sport sector. These changes have actually reflected drastic structural reformation in China's transition towards a consumption-based society, as well as the new generation of Chinese women's increasing education opportunities, growing financial independence, and shifting attitudes toward life style, sport, and health and fitness. Chinese women, especially those living in urban cities and aged between 25 and 45, are quickly emerging as the primary drivers of buying power in domestic consumption. It is reported that there are 480 million female consumers in China and Chinese women make almost 75% of household purchase decisions (Zhou, 2016). In addition, China's one-child families and the culture of grandparents offering childcare provide Chinese women with more time and capacity to pursue and achieve individual career aspirations (Yang, 2013).

From the elite sport perspective, a number of young female sport stars have emerged and become active in the public sphere, such as participating in public and community service activities, building and maintaining social media accounts, and engaging in live broadcasting on live-streaming platforms. For example, Fu Yuanhui, a Chinese female backstroke swimmer, attained preeminent public attention after the Rio Olympic Games, not because of her Olympic performance, but, rather, due to her exuberant and hilarious interviews and quirky talk about the menstrual cycles of female athletes (Phillips, 2016). Fu quickly became an "internet darling" and attracted millions of adoring fans (Siu, 2016). Her first one-hour online broadcast through Inke—a live-streaming app—attracted over 10 million internet viewers and brought over 100,000 RMB (about US$15,130) income (Jiang, 2016).

Other prominent examples of female sport stars include Ding Ning (table tennis player), Li Na (tennis player), and Xu Lijia (sailboat racer). The increasing popularity of this younger generation of female athletes seems to signal shifting Chinese public attitudes away from the "notorious obsession with 'robotic' gold medal-winning athletes" (Phillips, 2016, para. 12) toward focusing on the valorization of athletes as individual brands or celebrities (Ramzy, 2016). Furthermore, the transition toward a consumption-based sport economy has cultivated a growing number of sport spectators and fans with enormous spending power. The changing social perceptions among the Chinese public, along with the emergence of new sport consumers in China, have to some extent reconstituted and refashioned traditional Chinese gender roles around the role of social entrepreneurship, which largely stimulates and promotes female athletes' entrepreneurial interests and practices.

The professional and commercial sport sector has seen a similar pattern, whereby an increased number of female sport managers and entrepreneurs have emerged and engaged in quintessentially innovative sport-related business activities. Many female sport managers who enter the market now possess sport management or relevant business management degrees from western countries, domestic and foreign work experience, capabilities to leverage social relationships, and fluent English skills—all of which contribute to their competence in the development of technical knowledge and managerial skills, and ultimately career achievement. For example, the story of the CEO of Beijing Shougang Sports, Qin Xiaowen, is evidence of the entrepreneurial success of Chinese women sport managers. Qin originally worked in GASC as a middle-level female sport administrator for seven years. She then quit the state job and took an MBA program at a university in Washington State in the United States. After completing her degree program, Qin obtained a job in the United States and settled down in Portland. During her stay in the United States, she facilitated Sui Feifei's (a Chinese female basketball player) contract signing with the Women's National Basketball Association's (WNBA's) Sacramento Monarchs franchise. Qin's extensive social connection resources and savvy business skills allowed her to become the CEO of Beijing Shougang Sports (a State-owned enterprise that manages several professional sport clubs in Beijing) in 2016 (Ma, 2017). Her example is important, because it illustrates both how women sport managers are perceived to gain and embody industrial competency and the continuing legitimacy that is given to women's sport and the management of female athletes in China.

Conclusion

These are but a few examples of the changing landscape of the opportunities and challenges that face women in the Chinese sports industry. On the one hand, the sports industry has changed with the ebb and flow of *kai fang* reforms put in place from the early 1980s forward. Although China has transitioned toward a market economy, the country's old state-dominated sport system has stalled market reforms and retained stringent bureaucratic control (Yardley, 2012). All nation-wide sport-related activities and programs are subject to arbitrary decision-making in the development of sport policies, as well as discretionary managerial behaviors associated with the rigid sport bureaucracy.

This paradoxical blend of old and new, communism and capitalism, national and international knowledge, and technical systems has held both positive and negative consequences for women sport managers and managers of women's sport in China. The Chinese sports industry now features a unique blend of longstanding Confucian gender hierarchies and Mao-era gender progressiveness. Women are still significantly disadvantaged in hiring and promotion practices in major sport organizations, and yet current and former women athletes are often given priority in post-athletics professional training and job placement. New industrial logics based on *kai fang* reforms, economic globalization, and state-sponsored development through sport have all placed technical expertise at the center of industrial practices. Strong women athletes are heralded as the celebrity skin of the nation, and yet widely chided as leaders if they are deemed too soft or too hard. Although China has come a long way in the field of sport and has a unique story to tell the world about its sporting women, it still has a long way to go in terms of gender equality off the field.

Leader profile: Lijia (Lily) Xu

Lijia (Lily) Xu is the most famous Chinese female sailboat racer. Lily was born on August 30, 1987 in the city of Shanghai, China, and started sailing at the age of 10. She won her first National Championship title in the Optimist class in 1998, along with another four National, Asia, and World Championship titles in the same event in the following years. In 2005 Lily began racing the Laser Radial class and achieved champion titles in the 2006 World Championship, 2006 Asian Games, and 2009 National Games of China. In the 2008 Beijing Olympic Games, Lily obtained the Bronze medal in women's Laser Radial class and later she won the Gold medal in the 2012 London Olympic Games, becoming Asia's first dinghy sailing

Figure 23.2 Lijia (Lily) Xu

Gold medalist. In 2012, Lily was named the female winner of the 2012 ISAF Rolex World Sailor of the Year Awards.

Although she has experienced enormous athletic success, Lily has triumphed over considerable personal challenges. Born with one nearly deaf ear and one nearly blind eye, Lily was very shy and felt uncomfortable and unsure of herself around others in her childhood. In 1999, when she was 12 years old, she barely escaped death when during a training session she was pulled out to sea by a sudden storm off Fujian Province in China. Before the 2004 Athens Olympic Games, Lily was diagnosed with a giant-cell tumor of bone near her left knee and had to undergo six-hour-long surgery. In 2009, she had to take a break from the competition due to serious back injuries. Despite these dreadful obstacles, Lily never gave up and always embraced positive and optimistic thinking toward life. Her courage, endurance, determination, vision, and aspiration for success allowed her to not only gain individual athletic success but also earn achievements in promoting educational activities and programs around sailing.

After the 2012 Olympic Games, Lily took a Master's degree program in international management at the University of Southampton in the United Kingdom in 2014. During her Master's program, she published two books—*Follow the Olympic Champion to Study Sailing (Gen Ao Yun Guan Jun Xue Fan Chuan)* (Xu, 2015) and *Golden Lily: Asia's First Dinghy Sailing Gold Medalist* (Xu, 2016). The first one is a cartoon book that gives a step-by-step instruction guide on how to sail using an easy-to-read and entertaining method. Lily hopes this book can inspire young people's interest in sailing and motivate more people to participate in sailing. The second book—a sailing autobiography written in English—depicts an inspirational story of a young woman striving for success and achieving her dream, and shows Lily's independent and critical thoughts and insights about significant cultural differences around sport systems in China and western countries.

Despite these tremendous achievements, Lily never stopped pursuing her dreams. "My goal is always to make myself become a better person, no matter what kind of job I do and no matter which life stage I am at." She is currently taking a second Master's degree program in sport communication and journalism at Southampton Solent University in the UK, seeking to further her knowledge and career development in sport media after retirement from sailing. Meanwhile, she has started her personal internet radio program—*Sailing News (Fan Chuan Jia Yin)*—on Tingting FM—an online application launched by China Radio International. She has also been involved in making a film titled *The Medal Maker*. Her social media account has over one million followers. Carrying a more entrepreneurial aspiration of "being an excellent sport broadcaster and media producer," Lily has sailed across a new ocean in her life and has inspired more young Chinese women to participate in sailing and engage in the development of Chinese sailing business and industry.

Notes

1 According to Fan (2004), many young athletes, mostly girls, trained for 10–12 hours a day in those intensive training centers that primarily focused on athletics, gymnastics, swimming, football, basketball, volleyball, badminton, and table tennis.
2 All-China Sports Federation (ACSF) is a non-government, not-for-profit sport organization in China. It oversees various national sport associations in China.
3 "Small" sports refer to three small ball games—table tennis, badminton, and tennis; the "skill" focuses on the sports that require complicated skills and techniques; the "difficult" focuses on sports with a high level of difficulty; "female" refers to female athletes/sports; "a few" refers to individual sports (Xu, 2013).
4 Deng Yaping (born in 1973) is a famous table tennis player. She won four Olympic Gold medals and 14 other world championship titles. Yang Yang (born in 1976) is a well-known short track speed skater who won two Olympic Gold medals and 28 other world titles. Guo Jingjing (born in 1981) is a renowned diver. She was awarded four Olympic Gold medals and 10 world championship titles.

References

Adams, S. (2009). Chinese sexuality and the bound foot. In J. Peakman (ed.), *Sexual Perversions, 1670–1890* (pp. 246–275). London: Palgrave Macmillan.

Anonymous (2001). Women's choice: Home or work? *Beijing Review*, April 25. Retrieved from www.china.org.cn/english/2001/Apr/11788.htm.

Anonymous (2017). Tian Liang was uncovered by someone who was dismissed from the swimming team: Good for jumping and no high marks. *Best China News*, December 5. Retrieved from www.bestchinanews.com/Sports/18212.html.

Bowen, C.-C., Wu, Y., Hwang, C., & Scherer, R. F. (2007). Holding up half of the sky? Attitudes toward women as managers in the People's Republic of China. *International Journal of Human Resource Management*, **18**(2), 268–283.

Brownell, S. (1995). *Training the Body for China: Sports in the moral order of the People's Republic*. Chicago, IL: University of Chicago Press.

Brownell, S. (2005). Challenged America: China and America – women and sport, past, present and future. *International Journal of the History of Sport*, **22**(6), 1173–1193.

Cui, Y. (2007). Striving and thriving: Women in Chinese national sport organizations. *International Journal of the History of Sport*, **24**(3), 392–410.

Dong, J. (2017). Chinese retired female athletes face obstacles, opportunity as entrepreneurs, March 13. Retrieved from www.womenofchina.cn/womenofchina/html1/people/business/1703/2753-1.htm.

Dong, J. & Mangan, J. A. (2008). Olympic aspirations: Chinese women on top – considerations and consequences. *International Journal of the History of Sport*, **25**(7), 779–806.

Fan, H. (1997). *Footbinding, Feminism and Freedom: The liberation of women's bodies in modern China*. New York: Frank Cass.

Fan, H. (2003). Women's sport in the People's Republic of China: Body, politics and the unfinished revolution. In I. Hartmann-Tews & G. Pfister (eds), *Sport and Women: Social issues in international perspectives* (pp. 224–237). London: Routledge.

Fan, H. (2004). Innocence lost: child athletes in China. *Sport in Society*, **7**(3), 338–354.

General Administration of Sport of China (GASC) (2014). The cases of women career development in General Administration of Sport of China, January 16. Retrieved from www.sport.gov.cn/n4/n290/c327696/content.html

Harvey, D. (2007). *A Brief History of Aeoliberalism*. New York: Oxford University Press.

Hays, J. (2011). Chinese Olympic athletes: Women, perceptions, coaches and performance enhancing drugs, July. Retrieved from http://factsanddetails.com/china/cat12/sub79/item1007.html.

Jiang, S. (2016). Olympic swimmer makes huge splash in China's live-streaming world. *CNN*, August 15. Retrieved from www.cnn.com/2016/08/15/asia/china-live-streaming-fu-yuanhui/index.html

Jones, R. (1999). Sport in China. In J. Riordan & R. Jones (eds), *Sport and Physical Education in China* (pp. 1–19). New York: Routledge.

Leung, A. S. (2003). Feminism in transition: Chinese culture, ideology and the development of the women's movement in China. *Asia Pacific Journal of Management*, **20**(3), 359–374.

Liang, J. (2010). Table tennis legend Deng Yaping officially appointed Goso.cn president. *People's Daily*, September 26. Retrieved from http://en.people.cn/90001/90776/90882/7151013.html.

Lim, L. (2008). Many Chinese athletes find no glory in retirement. *National Public Radio*, July 22. Retrieved from https://www.npr.org/templates/story/story.php?storyId=92520419.

Liu, B., Li, L., & Yang, C. (2015). *Gender Equality in China's Economic Transformation*. Beijing: United Nations System in China.

Liu, K. (2014). Ups and downs of Chinese female retired athletes. *Shanghai Daily*, December 22. Retrieved from www.womenofchina.cn/womenofchina/html1/people/sportswomen/1412/2659-1.htm.

Ma, L. (2017). "Qin's governance" behind Marbury's contract renewal: Who's the women CEO of Shougang? *NetEase*, April 22. Retrieved from http://sports.163.com/17/0422/07/CIK0JM8V0005877V_mobile.html

NetEase (2009). A women's fight: 1984–2009. *NetEase*, October 21. Retrieved from http://sports.163.com/special/00052G99/honghong.html.

NetEase (2013). Iron women in sports. *NetEase Sports*, April 30. Retrieved from http://sports.163.com/photoview/0ACR0005/97644.html#p=8TKEPOA90ACR0005.

Phillips, T. (2016). "It's because I had my period": swimmer Fu Yuanhui praised for breaking taboo. *The Guardian*, August 15. Retrieved from https://www.theguardian.com/sport/2016/aug/16/chinese-swimmer-fu-yuanhui-praised-for-breaking-periods-taboo.

Phillips, T. (2017). In China women "hold up half the sky" but can't touch the political glass ceiling. *The Guardian*, February 13. Retrieved from https://www.theguardian.com/world/2017/oct/14/in-china-women-hold-up-half-the-sky-but-cant-touch-the-political-glass-ceiling.

Ramzy, A. (2016). The exuberant Chinese swimmer who has become a star at Rio. *The New York Times*, August 11. Retrieved from https://www.nytimes.com/2016/08/12/world/asia/china-olympics-fu-yuanhui-swimming.html?_r=0.

Ren, H. (2010). *China and the Olympic Movement: University lecture on the Olympics*. Barcelona: Centre d'Estudis Olímpics (UAB) (International Chair in Olympism [IOC-UAB]).

Riordan, J. & Dong, J. (1999). Chinese women and sport. In J. Riordan & R. Jones (eds), *Sport and Physical Education in China* (pp. 159–184). New York: Routledge.

Siu, P. (2016). Funny girl: China's "surprised" medal winner Fu Yuanhui becomes an instant internet darling. *South China Morning Post*, August 11. Retrieved from www.scmp.com/sport/china/article/2001645/funny-girl-chinas-surprised-medal-winner-fu-yuanhui-becomes-instant.

State Council (2014a). *State Council's Opinions on Accelerating the Development of Sports Industry and Promoting Sports Consumption* (guofa [2014] No. 46). Beijing: State Council.

State Council (2014b). *General Administration of Sport of China*, September 9. Retrieved from http://english.gov.cn/state_council/2014/09/09/content_281474986284050.htm.

Tencent (2016). The 28-year legend of iron women soldiers: Women athlete obtained first Olympic gold for Chinese army Games for 8 years in a row. *Tencent*, August 7. Retrieved from https://xw.qq.com/2016/20160807022211/BCP2016080702221100.

Theodoraki, E. (2004). Sport management reform, national competitiveness and Olympic glory in the People's Republic of China. *Managing Leisure*, **9**(4), 193–211.

Ting, Y. (2008). Women athletes' retired life: Various career paths ranging from participating in politics, teaching, to running business. *Sohu*, January 9. Retrieved from http://sports.sohu.com/20080109/n254538908_7.shtml.

World Bank Databank (2017a). Labor force participation rate, female (% of female population ages 15+) (modeled ILO estimate), China, 2016. Retrieved from https://data.worldbank.org/indicator/SL.TLF.CACT.FE.ZS?locations=CN.

World Bank Databank (2017b). Labor force participation rate, male (% of male population ages 15+) (modeled ILO estimate), China, 2016. Retrieved from https://data.worldbank.org/indicator/SL.TLF.CACT.MA.ZS?locations=CN.

Xinhua News Agency (2015). A new era for China's sports industry, December 23. Retrieved from http://news.xinhuanet.com/english/2015-12/23/c_134944723.htm.

Xinhua News Agency (2016). Olympic celebrity interview: Yang Yang: failure is an indispensable wealth. *Xinhua News Agency*, July 15. Retrieved from www.olympic.cn/museum/news/v/2016/0715/52455.html.

Xu, G. (2009). *Olympic Dreams: China and sports, 1895–2008*. Cambridge, MA: Harvard University Press.

Xu, J. (2013). Xu Jicheng: Gold Strategy cutting down three big balls; why do we need the National Games? *Xinhua News Agency*, September 5. Retrieved from http://sports.sohu.com/20130905/n385941792.shtml.

Xu, L. (2015). *Gen ao yun guan jun xue fan chuan* [Follow the Olympic Champion to Study Sailing]. Beijing, China: Publishing House of Electronic Industry.

Xu, L. (2016). *Golden Lily: Asia's first dinghy sailing gold medallist*. Leamington Spa: Fernhurst Books.

Yang, H. (2012). Urban women's gender discrimination issues in employment, September 6. Retrieved from www.womenofchina.cn/html/womenofchina/report/144652-1.htm.

Yang, K. (2013). In China, it's the grandparents who "lean in." *The Atlantic*, September 30. Retrieved from https://www.theatlantic.com/china/archive/2013/09/in-china-its-the-grandparents-who-lean-in/280097.

Yardley, J. (2012). *Brave Dragons: A Chinese basketball team and American coach, and two cultures clashing*. New York: Knopf.

Ye, J. (2017). China's sport sector could be the next big growth market. *South China Morning Post*, July 27. Retrieved from www.scmp.com/business/investor-relations/ipo-quote-profile/article/2104342/china-sports-sector-could-be-next-big.

Zhou, L. (2016). For domestic consumption, China's women are the biggest spenders, with most going online for their shopping sprees. *South China Morning Post*, March 8. Retrieved from https://www.scmp.com/news/china/policies-politics/article/1922290/domestic-consumption-chinas-women-are-driving-seat.

24
Women's involvement in sport governance
A case study of New Zealand Rugby

Gaye Bryham, Lesley Ferkins, Katie Dee, and Jacqueline Mueller

As with many other domains of sport, the lack of women's involvement within the formalized setting of governance has raised concern from scholars and policy-makers alike (Adriaanse, 2016; Henry & Robinson, 2010). Despite calls for greater gender diversity within sport governance, women are still strongly under-represented across international, national, and local levels (Burton, 2015; Sibson, 2010). The purpose of this chapter is to explore the topic of women's involvement in sport governance, and in doing so help explain why women are still largely absent from it, highlight the contribution women can make to it, and to suggest ways forward for research and practice. We do this by first providing some background about sport governance scholarship, which leads us to identify predominant theories that have been used to explain sport governance and gender dynamics. We particularly highlight institutional theory as a lens to examine women's involvement in sport governance, as well as considering the small number of studies that have focused on gender and sport governance. Next, we offer a contextualized account of women's involvement in sport governance by using New Zealand Rugby (NZR) to explore the forces that have influenced the governance of that sport. Institutional theory is used here to help explain this setting. We conclude by highlighting a landmark in the governance journey of NZR, the inclusion of the first women on the national board in 2016. Farah Palmer's backstory is offered as our leader profile after we conclude and offer future directions for research and practice.

Background to the study of sport governance

The field of sport governance scholarship has gained momentum over the past 15 years when organizational level governance has dominated the literature (O'Boyle & Shilbury, 2016). Sometimes referred to as "corporate governance," organizational governance focuses on the board grouping and/or individuals charged with the responsibility of governing sport organizations (Henry & Lee, 2004). Commonwealth countries such as Australia, New Zealand, Canada, and the United Kingdom, as well as Greece, Portugal, Spain, and Taiwan, where the sports systems are dominated by non-profit organizations, have been the primary contexts for investigation (Shilbury, Ferkins, & Smythe, 2013). Within these countries, scholars have found common topics and issues that have helped to strengthen our understanding of sport governance as a global concern (Hoye & Cuskelly, 2007; Hoye & Doherty, 2011). Early work established the role of the board (Inglis, 1997; Shilbury, 2001), and was followed by studies that considered the CEO–chairperson relationship (Hoye & Cuskelly, 2003), board member motivations (Hoye, 2007), board effectiveness and the link to organizational performance (Hoye & Doherty, 2011), and more recently a collection of studies that have centered on the strategic capabilities of boards (Ferkins & Shilbury, 2015). The issue of women's under-representation on sport boards is also a growing area of sport governance research across numerous countries (Adriaanse, 2016; Adriaanse & Schofield, 2013, 2014; Burton, Grappendorf, & Henderson, 2011; Claringbould & Knoppers, 2007, 2008, 2012; Schull, Shaw, & Khill, 2013; Shaw, 2006; Shaw & Slack, 2002), which seems to have gained momentum in the last five years.

Early working definitions of sport governance largely captured the organizational level view of governance within sport organizations. Although no agreed definition exists, most scholars consider that sport governance involves establishing a strategy or a direction, controlling the activities, and regulating the behavior of a sport organization (O'Boyle & Bradbury, 2013). Likewise, Ferkins, Shilbury and McDonald (2009, p. 245) defined sport governance as: "The responsibility for the functioning and overall direction of the organisation and is a necessary and institutionalised component of all sport codes from club level to national bodies, government agencies, sport service organisations and professional teams around the world." The establishment of such definitions and the focus at the board/organizational level has been influenced to a large extent by the study of governance within the business/for-profit sector (Ferkins, Shilbury, & McDonald, 2005). Perhaps it is the influence of an increasing focus on gender within the corporate/for-profit context of governance research that has encouraged and strengthened the more recent focus on this topic for sport scholars. More specifically, a number of studies in the corporate sector relating to women in governance have increasingly established the advantages of having women on boards (Fondas & Sassalos 2000; Geerat, Alm, & Groll, 2014; Zelechowski & Bilimoria, 2004). These studies have stated that a female presence on boards leads to improved governance and that boards with at least three women score higher in applying corporate strategy, conflict of interest rules/code of conduct, and more generally, bring a different voice to debates and decision-making (Fondas & Sassalos 2000; Geeraert, Alm, & Groll, 2014; Zelechowski & Bilimoria 2004). Furthermore, studies have established a positive link between the financial performance of a firm and board gender diversity (Geerat at al., 2014; Terjese, Sealy, & Singh, 2009). This burgeoning research agenda has seemingly provided a springboard for those researchers interested in the role of women within the sport governance context.

More recently, sport governance researchers have also turned their attention to a wider systemic view of governance, which involves not just the work of the board of an individual organization, but the way in which a network of organizations (e.g., within a sporting code) might work together. Taking this view, Shilbury et al. (2013) considered sport governance as a network of sport organizations that allocate resources, and exercise control and coordination. Underpinning this dual focus on both organizational and systemic governance, researchers have engaged a range of major theories to help explain the dynamics of sport governance. At the board and/or individual level, such theories have included agency theory, stewardship theory, institutional theory, leader-member exchange theory, and managerial hegemony theory (Ferkins, Shilbury, & O'Boyle, 2017; Hoye, 2004; Shilbury, 2001; Welty Peachey, Zhou, Damon, & Burton, 2015). Theories that have proven instructive at the organizational and system-wide level have included institutional theory, resource dependence theory, stakeholder theory, network theory, and inter-organizational relationships (Ferkins et al., 2017).

Institutional theory stands out as a multi-use theory across both individual and board groups, as well as at the organization level and system wide. In addition, Walker, Schaeperkoetter, and Darvin (2017) drew heavily on the notion of institutionalized practices in sport to help explain the over-representation of male leadership within sport organizations. In a general sense institutional theory provides some insight about why sport governance practice is seemingly repeated across sporting codes. Scott (2004) explains that institutional theory is a theory that reveals the deeper, more resilient aspects of a social structure (i.e., organization). More specifically, the theory is used to help explain the *processes* by which structures (e.g., rules, norms, routines) become established as authoritative guidelines that might dictate social behavior. In considering its application to sport, the ideas embedded within institutional theory help explain how sport organizations and the practice of governance seem resistant to change. As Ferkins and Kilmister (2012, p. 146) note, "Governance structures and decision-making are taken for granted, institutionalised, and thus resistant to change." This explains why there may be "a lack of incentives to explore new or improved ways of carrying out the board's business" (Ferkins & Kilmister, 2012, p. 146). The movement toward the involvement of women in sport governance, where men have previously dominated, may therefore be, in part, explained by the ideas captured by institutional theory. Next, we turn our attention to the small number of studies that have focused on women in sport governance.

Background to the study of women's involvement in sport governance

Worldwide we have seen a rise in women's participation in sport (Cunningham, 2008) and, more recently, in codes that have formerly been dominated by men (e.g., ice hockey, Australian Football League, rugby, cricket). In addition, at the 2016 Olympics, for example, women represented 45% of all athletes competing, compared with 44.3% at the 2012 Games (Adriaanse & Schofield, 2014; Donnelly & Donnelly, 2013; Burton & Leberman, 2017). The rise of women's on-field sport participation has not, however, been matched by off-field participation in governance (Adriaanse & Schofield, 2014; Burton & Leberman, 2017). Perhaps, it is the growing momentum in identifying the contribution women make to corporate boards (noted above), the continued under-representation of women on sport boards, and a seeming resistance for this to change that have led to a growing focus on the study of women's involvement in sport governance (Adriaanse, 2016; Adriaanse & Schofield, 2013, 2014; Burton et al., 2011; Claringbould & Knoppers, 2007, 2008, 2012; Schull et al., 2013; Shaw 2006; Shaw & Slack, 2002).

A recent study by Adriaanse (2016) examined the gender diversity in national sport organization's (NSOs') boards in 45 countries (referred to as "The Sydney Scoreboard Global Index of Participation" [SSGIP]) and identified three key indicators of global under-representation of women on sport boards. These indicators include the roles of chief executives, board chairs, and board directors. The authors of this and other studies advocated that a threshold of 30% women in these roles, or at least three women per board, is needed if we are to have some confidence that gender equity on sport boards is being advanced (Adriaanse, 2016; Adriaanse & Schofield, 2014). The SSGIP study, involving 1,600 NSOs, further revealed that the global mean for women directors was 19.7%, chairs of boards 10.8% and chief executives 16.3% – all below the 30% threshold (Adriaanse, 2016).

An enduring argument for increasing the number of women on sport boards has focused on the ethical dimension. Ahn and Cunningham (2017) argue that sport organizations have a responsibility to be inclusive from not only an ethical but also a social perspective. Central to the argument for fostering women's representation in governance is the fact that "women represent stakeholders who should be included (ethical principle) and that their inclusion increases the pool of talent available for selection into leadership positions (business principle)" (Adriaanse, 2016, p. 159). More recently, the case is being strengthened from an economic perspective on the basis that the inclusion of women not only increases the pool of talent available for selection into leadership positions, but also positively impacts a firm's financial performance (Post & Byron, 2015). As noted above, several studies about women's under-representation in sport leadership and governance have drawn heavily on institutionalized practices as a framework for understanding (Burton, 2015; Walker & Sartore-Baldwin, 2013; Walker et al., 2017). In the next section, we draw on the tenets of institutional theory and institutionalized practices to help understand why women have been largely invisible at the governance level of NZR. Through a case study approach, we seek to identify what forces came into play, to influence the appointment of the first women to the Board of NZR, in 2016.

Institutionalization of New Zealand Rugby governance: The forces against change

Rugby was first introduced to New Zealand in the late 1860s, with the first game played in 1870. The national body, now known as *New Zealand Rugby*, was established in 1892 (New Zealand Rugby, 2018). Females have long been excluded from participating in rugby union, and it was not until the 1980s that NZR began to have some involvement in the women's game (Carle & Nauright, 1999; Tucker, 2015). In 1998 the governing body officially recognized the first national women's rugby team, now known as the *Black Ferns*. This national side competed at the first World Cup in 1991 (New Zealand Rugby, 2018). What is referred to as "institutionalization" within sport could be one reason to explain the gender bias that has occurred within the sport of rugby union in New Zealand, as represented by the national body, NZR. The over-dominance of males in governance and leadership has resulted in what Walker et al. (2017, p. 33) refer to as institutionalized practices that have "valued male ideals, provided men with unquestioned power, and devalued women's contribution." Burton and Leberman (2017) advocate the importance of seeking to understand why such under-representation of women in leadership and governance established such a stronghold and the reasons it continues to reign – albeit with signs of change starting to occur – in some sporting domains. This raises the question as to what were the values and behaviors of the New Zealand rugby culture that created an institutional bias disadvantaging women's contributions in rugby governance. In this section we examine three concepts: gendered space; the notion of the "glass wall," and "glass ceiling"; and homologous reproduction; these may help to explain prevailing values and behaviors within the governance of NZR.

Gendered space

In an authoritative review of the literature pertaining to the under-representation of women in sport leadership (encompassing governance), Burton (2015) argues that sport should be viewed as a gendered space. This view of sport recognizes "gender as a fundamental aspect of organizational and social processes" (Burton, 2015, p. 156) which helps to reveal the issue of under-representation as well as the reasons for it. This approach is supported by Walker and Sartore-Baldwin (2013), who sought to understand the perspectives and attitudes of men's basketball coaches toward women in what they refer to as the "institution of men's college basketball and within the male-dominated organizational culture of sport" (Walker & Sartore-Baldwin, 2013, p. 303). Their findings allude to male sports as being gender exclusive, as well as hyper-masculine and resistant to change. There appear to be some parallels with the culture of such a longstanding male-dominated sport of rugby, as well as a relevance to a gendered view of sport advocated by Burton (2015).

In 2016, there was significant focus on women's rugby in New Zealand because the sevens Black Ferns team were serious Gold medal prospects for the 2016 Rio De Janeiro Olympics. Evidence indicates that female rugby players had to fight strong negative perceptions before being introduced into the Olympics (Adjepong, 2017; HSBC, 2017). One perception was that "rugby is a man's game," a carry-over from the early days of the sport. This judgment indicated that women were not physically able to handle the rigors of full contact sports, nor to have the temperament to attempt it (Corbett, 2016). This judgment also enabled another recurring negative perception, namely the labeling of rugby, among other traditionally defined male activities, as a lesbian sport based on the fact that the game contains large amounts of physical contact (Russell, 2007). As noted by Russell (2007), such a perception has potentially discouraged heterosexual women from competing in the game. Countering this, according to Griffin, McLellan, Presland, Rathbone, and Keogh (2017), Olympic inclusion accelerated global participation and. paired with the success of the Black Ferns, sevens has been a strong growth area in women's sport in New Zealand.

Several studies/authors (e.g., Burton, 2015; Burton et al., 2011; Burton & Leberman, 2017) have found that such inherent biases toward women in sport and sport leadership (which might often be subconscious) become more overt when sport is viewed as a gendered space. Anderson's (2009) article on understanding the maintenance of masculinity among stakeholders in sport also supports these assertions. He notes that: "Competitive team sports . . . exist as a microcosm of society's gendered values, myths and prejudices about gender" (Anderson, 2009, p. 4). Anderson also considers that competitive team sports condition males to show, value, and reproduce traditional ideas of masculinity. Such an explanation appears to fit with the game of rugby in New Zealand, which has seemingly promoted the "maintenance of masculinity" since being first established in the 1860s (Pringle, 2008). As pointed out by Theberge (1985) some 30 years ago, if we view sport as an institutionalized male preserve, then it enables us to better understand the male dominance within the sporting context.

The glass wall and the glass ceiling

A second factor that scholars have claimed contributes to the institutionalization of sport is referred to as the "glass wall" and the "glass ceiling" phenomenon (Walker, Bopp, & Sagas, 2011; Walker et al., 2017). Both terms are used to describe the institutionalized barriers that women face in organizations and in being appointed to leadership and governance positions in "men's sport" (Walker et al., 2017). Again, it is worth remembering that, in 2018, rugby is still a male-dominated sport in New Zealand and, as Burton and Leberman (2017, p. 37) state, it is the "sexist and hyper-masculine culture of men's sports, which supports the glass wall phenomenon." Farah Palmer's appointment to the Board of NZR in 2016 might be an example of the glass wall phenomenon. "It has taken more than a century but finally a woman has joined the upper echelons of New Zealand's rugby hierarchy" (McKendry, 2016, para. 1).

The glass wall and ceiling phenomena also convey the lack of opportunities available to women to progress upward in the leadership hierarchy of the organization (Burton & Leberman, 2017). An example of the glass ceiling being broken in rugby governance in New Zealand occurred in 2017, when the first women to chair a provincial rugby union board was appointed – Jane Duncan on the Buller Provincial Rugby Union. A *New Zealand Herald* reporter, Chris Rattue, referred to the appointment as "making history," and made reference to her as having "broken through the glass ceiling" (Rattue, 2017). Duncan's response to her appointment was:

It is changing times for women in New Zealand, especially in sport, but I really don't think this should come as a surprise. Maybe it's because rugby has a reputation for being male, pale and stale . . . I certainly never felt that way about rugby but there is increased awareness about women putting themselves forward for governance roles.

(Rattue, 2017, para. 6–7)

Homologous reproduction

A third contributor to the institutionalization of sport that has potentially resulted in under-representation of women in governance is what is referred to as homologous reproduction (Anderson, 2009). This idea helps to explain the tendency of male leaders to appoint to positions those akin to oneself, and in doing so replicate "the masculinized nature of their sport" (Anderson, 2009, p. 11). It would appear that the NZR board adopted a homologous reproduction approach in their appointments to governance for 124 years whereby male board members (of Provincial Unions) appointed/elected other men to the board who brought seemingly similar backgrounds and experiences. This, in turn, reinforced the institution of rugby favoring men over women in the governance of the sport. Figure 24.1, which is an image of the 2013 members of the NZR board, visually *indicates* the notion of homologous reproduction.

Challenges to institutionalization: Forces contributing to change

Just as there are forces against change that can in part be better understood by applying an institutional theory lens, so too are there forces that influence change. In this section we highlight some of these forces that we think have challenged the status quo, and indeed institutionalized processes within the governance of NZR.

Figure 24.1 The 2014 New Zealand Rugby board

Women's increasing participation and profile in rugby

World Rugby (formerly the International Rugby Board) labeled rugby the fastest growing women's sport in the world between 2012 and 2014. In addition, its development department announced that 23% of rugby participants were female in 2014 compared with 7% in 2009 (Corbett, 2016). In 2017, Rowan (2017) claimed that 25% of those participating in rugby globally were female.

New Zealand has also experienced a surge in the growth and interest in the women's game (Curtin, 2017). It is possible that this growth, as well as the profile and success of the Black Ferns (New Zealand women's 15 aside) and Black Ferns sevens teams, has begun to break down some of the earlier stigmas relating to women playing rugby, as well as their contribution to leadership off-field. Greater recognition by NZR for the development of women's rugby may also have played a role in contributing to a growing recognition that female participation in the governance of the sport also needs to change. This opportunity for change was recently highlighted by the Chair of NZR, Brent Impey, in a national newspaper article. Impey pointed out that NZR cannot afford to be "out of step with where the rest of society is going and I think that's being recognised" (McKendry, 2016, para. 11). He went on to say that:

> Of 155,000 players, 21,000 of them are women. It's my personal view that, particularly around women's sevens and the Olympics, it can become the No. 1 women's team sport in this country. It's just inconsistent to have those numbers and those ambitions without that group being represented at the governance level.
>
> *(McKendry, 2016, para. 12)*

Risk to the reputation of rugby: The glass cliff or glass wall/ceiling?

A second element that we consider has influenced change has been a perceived risk to the reputation of rugby in New Zealand. A number of off-field incidents have raised concern for the reputation of the game, leading to NZR initiating an independent review in 2016, referred to as the Respect and Responsibility Review (RRR). According to NZR:

> The recommendations provide all of rugby a pathway to continue to ensure everyone involved in the game has the right information and understanding with regards to respect and responsibility to enable them to make the right decisions. This includes ensuring that our attitudes towards women in rugby, diversity, respect, responsibility and inclusiveness are in keeping with a world leading sports organisation.
>
> *(New Zealand Rugby, 2017, para. 5)*

It is interesting to note that this review panel was chaired by a woman (Kathryn Beck), and five of the nine panel members were women. This raises the question of why, after more than 124 years of the dearth of women in positions of influence, did NZR appoint a panel that was proportionally opposite to what existed in the governance of the provincial unions and national board? Is this an example of the "glass cliff" or the start of the fracturing of the glass wall/ceiling (noted above)? As explained by Jackson and Parry (2011, p. 29), "Women are more likely than men to be appointed to leadership positions associated with an increased risk of failure and criticism because these positions are more likely to involve the management or organizational units that are in crisis." It is interesting that, in a study about the glass cliff, Haslam and Ryan (2008) found that women were associated with glass cliff appointments due to an underlying belief that women's particular capabilities were more or best suited to such situations.

Public expectations and pressures

In 2012, the New Zealand Human Rights Commission initiated a campaign challenging rugby over the lack of gender diversity on its national and provincial boards. A survey highlighted that, of the 26 provincial rugby unions in New Zealand, only 4 included a woman (McGregor, 2012; *New Zealand Herald*, 2017). The commissioner at the time, Dr. Judy McGregor. referred to rugby as "the last bastion of chauvinism" (Johannsen, 2016). This campaign highlighted the gender inequality that prevails in the country's "national sport" and in NZR, an organization that aspires to be world leading.

According to Gregor Paul of the *New Zealand Herald*, "such adverse publicity highlighted the lack of diversity in the governance at all levels of the game and ramped up NZ Rugby chairman Brent Impey's desire to bring a woman on to the previously all-male board" (Paul, 2016, para. 7). This campaign, combined with the issues and questions raised by the RRR (noted above), as well as the increase in women's participation in rugby, may have contributed to igniting the public voice and expression of expectations about gender diversity in rugby governance in New Zealand.

Breaking the glass wall/ceiling: A champion for change

Another critical factor that has seemingly influenced change may have been the leadership and influence of the Chairperson of NZR, Brent Impey. As expressed by Burton and Leberman (2017), change often comes when leaders and influencers inside the sport, who are mostly men, consider women as viable candidates for leadership in what are predominantly known as men's sports. The Chief Executive of New Zealand's government agency for sport, Sport New Zealand, also suggested that leaders from within the sport who are prepared to speak out and demand change are a critical step in the right direction (Johannsen, 2016). In an interview with the *New Zealand Herald*, Miskimmin was quoted as saying: "We've got a lot of women that want to go on boards, but we haven't got boards that are ready for women." He went on to say, "I do applaud Brent for standing up in what has been a fairly male-dominated sport, to say the world of rugby is different now and their decision-making processes should reflect that" (Johannsen, 2016, para. 18).

Could it be that Brent Impey is a champion for challenging the institutionalization of rugby in New Zealand and, with his leadership influence, is playing a key role in fracturing the glass wall and ceiling? Impey has been chair of the Board since 2014 and made publicly known his aspirations to ensure that the NZR board becomes more reflective of New Zealand society. He believed the appointment of at least one woman on the board was non-negotiable (McKendry, 2016). That moment came in 2016 when Farah Palmer was elected as the Maori representative on to the NZR board ending a 124-year all-male run. After the conclusion of this chapter, we provide a profile of Palmer and some context around her inclusion on to the board.

Conclusion and directions for research and practice

The chapter has explored the topic of women's involvement in sport governance using the lens of institutional theory and the situational context of rugby in New Zealand (i.e., NZR).

Although institutional theory is not the only theory to help us understand sport governance practice, as demonstrated in this case study, it is a useful theory to help explain the forces for and against change in governance practice within NZR in relation to women's involvement. The concepts of gendered space, glass wall/ceiling, and homologous reproduction help explain prevailing values and behaviors that have contributed to institutionalized practices where men have dominated the governance of rugby in New Zealand. Women's increasing participation and profile in rugby, the perceived risk to the reputation of rugby, public expectations, and pressures, and a champion for change have all seemingly challenged institutionalization processes and forces within the context of rugby in New Zealand.

Although we join a growing number of authors who have raised concern about the under-representation of women in sport governance, an appreciation for the influencing forces that underlie the resistance to change offers much opportunity to initiate change. We therefore advocate for greater momentum in research that embraces the ideas of institutional theory and institutionalized practices, and for those who are influential in the practice of sport governance to understand and recognize the forces for change at play within their specific sporting contexts. In particular, as Burton and Leberman (2017) note, much of the research pertaining to the glass wall and glass ceiling experiences in sport are in the context of coaching. Thus, there would be much to gain from future research focusing on sport leadership and governance in relation to these concepts.

Leader profile: Dr. Farah Palmer (based on work by Sophie Parker)

Farah Rangikoepa Palmer was born to Bruce Palmer and Judith Palmer on November 27, 1972 in Te Kuiti, New Zealand. In 1998, 2002, and 2006 she captained the Black Ferns, New Zealand's women's national rugby team, to victory in the Women's Rugby World Cup. She retired from her active playing career at the end of the 2006 season. With 35 caps for the national team between 1996 and 2006, she is New Zealand's second most appointed player after Anna Richards. In addition to being one of the greatest Black Ferns in history, Dr. Palmer also completed her PhD in 2001 and is employed by Massey University as a senior lecturer in management, with a focus on leadership issues in sport management. More specifically her research interests have involved gender issues in sport from a sociological or *kaupapa* Maori perspective, diversity issues in sport management and leadership, and Maori leadership and governance in sport and business (Massey University, 2018).

Palmer was recognized for her services to rugby when she was made an Officer of the New Zealand Order of Merit (ONZM) in 2007. She has obtained several accolades including, but not limited to, Women's Player of the Year 1998, International Women's Personality of the Year 2005, and she was the sixth woman to be inducted to the International Rugby Hall of Fame in 2014. On December 14, 2016 Palmer was elected as the Maori representative on to the NZR board. She had previously been an independent member of the New Zealand Maori Rugby Board for over a decade.

Despite her outstanding playing career, her contribution to Maori Rugby, and being unanimously elected by NZR's voting members, Palmer still expressed some concerns that her appointment could be seen as tokenism and said in an interview:

> I talked to lots of different people about it. One of the things that I was talking to people about is that I would be seen as a token gesture. I think there is an element of that, but someone has to be the one to break that stronghold. I feel that I am there because I have the skills and expertise that are needed.
>
> *(Eade, 2017, para. 7)*

The grounds for those doubts quickly dissipated as she received extensive support regarding her appointment from various sides, including Brent Impey, who stated in an interview with a local newspaper, "While Dr. Palmer becomes the first woman elected to NZR's Board in its almost 125 history, she clearly represented the best person for the role and the interests of Maori rugby" (Eade, 2017, para. 5). Another commentator (Jonathan Howe) offered:

> But make no mistake – this was not a decision done to tick a demographic box. Putting her legendary status to one side, Palmer has held executive positions on international and Maori rugby boards, making her uniquely qualified to thrive in such a role.
>
> *(Allblacks.com, 2016, para. 26)*

Palmer is eager to be a strong role model and calls on other women to follow in her footsteps. In an interview after her first board meeting she stated: "I do see this as opening the door to encourage other women to put themselves forward for board positions at provincial and Super Rugby level" (McKendry, 2016, para. 31). Palmer states that her approach will be predominantly collaborative but challenging where it needs to be (McKendry, 2016).

Acknowledgment

Thank you to Dr. Farah Palmer for her collaboration and Sophie Parker for her support work with this chapter.

References

Adjepong, A. (2017). "We're, like, a cute rugby team": How whiteness and heterosexuality shape women's sense of belonging in rugby. *International Review for the Sociology of Sport*, **52**, 209–222.

Adriaanse, J. A. (2016). Gender diversity in the governance of sport associations: The Sydney Scoreboard Global Index of Participation. *Journal of Business Ethics*, **137**, 149–160.

Adriaanse, J. A. & Schofield, T. (2013). Analysing gender dynamics in sport governance: A new regimes-based approach. *Sport Management Review*, **16**, 498–513.

Adriaanse, J. & Schofield, T. (2014). The impact of gender quotas on gender equality in sport governance. *Journal of Sport Management*, **28**, 485–497.

Ahn, N. Y. & Cunningham, G. B. (2017). Cultural values and gender equity on national Olympic committee boards. *International Journal of Exercise Science*, **10**(6), 857–874.

Allblacks.com (2016). Dr Farah Palmer elected to board of New Zealand Rugby. Retrieved from www.allblacks.com/News/30212/dr-farah-palmer-elected-to-board-of-new-zealand-rugby (accessed January 4, 2018).

Anderson, E. (2009). The maintenance of masculinity among the stakeholders of sport. *Sport Management Review*, **12**, 3–14.

Burton, L. J. (2015). Underrepresentation of women in sport leadership: A review of research. *Sport Management Review*, **18**, 155–165.

Burton, L. J., Grappendorf, H., & Henderson, A. (2011). Perceptions of gender in athletic administration: Utilizing the congruity to examine (potential) prejudice against women. *Journal of Sport Management*, **25**, 36–45.

Burton, L. J. & Leberman, S. (2017). *Women in Sport Leadership: Research and practice for change*. London: Routledge.

Carle, A. & Nauright, J. (1999). A man's game? Women playing rugby union in Australia. *Football Studies*, **2**, 55–73.

Claringbould, I. & Knoppers, A. (2007). Finding a "normal" woman: Selection processes for board membership. *Sex Roles*, **56**, 495–507.

Claringbould, I. & Knoppers, A. (2008). Doing and undoing gender in sport governance. *Sex Roles*, **58**, 81–92.

Claringbould, I. & Knoppers, A. (2012). Paradoxical practices of gender in sport-related organisations. *Journal of Sport Management*, **26**, 404–416.

Corbett, B. (2016). Strategic change in response to an environmental jolt: Rugby and the Olympic Games, Doctoral dissertation. Retrieved from National Library of Australia Database https://trove.nla.gov.au/version/246527620.

Cunningham, G. (2008). Creating and sustaining gender diversity in sport organizations. *Sex Roles*, **58**, 136–145.

Curtin, J. (2017). Before the "Black Ferns": Tracing the beginnings of women's rugby in New Zealand. *The International Journal of the History of Sport*, **33**(17), 2071–2085.

Donnelly, P. & Donnelly, M. K. (2013). *The London 2012 Olympics: A gender equality audit*. Toronto: Centre for Sport Policy Studies, Faculty of Kinesiology and Physical Education, University of Toronto.

Eade, S. (2017). Rugby legend and women's trailblazer Farah Palmer Manawatu Standard's person of the year. *Manawatu Standard*, January 2. Retrieved from https://www.stuff.co.nz/manawatu-standard/sport/87638141/Rugby-legend-and-womens-trailblazer-Farah-Palmer-Manawatu-Standards-person-of-the-year (accessed January 4, 2018).

Ferkins, L. & Kilmister, T. (2012). Sport governance. In S. Leberman, C. Collins, & L. Trenberth (eds), *Sport Business Management in New Zealand and Australia*, 3rd edn (pp. 137–159). Melbourne: Cengage Learning Australia Pty Ltd.

Ferkins, L. & Shilbury, D. (2015). Board strategic balance: An emerging sport governance theory. *Sport Management Review*, **18**, 489–500.

Ferkins, L., Shilbury, D., & McDonald, G. (2005). The role of the board in building strategic capability: Towards an integrated model of sport governance research. *Sport Management Review*, **8**, 195–225.

Ferkins, L., Shilbury, D., & McDonald, G. (2009). Board involvement in strategy: Advancing the governance of sport organizations. *Journal of Sport Management*, **23**, 245–277.

Ferkins, L., Shilbury, D., & O'Boyle, I. (2017). Leadership in governance: Exploring collective board leadership in sport governance systems. *Sport Management Review*. Advanced online publication DOI: 10.1016/j.smr.2017.07.007.

Fondas, N. & Sassalos, S. (2000). A different voice in the boardroom: How the presence of women directors affects board influence over management. *Global Focus*, **12**, 13–22.

Geeraert, A., Alm, J., & Groll, M. (2014). Good governance in international sport organizations: an analysis of the 35 Olympic sport governing bodies. *International Journal of Sport Policy*, **6**, 281–306.

Griffin, J. A., McLellan, C. P., Presland, J., Rathbone, E., & Keogh, J. W. (2017). Quantifying the movement patterns of international women's rugby sevens preparation training camp sessions. *International Journal of Sports Science & Coaching*, **12**, 677–684.

Haslam, S. A. & Ryan, M. K. (2008). The road to the glass cliff: Differences in the perceived suitability of men and women for leadership positions in succeeding and failing organizations. *The Leadership Quarterly*, **19**(5), 530–546.

Henry, I. & Lee, P. C. (2004). Governance and ethics in sport. In J. Beech & S. Chadwick (eds), *The Business of Sport Management* (pp. 25–41). London: Pearson Education.

Henry, I. & Robinson, L. (2010). *Gender Equality and Leadership in Olympic Bodies*. London: Loughborough University.

Hoye, R. (2004). Leader-member exchanges and board performance of voluntary sport organizations. *Nonprofit Management and Leadership*, **15**, 55–70.

Hoye, R. (2007). Commitment, involvement and performance of voluntary sport organization board members. *European Sport Management Quarterly*, **7**, 109–121.

Hoye, R. & Cuskelly, G. (2003). Board–executive relationships within voluntary sport organisations. *Sport Management Review*, **6**, 53–73.

Hoye, R. & Cuskelly, G. (2007). *Sport Governance*. Sydney: Elsevier.

Hoye, R. & Doherty, A. (2011). Nonprofit sport board performance: A review and directions for future research. *Journal of Sport Management*, **25**, 272–285.

HSBC (2017). The future of rugby: An HSBC report. Retrieved from https://www.google.co.uk/url?sa=t&rct=j&q=&esrc=s&source=web&cd=3&ved=0ahUKEwjsqKChg7DZAhWkBcAKHTHXDx4QFgg7MAI&url=http%3A%2F%2Fwww.hsbc.com%2F-%2Fmedia%2Fhsbc-com%2Fnewsroomassets%2F2016%2Fpdfs%2Fthe-future-of-rugby-an-hsbc-report.pdf&usg=AOvVaw2FLwq9G-46DOnx21300aVN (accessed February 18, 2018).

Inglis, S. (1997). Shared leadership in the governance of amateur sport. *AVANTE Journal*, **3**, 14–33.

Jackson, B. & Parry, K. (2011). *A Very Short Fairly Interesting and Reasonably Cheap Book about Studying Leadership*, 2nd edn. Thousand Oaks, CA: Sage.

Johannsen, D. (2016). Gender inequality could hit NZ Rugby in the pocket. *New Zealand Herald*. , May 12 Retrieved from www.nzherald.co.nz/sport/news/article.cfm?c_id=4&objectid=11638247.

Massey University (2018). Dr Farah Palmer. Retrieved from https://www.massey.ac.nz/massey/learning/colleges/college-business/school-of management/staff.cfm?stref=101630.

McGregor, J. (2012). *New Zealand Census of Women's Participation 2012*. Wellington: Human Rights Commission.

McKendry, P. (2016). New Zealand Rugby's newest board member Farah Palmer: Breaking through rugby's glass ceiling. *NZ Herald*, December 18. Retrieved from www.nzherald.co.nz/sport/news/article.cfm?c_id=4&objectid=11768340.

New Zealand Herald (2017). She's Got Game ep2: Why NZ Rugby needs women on their board. *New Zealand Herald*, May 12. Retrieved from www.nzherald.co.nz/sport/news/article.cfm?c_id=4&objectid=11637897.

New Zealand Rugby (2017). Respect and responsibility review. Retrieved from www.nzrugby.co.nz/what-we-do/rugby-responsibility/respect-and-responsibility review.

New Zealand Rugby (2018). Our board. Retrieved from www.nzrugby.co.nz/about-us/our-people/our-board (accessed January 4, 2018).

O'Boyle, I. & Bradbury, T. (2013). *Sport Governance: International case studies*. London: Routledge.

O'Boyle, I. & Shilbury, D. (2016). Exploring issues of trust in collaborative sport governance. *Journal of Sport Management*, **30**, 52–69.

Paul, G. (2016). Making history: Farah Palmer joins New Zealand Rugby's board. *NZ Herald*, December 15. Retrieved from www.nzherald.co.nz/sport/news/article.cfm?c_id=4&objectid=11767115.

Post, C. & Byron, K. (2015). Women on boards and firm financial performance: A meta-analysis. *Academy of Management Journal*, **58**(5), 1546–1571.

Pringle, R. (2008). "No rugby – no fear": Collective stories, masculinities and transformative possibilities in schools. *Sport, Education and Society*, **13**, 215–237.

Rattue, C. (2017). New Buller boss a woman keen to make big mark at her tiny union. *New Zealand Herald*, March 5. Retrieved from www.nzherald.co.nz/sport/news/article.cfm?c_id=4&objectid=11812127.

Rowan K. (2017). World Rugby to ensure that one third of board members are female. *The Telegraph*, November 23. Retrieved from www.telegraph.co.uk/rugby-union/2017/11/23/world-rugby-ensure-one-third-board-members-female.

Russell, K. (2007). Queers, even in netball?. Interpretations of the lesbian label among sportswomen. In C. Aitchison (ed.), *Sport and Gender Identities. Masculinities, Femininities and Sexualities* (pp. 106–121). Oxon: Routledge.

Schull, V., Shaw, S., & Kihl, L. (2013). If a woman came in . . . she would have been eaten up alive: Analyzing gendered political processes in the search for an athletic director. *Gender and Society*, **27**, 56–81.

Scott, W. R. (2004). Institutional theory. In G. Ritzer (ed.), *Encyclopedia of Social Theory* (pp. 408–414). Thousand Oaks, CA: Sage.

Shaw, S. (2006). Scratching the back of "Mr X": Analyzing gendered social processes in sport organizations. *Journal of Sport Management*, **20**, 510–534.

Shaw, S. & Slack, T. (2002). "Its been like that for Donkey's Years": The construction of gender relations and the cultures of sports organizations. *Culture, Sport, Society*, **5**, 86–106.

Shilbury, D. (2001). Examining board member roles, functions and influence: A study of Victorian sporting organizations. *International Journal of Sport Management*, **2**, 253–281.

Shilbury, D., Ferkins, L., & Smythe, L. (2013). Sport governance encounters: Insights from lived experiences. *Sport Management Review*, **16**, 349–363.

Sibson, R. (2010). "I was banging my head against a brick wall": Exclusionary power and the gendering of sport organizations. *Journal of Sport Management*, **24**(4), 379–399.

Terjesen, S., Sealy, R., & Singh, V. (2009). Women directors on corporate boards: A review and research agenda. *Corporate Governance: An International Review*, **17**, 320–337.

Theberge, N. (1985). Toward a feminist alternative to sport as a male preserve. *Quest*, **37**, 193–202.

Tucker, N. (2015). Going for gold: New Zealand women's elite rugby sevens in a new Olympic-era, Master's thesis, Massey University, Palmerston North, New Zealand. Retrieved from https://mro.massey.ac.nz/bitstream/handle/10179/7061/02_whole.pdf.

Walker, N., Bopp, T., & Sagas, M. (2011). Gender bias in the perception of women as collegiate men's basketball coaches. *Journal for the Study of Sports and Athletes in Education*, **5**, 157–176.

Walker, N. A. & Sartore-Baldwin, M. L. (2013). Hegemonic masculinity and the institutionalized bias toward women in men's collegiate basketball: What do men think? *Journal of Sport Management*, **27**, 303–315.

Walker, N. A., Schaeperkoetter, C., & Darvin, L. (2017). Institutionalized practices in sport leadership. In L. Burton & S. Leberman (eds), *Women in Sport Leadership: Research and practice for change* (pp. 33–46). London: Routledge,

Welty Peachey, J., Zhou, Y., Damon, Z.J., & Burton, L.J. (2015). Forty years of leadership research in sport management: A review, synthesis, and conceptual framework. *Journal of Sport Management*, **29**(5), 570–587.

Zelechowski, D.D. & Bilimoria, D. (2004). Characteristics of women and men corporate inside directors in the US. *Corporate Governance: An International Review*, **12**, 337–342.

25
Governance of college sport

Erianne A. Weight and Molly P. Harry

Women's sport participation at the collegiate level has steadily increased in the modern era. Governance and fan interest are, however, overwhelmingly male dominated. In response to issues of gender equity within the industry, members of the National Collegiate Athletic Association (NCAA), the predominant organization of intercollegiate athletics governance in the United States, have been prodded toward addressing inclusion and equity within the governance and participation opportunities in intercollegiate athletics. Specific measures taken include the NCAA designation of a Primary (now Senior) Woman Administrator in 1981, the organization of a Gender-Equity Task Force in 1993, and the development of the Emerging Sport Program in 1994. Currently, each of these initiatives is still in existence, because gender equity has not yet been reached. This chapter begins with a brief historical overview of college sport governance, then transitions to issues in intercollegiate athletics governance for women, discusses the work of the NCAA Gender-Equity task force, and concludes with issues of fan interest and financing, with a specific focus on women's basketball and softball.

Women's leadership and college sport governance

Federal legislation in the United States requires equal access and opportunity for women in employment and education (Title VII and Title IX). These laws have prompted significant growth in women's opportunities in education and sport participation (Acosta & Carpenter, 2014; Irick, 2015; Yiamouyiannis, 2009). Administration of college sport is, however, largely male dominated (Yiamouyiannis & Osborne, 2012). As mentioned in Chapter 2, the Association for Intercollegiate Athletics for Women (AIAW), at its peak (between 1971 and 1981), organized 41 championships in 19 sports across three competitive divisions. During this era, more than 90% of head athletics administrators and coaches of women's programs were female. After the hostile takeover of the AIAW by the NCAA in 1981 (Suggs, 2005; Wushanley, 2004), the administrative oversight quickly shifted to roughly 85% of athletic administrators being men with control over the men's and the women's programs (Acosta & Carpenter, 1992). This predominance of male leadership remains, although slow but steady increases in female leadership have continued. As of 2014, 23.3% of athletics directors were women, representing an all-time high since 1981, and 42% of women's teams and less than 3% of men's teams were coached by women (Acosta & Carpenter, 2014).

The landscape of gender equity in institutional leadership is important because institutions drive governance of intercollegiate athletics. The NCAA, as a governing body, functions to assist member institutions in the administration of college sport, which primarily includes the development, interpretation, and enforcement of rules, the development and protection of the NCAA brand, and the administrative organization of championships. The NCAA provides support for over 1000 institutions divided into three competitive divisions. Division I NCAA legislation, for instance, is overseen by a board of directors, which concentrates on oversight and strategic issues (Figure 25.1), and the Council, which makes the day-to-day policy and legislative decisions (Figure 25.2). The large administrative structure of the NCAA serves to support and enact the decisions made by the member-driven leadership boards and councils of the three competitive divisions.

Senior Woman Administrator (SWA)

One of the compromises from the 1981 merger of the AIAW and the NCAA was the creation of the Primary Woman Administrator (now Senior Woman Administrator or SWA). The SWA is the highest-ranking female in each NCAA conference office or athletics department (NCAA, 2017a).

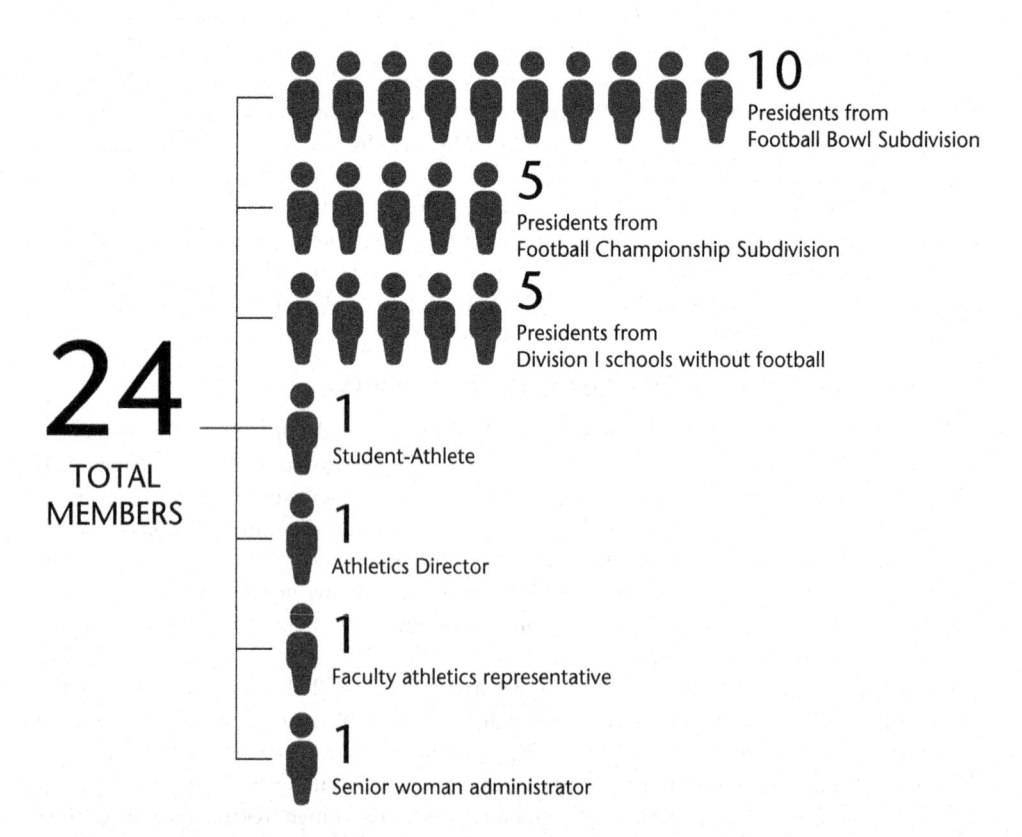

Figure 25.1 The NCAA Division I Board of Directors

Governance of college sport

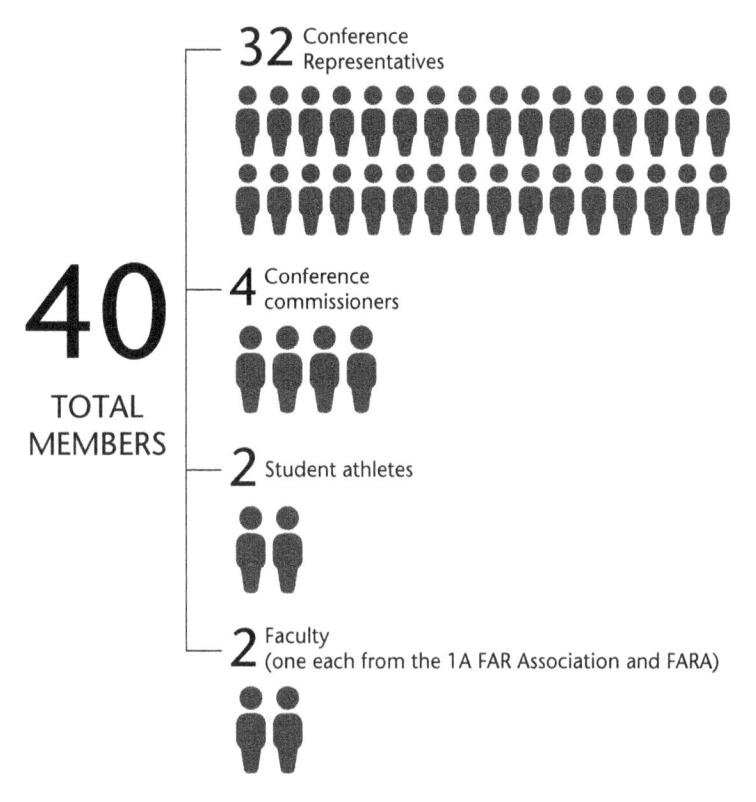

40 TOTAL MEMBERS
- 32 Conference Representatives
- 4 Conference commissioners
- 2 Student athletes
- 2 Faculty (one each from the 1A FAR Association and FARA)

Figure 25.2 Conference representatives may include athletics directors, conference administrators, senior woman administrators, or other athletics administrators or faculty athletics representatives

This title was created in 1981 to ensure the representation of women in leadership and business positions within college sports. Currently, SWAs are involved in a variety of senior-level decisions, and generally maintain sport oversight of both men's and women's revenue and nonrevenue sports.

The ideal outcomes of this designation include better decision-making due to the inclusion of more diverse perspectives, professional success for the SWAs, and an increased presence of women mentors and role models. SWAs at the institutional and conference levels believe that this designation facilitates the opportunity for the perspective of women to be considered in the management of athletic programs. However, few SWAs believe the title provides the chance for their perspective to be valued (NCAA, 2017a). Likewise, SWAs are more likely to have significant involvement in hiring process decisions, but less inclusion in financial decisions (NCAA, 2017a).

Misconceptions about the SWA role persist despite the salience of the position for nearly four decades. Many inside and outside athletics misinterpret the role of the SWA as the oldest woman administrator who oversees only women's sports or gender equity and compliance with Title IX. This is a common hurdle that women in these roles have to overcome, because even 50% of SWAs admit they do not understand their role within the institution or athletic department (NCAA, 2017a). Of current SWAs 84% believe, even with slow progress in representation and role ambiguity, that, if this role did not exist, some institutions would not have a female representative involved in the management and business of their athletics program (NCAA, 2017a).

Gender equity issues in intercollegiate athletics governance

Building on the research tracking the number of female participants, coaches, and administrators in college sport (e.g., Acosta & Carpenter, 2014; Irick, 2015; Lapchick, Hoff, & Kaiser, 2010), there is a body of literature that has identified workplace and personal barriers, in addition to strategies to address these barriers in an effort to increase gender representation in intercollegiate athletics administration. Specifically, workplace barriers identified in the literature include pay inequities, situations of homophobia and sexual harassment, issues related to the hiring process, and a lack of inclusivity in the work environment (Bruening & Dixon, 2008; Burton, Grappendorf, & Henderson, 2011; Dixon & Sagas, 2007; Greenhill, Auld, Cuskelly, & Hooper, 2009; Inglis, Danylchuk, & Pastore, 1996, 2000; NCAA, 2009; Yiamouyiannis, 2008). Personal barriers to a career in intercollegiate athletics administration have also been uncovered, including a lack of work–life balance, burnout, and a lack of interest in advancing in the industry (Cunningham, 2008; Grappendorf & Lough, 2006; Yiamouyiannis, 2008). Recommendations to address these barriers include mentoring/networking programs, training and education, time management support, and gender-neutral hiring policies (Kilty, 2006; Lough, 2001; NCAA, 2009; Weaver & Chelladurai, 2002; Yiamouyiannis, 2008).

NCAA Gender-Equity Task Force

The Gender-Equity Task Force was formed in 1993 to support and encourage gender equity at all NCAA institutions across all divisions. In the task force's words:

> An athletics program can be considered gender equitable when the participants in both the men's and women's sports programs would accept as fair and equitable the overall program of the other gender. No individual should be discriminated against on the basis of gender, institutionally or nationally, in intercollegiate athletics.
>
> *(NCAA, 2018a)*

In 1993, the task force successfully increased financial aid opportunities for female athletes, included gender equity as a component of Division I certification, increased representation of women in decision-making positions on NCAA committees and college campuses, and implemented the NCAA's emerging sports program for women (see Emerging sport program box below). However, after these accomplishments, the group did not reconvene again until 2014 (Stark-Mason, 2015). Currently, the Gender-Equity Task Force is a standing advisory group. Their findings and recommendations are presented annually to the NCAA president and Executive Committee, NCAA Division I Board of Directors, and the Committee on Women's Athletics. Current issues of interest that are likely to be addressed by the task force include implementing quality campus gender-equity plans, supporting the growth and retention of women coaches, education and prevention of sexual assault, and inclusion-centric hiring and retention practices (NCAA, 2018b).

> ## Emerging sport program
>
> Upon recommendation of the 1994 Gender-Equity Task Force, the NCAA created a list of emerging sports for women to help athletics departments increase participation opportunities. The list initially included nine emerging sports: archery, badminton, bowling, ice hockey, rowing, squash, synchronized swimming, team handball, and water polo. As of 2018, three of the original sports and two others have risen to championship status including beach volleyball, rowing, ice hockey, water polo, and bowling, whereas others have been added or removed from the list. Current emerging sports include equestrian, rugby, and triathlon. For a sport to rise to "emerging sport" status, it must meet the NCAA definition of a sport, cite 20 or more existing varsity or competitive club teams on college campuses, and demonstrate governing body support at the high school, professional, coach association, conference, or Olympic level. Once on the list, an emerging sport has 10 years to demonstrate steady progress toward championship status or meet the championship status requirement of being sponsored by 40 programs, with the exception of Division III only requiring 28 programs for team sports.

Gender-equity plans

Some keys to developing a successful and positive gender-equity plan include education, commitment, and communication (NCAA, 2018c). For the education component, the athletic department should assist people in understanding gender equity and Title IX because understanding facilitates commitment. Commitment should be modeled and encouraged by members of the athletic department and administrators across campus. Finally, communication should be constant and constructive. One suggestion for improved communication is the creation of an institution-based gender-equity committee with members coming from various parts of campus and offering diverse perspectives and experiences.

Women coaches

One recurring issue is the lack of women coaches coaching women's sport, which translates into mentorship and education about Title IX for female athletes (Staurowsky & Weight, 2011). Since the merger of the AIAW and the NCAA, the number of women coaching women's college teams has declined from 90% to a mere 40% (LaVoi & Silva-Breen, 2018). The trend of men replacing women as head coaches does not appear to be fading. From 2000 to 2014, NCAA schools created over 2,000 new head coaching jobs in women's sports, and over 65% of them went to men (Brown, 2016). These continued inequities certainly warrant consideration by the Gender-Equity Task Force.

Sexual assault education and prevention

With the recent exposure of sexual assault cases on university campuses nationwide involving several athlete-centric cases, this is an area the task force can embrace in an effort to address a critical need to facilitate clear systems that effectively punish perpetrators, protect victims, and encourage compliance with appropriate legislation. The task force could champion effective educational prevention programs and arrange speaking engagements to assist in educating the public and their campus community, not just those in athletics. It would also behoove the task force to have a current member who is an expert in the field of sexual assault, such as a researcher or mental health professional who specializes in the area.

Hiring and retention

A final area to consider is the need for a deliberate and intentional method that current college sport leaders can use to continue to grow the pool of qualified women interested in working in intercollegiate athletic administration. One SWA interviewed for this chapter put it this way:

> First starting out, it is hard to know what opportunities are available when you mostly see males working the jobs you want. Some women end up settling because they don't think they can get a particular job because only a man has held that position.

Women Leaders in College Sports (WLCS) is an organization that has been proactive in the development of future women leaders through education, leadership training, job posting, and networking opportunities (see https://www.womenleadersincollegesports.org). The development and cultivation of this education and mentorship network, consisting of women leaders in college sport, will help to support the next generation of women leaders. With more empowered women at the table, issues concerning gender inequities for athletes and leaders can be addressed through their unique voice.

Financial streams and fan support

As a governing body the NCAA is supported almost entirely by the television and marketing rights of the Division I Men's Basketball Championship. The Division I College Football Playoff (CFP) is also quite lucrative. However, it is independently operated, and the NCAA does not receive revenue from these events, though revenue is given to CFP-affiliated conferences. Of the 90 championship events that are sponsored by the NCAA, only 5 break-even or make a profit. Each of these is a men's sport (basketball, ice hockey, lacrosse, wrestling, and baseball) (Figure 25.3). At the campus level, the revenue streams are also driven predominantly by men's sports. As an example, in the 2018 Revenues and Expenses Report compiled by the NCAA, the Division I-Football Bowl Subdivision (most lucrative and expensive division) reported there were no women's programs where revenues exceeded expenses. This is down from 2004, when 3% of the women's basketball programs generated revenue. Conversely, 54% of football programs and 47% of men's basketball programs generate revenue greater than their expenses. As a result of the critical importance of financial sustainability within institutions of higher education that house intercollegiate athletics, and the ever-increasing costs to compete in college sport, many financial decisions are focused on how to maximize revenue, which translates into how to facilitate the competitive success of the men's basketball and football teams. As such, far more money is spent on men's sports than women's sports in every expense category (Fulks, 2016).

Only five NCAA championships (all in Division I) generate more money than they cost to run. There are 90 NCAA championships in total.

Despite college sport getting closer to achieving gender equity in sport participation, true equity will likely continue to elude most college athletic programs as long as the vast disparities remain in fan interest and financial support, which is predicated on sport

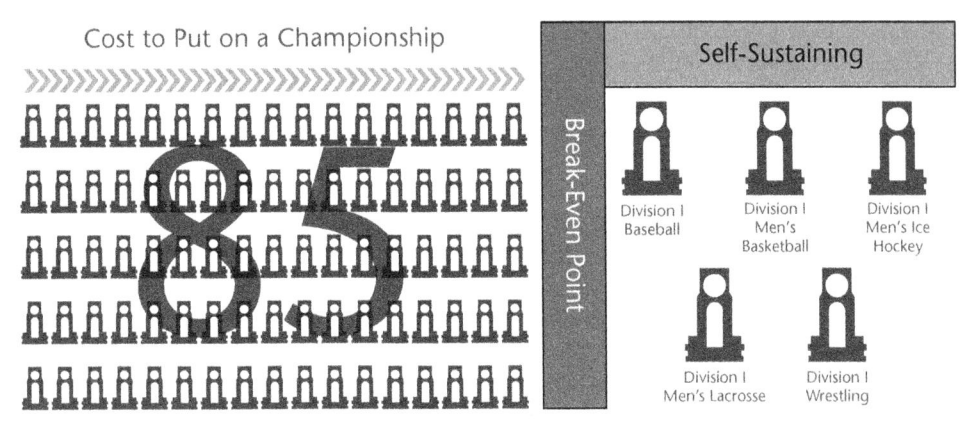

Figure 25.3 Profitable NCAA championships

visibility, marketing, and access. Unfortunately, research has demonstrated consistent and vastly inequitable coverage, promotion, and portrayal of women's sport, both on internally controlled websites, and in media outlets (e.g., Cahn, 2015; Cunningham, 2003; Eagleman, 2015; Fink, 2015; Rubin & Lough, 2015). The general shoulder-shrugging sentiment that has been pervasive since the inception of women's sport in the NCAA is evident in the following passage from the 1996 NCAA Gender-Equity Manual, with the concluding sentence reflecting the looming, but to-date ineffective threat of Title IX:

> Institutions typically have understaffed and under-funded sports information and marketing departments . . . . A common complaint by the women's teams is that they do not feel that they are provided the same level of marketing support as the men's teams . . . . A common institutional response is "market driven." In short, some Sports Information Directors believe they need to invest their limited resources in the areas that will generate the largest return on their investment. For many institutions, this means investing money and personnel in the marketing of the football and men's basketball team. Although this argument may be understandable from a business perspective, it fails to incorporate an institution's obligations under federal law.
>
> *(NCAA, 1996, p. 56–57)*

As long as there is a general industry belief that women's sports are a poor use of limited resources, and marketing efforts are funneled into the two sports and one gender that have historically demonstrated revenue potential, we are likely not going to witness significant change. Addressing efforts on how and why women's collegiate sport continues to struggle in expanding fan interest, and how to advance women's collegiate sport via fan support in the future, we now transition to an in-depth glimpse into two sports with revenue-generating potential.

Women's basketball

In the 2015–2016 season, 4,993 Division I female athletes competed in women's college basketball, a 17% increase since its addition to the NCAA's championship program in 1981–1982. Between 1990 and 2010, attendance and media interest increased in women's basketball, resulting in more viewership than any other women's intercollegiate sport (Ackerman, 2013); however. recent trends demonstrate that this growth is waning. Some critics believe this trend stems from the small number of women's college basketball programs achieving the highest level of competitive success; only 16 different teams in the last 20 years have played in the NCAA Women's Final Four championship game. Additional hypotheses include the limited media coverage provided for all women's sports, including women's college basketball. Research done by the Tucker Center for Research on Girls and Women in Sport found that, although 40% of athletes are female, only 4% of all sport media coverage is focused on women's sport (Tucker Center, 2013). When women's games are broadcast, they usually go head to head with the National Basketball Association (NBA) and men's college teams, causing them to get lost in the shuffle (Ackerman, 2013). Many female sport administrators have led the charge in efforts to grow and advance women's basketball, including Val Ackerman, Big East Conference Commissioner, and Tracie Hitz, NCAA Director of Championships and Alliances.

In 2013, Val Ackerman (see Leader profile) published the Division I Women's Basketball White Paper, a summary report of historical data, interviews, feedback, and observations on the landscape of Division I women's basketball. According to Ackerman, the overriding theme of the report was a "tremendous appetite for change in the way Division I women's basketball is played, marketed and managed" (Ackerman, 2013, p. 16).

To this end, Ackerman suggested a repositioning of women's basketball, with a focus on two tracks: the Heritage Track and the Innovation Track. While the former focuses on how to excel in shooting and ball handling, engage with fans, and lead women's college sport, the latter track highlights the uniqueness of women's basketball to jump-start a new age of growth for the sport (Ackerman, 2013, p. 33). Issues raised, such as the need for increased attendance through better marketing, along with incorporating more "high caliber sports business people," are addressed in a pilot program, titled the Women's Basketball Advancement Program, implemented by the NCAA in 2017. The committee, under Tracie Hitz, the Director of Championships and Alliances for the NCAA, consists of professionals with sport administration backgrounds who work with for-profit companies (NCAA, 2017b). These administrators serve as mentors to their institution's women's basketball programs and as liaisons with the NCAA committee pursuing the following goals: unite women's basketball programs, create one voice, improve marketing and branding best practices, and increase both game attendance and viewership (NCAA, 2017b).

The NCAA deemed the first year of the program a success with 20 participating schools seeing an increase in women's basketball attendance numbers (Nixon, 2018). In the 2018–2019 season, 30 schools participated in the second year of the pilot program. As these efforts continue, it will be important to monetize the increasing interest. Currently, as mentioned above, the financial bottom line for women's basketball is insufficient. Revenue generally rests on ticket sales, which are priced at low levels, leaving returns at a minimum. Diversifying the fan base to increase ticket sales and attendance has been described as a major and continuing priority by those working in the business of women's college basketball.

Softball

Softball is arguably one of the fastest-growing women's college sports with 6,042 athletes competing at the Division I level—more participants than women's college basketball. The interest sparked in college softball is in part due to media rights deals with ESPN, especially pertaining to the Women's College World Series (WCWS). ESPN began covering the WCWS in 2001. The 2015 and 2016 WCWS made national headlines because there were more viewers tuning in to watch women than the men's College World Series, their counterpart (Nyatawa, 2017). In 2017, both the men and the women broke viewership records when ESPN decided to broadcast most of the games on its main channel instead of ESPNU or ESPN2, and, in 2018, there was a slight decline in WCWS viewership, whereas the men hit their highest ratings since 2012 (Sports Media Watch, 2018). Over the last decade, players have improved, especially their speed and agility, making softball a more valuable product to air (Brunt, 2015). ESPN executives state that the faster-paced style of play and increased scoring, along with the fervor and excitement around the sport, especially during the WCWS, all appeal to the viewers at home and help keep fans engaged. Broadcasting the game showcases the positive attributes of the sport, which in turn helps softball grow as a sport. With more televised games, there are more opportunities for young female athletes to grow up watching, learning, and interacting with the sport of softball.

Growing women's sport

As we reflect on lessons learned from women's basketball and softball, it is clear that a combination of events, platforms, and initiatives is needed to grow women's sport. The NCAA, an individual sport, a piece of legislation, or any individual governing body do not have the innate power to transform the culture of sport participation and consumption, but, in concert, miraculous shifts can occur. In order for women's collegiate sport to make strides in generating fan support and engagement, and succeeding from a business perspective, the following actions are recommended:

- Improve the marketing of women's sport to create consistent messaging, generate excitement, and improve the fan experience.
- Focus on maximizing viewership of televised games, especially during the NCAA tournament and championship. The current Sunday/Tuesday game format is not desirable for fans and therefore not succeeding in the efforts to increase attendance and viewership. This model incorporates two weekdays, which makes it challenging for fans, especially families, to attend games due to work or school obligations. Women's sports are known to appeal to families, including children and parents as fans, so the current schedule compromises accessibility and the status of the sport as being fan friendly. Switching the format to Friday/Sunday offers the potential to put more fans in the stands, create new fans, and expand viewership through games broadcasts nationally.
- Combine business and marketing efforts for all women's sports. Bring coaches and administrators together to focus on current issues and outline strategies to address them. Creating connections between sports will reduce silos and barriers that prevent efficient use of resources and shared knowledge.
- Creating a sense of camaraderie within the athletic department, in which all coaches and athletes promote and support each other.
- Create ticket packages showcasing a variety of women's sports; offer the opportunity to appeal to more people, increase exposure for the less marketed sports such as field hockey and swimming, and bring in more fans to the larger women's sports of basketball and softball.

As research on the effects of participation in sport document the life-long impact competitive sport can have on an athlete's life (e.g., Weight, Bonfiglio, DeFreese, Kerr, & Osborne, 2018; Weight, Navarro, Smith-Ryan, & Huffman, 2016), it is increasingly important to maintain judiciousness in retaining and expanding opportunities for women to compete at the collegiate level. In addition to the positive impacts sport can have on post-graduation life satisfaction, long-term mental health, work engagement, and salary (e.g., Weight et al., 2016, 2018), participation in college sport can facilitate a pipeline for future industry leaders. As such, it is critical to fortify the programs and laws that support growth in collegiate women's sport and governance including Title IV and IX, the NCAA's Gender-Equity Task Force and Women Leaders in College Sport.

Acquiring resources will continue to be an evolving challenge in college athletics, making it increasingly necessary for coaches and administrators to act as entrepreneurs, financial guardians, and organizational stewards of women's sport. We must advocate for improved marketing and media coverage to generate financial support on a par with men's "revenue" sports and strive to achieve steady growth in participation numbers. In addition, we should seek to facilitate a culture within the industry that attracts, nurtures, and advances women coaches and leaders. Focusing on the sustainability of college women's sport and its continued growth requires a commitment to true gender equity, and the realization that opportunities to participate in sport equate to educational experiences that can propel and inspire generations of women. As we have learned from the history of the AIAW, which was dissolved, and Title IX, which has largely been under attack since inception, current governance structures do not guarantee future opportunities or experiences; as such, we must be mindful of what is, and what could be, the best governance structure to facilitate education through athletics.

Leadership profile: Val Ackerman, Commissioner, Big East Conference

Val Ackerman is the commissioner of the Big East Conference, and previously served as the founding president of the Women's National Basketball Association (WNBA) and President of USA Basketball, overseeing both the women's and the men's Olympic programs. She is an attorney and was a stand-out basketball player at the University of Virginia, where she served as a three-year captain and was the school's first basketball player to score 1,000 points. She graduated with a degree in political and social thought in 1981 and played one year of professional basketball in France before earning a law degree from UCLA in 1985. She has been widely recognized for her contributions to the sport industry and is one of the few leaders who has overseen both men's and women's sport at the collegiate, professional, national, and international levels.

After serving as a corporate and banking associate in a New York law firm, she joined the NBA in 1988 as a staff attorney and special assistant to the NBA commissioner David Stern. She then earned a series of promotions to Director. then Vice President of Business Affairs. before being named the WNBA's first President in 1996. After successfully launching the league in 1997, she oversaw operations for its first eight seasons before being elected President of USA Basketball for the 2005–2008 term.

Under her stewardship, USA basketball had an overall competitive record of 222-23, and two gold medals by both the men and the women in the 2008 Beijing Olympics. Ackerman also served two terms (2006–2010 and 2010–2014) as the US representative for men's and women's basketball on the Central Board of the International Basketball Federation (FIBA), the sport's world governing body. She has been widely recognized for her work and continues to serve in a variety of capacities to strengthen sport at every level.

References

Ackerman, V. (2013). Division I women's basketball white paper prepared for the NCAA, June 15. Retrieved from https://www.ncaa.org/sites/default/files/NCAAWBBWHITEPAPER_0.pdf.

Acosta, R. V. & Carpenter, L. J. (1992). As the years go by—Coaching opportunities in the 1990s. *Journal of Physical Education, Recreation & Dance*, **63**(3), 36–41.

Acosta, R. V. & Carpenter, L. J. (2014). Women in intercollegiate sport: A longitudinal, national study—thirty-seven year update—1977–2014. Unpublished manuscript. Available from www.acostacarpenter.org.

Brown, A. (2016). A man's game: Inside the inequality that plagues women's college sports. *Reveal*, May 5. Retrieved from: https://www.revealnews.org/article/a-mans-game-inside-the-inequality-that-plagues-womens-college-sports.

Bruening, J. E. & Dixon, M. A. (2008). Situating work–family negotiations within a life course perspective: Insights on the gendered experiences of NCAA Division I head coaching mothers. *Sex Roles*, **58**, 10–23.

Brunt, C. (2015). Women's softball grows as exposure, crowds increase. *USA Today*. Retrieved from https://www.usatoday.com/story/sports/college/softball/2015/06/01/womens-softball-grows-as-exposure-crowds-increase/28307743.

Burton, L., Grappendorf, H., & Henderson, A. (2011). Perceptions of gender in athletic administration: Utilizing role congruity to examine (potential) prejudice against women. *Journal of Sport Management*, **25**, 36–45.

Cahn, S. K. (2015). *Coming on Strong: Gender and sexuality in women's sport*. Champaign, IL: University of Illinois Press.

Cunningham, G. B. (2003). Media coverage of women's sport: A new look at an old problem. *Physical Educator*, **60**(2), 43.

Cunningham, G. B. (2008). Creating and sustaining gender diversity in sport organizations. *Sex Roles*, **58**, 136–145.

Dixon, M. & Sagas, M. (2007). The relationship between organizational support, work-family conflict, and the job-life satisfaction of university coaches. *Research Quarterly for Exercise and Sport*, **78**, 236–247.

Eagleman, A. N. (2015). Constructing gender differences: Newspaper portrayals of male and female gymnasts at the 2012 Olympic Games. *Sport in Society*, **18**(2), 234–247.

Fink, J. S. (2015). Female athletes, women's sport, and the sport media commercial complex: Have we really "come a long way, baby"? *Sport Management Review*, **18**(3), 331–342.

Fulks, D. L. (2016). *NCAA Division I Intercollegiate Athletics Programs Report, 2004–2015: Revenues and expenses*. Indianapolis, IN: National Collegiate Athletic Association.

Grappendorf, H. & Lough, N. (2006). An endangered species: Characteristics and perspectives from female NCAA Division I athletic directors of both separate and merged athletic departments. *Sport Management and Related Topics Journal*, **2**(2), 6–10.

Greenhill, J., Auld, C., Cuskelly, G., & Hooper, S. (2009). The impact of organizational factors on career pathways for female coaches. *Sport Management Review*, **12**, 229–240.

Inglis, S., Danylchuk, K. E., & Pastore, D. L. (1996). Understanding retention factors in coaching and athletic management positions. *Journal of Sport Management*, **10**, 237–249.

Inglis, S., Danylchuk, K. E., & Pastore, D. L. (2000). Multiple realities of women's work experiences in coaching and athletic management. *Women in Sport and Physical Activity Journal*, **9**(2), 1–26.

Irick, E. (2015) *NCAA Sports Sponsorship and Participation Rates Report*. Indianapolis, IN: National Collegiate Athletic Association .

Kilty, K. (2006). Women in coaching. *Sport Psychologist*, **20**, 222–234.

Lapchick, R., Hoff, B., & Kaiser, C. (2010). *The 2010 Racial and Gender Report Card: College sport*. Orlando, FL: The Institute for Diversity and Ethics in Sport.

LaVoi, N. M. & Silva-Breen, H. (2018). *Head Coaches of Women's Collegiate Teams: A comprehensive report on NCAA Division-I institutions, 2017–18*. Minneapolis, MN: Tucker Center for Research on Girls & Women in Sport.

Lough, N. (2001). Mentoring connections between coaches and female athletes. *Journal of Physical Education, Recreation and Dance*, **72**(5), 30–33.

National Collegiate Athletic Association (1996). *Achieving Gender Equity: A basic guide to Title IX and gender equity in athletics for colleges and universities*. Indianapolis, IN: NCAA.

National Collegiate Athletic Association (2009). 2008–2009 NCAA perceived barriers report: Gender equity in college coaching and administration. Retrieved from www.ncaapublications.com/productdownloads/BAR09.pdf.

National Collegiate Athletic Association (2017a). Optimization of the senior woman administrator designation. Retrieved from www.ncaa.org/sites/default/files/2018SWA_17-NCAA-1984_InclusionsSWAReport-20180402.pdf.

National Collegiate Athletic Association (2017b). Women's Basketball Advancement Program Overview, October 9. Retrieved from: https://www.ncaa.org/sites/default/files/2018DIWBKB_AdvancementProgramOverview_20171006.pdf.

National Collegiate Athletic Association (2018a). Gender equity and Title IX. Retrieved from www.ncaa.org/about/resources/inclusion/gender-equity-and-title-ix.

National Collegiate Athletic Association (2018b). Gender Equity Task Force. Retrieved from www.ncaa.org/governance/committees/gender-equity-task-force.

National Collegiate Athletic Association (2018c). Gender Equity planning best practices. Retrieved from www.ncaa.org/sites/default/files/Final%2Bonline%2Bversion.pdf.

Nixon, R. (2018). *Women's Basketball Advancement Program Participants for 2018–2019 Announced.* Indianapolis, IN: NCAA.

Nyatawa, J. (2017). College World Series draws millions of viewers, best ratings in years. *Omaha World-Herald*. Retrieved from https://www.omaha.com/sports/cws/college-world-series-draws-millions-of-viewers-best-ratings-in/article_a57ed84a-0bad-5752-8d3d-e440a4e40374.html.

Rubin, L. M. & Lough, N. L. (2015). Perspectives of Title IX pioneers: Equity, equality and need. *Journal of Intercollegiate Sport*, **8**(2), 109–130.

Sports Media Watch (2018). Women's College World Series Ratings. Retrieved from www.sportsmediawatch.com/tag/womens-college-world-series-ratings.

Stark-Mason, R. (2015). Reformed group aims to tip scales on equity. *NCAA Championship Magazine*, July 21. Retrieved from www.ncaa.org/champion/reformed-group-aims-tip-scales-equity.

Suggs, W. (2005). *A Place on the Team: The triumph and tragedy of Title IX*. Princeton, NJ: Princeton University Press.

Staurowsky, E. J. & Weight, E. A. (2011). Title IX literacy: What coaches don't know and need to find out. *Journal of Intercollegiate Sport*, **4**(2), 190–209.

Tucker Center (2013). *Media Coverage & Female Athletes*. Retrieved from https://video.tpt.org/video/tpt-co-productions-media-coverage-female-athletes.

Weaver, M. A. & Chelladurai, P. (2002). Mentoring in intercollegiate athletic administration. *Journal of Sport Management*, **16**, 96–116.

Weight, E.A., Bonfiglio, A., DeFreese, J.D., Kerr, Z., & Osborne, B. (2018). Occupational measures of former NCAA athletes and traditional students. *International Journal of Sport Management*, **19**(2), 1–26.

Weight, E.A., Navarro, K., Smith-Ryan, A., & Huffman, L. (2016). Holistic education through athletics: Health literacy of intercollegiate athletes and traditional students. *Journal of Higher Education Athletics and Innovation*, **1**, 38–60.

Wushanley, Y. (2004). *Playing Nice and Losing: The struggle for control of women's intercollegiate athletics 1960–2000*. Syracuse, NY: Syracuse University Press.

Yiamouyiannis, A. (2008). Occupational closure in intercollegiate athletics: Female head coaches of men's sport teams at NCAA colleges, Doctoral dissertation, George Washington University, Washington, DC. Retrieved from Proquest Digital Dissertations Database.

Yiamouyiannis, A. (2009). Gender equity, sport sponsorship, and participation. *New Directions for Institutional Research*, **144**, 43–52.

Yiamouyiannis, A. & Osborne, B. (2012). Addressing gender inequities in collegiate sport: Examining female leadership representation within NCAA sport governance. *Sage Open*, **2**(2), https//doi.org/10.1177/2158244012449340.

26
The evolution of women's rugby

Brittany Jacobs and Nicole Sellars

Utilizing an international perspective, this chapter explores the evolution of women's rugby by offering an in-depth review of its inception, expansion, and current success. Focusing on national and international sport organizations, this chapter addresses numerous areas of concern, including leadership challenges, women in governance, and future investment in women's rugby development. In addition, remarks on related issues of rugby participation and media coverage of women's rugby are made. Social role theory is used to frame the analysis, revealing the impact of sociological and cultural forces on women's rugby. By assessing the influence of societal structures and assumptions, the authors offer a foundation for understanding the historically difficult road faced by women in sport. The chapter is supplemented by a leader profile on Jennifer Gray, a World Rugby – Rugby Services Manager for North America, which emphasizes the importance of women in rugby as the sport grows within the larger sporting landscape.

No place for women in rugby

Women's rugby represents a unique sporting context in that the rules of the game are identical for both men and women. Despite the matching codes, the experiences of men and women within the rugby sporting structure have been markedly different since the sport's inception. Rugby is believed to originate from the Rugby School in England, where, in 1823, a student, disregarded the rules of soccer, picked up the ball in his arms, and ran with it, thus creating the distinctive feature of the game of rugby (Rookwood, 2003). From this point forward rugby grew rapidly in popularity and became known as an "establishment" sport for men and boys in England. Resulting from the gentile class that played the sport, rugby later became known as a "gentleman's sport," with a firm focus on the laws of the game and sportsmanship. It is important to note that the term "gentleman's sport" accurately describes the sporting environment of the time, because it was considered unladylike for women to participate in sport, particularly a sport with its foundation built on physical contact (Carle & Nauright, 1999). According to Hartmann-Tews and Pfister (2003, p. 267), "Views and values about sport have been androcentric right from the start, creating connotations of physical strength, muscularity, competition and masculinity," and rugby was no exception (Fields & Comstock, 2008).

Despite these presuppositions regarding who should participate in sport, there is record that, in 1887, at the Porta Royal School in Enniskillen, Northern Ireland, Emily Valentine played in an organized rugby match with her brothers (Palenski, 2015; World Rugby Museum, 2014). Unfortunately, her venture into the male-dominated rugby culture did not become a tipping point for women in rugby. In fact, during the same timeframe a women's rugby touring side was created in New Zealand, but, as a result of social pressures and public outcry, the team was disbanded before its first match (Crawford, 1987). Similarly, in England and France, women were reported to have played rugby in secret, because to do so in public would have been considered a faux pas. Nearly 100 years after rugby was invented, the first public women's rugby match was played at Cardiff Arms Park in Wales in 1917. The match featured the Cardiff Ladies competing against the Newport Ladies in the first public rugby match of its kind (Collins, 2015). Despite this foray into public play, women's rugby did not experience the growth seen by many other women's sports during this era (Lucas & Smith, 1982). Unlike tennis and golf, rugby was considered to be a sport too masculine for female participation, and those in the rugby community suggested that, if women were going to pursue sports at all, they, "should play soccer as it was a more feminine game than rugby" (Collins, 2015, p. 266). Decades later the masculine sentiments that surrounded the sport of rugby remained steadfast. In 1932 the President of the Rugby Football Union (RFU), England's governing body for rugby, noted that, "ours is a game not founded for women. It seems to me to be the only game today in which women cannot compete – thank goodness" (Collins, 2009, p. 91). These ideologies hindered women from entering what was considered to be a, "highly valued male terrain" (Thompson, 2003, p. 253) for years to come.

Social implications of women's rugby

Social role theory was developed in the latter half of the twentieth century as a way to ascribe specific social behaviors and characteristics to men and women. Typically associated with the division of labor, women have historically been assigned to communal, domestic, and feminine tasks, whereas men have been assigned a traditional gender role that is masculine, dominant, and agentic (Eagly, Wood, & Diekman, 2000). According to Hartmann-Tews and Pfister (2003, p. 8), "the social construction of gender produces a hierarchy and legitimizes marginalization and unequal treatment of women." In the case of sport, female athletes often abandon the traditional feminine social role in exchange for a more masculine one, where roles exist at the opposite ends of a gender spectrum and are mutually exclusive (Fallon & Jome, 2007; Hartmann-Tews & Pfister, 2003). A violation of this gender role is often met with criticism and discomfort because of cultural reliance on gender as an indicator of behavior. Take, for example, the influx of women into bodybuilding. Although the notoriety associated with female bodybuilding has grown in the last 20 years, a female athlete who is too bulky or muscular has, by society's standards, crossed over into the unsuitable realm of masculinity (McGrath & Chananie-Hill, 2009). Her hypermuscular physique leads society to assume she is a "mannish," steroid-using homosexual, regrettably blurring the lines across gender, sex, and sexuality (Halberstam, 1998; Lorber, 1996; Williams, 2000).

Women's rugby, like women's bodybuilding, is a sport in which women are ascribed to roles that are traditionally masculine. According to Potter (1999, p. 84), rugby "is diametrically opposed in its style and purpose to everything that traditional society has encouraged women to be." Female rugby players compete in the same game as male rugby players, including identical rules, the same high level of contact, and the same type of clothing (Howe, 2001). For male athletes, the expression of competitiveness, aggression, physical aptitude, and strength in rugby is assumed to be appropriate. For females playing the same game, those characteristics and behaviors are considered to be a disruption of their traditional, feminine gender role. Consequently, society's deeply held values reflected in social role theory have disadvantaged women's rugby by labeling players as rule-breakers and outsiders.

The image of women's rugby as a whole is also impacted by the values associated with social role theory. According to Howe (2001), the homo-negative mindset surrounding women's rugby has created an image issue. An already serious gender role violation by female rugby players to compete in a sport that is considered masculine is confounded by the assumption that women's rugby is strictly a lesbian sport. Thus, young female rugby players, sponsors, and fans may have a difficult time being associated with a sport that is not considered to be heteronormative. In the 1990s the Ladies Professional Golf Association (LPGA) suffered from being labeled as having a large lesbian fan base (Crossett, 1995; Howe, 2001). In an attempt to combat the homo-negative mindset and rebrand itself in the interest of sponsorship, the LPGA overtly celebrated and marketed the heterosexual relationships of its players, separating itself from lesbian fans. Intriguingly, the separation seems to have worked, and has likely contributed to the notable, long-term sponsorship success that the LPGA has experienced. Between 2016 and 2018, the LPGA signed more than 13 new marketing partners and eight title sponsors, including a string of agreements and extensions in early 2018 with companies such as Consumer Cellular, Dow Chemical Company, All Nippon Airways, and Umbel.

Women's rugby has not undergone such a rebranding to emphasize gender normality and, as an anti-establishment sport, some may argue that it should not. However, the growth and acceptance of women's rugby as an international sport is grounded in societal structures and ideals, as are all physical activities that generally marginalize women and look down on non-normative behaviors (Hartmann-Tews & Pfister, 2003). Thus, communities are inclined to discriminate against women's rugby because it challenges the traditional gender roles, behaviors, and characteristics that govern society. Intolerance is illustrated by the fact that women's rugby, especially in the United States, has had a difficult time attracting participants, viewers, and sponsors, and acquiring media coverage.

The emergence of women's rugby

Despite social pressures and stigmas, women's rugby finally began its rise to prominence in the 1960s. Women in the sport, although still maligned in much of the world, had begun to assert their right to play. As a result, rugby became an anti-establishment sport for women, where those looking to buck social and cultural norms found refuge. By 1972 four universities in the United States, Colorado State University, University of Colorado, University of Missouri, and University of Illinois, housed women's rugby teams, and the passage of Title IX that same year facilitated opportunities for women to participate in school-sanctioned sport (Brake, 2012; Nauright & Parrish, n.d.). In 1987 the USA women's national team was created and competed in their first match against Canada. This match was sanctioned by both the Canadian and the American Rugby Unions, making it the first internationally sanctioned women's rugby test match for either nation. Despite the progress made for women in sport to this point, the US Women's Rugby team was not permitted to wear the Eagle logo, which was considered to be the exclusive mark of the men's national team. As women's rugby in North America flourished throughout the 1980s, it was also gaining significant traction in the rest of the world. Thus, the creation of an international competition, the Women's Rugby World Cup, was a logical next step.

The first Women's Rugby World Cup (WRWC), held in Cardiff in 1991, was not sanctioned by the international governing body for the sport of rugby, the International Rugby

Board (IRB). In fact, the IRB refused to recognize the tournament and threatened to pursue copyright infringement lawsuits if their Rugby World Cup Logo was used (Bannerman, 2017). Despite the mounting odds, Deborah Griffin, Sue Dorrington, Alice Cooper, and Mary Forsyth – four players from the Richmond Rugby club in London, UK – had their minds set on breaking barriers (Bannerman, 2017). With a small staff and tight budget, they planned the first Women's World Cup (Rugby Football Union, 2017). Twelve teams competed in this groundbreaking event. The lack of sponsorship prospects meant that the teams paid their own way to the competition. Ultimately, the United States took home the gold medal and the rugby teams proved that women, too, deserved an opportunity to participate in elite rugby competitions. A further sign of support for the growing women's game came when the Rugby Football Union (RFU) waived the £30,000 bill that had resulted from the Women's World Cup (Englandrugby.com, 2017; Hitt, 2017). Seven years later the IRB began recognizing and sanctioning the event, making 1998 the first "official" Women's Rugby World Cup (Nauright & Parrish, n.d.). The event has become increasingly successful, with the 2017 WRWC in Dublin being broadcast in 120 countries, and selling out the pool matches so quickly that capacity at some of the venues was increased. As such, the "Women's Rugby World Cup is now regarded as a key event in the global sporting calendar that has grown from an invitational tournament to one with a robust qualification process, live broadcast, good attendances and an enthusiastic worldwide following" (World Rugby, 2017c, p. 1). This massive international tournament has created a significant buzz for women's rugby worldwide and highlights the necessity of considering rugby within the larger social context of women's sport.

Rugby participation

The current landscape of rugby is drastically different now than ever before for both men and women. In 2007, World Rugby reported that around 2.6 million people played rugby worldwide. In 2014, that number had nearly quadrupled to 9.1 million global competitors (World Rugby, 2016d). Although the growth of rugby at an international level is astonishing, there is a significant gap between the number of male players and the number of female players. Of the total 7.23 million registered and unregistered rugby players in the world in 2014, only 1.76 million were women. This begs the question, why aren't more females playing rugby?

Known during its beginnings as a gentleman's sport, rugby has had a seemingly difficult time garnering an international female representation comparable to other sports. To put participation numbers into perspective, approximately 6.5 million females played basketball in 2011 in America alone (Sports & Fitness Industry Association, 2012). Lemez, MacMahon, and Weir (2016) state that, in New Zealand, rugby yielded the highest sport participation numbers among secondary school students at 38,132. In a country with 148,483 registered rugby players in 2014, the proportion of children playing rugby in New Zealand is impressive to say the least. Lemez et al. (2016) suggest that the variance in youth participation is likely due to the exposure children have to a certain sport at a young age. In Canada, for example, where soccer is the leading participatory sport with over 850,000 registered players, children are likely exposed to soccer at an earlier age, which is reflected by participation numbers. The benefit of exposure as youth results in the opportunity to develop a specialized set of athletic skills, which can be improved throughout their adolescence and into college-age play. In addition, a lack of participation may be the result of the framing of women's rugby as an anti-establishment sport, void of gender conformity. For young women looking for athletic opportunities, the negative stigma associated with rugby may deter interest and, instead, steer female athletes toward heteronormative sports.

The National Collegiate Athletic Association (NCAA) has classified rugby as an emerging women's sport since 2002 (Lemez et al., 2016). Estimates of female rugby participation in the United States by the NCAA hover around 14,000, including both high school and college players. As an emerging sport, however, women's rugby is not solidified into intercollegiate athletic programs. Rather, the emergence means that the NCAA could, if they choose to, add rugby as a sanctioned championship sport when at least 40 varsity rugby programs exist (NCAA, n.d.). The trouble for many rugby programs is that, in addition to fighting for existence and funding, media attention is difficult to attain.

Media coverage of rugby, especially women's rugby, is scarce. Chase (2006) illuminated the lack of media attention given to women's rugby in the United States by stating, "Fox Sports World (now the Fox Soccer Channel) occasionally broadcasts rugby games . . . but the coverage of women's rugby is virtually nonexistent" (Chase, 2006, p. 230). Although rugby has grown since Chase's 2006 declaration, coverage of rugby, and specifically women's rugby, remains limited. If, as mentioned before, rugby participation is positively influenced by exposure at a young age, American rugby is at a disadvantage. At the international level, however, the popularity of rugby continues to rise. In 2016 women's rugby sevens was added to the summer Olympic Games in Rio De Janeiro, Brazil. This monumental event for the sport reflects how a blossoming relationship between national Olympic committees (NOCs) and World Rugby has begun to emerge (World Rugby, 2016a).

Rugby leadership

The lack of female leadership in rugby governance is an extension of the marginalization of female rugby competitors. Ryan and Dickson (2016) state that "from its inception, sport has been prudently segregated by gender, serving to normalize naturalistic views of the gendered body" (Dworkin & Messner, 1999, p. 4). In conjunction with the heteronormative customs related to competitive sport, men are more likely to be guided toward positions of leadership whereas women are pushed into supporting roles (Ryan & Dickson, 2016; Williams, 2013). Outlined in social role theory is the assumption that women should inhabit roles that are communal and subordinate whereas men maintain dominant roles. Sport organizations often reinforce this separation by placing men in situations where they are given the opportunity to influence decision-making and have authority and power over others. The trouble with practices like this is that women in sport organizations are left to watch from the sidelines as important decisions are made without their diverse input.

Cunningham and Sagas (2008) and Shaw and Frisby (2006) maintain that sports were created for able-bodied, white, heterosexual males. A deviation from this, then, would undermine the very foundation of sport. Although change is possible, there is concern that the marginalization of women in sport is based on taken-for-granted discourses. Alvesson and Billing (1997, p. 41) define discourses as socially constructed "statements, beliefs, and vocabularies . . . [where] certain beliefs are acted upon as true and therefore become partially true in terms of consequences." In sport organizations, discourses related to gender are reinforced and embedded, strengthening traditional gender roles that ascribe power to men (Hoeber, 2008). Discourses and norms become taken for granted when members of an organization no longer question them; they are perceived as true simply because they have been propagated and left uncontested (Cunningham, 2008).

The power and decision-making related to women's rugby has always been, and continues to be, in the hands of men. World Rugby (n.d.,a, p. 4) states that "a critical mass of around 30% representation" is needed for an optimum level of influence. So, for change to occur in women's rugby, 30% of its leadership should be female. Of the 20 organizations surveyed by World Rugby (n.d.,a), only one had female leadership representation above the 30% threshold. Instead of questioning discourses about females in authoritative positions in rugby, it seems that values of hegemony have been reinforced by the lack of promotion of women into leadership.

Investing in women's rugby

Despite the continued under-representation of women in rugby governance, World Rugby has set forth ambitious goals aimed at changing the landscape. According to the current strategic plan, World Rugby projects that:

> by 2025 rugby will be a global leader in sport, where women involved in rugby have equity on and off the field, are reflected in all strategy, plans and structures, making highly valued contributions to participation, performance, leadership and investment in the global game of rugby
>
> *(World Rugby, 2017c, p. 1)*

World Rugby has highlighted their commitment to women in rugby through the announcement of sweeping reform on their Council. The Council, which is the highest decision-making body within World Rugby, currently consists of 32 male representatives (World Rugby, n.d.,b). In an effort to expand the roles of women in the leadership and governance of rugby, the Council will be increased from 32 (male) members to 49 members, with the 17 new representatives to the council being women (World Rugby, 2017b). This new direction, with a strong focus on women's rugby, stems from the guidance of the Women's Advisory Committee. The Women's Advisory Committee was added to the World Rugby governance structure after previous reforms in 2015 (World Rugby, 2015). These monumental changes in governance and shifts in strategic focus underscore the importance of women's representation. The initial structural changes that created the Women's Advisory Committee have accentuated the importance of women's representation in rugby. As such, future developments can now include this perennially excluded group.

Female board members are incredibly important for the representation of women's issues but have also proven to be positively correlated with financial performance. Companies are 15% more likely to have financial returns above the national industry medians if they are in the top quartile for gender diversity (Hunt, Layton, & Prince, 2015). Beyond financial indicators of success, female board members have also been shown to be vigilant in board oversight which has shown to contribute to improved corporate governance (International Labor Organization, 2015). Thus, the drastic overhaul of the World Rugby Council has the potential to significantly impact the organization and, subsequently, other national rugby governing bodies. The Women's Rugby Leadership Council in the United States has recently lobbied for 35% female representation on their board and established a Women's Rugby Coaches Association, the first professional organization of its kind in American rugby (Rugby Americas North, 2017). Furthermore, both World Rugby and USA Rugby have added a General Manager of Women's Rugby to their organizational hierarchy (USA Rugby, 2017; World Rugby, 2016b), and the Australian Rugby union has appointed their first female Chief Executive Officer (CEO) who took office on January 15, 2018 (Australian Associated Press, 2017).

Rugby professionals are finally beginning to see women in rugby as an opportunity rather than a risk. These changes are timely as women's rugby continues to grow and become a tremendously marketable sporting property. According to the Chairman of World Rugby's Women's advisory committee, Bill Pulver, there were more new women playing the game of rugby than men in 2016 (World Rugby, 2017a). Beyond this, World Rugby notes that the women's game is growing at a rate of seven times that of the men's game (World Rugby, 2017a). With prolific growth, financial investment and media support of women's rugby must also increase. The success of the 2017 Women's Rugby World Cup in Dublin has led to Eurosport and NBC agreeing to broadcast the 2023 Women's Rugby World Cup. These broadcast partners are incredibly important to increasing awareness and legitimizing women's rugby as a viable investment opportunity.

Although stigma and social barriers still remain in many parts of the world, the changes in rugby's global governance indicate a willingness to grow and adapt. Beyond this, the participation numbers and recent trends in sponsorship indicate significant growth potential for women's rugby and create a sport rife with opportunity. It is now up to current and future sport managers to develop techniques to capitalize on the current momentum and to establish women's sport, specifically rugby, as a valuable entity in the sporting marketplace.

Leadership profile: Jennifer Gray – Regional Services Manager, World Rugby

Career in sport business

Having played rugby in college, Gray saw, firsthand, the lack of organizational and financial support afforded to her program. On entering the world of sport business, Gray knew that she

Figure 26.1 Jennifer Gray

wanted to be a part of the solution. She is now one of six Regional Rugby Services Managers working for World Rugby. She is the first American to have held one of these roles and is currently the only female to hold such a role. As a Rugby Services Manager, Gray oversees the Rugby Americas North Region, serving as a liaison between the region and World Rugby, and facilitating strategic development and planning. Before her work as a Regional Services Manager, she spent over 10 years working for USA Rugby. She began work with USA Rugby in the Referee Development Department, later led the Events Department, and ultimately served as the Director of Operations, overseeing all facets of business and game development operations. She has also worked as an editor and in a sports information department.

Suggestions for sport business professionals

Through these sport business experiences, Gray has found that it is incredibly important to have the confidence to back oneself. "If you have been hired for a role, you have the requisite knowledge and skills to get the job done," she says. "Trust yourself and what you know" (J. Gray, personal communication, December 5, 2017). As a young professional or someone moving into a new role, it can be easy to be overcome by self-doubt, but one cannot discount the contributions that you may be able to make to a sporting organization. To facilitate confidence in a new role or workplace Ms. Gray suggests that seeking good mentors can be invaluable. In most instances individuals will have to reach out to potential mentors – and be prepared for many to say no – but, once a good mentor has been found, they can be a limitless system of support.

Professional accomplishments

The value that Gray places on having a mentor is also reflected as she speaks about one of her biggest professional accomplishments. According to Gray, "building a culture of support and growth at USA Rugby was incredibly important to me. As a smaller NGB [national governing body] my colleagues and employees filled numerous roles and wore many hats, creating a culture that empowered employees to learn and grow and watching employees progress was one of my biggest professional accomplishments" (J. Gray, personal communication, December 5, 2017). She also noted that, being hired as the first American to fill one of the six Regional Services Manager positions for World Rugby, was a career highlight.

Inciting change in women's rugby

On reflecting on her career and her role within the rugby sporting context, Gray believes that numerous factors are necessary to start change. Within the amateur and Olympic structures change is slow and must be sought through the appropriate channels. Here it becomes important to understand the by-laws and charters of the organizations involved to petition for change. Inserting women into governance roles can help to advance change and encourage the inclusion of various viewpoints within the organizational system. Similarly, sport professionals must educate themselves so that they are fully aware of the opportunities that may exist or can help to create opportunity where opportunity is lacking. Ultimately, Gray suggests that female sport professionals must be persistent. As she says, "It only takes one yes" (J. Gray, personal communication, December 5, 2017). A single yes has the power to create a new role, change a governance structure, or cultivate funding, all of which can help to increase the stature of women's rugby.

The future of women in rugby

Within the last few years numerous positive changes have been made to facilitate the growth of women's rugby and to help ensure female representation in the governance of the game. World Rugby has recently voted to increase female representation on their Council to 34% (17 of 49 Council representatives). In her region (Rugby Americas North) incredible growth is also taking place. Gray said, "The World Cup Sevens will be hosted in San Francisco in 2018, which is a first for the region. At the grassroots level 45% of rugby participants in the 'Get into Rugby' program are women" (J. Gray, personal communication, December 5, 2017). Such monumental happenings suggest that "The future is wide open – it will be whatever we want to make it!" (J. Gray, personal communication, December 5, 2017).

Additional suggestions for success:

1   Have a global mindset – be a student of the world.
2   Relationships are important – build trust; to do so understand customs and traditions.
3   It does not matter where you come from – you can make a difference.

References

Australian Associated Press (2017). Raelene Castle becomes the first female chief executive of Rugby Australia, December 11. Retrieved from https://www.theguardian.com/sport/2017/dec/12/raelene-castle-set-to-be-first-female-chief-executive-of-rugby-australia.
Alvesson, M. & Billing, Y.D. (1997). *Understanding Gender and Organizations*. London: Sage.
Bannerman, L. (2017). Mary Forsyth, Sue Dorrington and Alice Cooper: The women who kicked off rugby World Cup, August 12. Retrieved from https://www.thetimes.co.uk/article/mary-forsyth-sue-dorrington-and-alice-cooper-the-women-who-kicked-off-rugby-world-cup-rczj5wrv2.
Brake, D. L. (2012). *Getting in the Game: Title IX and the women's sports revolution*. New York: NYU Press.
Carle, A. & Nauright, J. (1999). A man's game? Women playing rugby union in Australia. *Football Studies*, **2**(1), 55–73.
Chase, L. (2006). (un)disciplined bodies: A Foucauldian analysis of women's rugby. *Sociology of Sport Journal*, **23**(3), 229–247.
Collins, T. (2009). *A Social History of English Rugby Union*. London: Routledge.
Collins, T. (2015). *The Oval World: A global history of rugby*. London: Bloomsbury Publishing.
Crawford, S. (1987). One's nerves and courage are in very different order out in New Zealand: Recreational and sporting opportunities for women in a remote colonial setting, in J. A. Mangan & R. J. Park (eds), *From "Fair Sex" to Feminism*. London: Frank Cass.
Crossett, T. W. (1995). *Outsiders in the Clubhouse: The world of women's professional golf*. Albany, NY: SUNY Press.
Cunningham, G. B. (2008) Creating and sustaining gender diversity in sport organizations. *Sex Roles*, **58**(1), 136–145.
Cunningham, G.B. & Sagas, M. (2008). Gender and sex diversity in sport organizations: Introduction to a special issue. *Sex Roles*, **58**(1), 3–9.
Dworkin, S. & Messner, M. (1999) Just do . . . what?: Sport, bodies, gender. In M. M. Ferree, Lorber, J. & Hess, B. B. (eds), *Revisioning Gender*. Thousand Oaks, CA: Sage.
Eagly, A. H., Wood, W., & Diekman, A. B. (2000). Social role theory of sex differences and similarities: A current appraisal. In T. Eckes & H. M. Trautner (eds), *The Developmental Social Psychology of Gender* (pp. 123–174). Mahwah, NJ: Erlbaum.
Fallon, M. A. & Jome, L. M. (2007). An exploration of gender-role expectations and conflict among women rugby players. *Psychology of Women Quarterly*, **31**(3), 311–321
Fields, S. K. & Comstock, R. D. (2008). Why American women play rugby. *Women in Sport and Physical Activity Journal*, **17**(2), 8–18.
Halberstam, J. (1998). *Female Masculinity*. Durham, NC: Duke University Press.
Hartmann-Tews, I. & Pfister, G. (eds) (2003). *Sport and Women: Social issues in international perspective*. London: Routledge.

Hitt, C. (2017). The incredible journey women's rugby has taken to earn its place in the spotlight, August 9. Retrieved from www.walesonline.co.uk/news/news-opinion/incredible-journey-womens-rugby-taken-13451361.

Hoeber, L. (2008). Gender equity for athletes: Multiple understandings of an organizational value. *Sex Roles*, **58**(1), 58–71.

Howe, P.D. (2001). Women's rugby and the nexus between embodiment, professionalism and sexuality: an ethnographic account. *Football Studies*, **4**(2), 77–92.

Hunt, V., Layton, D., & Prince, S. (2015). *Diversity Matters*. London: McKinsey & Company.

International Labor Organization (2015). *Women on Boards: Building the female talent pipeline*. Geneva: International Labor Office.

Lemez, S., MacMahon, C., & Weir, P. (2016). Relative age effects in women's rugby union from developmental leagues to world cup tournaments. *Research Quarterly for Exercise and Sport*, **87**(1), 59–67.

Lorber, J. (1996). Beyond the binaries: Depolarizing the categories of sex, sexuality, and gender. *Sociological Inquiry*, **66**, 143–159.

Lucas, J. A. & Smith, R. A. (1982). Women's sport: A trial of equality. In R. Howell (ed.), *Her Story in Sport: A historical anthology of women in sports* (p. 239–265). West Point, NY: Leisure Press.

McGrath, S. A. & Chananie-Hill, R. A. (2009). "Big freaky-looking women": Normalizing gender transgression through bodybuilding. *Sociology of Sport Journal*, **26**(2), 235–254.

National Collegiate Athletic Association (NCAA) (n.d). Emerging sports for women. Retrieved from www.ncaa.org/about/resources/inclusion/emerging-sports-women.

Nauright, J. & Parrish, C. (n.d.). Cricket, rugby and soccer in the United States. Internal report, pp. 1–24. The Center for the Study of Sport and Leisure in Society – George Mason University.

Palenski, R. (2015). The lady footballers: Struggling to play in Victorian Britain [book review]. *Sporting Traditions*, **32**(1), 125.

Potter, J. (1999). Elegant violence? *Inside Rugby*, January.

Rookwood, D. (2003). A brief history of rugby, October 6. Retrieved from https://www.theguardian.com/sport/2003/oct/06/rugbyworldcup2003.rugbyunion6.

Rugby Americas North (2017). Former USA Eagle Kathy Flores on the state of the women's game, September 22. Retrieved from https://rugbyamericasnorth.com/former-usa-eagle-kathy-flores-state-womens-game.

Rugby Football Union (2017). The 1991 Women's Rugby World Cup trailblazers, August 1. Retrieved from www.englandrugby.com/news/features/the-1991-women-rugby-world-cup-trailblazers.

Ryan, I. & Dickson, G. (2016). The invisible norm: an exploration of the intersections of sport, gender and leadership. *Leadership*, **14**(3), 329–346.

Shaw, S. & Frisby, W. (2006). Can gender equity be more equitable?: Promoting an alternative frame for sport management research, education, and practice. *Journal of Sport Management*, **20**(4), 483–509.

Sports & Fitness Industry Association (2012). SGMA shows basketball is most played sport in US with 26.3 million participants. Retrieved from https://www.sfia.org/press/433_Over-26-Million-Americans-Play-Basketball.

Thompson, S. (2003). Women and sport in New Zealand. In I. Hartmann-Tews & G. Pfister (eds), *Sport and Women: Social issues in international perspective* (p. 252–265). London: Routledge.

USA Rugby (2017). USA Rugby appoints Emilie Bydwell as general manager of women's high performance, November 15. Retrieved from https://www.usarugby.org/2017/11/usa-rugby-appoints-emilie-bydwell-as-general-manager-of-womens-high-performance.

Williams, C. (2000). Hardcore: The radical self-portraiture of black female bodybuilders. In J. Frueh, L. Fierstein, & J. Stein (eds), *Picturing the modern Amazon* (pp. 104–116). New York: Rizzoli.

Williams, C. (2013). The glass escalator, revisited: Gender inequality in neoliberal times. *Gender and Society*, **27**(5), 609–629.

World Rugby (n.d.,a). Balancing the board: A toolkit to help increase women's representation on rugby boards. Retrieved from https://www.worldrugby.org/womens-rugby/development-plan?lang=en.

World Rugby (n.d.,b). World Rugby Council. Retrieved from https://www.worldrugby.org/organisation/structure/council?lang=en.

World Rugby (2015). Expanded game representation and independence at the heart of World Rugby governance reform. Retrieved from https://www.world.rugby/news/122987.

World Rugby (2016a). *Year in Review 2016*. Dublin, Ireland: World Rugby House.

World Rugby (2016b). Leading sports administrator appointed general manager for women's rugby, September 21. Retrieved from https://www.worldrugby.org/news/193715.

World Rugby (2016c). Women's Rugby World Cup 2017 overview, January 15. Retrieved from https://www.rwcwomens.com/tournament-overview.

World Rugby (2017a). World rugby women's plan 2017–25 [Video file], November 23. Retrieved from https://www.worldrugby.org/video/296303.

World Rugby (2017b). Beaumont hails historic governance reform to further gender balance in rugby, November 23. Retrieved from https://www.worldrugby.org/news/296055.

World Rugby (2017c). World Rugby Strategic Plan 2017–2025. Retrieved from https://www.worldrugby.org/womens-rugby/development-plan?lang=en.

World Rugby (2017d). *Year in Review 2017*. Dublin, Ireland: World Rugby House.

World Rugby Museum (2014). Emily Valentine – the first lady of rugby, August, 12. Retrieved from https://worldrugbymuseumblog.wordpress.com/2014/08/13/emily-valentine-the-first-lady-of-rugby.

27
Women and elite coaching in New Zealand
Challenges, benefits, and opportunities

Sarah Leberman and Jane Hurst

Introduction

New Zealand has a reputation of being a sporting nation. Sports such as rugby and netball have long been part of New Zealand culture and identity. Despite its small population of 4.8 million people (Statistics New Zealand, 2017), many New Zealand women athletes have achieved considerable success and recognition on the world sporting stage. In 2017, the Black Ferns, New Zealand's women's rugby team, won the Women's Rugby World Cup for the fifth time, and were crowned Rugby Team of the Year by the International Rugby Board (IRB). Other elite women athletes include Lisa Carrington, World and Olympic champion flatwater canoer, Sophie Pascoe, World and Paralympic champion swimmer, and Valerie Adams, World and Olympic champion shot putter. New Zealand also has internationally competitive female netball, hockey, football (soccer), and cricket teams. Their significant achievements on the world stage suggest that women's sport is in a strong position in New Zealand. However, scratching below this veneer of publicly celebrated success is a sporting environment that favors men.

Statistics demonstrate that New Zealand sport is a gendered domain. More boys and men participate in sport than women and girls (New Zealand Secondary Schools Sports Council, 2017; Sport New Zealand, 2015a). Although New Zealand has embraced professional sport, with a number of male sports teams competing in professional competitions both within New Zealand and overseas, there are no fully professional women's sports teams (Macdonald, 2017). At best, women participate at the elite level on a semi-professional basis, receiving relatively small retainers in comparison to the large salaries received by their male counterparts (Macdonald, 2017).

Gender discrepancies permeate all levels of New Zealand sport. Women remain under-represented at the governance and leadership level of most sporting organizations (Caldwell, 2017; Rainham, 2017). In New Zealand, steady progress has been made over the past 5 years, with 29 of New Zealand Olympic Committee-affiliated sporting organizations having 33% or more women board members in 2016. In contrast, women remain significantly under-represented at the elite coaching level. For example, at the 2008 Rio de Janiero and 2012 London Olympic Games, only 3 of the 43 New Zealand team coaches were women. Of the 44 coaches on the New Zealand team at the 2016 Rio Olympic Games, only 4 were women (Norman,

2017), despite the athlete gender representation being split 50/50. Although efforts are being made by New Zealand's national sporting agency, Sport New Zealand, as well as the country's various national sporting organizations, to increase female participation in sport generally, and to promote greater representation at the governance level, very little attention has been given to the paucity of women coaching at the elite level. This is concerning and an issue that needs specific attention and action if women are to participate fully at all levels of sport in New Zealand.

This chapter focuses on women in elite coaching, with reference to four team sports: cricket, hockey, football (soccer), and rugby union, all of which are played internationally by women. First, contextual information on the current status of women coaches in these sports in New Zealand is provided. Drawing on relevant literature, the challenges and opportunities faced by women coaches are then discussed. Finally, we conclude with recommendations for future research and action.

Current state of play in New Zealand

There are around 300,000 coaches in New Zealand, with most of these coaching at the foundation or grassroots level (Sport New Zealand Community Sport, 2016a). At the high performance or elite level, it is estimated that there are around 500 coaches (Sport New Zealand Community Sport, 2015). However, there is limited data available, particularly with respect to gender and ethnicity. Many national sports organizations have very little data about coaches and do not track coaches after they have completed training courses, resulting in a lack of information on the number of women coaching in New Zealand at any level. A survey in 2013 did conclude that, of the 6,000 adults surveyed, men were more likely than women to be volunteer coaches, with women more likely to be parent helpers (Sport New Zealand, 2015a).

In this section the national approach to the development of women coaches, as well as that adopted by four national sporting organizations, namely New Zealand Rugby, New Zealand Cricket, Hockey New Zealand, and New Zealand Football, is considered. Much of the information in this section has been sourced from publicly available reports and websites.

Sport New Zealand

The national approach to sport in New Zealand is governed by Sport and Recreation New Zealand (SNZ) under the Sport and Recreation New Zealand Act 2002. The purpose of this Act is to "promote, encourage, and support physical recreation and sport in New Zealand" (Sport and Recreation New Zealand Act 2002, section 3, see www.legislation.govt.nz/act/public/2002/0038/latest/DLM157117.html?src=qs) by establishing SNZ with the following functions, to:

(a) develop and implement national policies and strategies for physical recreation and sport;
(b) allocate funds to organizations and regional bodies in line with its policies and strategies;
(c) encourage participation in physical recreation and sport by Pacific peoples, women, older New Zealanders, and people with disabilities (Sport and Recreation New Zealand Act 2002, section 8, see www.legislation.govt.nz/act/public/2002/0038/latest/DLM157117.html?src=qs).

SNZ operates through three business arms: Community Sport, High Performance Sport New Zealand (HPSNZ), and Group Strategic Sport. It works with national sporting organizations to achieve the following strategic outcomes:

- More kids in sport and recreation;
- More New Zealanders involved in sport and recreation;
- More New Zealand winners on the world stage;
- Progress in all areas of a world-leading sport system (Sport New Zealand, 2015b, p. 31).

As part of developing a world-leading sport system, SNZ has as a strategic priority, working with national sporting organizations "to build world-leading coaching and high performance program leadership" (Sport New Zealand, 2015b, p. 26). This is further supported in its "High performance coaching plan 2011–2020" (High Performance Sport New Zealand [HPSNZ], 2011) and "Talent plan 2016–2020" (Sport New Zealand Community Sport, 2016b), which provide a focus on growing the coaching and leadership capability of coaches to provide high-performance athletes with the coaching they need to win. For example, the "Talent plan" promotes quality coaching as "crucial to long-term athlete success" and recognizes that "quality coaches understand the performance needs of the athlete and influence the people and the environment around the athlete" (Sport New Zealand Community Sport, 2016b, p. 6).

SNZ has a "Sport integrity framework" that has as a focus area "supporting diversity", recognizing that:

> Every Kiwi has the right to participate in sport and recreation within a welcoming and inclusive environment, and to be treated with respect, empathy and positive regard irrespective of age, ability, ethnicity, gender, national origin, race, religion, sexual orientation, political beliefs or socio-economic status.
>
> *(Sport New Zealand, n.d., p. 2)*

Despite the presence, functions, and strategic direction of SNZ, including the recognition of the importance of diversity, there is no national strategy or articulated strategic priority to encourage greater participation by women, at either the elite level of coaching or at the lower grassroots level, to create a pipeline of women in coaching. The strategies and plans simply do not address this issue. SNZ does support and promote greater participation by women at the governance level through a Women in Governance Program (Sport New Zealand, 2017b). HPSNZ runs a Coach Accelerator Program, which is designed to develop New Zealand coaches to become capable of producing world champions. However, although women have participated in this program, there were only five women (three from netball) selected for the program between 2014 and 2016, and, in 2017 only 2 of the 14 participants were women (High Performance Sport New Zealand, 2017). SNZ's diversity focus appears to be primarily aimed at increasing female participation at two levels: in playing sport and at the governance level, rather than the development of women coaches. Since 2010, there have been 157 carded coaches (highest level of coaches in New Zealand), of whom 32 (22%) have been women. Of these 22 are from netball and 5 from athletics.

Specific sports

In New Zealand, women are significantly under-represented in coaching women's national (elite) level rugby, hockey, football (soccer), and cricket. Only one of the four sports, cricket, has a female head coach of a women's national team. Three of the four sports, rugby, hockey, and football, have no women in their national coaching squads. As discussed below, there is a mixed strategic emphasis placed on increasing female participation in national or elite level coaching.

New Zealand Rugby

New Zealand has two elite women's rugby teams, namely the national team called the Black Ferns, and the Black Ferns Sevens, which competes in the Women's Sevens Series, a seven-a-side international rugby competition. Neither team is coached by women.

New Zealand Rugby's strategic plan (New Zealand Rugby, 2016) aims to increase participation in women's rugby to 21,000 by 2021 (from nearly 18,000 in 2014) and to have a clear coach development pathway for national teams (including the women's national team, the Black Ferns). It also aims to strengthen rugby in Auckland (New Zealand's largest city), with a strategic focus that "rugby is the sport of choice in wider Auckland" (New Zealand Rugby, 2016, p. 21). This includes a strategic measure to increase "female coaching numbers" in the Auckland area (New Zealand Rugby, 2015, p. 22). However, the strategy makes no mention of increasing the number of women coaches in other centers, such as Wellington and Christchurch, where women's rugby is also strong.

New Zealand Rugby has a strategy that specifically focuses on women's rugby: "This is our game: Women's rugby strategy 2015–2021" (New Zealand Rugby, 2015). This focuses on developing opportunities for women to play rugby. To support this, a dedicated team focused on women's rugby has been established, "tasked with creating opportunities for women to play which suit their needs and championing and building support for the women's game" (New Zealand Rugby, 2015, p. 10). Although it also recognizes the need to develop and retain the coaches to support women's rugby, it does not specifically focus on the development of women coaches at either the community or the elite level. It is unclear, therefore, what steps New Zealand rugby is taking to increase female participation in coaching at all levels, if any.

Hockey New Zealand

Field hockey in New Zealand has over 55,000 winter players, of whom 52% are women (Hockey New Zealand, 2017a). There is one elite-level women's team in New Zealand: the national women's team known as the Black Sticks Women, which has a male head coach and male assistant coaches. In 2016, there were over 5,400 active registered coaches, of whom 40 were coaching at the elite level (Hockey New Zealand, 2017a). However, it is unknown how many of these coaches are women.

Hockey New Zealand's strategic plan (Our 2020 strategy) has as a strategic goal, winning on the world stage, recognizing that "ultimately sport is about competing and winning" (Hockey New Zealand, 2016, p. 11). One stated way of achieving this is through a professional coaching pathway to develop a pool of national coaches (Hockey New Zealand, 2016). However, the strategy does not expand on how this will be implemented. A 2017 review found that there is a lack of a performance coaching program, which "results in an insufficient pool of great locally developed coaching talent available" (Hockey New Zealand, 2017c, p. 2). The strategy is also silent on the issue of developing women in coaching, particularly at the elite level. Therefore, although hockey has a wide appeal to women in New Zealand and gender equality is recognized as important by Hockey New Zealand, with the Board of Hockey New Zealand comprising six elected members (three men, three women) and two appointed members (Hockey New Zealand, 2017b), female participation in coaching appears to be a somewhat overlooked issue.

New Zealand Football

New Zealand Football, the governing body for football, has identified two strategic priorities specifically related to women in its strategic plan (New Zealand Football, 2016). The first is the development of women's football, with a goal of increasing participation from the current 27,000 participants to 33,000 by 2025. The second strategic priority is focused on the national women's team (called the Football Ferns), securing and maintaining a consistent top 10 FIFA ranking from 2019. The strategic plan recognizes the importance of investment in attracting, retaining, and developing coaches within the women's game, which includes full-time coaching staff for the women's national team. The strategic plan is supported by the "Whole of football plan" (New Zealand Football, 2017d), which specifically prioritizes an increase in the percentage of coaches which are women. Goals include:

- More qualified female coaches through women's specific courses;
- Better female coaches produced via the program mentoring (New Zealand Football, 2017d, p. 8).

In 2016, the Women's Football Committee was re-established. This committee is "responsible for advising and making strategic recommendations to the New Zealand Football Executive Committee on matters pertaining to women's football" (New Zealand Football, 2017a, p. 42). A Women's Development Manager leads the development of women's football. Attracting and retaining quality coaches has been identified as a key area of development (New Zealand Football, 2017d), with a recognition that, although a career in coaching is "now more appealing to women than it may have been in previous times, there is still a lack of females in coaching roles" (New Zealand Football, 2017b). To support this, women-only coaching courses have been run by New Zealand Football (New Zealand Football, 2017b). A 2017 women's only, senior level two, coaching course was attended by 32 women. In discussing this course, Women's Development Manager, Holly Nixon, emphasized the importance of developing women coaches:

> Women's football is a key strategic priority for New Zealand Football and developing female coaches is a vital part of that. We are looking to grow our pool of female coaches and develop them to an international level. It's important to do so as FIFA regulations now state that a female must be on the coaching team at all age-group FIFA Women's World Cups.
>
> *(New Zealand Football, 2017c)*

New Zealand Cricket

New Zealand has an elite women's cricket team competing internationally, known as the White Ferns, which also has a woman head coach. Although women's cricket has a long history in New Zealand, female involvement at all levels of the sport is low. New Zealand Cricket (NZC), the national organization, commissioned a research project in 2015 to enable it to better understand the reasons for this low level of participation. The subsequent 2016 Women and Cricket Report not only identified women as "having virtually no voice in the governance and leadership of cricket" (New Zealand Cricket, 2016, p. 12), but that there were also few women coaches. Specifically, fewer than 10% of coaches are female at the development, representative and high performance levels of the sport (New Zealand Cricket, 2016). The report recognized the need to increase and deepen the pool of players, coaches, officials, administrators, and fans. It made a number of governance and leadership recommendations, including to "gradually increase female presence in coaching and umpiring positions" (New Zealand Cricket, 2016, p. 11).

NZC has made significant strides in increasing female participation in the sport, in a short period of time. In 2017, NZC reported, for example, that female representation on the NZC Board has increased "from 11% in June 2016 to 33.3% in September 2017 (from one to three females, including the president)" (New Zealand Cricket, 2016, p. 11). In addition, increased funding has led to a growth in female participation by 11.7% in one season (New Zealand Cricket, 2017, p. 2). NZC has also adopted a new Inclusivity Policy and established a Women's Cricket High Performance Advisory Group (S. Beaman, personal communication, October 9, 2017). Although it is unclear what specific measures NZC is currently taking to increase the numbers of women coaches, it does appear to be making a strong commitment to enhancing female participation and involvement in all aspects of the sport.

Summary

This review points to a growing emphasis in New Zealand on encouraging greater participation by women at all levels of sport. This includes a specific focus by some sports on developing pathways for women seeking to break into the traditionally male-dominated domain of coaching, particularly at the development and elite levels. Although SNZ is silent on this issue, there are signs from at least two of the sports discussed, football and cricket, of a growing commitment at the strategic level to develop a coaching pathway for women to increase representation and improve gender equity.

Women as elite coaches: the benefits

Diversity at the leadership and governance level of any organization brings many financial and non-financial benefits. As well as enhancing financial performance, diversity increases the talent pool, enhances productivity and innovation, and improves employee retention (Badal & Harter, 2014; Catalyst, 2013; Dezsö & Ross, 2012; Joecks, Pull, & Vetter, 2013; Pellegrino, D'Amato, & Weisberg, 2011; Wagner, 2011). These benefits extend to sporting organizations, which research demonstrates achieve better performance outcomes when they adopt an inclusive culture and embrace diversity (Cunningham, 2009, 2011). Although considerable focus is often placed on the value of diversity within governance and management roles, this is equally important at the elite coaching level.

The social institution of sport, including coaching has traditionally been viewed as a male domain (Schull, 2016). The gender of coaches does matter, as explained by LaVoi (2016b, p. 3):

> Sport is one of the most visible and powerful social institutions in world [sic]. Individuals who are seen and known in the world of sports, like coaches, communicate who and what is relevant and valued (and what is not), and a majority of the time in every country in the world, these coaches are men.

Research demonstrates why women coaches matter. LaVoi (2016b) summarized some of the benefits attributed to women in coaching roles as follows:

- Women coaches are important role models and challenge stereotypes about women and leadership. Seeing women in leadership roles is important for women and girls. It demonstrates that coaching is a viable option for women and that they have the leadership skills to be effective and successful (Kane, 2016). It is also important for boys and men, because a woman coach teaches boys to respect women in leadership positions (Leberman & LaVoi, 2011).

They also provide a different perspective and are more likely to be strong advocates for equality and inclusion in the sporting domain.
- Women in coaching positions inspire and encourage other women and girls to pursue a coaching career. It is seen as a viable career option and as such, helps to grow the number of women in the coaching profession.
- Women coaches provide informal support networks to each other. They provide each other with "friendship, networking, career advice, mentorship, counselling, and help in navigating a male dominated workplace" (LaVoi, 2016b, p. 3). They are also more likely to improve the workplace environment and experience for women, because a more gender-balanced workforce reduces the likelihood of harassment and discrimination.

Women as elite coaches: the challenges

Although increasing the number of women in coaching positions brings many benefits to both the sporting organization and to women and girls, there are significant challenges to increasing the number of women in the coaching profession, particularly at the elite and professional levels. The Ecological–Intersectional Model developed by LaVoi (2016a) provides a framework for understanding these challenges and barriers to participation. This model examines the contexts that influence the careers of women coaches, namely the sociocultural, organizational, and interpersonal contexts. Overlaid are concepts of intersectionality and power. The relevance of each element to women in sport coaching is summarized below.

The sociocultural context includes the gender stereotypes associated with women, femininity, and leadership. Coaching is traditionally seen as a male domain and associated with heroic masculinity (Schull, 2016), which negatively impacts women who seek to pursue a career in coaching (Burton & LaVoi, 2016). At the organizational level, hiring practices often favor men, the existence of the "old boys club" disadvantages women seeking organizational progression (Shaw & Allen, 2009), and work practices promote male ways of working that do not recognize the complexities of women's lives and the need for flexibility, particularly when associated with the demands of family life (Burton & LaVoi, 2016). Recent research by Kerr and Cervin (2016) highlighted similar issues for elite female coaches within women's artistic gymnastics in Australia and New Zealand, highlighting the pervasiveness of coaching as a male activity. The interpersonal context recognizes the lack of supportive networks available to many women aspiring to a career in coaching and, at the personal level, women may struggle with the confidence needed to pursue a career within a gendered and unsupportive environment (Burton & LaVoi, 2016). Combined with these barriers, the concept of intersectionality highlights the additional challenges faced by women coaches when other factors are added to gender, such as race or sexuality (LaVoi, 2016a). Finally, the Ecological–Intersectional Model recognizes that sport and coaching is a social process that is laden with power (LaVoi, 2016a). The predominant gendered power imbalance at the governance level affects women at all levels of sport and influences how women coaches are perceived, supported, funded, and promoted.

Winning at all costs: searching for a different measure of success

Within New Zealand, much emphasis has been placed on increasing female participation at the playing and governance levels over the past 10 years. Although there are merits to this approach, research suggests that increased female participation in sport generally does not lead to more women in leadership positions (Schull, 2016). This is consistent with the Ecological–Intersectional model, which articulates how the challenges and barriers women coaches face are multi-dimensional and deeply entrenched in the fabric of society. Encouraging greater grassroots participation in sport generally, or in coaching specifically, is unlikely, on its own, to translate into more women transitioning to the elite level coaching. A radically different approach is needed.

Sports leadership sits within a dominant paradigm of "winning at all costs," which Burton and Leberman (2017) argue reinforces a model that privileges men. At the elite level, success is viewed through a lens of winning on the competitive sports field. In doing so, this reinforces the organizational structures and systems established to achieve that success, irrespective of whether they are inclusive and supportive of diversity. These structures prioritize and focus resources predominantly on successful male sports teams. They also reward coaches who can spend most of their time working in the office and out on the sports field, both in their hometown and through extensive periods of travel. This demands a level of commitment that may conflict with other priorities, such as family life and personal time. An expectation that a coach of an elite team will work excessive hours and prioritize work to win on the sports field favors those who can make this level of commitment, which will generally be men, who in general do not have responsibility for child care and other domestic responsibilities (Burton & Leberman, 2017).

Winning is important and desirable in competitive sport, particularly at the elite level. However, other factors are important in measuring success. For example, sport at all levels provides a positive influence in supporting economic development, health, social inclusion and equality (Burton & Leberman, 2017). In recognition of this, Burton and Leberman (2017) propose an alternative model to the model of "winning at all costs," called the Structure–Agency model. They advocate for a focus on both structural change (which is often slow) and agency-enhancing initiatives (which can be affected more quickly). This approach is also governed by a commitment to the adoption of quadruple top and bottom lines, namely social, economic, environmental, and cultural sustainability (Werbach, 2009), as a strategic guiding force. This focus on both structure and agency is seen as necessary to affect long-lasting change and, in the context of in sport leadership, will support women to start and remain in coaching. Coaching will then also be seen as a viable career choice for both women and men.

A national strategic approach to developing a pipeline of women coaches

LaVoi's (2016a) Ecological–Intersectional model confirms that a multi-layered approach is required to address the lack of women in coaching at all levels of sport. This is supported by the Structure–Agency model proposed by Burton and Leberman (2017). New Zealand lacks a national strategic commitment to the development of a pipeline of women coaches. The result is a piecemeal and haphazard approach by various sporting organizations, such as those described with reference to football, rugby, cricket, and hockey. Although some are undoubtedly committed to enhancing women's participation at all levels of sport, including coaching (such as New Zealand Cricket and New Zealand Football), a clear national strategic framework is also needed, which guides all national sports organizations in their strategic planning and program development, as well as funding decisions and allocation of resources.

The collection of robust data is a critical first step to establish a baseline that guides strategic actions and measures success. SNZ has acknowledged that more accurate and reliable participation information is required in order to gain a deeper understanding of its target participant groups (which includes women) (Sport New Zealand, 2017a). This needs to go further to include collecting accurate information about coaching participation at all levels of sport. SNZ, together with HPSNZ, can then create an evidence-based strategy focused on encouraging greater female participation in coaching and provide a clear pathway from participation to elite coaching.

Structural change also requires a commitment to coach development programs specifically tailored for women. Women-specific leadership programs have been shown to provide demonstrable benefits when they are conducted on a multi-organizational or sector-wide basis, and a long-term commitment is made to delivery of these programs (Harris & Leberman, 2012). In the sport sector, the Coaching Association of Canada (COC) is one of the few organizations in the world with a national program to develop women coaches at all levels of sport (Coaching Association of Canada, 2017; Robertson, 2016). New Zealand would benefit from a strategic commitment to developing a pipeline of women coaches, supported by an ongoing, fully funded, and multi-organizational leadership program delivered at the national level by SNZ and HPSNZ. Furthermore, women- and sport-specific coaching programs could then be delivered by individual sports to support this national strategic coaching program. This would provide a multi-layered approach to the development of women coaches, from the grassroots to elite levels.

Conclusion

HPSNZ has a performance-driven, athlete-focused, and coach-led system. The system appears to be working well for female athletes, but, in terms of providing leadership opportunities through coaching, it is not working for women. The Ecological–Intersectional model provides a framework to understand the multi-layered and complex reasons for this. When considered in combination with the Structure–Agency model, it is clear that a radically different approach is required. The responsibility for this initially sits with the national organizations responsible for promoting and supporting sport in New Zealand, namely SNZ and HPSNZ.

There is an urgent need for gender and ethnicity data on all coaches across all sports. This will enable evidence-based decision-making and provide baseline data against which to create, for example, an annual score card, such as that produced in the United States by the Tucker Centre for Research on Girls and Women in Sport. The value of women coaching also requires clear articulation, with pathways made visible and supported. Specific cross-code programs targeted at women coaches, from youth through to the elite level, will build networks and an infrastructure to highlight women coaches as role models.

Fundamentally, the structures within sport organizations need to change to enable women to reach their coaching potential. For example, central government funding should be tied to ensuring that all representative girls' and women's teams have at least one member of the coaching staff who is a woman. National sport organizations must start bringing through women as coaches and make this a priority, as British Cycling did after the London Olympics in 2012, which saw an increase in their female coaches by 70% in three years. Setting targets for women at the governance level, coupled with a women's governance program and mentoring, funded and supported by SNZ, has resulted in an increase in women board members within New Zealand. Urgent similar action is now required to redress the situation for women in elite coaching.

Leader profile: Haidee Tiffen

Tiffen is a former elite cricket player, who retired in 2009 and always wanted to have a career as a coach in the women's game. When playing, she worked through her coaching qualifications (completing the Level 2 coaching qualification) and studied to become a physical education teacher. On retirement, Tiffen completed the Level 3 coaching qualification, took a role as an assistant coach with the Canterbury Magicians, and went on two tours with the White Ferns (the national women's team). From 2013 to 2015, Tiffen was the head coach of the Auckland Hearts. In 2015, a part-time paid role as White Ferns' national team coach came open, which

Figure 27.1 Haidee Tiffen

involved touring and providing cricket-specific input into the players' individual performance plans (two and a half to three days a week). As the women's game has grown, Tiffen's role has progressed to 0.8, then to full time in 2016. Beating Australia in the T20 series in Australia in 2017 was a career highlight and a significant achievement for the team.

Tiffen is optimistic about the future for women coaches in cricket (personal communication):

> New Zealand Cricket is committed to succession planning from a coaching point of view. They are really encouraging, and want to help shape a pathway for women. I think that women do not see it as a career pathway. At this stage, our domestic coaches are part time and it is only really over the summer. The role is not paid well and there is work to be done in this space so that women can coach full time and can see a clear pathway.

Tiffen believes there are some exciting opportunities in the future for women's cricket in New Zealand because cricket is growing globally, with England and Australia leading the way.

References

Badal, S. & Harter, J. K. (2014). Gender diversity, business-unit engagement, and performance. *Journal of Leadership & Organizational Studies*, **21**(4), 354–365.

Burton, L. J. & LaVoi, N. M. (2016). An ecological/multisystem approach to understanding and examining women coaches. In N. M. LaVoi (ed.), *Women in Sports Coaching* (pp. 49–62). New York: Routledge.

Burton, L. J. & Leberman, S. (2017). New leadership: Rethinking successful leadership of sport organizations. In L. J. Burton & S. Leberman (eds), *Women in Sport Leadership: Research and practice for change* (pp. 148–161). New York: Routledge.

Caldwell, O. (2017). It's a long road to gender equality in New Zealand sport. *Stuff*, 24 September. Retrieved from https://www.stuff.co.nz/sport/95874944/its-a-long-road-to-gender-equality-in-nz-sport.

Catalyst (2013). Why diversity matters. Retrieved from www.catalyst.org/knowledge/why-diversity-matters.

Coaching Association of Canada (2017). Women in coaching. Retrieved from https://www.coach.ca/women-in-coaching-s16529.

Cunningham, G. B. (2009). The moderating effect of diversity strategy on the relationship between racial diversity and organizational performance. *Journal of Applied Social Psychology*, **6**, 1445.

Cunningham, G. B. (2011). The LGBT advantage: Examining the relationship among sexual orientation diversity, diversity strategy, and performance. *Sport Management Review*, **14**, 453–461.

Dezsö, C. L. & Ross, D. G. (2012). Does female representation in top management improve firm performance? A panel data investigation. *Strategic Management Journal*, **33**(9), 1072–1089.

Harris, C. & Leberman, S. (2012). Leadership development for women in New Zealand universities: Learning from the New Zealand women in leadership program. *Advances in Developing Human Resources*, **14**(1), 28–44.

High Performance Sport New Zealand (2011). New Zealand high performance coaching plan 2011–2020. Retrieved from https://www.hpsnz.org.nz/sites/all/modules/filemanager/files/Pubs_strats_reports/NZ_HP_Coaching_Plan_2011_2.pdf.

High Performance Sport New Zealand (2017). Coach accelerator programme. Retrieved from https://www.hpsnz.org.nz/coaches/coach-accelerator-programme.

Hockey New Zealand (2016). Our 2020 strategy. Retrieved from http://hockeynz.co.nz/Portals/30/Images/2016 Documents/170816 Hockey NZ Stategic Plan.pdf.

Hockey New Zealand (2017a). Annual report 2016. Retrieved from http://hockeynz.co.nz/Portals/30/2017 Documents/2016_Annual_Report_LowRes.pdf.

Hockey New Zealand (2017b). Hockey New Zealand – Stage 1 strategy delivery review. Retrieved from http://hockeynz.co.nz/Portals/30/2017 Documents/061017 HNZ SDR Stage 1 Report.pdf.

Hockey New Zealand (2017c). Our delivery review: What does success look like? Retrieved from http://hockeynz.co.nz/Portals/30/2017 Documents/061017 HNZ SDR Stage 1 Summary.pdf.

Joecks, J., Pull, K., & Vetter, K. (2013). Gender diversity in the boardroom and firm performance: What exactly constitutes a 'critical mass'? *Journal of Business Ethics*, **118**(1), 61–72.

Kane, M. J. (2016). A socio-cultural examination of a lack of women coaches in sport leadership positions. In N. M. LaVoi (ed.), *Women in Sports Coaching* (pp. 35–48). New York: Routledge.

Kerr, R. & Cervin, G. (2016). An ironic imbalance: Coaching opportunities and gender in women's artistic gymnastics in Australia and New Zealand. *International Journal of the History of Sport*, **33**(17), 2139–2152. https://doi.org/10.1080/09523367.2017.1283307.

LaVoi, N. M. (2016a). A framework to understand experiences of women coaches around the globe: The ecological–intersectional model. In N. M. LaVoi (ed.), *Women in Sports Coaching* (pp. 13–34). New York: Routledge.

LaVoi, N. M. (2016b). Introduction. In N. M. LaVoi (ed.), *Women in Sports Coaching* (pp. 1–9). New York: Routledge.

Leberman, S. & LaVoi, N. (2011). Juggling balls and roles, working mother-coaches in youth sport: Beyond the dualistic worker-mother identity. *Journal of Sport Management*, **25**(5), 474–488.

Macdonald, N. (2017). Girls just wanna get paid: Calling time on the undervaluing of women's sport. *Stuff*, 2 September. Retrieved from https://www.stuff.co.nz/sport/rugby/96239745/calling-time-on-the-undervaluing-of-womens-sport.

New Zealand Cricket (2016). Women and cricket: Cricket and women. Retrieved from https://nzc.nz/media/7756/nzcr_j000080_women-and-cricket-document_digital_d1.pdf.

New Zealand Cricket (2017). *Women & Governance Project*. Auckland, New Zealand.

New Zealand Football (2016). Strategic plan: Shaping football in New Zealand 2016–2025. Retrieved from www.nzfootball.co.nz/wp-content/uploads/2014/10/NZF-Strategy-2016-2025-Final-Branded.pdf

New Zealand Football (2017a). Annual report 2016. Retrieved from www.nzfootball.co.nz/wp-content/uploads/2017/06/NZF-Annual-Report_2016.pdf.

New Zealand Football (2017b). Calling all female coaches. Retrieved from www.nzfootball.co.nz/calling-all-female-coaches.

New Zealand Football (2017c). More female voices are likely to be heard on sidelines across the country as New Zealand Football continues to encourage women to try their hand at coaching and breaks down some of the barriers traditionally hindering them from doing so. Retrieved from www.nzfootball.co.nz/female-environment-brings-benefits.

New Zealand Football (2017d). Whole of football plan. Retrieved from www.nzfootball.co.nz/wp-content/uploads/2017/05/NZF-Whole-of-Football-Plan_Feb17.pdf.

New Zealand Rugby (2015). *This is Our Game: Women's rugby strategy 2015–2021*. Wellington, New Zealand.

New Zealand Rugby (2016). New Zealand rugby 2020: A bright future for rugby. Retrieved from http://files.allblacks.com/nzr2020/NZR-2020-Strategic-Plan-WEB.pdf.

New Zealand Secondary Schools Sports Council (2017). NZSSSC representation census 2016. Retrieved from www.nzsssc.org.nz/school-sport-data/nzsssc-census-reports.

Norman, L. (2017). *Gender & Olympic Coaching Report Card: What's changed since London 2012?* International Council for Coaching Excellence and Carnegie School of Sport, Leeds Beckett University.

Pellegrino, G., D'Amato, S., & Weisberg, A. (2011). The gender dividend: Making the business case for investing in women. Retrieved from www2.deloitte.com/content/dam/Deloitte/global/Documents/Public-Sector/dttl-ps-thegenderdividend-08082013.pdf.

Rainham, A. (2017). *Research into Women in Sport*. Women In Sport Aotearoa, New Zealand.

Robertson, S. (2016). Hear their voices: Suggestions for developing and supporting women coaches from around the world. In N. M. LaVoi (ed.), *Women in Sports Coaching* (pp. 177–222). New York: Routledge.

Schull, V. D. (2016). Female athletes' conceptions of leadership: Coaching and gender implications. In N. M. LaVoi (ed.), *Women in Sports Coaching* (pp. 126–138). New York: Routledge.

Shaw, S. & Allen, J. B. (2009). The experiences of high performance women coaches: A case study of two Regional Sport Organisations. *Sport Management Review*, **12**(4), 217–228.

Sport New Zealand (n.d.). Sport integrity framework. Retrieved from https://www.sportnz.org.nz/assets/Uploads/SportNZ-SportIntegrityFramework-Overview-sm.pdf.

Sport New Zealand (2015a). Sport and active recreation in the lives of New Zealand adults: 2013/14 active New Zealand survey results. Retrieved from www.srknowledge.org.nz/researchseries/active-new-zealand-20132014.

Sport New Zealand (2015b). Sport NZ Group Statement of Intent: 1 July 2015–30 June 2020. Retrieved from https://www.sportnz.org.nz/assets/Uploads/attachments/About-us/Sport-NZ-SOI-1-July-2015-30-June-2020.pdf.

Sport New Zealand (2017a). Sport NZ Group Statement of Performance Expectations: 1 July 2017–30 June 2018. Retrieved from https://www.sportnz.org.nz/assets/Uploads/SNZ-SPE-2017.pdf.

Sport New Zealand (2017b). Women in governance 2017. Retrieved from www.sportnz.org.nz/managing-sport/search-for-a-resource//women-in-governance-2017.

Sport New Zealand Community Sport (2015). Community sport strategy 2015–20. Retrieved from https://www.sportnz.org.nz/assets/Uploads/attachments/About-us/Com-Sport-Strategic-Plan.pdf.

Sport New Zealand Community Sport (2016a). New Zealand community sport coaching plan 2016–2020. Retrieved from https://www.sportnz.org.nz/assets/Uploads/Community-Sport-Coaching-Plan-2016-2020.pdf.

Sport New Zealand Community Sport (2016b). Talent plan 2016–2020. Retrieved from https://www.sportnz.org.nz/assets/Uploads/SportNZ-TalentPlan-v01.pdf.

Statistics New Zealand (2017). Top statistics, 22 November. Retrieved from www.stats.govt.nz/browse_for_stats/snapshots-of-nz/top-statistics.aspx.

Wagner, H. M. (2011). The bottom line: Corporate performance and gender diversity in the C-suite (2004–2008). Retrieved from http://papers.ssrn.com/sol3/papers.cfm?abstract_id=1980371.

Werbach, A. (2009). *Strategy for Sustainability: A business manifesto*. Boston, MA: Harvard Business Press.

Part V
Marketing and consumer behavior

28
Authentically communicating with women consumers
Examining successful (and non-successful) branding and marketing efforts

Brandon Brown and B. Nalani Butler

Speaking to a culture

When it comes to purchasing new products, what is it that you think influences consumers the most? Are consumers likely to purchase a new product because they have seen an informational television commercial? Is it because they have received, in some form or fashion, a free sample of the product? What about fliers or newspaper coupons? Could this be the number one reason why individuals purchase new products? Although all of these options seem viable, research suggests the number one reason why individuals purchase new products is because they have received a recommendation from a family member or friend (Marketing Charts, 2013). On the surface, such a response doesn't seem to raise any eyebrows. However, after reexamining the aforementioned possibilities, one can see there is a strong difference between the options. Television commercials, free samples, and coupons all have something in common – they are surface-level marketing tactics. On the other hand, when we think of a recommendation from a family member or friend, we begin to realize that this is not something conceived by a marketing team's efforts; rather, it is an option that is social in nature, and takes into consideration the importance of one's own culture and/or society.

Herein lies the importance of an individual's culture and/or society. Oftentimes, marketers believe they can get away with using surface-level marketing tactics (e.g., fliers or coupons) to attract individuals to their products. Yet, as research progresses, we are starting to find out that it takes more to truly influence a consumer's purchasing decision. Specifically, marketers have begun to realize the importance of understanding a consumer's society and/or place within a culture. As such, they have begun speaking to these cultures and/or societies as a means of developing better relationships with their consumers. Research suggests that, if an individual finds a product to be representative of their culture, then the consumer will value the product not for its worth or quality, but because it allows the consumer to better represent their own lifestyle (Arnould & Thompson, 2005).

There are countless products that represent the sentiment of lifestyle over quality. The popular "Beats by Dre" headphones may come to mind. If you speak with someone who understands headphone sound quality, they may be quick to tell you that "Beats by Dre" headphones are not all that great. In fact, in a recent 2017 Tech Radar article that ranked over-ear headphones on the basis of sound quality, "Beats by Dre" headphones failed to make the top 10 list (Pino, 2017). In 2014, *Time* magazine conducted a national study, ranking the best headphones on the basis of expert reviews, specifications, and various features (e.g., quality, frequency, sensitivity). "Beats by Dre" headphones were ranked second to last on a list that featured 18 different headphone brands (Taylor, 2014). Still, even with these rankings in mind, it likely doesn't surprise you that "Beats by Dre" headphones are *vastly* popular. They have been the number one selling headphone brand on the market over the last several years, and the company is valued at over US$3 billion (Lyles, 2015). Why is this? Why is the 17th best headphone product the number one selling headphone brand? It is likely because the headphone company, for consumers, is more than just a product that provides sound quality. To certain consumers, "Beats by Dre" headphones represent a certain lifestyle. Those who are wearing "Beats by Dre" headphones aren't wearing them because they provide quality sound, they are wearing them because they allow consumers to represent their lifestyle or culture through the brand. If, for example, a consumer would like to represent a lifestyle featuring determination, love, and strength, then they may look to consume "Beats By Dre" headphones due to the fact that Serena Williams wears these headphones, and epitomizes determination, love, and strength. These sentiments are reinforced by marketing consultant, David Deal. Deal says of "Beats by Dre" headphones, "electronics is almost an afterthought. Beats are cool, and they define what it means to be cool" (Klara, 2017). This example speaks to a larger point – individuals will consume a product, not for its quality, but also because it allows the consumer to better represent her or his culture.

What is culture?

If we know that culture is important for sport marketers, we must understand what defines a culture, and what constitutes a subculture. Culture, according to de Mooij (2004, p. 26) can be defined as a "set of shared beliefs, attitudes, norms, roles, and values found among speakers of a particular language who live during the same historical period of a specific geographic region." But culture doesn't simply stop there. Culture can be characterized by any number of commonalities, such as language, beliefs, or even food consumption habits (de Mooij, 2004). This is all important, because our best way to successfully market a product is to speak to an individual's culture. In that one of our main goals in this chapter is to understand women as consumers of sport, it would make sense then that we understand subcultures as they relate to gender.

A subculture is a subset of a particular culture; it is a group within a larger culture having a common set of shared values, roles, and/or beliefs (Schouten & McAlexander, 1995). As you know, in this handbook we have been speaking about a particular subculture – women. Therefore, for the purposes of this chapter, we highlight the importance of understanding this particular subculture. In doing so, we afford ourselves the opportunity to better comprehend the needs and wants of female consumers.

According to a 2017 report, women make purchasing decisions for over 90% of homes and vacations for a household, account for 60% of automobile purchasing decisions, and 51% of electronics purchasing decisions, and hold "half of America's wealth" (Conner, 2017, para. 1). In short, in terms of purchasing power, women are a powerful subculture. This is something that should not be overlooked. From time to time, marketing plans fail to realize the importance of this subculture and will rather speak to a whole group (or a completely different subculture), without taking into consideration the specific likes and dislikes of the female gender.

For marketing efforts to be successful they should correspond with the preferences of their targeted consumers, i.e., sport-marketing campaigns should be directly relatable to the intended consumer. This starts with research and an understanding that not all individuals within the same subculture uphold the exact same likes and/or dislikes. The more we understand that, the better we can authentically relate to each of our consumers.

As it relates to subcultures within gender, research suggests that there is a wide array of preferences for a number of different female consumers. These preferences depend on aspects such as age and/or race, for example. As an illustration, recent reports suggest female millennials carry an entirely different set of beliefs compared with the generation that preceded them (Meredith, 2017). Female millennials are digitally savvy consumers and are, for example, more likely to conduct research before purchasing products than non-millennial females. Furthermore, research indicates female millennials value beauty, see themselves as confident, and as such find "confident" brands attractive (Meredith, 2017). African–American females also have a unique set of values. According to reports, most African–American females prefer brands that are educational in nature, and those that support a cause (Nielsen, 2017). Successful sport-marketing and branding efforts will no doubt take research like this into account. If a marketer has in mind to attract African–American female consumers, for example, then the marketing campaign should feature a willingness to support a cause. If a sport marketer has in mind to attract millennial females, then the marketer should ensure that the sports brand embodies confidence and values beauty. Sport marketers should do this, not for the sake of their brand's worth, but because they should value beauty, for example, because valuing beauty adequately represents the valued characteristics of millennial females.

A failure to communicate

All of the above information is to say that consumers need to be properly understood. Understanding consumers allows a sport organization to grasp their likes, dislikes, needs, and wants, and therefore allows the brand to *authentically* communicate. If sport marketers are to understand their consumers, then they are likely to have a proper foundation for a successful sport-marketing campaign because they can speak to these preferences. But what happens if a marketing organization doesn't understand its consumers? What happens if an organization does not take into account their preferences, for example? If sport marketers fail to take into consideration consumer preferences, then their marketing strategy may end up backfiring. Later in the chapter there are examples of successful marketing campaigns that properly understand women. In this section, however, there is an examination of a number of marketing campaigns that failed to properly understand female consumers. The current section highlights these errors, and then provides a means for understanding them.

Of the many examples of marketing campaigns that have gone wrong, a number of them start with the flawed ideology of, "shrink it and pink it." This refers to the idea that all women will like anything pink. This is flawed logic that is then followed by the practice where a men's product is reduced in size and changed in color to then sell to women, creating the notion of shrink it and pink it. This cannot be further from the truth (Silverstein & Sayre, 2009). As mentioned earlier, not all women have the exact same interests and/or likes; among women, in particular, there are a countless number of subcultures, all of which uphold different tastes and preferences. It is no wonder then that, in 2009, the computer manufacturer Dell was fraught with negative reactions after releasing a new line of laptops, all of which were completely pink (Coughlin, 2017). The "shrink it and pink it" ideology did not work for Dell; sales for the pink line plummeted, and Dell eventually stopped production. Dell is not alone. Within the sports realm, several National Football League (NFL) teams offered diamond-encrusted jerseys as a means to attract female fans. These teams failed to understand their female fans, assuming that female fans would not only prefer diamonds on their jerseys, but would also be disinclined to purchase traditional jerseys. Unfortunately, it took a realization that the diamond-encrusted jerseys were not selling for these teams to stop production.

Any marketing campaign that is based on the assumption that women aren't intelligent and/or confident is sure to backfire. One example of this was the 2013 release of the "EPad Femme," a "female" iPad of sorts, which discounted personal preferences and intelligence. The Eurostar group, a European satellite and technology development company, created the produce and assumed that the EPad Femme would be attractive to females, not only by having apps centered around yoga, weight loss, and shopping, but also by having these apps already preinstalled, so as not to complicate the downloading procedure (Stern, 2013). The makers of the EPad Femme were bombarded with negative feedback due to their misunderstanding of female consumers. The Epad Femme, like Dell, eventually stopped production.

What do these examples have in common? First and foremost, these companies are violating a key concept that was mentioned earlier – these companies are not *authentically* speaking to the female culture! As the captain from the movie, *Cool Hand Luke* would say, "what we've got here is a failure to communicate!" Sure, some organizations make the mistake of thinking females like pink, and therefore would be persuaded to make a purchase on the basis of color. Yet research tells us women are intelligent consumers, and therefore value intelligent brands (Meredith, 2017). For example, women are much more likely to make a computer purchase on the basis of the computer's processing speed and available technology. And, although some marketers may want to trust their hunch that women enjoy shopping and yoga and enjoy products for their simplicity, this is not the case for all women. In fact, when research suggests that females prefer brands that exude confidence (Meredith, 2017), then the last thing women want to see is a brand essentially claiming they need help installing apps. This leads us to a very important lesson: simply having a hunch about an idea is not the equivalent to fully understanding one's consumer base. Authentic communication means communicating with a particular consumer on the basis of thoroughly understanding that consumer and their respective (sub) culture. If sport marketers fail to do this they may be in danger of losing business or, perhaps more importantly, they may be in danger of losing their consumer's trust. The question then becomes, "how can we better understand our consumers?" As we shall see, the answer to this question is twofold: research and staffing.

Research and staffing

If the question is, "how do we ensure that our sport marketing team is authentically communicating to a particular target market?", then the answer is twofold. Marketers should ensure that (1) they are conducting the proper research and (2) they are properly staffed with individuals who are representative of the target market, i.e., if a sport organization's goal were to create a branding campaign aimed at females, then the organization should be prepared to research female consumers and should have an ample number of females on staff. A recent study by the United Nation's Educational, Scientific, and Cultural Organization (UNESCO) shows that the vast majority of people within research and development roles are males. In particular, the study indicates that only 28.8% of researchers in the world are female (UNESCO, 2017).

Research in this case is not just laboratory science. We are referring to social science and understanding the causes of certain human phenomena. Specifically, as it relates to the sport industry, research is defined as:

a scientific, purposeful, systematic and rigorous method of collecting, analyzing, and interpreting data objectively or subjectively about some characteristic in order to gain new knowledge or add to the existing knowledge base of the field of sport organization management studies.

(Li, Pitts, & Quarterman, 2008, p. 4)

As it relates to sport, the social sciences, and understanding human behavior, this means that there is a way to understand certain aspects of human beings. If research is conducted correctly and put into a fitting context, we can understand what certain human beings like, dislike, favor, and even look down on. Therefore, we can say research is the medium that allows us to properly understand, and authentically communicate with, specific consumers. Research allows brand marketers to speak directly to intended consumers, so that consumers can say to themselves: "That brand gets me! The brand exudes confidence, and I am a confident person. It fits who I am!" This then comes with a number of benefits for both the consumer and the sport organization. The sport organization, in upholding a set of shared beliefs with the consumer, starts to garner trust from the consumer, and the consumer starts to build a relationship with the sport organization.

Perhaps one could argue that, if research is important, then the proper interpretation of said research is equally, if not more, important. This is where we can realize the importance of properly staffing an organization's marketing unit. A sport organization, for example, could have a vast set of data on female consumers, but, if all of the marketers in the sport organization are men, then the data may be misunderstood or misinterpreted. Having a diverse staff on an organization's marketing team is important for a number of reasons, but here we recognize its importance because having a diverse staff allows a marketing unit to properly represent the sport organization's target market. On-staff representatives of the target market can help a sport organization confirm plans before they are put into action, and can help formulate authentic thought processes for the sport organization while making said plans. It should come as no surprise that the EPad Femme was created without any female manufacturers or marketers on staff. Had several females been on staff during the process, they may have voiced concern, and things may have turned out differently.

We have now provided an adequate outline for properly and authentically communicating with a target market (in our case, female consumers). It is not only important to conduct research, but also to ensure proper staffing while creating sport marketing and branding campaigns. In doing so, sport organizations allow the consumer to feel as if they are being personally spoken to and valued. Whereas we could perceive the negative consequences of not adhering to these guidelines, it may be important for us to see examples of successful sport-marketing campaigns – campaigns that have become praiseworthy and popular in sports because of their effectiveness in reaching women consumers. In the next section we look at three such examples.

Sport marketing: Properly targeting women

Since the implementation of Title IX in 1972, there has been a consistent increase in sport participation among women and girls. With this progression in sport participation, there has also been an increase in television viewership of sports by women and girls. Women and girls like to play sports and watch sports, and female sport fans make up a big part of the sport marketing equation (Nielson, 2017). Furthermore, the wide variety of digital platforms has allowed women and girls to access the broadcast of their favorite games and to watch a variety of sports (Creedon, 2014). This has helped to increase fandom among females, and more companies and organizations have started initiatives to target female sport fans, create products based on the female consumer lifestyle, and market certain goods to a global female audience through sport-related media programming.

Historically the targeted consumer sport fans consisted of male consumers (IPG Media Lab, 2015). In today's society, women represent a substantial amount of the sport fan base (Brennan, 2013) and have the main purchasing power in the household (Danzinger, 2017). Research has shown us that that slapping pink on to a product will not suffice as a marketing strategy to girls and women (Docterman, 2014). This means that companies and organizations need to focus on how to strategically market and sell goods, services, and experiences to women as consumers in the twenty-first century (Silverstein & Sayre, 2009). Utilizing the proper ideals and tactics (i.e., research and staffing efforts), companies from all over the world are now using sport to sell non-sport-related products as well as sport-related products to women.

The three marketing campaigns that follow are used as noteworthy examples of how to market sport-related products and experiences to female consumers. All of these examples show how far companies and organizations will go in using sport as a way to attract women to their respective brands. These examples include: the Tampa Bay Buccaneers using outreach initiatives to target their growing female fan base, Lululemon Athletica Inc. tapping into grassroots efforts to promote their brand by using local brand ambassadors, and Proctor and Gamble focusing on combating gender stereotypes, while promoting their products to a socially conscience global audience.

"Go Red for Women": The case of the Tampa Bay Buccaneers

Female fans make up close to half of the NFL's fan base, meaning that women and girls like to watch football, be a part of football-related events, and purchase merchandise related to their favorite team (Salkowitz, 2018). Historically, the NFL has been dominated by male employees, but, more recently, females have started to slowly increase their representation in a number of NFL roles. We are seeing more women on the field as coaches and referees, women in prominent front office administrative roles, and now an increasing number of women as fans of NFL teams (Vrentas, 2017). One example that we will showcase is that of the Tampa Bay Buccaneers.

The Tampa Bay Buccaneers recognize the value that women and girls have provided for their franchise. The "Women of Red" campaign is a program created by the organization to celebrate female fans. The program does this through fan engagement initiatives involving access to exclusive events throughout the year, and enables fans to have access to unique content directly from the organization (Tampa Bay Buccaneers, 2017). This fan engagement program has been marketed toward female fans of all ages and is accessible to anyone who wants to join.

When the franchise first announced the outreach program, there was a backlash from some who were critical of how the Buccaneers were targeting their female consumers through promotions and advertising, for their "Women of Red" launch party. What offended some were references to "game day style tips" and "educational experiences focused on providing a better understanding of the game." The original kick-off for the first "Women of Red" launch party, referenced fashion, cooking, and Pinterest as buzzwords to hopefully get more female fans interested in attending this inaugural gathering (Auman, 2015). This was the launch of something big for the Buccaneers' organization, but it ended up backfiring because of the insensitive marketing tactics (Macur, 2015). This initial stereotypical marketing strategy suggested that women were more inclined to focus on fashion, what to post on Pinterest, and how to host football watch parties with unique NFL culinary creations for their partners, versus being an active football fan who enjoyed watching the game and being a part of the football culture (Block, 2015).

This initial backlash put a poor spotlight on the organization and, in the end, the entire organization pulled together to respond to the negative press by creating a fan experience in which gender stereotypes were not used to market to the female Buccaneer's fans.

As such, the Buccaneers' organization made a concentrated effort to address these concerns on site at the inaugural event and put protocols in place for future events, in which female fans were the target market. In doing so, the organization revised the initial event. The revised event featured a number of well-researched, gender-specific, target-marketing strategies. After conducting research on their consumer preferences, the Buccaneers' "Women of Red" party featured preferred food and drink choices such as Barefoot Wine and Stella Artois Cidre. These companies could activate a sponsorship contract by having on-site women brand ambassadors, who offered samples of unique beverage choices to women consumers. In fact, research shows that women who consume alcohol prefer tropical and berry-flavored alcoholic beverages in comparison to men. In addition, research shows that cider-flavored beverages are used by brewing companies as a gateway to buying beer and 75% of people who buy cider beer will end up buying beer or wine after consuming cider-flavored beer (Nielsen, 2015). In addition, a variety of non-traditional game day food options were provided in place of standard hotdogs and hamburgers, for female football fan consumers to try. The women were then asked to sample the food and provide feedback as a way to demonstrate that their input was valued by the Buccaneer's organization.

As a way to address their original faux pas, the Buccaneers marketed the event, knowing that their female consumers were well-informed football fans. The revised party offered women fans a chance to meet current players for an on-site question-and-answer session, and offered a virtual reality session to provide women fans a firsthand look at up and coming technology such as virtual reality headsets, which the quarterbacks used for training purposes. Furthermore, discounted Tampa Bay Buccaneers' merchandise was promoted by both male and female employees (Tampa Bay Buccaneers, 2017).

The event concluded on a high note with the General Manager, Jason Licht, directly addressing all of the attendees about the initial "Women of Red" controversy. Licht was able to have a fan discussion about football tips, in which he gave a behind-the-scenes look at the recruiting process for the 2015–2016 NFL season. In this, Licht utilized video footage and walked the crowd through the process of how scouting reports were used and why certain players were chosen over others for the Buccaneers' roster.

The Buccaneers were able to turn bad media publicity generated by poor decision-making, based on stereotypes and not proper market research, into a learning moment for other sport organizations looking to target more female sport fans. Since this debacle in 2015, the Buccaneers have been able to have successful "Women of Red" events every year, by using socially conscious marketing strategies.

This example shows how thoughtful market research is needed to make sure that organizations are using the right strategies to communicate with women. Word choices and the creation of event activations all play a role in communicating effectively with fans (Olenski, 2018), and more organizations need to be aware of these approaches as they begin to understand how to effectively reach their target market, which in this case was women. Although the marketing outreach may have good intentions, errors are common and some organizations suffer damaging and long-term consequences (Vilá & Bharadwaj, 2017). However, the Buccaneers' organization was able to put all hands on deck by addressing the issue head-on and reinventing the event just before doors opened. In fact, the "Go Red for Women" event is so appealing that they now face the issue of men crashing the event for the unique experience.

Lululemon: Athleisure apparel and empowering women consumers

The current progression of women being in leadership roles and having more opportunities with higher paying jobs has led to more independent financial freedom (Women in the workforce, 2009). There has been a slow, but steady, progression of more women entering the workforce and creating more opportunities for independent financial freedom (Graf, Brown, & Patten, 2018). Women are integrating and balancing work, life, and fitness into their daily routines (Stern, 2008), and more apparel and retail companies are starting to recognize and market to this burgeoning female demographic. Appealing to women who live an all-around active lifestyle is what has set Lululemon apart from historic brands like Nike and adidas (Danziger, 2017).

Lululemon was created and founded by Lululemon Athletica Inc. in Vancouver, British Columbia, Canada in late 1998. Lululemon has since grown to be one of the most popular women's athletic apparel brands in North America (Fromm, 2016). Lululemon focuses on the strength of independent women as consumers who can make their own choices. The company's efforts have been dedicated to educating and supporting women and girls leading healthy lifestyles, instead of marketing towards perceived weaknesses or insecurities often represented by stereotypical marketing campaigns (Garcia, 2017). Lululemon sells a wide variety of athletic apparel, and the products are designed for consumers who seek a health-conscious, fitness-based lifestyle. Women can feel comfortable making a purchase at a Lululemon retail store, knowing that they are valued by the company, and buying comfortable and stylish apparel signals their appreciation of how the company values women. This strategy of enclothed cognition is all about how clothing and apparel changes our mental state (Adam & Galinsky, 2012), which Lululemon uses to market to their female consumers.

Lululemon's empowerment marketing strategies have created a movement, and Lululemon has been able to create wearable clothes for women and girls on the go. Athletic wear is no longer limited to going to the gym, but has fallen into the casual wear category known as athleisure (Lee, 2016). Lululemon appeals to women looking to live a socially conscious lifestyle and is positioned to appeal to women at the grassroots level. In fact, women who purchase a product from Lululemon receive their garment in a reusable and recyclable eco-friendly tote bag, with empowering messages like, "hope is not a strategy and imperfect is perfect." The brand is built on loyalty and yoga-inspired apparel, but is starting to branch out to various other areas of the fitness market. For instance, Lululemon hosts running clubs, sponsors 5Ks, and creates community fitness classes in various cities worldwide.

Lululemon has made an effort to distinguish itself as a unique high-quality brand that understands women. The company's marketing campaigns have been exemplary in effectively communicating with their primary consumer base, and serve as a prime example of how marketing strategies can be developed to reach and value women as consumers (Tabuchi, 2016). In particular, Lululemon has found success in employing localized marketing strategies, rather than focusing their efforts on mass media marketing strategies (i.e., commercials, billboards, or print advertisements). Lululemon does not solely focus on using athletes, socialites, or models to market and promote their products, but rather local brand ambassadors. These ambassadors are usually yoga or fitness instructors, who are given samples of the Lululemon apparel to wear. In addition, the ambassadors help to promote the Lululemon brand through social media and personal interactions with the people who they instruct. As an outreach initiative, their grassroots campaigns have primarily targeted yoga and fitness studios within the radius of their retail stores (Soni, 2014). Examples of these outreach initiatives include offering free yoga classes at Lululemon retail stores, fundraising partnerships with local non-profit organizations, and fundraising partnerships with yoga or fitness studios. In having these opportunities, consumers can meet, and be surrounded by like-minded individuals, in a fitness and health-conscious environment. In fact, Lululemon creates socially conscious initiatives such as donating 100% of earned profit on International Day of Yoga, which is on June 21, to non-profit groups that promote yoga and meditation in low-income communities. Lululemon has been able to make a mark and has created a threat to well-known brands like Nike and Adidas, because of its micro-level target-marketing strategy at the grassroots level, and by focusing on marketing a holistic lifestyle of athleisure versus high-performance apparel, to female consumers.

This example shows how an athletic apparel company was able to use grassroots level lifestyle marketing to engage consumers on a local level through female empowerment. Lululemon is always keeping their brand fresh and new, by focusing on research that enables them to stay up to date with the needs and wants of women consumers, and by properly understanding, and authentically communicating with, their target market. In fact, Lululemon recently replaced former CEO Laurent Potdevin who resigned after allegations of ethical misconduct within the organization (Lublin, 2018). This resignation came about after the start of the #MeToo movement, in which women in corporate America and beyond started to use their voice to speak up and support survivors and victims of sexual harassment and assault, resulting in top-level male executives resigning because of past inappropriate interactions with employees (Farr, Hirsch, & Thomas, 2018).

Proctor and Gamble: #LikeAGirl and Thank You, Mom

Running and playing like a girl are no longer insults, but a stamp of approval, because of a brilliant campaign developed by Proctor and Gamble (P&G). In fact, P&G flipped the age-old approach by focusing on conquering demoralizing catch phrases and stereotypes linked to women and girls. They have done so by using sport to bring awareness to issues that face their female demographic. P&G has always focused on a wide range of females as consumers, from childhood to adolescence, and all the way to later adulthood. The "Always, Run Like a Girl Campaign" faced gender stereotypes head on, by touching on how a girl's self-confidence and self-esteem start to falter during puberty (Vagianos, 2015). P&G created the hashtag "#LikeAGirl" to bring awareness to their brand and to encourage people to be mindful of how they use these words when referring to girls. This campaign went viral, with the video receiving over 75 million global views on YouTube and over 290 million social impressions in the United States alone. P&G created a positive brand legacy through this campaign and has been able to continue to tap into the female consumer by focusing on the millennial women audience through socially conscious campaigns (Institute for Public Relations, 2013).

P&G also produced the, "Thank you, Mom" campaign, which gained momentum during the 2012 London Summer Olympic Games. P&G used the platform of sport to create an emotional appeal by valuing women as mothers. Through cross-cultural emotional marketing, they used storylines of strong women supporting their children as they pursued their dream of one day reaching the Olympics and overcoming adversity (Pritchard, 2017). This campaign did not focus on specific P&G products, but brought awareness to the fact that P&G is a socially conscious global brand, dedicated to bringing their products to mothers across the globe. Using this worldwide stage has continued on and P&G continued this campaign through the 2018 PyeongChang Winter Olympic Games. Please note that this campaign not only appeals to women, but also to men because of the sentimental framing of the campaign. P&G created marketing gold with "Thank you, Mom," because the reach of the campaign targets diverse age groups and demographics from all cultures around the world.

Conclusion

It is important that individuals realize the significance of communicating authentically. This is particularly true when communicating with individuals within particular cultures. Culture is not only an essential part of an individual's background, but also something that should be recognized within marketing campaigns. This chapter emphasizes this outlook by providing examples of culture's importance among female consumers of sport. As the chapter highlights, there have been a number of organizations that have misunderstood female sport consumers and, in turn, have lost out on potential business. Conversely, it showcases examples of organizations that could *authentically* speak to female sport consumers through market research, community outreach, and global appeal. Through trial and error, grassroots initiatives, and appealing to the heart, the chapter highlights examples of how professional sport teams, apparel companies, and global brands target the female audience by truly trying to understand the changing needs, likes, and preferences of the female sport consumer. Employing these methods not only allows female sport consumers to become receptive to such messages, but also allows this consumer base to support and ambassador the brand. This then should be a goal – to fully understand female sport consumers to the point where marketing campaigns can be authentically communicated, and duly received.

Leader profile: Anna Karefa-Johnson

Figure 28.1 Anna Karefa-Johnson
© Leigh Clifton 2017

Anna Karefa-Johnson is vice president, events and programming for the Ross Initiative in Sports for Equality (RISE). She previously served as regional director, events and programming – south.

Her work draws on 10 years of marketing experience in college and professional sports, most recently as the community outreach affinity manager for the Tampa Bay Buccaneers. Before that, Karefa-Johnson served as director of marketing for the Pac-12 Conference, overseeing branding and managing as many as 50 live events per year, including the Pac-12 Football Championship Game and Men's and Women's Basketball Tournaments. Clients for other events that she has produced range from Nike Basketball and the Cartoon Network to the LeBron James Family Foundation.

A California native, Karefa-Johnson interned in public relations with the Los Angeles Lakers and later with the Baltimore Ravens and NFL Players Association. She earned a Bachelor's degree in communication from the University of Southern California and a Master of professional studies degree in sports industry management from Georgetown University.

Karefa-Johnson's diverse background of having experience working in intercollegiate athletics and professional sports has allowed her to develop a skill set in which she is able to embrace all facets of the sport industry in an optimistic manner. She has been able to learn, grow, and craft a career she has always seen herself pursuing because of her openness and willingness to work in different environments.

Karefa-Johnson lets her work speak for itself and her level of professionalism is modeled through confidence and leading by example. She feels it is important to identify young female leaders and allow them to have access to spaces in which they are a part of the conversation. She makes it a point to include the feedback and opinions of women and girls, when making decisions around RISE and their outreach initiatives.

Karefa-Johnson was brought on board to RISE because of her unique ability to reimagine fan engagement by facilitating conversations about sport and social justice initiatives. Anna creates marketing campaigns around storytelling and first person accounts. She believes representation of marginalized populations is huge when getting a message out to the community and this is what sets her apart from the rest.

References

Adam, H. & Galinsky, A. (2012). Enclothed cognition. *Science Direct*. Retrieved from https://www.sciencedirect.com/science/article/pii/S0022103112000200.

Arnould, E. J. & Thompson, C. (2005). Twenty years of consumer culture theory: Retrospect and prospect. *Advances in Consumer Research*, **32**, 129–130.

Auman, G. (2015). Tampa Bay Buccaneers' women's outreach program sparks backlash, August 6. Retrieved from www.tampabay.com/sports/football/bucs/bucs-program-for-women-sparks-backlash/2240234.

Block, J. (2015). Tampa Bay Buccaneers create sexist website to teach women football. *HUFFPOST*. Retrieved from https://www.huffingtonpost.com/entry/tampa-bay-bucs-sexist_us_55c38764e4b0f1cbf1e3f72d.

Brennan, B. (2013). NFL raises its game with women consumers, September 4. Retrieved from https://www.forbes.com/sites/bridgetbrennan/2013/09/04/nfl-raises-its-game-with-women-consumers/#6346d2a28f58

Conner, C. (2017). Most businesses fall short with female consumers, new study reveals, April 15. Retrieved from https://www.forbes.com/sites/cherylsnappconner/2017/04/15/most-businesses-fall-short-with-female-consumers-new-study-reveals/#6a682315c9ed (accessed November 9, 2017).

Coughlin, J. F. (2017). How marketers badly misunderstand older female consumers, November 7. Retrieved from https://www.forbes.com/sites/nextavenue/2017/11/07/how-marketers-badly-misunderstand-older-female-consumers/#74ac2afca2fa (accessed November 10, 2017).

Creedon, P. (2014). Women, social media, and sport: Global digital communication weaves a web. *Television & New Media*, **15**(8), 711–716.

Danziger, P. N. (2017). Winning the sports retail race: Under Armour and Nike hit the wall. *Forbes*. Retrieved from https://www.forbes.com/sites/pamdanziger/2017/11/01/winning-the-sports-retail-race-under-armour-and-nike-hit-the-wall/#35486aa31a96.

de Mooij, M. (2004). *Consumer Behavior and Culture: Consequences for global marketing and advertising*. Thousand Oaks, CA: Sage Publications.

Docterman, E. (2014). The war on pink: GoldieBlox toys ignite debate. *Time*. Retrieved from http://time.com/3281/goldie-blox-pink-aisle-debate.

Farr, C., Hirsch, L., & Thomas, L. (2018). Lululemon CEO left in part because of relationship with female designer at the company. *CNBC*. Retrieved from https://www.cnbc.com/2018/02/06/lululemon-ceo-laurent-potdevin-had-inappropriate-employee-relationship.html

Fromm, J. (2016). The Lululemon lifestyle: Why millennials seek more than just comfort from athleisure wear. *Forbes*. Retrieved from https://www.forbes.com/sites/jefffromm/2016/07/06/the-lululemon-lifestyle-millennials-seek-more-than-just-comfort-from-athleisure-wear.

Garcia, T. (2017). Lululemon goes beyond yoga pants for sales growth, September 5. Retrieved from https://www.marketwatch.com/story/lululemon-goes-beyond-yoga-pants-for-sales-growth-2017-09-01.

Graf, N., Brown, A., & Patten, E. (2018). The narrowing, but persistent, gender gap in pay. *Pew Research Center*. Retrieved from http://www.pewresearch.org/fact-tank/2018/04/09/gender-pay-gap-facts.

Institute for Public Relations (2013). Always #Like a Girl: Turning an Insult into a Confidence Movement. *Always*. Retrieved from https://instituteforpr.org/wp-content/uploads/Always-LikeAGirl-Turning-an-Insult-into-a-Confidence-Movement.pdf.

IPG Media Lab (2015). Annual survey of the American Football consumer. Retrieved from https://www.ipglab.com/wp-content/uploads/2015/09/American_Football_Consumer-IPG-version-8.24.pdf.

Klara, R. (2017). How Beats used celeb marketing to become Millennials' favorite audio brand, January 3. Retrieved from www.adweek.com/brand-marketing/how-beats-used-celeb-marketing-become-millennials-favorite-audio-brand175314 (accessed November 20, 2017).

Lee, C. Y. (2016). Development of athleisure look design applying cut-out techniques. Unpublished Master's thesis, Dongduk Women's University, Seoul, Korea.

Lublin, J. S. (2018). Lululemon says CEO Laurent Potdevin has resigned, effective immediately, February 5. Retrieved from https://www.wsj.com/articles/lululemon-says-ceo-laurent-potdevin-has-resigned-effective-immediately-1517864962.

Lyles, T. (2015). The $3 billion deal for Dr. Dre's 'Beats' almost never happened, August 19. Retrieved from www.businessinsider.com/beats-by-dre-almost-never-happened-2015-8 (accessed November 20, 2017).

Macur, J. (2015). Buccaneers offer women a Modern N.F.L. lesson out of the '50s, August 6. Retrieved from https://www.nytimes.com/2015/08/07/sports/football/tampa-bay-buccaneers-womens-movement-shows-that-they-are-the-ones-that-need-help.html?_r=0.

Marketing Charts (2013). Family and friends still most trusted for shopping decisions, January 22. Retrieved, from https://www.marketingcharts.com/television-26423 (accessed November 20, 2017).

Meredith (2017). Meredith women 2020 female consumer report. Retrieved from www.meredith.com/marketing-capabilities/research.

Nielsen (2015). Nielsen Report: Sustainable selections: How socially responsible companies are turning a profit. Retrieved from https://www.nielsen.com/us/en/insights/news/2015/sustainable-selections-how-socially-responsible-companies-are-turning-a-profit.html.

Nielsen (2017). Nielsen report: African-American women: Our science, her magic. Retrieved from www.nielsen.com/us/en/insights/reports/2017/african-american-women-our-science-her-magic.html.

Olenski, S. (2018). The promises and pitfalls of socially conscious marketing, January 3. Retrieved from https://www.forbes.com/sites/steveolenski/2018/01/03/the-promises-and-pitfalls-of-socially-conscious-marketing/#4159977838ef.

Pino, N. (2017). The best over-ear headphones for 2017, November 16. Retrieved, from www.techradar.com/news/audio/portable-audio/best-over-ear-headphones-1280342 (accessed November 20, 2017).

Pritchard, M. (2017). P&G promotes love over bias, with latest "Thank You, Mom" campaign, November 2. Retrieved from https://www.olympic.org/news/p-g-promotes-love-over-bias-with-latest-thank-you-mom-campaign-1.

Salkowitz, R. (2018). Data shows women paid more attention to Super Bowl LII than men. *Forbes*. Retrieved from https://www.forbes.com/sites/robsalkowitz/2018/02/05/data-shows-women-paid-more-attention-to-super-bowl-lii-than-men/#75f93e535c4a.

Schouten, J. W. & McAlexander, J. H. (1995). Subcultures of consumption: An ethnography of the new bikers. *Journal of Consumer Research*, **22**, 43–61

Silverstein, M. J. & Sayre, K. (2009). The female economy. Retrieved from https://hbr.org/2009/09/the-female-economy.

Soni, P. (2014). Lululemon attempts to reinvigorate its interrupted growth model. Retrieved from http://marketrealist.com/2014/12/lululemon-attempts-reinvigorate-interrupted-growth-model/?utm_source=yahoo&utm_medium=feed&utm_content=toc-1&utm_campaign=lululemon-builds-brands-unique-marketing-strategies (accessed November 22, 2017).

Stern, M. (2008). The fitness movement and the fitness center industry, 1960–2000. *Business and Economic History*, Vol. 6. Retrieved from https://www.thebhc.org/sites/default/files/stern_0.pdf.

Stern, J. (2013). EPad Femme: A tablet designed for women fits the stereotype, March 19. Retrieved from http://abcnews.go.com/Technology/epad-femme-tablet-designed-women-fits-stereotypes/story?id=18759205 (accessed November 10, 2017).

Tabuchi, H. (2016). Products and competition stretch market for "Athleisure" clothing, March 25. Retrieved from https://www.nytimes.com/2016/03/26/business/products-and-competition-stretch-market-for-athleisure-clothing.html (accessed November 20, 2017).

Tampa Bay Buccaneers (2015). Red launch. Retrieved from www.buccaneers.com/redlaunch.

Tampa Bay Buccaneers (2017). Women of red. Retrieved from www.buccaneers.com/RED/index.html.

Taylor, B. (2014). 18 headphone brands ranked from worst to first, April 24. Retrieved from http://time.com/74886/best-headphones (accessed November 20, 2017).

UNESCO (2017). UNESCO report: UNESCO institute for statistics. Women in Science. Retrieved from http://uis.unesco.org/sites/default/files/documents/fs43-women-in-science-2017-en.pdf.

Vagianos, A. (2015). The reaction to #LikeAGirl is exactly why it's so important. *Huffington Post*, February 3. Retrieved from https://www.huffingtonpost.com/2015/02/03/why-like-a-girl-is-so-important_n_6598970.html.

Vilá, O. R. & Bharadwaj, S. (2017). Competing on social purpose. *Harvard Business Review*. Retrieved from https://hbr.org/2017/09/competing-on-social-purpose.

Vrentas, J. (2017). The women who are changing the face of the NFL, August 18. Retrieved from https://www.si.com/nfl/2017/08/16/themmqb-women-nfl-coaches-training-camp-bills-falcons-jets-49ers-vikings.

Women in the workforce (2009). Female power. *The Economist*. Retrieved from https://www.economist.com/briefing/2009/12/30/female-power.

29
Team identification in women's sport
What little we know

Elizabeth B. Delia

Understanding fan involvement in sport has important implications for sport organizations, including a range of attitudes and behaviors among sport consumers. As such, sport consumer behavior has been a topic of great importance to researchers over the years. For decades, scholars have utilized team identification to understand individuals' psychological connection to sport teams. As a result, we have a good understanding of how team identification influences a variety of attitudinal and behavioral outcomes, as well as the impact of identifying with a team on an individual's sense of self. However, nearly all studies of team identification to date have dealt with men's sport, essentially ignoring team identification in women's sport. In this chapter, the literature on team identification—including the very limited amount of knowledge we have of team identification in women's sport—is reviewed. As part of this review, figures on attendance and viewership of women's sport are presented, in part to illustrate how consumer involvement is far different in women's sport than in men's sport.

The theoretical foundation of team identification

Scholars use social identity theory to study team identification (Lock & Heere, 2017). According to social identity theory, an individual derives a greater sense of self from the perceived awareness, value, and emotional significance of belonging to a group (Tajfel & Turner, 1979). The social groups to which individuals perceive they belong contribute to their self-image by classifying themselves with group members and distinguishing themselves from non-group members. Individuals derive positive social identity from favorable comparisons between ingroups and outgroups. When a social identity is unfavorable, individuals will either strive to make the ingroup positive or leave the group if possible (Tajfel, 1974).

Social identity scholars acknowledge that social structures change based on economic, cultural, and historical circumstances, and thus are contextual and fluid (Abrams, 1999; Hogg & Abrams, 1988; Tajfel & Turner, 1979). The notion that social groups' defining features are susceptible to change highlights the importance of context in studying social identity (Hogg & Abrams, 1988). The social context in which a social identity is formed and maintained influences the meaning and significance of the identity (Abrams, 1999). Thus, in consideration of sport-related social identities, we should remember that they are not stable, but rather unfixed.

Team identification

Beyond understanding the theoretical underpinning of team identification, it is important to understand how team identification is often defined. Wann, Melnick, Russell, and Pease (2001) described team identification as the degree of psychological connection an individual may have with a sport entity. Others, such as Lock and Heere (2017), have defined team identification much more closely to social identity theory; these scholars explained that team identification involves a cognitive realization of a connection to a team that influences an individual's sense of self and a vested interest in the team's status, all of which has a degree of emotional value for the individual.

Traditionally, team identification has been assessed via surveys, using a scale such as the Sport Spectator Identification Scale (SSIS; Wann & Branscombe, 1993) or TEAM*ID (Heere & James, 2007a). Concerning the various scales that have been developed to measure team identification, some scholars have argued that a scale acknowledging the multidimensionality of team identification is necessary (Heere & James, 2007a), whereas others have contended that more simple unidimensional scales allow scholars to adequately assess identification with a sport team. Aside from team identification scales, other scholars have more recently used other means to assess team identification. If one is conducting qualitative research with individuals (e.g., interviewing, ethnography), it may be difficult to assess team identification via survey. In these instances, some have suggested that certain words, emotions, and/or behaviors may signal that an individual is identified with a team (e.g., Delia, 2017a). For example, an individual may routinely use the words "we," "us," "my," or "our" in describing a team, which signals that the individual feels they are part of that team (i.e., part of a group).

Once team identification has been assessed, why should sport entities care to know about it? Over the past three decades, scholars have found that team identification is positively related to various attitudes and behaviors, such that—generally speaking—individuals who are identified with a team typically exhibit more favorable behaviors toward organizations. This includes attitudes toward sponsors (Madrigal, 2001), team merchandise-purchasing behavior (Kwon & Armstrong, 2002), and amount paid to attend events (Wann & Branscombe, 1993). An individual's psychological connection to a team can also result in negative behaviors, such as fan aggression (Dimmock & Grove, 2005). For sport fans themselves, identifying with a team often yields social–psychological health (Wann, 2006); however, this can be periodically interrupted by identity threats, such as poor team performance or program scandal (Delia, 2017b; Doyle, Lock, Funk, Filo, & McDonald, 2017).

Separate from the influence of team identification on attitudinal or behavioral outcomes for organizations, some scholars have studied how such identification is developed over time (e.g., Doyle et al., 2017; Lock, Funk, Doyle, & McDonald, 2014; Lock, Taylor, & Darcy, 2011). Lock et al. (2011) suggested that other group identities, such as identification with the sport or one's place of origin, might influence the formation of identification with a new team. Investigating how team identification is developed and maintained during periods of poor performance, Doyle et al. (2017) found that tactics such as social mobility and creativity are used, illustrating that individuals may alter their perception of the focal identification object (team) in an effort to remain identified. Finally, in their research with fans of a new team, Lock et al. (2014) found that a new team might inherit meaning from the place where it is located or the history of the players on the new team. Collectively, these scholars have contributed to the team identification literature by illustrating the complexity of the concept.

Individuals often identify with multiple social groups, some of which may relate (Roccas & Brewer, 2002). Within sport, scholars have discussed the idea of a sport team as representative or symbolic of multiple group identities, including a city, state, or university (e.g., Heere & James, 2007b; Heere, James, Yoshida, & Scremin, 2011).

Scholars utilizing a self-categorization theory framework to study multiple group identities have suggested that individuals organize identities at different levels of abstraction (Turner, 1985). For example, an individual might be a resident of a city that has a soccer team and, as such, perceive group membership to the city and team. Thus, the team identity would be nested within the city identity. Lock and Funk (2016) suggested that individuals may identify with a sport entity at superordinate, subgroup, and relational levels, each of which fulfills different social needs, and they often operate together. Superordinate identification describes individuals' identification with a sport entity broadly, subgroup identification describes identification with a sub-section of team supporters (e.g., a section of fans within a stadium), and relational identification describes the interpersonal interactions that individuals have in less inclusive social groups (e.g., tailgating groups). Collectively, these various team-related identities enhance individuals' sense of self. The literature on multiple identities in team identification illustrates the complexity of individuals' identification with a sport entity, and lends support to the idea that identification with a team often includes one's relationships with others.

Despite the vast team identification literature, scholars have recently pointed to issues regarding the concept, such as the misuse of theoretical frameworks (Lock & Heere, 2017). In their conceptual work, Lock and Heere (2017) discussed how scholars have been inconsistent in studying team identification, particularly as it pertains to identity theory and social identity theory (Stets & Burke, 2000), and sought to provide clarity for scholars moving forward. The authors contended that social identity theory should be the prevailing theory used to examine team identification as a result of its focus on group membership. Identity theory should be reserved for examining a role identity, such as an individual's role as a fan of a team.

Another recent advancement in team identification focused on the meaning of team in team identification (Delia & James, 2017). Based on qualitative research with fans of two sport teams, Delia and James found that the meaning of team evolves due to environmental changes and personal experiences. They also determined that the meaning of team in team identification has three broad components—place, past, and present—each of which uniquely contributes to the identity.

Considering the recent advancements in team identification, it is evident that scholars are still aiming to improve the integrity of team identification, despite the vast literature that exists on the topic. This answers greater calls within the sport management discipline regarding the use of theory in research (e.g., Chalip, 2006). However, despite these advancements, another critical issue must be addressed.

Team identification in women's sport

Although efforts to improve the study of team identification should be celebrated, an additional issue must be acknowledged. In studying team identification over the past three decades, scholars have focused on individuals' identification with men's sport teams, largely ignoring team identification in women's sport. Indeed, nearly all of the empirical research on team identification has focused on men's sport. In a review of 157 journal articles examining team identification through 2017, only 3 dealt with women's sport.

One might wonder: how much does sport gender matter in terms of team identification? Could we simply take what we have learned about team identification in men's sport over the years and apply it to women's sport settings? To answer this question, we should consider what we do know about team identification in women's sport, as well as how the women's sport setting differs from that of men's sport in terms of consumer following. In the following paragraphs, each of these topics is addressed.

Although an overwhelming majority of scholarly research on team identification has been conducted in men's sport settings, we can look to a few studies that have been conducted in women's sport settings. In these studies, researchers have found that team identification positively influences basking in reflected glory (BIRGing) and expectations of team performance, and that those who are less identified with a team may care more about convenience factors in choosing to attend sporting events. These findings are consistent with similar studies of team identification in men's sport (e.g., Wann & Branscombe, 1990).

Madrigal (1995) conducted research to understand the relationship of cognition and affect to sporting event satisfaction at women's college basketball games. Specifically, he conducted survey research with 232 attendees (63.5% female, 36.5% male) over 4 women's basketball games at a university in the Midwest region of the United States. Respondents completed one questionnaire before the game and another immediately after the game. Team identification was measured using a nine-item scale informed by Wann and Branscombe's (1993) SSIS. Madrigal used structural modeling to test a model suggesting a causal link between fan cognition (team identification, expectancy disconfirmation, and quality of opponent) and satisfaction with attending the game, mediated by BIRGing (Cialdini, Borden, Thorne, Walker, Freeman, & Sloan, 1976), and enjoyment. Team identification was relatively high among respondents, with a mean score of 5.32 on a 7-point scale. Madrigal found that team identification, expectancy disconfirmation, and quality of the opponent had a significant and positive effect on individuals' BIRGing and enjoyment of the event. Concerning team identification specifically, identification with the team had the greatest effect on both BIRGing and enjoyment. In addition, those individuals with higher team identification (compared with those with lower or no identification) had greater expectations for the team before the start of the games. In all, Madrigal's (1995) study added support to the notion that more highly identified individuals are more likely to BIRG than lower identified (or not identified) individuals. As Madrigal (1995, p. 222) concluded:

> In sum, it appears that fans who view their association with a team as a more important facet of their self-identity tend to experience greater personal joy and seek greater individual association with the team when it experiences successful outcomes.

Fink, Trail, and Anderson (2002) conducted research to better understand the antecedents of team identification, informed by previous research suggesting that social psychological motives for consuming sport may be related to team identification (e.g., Sloan, 1989; Trail & James, 2001). Specifically, the purpose of their study was to examine the relationship between a variety of motives (vicarious achievement, acquisition of knowledge, esthetics, social interaction, drama/excitement, escape, family, and quality of physical skill of the participants) and identification. The authors also sought to understand whether gender differences existed concerning the paths between motives and identification. Fink et al. (2002) conducted their survey research with 364 attendees of 2 college basketball games at a university in the southern region of the United States; 168 surveys were completed at a men's game and 196 surveys at a women's game. In total, 53.8% of respondents were females. Team identification was assessed using the unidimensional Team Identification Index (TII: Trail & James, 2001), and motives were assessed using the Motivation Scale for Sport Consumption (MSSC: Trail & James, 2001). The authors used structural equation modeling to test the relationship between motives and identification. Unfortunately (for the purposes of learning about team identification in women's sport), the authors collapsed the data for analysis, reporting their findings from the men's basketball and women's basketball events collectively. None the less, they found that vicarious achievement explained the most variance in team identification (40%), and suggested that future research should consider the extent to which collective identification, symbolic representation, and other identities influence team identification.

In a third study of team identification within a women's sport setting, Lee, Branch, and Silva (2017) conducted research with attendees of a National Women's Soccer League (NWSL) game. Lee et al. sought to understand differences in game attributes and loyalty based on identification type (i.e., sport, team) with attendees of the NWSL FC Kansas City during the league's second season (2014). Identification with the sport (soccer) and team (FC Kansas City) were assessed using the Points of Attachment Index (PAI: Trail, Robinson, Dick, & Gillentine, 2003). Data were collected via online survey, and distributed through social media by players on the FC Kansas City team. A total of 265 completed surveys were deemed usable for analysis; 71.5% of respondents were female, and about two-thirds (68%) indicated they had experience playing soccer themselves. Considering identification scores, three groups were identified for a cluster analysis: serious fans (high team identification, high sport identification); soccer fans (moderate team identification, high sport identification); and local fans (moderate team identification, low sport identification). Based on these groups, the authors found that soccer fans and local fans considered convenience factors (stadium accessibility, parking) much more important for attending than serious fans. Among all respondents, game quality was the single most important factor indicated for attendance. Considering loyalty, not surprisingly serious fans were the most loyal, followed by soccer fans, and finally local fans.

Separate from team identification, some scholars have conducted research on individuals' motives to consume women's sport (e.g., Fink et al., 2002; Funk, Ridinger, & Moorman, 2003). Scholars have found that individuals' motives to consume women's sport do differ from men's sport, particularly concerning affordability, the influence of family and friends, and support for a cause. The notion that one's reason(s) for consuming women's sport may differ from those of men's sport indicates differences in what individuals are looking for in their consumption experience, which could inherently influence identification that often develops as a result of attending events. Unfortunately, because of the lack of research on team identification in women's sport, there is no research to support this idea. However, we can look to figures on sport attendance and viewership to further understand differences in men's and women's sport consumer behavior.

Women's sport attendance and viewership

Considering mainstream professional team sports such as basketball and soccer, we know that attendance of women's sport differs greatly from that of men's sport. In 2017, the Women's National Basketball Association (WNBA) regular season attendance averaged 7,716 (WNBA, 2017), compared with a 2017 National Basketball Association (NBA) regular season attendance average of 17,884 (NBA, 2017). Similarly, in 2016 the National Women's Soccer League (NWSL) regular season attendance averaged 5,558 (Goldberg, 2016), compared with a 2016 Major League Soccer (MLS) regular season average attendance of 21,692 (Carlisle, 2016). Considering both of these examples, it is obvious that, in both basketball and soccer, men's sport on average attracts a far larger number of spectators than women's sport. Television viewership appears to tell a similar story; the 2017 WNBA finals series averaged a 0.5 market rating, its highest in nearly 15 years (Spain, 2017), compared with a 2017 NBA finals series average market rating of 16.0, its highest in nearly 20 years (Holloway, 2017).

Of course, history could be thought to play a part in the discrepancy between women's and men's sport attendance and viewership, given that many men's sport leagues have existed far longer than women's leagues. Teams and leagues with a greater history to draw on influence consumer interest and motivation to attend, as well as fandom and identification, and team and/or league financial success. Perhaps, as a result, it is no secret that the consumer experience for women's sport is different to that of men's sport, given the limited time professional women's sport has existed in comparison to men's sport. Yet we have minimal data to illustrate how this difference translates to team identification in women's sport.

Consideration of attendance and viewership of women's professional sport leads to another question: who exactly is the women's sport attendee? Understanding the demographic characteristics of an organization's consumer base is often paramount in decisions pertaining to marketing, including segmentation and targeted marketing, branding, sponsorship, and promotion (e.g., Mumcu, Lough, & Barnes, 2016).

Scanning the women's professional sport landscape, a good amount of demographic information can be found on WNBA attendees via Sports Market Analytics (Table 29.1). Considering the gender of attendees, many people are often surprised to discover that a greater number of men attend WNBA contests than women. Looking at attendance figures from 2012 to 2015, more than half the attendees were male. This suggests that the prevalence of males consuming men's sport may carry over into women's sport—at least as far as it concerns professional basketball. WNBA attendees seem to range in age, however; typically most attendees fall between the ages of 18 and 49; in 2015, nearly half of all attendees were between the ages of 18 and 34, suggesting that the league may be gaining popularity with younger generations (e.g., millennials, Generation Z). This is promising for the future of the league, because adolescents and young adults mature into consumers with greater spending power. Finally, considering the income of WNBA attendees, most report an annual household income of US$50,000 or more, with about a quarter reporting an annual household income of US$100,000 or more.

Table 29.1 Demographic information for WNBA attendees and viewers

	2012	2013	2014	2015
Attendance/Viewership by gender (%)				
Female	23.2/41.8	45.6/44.9	44.0/37.4	30.4/40.1
Male	76.8/58.2	55.4/55.1	56.0/62.6	69.6/59.9
Attendance/Viewership by age group (%)				
13–17	5.3/7.4	7.7/6.4	4.5/6.2	18.9/7.3
18–34	19.4/16.5	37.0/25.7	35.5/18.0	47.3/23.3
35–49	54.0/21.3	21.2/15.2	18.5/22.4	26.1/27.4
50 or older	21.3/54.7	34.1/52.8	41.5/53.4	7.8/42.0
Attendance/Viewership by household income (%)				
<US$25,000	33.9/17.2	22.5/20.8	14.9/18.7	23.2/16.4
US$25,000–49,999	9.8/24.6	18.4/23.1	16.1/25.8	9.9/25.7
US$50,000–99,999	35.9/29.8	34.8/32.3	40.3/30.8	38.2/29.8
US$100,000 or more	20.4/28.5	24.3/23.8	28.7/24.8	28.6/28.2

Source: Sports Market Analytics – www.sportsmarketanalytics.com.

Demographic information like that on WNBA attendees can help paint a picture of who consumers of a given team or league are; however, very limited information like this is made available publicly on consumers of other women's professional sport. For example, Sports Market Analytics, a popular source for secondary research on sport consumers, lists demographic and psychographic attendance and viewership information on consumers in a range of men's professional sport leagues. However, with the exception of the limited WNBA data previously mentioned, there is no such information for women's professional sport.

It is a problem that we cannot access the same information on consumers of women's sport that we can for men's sport. In discussing the issue with one industry professional, they commented on the lack of viewership information in women's sport, stating, "There doesn't seem to be much out there. I suspect the reason is the universe is too small for any legitimate research company to produce data on a scientific sampling basis at a reasonable price." In reaching out to women's sport leagues directly for demographic information on their attendees, it was discovered that some do not even keep records of this type of information. It is a problem if our women's professional sport leagues are not endeavoring to understand who their consumers are—demographically, socioeconomically, psychographically, and so on. Do they not keep records of this information because they lack the resources to do so? How will these leagues or teams grow and expand their fan bases if details about such individuals are unknown or inadequately tracked? How can we fix this problem?

A path forward

The relative lack of both research on team identification in women's sport and data on women's sport consumer characteristics is unfortunate, but we should not be discouraged by this current state. As researchers, educators, students, and industry professionals, we can and should take steps to fill these gaps. In the remainder of this chapter, ideas for future research in this area are discussed.

Considering the lack of research on team identification in women's sport, perhaps a good starting point would be to engage in conversations with sport consumer behavior scholars and industry professionals to understand the extent to which others perceive this as a problem, and how we should address it. Although the lack of research on team identification in women's sport is quite evident, how often do scholars pause to think about this issue? Do they perceive particular sport settings, such as women's sport (compared with men's sport), as unique in terms of an individual's psychological connection to a team? What topics, if any, do scholars or practitioners believe should be investigated in women's sport settings?

Beyond engaging in conversations with others to address the lack of research, we should also get to work, conducting team identification research with fans of women's sport. Much of this effort, initially, could involve attempting to replicate key work that has been done on team identification in men's sport settings. We may not know the extent to which the women's sport setting differs in terms of identity until we have examined it. However, in the interest of women's sport—particularly, in hopes of growing opportunities for women in professional sport and improving the experiences of the fans who support women's sport—we should endeavor to conduct research in these settings regardless of whether or not differences are found from men's sport contexts. Understanding women's sport consumers and the influence of identification will only allow women's sport practitioners to make decisions pertaining to marketing and consumer behavior with greater confidence.

Considering specific topics to be studied within team identification, we still do not have a strong understanding of how a psychological connection to a women's sport team influences behavioral and attitudinal outcomes, nor do we know the extent to which an individual's identification with a women's sport team influences (or aligns with) his or her other social identities. Although scholars have recently acknowledged how multiple identities are at play in team identification (Delia, 2015; Lock & Funk, 2016), we could benefit from understanding how these multiple identities work in women's sport contexts. For example, it could be that, in instances where individuals feel as though identifying with a women's sport team allows them to support an opportunity for women (Funk et al., 2003), another external identity (e.g., feminist identity) may influence identification with the team. Understanding the relationships of these multiple identities could advance our theoretical understanding of identification in women's sport and could also be beneficial practically as sport teams consider best practices for marketing and promoting the women's sport consumer experience.

As mentioned, women's sport generally draws a smaller audience of consumers than men's sport. This, in turn, likely results in far fewer individuals who identify with a given women's sport team. If there are fewer people who identify with certain women's sport leagues or teams (compared with men's), does that change the nature of the team-related identity, compared with an identity associated with a men's sport team? We know that team identity is a social identity—it is a shared, collective identity that in part gets its significance and value from the group itself (Hogg & Abrams, 1988). The question concerning the study of team identification, then, is: What happens when that group is significantly smaller? Does the identity take on a different meaning or significance than in a comparable men's sport setting?

The preceding questions and ideas are just a handful of possible avenues of inquiry concerning identification among fans in women's sport. There are certainly more concepts and issues to be understood within this area. As scholars, students, and practitioners who are interested in women's sport, we must acknowledge that, from a consumer behavior perspective, we will never contribute to or advance the success of women's sport, compared with men's sport, unless we invest (at least) the same amount of time and energy into understanding who consumers of women's sport are, why they support women's sport, how it contributes to their sense of self, and what they are looking for in their experiences with women's sport.

Leader profile: Kerrilyn Curtin, Director of Market Research and Planning, LPGA

Kerrilyn Curtin is currently the Director of Market Research and Planning for the Ladies Professional Golf Association (LPGA), a position she has held since mid-2017. In this role, she oversees the market research efforts for the entire association, working on projects such as sponsor research (sales and recapping), television viewership, and fan research. Commenting on her position, she noted:

> One of the reasons I was excited to join the LPGA was to work with an organization that not only promotes women and young girls in sport but also promotes and advocates for women overall. The LPGA is successful in promoting confidence through sport and helping to mold the next generation of women leaders on the field, in the job force and the community. I am proud to have a small part in that.

Before working with the LPGA, Curtin worked for an innovative cross-platform research firm, Symphony Advanced Media, and also with NBC Universal as the Director of Research for Telemundo local affiliates across the United States. Before her time in the media industry, Curtin worked at Madison Square Garden, spending 10 years with the entity's market

Figure 29.1 Kerrilyn Curtin

research team, where she rose from Research Analyst to Director. Reflecting on her career path, Curtin noted:

> I got into market research by chance and quickly fell in love. I believe market research is the backbone of all business decisions, especially in the sports and media world. Market research provides the why to what makes fans who they are, and what makes sports so valuable to sponsors. There is a reason sponsors spend money to be associated with sport, and research helps to uncover that reason.

Curtin has spent time on the Board of Directors for the Commission on Sport Management Accreditation (COSMA) as the industry representative. As she explained, "Working with COSMA was an amazing experience in which I was able to get to know students and professors across the country, all of whom were looking to better their sport management program."

A native of Long Island, New York, Curtin earned a BS in Sport Management and Marketing from York College of Pennsylvania in 2003, and an MS in Sport Business from the State University of New York at Cortland in 2010. Her interest in working in sport stems from her own experiences as an athlete and sport fan. To this day, she tells the story of her first visit to Madison Square Garden as a child, when she told her father she would work there one day. The story illustrates how Curtin's ambition to succeed in the sport industry began early in life, and has continued only as she has established herself as an expert in market research.

References

Abrams, D. (1999). Social identity, social cognition, and the self: The flexibility and stability of self-categorization. In D. Abrams & M. A. Hogg (eds), *Social Identity and Social Cognition* (pp. 197–229). Oxford: Blackwell.
Carlisle, J. (2016). MLS sets average attendance record in 2016 as Seattle Sounders lead all clubs. Retrieved from www.espnfc.com/major-league-soccer/story/2980505/mls-sets-average-attendance-record-in-2016-as-seattle-sounders-lead-all-clubs.
Chalip, L. (2006). Toward a distinctive sport management discipline. *Journal of Sport Management*, **20**, 1–21.
Cialdini, R. B., Borden, R. J., Thorne, A., Walker, M. R., Freeman, S., & Sloan, L. R. (1976). Basking in reflected glory: Three (football) field studies. *Journal of Personality and Social Psychology*, **34**, 366–375.
Delia, E. B. (2015). The exclusiveness of group identity in celebrations of team success. *Sport Management Review*, **18**, 396–406.
Delia, E. B. (2017a). A digital ethnography of fan reaction to sponsorship termination. *European Sport Management Quarterly*, **17**, 392–412.
Delia, E. B. (2017b). March sadness: Coping with fan identity threat. *Sport Management Review*, **20**, 408–421.
Delia, E. B. & James, J. D. (2017). The meaning of team in team identification. *Sport Management Review*, **21**, 416–429.
Dimmock, J. A. & Grove, J. R. (2005). Relationship of fan identification to determinants of aggression. *Journal of Applied Sport Psychology*, **17**, 37–47.
Doyle, J. P., Lock, D., Funk, D. C., Filo, K., & McDonald, H. (2017). "I was there from the start": The identity-maintenance strategies used by fans to combat the threat of losing. *Sport Management Review*, **20**, 184–197.
Fink, J. S., Trail, G. T., & Anderson, D. F. (2002). An examination of team identification: Which motives are most salient to its existence? *International Sports Journal*, **6**, 195–207.
Funk, D. C., Ridinger, L. L., & Moorman, A. M. (2003). Understanding consumer support: Extending the Sport Interest Inventory (SII) to examine individual differences among women's professional sport consumers. *Sport Management Review*, **6**, 1–31.
Goldberg, J. (2016). National Women's Soccer League once again rising attendance numbers in 2016. Retrieved from www.oregonlive.com/portland-thorns/2016/11/nwsl_saw_rising_attendance_num.html.
Heere, B. & James, J. D. (2007a). Stepping outside the lines: Developing a multi-dimensional team identity scale based on social identity theory. *Sport Management Review*, **10**, 65–91.
Heere, B. & James, J. D. (2007b). Sports teams and their communities: Examining the influence of external group identities on team identity. *Journal of Sport Management*, **21**, 319–337.
Heere, B., James, J. D., Yoshida, M., & Scremin, G. (2011). The effect of associated group identities on team identity. *Journal of Sport Management*, **25**, 606–621.
Hogg, M.A. & Abrams, D. (1988). The social identity approach: Context and content. *Social Identifications: A social psychology of intergroup relations and group processes* (pp. 6–30). New York: Routledge.
Holloway, D. (2017). TV ratings: NBA finals is most watched since 1998. Retrieved from http://variety.com/2017/tv/news/tv-ratings-nba-finals-1202464230.
Kwon, H. H. & Armstrong, K. L. (2002). Factors influencing impulse buying of sport team licensed merchandise. *Sport Marketing Quarterly*, **11**, 151–163.
Lee, C., Branch, D. & Silva F. (2017). Examining women's soccer spectators on game attribute and loyalty. *Journal of Contemporary Athletics*, **11**, 97–109.
Lock, D. & Heere, B. (2017). Identity crisis: A theoretical analysis of "team identification" research. *European Sport Management Quarterly*, **17**, 413–435.
Lock, D. J. & Funk, D. C. (2016). The multiple in-group identity framework. *Sport Management Review*, **19**, 85–96.
Lock, D., Funk, D. C., Doyle, J. P., & McDonald, H. (2014). Examining the longitudinal structure, stability, and dimensional interrelationships of team identification. *Journal of Sport Management*, **28**, 119–135.

Lock, D., Taylor, T., & Darcy, S. (2011). In the absence of achievement: The formation of new team identification. *European Sport Management Quarterly*, **11**, 171–192.

Madrigal, R. (1995). Cognitive and affective determinants of fan satisfaction with sporting event attendance. *Journal of Leisure Research*, **27**, 205–227.

Madrigal, R. (2001). Social identity effects in a belief-attitude-intentions hierarchy: Implications for corporate sponsorship. *Psychology and Marketing*, **18**, 145–165.

Mumcu, C., Lough, N., & Barnes, J. C. (2016). Examination of women's sports fans' attitudes and consumption intentions. *Journal of Applied Sport Management*, **8**(4), 25–47.

National Basketball Association (NBA) (2017). NBA breaks attendance record for third straight season. Retrieved from www.nba.com/article/2017/04/13/nba-breaks-all-time-attendance-record-third-straight-season#.

Roccas, S. & Brewer, M. B. (2002). Social identity complexity. *Personality and Social Psychology Review*, **6**, 88–106.

Sloan, L. R. (1989). The motives of sports fans. In J. H. Goldstein (ed.), *Sports, Games, and Play: Social and psychological viewpoints*, 2nd edn, (pp. 175–240). Hillsdale, NJ: Lawrence Erlbaum Associates.

Spain, K. (2017). WNBA gets best TV ratings for finals since 2003. Retrieved from https://www.usatoday.com/story/sports/wnba/2017/10/05/wnba-gets-best-tv-ratings-finals-since-2003/736049001.

Stets, J. E. & Burke, P. J. (2000). Identity theory and social identity theory. *Social Psychology Quarterly*, **63**, 224–337.

Tajfel, H. (1974). Social identity and intergroup behavior. *Social Science Information*, **13**, 65–93.

Tajfel, H. & Turner, J. C. (1979). An integrative theory of intergroup conflict. In W. G. Austin & S. Worchel (eds), *The Social Psychology of Intergroup Relations* (pp. 33–47). Monterey, CA: Brooks/Cole.

Trail, G. T. & James, J. D. (2001). The motivation scale for sport consumption: Assessment of the scales psychometric properties. *Journal of Sport Behavior*, **24**, 108–127.

Trail, G. T., Robinson, M. J., Dick, R. J., & Gillentine, A. J. (2003). Motives and points of attachment: fans versus spectators in intercollegiate athletics. *Sport Marketing Quarterly*, **12**, 217–227.

Turner, J. (1985). Social categorization and the self-concept: A social cognitive theory of group behaviour. In E. Lawler (ed.), *Advances in Group Processes: Theory and research* (pp. 77–121). London: JAI Press.

Wann, D. L. (2006). Understanding the positive social psychological benefits of sport team identification: The team identification-social psychological health model. *Group Dynamics: Theory, research, and practice*, **10**, 272–296.

Wann, D. L. & Branscombe, N. R. (1990). Die-hard and fair-weather fans: Effects of identification on BIRGing and CORFing tendencies. *Journal of Sport & Social Issues*, **14**, 103–117.

Wann, D. L. & Branscombe, N. R. (1993). Sports fans: Measuring degree of identification with their team. *International Journal of Sport Psychology*, **24**, 1–17.

Wann, D., Melnick, M., Russell, G., & Pease, D. (2001). *Sport Fans: The psychology and social impact of spectators*. New York: Routledge Press.

Women's National Basketball Association (WNBA) (2017). WNBA scores highest attendance in six years during record-breaking season. Retrieved from http://pr.nba.com/wnba-metrics-2017.

30
Women are sport fans!
An examination of female sport fandom

Michelle Harrolle and Katie Kicklighter

On a warm spring day in sunny Florida on April 12, 1976, the chants and songs of the baseball stadium were ringing aloud, the scent of fresh popped popcorn were wafting in the air, and the wave had started to circle the stadium. It was my first Major League Baseball game. My grandfather had taken me out of school to watch the New York Yankees play a spring training game close to our home. When I looked into the crowd, I noticed a few other children in the stands lucky enough to be with their fathers and grandfathers. And, that's when I realized that I was the only fan in the stands who happened to be a young girl. This was just the way things were.

Today, sport fandom is no longer exclusively a man's world. Extraordinary social changes have allowed girls and women to become not only involved in, but also essential to, the sport industry. Although the importance of female fans is evident, a gap exists in the relationship between female fans, whose needs are not being met as consumers, and sport organizations, which are missing a significant potential revenue stream. To understand the fan as a primary stakeholder in the marketplace, it is essential to examine both the consumer and the business perspective of sport fandom. Therefore, this chapter examines the consumer behavior of female sport fans from a feminist viewpoint. To start, the chapter reviews the importance and definition of the female sport fan within the context of the cultural shifts that have led to increased opportunities for women to consume sport. Then, the stereotypes associated with female sport fandom are identified and discussed to illustrate the misconceptions that exist. Finally, by presenting literature on the similarities and differences between female and male sport fans, we hope to provide a better understanding of this customer segment while further providing implications for sport organizations.

Female sports fans: Why they matter

Reaching female sport fans becomes even more essential to sport organizations because studies show that women make up a large percentage of the sport consumer market (Bush, Bush, Clark, & Bush, 2005). For instance, in 2010, females made up 41% of the National Football League (NFL) fan base, 41% of Major League Baseball fans, 40% of National Basketball

Association fans, 37% of NASCAR fans, 36% of National Hockey League fans, and 40% of Major League Soccer fans (Funk, Alexandris, & McDonald, 2016). These statistics illustrate the depth of female sport fandom and the pressing need for sport organizations to understand their female fans and increase their sport consumption. However, many leagues and teams miss or fail to meet the needs of an entire customer segment because they do not understand the communication and marketing preferences of their female fans (Esmonde, Cooky, & Andrews, 2015).

Women have become the main purchasing decision-makers within their family units, determining or influencing 85% of all purchasing decisions, and buying more than 50% of products traditionally bought by men, including home improvement products, automobiles, and consumer electronics (Staurowsky, 2016). Hence, women are likely the primary purchasers of sport products including equipment, tickets, and other sport goods. Women's spending on sports logo apparel increased by US$1.3 billion from 2010 to 2011 across all eight major US leagues (Funk et al., 2016), illustrating the importance of understanding women as sport fans and consumers of sport. Marketers who can recognize the power and needs of the female sport fan will be more likely to engage and sell to this essential market segment.

Defining a "fan"

In seeking to define what today's female sport fan looks like, specifically the differences or lack thereof between men and women who identify as sport fans, we discover that no clear description exists to encompass the wide range of fandom seen throughout the industry. Esmonde et al. (2015, p. 41) supported this idea, stating: "There are no uniformly agreed upon meanings or purposes of sport fandom." One issue complicating the ability of scholars to define female fans is the limited inclusion of women as sport fans in the current scope of the literature. Society has historically looked at fans from a male perspective (Sveinson & Hoeber, 2016). Typically, strong fan identification has been interpreted as attending more games, being more knowledgeable about a team's players and history, and having persistent commitment to the team (James & Ridinger, 2002). These constructs are more commonly associated with male sport fans than female sport fans (Bush et al., 2005; James & Ridinger, 2002; McGinnis, Chun, & McQuillian, 2003).

There is a wide range of styles in which sport fandom can be expressed. Verbal, physical, and emotional displays differ based on the individual. McGinnis et al. (2003) stated that interpretations and meanings can be molded by the social environment and gender of the involved parties. As a result, no one, man or woman, will have the same interpretation of or reaction to their sport experience, making it increasingly difficult for marketers in the industry to reach fans. Regardless, our current definition of what it means to be a sport fan should be inclusive to reflect and represent the female voice.

Cultural shifts

The perceived differences between female and male sport fans and the questioned authenticity of females as sport fans are culturally based (McGinnis et al., 2003). Whiteside and Hardin (2011) stated that sports provide an arena for gender roles to be established, maintained, or challenged. Historically, sport has operated under a hierarchical and dualistic gender configuration which places a greater value on men as sport fans, likely inhibiting the ability of the industry

Women are sport fans!

to see girls and women as fans due to its separation of gender as different ranks of consumers (McGinnis et al., 2003). McGinnis et al.'s (2003) research further indicated that women's involvement in sports consumption is often met with resistance by men who feel that sport is their domain, noting the sport space as a traditional place of male bonding (Farrell, Fink, & Fields, 2011; McGinnis et al., 2003). Historically, many sports have not been an open and welcoming environment for female fans.

Several broader cultural shifts have opened the door for girls and women as sport fans, reflecting a need for a new definition of girls and women as fans, participants, and consumers of sport. The shifts lie in three key areas including education, employment, and access (Pope, 2017). Within these extensive cultural shifts, women have overcome specific barriers on the path to becoming authentic sport fans on a larger social scale. To illustrate the cultural shifts and explain the higher levels of influence on female fans, we have included a timeline with specific outcomes influencing the fandom of girls and women over the past century.

Based on research from Frantz (2017), Imbornoni (2017), and the National Women's History Project (n.d.), Figure 30.1 shows the historical markers that have affected the sport experience for women as fans. The expectation of traditional female roles, although relaxed in our current society, continues to influence women's decisions about sport. The transition of women to sport participants and sport fans has not been easy; many women have struggled to find acceptance in the sport space.

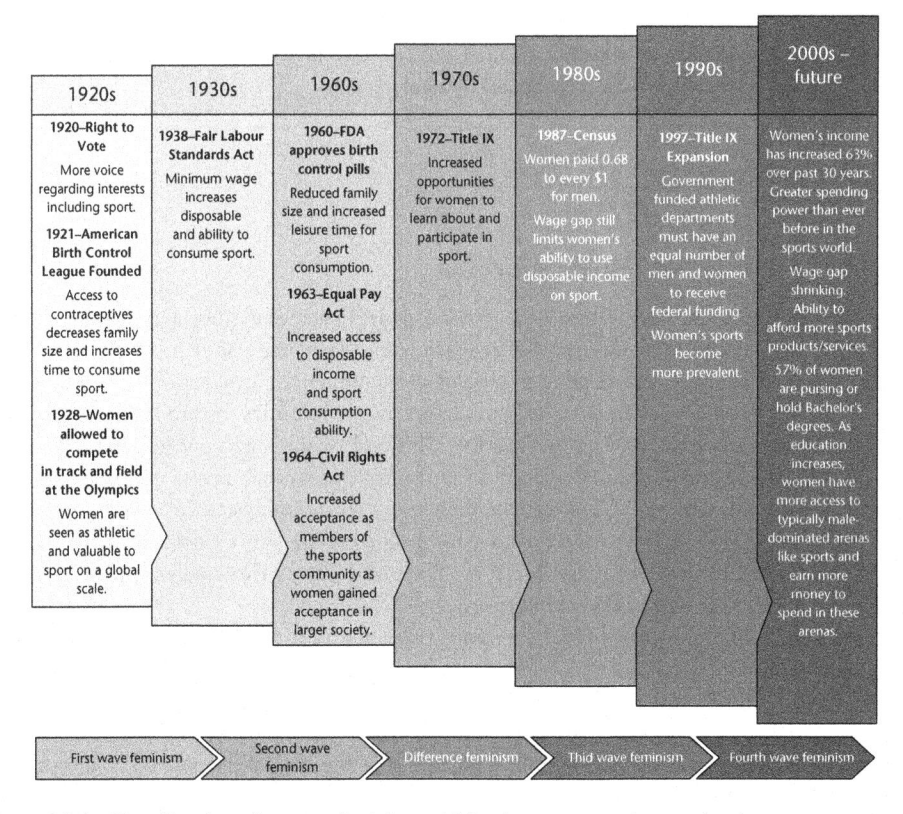

1920s	1930s	1960s	1970s	1980s	1990s	2000s – future
1920–Right to Vote More voice regarding interests including sport. **1921–American Birth Control League Founded** Access to contraceptives decreases family size and increases time to consume sport. **1928–Women allowed to compete in track and field at the Olympics** Women are seen as athletic and valuable to sport on a global scale.	**1938–Fair Labour Standards Act** Minimum wage increases disposable and ability to consume sport.	**1960–FDA approves birth control pills** Reduced family size and increased leisure time for sport consumption. **1963–Equal Pay Act** Increased access to disposable income and sport consumption ability. **1964–Civil Rights Act** Increased acceptance as members of the sports community as women gained acceptance in larger society.	**1972–Title IX** Increased opportunities for women to learn about and participate in sport.	**1987–Census** Women paid 0.68 to every $1 for men. Wage gap still limits women's ability to use disposable income on sport.	**1997–Title IX Expansion** Government funded athletic departments must have an equal number of men and women to receive federal funding. Women's sports become more prevalent.	Women's income has increased 63% over past 30 years. Greater spending power than ever before in the sports world. Wage gap shrinking. Ability to afford more sports products/services. 57% of women are pursing or hold Bachelor's degrees. As education increases, women have more access to typically male-dominated arenas like sports and earn more money to spend in these arenas.

First wave feminism → Second wave feminism → Difference feminism → Third wave feminism → Fourth wave feminism

Figure 30.1 Timeline for of women's rights within the context of sport fandom

> **Personal case study: Michelle Harrolle, PhD**
>
> I would like to share a personal case study of cultural changes that reflect the changing landscape of sports for girls and women. As a young girl, who was encouraged by her mother to pursue her dreams of swimming in college, I often found myself as the outsider. As a tween, I was stronger than everyone, was more athletic than the boys and girls, and embodied the current, modern example of an athletic girl. If you looked at my notably defined biceps and low body fat today, you would have seen an athlete. However, in the 1980s when the social norms for young girls did not include "the athlete" as a choice, life was tough. In middle school, the boys called me the "ox." I was called "crazy," for walking into high school as a freshman with wet hair from early morning practice. When the school paper gave out awards of the year, I was given an accolade that was disguised as the "dike" award. To this day, I remember running into the school counselor's office not truly understanding what that meant. While these times were difficult as the outsider, thankfully, society changed and social norms began to adjust in the 1990s. When I went off to college and became an All-American athlete in swimming, I was respected as an "athlete" and my athletic build was admired. My access to collegiate athletic events at a top 10 university was my introduction into sports and the catalyst of my current sport fandom. Now as a mother of an athlete, I make the majority of decisions pertaining to my son's sport participation, and I am the one in the household who purchases his favorite rock climbing shoes. While it may have been challenging growing up during this cultural shift, I relish where women have come from and where we are headed in terms of sport athleticism and fandom.

Transformation of the female sport fan

Since the 1990s, women have found greater control over their activities, and equality within sport (Pope, 2017). Consequently, the sport space is experiencing a shift in the line between masculinity and femininity, where gender is less likely to influence participation or consumption of sport (McGinnis et al., 2003). A significant change in the attitudes toward women's place in sport has occurred since the passing of Title IX. Girls and women are continuously expressing their increased interest in sports. An average of nearly 50% of women across multiple countries in the Americas, Europe, and Asia consider themselves to be interested or very interested in sports (Funk et al., 2016). In terms of participation, 40% of US sport participants are women (Kane & Maxwell, 2011). More than ever, it has become accepted for females to participate, be involved in, and be knowledgeable about sports.

Consequently, the number of female sport fans increased (Bush et al., 2005; James & Ridinger, 2002). Perhaps the most pressing statistic supporting the growth of women as sport fans and consumers of sport is the increase in the female NFL audience, up 3% from 2010 to 2011, compared with a 2% decrease in male audience size (Funk et al., 2016). With the increasing trend of female sport fandom, the importance of understanding the female sport perspective becomes more pressing for organizations.

The blurring of gender lines includes a narrowing of what McGinnis et al. (2003) called the spectator gender gap, because only 69% of men indicated they were interested or very interested in sports (Funk et al., 2016). Female fans may experience judgment about their decision to support a team, player, or sport in general, even with this positive transformation of attitudes, because some fan behaviors may continue to be seen as masculine, which conflicts with socially acceptable feminine behaviors (Sveinson & Hoeber, 2015). An expectation of the way women should behave in social settings exists that does not align with the typical behaviors displayed by male sport fans. Expectations for female fan behavior are related to gender schema theory, the idea that as a society we try to classify everything as male or female, which has carried over and had lasting effects on sport as it relates to communication with female fans (Staurowsky, 2016). Tension between gender identification and team identification will continue to play out in the sport space until women find equilibrium and acceptance (Sveinson & Hoeber, 2016).

Stereotypes and the current view of women as fans

Although it may be true that women exhibit sport fandom, the cultural shifts in sport have not altered the presence of stereotypes surrounding the female fan. Despite having an awareness of the need for an inclusive view, an apparent disconnect between the methods sport teams use to reach their female fans and provide for their interests prevails. Thus, looking at gender as it relates to attitudes, intentions, and behaviors surrounding the sport space is essential. The current view of women as sport fans is largely based on deeply embedded stereotypes and role expectations for women. Sveinson and Hoeber (2016) stated that female sport fans are seen as passive spectators who are inauthentic in their motives. Their study further discusses the idea that the "authenticity of fanship is associated with behaviors displayed by men" (Sveinson & Hoeber, 2016, p. 14).

The perception that women are not genuine in their interest in sports is a common theme throughout scholarly research. Female sport fans are assumed to be less knowledgeable, and to follow sport because of the social interaction opportunities it provides or due to their attraction to players (Pope, 2017). As a result, women experience segmentation in the sport marketplace by being placed into three main categories: the tomboy fan, the accessory fan, and the pink-and-proud fan, based on whether they reject, embrace, or accommodate femininity (Borer, 2009; Esmonde et al., 2015). Borer (2009) defined the tomboy fan as a female who has adopted stereotypically masculine attributes like consuming beer/hot dogs and wearing attire such as oversized T-shirts and jerseys, effectively rejecting feminine stereotypes and reinforcing male dominance in sport. Conversely, accessory fans do not care if they are recognized as real fans, instead accommodating femininity and accepting the uninformed and "in it for the players" stigma associated with being a female fan. Women who fall in the pink-and-proud classification embrace their femininity and challenge gender roles by asserting their place in sport as a true follower of the team while still asserting their femaleness. Again, we see that the evaluation of female fandom is based on an overarching tendency of society to classify fans according to male behaviors and typecast women as the stereotypical female sport fan.

Women not watching women

An additional notable and interesting point about female sport fan behavior is the failure of women to support women's sports. The lack of attention to women's sports could be a reflection of society's embedded beliefs on a larger scale of what is considered to be female. Correspondingly, most women's athletic events receive low ratings, a phenomenon believed to exist for three reasons: lack of coverage of women's sports, the framing of women's sports, and women's lack of leisure time. Women's sports are frequently positioned in the media against far more popular men's matches, making it difficult to attract an initial audience for the events (Whiteside & Hardin, 2011). In competing for prime air time and channels, women are not afforded the same media coverage as men's sports, and McGinnis et al. (2003) believe this is due to male dominance over sport production and distribution of women's sport. The lack of coverage can be linked to cultural framing as well. An implied inferior nature of women's sports leads to low production quality and the emphasized femininity of female athletes (Whiteside & Hardin, 2011). Only 6–8% of all sport media coverage includes women's sport (Kane & Maxwell, 2011), sending a clear message about the value that the media and sport industry place on women's sports. When female athletes do not receive the media attention they deserve, it proves difficult for females to increase their fandom. Perhaps a bigger question for sport marketers should be why they treat women's sports as inferior, and how they can more effectively promote the excitement and success of female athletes and women's sport.

Women as equal "fans"

Despite the supposed differences between men's and women's motivations, behaviors, and attitudes surrounding their sport fandom, we believe in the importance of recognizing that female fans may or may not be different from men. Regardless, female sport fans should not be seen as less important in the sport space. In the next two sections, we offer two contradictory perspectives and relevant literature on men and women as sport fans.

A study by End, Dietz-Uhler, Harrick, and Jacquemotte (2002) noted that women are just as likely as men to be sport fans. In fact, other researchers (James & Ridinger, 2002; McGinnis et al., 2003) have found that many similarities exist in the consumption patterns of male and female sport fans. For example, both men and women spend equal amounts of time attending sporting events (James & Ridinger, 2002). In addition, men and women have similar reactions to sport when controlling for interest (McGinnis et al., 2003). These overlaps indicate that women may not be as inauthentic as sport fans as was once thought by researchers. Again, we observe that the issues with female sport fandom may be a framing issue rather than a gender difference.

Women have rarely been asked for their perspective on what it means to be a sport fan. Thus, "there has been little opportunity to challenge the taken-for-granted and dominant viewpoints of what it means to be a fan" (Sveinson & Hoeber, 2015, p. 416). This lack of inclusion has prevented scholars and organizations from recognizing the sport identities held by women. Pope's (2012) research on hot and cool fans suggests that women can highly identify and have a deep commitment to sport. Her study drew on Giulianotti's "hot" and "cool" axis, in which hot fans see sport as central to their life and identity, whereas cool fans interacted with sport through media, but viewed the attendance of matches as leisure rather than part of their identity (Pope, 2012). With this in mind, industry leaders can feel confident in identifying females as fans and working on ways to better understand how to best reach them.

Differences between men and women

The counter-argument to the similarities between men and women as sport fans would suggest that, as a rule, men and women consume sport differently. Typically, male fans engage in more stereotypical sport fan behavior such as watching sport shows and listening to sport radio (Bush et al., 2005). Male fans spend more time discussing sports and watching on TV, show greater interest in sports, and possess more knowledge of sports, whereas women enjoy attending games, cheering, and watching with friends/family (James & Ridinger, 2002). Men often consume sports in an active–aggressive manner (McGinnis et al., 2003), whereas women report stronger attachment to a team rather than a sport in general (James & Ridinger, 2002).

These differences may be reflected in social identity theory, which states that highly identified individuals will feel greater group association (End et al., 2002). A study by James and Ridinger (2002) suggests that males' higher ratings on achievement, empathy, and knowledge measures provide a sport identity for men not shared by women. When asked about fandom, women offer more inclusive definitions than the norm as "one who legitimately enjoys the sport and the team, wears team colours and demonstrates positive support for the team" (Sveinson & Hoeber, 2015, p. 411). Women within the study believed that knowledge and attendance are secondary attributes of what it means to be a sport fan. Therefore, women may define their sport fandom differently to their male counterparts based on motives and behaviors (Sveinson & Hoeber, 2015). Other research (Bush et al., 2005) confirms that women do tend to see sport as a social event, but it is our belief that this does not make them less of a fan, a view that is supported by many other studies (Bush et al., 2005; Esmonde et al., 2015; Pope, 2017; Sveinson & Hoeber, 2015).

Implications for the sport industry

The research covered in this chapter illustrates why women should be considered authentic sport fans. The acceptance of sexist practices by sport fan communities opens the door to the continuation of female oppression because women are included only when they adhere to the very expectations that suppress their consumption of sport (Esmonde et al., 2015). Whether female fans display different behaviors, motives, or attitudes to male fans, sport organizations cannot continue to ignore the needs of such a significant customer segment. Many current marketing techniques within the industry follow the stereotypes of gender, an inaccurate and unattractive message. By making assumptions about female fans, sport organizations will continually fail to realize the potential revenue stream of this important and valuable market segment.

What not to do

To help maximize sales revenue, we have identified some communication strategies that we know do not work in attracting and retaining female sport fans. A delicate balance must be used when making a point to include women in the historically male sport space, because some approaches may segregate women even further (McGinnis et al., 2003). Thus, the stereotypical pink, bedazzled, and sexualized products, often utilized as sport-marketing techniques, are largely ineffective at connecting the brand with the female fan. Many of today's sport organizations have fallen for the "pink it and shrink it" method of marketing, where traditionally masculine products are colored pink and marketed to women, efforts that seek to infantilize, hyperfeminize, and hypersexualize the female sport fan (Esmonde et al., 2015). Not all women desire these kinds of products. Instead, teams need to promote goods and services that reflect the authenticity of women's fandom. Advertisements for sport should also reflect this authenticity.

Similarly, language is powerful and should be a major consideration when marketing to female sport fans. In sport, gendered adjectives are the norm, emphasizing the difference between male and female sports and the way sport marketers communicate with fans. The use of gendered adjectives supports the stereotypes between the sexes (Messner, Duncan, & Jensen, 1993). Examples of gendered communication in sport include what McGinnis et al. (2003) refer to as gender marking and infantilization. Gender marking occurs in the title of the tournaments (i.e., "the" championship for men versus the women's championship). Another example from McGinnis et al. (2003) is the men's Professional Golf Association (PGA) versus the Ladies Professional Golf Association (LPGA), which highlights the issue of infantilization such that female athletes are commonly referred to as girls or ladies, whereas male athletes are identified as men rather than boys (McGinnis et al., 2003; Messner et al., 1993). The industry's current framing of women in sport serves only to further distance girls and women as sport fans, thus providing another way to emphasize the "inauthenticity" of female fans and sustain the lack of inclusivity that can deter women from consuming sport.

A recent example of good intentions with questionable execution in regard to female athletes was the marketing campaign of the National Women's Soccer League (NWSL), "Pass the Ball." This advertisement featured celebrities such as Ellen DeGeneres, Julia Roberts, David Beckham, and Reese Witherspoon, who shared a public service announcement on the need for an increase in the support of female soccer athletes. The video presented messages of "saving the soccer players," a statement that paints the league as weak and in need of help, when in fact the organization is full of talented and strong women playing sport. McCauley (2017) added that DeGeneres takes away from the purpose of the content by saying, "Amazing athletes . . . see, notice she didn't say female athletes," instead of focusing on the incredible abilities of the women. Although their motive may have been in the right place, the NWSL sent a negative message for female sport fans, calling them to watch in support of women out of obligation, without acknowledging the players' skill, athleticism, and commitment to the game. In particular, no athletes or game play were shown in the clips (McCauley, 2017). The devaluing of women's sports reaffirms the gender roles that have been hard fought to alter and one day eliminate.

What to do

As discussed earlier, conventional gender structures are often deeply embedded in society (McGinnis et al., 2003), but, with the larger shifts seen on a cultural scale, the blurring of lines between masculinity and femininity will provide marketers with greater opportunities to capitalize on women sport fans as consumers. To satisfy the female sport fan, organizations must first realize that, even within the market, further segmentation can occur. Some women will display different consumer behavior to other women. Sport-marketing communication should be inclusive of all genders and all styles of female fandom. Ultimately, teams and organizations should tailor their messages to meet the needs of women, without classifying sport products as exclusively for women (Johnson & Learned, 2004). Strategies that follow this idea will provide the foundation to engage with female fans in meaningful ways, as demonstrated by a few organizations within the sport industry.

What should marketers do? They should look to the example of the Women's National Basketball Association (WNBA), which produced a great marketing campaign for the 2017 season titled "Watch Me Work"; this centered on a message dedicated to showing why women's basketball was a quality sport product (McCauley, 2017). The advertisements featured a number of women athletes such as Maya Moore and Candace Parker practicing, training, and playing basketball while highlighting the straightforward call to action: "watch me work." This message of empowerment is a marketing strategy that works well among the female fan base and market. By remaining transparent and not showcasing gender, the WNBA can communicate the idea that women's sports are viable as a consumer product and experience.

From a merchandise perspective, the NFL's "It's My Team" campaign provides another example of how sport organizations can successfully attract female fans. These print advertisements feature women from all backgrounds and social positions including Condoleezza Rice, Serena Williams, and DJ Kiss. The women within the photos are styled in various gear of their favorite NFL team, displaying the new apparel line that is based on extensive research driven by NFL female employees. In providing options beyond the stereotypical pink and smaller sizes, the NFL's new apparel strategy allows women to define their fandom on their own terms

(Jessup, 2012). By conducting research and not following stereotypes, the NFL could effectively develop an appealing product line and communicate with its women fans to drive sales. Female fans have responded with double-digit growth in women's apparel for four consecutive years, compelling the NFL to increase this product line by 30–35%, a quantitative show of the NFL's ability to understand female sport fans as a market (Dosh, 2013).

The future: What affect will data and analytics have on the female sports fan?

As a society, we have moved into the age of data analytics and sport organizations need to adapt accordingly. Within this chapter, we have defined the female sport fan, demonstrated the cultural shifts that have led to increased opportunities for women to consume sport, and shown how the stereotypes associated with female sport fandom have impacted sport organizations' ability to effectively communicate with these consumers. In addition, we examined a two-sided perspective on whether men or women really differ as sport fans, something that should continue to be studied by academia and sport organizations alike. From the academic perspective, sport-marketing research should include more data and research from a feminist perspective. This call is echoed by a number of scholars who have stated that the use of a feminist approach in sport fan research is important, including K. Toffoletti and P. Mewett who believe that female sports fandom has the potential to rewrite how we define sport fans (as cited in Sveinson & Hoeber, 2015). From the industry perspective, we recommend that sport organizations first develop meaningful research questions, conduct reliable research, and collect data of their own before designing a marketing strategy for their women fans. Teams and leagues should consult with professional researchers/consultants or academics to conduct this type of consumer behavior research.

The use of data analytics will prove valuable in drawing insights and understanding the consumer behavior of women sport fans without the bias of gender stereotypes. Technology will assist in removing assumptions from the marketing process and allow sport organizations to develop their own conclusions on whether differences truly exist between male and female sport fans, and how these differences should influence communication messages. Proper application of analytics to understand the growing amount of data available will eliminate inconsistencies in sport marketers' understanding of consumer behavior (Erevelles, Fukawa, & Swayne, 2016). Analysis of quality data can be used as a tool for conceptualizing what female fans look like (e.g., motives and needs) at all levels. Effectively using data and business intelligence to drive decision-making within sport organizations, including media coverage, merchandizing, and ticket sales will provide the greatest opportunities for meaningful change. Overall, it is crucial to acknowledge that women are a significant sport fan group that deserves attention and recognition within the sport industry as an authentic consumer segment.

Leader profile: Tracy West

As one of only four female tournament directors on the PGA Tour, the President of Copperhead Charities, and partner in ProLinks Sports, Tracy West leads the strategic and management efforts for the Valspar Championship. West was named one of Tampa Bay's Most Influential Women in Sports and *Tampa Bay Business Journal*'s Non-Profit Business Women of the Year. Similar to so many women executives in sport, West grew up immersed in sport and enjoyed watching golf on television with her father and grandfather on Sunday afternoons. "Sports was something to do with my family," said West. These shared experiences fostered her long-term interest in sport and inspired her to pursue a sport career.

Figure 30.2 Tracy West

Two major milestones shaped West's career path and leadership: founding her own company, Hayson Sports Group, and becoming a Tournament Director in the PGA Tour. "When all of the responsibility, the employees, the direction of the company, the risk, all of it rests on your shoulders, you grow as a leader," says West. At that time, only one other female director existed within the PGA. Now, female director positions are more prevalent because women like Tracy were trailblazers in the industry with of 5 of 48 PGA-sponsored tournament directors being female and an increasing number of women in elevated roles like Director of Sales and Tournament Chairman.

Over a distinguished career including 48 golf tournaments, West is most proud of the charitable contributions afforded from the proceeds of the golf tournaments. "Giving back to the community. That's what drives me. That's what keeps me motivated," says West. The Valspar Championship operates as a not-for-profit and, in 2017, the tournament raised US$2.4 million for charities including the All Children's Hospital, Chi Chi Rodriguez Foundation, First Tee, and Habitat for Humanity of Pinellas County, an organization in which West also serves as a board member.

From a business perspective, West believes sport should be a way to build relationships and increase revenue to allow organizations to create better fan experiences and increase community involvement. Women should embrace sport and, in particular, golf, as a way to use the sport to further their business careers. She feels that, when women don't play golf, they are missing out on the chance to build relationships in the corporate world by spending four hours on the golf course.

When asked about advancing women in sport, West expressed how her team provides mentorship and leadership to women who intern at her tournaments. She believes women starting their careers in sport need opportunities where they are given meaningful responsibilities and professional development. Being a mentor to Valspar Championship interns, serving on the first all women's advisory board to the local organizing committee for the Women's Final Four, and participating in speaking engagements through the Tampa Bay WISE chapter allows her to contribute to the growth of women in sport. Moreover, women and girls in sport are fortunate to have Tracy West as a leader in the industry!

References

Borer, M. I. (2009). Negotiating the symbols of gendered sports fandom. *Social Psychology Quarterly*, **72**(1), 1–4.

Bush, V., Bush, A., Clark, P., & Bush, R. (2005). Girl power and word-of-mouth behavior in the flourishing sports market. *Journal of Consumer Marketing*, **22**(5), 257–264.

Dosh, K. (2013). Women's apparel sales grow. *ESPNW*, September 13. Retrieved from www.espn.com/espnw/athletes-life/blog/post/7169/women-apparel-sales-grow.

End, C., Dietz-Uhler, B., Harrick, E., & Jacquemotte, L. (2002). Identifying with winners: A reexamination of sport fans' tendency to BIRG. *Journal of Applied Social Psychology*, **32**(5), 1017–1030.

Erevelles, S., Fukawa, N., & Swayne, S. (2016). Big data consumer analytics and the transformation of marketing. *Journal of Business Research*, **69**, 897–904.

Esmonde, K., Cooky, C., & Andrews, D. (2015). "It's supposed to be about the love of the game, not the love of Aaron Rodgers' eyes": Challenging the exclusions of women sports fans. *Sociology of Sport Journal*, **32**, 22–48.

Farrell, A., Fink, J., & Fields, S. (2011). Women's sport spectatorship: An exploration of men's influence. *Journal of Sport Management*, **25**(3), 190–201.

Frantz, C. (2017). Timeline: Women in sports. *Infoplease*. Retrieved from https://www.infoplease.com/spot/timeline-women-sports-0.

Funk, D. C., Alexandris, K., & McDonald, H. (2016). *Sport Consumer Behavior: Marketing strategies*. New York: Routledge.

Imbornoni, A. (2017). Women's rights movements in the U.S. *Infoplease*. Retrieved from https://www.infoplease.com/spot/womens-rights-movement-us-0.

James, J. & Ridinger, L. (2002). Female and male sports fans: A comparison of sport consumption motives. *Journal of Sport Behavior*, **25**(3), 260–278.

Jessup, A. (2012). How new marketing approaches helped the NFL achieve triple-digit growth in women's apparel sales, November 26. Retrieved from https://www.forbes.com/sites/aliciajessop/2012/11/26/how-new-marketing-approaches-helped-the-nfl-achieve-triple-digit-growth-in-womens-apparel-sales/#fdfde2d44342.

Johnson, L. & Learned, A. (2004). *Don't Think Pink: What really makes women buy—and how to increase your share of this crucial market*. New York: AMACOM.

Kane, M. & Maxwell, H. (2011). Expanding the boundaries of sport media research: Using critical theory to explore consumer responses to representation of women's sports. *Journal of Sport Management*, **25**(3), 202–216.

McCauley, L. (2017). NWSL whiffs with #PassTheBall campaign by refusing to sell its core product—great soccer, September 27. Retrieved from https://www.sbnation.com/soccer/2017/9/27/16374790/nwsl-pass-the-ball-ellen-degeneres.

McGinnis, L., Chun, S., & McQuillan, J. (2003). A review of gendered consumption in sport and leisure. *Academy of Marketing Science Review*, **5**, 1–24.

Messner, M., Duncan, M., & Jensen, K. (1993). Separating the men from the girls: The gendered language of televised sports. *Gender & Society*, **7**(1), 121–137.

National Women's History Project (n.d.). Timeline of legal history of women in the United States. Retrieved from www.nwhp.org/resources/womens-rights-movement/detailed-timeline.

Pope, S. (2012). "The love of my life": The meaning and importance of sport for female fans. *Journal of Sport and Social Issues*, **372**(2), 176–195.

Pope, S. (2017). *The Feminization of Sports Fandom: A sociological study*. New York: Routledge.

Staurowsky, E. (2016). *Women and Sport: Continuing a journey of liberation and celebration*. Champaign, IL: Human Kinetics.

Sveinson, K. & Hoeber, L. (2015). Overlooking the obvious: An exploration of what it means to be a sport fan from a female perspective. *Leisure Studies*, **34**(4), 405–419.

Sveinson, K. & Hoeber, L. (2016). Female sport fans' experiences of marginalization and empowerment. *Journal of Sport Management*, **30**(1), 8–21.

Whiteside, E. & Hardin, M. (2011). Women (not) watching women: Leisure time, television, and implication for televised coverage of women's sports. *Communication, Culture, and Critique*, **4**, 122–143.

31
Marketing women's professional tennis

Ashleigh-Jane Thompson

Gender equality in professional tennis

The worldwide competition structure of tennis and its increasing reputation in the Olympic Games serve to illustrate its global reach (Brouwers, Sotiriadou, & De Bosscher, 2015). It is the second most popular global sport after football (soccer), played in 190 countries, has 4.4 million fans and attracts 800 million television viewers globally (Brouwers et al., 2015). As former Women's Tennis Association (WTA) Chair Stacey Allaster argues, "having 10 different [countries] represented in the top 10 rankings shows how truly global tennis has become" (Marshall, 2011, para. 4). This increased globalization has led to further commercialization of the sport, its players, and events, leading to increased marketing-related opportunities (Brouwers et al., 2015). For example, recent figures serve to illustrate the growth of sponsorship spending in the sport (Figure 31.1).

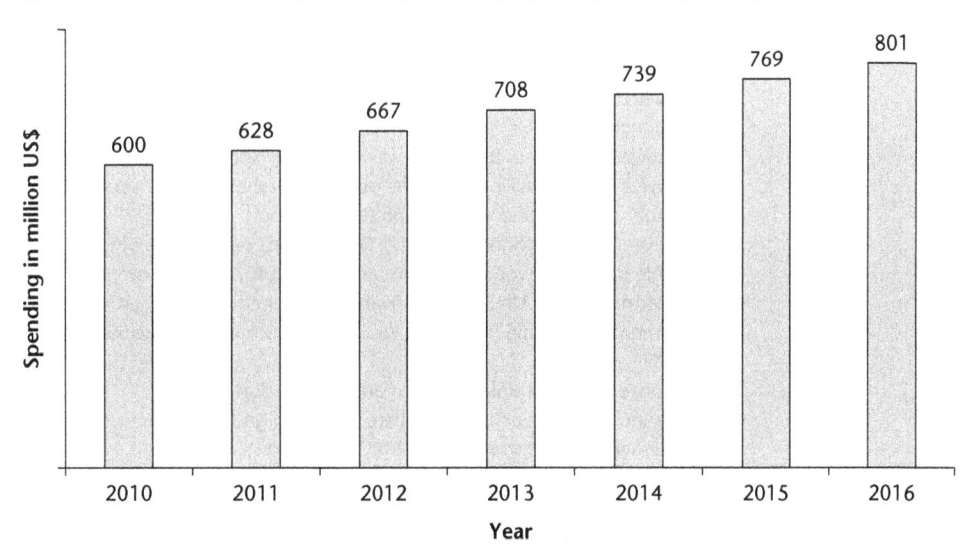

Figure 31.1 Tennis sponsorship spending worldwide from 2010 to 2016 (in million US dollars). Data from Statista (2016a)

Tennis serves as an interesting context within which to examine marketing efforts and social media use in promoting women's sport, because, for some, it is considered to be the "world's leading sport for women" (Walker, 2006, para. 4). It is one of the few popular sports in which men and women compete in the same tournaments and are awarded equal prize money in premier events.[1] As the principal organizing body of women's professional tennis, the Women's Tennis Association (WTA) is responsible for promoting the game and protecting the rights of its players. Table 31.1 summarizes the WTA's continuous efforts to achieve greater equality in tennis. In their discussion of marketing women's sport, Lough and Mumcu (2016) highlight the WTA and its success in enhancing the global status of women's tennis.

With an increase in the commodification of women's sport globally, and the reliance on sponsorship and endorsement money, there is an ever-present need for players to construct a socially acceptable image (Taylor, 2008). Some argue that no other sport has achieved this outcome better than women's tennis and the WTA (Lough & Mumcu, 2016; Taylor, 2008). Taylor (2008) claims that it is the glamour of women's tennis that has currently secured its reputation as the most marketable and profitable sport for women in the world. Nevertheless, there are still several significant impediments to the advancement of gender equality in the sport.

Certainly, it is a sport that has long been mired in accusations of sexism, marginalization, and overt gender bias. Demeaning treatment of women players is so widely accepted that many overlook what some top tennis officials say and do, given they rarely face any form of censure.

Table 31.1 Key moments of gender equality in women's tennis (based on information on the WTA's website)

Year	Key moments
1970	Start of women's professional tennis with nine players signing US$1 contracts to compete in the new women's tour, the Virginia Slims Series[a]
1973	Billie Jean King founds the WTA
	Equal prize money at the US Open
1974	WTA signs first-ever television broadcast contract, with US network CBS
1984	Equal prize money at the Australian Open
1990	First-ever US$1 million tournament in women's sports
2003	WTA launched the "Get In Touch With Your Feminine Side" Campaign
2005	Sony Ericsson becomes the Tour's worldwide title sponsor in a landmark six-year, US$88 million deal. The most comprehensive sponsorship in the history of tennis and women's professional sport
	Kim Clijsters, as the winner of the US Open Series, receives the biggest single payday in women's sports, and in any official tennis event
2006	WTA partnered with UNESCO to advance gender equality and promote women's leadership in society. Venus Williams named as the inaugural ZYX
2007	Equal prize money at Roland Garros and Wimbledon
2008	WTA launched the "Looking for a hero?" Campaign
2009	WTA launched the "Strong is Beautiful" Campaign
2013	WTA launched the "40 LOVE" Campaign
2014	WTA and media partner, PERFORM, signed a US$525 million, 10-year media rights extension, the largest media rights agreement in the history of women's sport

a Temporarily did not have equal prize money between 1996 and 2000.

For example, a statement made by former Indian Wells tennis tournament chief executive, Raymond Moore, highlights the continued dogma of male superiority in the sport. Before the women's final, Moore commented that women's tennis "rides on the coattails" of men's, and claimed, "if I was a lady player, I'd go down every night on my knees and thank God that Roger Federer and Rafael Nadal were born because they have carried this sport" (Newman, 2016, para. 8).

Although some point to the equal prize money paid at all major tournaments as a sign of the progressive movement to treat men and women equally in the sport, debates around pay equality continue, even embroiling leading male players. Frenchman Gilles Simon told reporters at Wimbledon that men's tennis is "ahead of women's tennis" because "they provide a more attractive show" (Associated Press, 2012, para. 5). Similarly, former world number one Novak Djokovic noted that, although he applauded women for fighting for equal prize money, men "should fight for more because the stats are showing that [they] have much more spectators on the men's tennis matches" (Newman, 2016, para. 7).

Before 2007, the All England Club's justification for unequal pay at Wimbledon appeared to center on gender demarcation (Taylor, 2008). In contrast, these comments focus on the belief that men's matches attract bigger audiences rather than any notion of inherent male athletic superiority. This justification is grounded in the belief that this leads to greater media and match revenue, creating a more impressive and popular spectacle than women's tennis. However, when it comes to the strategic marketing of such tournaments, the players are just one part of a larger commercialized sport system (Bouchet, Hillairet, & Bodet, 2013; Thompson, Martin, Gee, & Geurin, 2017a). Indeed, there exists a more complex sport–media–commercial nexus that is both influenced by, and influences, coverage, sponsorship, and advertising campaigns.

Unfortunately, actions at leading international tournaments also contribute to the continuation of gendered stereotypes and masculine hegemony within tennis. Connell (1995) states that masculine hegemony, as a social construct, guarantees (or is taken to guarantee) the dominant

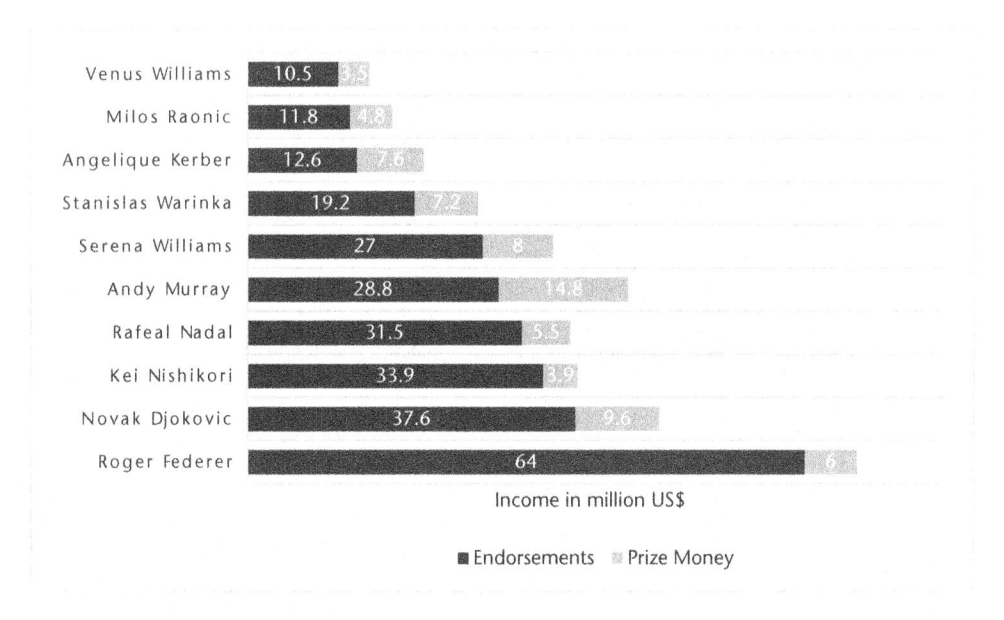

Figure 31.2 The highest-paid tennis players in 2016–2017 (in million US dollars). Data from Statista (2016b)

position of men and subordination of women. In post-match interviews, male players usually face questions about form, the game, and their performance on court. However, during the 2015 Australian Open, interviewers subjected American Serena Williams and Canadian Eugenie Bouchard to requests during their on-court interview that served to undermine their athletic performance and reinforce stereotypical gendered identities by focusing on their appearance. A (male) commentator asked Bouchard to twirl and tell the crowd about her outfit. A clearly embarrassed Bouchard acquiesced, but this interaction drew sharp criticism from tennis fans and commentators online, calling it out as "sexism" in the sport.

This was the second time the tournament had been embroiled in a global media frenzy about sexist gender representations in tennis. Bouchard was also at the center of a sexism row during the 2014 Australian Open when an on-court commentator questioned her after her quarterfinal win about her dream date. As Lough and Mumcu (2016) note, these actions not only belittle the athlete's success but also "thereby diminished the potential to build appreciation of the quality of the women's sport product" (Lough and Mumcu, 2016, p. 358). Thus, ultimately resulting in a frustrating cycle of self-perpetuation undermining women's sporting achievements.

In another example, the WTA itself courted controversy during Wimbledon in 2017 when it asked tennis fans, in an online poll, to choose the female player they thought was best dressed (Figure 31.3). By explicitly focusing on their appearance, this poll diverted much-needed attention away from the talent and athleticism of these players. In doing so, the WTA reinforced the notion that image is important for women playing sport and reinforced existing gender roles and power structures (Daniels & LaVoi, 2012).

Figure 31.3 WTA's tweet asking fans to vote on "Best Dressed" women at Wimbledon 2017

Media and marketing representations

The media play an instrumental role in shaping gendered sport representations and identities (Kian & Clavio, 2011) and, historically, sport media have focused much of their attention on men's sports (Fink, 2015). Lebel and Danylchuk (2009, p. 148) argued that today, "if something is not reported by the media, one might be justified to question whether the event actually took place." For women's sport this is particularly troubling given the lack of mainstream media attention women's sport receives (see Fink, 2015). Moreover, when the media does cover it, the trivialization and sexualization of women's sport constitutes a denial of power for sportswomen (Quayle et al., 2017). For example, women are trivialized when portrayed in situations that focus on aspects of their behavior, femininity, and personal lives rather than their contributions and performances as talented athletes. Similarly, they are sexualized, either overtly or covertly, by focusing on their physical attractiveness. In such cases their female athleticism is downplayed, devalued, or ignored.

Although some may argue that gender pay parity is a significant milestone in achieving greater gender equality in the sport, women's tennis is still far from being on a par with men's tennis. Unfortunately, it's not only those within the sport contributing to the continued gender disparity. Research is replete with examples of instances that highlight where sport media and marketers serve to "coerce female athletes to adhere to heterosexual, hyper-feminine scripts" (Fink, 2012, p. 50), by producing hypersexualized portrayals. These representations serve to undermine and trivialize their athletic endeavors, and are most commonly achieved through gender marking, sexualization of female athletes, and familial references (see Lough & Mumcu, 2016). Within professional tennis, former Wimbledon champion Martina Hingis is credited with openly acknowledging the role of the media and marketing in framing women's tennis, noting "it's business that wants this from us, and we're playing the game, me and Anna and Venus. We're the Spice Girls of tennis" (Finn, 1998, para. 6).

As acknowledged earlier, compared with some sports female tennis players do receive greater media coverage; however, differences still exist in the amount, type, and content (Quayle et al., 2017; Yip, 2016). The media's (re)presentation of female players and women's tennis has contributed to a continued inequality and sustained male hegemonic dominance by "activating negative stereotypes and providing prejudicial treatment" (Lough & Mumcu, 2016, p. 363) of female players, matches, and events. For example, analyses of British newspaper coverage of female players in the 2000 Wimbledon Championships found that the male journalists' coverage marginalized and devalued women by comparing their accomplishments and athleticism with those of men (Vincent, 2004; Vincent, Pedersen, Whisenant, & Massey, 2007). In addition, much of the coverage often focuses on their physical appearance (Kian & Clavio, 2011; Vincent, 2004; Vincent et al., 2007). As recently as the 2018 Australian Open, officials scheduled men's matches to coincide with host broadcaster Seven's primetime, thereby propagating the notion of women's tennis as an inferior and less marketable product.

Coupled with such gendered media representations, Kane and Maxwell (2011) found women's sports and female athletes have also been marketed and depicted in advertising promotions in ways that utilize their sex appeal. Consequently, many times athletes selected for marketing campaigns and product endorsements aren't the top-ranked, but rather those deemed to be the 'prettiest' (Fink, 2012). Certainly, this has been the case in tennis. Many cite the well-known example of Anna Kournikova, who never won a WTA singles title but was "the centre of the media's attention because of her beauty" (Yip, 2016, p. 4). Such findings serve to underpin the notion that their heterosexuality and heterosexual appeal are more important than their athletic talents. Former Wimbledon Champion Marion Bartoli can vouch for the notion that women are still judged first on their physical appearance, after the following comment from a BBC tennis commentator:

> I just wonder if her dad did say to her when she was 12, 13, 14: "Listen, you're never going to be a looker, you are never going to be somebody like a Sharapova, you're never going to be 5-foot-11, you're never going to be somebody with long legs, so you have to compensate for that."
>
> *(O'Carroll, 2013, para. 7)*

Although it resulted in 700 complaints it is unimaginable to consider such a comment being directed toward a male player. Importantly, however, for women's sport, research has shown that a "sex sells" approach can be detrimental to a female athlete and women's sport (see Fink, 2012).

Consequently, marketers have not traditionally portrayed women in sports advertising showcasing characteristics like hard work and athletic performance. However, the WTA has undertaken a raft of global marketing and promotional campaigns aimed at promoting the quality of the professional women's tennis tour and improving the image of their players, by showcasing them as highly skilled and dedicated athletes (see Table 31.1). The "Strong is Beautiful" campaign is one of the most notable WTA campaigns in recent years. Stacey Allaster commented that "the unique combination of athleticism, strength and determination on the court and success, interests and inner beauty off the court is what makes women's tennis so attractive to millions around the world" (Lawrence Corbett, 2014, para. 6).

However, although campaigns such as these provide an opportunity to challenge, and indeed change, the portrayal of women in professional tennis, there remains the issue that less money is invested in the promotion of women's sport (Lough & Mumcu, 2016). Unfortunately, this reinforces a common perception that women's sports are inherently less interesting and exciting, resulting in a cycle of self-perpetuation. However, with the emergence of social media the WTA and its players themselves now have an opportunity to change this. The following sections highlight marketing efforts and social media utilization that serve to change this dynamic and positively promote women's professional tennis.

Social media use to promote professional women's tennis

Online social media platforms are becoming increasingly integrated into people's everyday lives. We Are Social's Global Digital report (Kemp, 2018) reveals:

- The number of active social media users in 2018 is 3.196 billion, up 13% year on year.
- Facebook users aged 65 and above increased by almost 20% in the past 12 months.
- 58% of Facebook and 61% of Instagram users are aged 18–34.
- The number of global Instagram users is up by a third.
- Facebook (2,167 million), YouTube (1,500 million), and Instagram (800 million) have the highest number of active users.
- A "brand's community" has the potential to become its most asset.

Arguably, social media are also now an integral part of modern sports. As a result, sport marketers have taken a growing interest in social media platforms, developing various social strategies to connect with consumers. With the emergence of social media, the sport industry is now seeking to capitalize on these platforms to reach fans more directly than ever before. Although in the past athletes relied on traditional media and, more recently, official websites to communicate with fans, they now also maintain an official presence on various social media platforms such as Facebook, Twitter, YouTube, Instagram, and Snapchat.

Social media research has shown that these platforms are valuable marketing communication tools. Scholars have suggested that the benefits of social media use may include, but are not limited to, developing social connections, direct communication of brand image, and enhanced loyalty (Naraine & Parent, 2016; Thompson, Martin, Gee, & Geurin, 2017b; Walden & Waters, 2015). Furthermore, the current generation of "net-users" demands two-way communication, necessitating a connection with them via these channels. Research suggests that failure to do so may result in a loss of fans, competitive advantage and the benefits that social media provide (Thompson et al., 2017b).

Social media are having a profound effect on tennis (Thompson et al., 2017a, 2017b), and for women's professional tennis it's even more valuable. The women are no longer forced to rely on traditional media determining their "news value" and framing their coverage. The significance and importance of this link to the inherent value sport properties derive from the attention they garner (Lough & Mumcu, 2016). Figure 31.4 showcases the tennis players with the highest social media followers as of January 2018. Of note here is that six of the top ten are women. Such high levels of social media activity provide quantifiable evidence of a viable audience interested in women's professional tennis (and its players) and its value as a legitimate sport product (Lough & Mumcu, 2016). Moreover, in today's commercialized sporting landscape, demonstrated popularity can be leveraged into lucrative sponsorships, larger purses, and, for tournaments, a "must attend" attitude by players and spectators (Schoenstedt & Reau, 2013).

Notably, particularly for a global sport such as tennis, social media have transcended geographic barriers. As Qualman (2012, p. 2) asserts, "social media is global in nature . . . [and supports] global connectivity." If used proactively, the global reach and possible increased exposure afforded by social media extends the marketing and sponsorship potential for women's players (Thompson et al., 2017a). Coupled with this, these platforms have dramatically changed the communication landscape, allowing players now to communicate directly with various

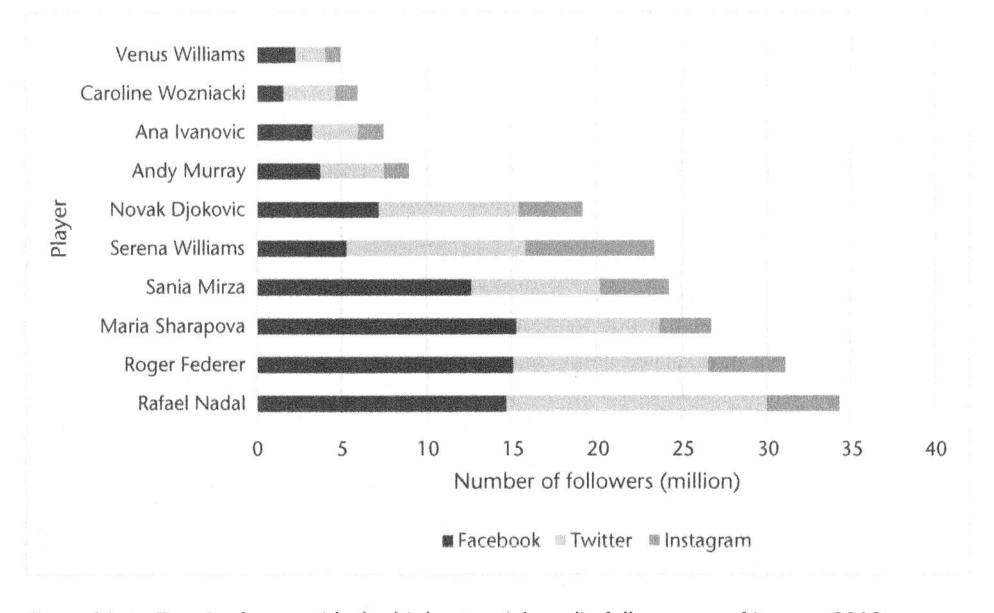

Figure 31.4 Tennis players with the highest social media followers as of January 2018.

stakeholders, which can be leveraged to develop relationships with both current and potential fans, and in so doing, enhance the players', tournaments', and WTA's marketing value.

In line with this, one of the key marketing benefits of social media is the opportunities they present for positive brand-building endeavors (Davies & Mudrick, 2017; Thompson et al., 2017a, 2017b). From a branding context, research shows that social media can affect consumer perceptions, and potentially influence consumptive behaviors (Thompson et al., 2017b). For women's professional tennis, which has struggled to gain legitimate mainstream media attention and coverage in the past, such branding benefits may be achieved through direct communication opportunities with an increasing online audience, enabling much greater interactivity between key stakeholders and their fans (Thompson et al., 2017b). Furthermore, Coche (2016) concluded that, as journalists often look to social media for breaking stories, women should look to platforms like Twitter in the search for exposure.

Increasing exposure is important to secure additional avenues for promotion and revenue generation through potential sponsorship and endorsement opportunities (Lough & Mumcu, 2016). Indeed, in 2017 retired former tennis No. 1. Ana Ivanovic was included in an Adidas campaign that identified 25 social media influencers Adidas hoped would assist their brand to increase its female sporting goods market share (Weiss, 2017). Successful social media activation assists women's professional players, no matter their rank, in developing their brand as an athlete, raising their profile and gaining this exposure (Davies & Mudrick, 2017; Geurin-Eagleman & Burch, 2016; Thompson et al., 2017a, 2017b). For example, during the 2013 Australian Open, American Sloane Stephens posted tweets to her followers with clues to the location of balls she had hidden around the venue (Figure 31.5), and those lucky enough to find them were treated to two box tickets to watch her match (Stephens, 2013).

This initiative saw her engaging with more people and increasing her awareness. Social media consultant C. James (personal communication, January 12, 2013), considers this a particularly successful execution:

> She quadrupled her fan base over 24 hours at one stage. She talked to people and improved her awareness. Sponsorship these days is tough to get, it's all about having a profile, and social media is where your profile is at now. It's not enough to have a website or do a photo-shoot; people want to see a relationship between the person they're sponsoring and their fans.

Similarly, in 2012 Brit Laura Robson, then ranked 89th in the world, used Twitter to successfully raise her public profile. As tennis writer Ben Rothenberg (2012, para. 6) stated, "Her sensibilities about social media have made her a dominant online force, outranking the top American male players John Isner and Mardy Fish." Her authentic approach to social media resulted in a posting style that presented an image of "normalcy" that translated into relatability, and saw her online popularity outpace her on-court results and ranking.

Moreover, by going beyond the arguably limited interaction of traditional media, social media provide largely unparalleled communication tools that can assist stakeholders involved in women's professional tennis to strengthen their relationships with fans (Abeza, O'Reilly, & Reid, 2013; Thompson et al., 2017a). Relationships can be strengthened through prolonged, authentic engagement that motivates increased consumptive behaviors and loyalty (Thompson et al., 2017a). One of the keys to using social media successfully is the need for continual communication and, as the name suggests, *social* interaction. Research has shown that the overwhelming responses to *why* people use social platforms are intrinsic in nature. They do so to feel connected, to learn and be inspired, and not because there is a reward to be received (Clavio & Kian, 2010; Thompson et al., 2017b).

> Sloane Stephens ✓
> @SloaneStephens
>
> Hey all! I am hiding this ball on-site at the @AustralianOpen . Find it & win 2 box Tix to my match 2mrw. Clue to come
>
> 7:45 PM - 21 Jan 2013

Figure 31.5 Sloane Stephens' tweet letting followers know about a competition to win tickets to her payer's box

Furthermore, although in the past, traditional media mediated such efforts, fans now have unprecedented access to their sporting idols, and as a result fans demand "insider perspectives" or "behind the scenes" insight that they are unable to get elsewhere (Thompson et al., 2017b). For professional women's tennis, social media have uniquely changed the relationship between the fan and tournaments and players. Showing authenticity and personality in posts proves popular, and so too do behind-the-scenes snapshots to which traditional media are not privy. According to a senior tennis social media consultant, the key to maintaining a strong social media presence comes back to people needing to have an authentic relationship with their fans, and in doing so players are more likely to be commercially viable, or commercially powerful (C. James, personal communication, January 12, 2013). Leading players have recognized the importance of this and are looking to maximize their efforts in building their online profile. For example, Maria Sharapova, one of the leading female athletes on social media, has publicly acknowledged the importance of interacting with fans via social media, stating:

> I tell them about what I'm doing, I log in on my phone and I report to them where I'm traveling from, my ideas and thoughts. Interacting with my fans is so important. I have a lot of them and I'm very thankful for that, and I really want them to have accessibility because I think they're important.
>
> *(Morely, 2011, para. 15)*

In addition, those involved in women's tennis can leverage social media to build an online community for their fans. Fostering feelings of community may aid in brand building efforts and ultimately lead to increased consumptive behaviors (Clavio & Kian, 2010; Thompson et al., 2017a, 2017b). Players and officials have promoted women's tennis to a larger audience through the creative use of hashtags to further "build" these online communities. One such example is French player Caroline Garcia, who has fostered her own fan community or "team" using #FlyWithCaro. Importantly, if the communities of women's professional tennis (i.e., players, tournaments, and WTA) on social media continue to grow, and in fact surpass men's tennis, traditional media outlets may give more weight to the importance of providing tennis fans with more equitable women's coverage (Vann, 2014).

As we've seen, traditional media journalists and editors had power in how women in sport were conveyed to the public. However, with the emergence of social media many sport scholars have suggested that we may experience an era of change, whereby stereotypical notions of gender and sexuality that have dominated the portrayal of female athletes will be increasingly challenged. Women now can speak out directly, and present their own image to fans, providing athletes with an opportunity to challenge the media's framing and promote women's sport in legitimate ways (LaVoi & Calhoun, 2013). This is something particularly significant for women's tennis, because the women athletes seek to break free from the overtures of hegemonic masculinity that have been so ingrained in the sport. Indeed, recent research has revealed that social media are being used to contest masculine hegemony that has prevailed in sport broadly for decades (Coche, 2016).

Moreover, women's professional tennis players are increasingly turning towards social media and bypassing traditional media sources to break news stories and make official statements, thereby reducing the reliance on gatekeepers in traditional media, many of whom are male (LaVoi & Calhoun, 2013). For example, in 2016 Ana Ivanovic used Facebook Live to announce her retirement from professional tennis to 2.4 million viewers. In her opening remarks, Ivanovic addressed why she had taken this approach, stating, "I haven't announced it anywhere else because I think you deserve to hear it first" (Ivanovic, 2016). Players have also turned to this platform in crises. In 2016, after a press conference announcing that she had tested positive for a banned substance, Maria Sharapova used her official Facebook page to update fans on the status of the Court of Arbitration for Sport appeal ruling. In a study examining fan responses to her Facebook post, results revealed that social media may be a valuable site for female athletes to engage in image repair work by making supportive messages likely and acutely visible to the public (Pegoraro, Thompson, & Frederick, 2017).

Although, in the past, players (and women's tennis organizations) would have released such statements through a formal "traditional" media channel, they can now deliver such content directly to fans. This illustrates a clear shift in both sport consumption and the sport–media nexus, particularly through social media. The point of note here is that players and women's tennis organizations can now attempt to control their own online image (i.e., self-branding) and promotion, through engaging with and through social media (Thorpe, Toffoletti, & Bruce, 2017), and by producing content that increases interest in and respect for women's tennis.

In addition, social media allow women's professional tennis to leverage opportunities for additional revenue and marketing opportunities (LaVoi & Calhoun, 2013; Thompson et al., 2017a). As Lough and Mumcu (2016) argued, previous efforts to achieve this have been hampered by diminished brand exposure suggesting, to effectively promote women's sport, more targeted tactics are required. Social media provide this capacity for women's tennis with free distribution to a targeted audience (i.e., fans that want to follow), which allows for more alignment with potential sponsors. Moreover, players, tournaments, and the WTA use social media not only to engage with fans but also to activate sponsorships and increase their own and their endorsers' brand awareness (Thompson et al., 2017a).

As Stacey Allaster notes, the growth the WTA previously experienced across their digital channels has positively affected the WTA's player, tournament and sponsor businesses (Emmett, 2014). Consequently, digital engagement should remain as one of the organization's key strategic priorities. The use of digital technology and social media will continue to enhance fan engagement opportunities that will be of critical importance in the continued fight for consumer's limited time and discretionary income. In acknowledgment of the growing importance of social (and digital) media, in 2016 the WTA announced the launch of WTA Networks, a dedicated digital and marketing division created to enhance the sports promotional efforts and attract fans and sponsors (WTA, 2016).

Conclusion

As previous research has shown, sport media and marketing have traditionally favored men's tennis, prolonging the stereotypical gendered notion of tennis as a bastion of masculine hegemony. To overcome this and ensure the growth of women's professional tennis, those involved in the sport must take ownership of their story and the presentation of their image, differentiating themselves from their male counterparts. Moreover, greater attention and understanding of the next generation of fans are required. Women's professional tennis needs to look at innovative strategies for engaging the youth market.

Social media provide professional women's tennis with the opportunity to, at least in part, address some of these issues. Although women's tennis has previously been underexposed and underinvested in, now through promotional efforts and opportunities with social media, times are changing. As professional women's tennis appears to have astutely realized, the future of sports consumption lies in the digital sphere, and it is likely that women's sport will experience their greatest rewards through this space. What we are currently experiencing is arguably just the beginning of what may be a sea change not only for the WTA and its players, but also for women's sport in general.

Leader profile: Karl Budge, Director, The LIVE Experience

Karl Budge acknowledges that he's taken a different route to most in the industry, having left school at 16. He credits his initial work with a sports marketing agency for opening the door to his first tennis-related role as a Sponsorship Manager for Tennis Australia, where he managed several of their commercial partnerships and business development for the Australian Open. After this, he moved to London to join the WTA as Director of Sales and Marketing and was instrumental in the organization's transition into new markets with the successful delivery of the season-ending championships in Istanbul. This success led to his relocation to the WTA's Beijing office to lead initiatives to drive growth in the Asia Pacific region. At 27, he became the youngest Tournament Director in the world, when he was approached about the Tournament Director role for the ASB Classic, and considers this to be, without question, the best move of his career. Under his direction, the ASB Classic has grown from strength to strength and is now established as the most commercially successful event of its tier on both the ATP and WTA Tours. It has won best event for its tier four years in a row and has, for five consecutive years, set crowd attendance and net profit records. In 2017, he also set up his own sports

Figure 31.6 Karl Budge

marketing agency, which works with rights holders and brands on all things sponsorship, sports, and entertainment.

Within his various roles, Budge has made significant contributions to the business of women's sport. Through his roles with the WTA he was instrumental in exposing new markets to how engaging, empowering, and entertaining women's tennis is and played a key role in the growth of women's tennis throughout Asia and the Middle East. He has also been involved in laying a foundation to drive investment in and promotion of women's tennis. During his time with the WTA, the organization signed more than US$15 million of new commercial revenues. This, coupled with significant gains in rights fees to host the season-ending championships and a record-setting broadcast deal, provided greater stability and a platform to invest in the WTA's athletes, brand, and promotion of women's tennis. A governance role with the WTA Tour afforded a great platform to influence change for players, officials, tournaments, and the tour itself. Specifically, Budge was very passionate about advancing investment in athlete support. In his current role, he's passionate about showing that a women's event can outshine its male counterparts. Although the ASB Classic now falls under the one name, ultimately it is still two separate events – a women's WTA event and a men's ATP event. The men's event had always been the standout in popularity and revenue. However, this changed under Budge's leadership with the women's event, with three out of the last five years achieving greater domestic broadcast viewership and spectator numbers than the men's event.

Note

1 Female players still receive significantly less prize money in lower-tier (less visible) tournaments than men, however.

References

Abeza, G., O'Reilly, N., & Reid, I. (2013). Relationship marketing and social media in sport. *International Journal of Sport Communication*, **6**(2), 120–142.

Associated Press (2012). *Gilles Simon: Men should make more*. Retrieved from www.espn.com.au/tennis/wimbledon12/story/_/id/8100886/players-debate-equal-prize-money-tennis.

Bouchet, P., Hillairet, D., & Bodet, G. (2013). *Sport Brands*. Oxon: Routledge.

Brouwers, J., Sotiriadou, P., & De Bosscher, V. (2015). Sport-specific policies and factors that influence international success: The case of tennis. *Sport Management Review*, **18**, 343–358.

Clavio, G. & Kian, T. M. (2010). Uses and gratifications of a retired female athlete's Twitter followers. *International Journal of Sport Communication*, **3**(4), 485–500.

Coche, R. (2016). Promoting women's soccer through social media: How the US Federation used Twitter for the 2011 World Cup. *Soccer & Society*, **17**(1), 90–108.

Connell, R. W. (1995). *Masculinities*. Sydney: Allen & Unwin.

Daniels, E. A. & LaVoi, N. M. (2012). Athletics as solution and problem: Sports participation for girls and the sexualisation of female athletes. In T. A. Roberts & E. L. Zubriggen (eds), *The Sexualisation of Girls and Girlhood* (pp. 63–83). New York: Oxford University Press.

Davies, M. & Mudrick, M. (2017). Brand management in a niche sport: A case study of an LPGA golfer's use of Instagram. *Global Sport Business Journal*, **5**(1), 1–22.

Emmett, J. (2014). The WTA in Singapore: how women's tennis measures parity in dollars. Retrieved from www.sportspromedia.com/magazine_features/the_wta_in_singapore_how_womens_tennis_measures_parity_in_dollars.

Fink, J. (2012). Homophobia and the marketing of female athletes and women's sport. In G. B. Cunningham (ed.), *Sexual Orientation and Gender Identity in Sport: Essays from activists, coaches and scholars* (pp. 49–60). College Station, TX: Centre for Sport Management Research and Education.

Fink, J. (2015). Female athletes, women's sport, and the sport media complex: Have we really "come a long way baby"? *Sport Management Review*, **18**(1), 331–342.

Finn, R. (1998). Game, set, glamour. Retrieved from www.nytimes.com/1998/11/22/style/game-set-glamour.html.

Geurin-Eagleman, A. N. & Burch, L. M. (2016). Communicating via photographs: A gendered analysis of Olympic athletes' visual self-presentation on Instagram. *Sport Management Review*, **19**(2), 133–145.

Ivanovic, A. (2016). Ana Ivanovic was live [Video file], December 29. Retrieved from https://www.facebook.com/anaivanovic/videos/1734062939942542.

Kane, M. J. & Maxwell, H. D. (2011). Expanding the boundaries of sport media research: Using critical theory to explore consumer responses to representations of women's sports. *Journal of Sport Management*, **25**(3), 202–216.

Kemp, S. (2018). Digital in 2018: Essential insights into internet, social media, mobile, and ecommerce use around the world. Retrieved from https://wearesocial.com/blog/2018/01/global-digital-report-2018.

Kian, E. M. & Clavio, G. (2011). A comparison of online media and traditional newspaper coverage of the men's and women's U.S. Open tennis tournaments. *Journal of Sports Media*, **6**(1), 55–84.

LaVoi, N. M. & Calhoun, A. S. (2013). Digital media and female athletes. In A. C. Billings & M. Hardin (eds), *Handbook of Sport and New Media*. New York: Routledge.

Lawrence Corbett, M. (2014). Is the WTA's focus on image good or bad for women's tennis? Retrieved from http://bleacherreport.com/articles/2137065-is-the-wtas-focus-on-image-good-or-bad-for-womens-tennis.

Lebel, K. & Danylchuk, K. (2009). Generation Y's perceptions of women's sport in the media. *International Journal of Sport Communication*, **2**(2), 146–163.

Lough, N. & Mumcu, C. (2016). Marketing women's sports: A European versus North American perspective. In S. Chadwick, N. Chanavat, & M. Desbordes (eds), *Routledge Handbook of Sports Marketing* (pp. 355–368). Milton Park, Oxon: Routledge.

Marshall, A. (2011). Tennis' global evolution is bringing the sport to new markets: An analysis. Retrieved from http://bleacherreport.com/articles/594875-the-global-evolution-of-tennis-is-bringing-the-sport-to-new-markets-an-analysis.

Morely, G. (2011). Serving social media or backhanded marketing? Retrieved from http://edition.cnn.com/2011/SPORT/tennis/05/04/tennis.sharapova.federer.nadal/index.html.

Naraine, M. L. & Parent, M. M. (2016). "Birds of a feather": An institutional approach to Canadian National Sport Organizations' social-media use. *International Journal of Sport Communication*, 9(2), 140–162.

Newman, P. (2016). Djokovic slammed for saying men should be paid more than women. Retrieved from www.independent.co.uk/sport/tennis/novak-djokovic-slammed-for-saying-men-should-be-paid-more-than-women-a6945016.html.

O'Carroll, L. (2013). John Inverdale's Marion Bartoli comments 'wrong', says BBC news chief. Retrieved from https://www.theguardian.com/media/2013/jul/09/john-inverdale-marion-bartoli-bbc.

Pegoraro, A., Thompson, A., & Frederick, E. L. (2017). Response to female athlete transgressions: Does gender matter? Paper presented at the 10th Summit on Communication and Sport, Phoenix, AZ.

Qualman, E. (2012). *Socialnomics: How social media transforms the way we live and do business*, 2nd edn. Hoboken, NJ: John Wiley & Sons.

Quayle, M., Wurm, A., Barnes, H., Barr, T., Beal, E., Fallon, M., et al. (2017). Stereotyping by omission and commission: Creating distinctive gendered spectacles in the televised coverage of the 2015 Australian Open men's and women's tennis singles semi-finals and finals. *International Review for the Sociology of Sport* 54(1). https://doi.org/10.1177/1012690217701889.

Rothenberg, B. (2012). Robson popular beyond her rank. Retrieved from www.nytimes.com/2012/08/31/sports/tennis/laura-robson-kim-clijsterss-us-open-conqueror-to-face-li-na.html?_r=1&ref=sports.

Schoenstedt, L. J. & Reau, J. (2013). Ladies first, men second: The 2010 Western & Southern Financial Group Masters and Women's Tennis Open and use of social media marketing. *Journal of Sports Media*, 8(1), 87–116.

Statista (2016a). Tennis sponsorship spending worldwide from 2010 to 2016 (in million U.S. dollars). Retrieved from https://www.statista.com/statistics/380296/tennis-sponsorship-spending-worldwide.

Statista (2016b). The world's highest-paid tennis players in 2016–17 (in million US dollars). Retrieved from https://www.statista.com/statistics/201486/wages-of-the-worlds-highest-paid-tennis-players.

Stephens, S. [SloaneStephens] (2013). Hey all! I am hiding this ball on-site at the @AustralianOpen. Find it & win 2 box Tix to my match 2mrw. Clue to come [Tweet], January 22. Retrieved from https://twitter.com/SloaneStephens/status/293565017796775936.

Taylor, S. (2008). Game, sex and match: sexism, heterosexism and homophobia in women's tennis [online]. In T. V. Hickie, H. Deborah, J. Scutt, & A. Hughes (eds), *Essays in Sport and the Law* (Vol. 24, pp. 147–160). Melbourne: Australian Society of Sports History. Retrieved from https://search.informit.com.au/documentSummary;res=IELHSS;dn=990225919504006.

Thompson, A., Martin, A. J., Gee, S., & Geurin, A. N. (2017a). Fans' perceptions of professional tennis events' social media presence: Interaction, insight, and brand anthropomorphism. *Communication & Sport*, 5(5), https://doi.org/10.1177/2167479516650442.

Thompson, A., Martin, A. J., Gee, S., & Geurin, A. N. (2017b). Managing social media marketing to develop event brand relationships: Perceived benefits, strategies and challenges. *International Journal of Sport Management*, 18(4), 488–515.

Thorpe, H., Toffoletti, K., & Bruce, T. (2017). Sportswomen and social media: Bringing third-wave feminism, post feminism, and neoliberal feminism into conversation. *Journal of Sport and Social Issues*, 41(5), 359–383.

Vann, P. (2014). Changing the Game: The role of social media in overcoming old media's attention deficit toward women's sport. *Journal of Broadcasting & Electronic Media*, 58(3), 438–455.

Vincent, J. (2004). Game, sex and match: The construction of gender in British newspaper coverage of the 2000 Wimbledon Championships. *Sociology of Sport Journal*, 21(4), 435–456.

Vincent, J., Pedersen, P. M., Whisenant, W. A., & Massey, D. (2007). Analyzing the print media coverage of professional tennis players: British newspaper narratives about female competitors in the Wimbledon Championships. *International Journal of Sport Management and Marketing*, 2(3), 281–300.

Walden, J. & Waters, R. D. (2015). Charting fandom through social media communication: A multi-league analysis of professional sports teams' Facebook content *PRism*, 12(1), 1–18.

Walker, A. (2006). UNESCO and Sony Ericsson WTA Tour announce global partnership to advance gender equality. Retrieved from http://portal.unesco.org/en/ev.php-URL_ID=35640&URL_DO=DO_TOPIC&URL_SECTION=201.html.

Weiss, R. (2017). Adidas hires social media stars to double women's market share. Retrieved from https://www.bloomberg.com/news/articles/2017-03-14/adidas-hires-social-media-stars-to-double-women-s-market-share.

Women's Tennis Association (WTA) (2016). WTA to launch new digital and social platform to take fans on tour. Retrieved from www.wtatennis.com/news/wta-launch-new-digital-and-social-platform-take-fans-tour.

Yip, A. (2016). Deuce or advantage? Examining gender bias in online coverage of professional tennis. *International Review for the Sociology of Sport*, **53**(5), 517–532.

32
Sexism in marketing women's sport and female athletes
Ineffective and harmful

Janet S. Fink

Introduction

On Sunday, August 20, 2017, I settled in to watch the Solheim Cup. Every two years the Solheim Cup pits LPGA (Ladies Professional Golf Association) golfers from the United States against those from Europe. The tournament has existed since 1990 and is similar in structure to the PGA's Ryder Cup, featuring four foursomes or four fourballs on the first and second days, and 12 single matches on the final day. The 2017 tournament featured truly magnificent golf with athletes from both teams pulling off amazing shots and clutch putts again and again (Soebel, 2017). Although the United States led 10.5–5.5 going into Sunday's final round of singles matches, nearly all of the contests between golfers were close, and people noticed. In fact, Sunday's round was the most watched women's golf tournament on cable TV in 8 years with nearly 800,000 viewers, and the tournament garnered 7.3 million viewers over the 3 days (Golf Channel Public Relations, 2017).

However, the Golf Channel's coverage only ran from 10:30am to 4:10pm on Sunday. I watched the United States seal the win with rookie Angel Yin's five-foot put with seven matches still in contention. Just as I was looking forward to the final players in the singles matches finish out their rounds, listen to interviews with the players, and watch the presentation of the trophy, coverage was aborted. Instead of sticking with the coverage of the Solheim Cup, the Golf Channel decided instead to switch to the final round of the Dick's Sporting Goods *Champions* tour. The Champions tour features *retired* PGA golfers and this particular event was a regular yearly contest that is part of the Champions tour. Sadly, the only people who got to see the end of the Solheim Cup, interviews with the players and captains, and the presentation of the trophy were those in attendance because there was no live coverage of it anywhere on television or other media. This would never happen to the men's Ryder Cup; even if the tournament's outcome were known, it would be shown in its entirety. Why would the Golf Channel leave the Solheim Cup, an every-other-year event featuring many of the world's top golfers, for a regularly scheduled Champions Tour event, especially given that the Solheim cup generated outstanding viewership metrics? This is just one of many examples of how women's sport and female athletes are treated differently by the sports media commercial complex. Ironically, had the Golf Channel aired the trophy ceremony, viewers would have heard this from team captain, Julie Inkster,

"We don't get what credit we're due," she said, with Solheim Cup in hand. "If we play well, the courses are too short. If we don't play well, we're not good enough."

"These ladies behind me, and even the European team, are amazing golfers. They play with power. They play with finesse . . . I hope people are starting to recognize how good they are . . . I just think as women golfers we always get shortchanged and it irks me," she said. "Even from the PGA Tour down, I just don't think we get really the respect we deserve."

(Coffin, 2017, para. 2)

Certainly, this isn't just a golf problem; it spans all sports. Sport is a traditionally male domain that reinforces gendered power relationships and the patriarchal power structure so firmly embedded in our culture (Bryon, 1987). Although women have made much progress in the world of sport, particularly in terms of participation rates, women's sport and female athletes are treated differently and often detrimentally. As Meân and Kassing (2008) note, even in the post-Title IX era of sports, females are rarely celebrated exclusively for their athleticism because "gender remains the primary categorization of women athletes, re/producing female athletes as women who play sport rather than as athletes first and foremost" (Meân and Kassing, 2008, p. 127). Perhaps no aspect of modern-day sport exemplifies this more than the sport media commercial complex – from marketing campaigns, to media coverage, to sponsorship decisions, the sport–media–commercial complex has enormous influence on framing how society views women's sport and female athletes (Fink, Kane, & LaVoi, 2014; Kane & Maxwell, 2011; Messner & Montez de Oca, 2005), and continually undermines the progress of women's sport and female athletes.

This chapter uses a critical feminist perspective to examine the marketing of women's sport and female athletes. Critical feminist theory proposes that there are unequal power relationships based on gender that result in the marginalization and debasing of women as a means to further solidify the patriarchal power structure. It asserts that gendered hierarchies are entrenched in (sport) culture and normalized in order to further advantage dominant groups (Hoeber, 2007). Critical feminist theorists probe taken-for-granted assumptions that are gender based in order to challenge the gendered hierarchies in an attempt to disrupt the existing state of affairs (Hoeber, 2007; Fink et al., 2014). As Kane (2011, para. 4) noted, sport is "one of the most powerful economic, social, and political institutions on the planet." Or, as McDonagh and Pappano (2008, p. 1) forcefully proclaim, "Sports matter." Sport's universal draw, appealing to different age groups, social classes, cultures, etc., translates into a powerful tool for socialization (Fink, 2008). If these gendered power differentials and taken-for-granted assumptions are not contested in sport, they will not only impact women's lives within sport, but also constrain their social, economic, and political opportunities outside of sport as well (McDonagh & Pappano, 2008; Fink, 2015a). Therefore, critical examination of the sport industry is a vital tool for advancing women's status in society at large.

This chapter focuses on sexism in the *marketing* of women's sport and female athletes, while acknowledging that such marketing does not operate in a vacuum. Certainly, marketing, media, and sponsorship are unequivocally intertwined with each impacting the other – as Fink (2015b, para. 4) stated, "Audiences grow with media hype, making sponsorship more appealing, while sponsorship support (and activation) increases consumer awareness and, subsequently, media attention." Marketing campaigns are created to appeal to assumed audience preferences, preferences influenced by media coverage and sponsorship. Thus, the fact that marketing campaigns for women's sport and female athletes often focus on attributes unrelated to their athleticism is impacted by, and impacts, differential media coverage and sponsorship decisions.

The assumption that sex sells

There has been a long-held assumption in the world of sports that the best (and perhaps only) way to market women's sport and female athletes is to focus on traditional standards of femininity and heterosexuality (LaVoi & Kane, 2011). This allows for females to participate in sport, but not overly threaten standard gender norms (Kane, LaVoi & Fink, 2013). Many who work in the marketing of women's sport and female athletes create and perpetuate this view (Kane, 2011). For example, Scott Becher, president of Sports and Sponsorships, said, when contrasting the marketability of similarly talented Olympic soccer players, Hope Solo and Abby Wambach, "Of course [appearance plays a role]. . . . With Hope, and this has nothing to do with Abby or anyone else, but don't you think there is a kind of a sexy appeal to her looks?" (Merrill, 2011, para. 11). Leonard Armato, a nationally acclaimed marketer and brand strategist, was even more blunt when speaking about female athletes in ESPN's *Nine for IX's* "Branded" episode:

> What makes a woman valuable? Her currency is how attractive she is. That's really the bottom line. Don't shoot me for it . . . but if you want to be successful as a woman, who is an athlete, sex appeal has to be part of the equation.
>
> *(ESPN Films, 2013)*

Such statements reinforce Meân and Kassing's (2008) contention that female athletes are still not appreciated for their athletic ability alone and are "othered" as *female* athletes (Krane, Choi, Baird, Aimar, & Kauer, 2004). Coupled with this, female athletes must be attractive, even sexy, to be deemed successful. Such pervasive attitudes clearly impact the marketing of women's sports and female athletes. For example, compared with their male counterparts, female athletes are much less likely to receive endorsement deals, receive far less in endorsement earnings, and the top female earners typically exhibit traditional ideals of femininity (Fink et al., 2014). In addition, most female athletes with the largest endorsement deals participate in what Metheny (1965) categorized as "female-appropriate sports," typically individual sports that feature "aesthetically pleasing" movements and feminine attire (e.g., tennis, figure skating). Few who receive endorsements compete in Metheny's "sex-inappropriate" sports, typically team-oriented sports that involve physical contact or bodily intimidation of the opponent (e.g., basketball, soccer). Of the female athletes in the top 10 in endorsement earnings in 2017, 8 are tennis players, all are attractive, and nearly all exhibit traditionally feminine characteristics (Badenhousen, 2017). Only two, Danica Patrick and Ronda Rousey, compete in traditionally "sex-inappropriate sports." Serena Williams, the top endorsement earner among the women, made US$19 million in endorsements; in contrast, the top male endorsement earner, Roger Federer, earned three times that amount, US$58 million (Badenhousen, 2017). Furthermore, there were no team sport athletes in the women's top 10; however, on the men's side, there were 4 basketball players, 2 soccer players, and a football player in the men's top 10 (Badenhousen, 2017). There is undoubtedly a double standard operating here; to be considered for lucrative endorsement deals, female athletes are much more likely to be considered if they embody traditionally feminine traits and compete in "female-appropriate" sports whereas, for male athletes, athleticism is by far the most important factor.

Some marketing campaigns for women's sport leagues also appear to reinforce the notion that female athletes must be attractive, traditionally feminine, and/or hypersexualized to be relevant. The Women's Tennis Association (WTA) recently ran a campaign titled "Strong is Beautiful" in which the players were on the court playing tennis, but in evening gowns/cocktail dresses, in full make-up with provocative images and verbal messages provided by the athlete in the background. For example, in a clip featuring Victoria Azarenka she says, "I like to hit the ball hard. CRUSH IT! And if the ball comes back, then it's trying to tell me something. How about a little harder?" (Women's Tennis Association, 2012; Fink, 2015a). The ShopRite Classic, an LPGA tour event, recently came under fire for conducting a Twitter poll to choose its sponsor exemptions. The four golfers in the poll, Blair O'Neal, Sharmila Nicollet, Carly Booth, and Susan Benavides, could all certainly be deserving of an exemption, but, as Alverez (2017, paras. 16 and 25) said, "But let's cut through the baloney. None of the ladies in the poll struggle in the looks department. They're all uniquely beautiful, and all have a strong male fan base. . . . It's gimmicky, erring on the side of tacky, and despite what Erensen believes is creative thinking, it's just a new way of exploiting women."

An even more disturbing trend is occurring in the sporting goods industry because sport organizations are foregoing female athletes in their advertising campaigns, opting instead for models and non-sport celebrities. Under Armour was the first to go this route with the use of Gisele Bundchen, a model, in their "I Will" campaign. Nike signed a lucrative deal to model Karlie Kloss and Puma signed Rihanna to be the face of its women's fitness line. Although all may be fit and even athletic, they certainly didn't compete at an elite level in the sports most little girls grow up playing (e.g., soccer, basketball) (Armato, 2015). It sends a strong message to girls and women consuming sporting goods – we encourage you to be fit, but in the course of exercise and playing sports, appearance matters most.

Perhaps the fact that female athletes are not celebrated solely for their athleticism is the reason corporate sponsors are hesitant to become partners with women's sports leagues. Sport sponsorship spending in 2017 in North America is projected to be US$15.7 billion (ESP Sponsorship Report, 2017); and yet, less than half of one percent is spent on women's sport (Fink, 2015b). Corporate executives will argue that they make sponsorship decisions solely based on return on investment (ROI). But this argument is difficult to believe in light of these facts:

> Women make up 58 percent of participants at running events; Women control 70 to 80 percent of consumer purchases. Women purchase more than 50 percent of traditionally male products, 68 percent of automobiles, and control more than 60 percent of all personal wealth in the United States.
>
> *(Fink, 2015b, para. 4)*

It seems that sponsoring women's sports leagues could be an incredible opportunity for many brands to connect with the female consumer and, yet, they fail to jump into the sponsorship of women's sports. As Women's Professional Fastpitch Commissioner, Cheri Kempf (2016, para. 5), says:

> Here's what brands do, from what I can see. They target the female audience, but they target that audience through male sport. . . . I think we have a tremendous amount to offer at an economical position right now, and it's so much not on their radar. In 90 percent of the cases, it seems they're not even considering it. It's like you're asking them to go to the moon.

Suggesting that the sponsorship of women's sports provides a great opportunity is not a new idea; Lough and Irwin recommended it in 2001. And yet, 16 years later, corporate executives still react as if you've asked them "to go to the moon" when offering such advice.

Female athletes' perspectives

Although corporate executives continue to drum the "sex sells" message, a few recent studies show that female athletes would overwhelmingly prefer to be recognized for their athletic competence in media, marketing, and endorsement campaigns (Fink et al., 2014; Kane et al., 2013; Krane et al., 2010). Still, many of the athletes seemed to have internalized the message that "sex sells" women's sport. In addition, it is clear that many feel the need to present the dual identity of being traditionally feminine in conjunction with their athleticism.

Krane et al. (2010) incorporated creative methodology to determine how female athletes would prefer to be depicted. They asked 20 female college athletes to participate in a photo shoot in which the athletes had complete control over how they would be portrayed. The resulting photos robustly featured the athletes' strength and power, a departure from earlier research and the common depictions of female athletes in the media, endorsements, and marketing campaigns. The authors suggested this was the result of the minimized social constraints the research setting offered. When free from any social pressure, they chose to portray their strength and power.

Later work by Kane et al. (2013) and Fink et al. (2014) produced slightly different results. Kane et al. (2013) interviewed 36 female intercollegiate athletes competing in "sex-appropriate" (e.g., tennis, track and field, swimming) and "sex-inappropriate" (e.g., basketball, hockey, softball) sports. They were presented with four photos of athletes in their sport depicting: athletic action/competence (on court action photo), mixed message (off court, dressed up, but with athletic marker), sexy/classy lady (off court, dressed up, no athletic marker), soft porn (off court, posed image that sexualizes the athlete), and asked which photo: (a) best represents how you would like to be portrayed, (b) best represents your sport, (c) best increases interest in your sport, and (d) best increases respect for your sport? The vast majority of respondents across all of the sports chose the competence photo to answer all four questions. They were immensely proud of their athleticism, hard work, and athletic accomplishments and felt the competence photos depicted that best.

It is interesting, however, when answering the first question, that half of the participants asked if they could pick two photos, and chose the competence photo along with either the mixed message or sexy/classy lady photo, providing strong evidence of wanting, or feeling the need, to present a dual identity. This was particularly prevalent among the team (i.e., sex-inappropriate) sport athletes, one of whom said, "I definitely want to be portrayed as a competitor . . . as bold and fierce . . . but then maybe be portrayed [like the mixed message image] because I like to dress up and look cute" (Kane et al., 2013, p. 20). This need to express a dual identity is not a new finding; Krane (2001, p. 2) noted, "Within women's sport environments, females continue policing themselves, emphasizing the importance of balancing the perceptions of masculine athleticism with feminine appearance." However, the durability and strength of such attitudes, particularly among the team sport athletes, suggest that little has changed since 2001.

Remarkably, 86% of the athletes responded affirmatively when asked if they thought sex sells women's sport. Qualitative analysis revealed that they deemed men as the primary target market for women's sports and they thought that sexualizing the athletes was the best way to get men's attention and attract them to the sport. As one athlete noted:

> Definitely. I think that's the only way we can draw attention. Sports is more geared toward guys anyway . . . so the only way for us to get attention is to be portrayed like that, in a bikini or completely naked because I almost think that's the only way for them to really care about women's sports or to have any interest in it.
>
> *(Kane et al., 2013, p. 22)*

Thus, it appears that many of the athletes in the study internalized the assumption that sex sells women's sport.

Fink et al. (2014) produced similar findings when they asked female athletes how they would like to be depicted in endorsement campaigns. Again, the vast majority of participants chose competence, but there were many who asked if they could choose two photos in order to highlight their femininity as well as their competence. The qualitative analysis revealed that athletes in team sports were more likely to emphasize words like "normal" when explaining their choice of two photos and/or suggest they did not want to be viewed as butch or gay if they were portrayed only as athletically competent. Furthermore, most of the athletes just accepted the notion that, to obtain corporate sponsorship as a female athlete, one had to project a feminine and heterosexual image. As one player noted, "If you're going to make it big you want to [appear] as pretty as possible so that you can make more money and further your career" (Fink et al., 2014, p. 214).

Conflicting evidence

Although the sports–media–commercial complex continues to advocate the notion that the most effective way to sell women's sport is to focus on the athletes' sex appeal or attractiveness, results from recent research disputing this long-held assumption. Fink, Cunningham, and Kensicki (2004) designed an experimental analysis in which they manipulated the skill level and attractiveness of a female athlete used in promotional materials for an intercollegiate softball event. Results showed that the athlete's skill level, rather than her attractiveness, was the most important component in predicting fit for the event and subsequently led to greater attendance intentions. Cunningham, Fink, and Kenix (2008) replicated the study in a tennis setting. The results indicated that attractiveness and skill level were both important predictors of fit for the event and attendance intentions.

Fink, Parker, Cunningham, and Cuneen (2012) manipulated the sport in which the female endorser competed (boxing versus tennis) to determine its effect on participants' perceptions of the endorsers' source credibility characteristics, fit, and purchase intentions. There were no significant differences on ratings of endorser expertise or trustworthiness; however, even though the same athlete was pictured in the two different sport settings, attractiveness ratings for the boxer were slighter lower than those of the tennis player, albeit explaining only 2% of the variance. In addition, there were no significant differences by sport on endorser/product fit or purchase intentions, which suggests that female athletes participating in more traditionally masculine sports can also be effective endorsers.

Kane and Maxwell (2011) conducted focus groups with actual sport fans in which the participants were presented with six different media images of female athletes. The different types of images ranged from "athletic competence" (pictures of the athletes in action) to "the girl next door" (wholesome image of athlete with no athletic marker) to "soft pornography" (images that sexually objectified the female athletes). The sport fans spanned a variety of ages (18–54) and included both men and women. The female sport fans, and older males, indicated that the depictions of athletic competence were the most likely to generate their interest for the sport. In fact, these two groups were actually offended by the sexualized photos, suggesting such images would alienate these fans. Finally, the young males in the study deemed some of the sexualized images to be "hot," but conceded that the depictions would not entice them to attend the women's sport event (Fink, 2015a).

A similar study was conducted by Antil, Burton, and Robinson (2012). They carried out focus groups with men and women (aged 14–61) in which they uncovered participants' judgments of female endorsers in different types of marketing campaigns. All of the participants in their study responded negatively to endorsements that sexualized female athletes. This was particularly true for female participants. It led the authors to speculate that female athletes are not less effective as endorsers because of their gender, but instead endorser effectiveness may be the result of how such endorsements are typically designed and communicated (Fink, 2015a).

Deleterious effects of sexualized depictions of female athletes

Although the studies above question the validity of the notion that sex sells women's sport, other research shows that such marketing strategies actually have adverse effects in a variety of ways. For example, Daniels (2012) presented different depictions of female athletes and models (sexualized to athletic action shots) to 350 adolescent girls and 225 college-aged females. She found the sexualized images prompted more negative self-objectification among the participants. Daniels and Wartena (2011) conducted a similar study with adolescent boys, in which the boys were grouped in three photographic conditions: sexualized athletes, performance athletes, and sexualized models. The boys responded to the sexualized female athlete photo in ways that objectified the female athlete by focusing on her appearance and attractiveness, rather than focusing on what she was (an athlete). Furthermore, this depiction elicited negative or neutral commentary about her athleticism. In contrast, the boys' reactions to the performance athlete photos focused on their athletic performances and were positive in nature. They noted: "These patterns demonstrated that sexualized images of female athletes are especially problematic and may contribute to the devaluation of female athleticism" (Daniels & Wartena, 2011, p. 576).

This contention received support in other studies as well. Fink (2010) and Knight and Giuliano (2001) found that depictions of *both* male and female athletes that highlighted their appearance or sex appeal resulted in significantly lower ratings of their athleticism compared with when they were shown in an athletic action photo. Thus, such depictions are harmful to any athlete. But as Fink (2015a) noted, male athletes are rarely depicted in this manner, whereas female athletes are routinely represented in this way by the sports–media–commercial complex. Thus, the longitudinal impact of such depictions for female athletes must be immense.

Relatedly, Greenwell, Simmons, Hancock, Shreffler, and Thorn (2017) conducted an experiment in a mixed martial arts setting, in which they manipulated how the female fighter was presented in the advertisement (sexualized, neutral, combat) to determine effects on attitudes toward the advertisement, event, and athlete brand. In contrast with previous work, the sexualized photo of the female athlete resulted in more positive attitudes about the advertisement and the event, particularly among men. However, the sexualized images resulted in lower measures of the athlete's image. The authors cautioned:

> sexualized imagery may be effective in attracting males to events in the short-term but may have longer lasting effects on how the female athletes are viewed as their brand image affects how athletes are positioned with not only consumers but also with event promoters, sponsors, and media. Further, this type of presentation may have long-term effects on promoters. . . . Therefore, in the long-term, it may be better to avoid the sexualized imagery.
> *(Greenwell et al., 2017, p. 541)*

Angelini (2008) conducted an interesting study to determine whether the different media coverage afforded to female athletes impacts perceptions of their athletic ability. He had participants watch men and women's televised sporting events. He obtained self-reports of their excitement level during the event, but he also collected actual physiological measures of excitement. It is interesting that the participants' self-report measures did not match their physiological measures – participants reported greater levels of excitement during the men's event; however, the physiological measures showed no significant differences between the two events. He suggested this offered proof that individuals have been socialized to believe that male athletes are innately more exciting and that a response bias has been built, in part, by the manner in which female athletes have been historically depicted and marketed (Fink, 2015a).

Conclusion

Thus, not only is the "sex sells" strategy in women's sport ineffective, but it also appears to damage society's perceptions of female athletes. If we continue to market female athletes based on sex appeal/appearance, these athletes will never be recognized, or given credit for, their tremendous athletic ability. As Kane (2011, para. 10) said, "Sex sells sex, not women's sports." We should market the reality of women's sports, rather than trying to focus on or manufacture sex appeal. We should market women's sports like we market men's sports. As Kane (2011) said, in discussing the popularity of the women's Final Four:

> Coverage of the women's Final Four bears a remarkable resemblance to that of the men's – a focus on great traditions, conference rivalries (Duke vs. North Carolina), legendary coaches (Pat Summitt vs. Geno Auriemma) – and, most important, showcasing sportswomen as physically gifted, mentally tough, grace-under-pressure athletes.
>
> *(Kane, 2011, para. 11)*

As this chapter revealed, these long-held (erroneous) assumptions about marketing women's sport and female athletes are detrimental in so many ways. Marketing, league and sponsor executives need to understand that core sport consumers care about talent, not sex appeal, when it comes to women's sport. Research indicates it would be a much more successful tactic.

Leader profile: Cheri Kempf

Cheri Kempf, Commissioner of National Professional Fastpitch (NPF), exudes a contagious enthusiasm when discussing her league and women's professional sport in general. "We're so close, I just think we're so close to really breaking through . . . there is a real market for our product," Kempf said when discussing her league. "This has been proven at the intercollegiate level, and I believe it shouldn't take much to see it at the professional level," she said. Kempf has been heavily involved in softball her entire life. She was a standout pitcher for Missouri Western State, earning the National MVP award and leading her team to the national championship. She was a pitcher for the 1992 National Team which won a gold medal in the World Cup in Beijing China, and as a professional player was a two-time Women's Majors National Champion as part of the Raybesto's Brakettes of Stratford, Connecticut.

In fact, Kempf sites the relationships she formed through her playing days as the foundation for her successful career and road to Commissioner. "You know, some of the people I still work with I knew at age 12 because we competed against one another," Kempf explained. After her successful playing career, Kempf founded Club K, where she was lead instructor at the women's fastpitch training facility – a facility that grew to be the largest of its kind in the world. She also used her experience to write a book, *The Softball Pitching Edge*, which has been produced in video.

Figure 32.1 Cheri Kempf
Photo courtesy of National Pro Fastpitch

She credits her connections to her work as a television analyst for both professional and intercollegiate softball spanning numerous outlets from ESPN, to MLB Network, to Comcast Sports.

Kempf became commissioner of the NPF in 2007 and has championed significant growth of the league. In 2017, the league featured six teams with one, the Beijing Eagles, an affiliate team originating in China. Nearly 150 games in the 2017 season were aired on NPFTV, and people from over 120 countries consumed the live events through NPFTV as well as The Olympic Channel, Flow Softball, Facebook Live, and MLB.com. NPFTV generated close to US$50,000 in subscription revenue and there were over 150,000 unique viewers over all streaming channels. Kempf was also excited to announce the landing of the NPF's first non-endemic sponsors, something she sees as vital to the growth of the league.

When asked if she could name one thing that would push the league to the heights of success she envisions, Kempf didn't hesitate, "Exposure, we need exposure. You know, I'm not much of a TV watcher. But lately, seemingly every day over numerous platforms, I've been bombarded with messages about a new show, The Good Doctor . . . so now I want to watch it! We need that exposure in many forms, multi-media, in venue, and a broader coverage not just in the United States, but globally." Her passion is palpable as she assured me, "We are going to get there." With people like Cheri Kempf trailblazing the way, I'm sure we will.

References

Alverez, A. (2017). LPGA's Twitter poll to award event entry is exploitation not creative thinking, May 4. Retrieved from www.theguardian.com

Angelini, J. R. (2008). Television sports and athlete sex: Looking at the differences in watching male and female athletes. *Journal of Broadcasting and Electronic Media*, **52**, 16–32.

Antil, J. H., Burton, R., & Robinson, M. J. (2012). Exploring the challenges facing female athletes as endorsers. *Journal of Brand Strategy*, **1**, 292–307.

Armato, L. (2015). What happened to endorsements for actual female athletes? *SportsBusiness Journal*, March 2–8, p. 35.

Badenhousen, K. (2017). Serena Williams heads the highest paid female athletes in 2017, August 14. Retrieved from www.forbes.com.

Bryon, L. (1987). Sport and the maintenance of masculine hegemony. *Women's Studies International Forum*, **10**, 349–360.

Coffin, J. (2017). Inkster: Women's golf doesn't get the credit we're do, August 20. Retrieved from www.golfchannel.com

Cunningham, G.B., Fink, J.S., & Kenix, L.J. (2008). Choosing an endorser for a women's sporting event. The interaction of attractiveness and expertise. *Sex Roles*, **58**, 371–378.

Daniels, E. A. (2012). Sexy versus strong: What girls and women think of female athletes. *Journal of Applied Developmental Psychology*, **33**, 79–90.

Daniels, E. A. & Wartena, H. (2011). Athlete or sex symbol: What boys think of media Representations of female athletes. *Sex Roles*, **65**, 566–579.

ESP Sponsorship Report (2017). Sponsorship spending forecast, continued growth around the world, January 4. Retrieved from www.sponsorship.com.

ESPN Films (2013). *Nine for IX: Branded*. ESPN Films.

Fink, J. S. (2008). Gender and sex diversity in organizations: Concluding comments. *Sex Roles*, **58**, 147–148.

Fink, J. S. (2010). Using athletes to advertise their sport: A comparison of male and female athletes and the notion that "sex sells". *Proceedings from the North American Society for Sport Management (NASSM)*. Miami, FL.

Fink, J. S. (2015a). Female athletes, women's sport, and the sport media commercial complex: Have we really "come a long way, baby?" *Sport Management Review*, **18**, 331–342.

Fink, J. S. (2015b). Sponsorship for women's sports presents untapped opportunity. *SportsBusiness Journal*, November 2–8, p. 15.

Fink, J. S., Cunningham, G. B., & Kensicki, L. J. (2004). Using athletes as endorsers to sell women's sport: Attractiveness versus expertise. *Journal of Sport Management*, **18**, 350–367.

Fink, J. S., Kane, M. J., & LaVoi, N. M. (2014). The freedom to choose. Elite female athletes' preferred representations within endorsement opportunities. *Journal of Sport Management*, **28**, 207–219.

Fink, J. S., Parker, H. M., Cunningham, G. B., & Cuneen, J. C. (2012). Female athlete endorsers. Determinants of effectiveness. *Sport Management Review*, **15**, 13–22.

Golf Channel Public Relations (2017). Golf Channel's Sunday Solheim Cup coverage most-watched women's golf telecast on cable in eight years, August 23. Retrieved from www.thegolfchannel.com.

Greenwell, C., Simmons, J. M., Hancock, M., Shreffler, M., & Thorn, D. (2017). The effects of sexualized and violent presentations of women in combat sport. *Journal of Sport Management*, **31**, 533–545.

Hoeber, L. (2007). Exploring the gaps between meanings and practices of gender equity in a sport organization. *Gender, Work and Organization*, **14**, 259–280

Kane, M. J. (2011). Sex sells sex, not women's sports. *The Nation*, August 15, pp. 28–29.

Kane, M. J., LaVoi, N. M., & Fink, J. S. (2013). Exploring elite female athletes' interpretations of sport media images: A window into the construction of social identity and "selling sex" in women's sports. *Communication & Sport*, 1–30.

Kane, M. J. & Maxwell, H. D. (2011). Expanding the boundaries of sport media research: Using critical theory to explore consumer responses to representations of women's sports. *Journal of Sport Management*, **25**, 202–216.

Kempf, C. (2016). NPF commissioner seeks sponsor to say 'Yes, there is value here'. *SportsBusiness Journal, May 9-15*, May 9, p. 14.

Krane, V. (2001). We can be athletic and feminine, but do we want to? Challenging hegemonic femininity in women's sport. *Quest*, **53**, 115–133.

Krane, V., Choi, P. Y. L., Baird, S. M., & Aimar, C. M. (2004). Living the paradox: Female athletes negotiate femininity and masculinity. *Sex Roles*, **50**, 315–329.

Krane, V., Ross, S. R., Miller, M., Rowse, J. L., Ganoie, K., Andrzejczyk, J. A., & Lucas, C. B. (2010). Power and focus: Self-representation of female college athletes. *Qualitative Research in Sport and Exercise*, **2**, 175–195.

Knight, J. L. & Giuliano, T. A. (2001). He's a Laker, she's a looker: The consequences of gender-stereotypical portrayals of male and female athletes by the print media. *Sex Roles*, **45**, 217–229.

LaVoi, N. M. & Kane, M. J. (2011). Sociological aspects of sport. In P. Pedersen, J. B. Parks, J. Quarterman, & L. Thibault (eds), *Contemporary Sport Management* (pp. 372–391). Champaign, IL: Human Kinetics.

Lough, N. L. & Irwin, R. L. (2001). A comparative analysis of sponsorship objectives for U.S. Women's sport and traditional sport. *Sport Marketing Quarterly*, **10**, 202–211.

McDonagh, E. & Pappano, L. (2008). *Playing with the Boys: Why separate is not equal in sports*. New York: Oxford University Press.

Meân, L. J. & Kassing, J. W. (2008). "I would just like to be known as an athlete": Managing hegemony, femininity, and heterosexuality in female sport. *Western Journal of Communication*, **72**, 126–144.

Merrill, E. (2011). Hope Solo dealing with the stars, September 26. ESPN. Retrieved from http://espn.go.com/espnw.

Messner, M. & Montez de Oca, J. (2005). The male consumer as loser: Beer and liquid ads in megasports media events. *Journal of Women in Culture and Society*, **30**, 1879–1909.

Metheny, E. (1965). Symbolic forms of movement. The feminine image in sport. In E. Metheny (ed.), *Connotations of Movement in Sport and Dance* (pp. 43–56). Dubuque, IA: Brown.

Soebel, J. (2017). Week 18: Solheim Cup delivers plenty of punch, August 20. Retrieved from http://espn.go.com.

Women's Tennis Association (2012). The strong is beautiful celebrity campaign. Retrieved from: https://www.wtatennis.com/news/strong-beautiful-celebrity-campaign.

33
You're just not our type
An examination of the obstacles faced by women athlete endorsers

Ted B. Peetz

When tennis superstar Roger Federer stepped on to the famed grass courts of Wimbledon in 2018, something was noticeably different. Although he still wore the customary Wimbledon all-white tennis attire, for the first time in 20 years, his clothes were missing the Nike "swoosh." The player, the "swoosh," and his customized "RF" logo had become synonymous with tennis excellence. This tournament, however, marked a new era for Federer, having signed a roughly US$300 million, 10-year endorsement contract with outerwear brand Uniqlo (Perrotta, 2018). Uniqlo and Federer's deal epitomizes the significance companies place on celebrity athlete endorsers to positively affect their brands. Although the impact of endorsement deals is often debated, it has generally been shown these agreements, at a minimum, create "fair-value" contracts (Fitzel, McNeil, & Smaby, 2008). Peetz and Lough (2016, p. 127) noted, "Although the cost of using this marketing strategy has risen exponentially over the years, the goals of using celebrity athletes have remained the same: grab the consumer's attention, create positive associations with the product or service, and positively impact revenue." With companies tapping into the ability of superstars to penetrate saturated media markets, athletes like Federer have benefited greatly. In a 12-month span from 2017 to 2018, Forbes estimated that the top 100 highest-paid athletes derived 23% of their cumulative US$3.8 billion earned from endorsements and appearances (Forbes, 2018). However, further examination of this list reveals another startling statistic: not a single woman athlete appears in the Top 100. This chapter aims to examine endorsement theories and undercover the potential barriers that have led to the glaring under-representation of women athletes within this promotional strategy.

Celebrity athlete endorsement overview

The practice of using celebrities to promote products, services and ideas has been widespread for most of the twentieth century. Endorsements have been referred to as "personality sponsorships" because they have similarities to the broader marketing tactic. Although comparable in their approach to generating positive brand associations, endorsements differ from sponsorships in their ability to reach target markets in a more direct manner (Peetz & Lough, 2016). McCracken (1989, p. 30) defined a celebrity endorser as "an individual who enjoys public recognition and who uses this recognition on behalf of a consumer good by appearing with it in an advertisement." When examining the media landscape it is nearly impossible to avoid celebrity endorsers because they are featured in roughly one out of five television advertisements (Agrawal & Kamakura, 1995). Athletes, in particular, have been an extremely popular form of celebrity endorser for advertisers. Belch and Belch (2013) found, in a content analysis of magazine advertisements, that athletes were used in 27% of advertisements featuring a celebrity, second only to actors and actresses at 34%. Investigations into the effectiveness of celebrity athlete endorsers have mainly examined factors and the culturally acquired meanings associated with the athletes through four specific models. These theoretical models provide a framework to examine the potential reasons for the disproportionately low number of female endorsers used in this form of marketing communication.

Source credibility

Source credibility has been defined as "the believability of the endorser, spokesperson or individual in an advertisement" (Clow, James, Sisk, & Cole, 2011, p. 25). Ohanian (1990) adds that source credibility is a communicator's ability to evoke positive attitude changes from the receiver of the message. The source credibility model encompasses three critical effects of a source on brand attitudes, purchase intent, and attitude toward the message (Amos, Holmes, & Strutton, 2008). Source credibility is a multidimensional concept. When the source credibility model was first developed it included two primary factors: trustworthiness and expertise (Hovland Janis, & Kelley, 1953). Attractiveness was added as a factor to this model and has become commonplace in literature on the subject (McGuire, 1969; Ohanian, 1990). It seems intuitive that these three factors formed the early foundation for investigation into this concept. When asking a marketing practitioner to name qualities they would seek out in an endorser – trustworthiness, expertise, and attractiveness – all would likely be high on the list. Ultimately, a consumer's perception of these factors plays a key role in message effectiveness (Hovland et al., 1953; Ohanian, 1991) and in optimizing the consumer's ability to process the message (Carrillat, D'Astous, & Charette Couture, 2015). Based on this rationale, it seems logical to ask this question: is the reason for the severe lack of women athlete endorsers a credibility issue? An examination into the factors included in the source credibility model provides a lens to analyze this question.

Expertise, trustworthiness, and attractiveness

Wang and Scheinbaum (2018, p. 18) note that "an endorser's expertise is akin to the source's qualification, which directly influences the level of conviction to persuade consumers to purchase that which is endorsed." Societal expectations of appropriate gender norms may influence how a woman athlete's "qualification" or expertise is viewed within her particular sport. Athletics, in general, is still viewed as a predominately male domain and research has shown that qualifying sports as masculine or feminine can affect attitudes about those competing in them (Kane, 1987, 1988, Fink, Parker, Cunningham, & Cuneen, 2012). Krane (2001, p. 116) noted, "Sportswomen tread a fine line of acceptable femininity . . . engaging in athletic activities is empowering, yet maintaining an acceptable feminine demeanor is disempowering." Marketers add to what has been described as the "female/athlete paradox" by promoting traditional female stereotypes in their advertising (Krane, Choi, Baird, Aimar, & Kauer, 2004; Ross & Shinew, 2008). When females are portrayed in ways that trivialize their athletic accomplishments (e.g., in a sexual nature for an advertisement) it can undermine how consumers perceive their level of competence or expertise. Therefore, in an effort to maximize the impact of an athlete endorser, marketers may want to reconsider emphasizing looks over athletic substance. On an individual level, this marginalization may also suppress a female athlete's ability to develop her own personal brand (Lobpries, Bennett, & Brison, 2018). Without a distinctive personal brand, processing marketing messages from that celebrity becomes more difficult. In fact, it can limit the level of celebrity that individual can achieve and ultimately call into question an endorser's expertise and trustworthiness (Antil, Burton, & Robinson, 2012). Consumers tend to reject arguments in ads featuring a source perceived to have low credibility (Grewal, Gotlieb, & Marmorstein, 1994). If companies are unsuccessful in projecting a certain level of expertise from their women athlete celebrity endorsers, they set those athletes up to fail in reaching the company's advertising objectives.

The growth of an athlete endorser's reputation and credibility inherently raises awareness that they can make valid assertions (McCracken, 1989). Trustworthiness is an aspect of the source credibility scale that focuses on "a listener's trust in a speaker" (Ohanian, 1990, p. 41). Priester and Petty (2003) examined this factor using figure skaters Nancy Kerrigan and Tonya Harding, who were likely to be perceived very differently on the factor of trustworthiness, as endorsers of a fictitious roller blade product. The results of the study showed that, if an endorser were perceived to be highly trustworthy, a consumer could not scrutinize the advertising message as intensely and instead, "unthinkingly accept the conclusion as valid" (Priester & Petty, 2003, p. 409), whereas, if the endorser was viewed as untrustworthy, respondents scrutinized the advertisement to a greater degree. It is intuitive that an individual would be more positive in their response to a message from a trustworthy source rather than an untrustworthy source. One way to increase trustworthiness is to pair an athlete with a product that they are known to use or would naturally engage with based on the sport they play. As this connection increases so does the believability of the endorser (Atkin & Block, 1983). Research has found, however, that female athletes cannot rely on athleticism alone to establish congruence with a product. Lobpries et al. (2018), who interviewed elite female athletes and agents, found that sportswomen need athletic ability and "something else" to develop a memorable brand. "While both athlete and agent respondents expressed the need for female athletes to perform well and do something else to bolster their brand, all of the athletes interviewed believed male athletes did not face the same barrier to building a brand" (Lobpries et al., 2018, p. 12). It appears that advertisers, whose decision makers are overwhelmingly male, have the belief that women athletes need to work harder to establish baseline factors of credibility, such as trustworthiness. Ultimately, this hurdle can negatively impact marketers' decisions to choose women athletes as endorsers of their products and has contributed to their lack of endorsement opportunities.

Attractiveness is another factor associated with source credibility. A casual inspection of advertisements shows that attractiveness is a highly sought after trait in celebrity endorsers. It is widely assumed that being attractive helps persuasively convey a message (Dion, Berscheid, & Walster, 1972). An endorser who is viewed as attractive will be more effective endorsing products that are related to being attractive, for example cosmetics, which results in greater perceived endorser credibility toward the advertisement (Kamins, 1990). For example, when tennis player Maria Sharapova signed on as the face of Avon Luck, a fragrance for men and women, her "sophisticated beauty" was mentioned as a reason (Prior, 2014). Due to the nature of athletics, some athletes may be perceived to be attractive endorsers based on physical appearance and body shape (Boyd & Shank, 2004). However, attractiveness is a subjective term and not all consumers assess it in the same way. The many ways this factor has been operationalized has led to some confusion. For example, personality, lifestyle, and intellectual skills have also been used as items included in the attractiveness concept (Erdogan, 1999). Carlson and Donovan (2017, p. 186) found that "reputation may be more important than attractiveness in predicting the extent to which fans identify with an athlete." For example, if a consumer is highly identified as a fan of soccer, United States Women's National Team member Alex Morgan's reputation would be a key persuasive attribute in her endorsement, whereas attractiveness would be more marginal to the outcome. In this situation it would appear that the old adage of "sex sells" is counterproductive because a valued reputation has been shown to more likely persuade consumers of the marketing message (Ohanian, 1991). When analyzing female athlete endorsers, the factors associated with the competence of the athlete appears to be one that marketers often downplay, which is a critical error, because the factor plays such an important role in efficacy of the endorser.

Source attractiveness

It can be confusing to describe the source attractiveness model because the attractiveness factor is not actually included. McGuire (1985) developed the source attractiveness model, which theorized an endorser's effectiveness was based partially on the attributes of similarity, likability, and familiarity. The factors included in this model have been shown to enhance the target audience's perception of an advertisement (Baker & Churchill, 1977) and increase purchase intentions (Petroshius & Crocker, 1989). This model provides another intriguing lens to examine challenges faced by women athletes within this marketing strategy.

Similarity, likability, and familiarity

According to the source attractiveness model, similarity can be described as a supposed feeling of closeness or alikeness someone feels with the source (Erdogan, 1999). This feeling can occur on a number of different levels. For example, Desphande and Stayman (1994) found that an endorser's ethnicity affected a respondent's perception of trustworthiness and as a result brand attitudes. The researcher hypothesized that this occurred because people trust individuals who are similar to them. In addition to surface level similarities, people can perceive they are similar to an endorser based on traits such as personality, beliefs, background, or lifestyle (Cialdini, 2007). Therefore, similarity of an endorser to the target audience is an important consideration in advertising (Feick & Higie, 1992). Some researchers have argued that this trait can be underutilized when dealing with female athlete endorsers, especially when targeting mothers or older consumers. Antil et al. (2012) noted that mothers, who control most of a household's purchasing power, can feel alienated when the similarity factor is not met. In their study, they showed that age of the endorser caused women to feel a lack of connectedness between the athlete and themselves, which diluted the effectiveness of the endorsement. The authors also noted how the endorsers, where used, could play a role in their evaluation from an older demographic. They suggest advertisers should downplay sexual appeal and physical attractiveness and focus more on parallel traits associated with an older age group like determination, hard work, and the ability to balance work and family (Antil et al., 2012).

The likability attribute is another factor within the source attractiveness model. A very popular method currently used to evaluate endorsers is the Performer Q-Rating (Q-score) which is compiled by Marketing Evaluations Incorporated (Knott & St. James, 2004). These scores are based on a simple ratio of likability and familiarity. It is easy to assume that one would prefer to hear endorsement messages from someone they liked rather than from someone they did not. Researchers have suggested that, if an athlete can increase their rating by as little as one Q-score point they could see an aggregate increase in their endorsement value between US$750,000 and US$1 million (Rascher, Eddy, & Hyun, 2017).

An endorser's ability to raise their Q-score is greatly enhanced by their exposure or familiarity with an audience. Familiarity or being a known entity is critical in developing the persuasive power of an endorser. When a celebrity is clearly recognizable they can attract attention more easily. Grabbing a consumer's attention and breaking through the "clutter" is considered one of the main roles of an endorser. It is interesting that, when a celebrity's familiarity and status is extremely high, endorsed products can get lost in the promotion. Evans (1988, p. 35) referred to this phenomenon as the "vampire effect" when powerful celebrities "suck the lifeblood of the product dry; the audience remembers the celebrity but not the product." Achieving this intense level of familiarity is exceptionally more difficult for female athletes due to the lack of coverage they receive in the media. For example, in an analysis of women's sport coverage from ESPN's SportsCenter and Fox Sports 1's Fox Sports Live, Billings and Young (2015) found that less than 1% was devoted to women's sports. This research supports the argument on the lack of familiarity some consumers have when examining female athlete endorsers. Peetz, Parks, and Spencer (2004) found that the odds of a respondent correctly identifying male athletes was almost four times the odds they would correctly identify female athletes. An explanation for these findings included media exposure and the resulting higher profile male athletes achieve in American culture. The remarkably disproportionate coverage of women athletes plays a crucial role in the overall effectiveness they can have as endorsers. As Antil et al. (2012, p. 301) explain:

> This relative lack of awareness and familiarity is important for two major reasons. First, to be a celebrity, by definition the person must be well known enough to people. If one considers the ... common components of the source attractiveness model ... one could say familiarity trumps the others as without enough awareness one is not a celebrity so the other components become inconsequential.

The source credibility and source attractiveness models provided a framework to examine factors associated with endorser effectiveness. These models were used to highlight the mistakes made by marketers and show barriers sportswomen face in gaining greater relevance within this promotional strategy. Although the two models provide a foundational level of understanding on idealized endorser characteristics, they fail to present the complete picture. The transfer of meaning process (McCracken, 1986) and the match-up hypothesis (Mowen, Brown, & Schulman, 1979) are two additional theories that are frequently used when analyzing endorser effectiveness. As Belch and Belch (2001, p. 181) noted, "a celebrity's effectiveness as an endorser depends on the culturally acquired meanings he or she brings to the endorsement process." These two models are explored further in the following sections to help explain the additional obstacles women athletes face in acquiring endorsement opportunities.

Transfer of meaning process

The transfer of meaning process is based on the notion that celebrities are associated with certain culturally acquired meanings and that those meanings can be transferred to products. The effectiveness of an endorsement depends on the successful transfer of meaning from the endorser to the product and finally the consumer transferring those meanings to their own sense of self (McCracken, 1989). The first stage of the process is finding an endorser that embodies the cultural meanings with which a company wants to align. For example, if a company wanted their product to convey a youthful and fun image, they could choose an athlete like snowboarder and Olympic Gold medalist, Chloe Kim. In the second stage of the process, Kim's culturally constructed meaning is transferred to the consumer good through imagery and/or language. The final stage in the process is when the acquired meaning transfers from product to consumer. The act of wearing a product endorsed by an athlete like Chloe Kim may strengthen the consumer's self-image (McCracken, 1986). "Those in need of self enhancement are often those in need of the meanings created by celebrities" (St. James, 2010, p. 6). The transfer of the meaning process has been shown to be particularly powerful in groups that are still developing a sense of self, such as teenagers (Adams-Price & Green, 1990). It is also interesting to note that specific athletes resonate with certain demographics based on the cultural atmosphere of that time period. For example, tennis player Billie Jean King resonated with the women's liberation movement of the 1960s and 1970s. Although transformational athletes like King exist for almost every modern generation, the issue faced by most sportswomen is the continuous lack of media coverage and related exposure, which reduces their opportunities to cultivate their own culturally significant meaning. Researchers have, however, theorized that, due to the dramatic increase in sport participation opportunities for women over the last 40 years, endorsement opportunities would increase (Veltri & Long, 1998). Indeed, unprecedented moments have occurred that would suggest a change in attitudes and opportunities for female endorsers, such as the FIFA Women's World Cup or Olympic success. Unfortunately, many of these events lack the continuous media coverage afforded to male-dominated sports, which then results in diminishing the impact of these women's successes over time.

Musto, Cooky, and Messner (2017) introduced the idea of "gender-bland sexism" which can be extended to women in sports. The authors note that even when covered, women's sports are often portrayed in an uninspired way, which can make women's athletic accomplishments seem dull compared with those of men. This particular type of reporting, in both duration and intensity, hinders the cultural value women athletes are able to create. As Lobpries et al. (2018, p. 8) stated, "or female athletes . . . the availability of resources and status needed to enhance brand equity could hinder their ability to leverage effective branding strategies." Applied to the transfer of meaning process, female athletes have a more difficult time establishing the criteria to elicit reaction from the first stage of this process. Without strong culturally acquired meanings to transfer, the process becomes weakened or non-existent, thus limiting opportunities for female endorsers.

Match-up hypothesis

The match-up hypothesis (Mowen et al., 1979) is a theoretical framework that examines the appropriateness of endorser-brand fit and how that fit influences consumer evaluations of the advertisement and brand. When using a "match-up" selection method, a company would choose an endorser based on the amount of fit or commonality it had with a brand or product such as a golfer endorsing a brand of golf clubs. Although attractiveness is often viewed as a persuasive factor in advertising, Fink, Cunningham, and Kensicki (2004) found an endorser's attractiveness had little impact when a match-up between endorser and product did not have a logical link to what was being endorsed. In their study, they analyzed the attractiveness of an endorser on an event, the National Collegiate Athletic Association (NCAA) National Softball Championship, and found that a weak link was created which reduced the effectiveness of the endorsement. In this case, the attractiveness of the endorser had no impact on how well the games would be played and therefore made for a less effective endorser than someone who was seen as an expert on the game. This idea also mirrors the concept of identification, which can be seen to be equally important to the "fit" of the endorsement (Carlson & Donovan, 2013, 2017). When a consumer's sense of self, or their identification, connects with that of the endorser, high identification is achieved. "This connection can be very influential on consumer intentions" (Carlson & Donovan, 2017, p. 177). Misra and Beatty (1990) supported the match-up hypothesis with findings showing that brand recall and fondness towards the brand increased when the endorser and product had congruence. Premeaux (2005) examined endorser effectiveness and consumer perceptions in relation to the AIDA (attention, interest, desire, action) framework and the match-up hypothesis. The study concluded, "The main effect was the ability of the celebrity endorser to get and hold attention" (Bailey, 2007, p. 88). However, other findings for the match-up hypothesis do not support these claims. For example, Kamins (1990) did not find support for the match-up hypothesis for the critical measures of brand attitude and purchase intentions. Others have warned of the "vampire effect," already discussed, where one's celebrity can overpower the fit with a product or brand in an endorsement (Evans, 1988).

In a highly controlled experimental study, Fink, Parker, Cunningham, and Cuneen (2012, p. 21) showed that "female athletes in gender 'inappropriate' sports are still perceived to be statistically less attractive than their counterparts in more traditionally held gender 'appropriate' sports." In terms of the athlete product match-up, however, the source traits of the athletes' perceived expertise and trustworthiness were not viewed negatively, regardless of the sport in which they participated. Further examination into the role that gender "norms" play in the match-up hypothesis are warranted, but it appears that the barriers faced by women athletes in creating a fit with a product may go beyond simply excelling in their sport. Marketers play a vital role in expanding the use and appreciation for women athletes in the endorsement process, going beyond a cursory acknowledgment and instead fully embracing their potential as effective marketing vehicles. As companies begin more purposeful engagement with women athlete endorsers, they may realize they have a significant function in developing cultural meanings associated with that athlete. Although male athletes oftentimes have multiple avenues to develop their culturally acquired meaning, this meaning can be varied and lack cohesiveness for a particular brand. On the other hand, some female athletes have significantly less powerful, culturally acquired meaning due to their lack of exposure and marketing opportunities. If marketers embrace the development of a woman athlete's personal brand, they can work toward crafting a fixed meaning that aligns specifically to their product. Creating a tailored "fit" between athlete and brand sounds like a marketer's dream and may be easier than using an endorser who promotes multiple products across multiple categories.

Conclusion

Tremendous strides have been made in women's sport over the last 40 years, including dramatic increases in participation rates, prize money, and professional opportunities. This chapter has shown, however, that the utilization in endorsement strategy is one aspect that has remained elusive for the vast majority of women athletes. In exploring this phenomenon, this chapter examined traditional endorsement theories and models to show how underutilized women have been in this marketing strategy.

The source credibility model highlighted how women athletes are often depicted in advertisements in ways that marginalize their abilities and accomplishments. Marketers hoping to benefit from the expertise, trustworthiness, and attractiveness of an endorser need to focus on emphasizing these traits in their athlete endorsers, regardless of gender. Unfortunately, most marketing campaigns featuring women athletes have relied on tired, old-fashioned, and lazy clichés, which minimize their impact. Additional hurdles faced by women athletes appear in the source attractiveness model. As women's sport receives such a small percentage of media coverage, these athletes have struggled to gain a notoriety and build personal brand power sought after by advertisers. However, sportswomen are uniquely positioned to utilize source attractiveness traits, such as similarity, to influence certain target markets. Marketers that acknowledge and position female athlete endorsers toward these underserved markets are likely to reap substantial rewards, by cutting through clutter and communicating more authentically with consumers.

Marketers have a long way to go to fully harness the potential benefits of utilizing women athletes as endorsers. A shoe company signing a women's basketball player to an endorsement contract is one thing, the extent to which they embrace and activate the endorsement another. When determining fit or which woman athlete might be a charismatic endorser for their products, marketers need to be at the forefront of maximizing the elements associated with the theories and models mentioned in this chapter. By simply applying classic marketing endorsement theories and making an earnest attempt to place female athletes on a comparable plane, marketers have the potential to create significant and positive change to advance the business of women's sport.

References

Adams-Price, C. & Greene, A. J. (1990). Secondary attachments and adolescent self-concept. *Sex Roles*, **22**, 187–198.
Agrawal, J. & Kamakura, W. A. (1995). The economic worth of celebrity endorsers: An event study analysis. *Journal of Marketing*, **59**(3), 56–63.
Amos, C., Holmes, G., & Strutton, D. (2008). Exploring the relationship between celebrity endorser effects and advertising effectiveness: A quantitative synthesis of effect size. *International Journal of Advertising*, **27**(2), 209–234.
Antil, J. H., Burton, R., & Robinson, M. J. (2012). Exploring the challenges facing female athletes as endorsers. *Journal of Brand Strategy*, **1**, 292–307.
Atkin, C. & Block, M. (1983). Effectiveness of celebrity endorsers. *Journal of Advertising Research*, **23**(1), 57–62.
Bailey, A. A. (2007). Public information and consumer skepticism effects on celebrity endorsements: Studies among young consumers. *Journal of Marketing Communications*, **13**(2), 85–107.
Baker, M. & Churchill, G. (1977). The impact of physically attractive model on advertising evaluation. *Journal of Marketing Research*, **14**, 538–555.
Belch, G. E. & Belch, M. A. (2001). *Advertising and Promotion: An integrated marketing communication perspective*, 5th edn. New York: Irwin/McGraw Hill.
Belch, G. E. & Belch, M. A. (2013). A content analysis study of the use of celebrity endorsers in magazine advertising. *International Journal of Advertising*, **32**(3), 369–389.
Billings, A. C. & Young, B. (2015). Comparing flagship news programs: Women's sport coverage in ESPN's SportsCenter and Fox Sports 1's Fox Sports Live. *Electronic News*, **9**(1), 3–16.
Boyd, T. C. & Shank, M. D. (2004). Athletes as product endorsers: The effect of gender and product relatedness. *Sport Marketing Quarterly*, **13**(2), 82–93.
Carlson, B. D. & Donovan, D. T. (2013). Human brands in sport: Athlete brand personality and identification. *Journal of Sport Management*, **27**, 193–206.
Carlson, B. D. & Donovan, D. T. (2017). Be like Mike: The role of social identification in athlete endorsements. *Sport Marketing Quarterly*, **26**, 176–191.
Carrillat, F. A., D'Astous, A., and Charette Couture, M. (2015). How corporate sponsors can optimize the impact of their message content. *Journal of Advertising Research*, **15**(3), 255–269.
Cialdini, R. B. (2007). *Influence: The psychology of persuasion*. New York: Harper Collins.
Clow, K. E., James, K. E., Sisk, S.E., and Cole, H. S. (2011). Source credibility, visual strategy and the model of print advertisement. *Journal of Marketing Development and Competitiveness*, **5**(3), 24–31.
Desphande, R. & Stayman, D. (1994). A tale of two cities: Distinctness theory and advertising effectiveness. *Journal of Marketing Research*, **31**(1), 57–64.
Dion, K., Berscheid, F., & Walster, E. H. (1972). What is beautiful is good. *Journal of Personality and Social Psychology*, **24**, 285–290.
Erdogan, B. Z. (1999). Celebrity endorsement: a literature review. *Journal of Marketing Management*, **15**(3), 291–314.
Evans, R. B. (1988). *Producing and Creativity in Advertising*. London: Pitman Publishing
Feick, L. & Higie, R. A. (1992). The effects of preference heterogeneity and source characteristics on ad processing and judgments about endorsers, *Journal of Advertising*, **21**(2), 9–24.

Fink, J. S., Cunningham, G. B., & Kensicki, L. J. (2004). Using athletes as endorsers to sell women's sport: Attractiveness versus expertise. *Journal of Sport Management*, **18**, 350–367.

Fink, J. S., Parker, H. M., Cunningham, G. B., & Cuneen, J. (2012). Female athlete endorsers: Determinants of effectiveness. *Sport Management Review*, **15**, 13–22.

Fitzel, J., McNeil, C. R., & Smaby, T. (2008). Athlete endorsement contracts: The impact of conventional stars. *International Advances of Economic Research*, **14**, 247–256.

Forbes (2018). The world's highest-paid athletes. Retrieved from https://www.forbes.com/athletes/#1aaf884055ae (Accessed July 13, 2018).

Grewal, D., Gotlieb, J., & Marmorstein, H. (1994). The moderating effects of message framing and source credibility on the price-perceived risk relationship. *Journal of Consumer Research*, **21**(1), 145–153.

Hovland, C. I., Janis, I. K., & Kelley, H. H. (1953). *Communication and Persuasion*. New Haven, CT: Yale University.

Kamins, M. A. (1990). An investigation of the match-up hypothesis in celebrity advertising: When beauty may be only skin deep. *Journal of Advertising*, **19**(1), 4–13.

Kane, M. J. (1987). The "new" female athlete: Socially sanctioned image or modern role of women? *Medicine and Sport Science*, **24**, 101–111.

Kane, M. J. (1988). The female athletic role as a status determinant within the social-systems of high school adolescents. *Adolescence*, **23**, 253–264.

Knott, C. L. & St. James, M. (2004). An alternative approach to developing a total celebrity endorser rating model using the analytic hierarchy process. *International Transactions in Operational Research*, **11**, 87–95.

Krane, V. (2001). We can be athletic and feminine, but do we want to? Challenging hegemonic femininity in women's sport. *Quest*, **53**, 115–133.

Krane, V., Choi, P. Y. L., Baird, S. M., Aimar, C. M., & Kauer, K. J. (2004). Living the paradox: Female athletes negotiate femininity and muscularity. *Sex Roles*, **50**, 315–329.

Lobpries, J. Bennett, G., & Brison, N. (2018). How I perform is not enough: Exploring branding barriers faced by elite female athletes. *Sport Marketing Quarterly*, **27**, 5–17.

McCracken, G. (1986). Culture and consumption: A theoretical account of the structure and movement of the cultural meaning of consumer goods. *Journal of Consumer Research*, **13**(1), 71–84.

McCracken, G. (1989). Who is the celebrity endorser? Cultural foundations of the endorsement process. *Journal of Consumer Research*, **16**, 310–321.

McGuire, W. J. (1969). The nature of attitudes and attitude change. In Lindzey, G. and Aronson, E. (eds), *Handbook of Social Psychology*, 2nd edn (pp. 136–314). Reading, MA: Addison-Wesley, .

McGuire, W. J. (1985). Attitudes and attitude change. In G. Lindzay & E. Aronson (eds), *Handbook of Social Psychology*, Vol. 2 (pp. 233–346). New York: Random House.

Misra, S. & Beatty, S. E. (1990). Celebrity spokesperson and brand congruence: An assessment of recall and affect. *Journal of Business Research*, **21**(2), 159–173.

Mowen, J. C., Brown, S. W., & Schulman, M. (1979). Theoretical and empirical extensions of endorser effectiveness. In N. Beckwith et al. (eds), *Marketing Educators Conference Proceedings* (pp. 258–263). Chicago, IL: American Marketing Association.

Musto, M., Cooky, C., & Messner, M. A. (2017). "From frizzle to sizzle!" Televised sports news and the production of gender-bland sexism. *Gender & Society*, **3**(5), 573–598.

Ohanian, R. (1990). Construction and validation of a scale to measure celebrity endorsers' perceived expertise, trustworthiness, and attractiveness. *Journal of Advertising*, **19**(3), 39–52.

Ohanian, R. (1991). The impact of celebrity spokespersons' perceived image on consumers' intentions to purchase. *Journal of Advertising Research*, **31**(1), 46–54.

Peetz, T. B. & Lough, N. L. (2016). Celebrity athlete endorsers: A critical review. In N. Chanavat, S. Chadwick, & M. Debordes (eds), *Routledge Handbook of Sport Marketing*. Milton Park: Taylor & Francis.

Peetz, T. B., Parks, J. B., & Spencer, N. (2004). Sport heroes as sport product endorsers: The role of gender in the transfer of meaning process for selected undergraduate students. *Sport Marketing Quarterly*, **13**, 141–150.

Perrotta, T. (2018). Roger Federer leaves Nike, snags $300 million deal to wear Uniqlo. *Wall Street Journal*, July 2. Retrieved from https://www.wsj.com/articles/federer-leaves-nike-snags-300-million-deal-to-wear-uniqlo-1530541948

Petroshius, S. M. & Crocker, K. E. (1989). An empirical analysis of spokesperson characteristics on advertisement and product evaluations. *Journal of the Academy of Marketing Science*, **17**, 217–225.

Premeaux, S. R. (2005). The attitudes of middle class male and female consumers regarding the effectiveness of celebrity endorsers, *Journal of Promotion Management*, **11**(4), 33–48.

Priester, J. R. & Petty, R. E. (2003). The influence of spokesperson trustworthiness on message elaboration, attitude strength, and advertising effectiveness, *Journal of Consumer Psychology*, **13**(4), 408–421.

Prior, M. (2014). Sharapova to front Avon Luck scents, June 11. Retrieved from http://link.galegroup.com/apps/doc/A371610406/AONE?u=tel_a_belmont&sid=AONE&xid=15fe64bc.

Rascher, D., Eddy, T., & Hyun, G. (2017). What Drives Endorsement Earnings for Superstar Athletes? *Journal of Applied Sport Management*, **9**(2).

St. James, M. (2010). Female sports celebrities targeting female teenagers: A content analysis of magazine advertising. *Journal of Business and Economic Research*, **8**(3), 1–13.

Ross, S. R. & Shinew, K.J. (2008). Perspectives of women college athletes on sport and gender. *Sex Roles*, **58**, 40–57.

Veltri, F. R. & Long, S. A. (1998). A new image: Female athlete-endorser. *Cyber-Journal of Sport Marketing*, **2**(4). Retrieved from http://ruby.fgcu.edu/courses/tdugas/ids3301/acrobat/womenendorsements.pdf.

Wang, S. W. & Scheinbaum, A. C. (2018). Enhancing brand credibility via celebrity endorsement: Trustworthiness trumps attractiveness and expertise. *Journal of Advertising Research*, **58**(1), 16–31.

34
Sponsorship of women's sport

Nancy Lough and Greg Greenhalgh

History of sponsorship in sport

The history of sport sponsorship can be dated back to the Roman Empire. Politicians, or tyrants, would sponsor athletic events (horse racing, running, boxing, gladiator fights, etc.) to please the public and enhance their own image (Mullin, Hardy, & Sutton, 2014). More recently, sport sponsorship has been viewed as a way for corporations to align themselves with a sport property in an effort to gain a competitive business advantage. However, sport sponsorship has not always been used as a strategic marketing tool. In the early years of sponsorship, the decision to support a sport financially was made by a top executive who held a vested interest in that sport. As investments in sponsorship increased, the need to justify these relationships grew, resulting in more strategic approaches. As a result, sport sponsorship has a variety of definitions, most of which emphasize that sponsorship is an investment by a corporation in an activity (sport property) in exchange for access to the commercial potential of being associated with that activity (Meenaghan, 1991). In today's environment, companies use sponsorship in an effort to distinguish their brand from competitors and establish some competitive advantage (Chanavat & Desbordes, 2014).

Two major events catapulted the popularity of sport sponsorship as a way for companies to accomplish marketing, communications, and public relations objectives: (1) a ban on advertising by tobacco companies in the UK (1965), the USA (1971), and Canada (1972) (Dewhirst & Hunter, 2002); and (2) the success of the sponsorship program for the 1984 Los Angeles Olympic Games (Irwin, Sutton, & McCarthy, 2008). The tobacco advertising bans created a market where an entire industry had substantial marketing budgets with few places to spend those dollars. Many tobacco companies realized they could get several of the same benefits attained from advertising plus numerous other benefits by sponsoring sport properties, namely Indy Car teams where multiple logos were prominently displayed on race cars. Women's sport was a direct beneficiary of the tobacco advertising ban, because Virginia Slims, a cigarette brand designed to appeal to women, agreed to sponsor the newly forming Women's Tennis Association (WTA) in 1973. The WTA needed financial backing and offered an avenue for Virginia Slims to communicate with women who were not only following tennis but were actively engaged in the women's movement of the 1970s.

After the bans on tobacco advertising, the success of the 1984 Olympic Games sponsorship program demonstrated that, if properly managed, sponsorship could be a major revenue generator for sport properties while attaining key marketing objectives for companies. Before the 1984 Olympic Games, host cities incurred enormous debt that often lasted for decades beyond their Olympic competition. In an effort to prevent debt, Peter Ueberroth, Los Angeles Olympic Organizing Committee President, initiated a corporately subsidized Olympics. To avoid clutter and provide product exclusivity only 30 sponsors were allowed, which enabled Ueberroth to develop relationships with corporate partners, in which both parties achieved the benefits desired. For women's sport, the 1984 Games in Los Angeles featured several firsts, including the first women's marathon. Running shoe companies, who were also young as businesses, found sponsorship attractive because attention was paid to the top American marathoner, Joan Benoit. By winning the Gold medal, Benoit helped sponsors attain the goodwill and brand identity they desired among runners, while also supporting a historic event for women in sport.

Following these two major events, sport sponsorship exploded across the sport landscape over the next three decades. In 1990, an annual growth rate of 15% was predicted for sponsorship spending. By 1997, US$5.9 billion was spent on sponsorship among North American companies, followed by US$6.8 billion in 1998. The anticipated increase in sponsorship investment continued throughout the next decade. By 2008, North American companies were projected to increase spending by 11.7%, reaching US$14.93 billion according to IEG Sponsorship Report's (2006) 22nd annual industry forecast. Global spending on sport sponsorship also increased dramatically to the unprecedented level of US$37.7 billion in 2008, an 11.9% increase over 2007, when US$33.7 billion was reached (Lough, 2009). By 2017, sport sponsorship spending in North America totaled US$15.7 billion, nearly half of what was spent globally (IEG sponsorship.com, 2018). Today, within North America, sport properties without corporate partners are viewed as second rate and of little significance (Lamont & Dowell, 2007).

As more companies developed an interest in sport sponsorship, and as more sport organizations pursued sponsorship relationships, previously overlooked options like women's sports became increasingly attractive as a means to cut through the clutter of more mainstream sport sponsorships. For example, in 1992 sponsorship investments in women's sport reached US$285 million in the United States, which was an unprecedented new high mark. Five years later, that figure had more than doubled to US$600 million. Before 1997, sponsorship money spent on women's sport was primarily allocated to the Ladies Professional Golf Association (LPGA), WTA, and figure skating (Lough, 1996). However, the 1996 Olympic Games served as a major catalyst for corporate investment in women's sport, with new women's sport properties like the Women's National Basketball Association (WNBA) and US Women's National team (soccer) emerging as viable sponsorship options.

The 1999 FIFA Women's World Cup Soccer Tournament, held in the United States, was a watershed event in women's sport, although securing sponsorship was not easy. For the sponsors who invested in 1994 when the United States hosted the FIFA (men's) World Cup, the elimination of the American men's team resulted in a minimal return on their investment. In contrast, the successful run to the championship for the US women's team in 1999 elicited a tide of emotion that created substantial financial success for sponsors and event organizers. In these contrasting examples, the corporations who passed on sponsorship of the women's World Cup, due to unrealized returns from the men's World Cup, lost out. Meanwhile, valuable benefits accrued for those corporations who were willing to support the women in 1999 (Lough & Greenhalgh, 2014). The success for sponsors was so significant that the Women's United Soccer Association, the first women's professional soccer league in the United States, was created in 2000.

More recently, innovative sport properties such as the LPGA have expanded their media platforms and increased their sponsorship activation efforts, resulting in new partnerships and expanded earning for players. The LPGA remains one of the few sport options that experienced double-digit television growth in the United States after 2005, resulting in substantially higher prices for sponsors. Tournament title sponsors paid as much as US$100,000 for a three-year contract in 2005 compared with their previous commitment of only US$15,000. The sevenfold increase in fees was attributed to the LPGA's first female commissioner, Carolyn Vesper Bivens, and her ability to communicate how the value offered to sponsors had increased in parallel with expanded service and brand exposure. In the other sport deemed culturally gender appropriate, the WTA recently translated the popularity of tennis into significant sponsorship and media deals. A 10-year, US$525 million media rights deal was signed in 2015 with PERFORM, making history as the single largest media rights and production deal to date in women's sports. With equal broadcasting at major tennis tournaments for men's and women's events, and highly valued individual players like Serena Williams, this notable sponsorship deal demonstrated the leadership of the WTA and also contributed to the developing momentum for sponsorship opportunities in other women's sports (Labrie, 2016).

Sponsorships in these two individual sports provide the earnings for players who win tournaments. In 2017, 16 players on the LPGA Tour made US$1 million or more, whereas 37 players on the WTA tour achieved this level. In 2017, Venus Williams topped the earnings list in women's tennis, earning US$5.5 million from reaching two major finals, at Wimbledon and the Australian Open, and finishing runner-up at the year-end WTA Finals. South Korean golfer Sung Hyun Park, winner of the Women's US Open, led the LPGA money list in 2017 with US$2.3 million in prize money (Rossingh, 2017). Yet, women's golf and tennis enjoy the benefits of being considered gender-appropriate sports. For team sports, or combat sports such as boxing or mixed martial arts, women are considered to be violating the gender norm.

Sexism in sponsorship

One reason why corporate sponsors have been hesitant to invest as partners with women's sports properties and leagues is the fact that female athletes have not been celebrated solely for their athleticism. Acceptance of women as athletes has improved over time, yet sexism remains as one salient explanation for the limited investment in women athletes and women's sports. For example, not one woman athlete made the Forbes Top 100 highest-paid athletes list in 2017–2018. The top 100 highest-paid athletes were estimated to have derived 23% of their cumulative income from the US$3.8 billion earned from endorsements and appearances (Forbes, 2018). The startling statistic of not one woman athlete appearing in this list of 100 points directly to the gender binary that overvalues the marketing potential offered by male athletes, while undervaluing women athletes and women's sport. Even with sport sponsorship spending in North America projected to eclipse US$15 billion (IEG sponsorship.com, 2018) the amount allocated to women tends to be miniscule, given that reports show less than half of one percent of sponsorship spending going directly to women's sport (Fink, 2015).

Sexism is also apparent in the media coverage allocated to women's sport and women athletes. In essence, the undervaluing of women's sports and athletes is evident in editors' choices not to provide coverage, which effectively renders female athletes and women's sport invisible. In their 25-year longitudinal content analysis study, Musto, Cooky, and Messner (2017) found that women's sport received about 3% of the televised sports highlights and coverage. Similarly, Fox Sports Live was found to allocate less than 1% of its coverage to women's sports (Billings & Young, 2015). The result is invisibility and lack of fan accessibility, which diminishes the value of women's sport, and thereby eliminates marketing opportunities for companies that seek to align their brand as a sponsor with the brand of the league, team, or athlete.

Although some may argue this is not sexism, the definition of the term would suggest otherwise. Sexism is described as prejudice, stereotyping, or discrimination, typically against women, on the basis of sex (*Oxford English Dictionary*, 2018). Quite simply, prejudicial attitudes of sport editors have been correlated with stereotyping behaviors manifest in the attitudes that women's sport is not interesting, not exciting, and not worthy of coverage (Hardin, 2013). The result of this attitude, the allocation of 95–99% of media coverage for men's sport, illustrates the discrimination that women in sport face. Further support from Frisby (2017) was offered in her analysis of the two most recognized sport magazines, *Sports Illustrated* and *ESPN the Magazine*, in which women athletes were represented on their covers about 6% of the time and, even when the most well-known female athletes competed at major events like the US Open (tennis), women received only a fraction of the coverage from national news outlets (Kian & Clavio, 2011). These sexist practices result in diminished prize money in tournament offerings due to lower sponsorship valuations, and/or lower salaries on teams and in professional leagues, as well as fewer endorsement options.

Why sponsors need women's sport

Women's sport has been underfunded globally due to limited commercial investment (Farrell, Fink, & Fields, 2011). For women's sport to advance and succeed on the level of other mainstream sports, support in the form of corporate sponsorship and investments is necessary. What has remained a mystery is why companies have yet to realize the potential value that women's sport offers. When data shows that women are most often the primary purchasers of sport products in all categories, including equipment, tickets, and sporting goods, and recent research has revealed women are responsible for up to 70% of the National Football League's (NFL's) licensed product purchases (Bush, Bush, Clark, & Bush, 2005), the importance of women as consumers and fans of sport is clear. Scarborough Sports Marketing reported that since 1998 the percentage of women identifying as avid sports fans increased 29%, resulting in 50 million women avidly following sports (Bush et al., 2005). Clearly there is a market for sport among women. Yet, scholars have also shown motives to consume women's sport differing from those for men's sport. Women's sport offers affordability, is more influenced by family and friends, and can be tied to support of a cause more readily than men's sport (Fink, Trail, & Anderson, 2002; Funk, Ridinger, & Moorman, 2003). Thus, sponsors need women's sport because women's sport will open up marketing channels to reach women consumers, as well as broaden opportunities for differentiation and the realization of distinct marketing objectives and goals.

Sponsorship objectives

The pressure placed on sport properties to secure sponsors has significantly increased and corporations now view sponsorship as a way to create brand value. However, during the early days of modern sponsorship, most companies lacked a strategic plan and failed to use sponsorship as a vehicle to achieve their marketing objectives. As noted by Copeland, Frisby, and McCarville (1996), during the 1960s and 1970s many sponsors viewed sponsorship as a form of philanthropy and corporations would select the sport organization(s) they wanted to sponsor based on intuition or the interests of the sponsor's CEO or marketing director. However, those motives have changed and companies are now looking to use sport sponsorship as a way to create or enhance brand value (Lough & Irwin, 2001). With these new expectations of sponsors, sport properties have had to become more aware of the objectives sponsors are looking to achieve in order to best serve their corporate partners.

Due to the immense pressure placed on sport properties to understand the goals and expectations of potential sponsors, there has been an abundance of research on corporate sport sponsorship objectives. Yet, it is difficult to classify corporate sponsorship objectives in a clear-cut way because companies frequently have a number of overlapping and interacting objectives within one sponsorship relationship (Mullin, Hardy, & Sutton, 2007). Even after a thorough review of academic writing and empirical research combined with practical findings, Mullin et al. (2007) found no specific single corporate objective dominated the decision-making process concerning whether or what sport property to sponsor. Some of the most commonly cited sport sponsorship objectives include increasing corporate awareness, increasing target market awareness, enhancing company image, becoming involved in the community, building trade relationships, enhancing employee relations, and increasing sales/market share (Ferreira, Hall, & Bennett, 2008; Irwin et al., 2008; Stotlar, 2009).

Although a number of objectives have been identified, measuring these objectives has proven extremely difficult. As noted by Copeland et al. (1996), one major difficulty in measuring the effectiveness of a given sponsorship is the fact that sponsorships do not live in a vacuum. For instance, a sponsor noticing an increase in sales may be able to attribute these results to the sponsorship, but the company is likely performing other marketing and promotional tactics that may also be (or are solely) contributing to the increase in sales. Therefore, the ability to demonstrate that a sponsorship is enhancing brand value is difficult at best. For these reasons, most of the early attempts to measure or determine the effectiveness of sport sponsorship were limited to measuring media equivalencies (Berkes, Nyerges, & Vaczi, 2009). Generally speaking, media equivalency measures assess the amount of exposure a sponsoring brand's logo was in focus during the telecast of a sporting event and equate that exposure to what it would have cost the sponsor to buy traditional advertising to reach a similar number of viewers at a similar time. This form of sponsorship evaluation was advantageous for large sporting events with a strong television following, but fell well short in assessing the numerous other benefits that can be provided through sport sponsorship. Furthermore, as noted above, many sponsors look to achieve a variety of sponsorship objectives and simply gauging sponsorship effectiveness via media equivalencies undermines the impact of sponsorships aimed at achieving objectives beyond increasing the awareness level of the sponsoring company.

Work by Greenhalgh and Greenwell (2013a) investigated the objectives of companies currently engaged in a sponsorship of a niche sport. As outlined below, most women's sport properties fall within the niche sport moniker. Miloch and Lambrecht (2006) defined niche sports as sports that are not mainstream and do not appeal to a mass audience. Within North America, niche sports include: tennis, lacrosse, bowling, fishing, curling, horse racing, action/extreme sports, archery, cycling, mountaineering, and snow sports. In a more comprehensive definition of niche sports, Rosner and Shropshire (2004) classified niche sports into four distinctive categories: (1) minor leagues: these leagues do not represent the top level of professional competition within the given sport; 2) emerging sports that represent the top level of competition in their respective sport but lack the financial success and media coverage to make them mainstream, for example Major League Lacrosse (MLL) or the X Games; (3) indoor variations of traditionally outdoor sports such as the Arena Football League or the Professional Arena Soccer League; and (4) gender-specific leagues that offer women the opportunity to participate in their own league such as World Team Tennis, and the WBNA (Rosner & Shropshire, 2004). These four categories, although not necessarily exhaustive or mutually exclusive of all niche sports, provide insight into the fact that the term "niche sports" encompasses a vast array of eclectic sports. However, within both the Miloch and Lambrecht (2006) and Rosner and Shropshire (2004) definitions, one could clearly argue that women's sport fits within the broader definition of niche sport.

It is important to note that women's sport fits within the broader landscape of niche sport because this allows for women's sport administrators to borrow from the still scant research on niche sport. Yet, it must also be noted that all sport properties live in a dynamic environment and can evolve from niche to mainstream. Some may argue Major League Soccer and the Ultimate Fighting Championship have made, or are currently making, the transition towards a "mass appeal." Furthermore, we have witnessed certain athletes, and in particular female athletes, transform what would be a niche event into a more mainstream endeavor due to their personal star power (e.g., Ronda Rousey).

As noted earlier, niche sports, and in turn women's sports, typically do not receive the mainstream media attention, or large-scale crowds realized by the NFL, NBA, and MLB and, as a result, major corporations have been less likely to engage in sponsorship relationships with these niche sports. It is of interest that Brenner (2003) noted the Core Tour, Long Drivers of America, Wal-Mart FLW Outdoors Tour, and the International Mountain Bike Association have been able to draw many major corporate sponsors including Re/Max International, Fuji Film U.S.A., Nokia, and Subaru of America. The lack of empirical research on niche sport sponsorship has led to anecdotal claims, by both academics and practitioners, as to the rationale for corporation's engagement in niche sport sponsorship relationships. The literature has identified four main reasons sponsors engage in niche sport sponsorship relationships. These reasons include cost-effectiveness (Fullerton, 2010; Hanas, 2007; Williams, 2001), more refined target market (Brenner, 2003; Greenwald & Fernandez-Balboa, 1998; Milne, McDonald, Sutton, & Kashyap, 1996; Stotlar, 2009; Tripodi, 2001), niche sport property flexibility (Hanas, 2007; Jones, 2008; Livingstone, 2009; Rovell, 2009; Williams, 2001), and decreased niche sponsorship clutter (Amis, Slack, & Berrett, 1999; Greenwald & Fernandez-Balboa, 1998; Lough, 1996; Lough & Irwin, 2001; Maxwell & Lough, 2009; Shank, 2005; Tripodi, 2001). Clearly, there must be cogent reasons why these companies choose to sponsor niche sports. According to Greenhalgh and Greenwell (2013b), niche sports offer sponsors a cost-effective alternative to mainstream sport sponsorship, a more refined target market, more flexibility in their ability to help sponsors achieve their objectives, and decreased clutter because there are typically fewer total sponsors of niche sports compared with mainstream sports, Minor League Baseball notwithstanding.

Niche sport properties would be wise to embrace these differences because they have been found to be competitive advantages. We have witnessed the WNBA embrace this flexibility with respect to sponsorship as they allowed sponsors to place logos on their game jerseys starting in 2011. Although this is rather commonplace in Europe, this innovative move marked the first team sport in North America to adapt this line of sponsorship inventory. The financial benefits associated with jersey sponsorships have been touted as a main reason many WNBA teams have remained fiscally solvent (Mandell, 2017). Not only is this a great example of niche sport flexibility, but it also allows these jersey sponsors to cut through the clutter of all other forms of sponsorship associated with the WNBA teams. Interestingly, the NBA began including jersey sponsorships for the 2017–2018 season.

In conjunction with some of the benefits niche sports can provide sponsors is the fact that sponsorship evaluation has progressed. Many sponsors are moving beyond simply measuring media equivalencies to more sophisticated measures of the effectiveness the sponsorship had in obtaining their particular marketing-based objectives. This can be viewed as a very positive progression for most niche sports because they were unable to compete with mainstream sports with respect to audience size and media attention. However, we are now seeing sponsors assessing the ability of a sponsorship to move web traffic from the sponsored team's webpage to the sponsors' webpage via a link on the team's site. Furthermore, sponsors can also track the sales created from those consumers who came directly from the team's webpage. This level of assessment was something not available to sponsors before the internet boom. One could easily see how this same formula for website traffic spills over to all forms of social media. Although most niche sport properties do not have the volume of web traffic or social media followership compared with their mainstream counterparts, they can often provide a more targeted demographic of potential consumers to their sponsors. For example, Subaru chose to sponsor the International Mountain Bike Association rather than advertise during the Super Bowl. Subaru's justification was that only 10% of the millions of Super Bowl viewers fit the demographic profile of the typical Subaru driver, whereas nearly all of the 32,000 International Mountain Bike Association members fit Subaru's profile (Brenner, 2003). Here we can see that sponsors are becoming savvier in their sponsorship selection, understanding that bigger is not always better. Niche sport properties can use this information when selling sponsorships so long as they can accurately describe their average fan from a demographic and psychographic perspective.

Sponsorship objectives in women's sport

Corporate partners use sponsorships as part of their overall marketing strategy, seeking fit and alignment with their target audience, brand image, and product function. In this process, audience characteristics and fan passion are utilized to present the fit and alignment. Audience characteristics often include size, demographics, geographic data, purchase behavior, brand preferences, and attitudes. Fan passion refers to points of attachment, source and level of passion, and fan behavior. In pursuing corporations for potential sponsorships, major league sport organizations have an advantage, because there is syndicated data on their fans' affinity, loyalty, brand preferences, consumption patterns, and demographics. However, women's sport organizations often lack this information. Gaining this information would allow women's sport properties to prepare more targeted sponsorship proposals, providing relevant sponsorship messaging, manifesto, and activation efforts that the potential partners seek.

Consistently, corporations argue that return on investment is the basis for their decisions on sponsorship investments. Yet this argument is increasingly losing validation given the statistics on women as consumers. For example, the majority, or 58%, of running event participants are women. Yet most race sponsors are more often targeting men, as opposed to strategically communicating with women. We've known for years that women are responsible for between 70% and 80% of all consumer purchases, and women purchase 68% of automobiles as well as more than 50% of traditionally male products. Perhaps even more intriguing is the recent statistic showing "women control more than 60 percent of all personal wealth in the U.S." (Krasney, 2012, para. 4). Thus, a viable and valuable market comprising women consumers exists and is available for sponsors to tap into. Plus, men account for half of the fan base and audience of most women's sports, creating an even wider market potential for sponsors who invest in women's sport (Nielsen, 2018). Still there is strong evidence to support the marketing of women's sport to women consumers. The opportunity cost represented in all of these figures could be realized through sponsorship, which in fact would assist sponsors in cutting through the clutter of traditional advertising, especially in sport. In essence, multiple marketing objectives have been realized through innovative relationships with women's sport, including increasing target market awareness, enhancing the sponsor's image, becoming involved in the community, and increasing sales/market share.

Sponsorship conceptual framework

In marketing, the AIDA model (Figure 34.1), which depicts awareness, interest, desire, and action (Mullin et al., 2014), has long been perpetuated as a way to move consumers along a continuum toward purchase intention – a key goal of effective marketing. This model can also be applied to depict the crucial role media coverage plays relative to sponsorship. Sport media have long argued that they cover the sport in which their readers or viewers have expressed an interest. Meanwhile scholars have argued that media coverage effectively "builds audiences," because their coverage communicates to consumers the content that is worthy of their time for consumption (Messner, Duncan, & Wachs, 1996). The traditional relationship works to increase interest in mainstream (men's) sport such as the NFL, MLB, and NBA due to the incessant coverage on ESPN and within major news outlets, consistently building the audience for men's sport. Yet the same cannot be said for women's sport. With studies showing a range between 1% and 6% of all sport media allocated to women's sport (Billings & Young, 2015; Frisby, 2017; Kian & Clavio, 2011; Musto et al., 2017), the lack of media coverage leads to a failure in generating awareness, the first step on the continuum. The lack of awareness then limits interest, the second step on the continuum, which actively diminishes the value potential offered by women's sport. Meanwhile the awareness and resulting interest granted to mainstream sport, with 94–99% of the allotted media coverage, effectively bolsters the value proposition of these mainstream men's sports by creating desire among consumers and thus enhancing attractiveness to sponsors.

Thus, the starting point on the AIDA continuum model is quite distinct for a women's sport property compared with their mainstream competitors. With a lack of awareness, interest must be organic. If interest is not fostered, then desire is flat with no resulting action. For women's sport the continuum can be viewed more as a cycle. Interest is evident by women's sport consumers seeking information and coverage of women's sport through social media or new content-specific platforms. Desire is satiated and action is fostered when women sport consumers can access content, and can actively follow their favorite sport or female athlete. For

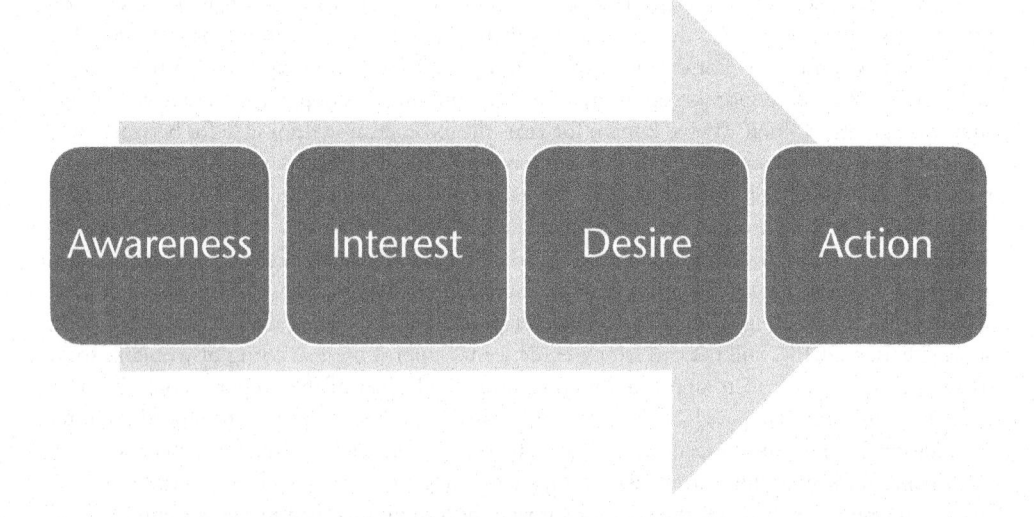

Figure 34.1 The attention, interest, desire, action (AIDA) continuum model

example, fans of the WNBA can purchase the WNBA League Pass to watch games played by every team in the league, or they can purchase a pass to watch their favorite team all season. In 2016 the WNBA League Pass saw a 24% increase in subscriptions, and website traffic increased 22% for average monthly unique visitors (WNBA, 2016). Further evidence of women's sport fans seeking digital content is notable in the growth of ESPNW, the website dedicated to women's sport, where page views increased 71% year to year with 19.8 million views per month (Glass, 2016). In each of these cases, we see evidence of the AIDA cycle wherein consumers first demonstrate interest, followed by desire, leading to the action of accessing content or attending events, which then leads to more awareness among other fans and the media of the growing interest in women's sport.

Building the case for women's sport sponsorship

There are several reasons why corporations would be wise to pay heed to the emerging benefits associated with sponsoring women's sports. Nielsen (2018) found women's sport to be more inspiring, progressive, family oriented, clean, and less money driven compared with men's sport. They also found that 84% of sports fans are interested in women's sport, which was evenly split with 51% of men and 49% of women interested in viewing more women's sport. This is important for two reasons: first, it debunks the perception that only women are interested in women's

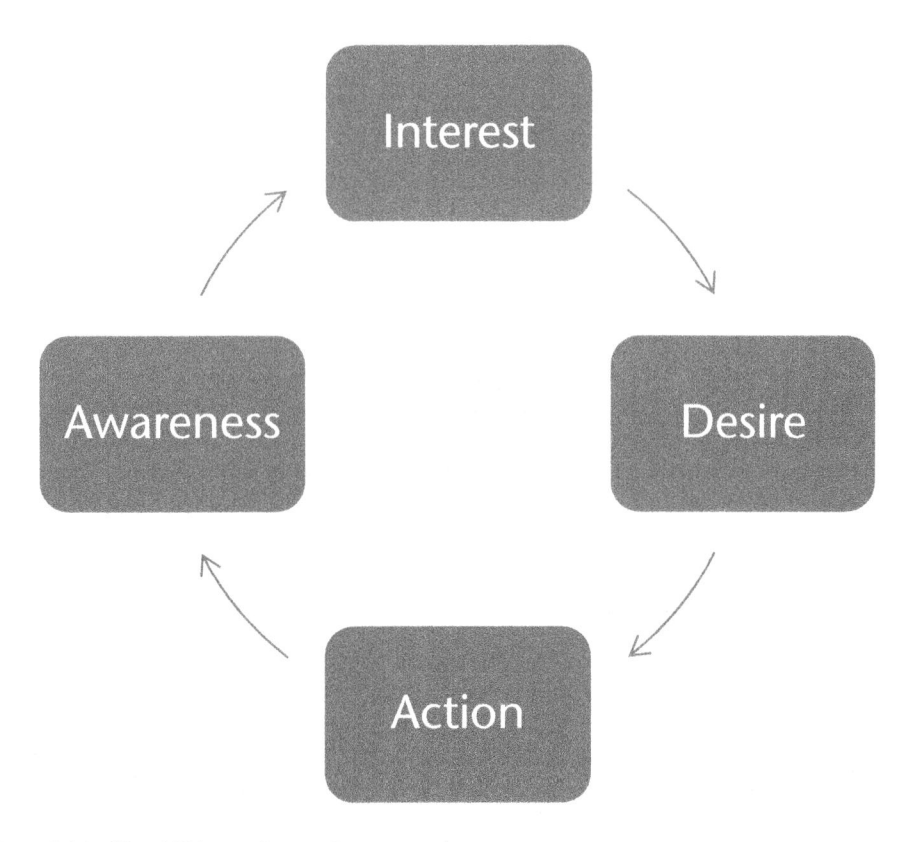

Figure 34.2 The AIDA continuum for women's sport

sports, and, second, it demonstrates that the primary decision-maker for most household spending (women) is a captive audience during these events. Hence, women's sport organizations should be capable of providing a very lucrative audience to their corporate partners.

Not only has women's sport attracted appealing audiences, but also these audiences have become robust in some instances. For example, the 2018 Liga MX Femenil drew 51,000 fans and the Women's FA Cup final between Chelsea and Arsenal drew 43,000 attendees and 1.6 million viewers in the same year (Nielsen, 2018). Similar occurrences have happened in Australia where the newly created women's division of the Australian Football League (AFL) was able to attract a capacity crowd of 24,500 fans (even having to turn away 2,000 fans because admission was free). This trend of filling stadiums to capacity was commonplace throughout their inaugural season in 2017 (Jarrett, 2017). Clearly, there is an appetite for women's sport and the sponsorship dollars will follow. The surge in attendance and viewership of women's sport are typically accompanied by a precursor of enhanced media coverage. Specifically, we witnessed an uptick in interest and sponsorship of field hockey in Britain after the women's team won Gold during the 2016 Olympics. The Gold medal game was broadcast live on the BBC during primetime (Nielsen, 2018), providing the exposure needed to foster desire among fans to tune in. Further supporting this notion is the fact that "45% of the general population across eight markets (U.S., UK, France, Italy, Germany, Spain, Australia and New Zealand) would consider attending live women's sports events, while 46% say they would watch more if more women's sports was accessible on free TV" (Nielsen, 2018, p. 12). Many companies have begun to act in this space because sponsorship of women's sports has increased both in the number of sponsorship deals signed (37% increase from 2013 to 2017) and in the monetary size of the deals (49% increase between 2013 and 2017) (Nielsen, 2018).

Conclusion

The business of sport sponsorship is somewhat mysterious. On rare occasions when new deals are announced, terms are often not disclosed. The sponsor's desired objective or audience is probably mentioned, yet rarely is the strategy revealed. And yet, the sponsorship business is the single largest component of revenue globally for sport organizations. Clearly, success in the business of sport depends on sponsorship. For women's sports to become established as a viable option for sponsorship investments, visibility must continue to increase. Sponsors always want to know about "eyeballs," the industry term for who the likely viewers will be who see the sponsor's brand at the sporting event or in a broadcast. We now have increasing evidence that the viewership for women's sports is substantial and growing globally. Changing the narrative to one in which women's sport is known for the unique value it offers is a good start. The media, rights holders and sponsors all have a key role in creating the platforms for women's sport to flourish in the future.

Leader profile: Megan Kahn, Executive Director, WeCOACH

A former collegiate basketball player, NCAA Division I assistant coach and athletic administrator, Megan Kahn now serves as Executive Director of WeCOACH. Since August 2016, she has quickly elevated the reach of WeCOACH by developing new programming and resources for women coaches across all sports and all levels. WeCOACH has become the premier nonprofit organization focused on recruiting, advancing, and retaining women in the coaching profession. At a time when female participation in sports continues to increase, barriers still exist for women to enter and stay in the coaching profession.

Figure 34.3 Megan Kahn

> "With WeCOACH being a young organization (founded in 2011), we had plenty of challenges early on in gaining sponsorship exposure. Now that we are steadily growing, we have begun attracting the attention of regional and national sponsors," said Kahn. "It makes a strong social statement for a brand to align with WeCOACH. Because our work is directly impacting the coaches (who are the role models of today's student-athletes). By becoming a corporate sponsor of WeCOACH, a brand's support is indirectly influencing future female leaders."

WeCOACH has leveraged a national partnership with global brand leader, Adidas, as well as several other companies, including the NCAA, ARMS Software, and Morgan Stanley to name a few.

> "One of the challenges is identifying companies whom we think will align with our mission in this overcrowded space – it's a very competitive market seeking funding. Now in the executive director role, I spend a significant amount of time looking for areas of overlap and cultivating authentic relationships and partnerships," said Kahn.

Kahn also has her own consulting company, KAHNSULTING, specializing in championship management and administration. She served as the 2015 and 2019 NCAA Division I Women's Basketball Final Four tournament manager, overseeing game operations in Tampa

Kahn's earlier administrative career included positions at the Atlantic 10 Conference office (A-10), where she oversaw both men's and women's basketball operations during her four-year tenure. Before the A-10, Kahn started her career in women's basketball administration at the Atlantic Coast Conference office (ACC).

Kahn continues to be active in the Tampa Bay community as a founding committee member of the Women in Sports and Events (WISE) chapter, as well as a local advisory committee member for the 2019 NCAA Women's Basketball Final Four. She is a lifelong seeker of professional growth, having attended the National Collegiate Athletic Association (NCAA) Women Coaches Academy (2004), National Association of Collegiate Women Athletics Administrators (NACWAA)/ Higher Education Resource Services (HERS) (2006), now known as Institute for Administrative Advancement, and the Sports Management Institute (2011–2012).

When asked about her desire to advance women in sport, Kahn shared her intentions

> From the time I finished my collegiate playing career, I knew my path would entail being a role model and having an impact on women in the business. It's important for young girls to see other women succeeding – that includes on the sidelines, in front offices, as athletic trainers, or strength and conditioning coaches. We have a responsibility to reach back and pull others along, serve as mentors and give other young women opportunities to get experience. I feel so blessed to wake up every day knowing our work is making a real difference in the lives of female coaches.

References

Amis, J., Slack, T., & Berrett, T. (1999). Sport sponsorship as distinctive competence. *European Journal of Marketing*, **33**(3/4), 250–272.

Berkes, P., Nyerges, M., & Vaczi, J. (2009). The changing of the sponsorship market. *Sportwissenschaft*, **39**, 35–44.

Billings, A. C. & Young, B. D. (2015). Comparing flagship news programs: Women's sport coverage in ESPN's SportsCenter and FOX Sports 1's FOX Sports Live. *Electronic News*, **9**(1), 3–16.

Brenner, S. (2003). Emerging sports sponsors find value below the radar. *SportsBusiness Journal*, September 15. Retrieved from: www.sportsbusinessjournal.com/index.cfm?fuseaction=article.preview&articleID=33191.

Bush, V., Bush, A., Clark, P., & Bush, R. (2005). Girl power and word-of-mouth behavior in the flourishing sports market. *Journal of Consumer Marketing*, **22**(5), 257–264.

Chanavat, N. & Desbordes, M. (2014). Towards the regulation and restriction of ambush marketing? The first truly social and digital mega sports event: The Olympic Games, London 2012. *International Journal of Sports Marketing & Sponsorship*, **15**(3), 2–11.

Copeland, R., Frisby, W., & McCarville, R. (1996). Understanding the sport sponsorship process from a corporate perspective. *Journal of Sport Management*, **10**(1), 32–48.

Dewhirst, T. & Hunter, A. (2002). Tobacco sponsorship of Formula One and CART auto racing: Tobacco brand exposure and enhanced symbolic imagery through co-sponsors' third party advertising. *Ad Watch*, **11**, 146–150.

IEG sponsorship.com (2018). *What sponsors want and where dollars will go in 2018*. Retrieved from www.sponsorship.com/IEG/files/f3/f3cfac41-2983-49be-8df6-3546345e27de.pdf.

Farrell, A., Fink, J., & Fields, S. (2011). Women's sport spectatorship: An exploration of men's influence. *Journal of Sport Management*, **25**(3), 190–201.

Ferreira, M., Hall, T. K., & Bennett, G. (2008). Exploring brand positioning in a sponsorship context: A correspondence analysis of the Dew Action Sports Tour. *Journal of Sport Management*, **22**, 734–761.

Fink, J. S. (2015). Female athletes, women's sport, and the sport media commercial complex: Have we really "come a long way, baby"? *Sport Management Review*, **18**(3), 331–342.

Fink, J. S., Trail, G., & Anderson, D. (2002). An examination of team identification: Which motives are most salient to its existence? *International Sports Journal*, **6**(2), 195–207.

Forbes (2018). The world's highest-paid athletes. Retrieved from https://www.forbes.com/athletes/list.

Frisby, C. M. (2017). Sacrificing dignity for publicity: Content analysis of female and male athletes on *Sports Illustrated* and *ESPN the Magazine* covers from 2012–2016. *Advances in Journalism and Communication*, **5**(2), 120–135.

Funk, D., Ridinger, L., & Moorman, A. (2003). Understanding consumer support: Extending the sport interest inventory (SII) to examine individual differences among women's professional sport consumers. *Sport Management Review*, **6**, 1–32.

Fullerton, S. (2010). *Sports Marketing*, 2nd edn. New York: McGraw-Hill Irwin.

Glass, A. (2016). How espnW harnesses the power and importance of a woman's voice. Forbes, October 17. Retrieved from https://www.forbes.com/sites/alanaglass/2016/10/17/how-espnw-harnesses-the-power-and-importance-of-a-womans-voice/#7b191ef256c5.

Greenhalgh, G. & Greenwell, T. C. (2013a). What's in it for me? An investigation of North American professional niche sport sponsorship objectives. *Sport Marketing Quarterly*, **22**, 101–112.

Greenhalgh, G. P. & Greenwell T. C. (2013b). Professional niche sports sponsorship selection criteria. *International Journal of Sports Marketing & Sponsorship*, **14**, 77–94.

Greenwald, L. & Fernandez-Balboa, J. (1998). Trends in the sport marketing industry and in the demographics of the United States: Their effect on the strategic role of grassroots sport sponsorship in corporate America. *Sport Marketing Quarterly*, **7**(4), 35–47.

Hanas, J. (2007). Going pro: What's with all these second-tier sports? *Advertising Age*, **78**(5), S3.

Hardin, M. (2013). Want changes in content? Change the decision makers. *Communication & Sport*, **1**(3), 241–245.

IEG Sponsorship Report (2006). Projection: Sponsorship growth to increase for fifth straight year. Retrieved from www.sponsorship.com/iegsr/2006/12/25/Projection--Sponsorship-Growth-To-Increase-For-Fif.aspx.

Irwin, R. L., Sutton, W. A., & McCarthy, L. M. (2008). *Sport Promotion and Sales Management*. Champaign, IL: Human Kinetics.

Jarrett, N. (2017). Aussies on the rise: The growth of women in sports in Australia, December 4. Retrieved from https://www.womenssportsfoundation.org/sports/aussies-rise-growth-women-sports-australia.

Jones, R. (2008). Advertise creatively with offbeat sports. Entrepreneur.com. Retrieved from www.entrepreneur.com/article/printhis/193762.html.

Kian, E. M. & Clavio, G. (2011). A comparison of online media and traditional newspaper coverage of the men's and women's US Open tennis tournaments. *Journal of Sports Media*, **6**(1), 55–84.

Kransey, J. (2012). Inforgraphic: Women control the money in America. *Business Insider*. Retrieved from https://www.businessinsider.com/infographic-women-control-the-money-in-america-2012-2?op=1.

Labrie, C. (2016). Exxon, Soccer United Marketing and sponsorship of women's sports. Retrieved from www.excellesports.com/news/author/christina-labrie.

Lamont, M. & Dowell, R. (2007). A process model of small and medium enterprise sponsorship of regional sport tourism events. *Journal of Vacation Marketing*, **14**(3), 253–266.

Livingstone, S. (2009). PBR stays in saddle. *USA Today*. Retrieved from http://usatoday.com/sports/2009-01-14-tough-economy-impact_N.htm.

Lough, N. (1996). Factors effecting corporate sponsorship of women's sport. *Sport Marketing Quarterly*, **5**(2), 11–19.

Lough, N. (2009). Sponsorship and sales in the sport industry. In S. Gillentine & B. Crow (eds), *Foundations of Sport Management*, 2nd edn (pp. 145–159). West Virginia: Fitness Information Technology.

Lough, N. & Greenhalgh, G. (2014). Sponsorship and sales in the sport industry. In S. Gillentine & B. Crow (eds), *Foundations of Sport Management*, 3rd edn. West Virginia: Fitness Information Technology.

Lough, N. L. & Irwin, R. L. (2001). A comparative analysis of sponsorship objectives for U.S. women's sport and traditional sport sponsorship. *Sport Marketing Quarterly*, **10**(4), 202–211.

Mandell, N. (2017). Sponsors logos everywhere? WNBA unveils plan to boost how many fans see per game, November 9. Retrieved from https://ftw.usatoday.com/2017/11/wnba-court-jerseys-sponsors.

Maxwell, H. & Lough, N. (2009). Signage vs. no signage: An analysis of sponsorship recognition in women's college basketball. *Sport Marketing Quarterly*, **18**, 188–198.

Meenaghan, T. (1991). The role of sponsorship in the marketing communications mix. *International Journal of Advertising*, **10**, 35–47.

Messner, M., Duncan, M., & Wachs, F. (1996). The gender of audience building: Televised coverage of women's and men's NCAA basketball. *Sociological Inquiry*, **66**(4), 422–440.

Miloch, K. S. & Lambrecht, K. W. (2006). Consumer awareness of sponsorship at grassroots sport events. *Sport Marketing Quarterly*, **15**(3), 147–154.

Milne, G. R., McDonald, M. A., Sutton, W. A., & Kashyap, R. (1996). A niche-based evaluation of sport participation patterns. *Journal of Sport Management*, **10**, 417–434.
Mullin, B. J., Hardy, S., & Sutton, W.A. (2007). *Sport Marketing*, 3rd edn. Champaign, IL: Human Kinetics.
Mullin, B.J., Hardy, S., & Sutton, W.A. (2014). *Sport Marketing*, 4th edn. Champaign, IL: Human Kinetics.
Musto, M., Cooky, C., & Messner, M. A. (2017). "From fizzle to sizzle!" Televised sports news and the production of gender-bland sexism. *Gender & Society*, **31**(5), 573–596.
Nielsen (2018). The rise of women's sports. Retrieved from https://www.nielsen.com/content/dam/corporate/us/en/reports-downloads/2018-reports/the-rise-of-womens-sports.pdf.
Oxford English Dictionary (2018). Sexism. Retrieved from https://www.oxforddictionaries.com.
Rosner, S. & Shropshire, K. L. (eds) (2004). *The Business of Sports*. Sudbury, MA: Jones & Bartlett Publishers.
Rossingh, D. (2017). Want to make a good living in sport? Take up golf. CNN, November 14, 2017. Retrieved from www.kitv.com/story/36838440/want-to-make-a-good-living-in-sporttake-up-golf.
Rovell, D. (2009). NFL teams selling space on practice jerseys. Retrieved from www.cnbc.com/id/31082521.
Shank, M. (2005). *Sports Marketing: A strategic perspective*. Upper Saddle River, NJ: Pearson Prentice Hall.
Stotlar, D. K. (2009). *Developing successful sport sponsorship plans*, 3rd edn. Morgantown, WV: Fitness Information Technology.
Tripodi, J. A. (2001). Sponsorship – A confirmed weapon in the promotional armory. *International Journal of Sports Marketing & Sponsorship*, March/April, 1–20.
Williams, P. (2001). Minor leagues play major competitive role. *SportsBusiness Journal*, January 15. Retrieved from www.sportsbusinessjournal.com/index.cfm?fuseaction=article.preview&articleID=8964.
Women's National Basketball Association (WNBA) (2016). WNBA's record-breaking season scores highest attendance in five years, September 21. Retrieved from https://www.wnba.com/news/record-breaking-attendance-five-years-digital-social-retail.

Part VI
Media and technology

35
Social media and women's sport
What have we learned so far

Ann Pegoraro, Katie Lebel, and Alanna Harman

When Serena Williams won Wimbledon in July 2015, author J. K. Rowling took to Twitter to express her fandom: "I love her," she wrote. "What an athlete, what a role model, what a woman!" (Bacle, 2015, para. 1). Of course, other fans took the time to chime in and reply to Rowling's tweet. One Twitter user responded, "ironic then that main reason for her success is that she is built like a man" (Bacle, 2015, para. 2). What happened next was an epic Twitter take down by Rowling who slammed that Twitter user in her response: "She is built like a man," Rowling replied along with a photo of Williams wearing a form-fitting red dress. "Yeah, my husband looks just like this in a dress. You're an idiot." (Bacle, 2015 para. 3). This very public unveiling of Twitter abuse serves to illustrate the types of dialogue around women athletes that occur every day on social media platforms.

Although women athletes have long been subjected to inequitable, often inferior media coverage in comparison to men (Cooky, Messner, & Musto, 2015), the rise of digital platforms has brought with them a whole new set of challenges, including new outlets for harassment. But these platforms have also provided new opportunities for women's sport coverage and the hope of a more democratized portrayal of these women as athletes. The traditional media portrayals of women in sport have historically emphasized femininity and heterosexuality over athletic competence (e.g., Fink & Kensicki, 2002; Knight & Giuliano, 2003; Krane et al., 2010). As digital media opportunities have increased, many hoped women's representation in sport might showcase more of their athletic abilities and strength, but, to date, the results of this remain mixed. Although the digital media landscape has in some cases provided an outlet for increasing the coverage of women's sport, it has also reflected deeply engrained female stereotypes and, at times, revealed an ugly, vicious, and patriarchal digital culture (e.g., Clavio & Eagleman, 2011; Hum, Chamberlin, Hambright, & Bevan, 2011; Kane, LaVoi, & Fink, 2013; Lebel & Danylchuk, 2014).

This chapter presents results from several research projects related to women in sport and their interaction with social media platforms, with the goal of providing a comprehensive look at the issues faced by sportswomen on social media. To start with, a brief background on the media inequities faced by sportswomen is presented to set the stage for what has or has not changed with the advent of social media platforms. Social media afford us the ability to look at both athletes' use of these platforms and also the audiences' responses to these athletes.

Therefore, the next section provides insight into these responses and includes a thematic analysis of audience comments to illustrate the types of engagement various digital presentations motivate among audiences. In addition, a discussion of fandom in the digital world around women's sport is included. Finally, we look at the experience of women sport journalists in the digital space. In total, this chapter seeks to provide a deeper understanding of the conversation around women in sport in digital spaces, while generating insight into the negotiation of gender in digital media.

Media coverage of women's sport

Over the past few decades, women have made significant inroads in sports participation, with more opportunities to participate than ever before (Women's Sport Foundation, 2011). During this same time period, the media coverage of women's sports did not see any similar gains, and overall this coverage remains disproportionately low. Recent research indicated that, although women make up 40% of all sport participants in North America (Kane, 2013), women's sport receives just 2% of total sport media coverage (Cooky et al., 2015). When looking deeper into the 2% of media coverage, one finds that the portrayal of women athletes is often quite gendered. As noted by Mean and Kassing (2008, p. 127), "gender remains the primary categorization of women athletes, re-producing female athletes as women who play sport rather than as athletes first and foremost." This gendering of women athletes results in them often referred to as mothers by the media, usually with visuals and stories that focus on their femininity as opposed to their athletic abilities and achievements. It is heartening that recent work by Cooky et al. (2015) suggests that sexualized coverage of women athletes is dissipating, although the authors also noted that media outlets still cover women's sports in a way that conforms to conventional gender norms (e.g., media are more likely to cover "gender-appropriate" sports like gymnastics or tennis).

Researchers have spent significant time investigating the differences in traditional media coverage for men and women athletes, producing a significant body of research that mostly reaches the same conclusion: men athletes are portrayed as more powerful and dominant and women athletes are depicted less as athletes with more frequent mentions of their families or personal lives (e.g., Knight and Giuliano 2002, 2003). Much of this research has analyzed the visuals produced by mass media around women athletes, both through broadcast media and photographs in print media (e.g., Angelini, MacArthur, & Billings, 2012; Billings & Angelini, 2007; Fink & Kensicki, 2002; Hardin, Lynn, & Walsdorf, 2005; Jones 2006).

In their 2011 work, Kane and Maxwell highlighted the far-reaching influence of the "sports media commercial complex" in framing how society perceives women's sport. Previous studies demonstrated that the media portrayal of women athletes can have substantial social impact in terms of the acceptance of women athletes in society and economic outcomes in terms of their marketability as elite athletes (Kim, Walkosz, & Iverson, 2006). Although research on the representation of women athletes in traditional media outlets shows little evidence of the progress of women's equality in sport—the rising popularity of social media platforms has offered women athletes a new and potentially promising opportunity to connect with the world.

The rise of social media has also attracted researchers to study the portrayal of women athletes on these new platforms. In one of the first studies conducted on the media coverage in the digital world, Jones (2013) investigated visual coverage of the 2008 Olympic Games on digital sites, finding that men athletes were 1.6 times more likely to be the subject of photographs on these sites. Researchers have also investigated gender portrayal and gender performance on social media platforms. In their study, Clavio and Eagleman (2011) focused on the 10 most popular sport blogs in the United States for their study on photographic coverage of athletes. As with Jones (2013), these authors also found that men received significantly more photographic coverage than did women. In addition, Clavio and Eagleman (2011, p. 295) discovered that photos of women athletes were "far more likely to be sexually suggestive in nature." In their analysis of women and men tennis players' use of Twitter, Lebel and Danylchuk (2012) found that both men and women utilized candid portrayals in their content more than calculated ones focused on marketing. Overall, the authors discovered that men utilized the role of super fan (e.g., informal discussion of sport) most often, whereas women utilized the brand manager role (e.g., formal, brand-conscious acknowledgments) more often than men, indicating a persistence of hegemonic values. In addition, in their study of Instagram feeds of both men and women professional athletes, Smith and Sanderson (2015) found that women athletes utilized more active photos on their Instagram accounts than men athletes, a finding that counters previous research, which indicated that women athletes were more likely to be shown in a passive role (i.e., on the sidelines). Perhaps this study demonstrates that women athletes are using social media platforms to counteract traditional media narratives and portray themselves as the athletes that they are (e.g., Hardin et al., 2002).

In her more recent work, Bruce (2016) found that the utilization of social media has led to the emergence of two new rules for sportswomen: *our voices* and *pretty and powerful*. Social media have allowed women athletes to gain control of communicating their "sporting truths" (Bruce, 2016, p. 369) to the masses, thereby providing *our voices*. In addition, Bruce (2016) found that social media platforms allow for discourse to appear that stresses the notion that femininity is empowering, which is in "stark contrast to sexualization" (Bruce, 2016, p. 369), which has permeated traditional media coverage of women athletes for several decades. This is what she refers to as "pretty and powerful" (Bruce, 2016). Traditional media have portrayed women athletes as feminine first and as an athlete second. The rise of social media has allowed women athletes to embrace their femininity, as well as their physical competence, as complementary rather than exclusionary. We see top women athletes such as Serena Williams embracing this dual role, as demonstrated through the images they post to their own social media feeds. Indeed the sharing of images from the ESPN Body Issue by athletes such as Sue Bird on their social media channels [@S10Bird (2018, June 25) #Body10 in motion. Twitter post retrieved from https://twitter.com/s10bird/status/1011282583483768832] illustrate how these athletes embrace the dual nature of pretty and powerful, perhaps dispelling the notion they feel exploited through these types of portrayals. Therefore, the emergence of these new roles afforded women athletes on social media platforms makes it particularly interesting to examine how social media users respond to these portrayals.

Athletes in the digital landscape: Fans' responses

One of the key drivers behind the success of social media in sport has been the novelty of extending athletes the ability to bypass media and communicate directly with the public (Pegoraro, 2010). Although the relative novelty of social media's influence on sport remains difficult to quantify, a recent Forbes' article suggested that professional soccer star Ronaldo, currently the most followed athlete on social media, generated US$500 million in value for Nike through his social media properties in 2016 (Badenhausen, 2017). The social media insight platform, Hookit, tracks the social media activity of athletes based on metrics of influence, engagement, and interactions (likes, comments, shares re-tweets, and views on videos). As of November 2017, Hookit calculated that the Top 10 most followed athletes in the world had a combined 1,086,900,000 total followers on Facebook, Twitter, and Instagram, demonstrating the magnitude of the interest that fans and followers on these platforms have for athletes. Table 35.1 illustrates the social footprint of the most-followed athletes in the world. Hookit measures engagement by dividing the total number of interactions by the total number of fans following a particular athlete. Interactions were measured by combining the total number of likes, comments, and re-tweets each athlete post received (Hookit, 2017). It should be noted that only one woman athlete is in the Top 10, but that, in the previous months, the Hookit evaluation has shown that no women athletes made the Top 10. Personal trainer Kayla Itsines from Australia appears as the number seven position with 24.9 million followers on the lists as the highest positioned sportswoman (Hookit, 2017). The next woman athlete on the list is Serena Williams and she appears at the 32nd position.

As we can see from Table 35.1, athletes on social media get a lot of interaction from fans, but most of this interaction occurs around male athletes. Although women athletes attract less interaction, it is still important to explore what these responses look like for women athletes. To accomplish this, we analyzed the responses to posts of four top women athletes on the social media platform Instagram. Fan comments were thematically analyzed to investigate the responses to different types of posts. On first look, the results indicated that images that portrayed the four women athletes in a more sexualized way drew a larger number of responses (e.g., likes, comments), seemingly reinforcing the way traditional media have framed women athletes. However, on a more in-depth review of content within the comments on these posts, we found different types of fan responses. The sexualized images actually tended to evoke comments focused on the "beauty" of the athlete, whereas images that showed the women displaying their athletic competence were linked to inspiration and respect for the athlete. Although sexualized images may receive the greatest number of interactions from fans (e.g., likes and comments), these interactions were focused on the beauty of the athlete and not on their athletic ability, so these types of posts were unlikely to enhance the credibility of a woman athlete's "athletic brand." Conversely, images that display the athletic competence of a woman athlete may be of significant benefit to these athletes because fans demonstrated both acknowledgment and acceptance of the athletic prowess of these women. Given the rise of use of visually based platforms such as Instagram, these findings illustrate important implications for the personal branding strategies of women athletes in the construction of their digital brands. Perhaps, most

Table 35.1 The social footprint of the Top 10 athletes as measured by Hookit, November 2017

Athlete	Followers (millions)	New followers (millions)	Total posts	Engagement (%)	Total interactions (millions)
Cristiano Ronaldo	303.9	4.4	99	0.90	269.4
Dwayne "The Rock" Johnson	96.4	640,200[a]	77	3.00	223.2
Neymar da Silva	181.2	2.6	68	0.70	89.8
Conor McGregor	35.6	514,700[a]	44	3.30	51.5
Ronaldinho Gaúcho	79.5	1.1	129	0.50	47.9
Virat Kohli	73.9	1.7	90	0.60	39.6
Kayla Itsines	24.9	1.0	720	0.20	38.9
Sachin Tendulkar	58.8	1.2	88	0.70	38.0
Sergio Ramos	57.2	746,600[a]	79	0.80	34.7
Lionel Messi	175.5	1.4	31	0.50	29.3

a These numbers are in the thousands, not millions.

notably, it appears to be in the best interest of women athletes to embrace their strength and celebrate their athletic capabilities, because these images evoke the most positive responses from their fans.

Women's sport fandom in the digital world

The growth of the internet, especially the interactive capabilities of Web 2.0, has afforded sport fans increased opportunities to interact with other fans, teams, and athletes (Pegoraro, 2013). These various avenues (e.g., forums, social media platforms) allow fans a multitude of new environments in which to engage in fandom-related activities and connect with other fans. In the one-to-many broadcast model of sport (e.g., televised sport), sport fans have acted as consumers of sport-related content and have not been involved in how the content is shaped and presented (Sanderson & Kassing, 2011). The unique characteristics of Web 2.0 that allow for users to participate as both the creators and the consumers of content present a ripe area for scholars to investigate this new type of sport fandom behavior (Clavio, 2008).

Fan-created content is often referred to as user-generated content (UGC) and defined as "media content created or produced by the general public rather than by paid professionals and primarily distributed on the Internet" (Daugherty, Eastin, & Bright, 2008, p. 16). UGC can exist in diverse forms, including content uploaded to social media platforms such as: Facebook or Twitter; comments in online forums; team- or sport-specific blogs; videos uploaded to file-sharing sites such as YouTube; and information contributed to pages on Wikipedia (Glickman & Fingerhut, 2011). Today, sport fans increasingly drive the production of sport-related content on these platforms.

With respect to women's sport fans in this new digital world, the question is what does this content look like? Antunovic and Hardin (2015) explored women's sport blogs and found that women tend to conceptualize sport differently to men. Previous research found that male sport blogs tend to be dominated by discussions centered on power and performance in sport (Messner, 2013). In their study, Antunovic and Hardin (2015) found that, although women fans discuss power and performance, they also framed sport in "empowering and inclusive ways that facilitated women's physical and emotional development as an avenue for relationship building" (Antunovic & Hardin, 2015, p. 669).

Twitter has also been a subject of study as researchers have investigated the use of this platform by women sport fans. Heinecken (2015) studied the postings and followers of @SoccerGirlProbs—an anonymous Twitter account that used humor to portray the everyday struggles of girls who play soccer. This investigation lead to the author concluding that Twitter provides "a forum for female sport fans to construct their identities in relation to other users and demonstrate their membership in a distinct affinity group marked by a shared reality" (Heinecken, 2015, p. 3).

Social media platforms also offer the potential to attract attention to women's sport, attention that has been inadequately provided by traditional media. One of the affordances of Twitter and Instagram is the ability to collate conversations into a larger voice through the use of common hashtags. For women's sport and its fans, using hashtags can be particularly powerful in drawing attention to gender issues; it can also provide women athletes with an opportunity to share and discuss their personal experiences with sport. One of the fastest growing social media platforms in the last few years has been Instagram, a visually based medium in which users can upload pictures, videos, create stories, and engage with similar content shared by other users. Duggan, Ellison, Lampe, Lenhart, and Madden (2015) indicated that roughly half (53%) of internet-using young adults aged 18–29 use Instagram and 26% of all adults online use the platform. In addition, half of all Instagram users (49%) use the site daily (Duggan et al., 2015).

In previous research investigating the visual representation of women athletes, researchers have found that sportswomen are often portrayed through images that emphasize their femininity and heterosexuality more than their athletic competence (e.g., Jones, 2006; Daniels & Wartena, 2011; Weber & Barker-Ruchti, 2012). These portrayals serve to reaffirm traditional notions of femininity and heterosexuality. As noted by Kane and Maxwell (2011), the focus on sexuality of women athletes perpetuates the notion that sexualizing these athletes is the only way to generate fan interest, primarily from male fans, and ultimately leading to the conclusion that sexualizing athletes is the only way to sell women's sports. Essentially, traditional media have reinforced the notion that, although women can be fully engaged in competitive sports, they must do so in ways that do not threaten conventional gender norms (Boyle, Millington, & Vertinsky, 2006).

Following the lead of the various scholars who have analyzed the role traditional media plays in reinforcing gender stereotypes, researchers have now turned their efforts to examining the portrayal of women athletes by individual users through UGC via social media platforms. For example, researcher has focused the portrayal of women athletes on blogs (e.g., Clavio & Eagleman, 2011), Twitter (e.g., Lebel & Danylchuk, 2012), and Instagram (Geurin-Eagleman & Burch, 2016; Smith & Sanderson, 2015), all from the point of view of the athlete.

In one of the first studies to investigate fan UGC, Pegoraro, Comeau, and Frederick (2017) examined how fans demonstrated their fandom, by engaging with two hashtags associated with the 2015 FIFA Women's World Cup of Soccer—#FIFAWWC, the official hashtag for the event, and #SheBelieves created by the US Soccer Federation in support of the American women's team. Images shared by fans on both hashtags throughout the month-long tournament were collected and then analyzed to determine how fans utilized these hashtags to frame the women soccer players. The results revealed that UGC shared primarily portrayed women athletes as athletically competent, with almost 90% of posts on either hashtag portraying athletes in either action or preparing for athletic action (Pegoraro et al., 2017). Even though this is one of the first studies to focus on fans' UGC in relation to the framing of women athletes, the findings demonstrate that social media can provide users with an opportunity to challenge gender stereotypes generated by traditional media. In addition, this study demonstrates that fans are willing to create and capable of creating their own frames around women athletes (Pegoraro et al., 2017).

Researchers have also been able to distinguish that fans of women's sport use social media in different ways to practice their fandom. As Toffoletti (2017, p. 119) explains the "feminist potential of social media lies in its ability to increase the profile of women fans and women's sport, allowing women to search the relatively unfiltered medium of social media to advocate for women's sport." Research has only begun to broaden our understanding of how women fans of women's sport use digital media, and many opportunities exist for researchers to explore the relatively untapped potential of social media to facilitate women's practices of sport fandom. Social media platforms are constantly evolving to meet the needs of users of all types. These changes provide increasing avenues for researchers to investigate women's sport and fans' use of these platforms.

Women sport journalists' experiences in the digital realm

The media have long been regarded as a socializing agent (Gerbner, 1998), and the lens through which the media presents "reality" can have a confirming affect for those who belong to powerful majority groups (van Dijk, 1995), and a detrimental effect on those who are portrayed in unbecoming ways (Cohen & Young, 1981). Hetsroni and Lowenstein (2014, p. 377) suggested that "the process through which the contents are chosen is intentionally selective, prioritizing certain societal segments," thus reflecting only certain members of society. Non-representation or under-representation of certain groups, including women, has been described as *symbolic annihilation* (Tuchman, 1978). The stark under-representation of women in the media was first highlighted in the 1968 Kerner Commission's Report and continues to be an unresolved issue (Women's Media Center, 2015).

The presence of women in the sport media realm is truly in its infancy, because it took until 1975 before a "female [Phyllis George] had a prominent role in network sports broadcasting" (Mead, 2010, para. 2), and it wasn't until 1978 when a federal judge ruled that banning women reporters from locker rooms was a violation of the 14th Amendment (*Ludtke v. Kuhn* 1978). When the legal barriers limiting women reporters' access to players to conduct interviews were eliminated, the number of women reporters increased but not at rates proportional to men reporters, because today women still represent only 10–20% of the sports media (Lapchick, 2014). This under-representation of women in the field of sport journalism is further compounded by the dearth of on-air opportunities that are available for women. In televised sport broadcasts women sport journalists are frequently relegated to sideline reporting, with very limited timeframes for interviews or opportunities to demonstrate intricate knowledge of sport. In the history of the National Football League (NFL), the most dominant sport league in North America, only four women have had the opportunity to provide color commentary, and only one did so during the regular season (Deitsch, 2016). In terms of major televised sport events, it was not until the 2014 Sochi Olympic Games that a woman, Meredith Vieira, anchored NBC's primetime coverage of the Games solo, and this came about only because of a health issue experienced by the lead male journalist, Bob Costas.

Although there has been an increase in the number of women sport journalists, just having an identifiable presence in this industry is not enough to support the pursuit of equality where women are perceived and treated as equals among their male counterparts. The continued existence of popular lists that document the "Hottest Female Sports Reporters" (e.g. Top 10 Hottest ESPN Reporters https://www.trendrr.net/14721/hottest-most-famous-espn-reporters-beautiful-sports-news-anchors) perpetuates cultural norms that emphasize the appearance of women sport reporters and often prioritizes appearance as just important, if not more important, than their journalistic skill.

The ill treatment of women sport journalists is further heightened in this digital age. As cable networks expand their broadcasting to the digital realm, there are expectations that journalists will also engage in the digital arena (Gibbs & Haynes, 2013). Although this new platform provides opportunities for women sport journalists, the very nature of the platforms that allow two-way interaction between consumers and journalists has in fact also served to exacerbate the attitudes of some sport fans toward women in sport media. When one takes a minute to scan through comments on social media, the disparity in how fans treat male journalists versus their counterparts becomes abundantly clear.

In 2016, when sexual assault allegations were brought against Patrick Kane of the NHL, Julie DiCaro, a radio anchor and columnist for CBSChicago.com and *Sports Illustrated*'s The Cauldron, drew on her 15-year career in criminal and family court to report on the case. Just by doing her job, reporting on these allegations, DiCaro instantly found herself the target of severe online harassment, receiving as many as 30 harassing tweets a day (Ryan, 2016). DiCaro and fellow Chicago sport journalist Sarah Spain appeared in a public service announcement entitled #MoreThanMean, a parody of Jimmy Kimmel's "Mean Tweets" to highlight the harassment experienced by women in sport media. The tweets, read by unsuspecting male participants, were so offensive in nature that they required a graphic language warning and many of the tweets also referenced criminal acts against the women journalists. Despite this vulgar language, the public service announcement has garnered over four million views on YouTube.

In October 2015, Jessica Mendoza, an Olympic gold and silver medal-winning softball player for Team USA, became the first women analyst for a nationally televised MLB postseason game (Boren, 2016). This move to add a woman journalist to an MLB broadcast was not well received by spectators or her peers. In particular, Mike Bell, a sport talk radio host on Atlanta's CBS Sports affiliate, trolled Mendoza on Twitter. His tweets focused on Mendoza's appearance and her inability to actually call an MLB game because she had never played in the league. "You tell us Tits McGhee when you're up there hitting the softball you see a lot of 95 mile an hour cutters?' and "Really? A women's softball slugger as guest analyst on MLB Wildcard Game? Once again ESPN too frigging cute for their own good," Bell's Twitter rant included over 10 tweets of a similar nature (Glasspiegel, 2015).

Sadly, these examples are not unique because most women sport journalists have indicated that most of the online engagement they receive from fans is highly critical of their appearance and falls in the domain of harassment (Harbison, 2016). In today's political climate, the opinions expressed on social media have caused sponsors to cease relationships and even forced the hand of major corporations to terminate public personas (e.g., Bill O'Reilly). On the other hand, corporations have been seen to excel as a result of their conservative views; for example, Chick-fil-A saw an increase in sales, despite public backlash at the company's president's stance against same-sex marriage (Kim, 2012). Although sport networks cannot fire their consumers for their public statements in the digital domain, it is possible that these networks are listening and perpetuating homogeneous, hegemonic reproductions within the sport media industry as a means of appeasing their fans, thereby perpetuating the cycle of abuse and lack of opportunities for women in the sport media. In contrast, what if we imagine the possibilities for future generations if they were given greater opportunity to both consume women's sport and see it presented by knowledgeable female sport personalities? The increased presence of strong women role models, who are viewed as credible sources of sport information and respected accordingly for the quality of their work, has the potential to change societal expectations and cultivate gender equality in sport.

Conclusion

The emerging and ever-changing digital world has had a profound effect on women's sport. Athletes can now directly interact with fans and fans can use social media to express their fandom. Indeed, the negotiation of gender, athletic identities and fandom all play out in the digital world. The revolutionary nature of social media extends beyond the reach of traditional media outlets to more diverse audiences, giving voices to previously marginalized groups such as women athletes and their fans. With strong leadership from elite sportswomen springs the potential to capitalize on the affordances of social media platforms to attract new audiences to women's sport. These new audiences will help to drive potentially lucrative marketing opportunities, and perhaps a leveling of the field for women athletes who previously have not had the same opportunities as their male counterparts. Overall, the light that social media shine on women's sport can help to achieve the ultimate goal of positive societal acceptance for women athletes and women's sport. This is what the possibilities of social media can provide if capitalized on.

With these possibilities also comes a downside. As the research in this chapter has highlighted, many times the experiences of women athletes and other women in sport business have not been positive. Social media often provide an amplification of a dominant point of view on social issues, and this can be seen in relation to women athletes. The negative reactions to women athletes, and the reinforcing of gender norms, have been seen in most of the research to date. However, there are also positive aspects to research related to fans and their UGC related to women athletes. Therefore, although the results to date have not all been positive for both athletes and journalists, the opportunity still remains for social media to provide a re-negotiation of concepts of femininity that could prove to be a valuable key to unlocking the time-honored tradition of hegemony in sport. Although it is true there exists a dark side to social media, a sustained vigilance to monitor and dissuade this negativity, combined with a concerted effort to promote athletic success and women's equality in sport, has the potential to go a long way toward ensuring this cultural shift bends in the right direction.

Leader profile: The GIST

Brief biography

The GIST is an audience engagement company that creates sport news, experiences, and community for women and casual sports fans. The GIST's mission is to level the playing field by empowering and connecting women through sports.

Q1: What inspired you to create The GIST?

The three of us co-founders met while studying business at Queen's University. After graduating in 2014 we moved to Toronto and started working in different sectors within the financial services industry.

Figure 35.1 Founders of the GIST: Ellen Hyslop, Roslyn McLarty, and Jacie deHoop

After a few years of living and working in Toronto there was something we noticed—sports are a social currency in our society. Sports can be an incredible equalizer and have the unique ability to unite people regardless of age, gender, race, or religion. Sports are a part of our culture and they build relationships.

However, we also noticed that sports and sport talk can be incredibly exclusionary and that women, in particular, felt left out of the sport conversation and community. This stems from the fact that there is a lack of diversity in the sport industry today, as the majority of sport media are created by, and cater for, men and avid sport fans. When you don't identify as either of those people it's easy to feel like you're on the outside looking in. So, we decided to launch The GIST—a source for sports that is created by women, for women.

Q2: Why do you think females need sport content delivered in a different format?

It is no secret that many women (not all, but some) feel disenfranchised with sports and feel that it is a "guy's thing." We wanted to better understand this social problem and found that there is an immense lack of diversity in the sports industry today.

First, only 14% of sport journalists are female. As a result, sport content is largely written by men, for men, and an avid sport fan. Second, only 4% of sport media coverage is on female athletes, and only 0.4% of sponsorship funding goes toward female athletes.

As a result, it's no wonder so many women feel that current sport news is unrelatable and not made for them. So, we provide sport news, content, and experiences through platforms that are made specifically for women. A platform that they can feel is "for them." We focus on contextualization, providing a narrative, and providing a female tone and perspective to the goings on in the sports world.

Q3: What have been your biggest challenges as you've ventured into the social media space?

Social media are a very interesting space that we are still learning about. It has been an incredibly powerful tool to deliver content to where our audience is already scrolling, to build an online community and help us grow.

Although social media may seem like a straightforward tool that we all use personally, to leverage all the benefits it provides requires a significant amount of time. This is mostly due to the different audiences on each platform that need to be catered for. The challenge is providing a holistic, consistent brand experience—from the visuals to the tone—so that each user feels that they are communicating with the same GIST across multiple platforms.

Q4: What is your advice to women in sport who might be looking to follow your lead and authentically embrace female audiences?

Our largest piece of advice would be to go for it—there is a market for a more diverse sports industry and the female audience should be embraced and invested in.

Our initial success has shown that there is demand from *both* women and men to consume sport news from a female perspective and that there is a market out there for a more diverse and inclusive sport industry.

References

Angelini, J. R. MacArthur, P. J., & Billings, A. C. (2012). What's the gendered story? Vancouver's prime time Olympic glory on NBC. *Journal of Broadcasting & Electronic Media*, **56**(2), 261–279.

Antunovic, D. and Hardin, M. (2015). Women and the blogosphere: Exploring feminist approaches to sport. *International Review for the Sociology of Sport*, **50**(60), 661–677.

Bacle, A. (2015). J.K. Rowling shuts down a Serena Williams hater with one perfect tweet *Entertainment Weekly*, July 11. Retrieved from http://ew.com/article/2015/07/11/serena-williams-jk-rowling-tweet.

Badenhausen, K. (2017). Ronaldo beats Messi by 800% when it comes to return on social media for their brands, February 23. Retrieved from https://www.forbes.com/sites/kurtbadenhausen/2017/02/23/ronaldo-beats-messi-by-800-when-it-comes-to-return-on-social-media-for-their-brands/?utm_source=TWITTER&utm_medium=social&utm_content=823145558&utm_campaign=sprinklrForbesMainTwitter#18fda9f7401b (accessed October 14, 2018).

Billings, A. C. & Angelini, J. R. (2007). Packaging the Games for viewer consumption: Gender, ethnicity, and nationality in NBC's coverage of the 2004 Summer Olympics. *Communication Quarterly*, **55**(1), 95–111.

Boren, C. (2016). Fox Sports Radio tweets ESPN's Jessica Mendoza would be fired 'if she was a man', May 9. Retrieved from https://www.washingtonpost.com/news/early-lead/wp/2016/05/09/fox-sports-radio-tweets-espns-jessica-mendoza-would-be-fired-if-she-was-a-man/?utm_term=.19bff846a3a8 (accessed October 14, 2018).

Boyle, E., Millington, B., & Vertinsky, P. (2006). Representing the female pugilist: Narratives of race, gender, and disability in Million Dollar Baby. *Sociology of Sport Journal*, **23**(2), 99–116.

Bruce, T. (2016). New rules for new times: Sportswomen and media representation in the third wave. *Sex Roles*, **74**, 361–376.

Clavio, G. (2008). Uses and gratifications of Internet collegiate sport message board users. *Dissertation Abstracts International*, **69**(8). [ProQuest Digital Dissertations database (Publication No. AAT 3319833).

Clavio, G. & Eagleman, A. N. (2011). Gender and sexually suggestive images in sports blogs. *Journal of Sport Management*, **7**, 295–304.

Cohen, S. & Young, J. (1981). *The Manufacture of News. Deviance, social problems, and the mass media.* Beverly Hills, CA: Sage.

Cooky, C., Messner, M., & Musto, M. (2015). "It's dude time!" A quarter century of excluding women's sports in televised news and highlight shows. *Communication & Sport*, **3**(3), 261–287.

Daniels, E. & Wartena, H. (2011). Athlete or sex symbol: What boys think of media representations of female athletes. *Sex Roles*, **65**(7/8), 566–579.

Daugherty, T., Eastin, M. S., & Bright, L. (2008). Exploring consumer motivations for creating user generated content. *Journal of Interactive Advertising*, **8**(2), 16–25.

Deitsch, R. (2016). Uphill battle for women in NFL play-by-play role may soon reach a turning point, August 24. Retrieved from https://www.si.com/nfl/2016/08/24/nfl-women-announcers-beth-mowins-kate-scott (accessed October 14, 2018).

Duggan, M., Ellison, N. B., Lampe, C., Lenhart, A., & Madden, M. (2015). Social media update 2014, *Pew Research Center*. Retrieved from www.pewinternet.org/2015/01/09/social-media-update-2014 (accessed October 14, 2018).

Fink, J. S. & Kensicki, L. J. (2002). An imperceptible difference: Visual and textual constructions of femininity in *Sports Illustrated* and *Sports Illustrated for Women*. *Mass Communication and Society*, **5**(3), 317–339.

Gerbner, G. (1998). Cultivation analysis: An overview. *Mass Communication and Society*, **1**, 175–194.

Geurin-Eagleman, A. N. & Burch, L. M. (2016). Communicating via photographs: A gendered analysis of Olympic athletes' visual self-presentation on Instagram. *Sport Management Review*, **19**(2), 133–145.

Gibbs, C. & Haynes, R. (2013). A phenomenological investigation into how Twitter has changes the nature of sport media relations. *International Journal of Sport Communication*, **6**, 394–408.

Glasspiegel, R. (2015). Here's the Twitter rant about ESPN's Jessica Mendoza that got an Atlanta radio host suspended, October 7. Retrieved from http://thebiglead.com/2015/10/07/mike-bell-jessica-mendoza-twitter-suspended (accessed October 14, 2018).

Glickman, L. & Fingerhut, J. (2011). User-generated content: Recent developments in Canada and the U.S. *Internet and E-Commerce Law in Canada*, **12**(6), 49–76.

Harbison, M. (2016). Female media pros often face gender backlash, online harassment, May 19. Retrieved from http://mediaschool.indiana.edu/news/female-media-pros-often-face-gender-backlash-online-harassment (accessed June 14, 2017).

Hardin, M., Lynn, S., Walsdorf, K., & Hardin, B. (2002). The framing of sexual difference in SI for kids editorial photos. *Mass Communication & Society*, **5**(3), 341–359.

Hardin, M., Lynn, S., & Walsdorf, K. (2005). Challenge and conformity on contested terrain: Images of women in four women's sport/fitness magazines. *Sex Roles*, **53**(1/2): 105–117.

Heinecken, D. (2015). So tight in the thighs, so loose in the waist: Embodying the female athlete online. *Feminist Media Studies*, **15**(6), 1035–1052.

Hetsroni, A. & Lowenstein, H. (2014). Is she an expert or just a woman? Gender differences in the presentation of experts in TV talk shows. *Sex Roles*, **70**, 376–386.

Hum, N., Chamberlin, P., Hambright, B., & Bevan, J. (2011). A picture is worth a thousand words: A content analysis of Facebook profile photographs. *Computers in Human Behavior*, **27**(5), 1828–1833.

Hookit (2017). Hookit Index Top 100, December. Retrieved from: www.hookit.com/ranks (accessed December 1, 2017).

Jones, D. (2006). The representation of female athletes in online images of successive Olympic Games. *Pacific Journalism Review*, **12**(1), 108–129.

Jones, D. (2013). "Online coverage of the 2008 Olympic games on the ABC, BBC, CBC and TVNZ." *Pacific Journalism Review*, **19**(1), 244–263.

Kane, M. J. (2013). The better sportswomen get, the more the media ignore them. *Communication & Sport*, **1**(3), 231–236.

Kane, M. J., LaVoi, L. M., & Fink, J. S. (2013). Exploring elite female athletes' interpretations of sport media images: A window into the construction of social identity and "selling sex" in women's sports. *Communication & Sport*, **1**(3), 269–298.

Kane, M. & Maxwell, H. (2011). Expanding the boundaries of sport media research: Using critical theory to explore consumer responses to representations of women's sports. *Journal of Sport Management*, **25**, 202–216.

Kerner, O. (1968). *Report of the National Advisory Commission on Civil Disorder*. New York: Bantam Books.

Kim, S. (2012). Chick-fill-A benefited from summer's gay marriage flap with more customer visits, October 25. Retrieved from http://abcnews.go.com/Business/chick-fil-benefited-summers-gay-marriage-debate/story?id=17562204 (accessed October 14, 2018).

Kim, E., Walkosz B. J., & Iverson J. (2006). USA Today's coverage of the top women golfers, 1998–2001. *The Howard Journal of Communications*, **17**, 307–321.

Knight, J. L. & Giuliano, T. A. (2002). He's a Laker, she's a looker: The consequences of gender-stereotypical portrayals of male and female athletes by the print media. *Sex Roles*, **45**(3/4): 217–229.

Knight, J. L. & Giuliano, T. A. (2003). Blood, sweat, and jeers: The impact of the media's heterosexist portrayals on perceptions of male and female athletes. *Journal of Sport Behavior*, **26**(3): 272–284.

Krane, V., Ross, S., Miller, M., Rowse, J., Ganoie, K., Andrzejczyk, J., et al. (2010). Power and focus: Self-representation of female college athletes. *Qualitative Research in Sport and Exercise*, **2**, 175–195.

Lapchick, R. E. (2014). The 2014 associated press sports editors racial and gender report card. Retrieved from http://nebula.wsimg.com/038bb0ccc9436494ebee1430174c13a0?AccessKeyId=DAC3A56D8FB782449D2A&disposition=0&alloworigin=1 (accessed October 14, 2018)

Lebel, K. & Danylchuk, K. (2012). How tweet it is: A gendered analysis of professional tennis players' self-presentation on Twitter. *International Journal of Sport Communication*, **5**, 461–480.

Lebel, K. & Danylchuk, K. (2014). Facing off on Twitter: A generation Y interpretation of professional athlete profile pictures. *International Journal of Sport Communication*, **7**(3), 317–336.

Ludtke v. Kuhn, 461 F. Supp. 86 (S.D. NY. 1978).

Mead, D. (2010). Twelve women who pioneered the era of female sports broadcasters, August 21. Retrieved from http://bleacherreport.com/articles/440556-twelve-women-who-pioneered-the-era-of-female-sports-broadcasters (accessed October 14, 2018).

Mean, L. J. & Kassing, JW. (2008). "I would just like to be known as an athlete": Managing hegemony, femininity, and heterosexuality in female sport. *Western Journal of Communication*, **72**, 126–144.

Messner, M. (2013). Reflections on communication and sport: On men and masculinities. *Communication & Sport*, **1**, 113–124.

Pegoraro, A. (2010). Look who's talking-athletes on Twitter: A case study. *International Journal of Sort Communication*, **3**(4), 501–514.

Pegoraro, A. (2013). Sport fandom in the digital world. In P. Pedersen (ed.), *The Routledge Handbook of Sport Communication* (pp. 248–258). New York: Routledge.

Pegoraro, A., Comeau, G., & Frederick, E. (2017). #SheBelieves: Fans' use of Social Media to frame the US Women's Soccer Team during #FIFAWWC. *Sport and Society*, **21**(7), 1063–1077.

Ryan, S. (2016). WSCR's Julie DiCaro a lightning rod on local sports media scene, June 20. Retrieved from www.chicagotribune.com/sports/ct-julie-dicaro-wscr-spt-0621-20160620-story.html (accessed October 14, 2018).

Sanderson, J. & Kassing, J. W. (2011). Tweets and blogs: Transformative, adversarial and integrative developments in sport media. In A. Billings (ed.), *Sports Media: Transformation, integration, consumption* (pp. 114–27). New York: Routledge.

Smith, L. R. & Sanderson, J. (2015). I'm going to Instagram it! An analysis of athlete self-presentation on Instagram. *Journal of Broadcasting and Electronic Media*, **59**(2), 342–358.

Toffoletti, K. (2017). *Women Sport Fans: Identification, participation, representation.* New York: Routledge

Tuchman, G. (1978). *Making News: A study in the construction of reality.* New York: Free Press.

van Dijk, T. A. (1995). Discourse semantics and ideology. *Discourse and Society*, **6**, 243–289.

Weber, J. & Barker-Ruchti, N. (2012). Bending, flirting, floating, flying: A critical analysis of female figures in 1970s gymnastics photographs. *Sociology of Sport Journal*, **29**(1), 22–41.

Women's Media Center (2015). WMC status of women in U.S. media 2015. Retrieved from http://wmc.3cdn.net/83bf6082a319460eb1_hsrm680x2.pdf (accessed October 14, 2018).

Women's Sport Foundation (2011). *Women's Sports & Fitness Facts & Statistics.* East Meadow, NY: Women's Sports Foundation.

36
Female athletes find a place for expression on Instagram

Lauren M. Burch and Matthew H. Zimmerman

As mainstream media coverage of female athletes has declined over the years, the comparatively few examples of such coverage that exist often present subjects as sexualized, or in traditional gendered roles such as motherhood (Cooky, Messner, & Musto, 2015). Although media reports have often concentrated on female athletes' physical attractiveness, there has also been a reluctance to cover those athletes who do not fit traditional feminine roles (Kaskan & Ho, 2016). Public response to such depictions has been shown to divide along gender lines, because male audiences prefer a more traditionally feminine depiction of woman athletes, whereas female audiences appreciated when a woman athlete was shown to be strong and engaging in sport as physical activity (Jones & Greer, 2011). These media representations of female athletes can affect perceptions, because examples of athletic prowess inspire respect for accomplishments whereas sexualized depictions lead to objectification (Daniels & Wartena, 2011).

Recently, social media including words and profile photos have become an important aspect of self-presentation (Leary & Kowalski, 1990) and brand presentation for athletes (Lebel & Danylchuk, 2014). The use of social media by individual female athletes offers the opportunity to present their preferred image to their fans, as opposed to other media having sole control of the athlete's image (Shreffler, Hancock, & Schmidt, 2016). In contrast to more gendered depictions by mainstream media gatekeepers, female athletes have a tendency to present themselves online in more traditionally athletic situations (Shreffler et al., 2016; Smith & Sanderson, 2016). Notably, athletes who present themselves in a sport-related manner on social media receive a favorable response from other users who engage with the athlete's online content (Jones & Greer, 2011; Lebel & Danylchuk, 2014).

In this chapter, we intend to undertake a review of a group of female athletes' personal Instagram accounts. When a prominent female athlete posts on Instagram, examination of fan responses to a particular type of post can be beneficial to forming a more complete understanding of what kinds of self-presentations lead to the highest number of positive reactions. In addition, such an examination may provide a template for how female athletes might best be presented online, both by the athletes themselves and by the organizations with which they are associated.

Inherent to the concept of self-presentation is the notion that individuals place importance on how they are viewed and evaluated by others (Leary & Kowalski, 1990). The study of self-presentation is attributed to sociologist Erving Goffman, who was interested in self-presentation as it applies to social structures, or the construction of social reality. In the book *The Presentation of Self in Everyday Life*, Goffman (1959) highlights how individuals create their social reality through the adoption of identities based on how they wish to be perceived by a particular audience or in a specific situation. Utilizing the framework of an actor navigating between the "front stage" and the "back stage" during a performance, Goffman stated that people employ these same tactics in daily interactions as a form of self-presentation (Bortree, 2005).

A front-stage form of self-presentation takes place before an audience that is somewhat less known, and is a more constructed, idealized version of the self, whereas back-stage self-presentation is delivered to a more personal audience, and is thus more candid, offering a glimpse behind the curtain (Dominick, 1999). In both a front-stage and a back-stage performance, however, according to Marshall (2010, p. 39), "Performance of the self was a conscious act of the individual and required careful staging to maintain the self – a composed and norm-driven construction of character and performance." As Geurin-Eagleman and Burch (2016) noted, the use of Instagram can be an important aspect of public brand management for athletes. Considering this, the individual athlete must remain conscious of how each posting can affect their own brand, as well as that of their sport. In addition, people who post on social media might be seen as representative of others of similar backgrounds, with their own branding potentially affecting outsiders' perceptions of large groups of like individuals (Kaskan & Ho, 2016; Marshall, 2010; Murray, 2015).

In the early 2000s, the development of social networking sites facilitated the presentation of self in an online environment. Initially, these online environments included chat rooms or message boards (Mehdizadeh, 2010), but expanded to include such platforms as MySpace, Facebook, Twitter, and Instagram (Bortree, 2005; Hancock & Toma, 2009; Papacharissi, 2002). Although not preferred compared with face-to-face interactions, online environments did present the opportunity to control social reality and self-presentation (Mehdizadeh, 2010). For example, individuals could employ various strategies such as ingratiation, competence, intimidation, exemplification, and supplication in self-presentation in order to shape perceptions (Jones, 1990). Early studies examining online self-presentation found that individuals embedded these strategies or cues in text to portray themselves in certain ways, often including personal information, or discussions about their daily lives (Bortree 2005; Ellison, Heino, & Gibbs, 2006).

Later studies of online dating sites incorporated the utilization of photographs into online self-presentation with differences found in presentation based on gender. A study by Hancock and Toma (2009) found that women's photographs were considered less reliable than men's photographs, a finding attributed to a specific self-presentation tactic employed by women to establish physical attractiveness. The use of photographs as a form of self-presentation was incorporated into new media platforms such as Facebook. Specifically, the researchers used profile photos to analyze online self-presentation and also how gender is represented on Facebook by examining the number of profile photos, posed or candidness features of the photo, and how "appropriate" the photo was considered to be (Hum, Chamberlin, Hambright, Portwood, Schat, & Bevan, 2011). Other new media platforms, such as Twitter, have also been examined in regard to online self-presentation. As Twitter is a microblogging platform, the content produced by individuals was studied to determine self-presentation to particular audiences. It was found that individuals produced content to target difference audiences, conceal certain subject matter, and project authenticity (Marwick & Boyd, 2011). As individuals produced this content with a specific objective in mind, they were simultaneously creating an imaginary or ideal audience, and a constructed sense of self online to conform to this audience.

The ability to construct an online identity of the individual's choosing, while also communicating directly with a specific audience, presents an attractive proposition for individuals such as celebrities, including athletes, to utilize social media platforms. Self-presentation is the core element of celebrity, and social media provide a platform for presentation to the world (Marshall, 2010). Through a qualitative examination of celebrity messages on various social media platforms, Marshall (2010) proposed that self-presentation online has evolved due to its increasingly sophisticated use by celebrities to deliver a desired presence. This evolution involves the expansion of Goffman's (1959) original conceptualization of self-presentation as a dichotomous front-stage or back-stage performance to include utilizations such as the intercommunicative self, the para-social self, and the private self for public presentation.

Within a sport-specific setting, there has been a recent expansion of studies examining self-presentation by athletes on social media. An early study by Pegoraro (2010) examined athlete utilization of Twitter, and found that the primary discussion centered on athletes' private lives, which corresponded with a more back-stage performance. Along similar lines, a study by Hambrick, Simmons, Greenhalgh, and Greenwell (2010) also looked at the content produced by professional athletes on Twitter. The second, most widely employed usage was diversion, which included sharing stories about friends or family, again constituting a back-stage performance (Hambrick et al., 2010). Specifically employing the framework of self-presentation, Lebel and Danylchuk (2012) examined the use of Twitter by professional tennis players. Results indicated the usage of back-stage performances, specifically involving conversational elements by both male and female players.

Burch et al. (2014) examined differences in content produced by male and female athletes on Twitter, and found both male and female athletes utilized Twitter to portray themselves as a normal, everyday individual. These back-stage portrayals involved the discussion of their personal, or everyday, lives. Expanding the analysis of self-presentation to social media platforms other than Twitter, Geurin-Eagleman and Clavio (2015) focused on how niche and mainstream athletes employed Facebook and found that, due to the need to increase promotional efforts, niche athletes relied more heavily on social media, and employed more back-stage performances that discussed their personal lives. Although the sample examined included an equal number of male and female athletes in both the mainstream and the niche groups, no difference was found in the utilization of backstage performances between male and female athletes. Conversely, in a study examining athlete self-portrayals on Instagram by Geurin-Eagleman and Burch (2016) results indicated an overall utilization of back-stage performances by athletes through the sharing of personal photos or photos taken in a private setting. In addition, when examining differences in photographs shared by gender, it was found that female athletes were more likely to engage in backstage performances than male athletes In addition, Geurin-Eagleman and Burch (2016) found that female athletes posted more photos of a personal nature, although business-related photos were more popular with users. Last, although the athletes examined posted comparatively fewer photos of a sexual nature, and there was no difference between male and female athletes utilizing this post type, sexually suggestive photos generated statistically significant more likes and comments than other post types.

Taking into consideration the continued development of research focusing on athlete self-portrayals on social media, this chapter expands this line of research by determining whether previous trends toward back-stage performances by female athletes are likely to continue, and if/how backstage performances impact fan interest and engagement with the athlete's personal brand. To this end, the authors first seek to determine the type of content in the Instagram posts, including the level of fan interaction and/or engagement present in the posts. In addition, the effects of photo type and hashtag usage is probed. Finally, this study examines the presence and type of self-presentation strategies, and such strategies' effect on user engagement.

To examine how female athletes are utilizing social media for self-presentation purposes, researchers employed a content analysis of the top 10 most-followed female athletes with public accounts on Instagram. This methodology was selected due to its systematic and replicable process for analyzing static content (Riffe, Lacy, & Fico, 2013). Given the fact that photographs are posted on Instagram for public consumption, this is an unobtrusive analysis process (Creswell, 2013; Wimmer & Dominick, 2013). Consistent with previous studies employing this methodology when examining social media platforms, the most recent 50 photos from each of the top 10 most-followed female athletes, at the time of data gathering on Instagram, were examined (Geurin-Eagleman & Burch, 2016).

To guide the coding of Instagram posts pertaining to self-presentation strategies, a codebook and coding protocol were developed based on previous content analyses focusing on this specific social media platform (Geurin-Eagleman & Burch, 2016), and theoretical framework (Lebel & Danylchuk, 2012). Variables for analysis included the 10 variables previously employed by Geurin-Eagleman and Burch (2016) and were: Coder ID, Athlete's Name, Photo or Video, Single or Multiple Photos, Date the Photo/Video Was Taken, Number of Likes, Number of Comments, Photo Caption, Number of User Tags (indicated by the usage of @), Number of Hashtags (indicated by the usage of #), the Main Content of the Photo, and whether or not the athlete was in the photo. The main content of the photo included categories for relating to the athlete's personal life, relating to the athlete's own business life, relating to the athlete's sport (but not relating to the athlete), other sports or athletes, reposting content by fans, pop culture or landmark photos, and internet memes. If the athlete was present in the photo, then an additional variable determining type of photo was coded, which included athletic action, dressed but not posed, non-sport setting, sexually suggestive, and combination.

To determine the self-presentation strategy employed in the photo, an additional variable was coded to highlight whether it was a front-stage or back-stage performance based on the categories defined by Lebel and Danylchuk (2012). Sub-variables for each type of presentation (i.e., front stage or back stage) were incorporated to provide greater specificity. Front-stage performances included acting as a publicist (e.g., promotion or publicity), the superintendent (e.g., maintaining presence), the fan aficionado (e.g., fan interaction), and brand manager (e.g., formal acknowledgments associated). Back-stage performances included the categories of the conversationalist (e.g., interactions with athletes, celebs, family, friends), the sports insider (e.g., behind-the-scenes information), the behind-the-scenes reporter (e.g., favorite movies, hobbies), the super fan (e.g., non-sport discussions), the informer (e.g., general information sharing), and the analyst (e.g., general statements or opinions) (Lebel & Danylchuk, 2012).

The list of the top 10 most-followed female athletes on Instagram was based on follower figures provided in Pledgesports (2017) and follower numbers were verified by the researchers in November 2017. To capture the most relevant utilization of photos and presentation strategies, the most recent 50 Instagram posts from each athlete were analyzed. Thus, the sample size for analysis consisted of 500 posts ($n = 500$). These female athletes were selected due to the fact most of their mainstream coverage derives from major events (e.g., tennis championships, Olympic participation) or because they represent niche sports (e.g., mixed martial arts and professional wrestling). Thus, utilization of social media for self-presentation and promotion purposes may be necessary to remain visible and relevant in non-competition times, or in a sport that does not receive mainstream media coverage (Mahoney, Hambrick, Svensson, & Zimmerman, 2013). As the photo caption may provide insight into the photo type or self-presentation strategy, athletes who provided captions in English were selected, given the coders are both native English speakers. The list of female athletes and their number of Instagram followers is provided in Table 36.1.

Table 36.1 Athlete Instagram accounts

Athlete's name	Country	Sport	Instagram followers (millions)[a]
Ronda Rousey	USA	Mixed martial arts	9.7
Serena William	USA	Tennis	7.1
Nikki Bella	USA	Professional wrestling	6.6
Brie Bella	USA	Professional wrestling	5.4
Alex Morgan	USA	Soccer	5
Paige	USA	Professional wrestling	4.2
Natalie Eva Marie	USA	Professional wrestling	3.8
Sania Mirza	India	Tennis	3.7
Simone Biles	USA	Gymnastics	3.5
Maria Sharapova	Russia	Tennis	2.9

a Instagram followers at the time of data collection.

Photographs were coded by two individuals with previous experience in the content analysis methodology. Intercoder reliability, which ascertains coders interpret the variables in a consistent and replicable manner, was established through an independent coding of a sub-sample of 10% of the dataset. This is consistent with intercoder reliability guidelines established by Riffe et al. (2013). Thus, each coder independently coded 50 photographs. In addition to percentage agreements above 80% (Riffe et al., 2013), Cohen's kappa values were calculated to determine chance agreement between coders (Wimmer & Dominick, 2013). All 14 variables obtained Cohen's kappa values above the 0.70 threshold needed to establish intercoder reliability. After the establishment of intercoder reliability, the remaining 450 photos were divided equally and coded independently.

First, researchers focused on the content of photographs posted by female athletes on Instagram. The results indicated that, with regard to content, personal life photos were the most widely utilized, appearing in 51.8% ($n = 259$) of total photographs. This was followed closely by photographs focusing on the athletes' professional lives at 44.8% ($n = 224$) of the sample. Table 36.2 contains the percentages and counts of each photo content type.

Athletes appeared in 86.6% ($n = 433$) of photographs in the dataset. When an athlete appeared in a photo, the most prevalent image was a non-sport setting, representing 68.2% ($n = 341$) of the dataset. The remaining four categories of photographs that featured athletes were all utilized in less than 10% of the dataset. Table 36.3 contains the full breakdown of types of photos in which athletes appeared.

Table 36.2 Photo type and usage

Type	Count	Percentage
Personal	259	51.8
Professional	224	44.8
Internet	9	1.8
Other sport	4	0.8
Fan content	4	0.8
Pop culture	0	0.0
Sport	0	0.0
Total	500	

Table 36.3 Athlete's appearance in photo

Type	Count	Percentage
Non sport	341	68.2
Action	39	7.8
Dressed but posed	35	7.0
Sexually suggestive	12	2.4
Combo	6	1.2
Total	433	

With regard to fan interaction, as measured through likes and comments for each type of photo content, results of a one-way analysis of variance (ANOVA) of photo content on the number of likes was significant at the $P < 0.00$ level [$F(4, 495) = 7.65$, $P = 0.000$]. Post-hoc analysis, consisting of Tukey's honestly significant difference (HSD) to determine differences between groups, was conducted and indicated a statistically significant higher number of mean likes for photos relating to athletes' personal lives (mean = 167,579.59, standard deviation [SD] = 191,596.60) and likes for photos relating to an athletes' business lives (mean = 99,905.62, SD = 77,302.46). Table 36.4 contains the means and standard deviations for all conditions.

There was no significant difference found with regard to photo content and number of comments. Bivariate correlation analysis revealed a statistically significant positive relationship between the number of likes and comments [$r(498) = 0.39$, $P < 0.000$].

Next, the authors examined the relationship between the utilization of hashtags (indicated by the use of #) and user tags (indicated by the use of @) on the number of likes and comments. There was a small negative correlation between the number of hashtags and the number of likes found through bivariate correlation analysis [$r(498) = -0.16$, $P < 0.000$]. This indicates that as the number of hashtags used increased and the number of likes decreased. The utilization of user tags was not found to correlate with the number of likes. In addition, no correlation was found between the number of user tags and hashtags and the number of comments.

Furthermore, the researchers asked whether the type of photo increased or decreased fan engagement, as measured by likes and comments. ANOVA results revealed no significant effect from the type of photo and the number of likes or comments. The mean number of likes and comments for each photo type are provided in Table 36.5. It should be noted that the sexually suggestive photo type received the highest mean likes and comments, respectively (mean = 167,235.83, SD = 96,740.40; mean = 1,363.33, SD = 1,407.39). Notably, it was impossible to determine with any reliable accuracy the gender of the individual users who followed the athlete accounts, or the users who gave likes to the posts.

Table 36.4 Mean likes for photo content

Photo type	Count	Mean	Standard deviation
Personal	259	167,579.59	191,596.60
Professional	224	99,905.62	77,302.46
Internet	9	40,913.78	20,744.61
Other sport	4	89,604.75	50,538.46
Fan	4	46,420.50	16,240.45
Pop culture	0	0	0

All values significant at $P < 0.00$.

Table 36.5 Mean likes and comments for photo type

Photo type	Count	Likes Mean	SD	Comments Mean	SD
Non-sport	341	146,155.54	173,879.88	1,079.33	3,728.09
Action	39	125,134.69	79,624.29	544.41	447.58
Posed	35	117,397.85	75,059.74	583.34	832.42
Sexually suggestive	12	167,235.83	96,740.40	1,363.33	1,407.39
Combo	6	71,389.33	21,807.17	523.83	532.06

Pertaining to the types of self-presentation strategies employed by athletes on Instagram, the athletes examined utilized back-stage performances (58.0%, $n = 290$) slightly more frequently than front-stage performances (42.0%, $n = 210$). Table 36.6 illustrates the counts and percentages for all self-presentation sub-strategies.

When employing backstage performances, athletes were operating as a behind-the-scenes reporter most frequently at 35.6% ($n = 178$) of the total dataset. The conversationalist was utilized second most often, at 19.6% ($n = 97$) of the photographs. The sport insider (2.8%, $n = 14$), informer (0.02%, $n = 1$), super fan (0.00%, $n = 0$), and analyst (0.00%, $n = 0$) were used less frequently.

In photographs where athletes were employing front-stage performances the most widely utilized strategy was the publicist, which was used in 41.2% ($n = 207$) of all posts. In addition, this was the most widely utilized presentation strategy by athletes, in terms of both front-stage and back-stage performances overall. The remaining front-stage strategies of superintendent (0.04%, $n = 2$), fan aficionado (0.02%, $n = 1$), and brand manager (0.00%, $n = 0$) were not highly utilized in posts.

Finally, researchers asked whether the various self-presentation sub-strategies impacted fan engagement as measured through likes and comments. ANOVA revealed significant differences in the self-presentation sub-strategy and the number of likes at the $P < 0.000$ level [$F(6, 493) = 17.22, P = 0.000$]. Tukey's HSD post-hoc test revealed a statistically significant higher number of mean likes for photos utilizing the backstage self-presentation sub-strategy

Table 36.6 Self-presentation sub-strategies in photos

Backstage performances	Count	Percentage
Behind the scenes	178	35.6
Conversationalist	97	19.4
Sport insider	14	2.8
Sport informer	1	0.2
Analyst	0	0.0
Super fan	0	0.0
Front-stage performances		
Publicist	207	41.4
Superintendent	2	0.4
Fan aficionado	1	0.2
Brand manager	0	0.0
Total	500	

of the conversationalist (mean = 260,511.28, SD = 266,471.71) than the front-stage self-presentation sub-strategy of the publicist (mean = 100,729.58, SD = 80,639.63). In addition, post-hoc analysis indicated a statistically significant higher number of mean likes for photos utilizing the backstage self-presentation sub-strategy of the conversationalist (mean = 260,511.28, SD = 266,471.71), and other backstage self-presentation sub-strategies of behind-the-scenes reporter (mean = 107,274.72, SD = 84,401.35) and the sport insider (mean = 73,990.21, SD = 30,118.41). Table 36.7 provides the mean number of likes for each self-presentation sub-strategy. There was no significant effect from the self-presentation sub-strategies on the number of comments.

One noteworthy finding is that, although the publicist was the most utilized sub-strategy in terms of counts ($n = 207$), it was not the most interactive in terms of mean likes or comments. The self-presentation strategy that garnered the highest mean likes (mean = 260,511.28, SD = 266,471.71) and comments (mean = 1,791.28, SD = 4,039.93) was the conversationalist sub-strategy.

Discussion

The importance for female athletes to take the opportunity to present a more complete view of their lives on social media is clear, because there is the potential for the more stereotypical portrayals of female athletes to negatively affect not only the views of other female athletes, but also those of non-athletes (Kaskan & Ho, 2016). As previous research (e.g., Geurin-Eagleman & Burch, 2016; Geurin-Eagleman & Clavio, 2015) has indicated, the use of Instagram to post photos of a personal nature is an opportunity for individual athletes to show more personality than simply being seen as physically impressive athletes. This study of ten female professional athletes' use of Instagram featured posts by athletes from seven different sports. Although not examined as part of this study, it would be beneficial to examine differences in utilization between female athletes based on their sport category (i.e., team sports, individual sport). The individual athletes' feeds overwhelmingly featured personal and professional posts, with other types (i.e., internet, other sport, fan content) combining for less than 4% of all posts. Supporting previous research (Daniels & Wartena, 2011; Jones & Greer, 2011; Lebel & Danylchuk, 2014), sexually suggestive poses were only 2.4% of the sample posted by the athletes themselves. However, some previous research (Shreffler et al., 2016; Smith & Sanderson, 2016) was contradicted by the comparative lack of action shots, which made up only 7.8% of the sample. Notably, more than two-thirds of the content examined for this chapter featured athletes in non-sport situations. It can be surmised that much of the examined individuals' followings on social media would result from their status as athletes. However, as previous research showed, athletes often prefer

Table 36.7 Mean likes for self-presentation sub-strategies

Sub-strategy	Count	Mean	SD
Publicist	206	100,729.58	80,639.63
Behind the scenes	178	107,274.72	84,401.35
Conversationalist	98	260,511.28	266,471.71
Sport insider	14	73,990.21	30,118.41
Superintendent	2	76,666.50	27,620.30
Informer	1	59,995.00	–
Fan aficionado	1	69,808.00	–

to post photos including sponsors (Geurin-Eagleman & Clavio, 2015; Pegoraro, 2010) or more examples of life away from athletic competition (Geurin-Eagleman & Burch, 2016). Here, users responded to the personal content to a high degree, indicating that these small windows into the real life of individual athletes were appreciated by their followers. The contrast here with images presented by mainstream media is noteworthy, because media tend to seek to cover athletes who are perceived as traditionally attractive physically, with athletic accomplishments sometimes proving to be a secondary concern (Cooky et al., 2015; Daniels & Wartena, 2011; Kaskan & Ho, 2016).

The use of a personal Instagram account to show both publicist and behind-the-scene images indicates that the athletes sought a balance between disseminating informational messages and personal messages. As a publicist, the athletes can inform followers of their events, giveaways, and other brand interaction opportunities. With presentation of behind-the-scene images, a more intimate portrayal is given, with followers receiving what can be identified as insider information, secret moments captured and posted for their followers (Geurin-Eagleman & Burch, 2016). This allows the follower to feel a perception of a more personal connection with the athletes, learning about what the athlete presents in real life, as opposed to just the frontstage athletics-related events. The user can see that the athlete, who might be presented in their athlete role as being larger than life, might also enjoy similar activities and interests as their fans and the general public. In this way, the athlete is humanized for the follower, because social media are used to disseminate messages ranging from joyful to contrite (Romer, 2017).

From a technical standpoint, the decrease in number of post likes as the number of hashtags increased can be attributed to simple online etiquette. Hashtags are usually utilized on social media when a user is attempting to engage in a larger conversation which may not include only people whom a user may be following or who may be following the user (Billings, Burch, & Zimmerman, 2014). However, although Instagram offers a limitless space for text on each post, including the opportunity for multiple hashtags for each post, writers from internet-savvy outlets, including Hootsuite and Mashable, have noted that an overuse of hashtags in Instagram posts can irritate followers (LePage, 2017; Romano, 2014).

There are potential negatives connected with the use of Instagram for personal messages, because social media use also can lead to unwanted attention for female athletes (Geurin, 2017). Despite the low number of photos in this study that were categorized as sexually suggestive, this type of post received the highest number of mean likes and comments. Although this chapter does not include an examination of the gender of the users who reacted to the photos, research has found that males showed more interest when an article and photo depicted a female athlete in a more feminine way. By comparison, male participants rejected depictions of female athletes that did not fit what were previously held to be standard expectations with regard to gender stereotypes (Jones & Greer, 2011). In various media, female athletes have been treated as inferior to males. This has included a higher level of objectification compared with male athletes, as well as assumptions that female athletes are limited to certain societal roles (Kaskan & Ho, 2016). Through the use of social media, including Instagram, female athletes can counter these portrayals, and seek to alter perceptions to create a fuller picture of themselves as individuals with interests away from athletic competition.

Leader profile: Andrea Canales

Andrea Canales is a longtime sports journalist who has seen the transformation of media from a traditional print-based model to the online world. Canales' career has included stops at SI.com, ESPN.com, Top Drawer Soccer, and Goal.com, where she has covered Major League Soccer as

Figure 36.1 Andrea Canales
Photo courtesy of Andrea Canales

well as the US and Mexico men's and women's national teams. Canales also maintains an active Twitter presence (@soccercanales), where she shares thoughts and engages in discussions with a steadfast refusal to "stick to sports."

As the first female editor of one of international soccer media company Goal.com's many national sites, starting in 2008, Canales was part of conference calls with other site editors from around the globe.

"It was a little nerve-wracking. I have to say that I didn't enjoy my tenure at Goal.com as much as I could have, because I was always feeling the pressure to prove myself," Canales said. "I had to get up earlier, I had to work harder. I wanted our site to be the cleanest, most accurate, the best. I really had that chip on my shoulder that I had to prove myself."

And since Canales, who earned her undergraduate and Master's degrees at La Sierra University, and whose colleagues couldn't see her, there was a case or two of mistaken identity.

"It turned out that a good half of the editors (for the other editions) didn't know I was female, because Andrea is a male name in Italian," Canales said. "The Italian guy was super-friendly with me. He thought I was a guy the whole time, with a weird voice."

After three years with Goal, new ownership announced a plan to include more video, and Canales left in 2011. Soon, she was back at ESPN.com, where she had freelanced soccer articles before the Goal.com stint.

But, unlike before, social media usage and interaction were now part of sports journalism, as well as the life of an athlete. Canales noted that, with changes in sports media, the chance for an athlete to be on social media has also become the main window for fans to get to know them.

"I do think it's kind of interesting, the way social media affects the way even I as an objective soccer reporter relate to these athletes," Canales said. "And I imagine it's the same, in some ways, for the public at large, that you feel a certain intimacy, or more a sense of understanding of certain aspects of athletes' lives."

Such personal connections can form as athletes reveal more of their everyday experiences. US National Team forward and 2015 FIFA Women's World Cup Champion Sydney Leroux shared photos of her leg injuries to illustrate the problems with playing soccer on turf and also shared details about her life journey away from the sport.

"I'm not in the shape Sydney Leroux is, but with getting pregnant and your body changes, and you have a child," Canales said. "And you're trying to find time to get fit again, start your life again. Yet, you're excited to see your child developing."

Ultimately, Canales has seen the role and types of media shift as athletes take the opportunity to chronicle their own lives, bypassing tradition media outlet gatekeepers. However, Canales wonders whether there might be more to each Instagram story, so to speak.

"We don't have the stories that would explain things about these athletes. Instead, we have these images, and we feel like we know them, but the explanations that articles used to provide for us no longer exist."

References

Bortree, D. S. (2005). Presentation of self on the Web: An ethnographic study of teenage girls' weblogs. *Education, Communication & Information*, **5**(1), 25–39.

Billings, A. C., Burch, L. M., & Zimmerman, M. H. (2014). Fragments of us, fragments of them: social media, nationality and U.S. perceptions of the 2014 FIFA World Cup. *Soccer & Society*, **16**(5–6), 726–744.

Burch, L.M., Clavio, G., Eagleman, A.N., Major, L.H., Pedersen, P., Frederick, E.L., & Blaszka, M. (2014). Battle of the sexes: Gender analysis of professional athlete tweets. *Global Sport Business Journal*, **2**(2), 1–21.

Cooky, C., Messner, M. A., & Musto, M. (2015). "It's dude time!": A quarter century of excluding women's sports in televised news and highlight shows. *Communication and Sport*, **3**(3), 261–287.

Creswell, J. W. (2013). *Research Design: Qualitative, quantitative, and mixed method approaches*, 4th edn. Thousand Oaks CA: Sage.

Daniels, E. A. & Wartena, H. (2011). Athlete or sex symbol: What boys think of media representations of female athletes. *Sex Roles*, **65**(7–8), 566–579.

Dominick, J. R. (1999). Who do you think you are? Personal home pages and self-presentation on the World Wide Web. *Journalism & Mass Communication Quarterly*, **76**(4), 646–658.

Ellison, N., Heino, R., & Gibbs, J. (2006). Managing impressions online: Self-presentation processes in the online dating environment. *Journal of Computer-Mediated Communication*, **11**, 415–441.

Geurin, A. N. (2017). Elite female athletes' perceptions of new media use relating to their careers: A qualitative analysis. *Journal of Sport Management*, **31**(4), 345–359.

Geurin-Eagleman, A. N. & Burch, L. M. (2016). Communicating via photographs: A gendered analysis of Olympics athletes' visual self-presentation on Instagram. *Sport Management Review*, **19**(2), 133–145.

Geurin-Eagleman, A. N. & Clavio, G. (2015). Utilizing social media as a marketing communication tool: An examination of mainstream and niche sport athletes' Facebook pages. *International Journal of Sport Management*, **13**, 143–159.

Goffman, E. (1959). *The Presentation of Self in Everyday Life*. New York: Anchor Books.

Hambrick, M. E., Simmons, J. M., Greenhalgh, G. P., & Greenwell, C. (2010). Understanding professional athletes' use of Twitter: A content analysis of athlete tweets. *International Journal of Sport Communication*, **3**, 454–471.

Hancock, J. T. & Toma, C. L. (2009). Putting your best face forward: The accuracy of online dating photographs. *Journal of Communication*, **59**, 367–386.

Hum, N. J., Chamberlin, P. E., Hambright, B. L., Portwood, A. C., Schat, A. C., & Bevan, J. L. (2011). A picture is worth a thousand words: A content analysis of Facebook profile photographs. *Computers in Human Behavior*, **27**, 1828–1833.

Jones, A. & Greer, J. (2011). You don't look like an athlete: The effects of feminine appearance on audience perceptions of female athletes and women's sports. *Journal of Sport Behavior*, **34**(4), 358–377.

Jones, E. E. (1990). *Interpersonal Perception*. New York: W. H. Freeman

Kaskan, E. R. & Ho. I. K. (2016). Microaggressions and female athletes. *Sex Roles*, **74**(7–8), 275–287.

Leary, M. R. & Kowalski, R. M. (1990). Impression management: A literature review and two-component model. *Psychological Bulletin*, **107**(1), 34–47.

Lebel, K. & Danylchuk, K. (2012). How tweet it is: A gendered analysis of professional tennis players' self-presentation on Twitter. *International Journal of Sport Communication*, **5**, 461–480.

Lebel, K. & Danylchuk, K. (2014). Facing off on Twitter: A Generation Y interpretation of professional athlete pictures. *International Journal of Sport Communication*, 7, 317–336.

LePage, E. (2017). The do's and don't's of how to use hashtags. Hootsuite Blog, March 10. Retrieved from https://blog.hootsuite.com/how-to-use-hashtags.

Mahoney, T. Q., Hambrick, M. E., Svensson, P. G. & Zimmerman, M. H. (2013). Examining emergent niche sports YouTube exposure through the lens of the psychological continuum model. *International Journal of Sport Management and Marketing*, **13**(3–4), 218–238.

Marwick, A. & Boyd, D. (2011). To see and be seen: Celebrity practice on Twitter. *Convergence: International Journal of Research into New Media Technologies*, **17**(2), 139–158.

Marshall, D. P. (2010). The promotion and presentation of the self: Celebrity as marker of presentational media. *Celebrity Studies*, **1**(1), 35–48.

Mehdizadeh, S. (2010). Self-presentation 2.0: Narcissism and self-esteem on Facebook. *Cyberpsychology, Behaviour, and Social Networking*, **13**(4), 357–364.

Murray, D. C. (2015). Notes to self: The visual culture of selfies in the age of social media. *Consumption Markets & Culture*, **8**(6), 490–516.

Papacharissi, Z. (2002). The presentation of self in virtual life: Characteristics of personal home pages. *Journalism & Mass Communication Quarterly*, **79**(3), 643–660.

Pegoraro, A. (2010). Look who's talking – athletes on Twitter: A case study. *International Journal of Sport Communication*, **3**, 501–514.

Pledgesports (2017). 10 Most followed female athletes on Instagram. https://www.pledgesports.org/2017/06/10-most-followed-female-athletes-on-instagram.

Riffe, D., Lacy, S., & Fico, F.G. (2013). *Analyzing Media Messages: Using quantitative content analysis in research*, 3rd edn. Mahwah, NJ: Lawrence Erlbaum Associates, Inc.

Romano, A. (2014). Nobody wants to see your excessive hashtags on Instagram. Mashable, August 20. Retrieved from http://mashable.com/2014/08/20/hashtags-on-instagram/#9VgIMUBXiZqY.

Romer, I. L. (2017). Orlando City Soccer Club's Alex Morgan apologizes for Disney World incident. *Orlando Sentinel*, October 4. Retrieved from www.orlandosentinel.com/sports/orlando-pride-soccer/os-sp-alex-morgan-disney-world-20171004-story.html.

Shreffler, M. B., Hancock, M. G., & Schmidt, S. H. (2016). Self-presentation of female athletes: A content analysis of athlete avatars. *International Journal of Sport Communication*, **9**, 460–475.

Smith, L. R. & Sanderson, J. (2016). I'm going to Instagram It! An analysis of athlete self-presentation on Instagram. *Journal of Broadcasting and Electronic Media*, **59**(2), 342–358.

Wimmer, R. D. & Dominick, J. R. (2013). *Mass Media Research: An introduction*, 10th edn. Belmont, CA: Thomson Wadsworth.

37
Transforming sporting spaces into male spaces
Considering sports media practices in an evolving sporting landscape

Erin Whiteside

Shortly after leading the University of South Carolina to the 2017 women's basketball National Collegiate Athletics Association (NCAA) national championship, head coach Dawn Staley appeared in front of an overflowing media room, wearing the net as a trophy around her neck. Famous fans, including Magic Johnson and former President Bill Clinton, tweeted their congratulations to the legendary player and coach. Meanwhile, nearly four million viewers watched the game live on television – a 20% increase from the previous year – and a record number of people live-streamed what NCAA.com called the "spectacular event," pointing to a growing and increasingly varied future of mediated women's sports consumption (Hobson, 2017, para. 1). Indeed, the championship unfolded in a media glare that in many ways represents the gains women's sports in general have made since Staley's time as a player several decades earlier.

Although this narrative highlights the increased status enjoyed by women in sport media, it also raises questions about the future of coverage surrounding female athletes. If girls and women are indeed celebrated in a variety of contexts, why are media moments like Staley's still few and far between? Indeed, despite the exponential growth in girls' and women's sports participation in a post-Title IX world, along with a shifting cultural landscape that has become accommodating to the notion of female athleticism, sports media are still a space where girls and women in sports, and femininity and feminine values in general, are *not* valued. Female athletes continue to face challenges in attracting not just coverage alone, but coverage that depicts them as legitimate players in the sport media landscape. Given this tension, this chapter seeks to outline the trajectory of growth and change in coverage practices of girls' and women's sports, while contextualizing that assessment in both the theoretical orientation of those conducting the assessments and the social landscape of the era in which the coverage appears. It finishes with a discussion of the questions scholars and advocates should address moving forward in a contemporary sporting landscape where, like the spectacle surrounding Staley's moment suggests, that girls and women in sport have "made it."

The ideological work of sports journalism

Staley's post-game celebration in front of countless cameras, and her team's prominence in the sport media that evening, which included highlights showcasing women muscling under the basket for rebounds, sprinting down the court for layups, and other raw displays of speed, power, and strength, is symbolically significant in that those examples illustrate a challenge to the common assumptions in sport that define the game's most valued attributes as *essentially* male. Indeed, sports have been critiqued for offering a platform for the expression and celebration of "hegemonic masculinity," a term that describes a pattern of practice that not only privileges a version of masculinity that emphasizes traits such as power, size, and brute force, but also normalizes those attributes as natural to men (Connell & Messerschmidt, 2005). The implications of both connecting certain characteristics with men and masculinity in the public consciousness, and culturally elevating those characteristics as essential to the authentic athlete, provides a logic for the exclusion of women from sporting spaces (e.g., Messner, Dunbar, & Hunt 2004). This exclusion can be reinforced through a variety of processes that directly involve female athletes, including through editorial decisions that render girls and women invisible in sport media, to media representations that construct female athletes as an inferior "other" in sporting spaces. Boyle, Rowe, and Whannel (2010, p. 245) write that sports reporters and journalists are "key cultural narrators," in that they wield a tremendous amount of power in contributing to cultural discourses about what the symbolic practices on display in sporting spaces *mean*. In particular, sport media are important sites of cultural production in relation to identity, especially in terms of gender (Meân, 2014).

Furthermore, as Fink (2015, p. 331) writes, even though we appear to be in an age of celebration in regard to the female athlete, "very little has changed with respect to the media coverage, marketing and promotion of female athletes and women's sport." Thus, evaluating sport media practices, and how female athletes are represented, is critical to understanding the process by which women's status in sporting spaces more generally is understood, as well as for providing opportunities for rethinking how we might imagine a more inclusive sporting landscape.

Sports media's role in constructing women as the athletic other

(In)Visibility

The year 1972 represented a monumental one in the development of girls and women in sport, as Title IX of the Educational Amendments was signed into law, mandating that girls and women at federally funded institutions would have equitable access and resources to school-sponsored programs. Although athletics was not explicitly mentioned in the legislation, it was women's sport advocates who first pushed for protections under the law, and since then Title IX has become synonymous with the growth of girls' and women's sports in the United States.

Title IX is grounded in liberal feminist logic in that its ontological position – that is, the major assumptions regarding the nature of reality – is guided by the notion that women and men are more alike than different (Birrell, 2000). Liberal feminists, recognizing this assumption, then turn their attention to investigating why men's and women's experiences are often markedly different; furthermore, policy and related activism is, then, considered successful when it enables "women to compete equally with men" (Tong, 1998, p. 33). In sports media, part of that opportunity comes via representation and what simple visibility signals to the public about the status and legitimacy of women's sports.

Stagnation in growth

The amount of coverage dedicated to girls' and women's sports has not paralleled the exponential growth of female athletic participation in the immediate years post-Title IX, however. In his analysis of *Sports Illustrated* coverage, for instance, Bishop (2003) documented the lack of attention the magazine dedicated to women's sports both before and after Title IX's passage. For instance, in 1956, 4.3% of the articles focused on women's sports, in 1972 that figure rose to 4.7%, and by 1996 had fallen to 3.3% after reaching highs of 9.1% and 9.6% in 1992 and 1994, leading the author to conclude that "SI does not yet reflect the growing popularity of women's sports" (Bishop, 2003, p. 192).

In recent years, however, quantity totals have begun to change in ways that reflect a growing appreciation for girls' and women's sports in the United States. Still, it is not uncommon for scholars to begin a conversation on the state of contemporary media coverage of female athletes by broadly asserting that female athletes are generally overlooked and undervalued by members of sport media. At the national level, that statement is largely accurate, and sport journalists continue to render female athletes invisible, as reflected in the most recent edition of a 25-year longitudinal content analysis study that showed that about 3% of televised sports highlights and coverage focuses on women's sports (Musto, Cooky, & Messner, 2017). That research, which focuses on ESPN's marquee show *SportsCenter* and the sports content on three Los Angeles affiliate news stations, aligns with other work evaluating the quantity of women's sports coverage in national media. For example, the United States' most prominent sports magazines, *Sports Illustrated* and *ESPN the Magazine* feature female athletes on their covers about 6% of the time (Frisby, 2017), Fox Sports Live dedicates less than 1% of its coverage to women's sports (Billings & Young, 2015), and even when prominent female athletes compete at a well-known event such as the US Tennis Open, women continue to receive but a fraction of the coverage from national news outlets (Kian & Clavio, 2011). What Musto et al. (2017, p. 579) call the "silence" among such sport media outlets on women's sports contributes to the normalization of such practices, in that, over time, the absence of women in such high-profile media coverage becomes routine and accepted. Furthermore, such invisibility undermines potential challenges to commonsense assumptions that equate authentic athleticism to being essentially male. Such logic has long provided the justification for women's exclusion among decision-makers in sport media, the large majority of whom are white and male (Hardin, 2013).

Points of divergence

Although it is popular to lament the paucity of coverage of female athletes in sport media, there are numerous instances in which girls and women do receive higher rates of coverage than what is often seen in national media trends, and it is now more precise to assert that, in some instances, women continue to be overlooked, whereas, in others, sports journalists and reporters provide coverage amounts that align with the goals of women's sports advocates. Such shifts in trends are most notable during the Olympics, an event that has generated an increased amount of women's sports coverage in recent years, with 53% of NBC's primetime coverage dedicated to female athletes during the 2016 Summer Olympics (Coche & Tuggle, 2017) and nearly half (47.7%) during the 2014 Sochi Winter Olympic Games (MacArthur, Angelini, Billings, & Smith, 2016). Although it can be tempting to singularly praise such equity, scholars argue that nationalistic narratives drive coverage of international events, making the coverage less about the triumph of female athletes and more about the celebration of the home country (Wensing & Bruce, 2003). Furthermore, as Billings, Angelini, MacArthur, Bissell, and Smith

(2014) argue, Olympics broadcasting coverage of female athletes centers around sports that align with normative femininity -- the most obvious example reflected in the high rates of coverage dedicated to beach volleyball and gymnastics. The sports themselves showcase body types that align with normative male (hetero)sexual appeal, feature athletes wearing tight uniforms, and do not include bodily contact. Taken together, the high levels of coverage of these sports may be a function of perceived "gender appropriateness" rather than an overall shift in acceptance of diverse female athleticism (Billings et al., 2014, p. 49). Kane and Maxwell (2011, p. 203) argue that these production decisions are a product of "cultural stereotypes" by media gatekeepers, who believe that large audiences are dependent on coverage that reflects normative gender assumptions. Their work evaluating audience interpretation of various sportswomen images contradicts such assumptions, writing that "image[s] associated with athletic competence ... prompted the greatest interest in women's sports" among participants in their study (Kane & Maxwell, 2011, p. 208).

Other fissure points that challenge the logic of invisibility of women's sports may also be appearing. Whiteside and Rightler-McDaniels (2013), for instance, argue that local sports media may be an important space in which the goals of such outlets align with those of women's sports advocates; they suggest that community-oriented journalism in the form of smaller news outlets is dedicated to highlighting its local members, including its female athletes. Their research bears out this hypothesis, as girls' high school basketball receives about a third of local coverage, which dwarfs what is seen at national levels. Similarly, Bruce and Hardin (2014, p. 314) point to social media as a potentially liberating space for select female athletes to attract vibrant and sustainable fan followings on their own terms, and ultimately "prove interest to mainstream media gatekeepers."

Historical connections to the marginalization of women's sports in media

The logic of evaluating the amount of coverage that women's sports receives rests on the assumption that visibility equates, to some degree, with legitimacy. Yet, even if women do receive coverage, their presence in sport media texts does not always connote credibility and authenticity as athletes. Sport media representations that assign an inferior status to female athletes trace back to the emergence of sport journalism and the historical connection of sports as a space for the expression and celebration of idealized masculinity. For instance, Cahn (2015) writes that, during the 1920s, when women more generally were asserting themselves in spheres previously understood as open only to men, media accounts of female athletes often reminded readers about the so-called natural gender order and the inherent threat that women's athletic achievements posed to that way of life. As an example, Jhally and Earp (2013) recall the widespread adoption of the bicycle and related media accounts that worried about women adopting so-called ' "bicycle face' – a physical condition marked by 'peculiarities' including 'pale complexion' and an 'anxious expression'." Other female athletes became media darlings because they were seen as representing what Guttmann (1991, p. 146) describes as "respectable heroines," or women whose athletic achievements did not challenge their femininity. Indeed, as Cahn (2015) documents, when women's sports were positioned as valuable, it was because they were seen as able to "enhance the sexual appeal of young women, at the same time heightening the viewing pleasure of audiences entranced by attractive competitors" (Cahn, 2015, p. 77). Sexuality continued to be a concept around which women's sports was understood as valuable or threatening as organized women's sports grew, but, by the 1950s, concerns of the effect of sport's perceived masculine qualities on women began to dominate the public discourse. As one *New York Times*' writer opined in 1953, "There's nothing feminine or enchanting about a girl with beads of perspiration in her alabaster brow" (Jhally & Earp, 2013). Such characterizations brought into public discourse a concern that sport participation would "masculinize" women, an argument that provided the logic for engaging in homophobic rhetoric, and media coverage began to echo those concerns (Lenskyj, 2003).

Protecting sporting spaces as male spaces

Emphasizing femininity

When *Sports Illustrated* launched its (now defunct) *Sports Illustrated for Women*, it featured a pregnant Sheryl Swoopes in full makeup, smiling for the camera in what Fink and Kensicki (2002, p. 335) described as an "overt attempt to focus on femininity." Swoopes' pose, which highlighted attributes such as makeup, and painted fingernails that are typically coded as feminine, is one strategy that Duncan (1990) argues members in sport media use to emphasize *sexual difference* between male and female athletes. The term refers to strategies that transform the social constructs of femininity and masculinity into attributes that appear "natural and real" (Duncan, 1990, p. 25). Scholars working on this area have largely adopted the work of Antonio Gramsci's notion of hegemony to explain the process by which dominant ideology functions to establish "consent" among those in a given community on the status of given social arrangements (Duncan, 1990, p. 23). Underpinning this perspective is the assumption that social arrangements in sports serve patriarchal interests by constructing a vision of sports as a space vital to the interests of men, and simultaneously best served by natural displays of masculinity. Duncan (1990, p. 25) argues that this social construction is facilitated by images that emphasize sexual difference, or those that showcase masculinity and femininity in ways that invite the viewers to see those differences as "natural and real," and distinct to men and women, respectively. She suggests this process happens through the deployment of certain techniques in visual communication, including pose, body positioning, references to emotional displays, camera angles, and visual groupings. Such examples continue to manifest themselves in sports media today; a recent analysis of *Sports Illustrated* and *ESPN the Magazine*, for instance, found that cover shots of female athletes routinely emphasize the (hetero)sexuality of female athletes; furthermore, female athletes were more often shot while smiling compared with men, who were conversely "depicted with facial expressions that could be read as having serious intent, such as a determination to win" (Duncan, 1990, p. 14). Such outlets have a long institutional history of catering to men's sports and male audiences, which might partly explain the findings. Other research exploring similar trends in emerging media platforms has, however, yielded similar results and, as Clavio and Eagleman (2011, p. 301) write, "conventional media mores regarding images of female athletes in sport have informed the digital sphere."

Wasike's (2017) study also referenced another of Duncan's (1990) attributes regarding the production of sexual difference: body positioning. In his research, female athletes on the cover of these two magazines were depicted in passive poses that emphasize submissiveness and weakness, two traits that simultaneously fail to connote athleticism, and leave in place shared assumptions about incompatibility between women and sport.

Production techniques

Jones and Greer (2012, p. 616) argue that strength and athleticism can be communicated as natural to men in other, more subtle, ways, as well. In their study of Olympics coverage, for instance, they found that broadcasters more frequently used low camera angles when shooting male snowboarders compared with female snowboarders, "giving them the appearance of size and might." Other research has pointed to the deployment of production techniques that convey excitement – such as the use of quick shots, varied angles, and the use of new camera technology – being used more frequently with men (Greer, Hardin, & Homan, 2009). Meân (2014) suggests that digital media enable new ways in which women's inferior status can be communicated via the technology available through online platforms. Incorporating multi-media elements into coverage, for instance, impacts production values and conveys a sense of "dynamic, spectacular, action-oriented, eventful and newsworthy coverage," elements that continue to be lacking too often in mediated women's sports representation (Meân, 2014, p. 335). Whiteside and Stamm (2018) identified the increased rate by which athletic communications officials used entertaining GIFs in Twitter posts about male athletes, compared with female athletes, a digital media production technique that conveys importance and attracts attention among audience members. Musto et al. (2017), acknowledging a shifting gender landscape where outright sexism is considered taboo, argue that contemporary coverage might be marked by what they term "gender-bland sexism." Such coverage may not blatantly delegitimize female athletes, but simultaneously fails to invite audiences to see girls' and women's sport as worthwhile through the lack of production techniques that convey excitement, drama. and energy.

Uneven descriptors

Along with visual cues, sport coverage can reaffirm sexual difference by similarly emphasizing so-called masculine and feminine traits through writing and commentary that highlight so-called natural gendered differences. Such inequities became part of the international conversation on gender and sport during the 2018 Winter Olympic Games when sports journalists began questioning why commentators referred to women competing in figure skating as "ladies" but referenced their male counterparts as simply "men" – instead of the equivalent "gentlemen" (Brennan, 2018). This example of uneven labeling is a type of "gender marking," a linguistic practice that often involves using the qualifier "women" to refer to women's sports but fails to use similar qualifiers in male versions of the sports (e.g., Fink, 2015). Doing so positions male athletes as the standard in a given sport and is part of the wider process in equating authentic athleticism with masculinity.

Scholars have further argued that the conflation of masculinity and athleticism happens in part through the uneven distribution of strength and power adjectives when referring to male and female athletes (e.g., Billings & Eastman, 2003; Fink, 2015, Kian & Clavio, 2011). Descriptors can also be used to infantilize female athletes by suggesting they are not serious competitors. Eagleman (2015, p. 239), for instance, argues that the lack of language in newspaper articles that highlighted technical aspects of gymnastics during the 2012 Summer Olympics rendered female gymnasts as "children on a playground" compared with their more serious male counterparts.

Representations that highlight women's strength and power disrupt that process, and Wolter (2015a) argues that espnW represents one space in which counter-hegemonic narratives may be challenging commonly held assumptions. Her study highlighted greater instances of references to athletic prowess in articles about women compared with articles about men; as she writes, the texts powerfully connote a vision of "serious, competent sportswomen" (Wolter, 2015a, p. 186).

Connecting content to the producers

Given the complex and varied ways in which the female athletic subject is produced and understood through sporting discourses, scholars have raised the question of whether a more diverse group of sport media professionals might redirect discourses in ways that are ultimately more liberating and empowering for girls and women in sports. That may be a challenge, given the minority status that women occupy in the sport media industry; for instance, the most recent edition of a longitudinal study assessing gender and racial diversity, among Associated Press Sports Editor-member outlets, found that women comprised 10% of all sports editors and 11.5% of all reporters Women have most opportunity in copy-editing and design positions, where they comprise 20% of all staffers (Lapchick, 2018).

Research exploring attitudes among those working in sport media have identified differences toward women's sports that fall along gender lines, providing a logic for increasing the number of women working in sport media as a possible solution to the problem of continuing inequities in coverage (Hardin, 2013). Part of that redirection may come through gatekeeping and framing decisions which include story selection, source choices, and other journalistic processes that shape the overall message. In coverage of Title IX, for instance, research has noted that female reporters consult female sources at a higher rate compared with male reporters (Hardin, Simpson, Whiteside, & Garris, 2007). The prominence of more female sources in sport media may direct discourses in ways that may center female athletes in discussions about sports in general. In the case of Title IX coverage, Roessner and Whiteside (2016) argue that coverage prioritized female athletes in the discussion, which moved Title IX-related discourses in ways that may reshape how female athletes are understood in the public consciousness. Similarly, following his longitudinal analysis of Title IX coverage, Kaiser (2011) identified several different frames, including one that he labeled the "advocacy frame." This particular frame represents a sharp departure from narratives that position girls and women as villains and unwanted intruders in sporting spaces. Significantly, female reporters were more likely than men to incorporate the advocacy frames during certain time eras within his study. Furthermore, female reporters may be more apt to resist common techniques that marginalize girls and women in sports through framing practices that highlight their athleticism to a greater degree compared with that of male reporters (Kian & Hardin, 2009).

Yet, simply suggesting that an "add-women-and-stir approach" is the solution to addressing problematic trends in the coverage of female athletes is shortsighted, because it fails to address the ways in which gender functions as an organizing principle in sport media (Kian & Hardin, 2009, p. 186). Indeed, women working in sport media represent a minority of the profession. In such a "token status," women face risks in directly contradicting dominant values guiding decision-making and content production (Hardin & Shain, 2006). Furthermore, research has suggested that female reporters may consent to a hegemonic system that contributes to their own marginalization through the adoption of values and work routines that simultaneously disenfranchise women and question their own status in the workplace (Whiteside & Hardin, 2013).

Girl power and sport media

Perhaps no image in women's sports is as iconic as the 1999 cover of *Newsweek Magazine* featuring Brandi Chastain. Photographers captured the star soccer player moments after she ripped off her shirt to reveal a Nike-branded sports bra, and fell to the ground with her arms outstretched, celebrating her game-winning shot for Team USA in that year's World Cup. Chastain's energy and emotion are palpable in the cover shot, but what arguably gave the image its traction in the public consciousness was, however, the bold headline screaming "Girls Rule!," which was placed above Chastain's figure. The rhetoric of the headline and Chastain herself symbolize an important moment for girls and women in sports. In asserting that "Girls Rule," *Newsweek* symbolically transformed female athletes from an object of derision to one of empowerment and represented what Cooky (2010, p. 211) calls a "cultural shift in the landscape of girls and women sport."

That shift was part of a larger movement often called "girl power" or "popular feminism," a cultural discourse that draws "on a quasi-feminist vocabulary which celebrates female freedom and gender equality" (McRobbie, 2008, p. 532), and is reflected largely in popular culture spaces, including music, television, film, as well as sports. The *Newsweek* cover symbolically acknowledged that seemingly progressive step toward equality by providing female athletes a platform to claim space in what had historically been culturally understood as exclusively male territory. Furthermore, Chastain's image represented what Gonick (2006) describes as the so-called "new girl" of the girl power movement, or one who embraces assertiveness, sexual liberation, and is far divorced from the constraints of normative femininity, especially that which dictates a kind of passive, subservient, and demure subjectivity.

These narratives have been especially salient in sports advertising, where brands like Nike, Reebok, and others promise liberation and empowerment through the act of both consumption and aesthetics. Cooky (2010) points to a campaign by Reebok that showcased female athletes dismantling oppression via their athletic accomplishments as evidence of such rhetoric; in one spot, for instance, a serious Venus Williams confronts the viewer with the tagline "It's a Man's World" – with a bright red line crossing out the text, suggesting to the audience that such patriarchal understandings of sport are no longer welcome. As numerous scholars have pointed out, however, such discourses do not challenge inequities, but rather reassure girls and women that the opportunity exists for them to "have it all," a logic that simultaneously mutes future political resistance. Thus, although the phrase "girl power" evokes a strong and liberated connotation, scholars caution that related discourse is grounded in ideals of individualism and self-help that push aside any acknowledgment of existing gendered barriers. From this perspective, women who do not "rule" have only themselves to blame, a logic that exposes the limitations of girl-power rhetoric and betrays its empowering potential (Cooky, 2010; Whiteside & Roessner, 2018). For these reasons, scholars argue that such discourses are post-feminist in that, although choice and agency are celebrated as rightly available to girls and women, the context by which that choice happens is ignored, thus placing any blame on failures or shortcomings among girls and women squarely and solely on their own shoulders (McRobbie, 2008).

This context is significant for interpreting the evolution of discourse related to girls and women in sports media through the 1990s and to contemporary times. Wolter (2015b, p. 359) uses a critical discourse analysis to argue that espnW, while promising a space of liberation and empowerment for sportswomen, simultaneously draws on post-feminist discourses in what she describes as coverage reflecting "obsessional preoccupations with the body as a means to represent femininity." Lynn, Hardin, and Walsdorf (2004) point to advertising images in sports and fitness magazines as another example of post-feminist narratives, where ideals of fitness are co-opted by commercial interests to simultaneously celebrate a hetero-normative aesthetic, designed to please the male gaze. Scholars have also interrogated the ideological work that girl-power rhetoric accomplishes in suggesting that inequity in sport is an "historic relic," rendering future potential activism on behalf of female athletes as unnecessary; such narratives were at the forefront of coverage celebrating Title IX's fortieth anniversary, an event covered heavily by myriad sports media outlets, including industry leaders such as *Sports Illustrated* and *ESPN* (Whiteside & Roessner, 2018). In coverage of the law in 2012, sports and news outlets, in alignment with girl-power discourses, touted the visibility of female athletes and celebrated the gains, simultaneously rendering invisible existing inequities, especially those organized along racial, class, and sexuality lines.

Conclusion and avenues for future research

Dawn Staley's moment in the media glare can be read simultaneously as reflective of all that women's sports has accomplished, as well as a narrative vulnerable to co-optation by patriarchal interests that may point to the example as evidence of a post-gender sporting world. As Whiteside and Roessner (2018) caution, discourses about the United States representing an age of girl power are dangerous, in that they obscure lingering inequities, especially in terms of how most of the advancements made in sport participation have been experienced by white middle- and upper-class girls and women, who simultaneously adhere to a hetero-normative aesthetic. Indeed, as Fink (2015) argues, although little has changed in the past 15 years of sport media coverage despite strong advocacy records, scholars must continue to adapt their line of inquiries to reflect the pressing needs of all girls and women in sport. Perhaps most useful would be the incorporation of more intersectional analyses – those that consider the myriad ways sexism and oppression may be experienced by diverse groups of girls and women in sport media. Thus, although comparisons examining representations between male and female athletes are useful for continuing to think about how sporting spaces are normalized as male spaces, in an age where female athletes are often publicly celebrated, it will also be important to think about who benefits from those discourses and why, and what the operation of those narratives might mean for the creation of hierarchies among women. Kim, Walkosz, and Iverson's (2006) piece examining differences in coverage among golfers representing different ethnicities, McDonald's (2002) work questioning hetero-normativity in women's professional basketball, and Spencer's (2004) piece examining the gendered and racial discourses surrounding tennis's Williams' sisters all provide apt examples of intersectional work that can, as McDonald (2002, p. 381) writes, "make the familiar strange," and provide insight into what the concept of "woman" means in sporting spaces.

Leader profile: Vicki Michaelis

When Vicki Michaelis entered the press room at a University of Miami men's basketball media event in the early 1990s, she thought her day would unfold as it usually did. But that day Linda Robertson from the *Miami Herald* also happened to be there, spotted the relatively new reporter and headed over for an introduction. Robertson also told Michaelis about the Association for Women in Sports Media (AWSM), an important advocacy and networking group.

Michaelis, a longtime Olympics reporter for *USA Today*, looks back on that chance meeting as evidence of the power of networking, something critical to success for women working in the male-dominated sport media industry.

"What has always worked, worked for me," Michaelis says. "Women reaching out to other women saying, 'hey, here's this thing, you might want to check it out.' We support each other, we help each other and that's how I got involved."

It was through AWSM connections that Michaelis learned about the position at *USA Today*, where, in 2000, she became just one of five individuals in the United States on a full-time Olympics beat, covering some of the planet's most elite athletes in a wide variety of sports.

Michaelis, who started at the *Palm Beach Post* covering high school sports before rising to become the lead Miami Heat beat reporter, left Miami in 1995 for *The Denver Post* where she covered CU (Colorado Buffaloes) football, the Denver Nuggets, and the Olympics. During that time, she also built her network with AWSM and became the organization's president in 2006. AWSM has long advocated on behalf of female sport reporters, and Michaelis says that, although the industry has become more welcoming to women, they still face a host of challenges every

Figure 37.1 Vicki Michaelis

day, including perceptions that they are less knowledgeable about sports, and must meet a hetero-normative aesthetic.

She points to the decision-makers, many of whom are men, as holding the power to change those perceptions and norms. She also believes that changes in the amount and type of girls' and women's sports coverage are a direct outcome of whom those decision-makers are.

As she explains, "More women making the decision of what gets posted, what gets covered makes a difference. And if those people are women, then you'll see some difference."

With the help of individuals like Michaelis and organizations such as AWSM, that change may become more likely every day.

References

Billings, A. C., Angelini, J. R., MacArthur, P. J., Bissell, K., & Smith, L. R. (2014). (Re) calling London: The gender frame agenda within NBC's primetime broadcast of the 2012 Olympiad. *Journalism & Mass Communication Quarterly*, **91**(1), 38–58.

Billings, A. C. & Eastman, S. T. (2003). Framing identities: Gender, ethnic, and national parity in network announcing of the 2002 Winter Olympics. *Journal of Communication*, **53**(4), 569–586.

Billings, A. C. & Young, B. D. (2015). Comparing flagship news programs: Women's sport coverage in ESPN's SportsCenter and FOX Sports 1's FOX Sports Live. *Electronic News*, **9**(1), 3–16.

Birrell, S. (2000). Feminist theories for sport. In J. Coakley & E. Dunning (eds), *Handbook of Sports Studies* (pp. 61–76). Thousand Oaks, CA: Sage.

Bishop, R. (2003). Missing in action: Feature coverage of women's sports in *Sports Illustrated*. *Journal of Sport and Social Issues*, **27**(2), 184–194.

Boyle, R., Rowe, D., & Whannel, G. (2010). "Controversy? Questions for sports journalism. In S. Allen (ed.), *The Routledge Companion to News and Journalism*, New York: Routledge.

Brennan, C. (2018). When it comes to figure skating, Olympic officials need to come out of the dark ages. Usatoday.com, February 20. Retrieved from https://www.usatoday.com/story/sports/columnist/brennan/2018/02/20/2018-winter-olympics-figure-skating-women-athletes-ioc/357498002.

Bruce, T. & Hardin, M. (2014). Reclaiming our voices: Sportswomen and social media. In A. Billings & M. Hardin (eds), *Sport and New Media* (pp. 311–319). London: Routledge.

Cahn, S. K. (2015). *Coming on Strong: Gender and sexuality in women's sport*. Chicago, IL: University of Illinois Press.

Clavio, G. & Eagleman, A. N. (2011). Gender and sexually suggestive images in sports blogs. *Journal of Sport Management*, 25(4), 295–304.

Coche, R. & Tuggle, C. A. (2017). Men or women, only five Olympic sports matter: A quantitative analysis of NBC's prime-time coverage of the Rio Olympics. *Electronic News*. Advance online publication. doi.org/10.1177/1931243117739061

Connell, R. W. & Messerschmidt, J. W. (2005). Hegemonic masculinity: Rethinking the concept. *Gender & Society*, 19(6), 829–859.

Cooky, C. (2010). Understanding popular culture images of "girl power!" and sport. In S. Prettyman and B. Lampman (eds), *Learning Culture Through Sports: Perspectives on society and organized sports* (pp. 210–226). Lanham, MD: Rowman & Littlefield.

Duncan, M. C. (1990). Sports photographs and sexual difference: Images of women and men in the 1984 and 1988 Olympic Games. *Sociology of Sport Journal*, 7(1), 22–43.

Eagleman, A. N. (2015). Constructing gender differences: Newspaper portrayals of male and female gymnasts at the 2012 Olympic Games. *Sport in Society*, 18(2), 234–247.

Fink, J. S. (2015). Female athletes, women's sport, and the sport media commercial complex: Have we really "come a long way, baby"? *Sport Management Review*, 18(3), 331–342.

Fink, J. S. & Kensicki, L. J. (2002). An imperceptible difference: Visual and textual constructions of femininity in *Sports Illustrated* and *Sports Illustrated for Women*. *Mass Communication & Society*, 5(3), 317–339.

Frisby, C. M. (2017). Sacrificing dignity for publicity: Content analysis of female and male athletes on "Sports Illustrated" and "ESPN the Magazine" covers from 2012–2016. *Advances in Journalism and Communication*, 5(2), 120–135.

Gonick, M. (2006). Between "girl power" and "reviving Ophelia": Constituting the neoliberal girl subject. *NWSA Journal*, 18(2), 1–23.

Greer, J. D., Hardin, M., & Homan, C. (2009). "Naturally" less exciting? Visual production of men's and women's track and field coverage during the 2004 Olympics. *Journal of Broadcasting & Electronic Media*, 53(2), 173–189.

Guttmann, A. (1991). *Women's Sports: A history*. New York: Columbia University Press.

Hardin, M. (2013). Want changes in content? Change the decision makers. *Communication & Sport*, 1(3), 241–245.

Hardin, M. & Shain, S. (2006). "Feeling much smaller than you know you are": The fragmented professional identity of female sports journalists. *Critical Studies in Media Communication*, 23(4), 322–338.

Hardin, M., Simpson, S., Whiteside, E., & Garris, K. (2007). The gender war in US sport: Winners and losers in news coverage of Title IX. *Mass Communication & Society*, 10(2), 211–233.

Hobson, J. (2017). 2017 Women's Final Four thrives in Dallas. Ncaa.com, April 12. Retrieved from https://www.ncaa.com/news/basketball-women/article/2017-04-10/2017-womens-final-four-thrives-dallas.

Jhally, S. (producer), & Earp, J. (director) (2013). Not just a game. [Motion Picture] United State of America: Media Education Foundation.

Jones, A. & Greer, J. (2012). Go "Heavy" or go home: An examination of audience attitudes and their relationship to gender cues in the 2010 Olympic Snowboarding Coverage. *Mass Communication and Society*, 15(4), 598–621.

Kane, M. J. & Maxwell, H. D. (2011). Expanding the boundaries of sport media research: Using critical theory to explore consumer responses to representations of women's sports. *Journal of Sports Management*, 25, 202–216.

Kaiser, K. (2011). Gender dynamics in producing news on equality in sports: A dual longitudinal study of Title IX reporting by journalist gender. *International Journal of Sport Communication*, 4(3), 359–374.

Kian, E. M. & Clavio, G. (2011). A comparison of online media and traditional newspaper coverage of the men's and women's US Open tennis tournaments. *Journal of Sports Media*, 6(1), 55–84.

Kian, E. M. & Hardin, M. (2009). Framing of sport coverage based on the sex of sports writers: Female journalists counter the traditional gendering of media coverage. *International Journal of Sport Communication*, 2(2), 185–204.

Kim, E., Walkosz, B. J., & Iverson, J. (2006). *USA Today*'s coverage of the top women golfers, 1998–2001. *Howard Journal of Communications*, **17**(4), 307–321.

Lapchick, R. (2018). The 2018 Associated Press Sports Editors race and gender report card. The Institute for Diversity and Ethics in Sport (TIDES). Retrieved from https://www.tidesport.org/associated-press-sports-editors.

Lenskyj, H. (2003). *Out on the Field: Gender, sport and sexualities*. Toronto: Women's Press.

Lynn, S., Hardin, M., & Walsdorf, K. (2004). Selling (out) the sporting woman: Advertising images in four athletic magazines. *Journal of Sport Management*, **18**(4), 335–349.

MacArthur, P. J., Angelini, J. R., Billings, A. C., & Smith, L. R. (2016). The dwindling Winter Olympic divide between male and female athletes: The NBC broadcast network's primetime coverage of the 2014 Sochi Olympic Games. *Sport in Society*, **19**(10), 1556–1572.

McDonald, M. G. (2002). Queering whiteness: The peculiar case of the Women's National Basketball Association. *Sociological Perspectives*, **45**(4), 379–396.

McRobbie, A. (2008). Young women and consumer culture: An intervention. *Cultural studies*, **22**(5), 531–550.

Meân, L. J. (2014). Sport websites, embedded discursive action, and the gendered reproduction of sport. In A. C. Billings, & M. Hardin (eds), *Routledge Handbook of Sport and New Media* (pp. 331–341). London: Routledge.

Messner, M., Dunbar, M., & Hunt, D. (2004). The televised sports manhood formula. In D. Rowe (ed.), *Critical Readings: Sport, culture and the media* (pp. 229–245). Berkshire, EN: Open University Press.

Musto, M., Cooky, C., & Messner, M. A. (2017). "From fizzle to sizzle!" Televised sports news and the production of gender-bland sexism. *Gender & Society*, **31**(5), 573–596.

Roessner, A. & Whiteside, E. (2016). Unmasking Title IX on its 40th birthday: The operation of women's voices, women's spaces, and sporting myth narratives in the commemorative coverage of Title IX. *Journalism*, **17**(5), 583–599.

Spencer, N. E. (2004). Sister act VI: Venus and Serena Williams at Indian Wells: "Sincere fictions" and white racism. *Journal of Sport and Social Issues*, **28**(2), 115–135.

Tong, R. P. (1998). *Feminist Thought*, 2nd edn. Boulder, CO: Westview Press.

Wasike, B. (2017). Jocks versus jockettes: An analysis of the visual portrayal of male and female cover models on sports magazines. *Journalism*. Advance online publication: doi.org/10.1177/1464884917716818.

Wensing, E. H. & Bruce, T. (2003). Bending the rules: Media representations of gender during an international sporting event. *International Review for the Sociology of Sport*, **38**(4), 387–396.

Whiteside, E. & Hardin, M. (2013). The glass ceiling and beyond: Tracing the explanations for women's lack of power in sports journalism. In P. Pederson (ed.), *Routledge Handbook of Sport Communication* (pp. 146–154). London: Routledge.

Whiteside, E. & Rightler-McDaniels, J. L. (2013). Moving toward parity? Dominant gender ideology versus community journalism in high school basketball coverage. *Mass Communication and Society*, **16**(6), 808–828.

Whiteside, E. & Roessner, A. (2018). Forgotten and left behind: Political apathy and privilege at Title IX's 40th anniversary. *Communication & Sport*, **6**(1), 3–24.

Whiteside, E. & Stamm, J. (2018). Animating women's sports: Social media, gender and evolving techniques for constructing the legitimate and authentic athlete. Paper presented at the Association of Educators in Journalism & Mass Communication, Washington DC.

Wolter, S. (2015a). A quantitative analysis of photographs and articles on espnW: Positive progress for female athletes. *Communication & Sport*, **3**(2), 168–195.

Wolter, S. (2015b). A critical discourse analysis of espnW: Divergent dialogues and postfeminist conceptions of female fans and female athletes. *International Journal of Sport Communication*, **8**(3), 345–370.

38
Netball
Carving out media and corporate success in the game for all girls

Margaret Henley and Toni Bruce

Introduction

In this chapter, we discuss how netball achieved its status as the premiere women's sport in New Zealand, with high participation rates, a strong financial base, significant corporate support, an appealing television rights package, and national recognition. We also identify potential risks that may lead to netball slipping from its currently secure position of cultural, corporate, and media dominance. We profile Kate Buchanan, who leads corporate and media activities for New Zealand's most successful netball franchise, the Southern Steel.

Throughout, to situate netball in a broader national sporting context, we compare netball with rugby because each sport is historically strongly associated with only one gender and seen as *the* nationally important sport for that gender.

With over 20 million players in 80 nations, netball is a rare international team sport played almost exclusively by women. Although thriving, it faces potential rifts within the international netball community, focused on tensions between innovation and tradition, and between funding for grassroots participation and funding for elite levels of the game. Netball is played at all levels, from primary school to international Golden Oldies festivals that may include players into their 80s, and now includes the predominantly social variant of indoor netball for women, mixed and men's teams. Major netball-playing nations offer semi-professional, within-nation leagues, and international competitions include the quadrennial Netball World Championships and Commonwealth Games, semi-annual Fast5 World Series, and test matches between nations.

Netball in New Zealand

Despite netball's history as the major female team sport in many Commonwealth nations, its role in physically empowering generations of girls and women, and its "tremendous impact" on New Zealand's "overall sporting culture" (Andrew, 1997, p. 1), there is a remarkable dearth of research on netball's place in the social construction of gender and sport (compare Marfell, 2011, 2016; Nauright & Broomhall, 1994; Russell, 2007; Tagg, 2014a, 2014b; Taylor, 2001a, 2001b; Treagus, 2005), or on netball as a mediated product (compare Bruce, 2013a; Henley, 2004a, 2004b, 2012; Needs, 2017; Vann, 2014; Vann, Woodford, & Bruns, 2015), and virtually nothing in the areas of sports business, sponsorship, or management (compare Charbonneau & Garland, 2006; Garland & Ferkins, 2003). This startling absence, considering netball's significance in women's lives for over 100 years, is a potent example of the broader public marginalization of women's sporting activities. Netball has long been accepted as *the* appropriate sport for women (Andrew, 1997; Henley, 2012; Marfell, 2016). As early as the 1920s, news media were calling it "eminently suitable for every girl" (Nauright & Broomhall, 1994, p. 394) and the "national game . . . for women" (Nauright & Broomhall, 1994, p. 389).

Current participation statistics demonstrate the ongoing power of this belief: netball had the most participants of 90 high school sports played in New Zealand in 2017, despite 97% of players being girls (New Zealand Secondary Schools Sports Council, 2017), and it remains the highest participation team sport in the 16- to 24-year age group (Sport New Zealand, 2015). For many women, playing and consuming netball is "a space of immense joy and insurmountable pleasure," not least because of its overwhelmingly "women-onlyness" (Marfell, 2016, p. 224). This relatively secure grassroots base is a reflection of the importance the game still represents in the lives of girls and women. In addition, its positioning within evolving discourses of femininity, alongside years of "resourceful tactics and socially astute struggle" by netball administrators to convince broadcast media of netball's televisual value, have led to its current position of high television and public visibility (Henley, 2012, p. iii), and financial success.

There seems little doubt that netball's current success is built on its ability to secure consistent live broadcast coverage of elite levels of the game. Both authors have independently argued that netball provides an important antidote to persistent media inattention to women's sport, and shows that, under certain conditions, sportswomen can be seen as valued contributors to sport (Bruce, 2013b; Henley, 2012). For example, Henley's ongoing analysis clearly explains netball's "hard fought migration from the rarely mediated anonymity of the back courts to the centrality of the primetime television screen" (Henley, 2012, pp. 4–5; see also Henley, 2004a, 2004b). Henley found that this migration owes much to the determination of early netball administrators, whose intuitive understanding of netball's strong cultural roots, and belief that women's sport should be valued as much as the dominant men's sports, led to netball achieving the status of "a major New Zealand sport" by the 1970s, and its elevation in the 1980s to one of only four sports identified by the state broadcaster Television New Zealand (TVNZ) as nationally important enough to receive full broadcast sponsorship and a rights payment (Henley, 2012). Since then, and largely as a result of an intense rivalry with Australia, grounded in many close battles for the world number one ranking, which articulates the sport and its players to valued discourses of nationalism (Henley 2004a, 2004b), netball has carved out its place as the most financially successful women's sport in New Zealand.

In contrast, netball in Australia is a "niche" or "marginal" sport, "crowded out" by competing sports, and until 2017 able to achieve only "a precarious hold on commercial free-to-air broadcast airtime" (Vann et al., 2015, p. 117). Indeed, in recent decades, the elite levels of Australian netball have been financially supported by television rights negotiated by Netball New Zealand (NNZ) to the tune of "more than NZ$10 million in broadcast revenue" (Johannsen, 2016b, para. 7). Netball's high visibility on New Zealand television is matched by its status as the most-covered women's sport in print media. Numerous studies have demonstrated that netball "is rare in terms of its status and visibility," even if levels of netball coverage (4% across one year) remain far below those of men's rugby (20% across one year) (Bruce, 2013b, p. 261). Such findings may explain the netball fans' dissatisfaction with news coverage: less than 10% in a recent survey turned to print or television news as sources of information about major netball events (Needs, 2017).

Elite netballers enjoy a high public profile, including regular appearances on celebrity shows like "Dancing with the Stars," and rating highly in Readers' Digest Most Trusted surveys

(Bruce, 2009; Marfell, 2016). Many have a dedicated fan base on social media (Needs, 2017; Vann, 2014; Vann et al., 2015). As Marfell (2016, p. 8) explained, "Live match broadcasts and television advertisements featuring the national team, the Silver Ferns, have increased the visibility of netball and its elite players, sometimes to the point of making these women household names." Netball has consistently attracted "corporate sponsorship far in excess of that for any other women's sports organisation" (Andrew, 1997, p. 2). In two small studies with the public and students, "female celebrity athletes outperformed their male counterparts as potential endorsers", with a netballer as the "best fit" based on trustworthiness, expertise, and attractiveness (Charbonneau & Garland, 2006, p. 31; see also Garland & Ferkins, 2003).

Television ratings for live games have proven that netball can attract large audiences (Henley, 2004b). For example, ratings for TVNZ's free-to-air broadcasts regularly exceeded those for the national men's rugby team in 1999 and the early 2000s. According to AC Nielsen television ratings in 1999, the New Zealand versus Australia 1999 Netball World Championship final attracted over one million viewers (from a population of just over 3.8 million), and this broadcast became one of the highest rated programs in New Zealand's television history. It was seen as a "watershed day for netball" that led to an unprecedented broadcast rights fee of NZ$500,000 per annum from TVNZ (Henley, 2012, p. 268)—even if it was half the amount sought and paled in comparison to the rumored NZ$19.6 million TVNZ paid to screen the 1999 men's Rugby World Cup. This income closely followed NNZ's first major jump in corporate sponsorship income of over NZ$730,000 in 1994 (Andrew, 1997). Thus, at the end of the 1990s, Andrew (1997, p. 62) was able to argue that "the influx of corporate sponsorship capital and an increasingly aggressive marketing strategy have increased the visibility of netball to an unprecedented extent. Netball has grown from 'a good game for girls' into an exciting, media-accessible, spectator sport."

Going semi-professional: The trans-Tasman[1] ANZ Championship (2008–2016)

To understand both the financial success and the potential risks for netball, we discuss the nine-year, trans-Tasman ANZ Championship. In 2006, NNZ and Netball Australia joined forces to approach Sky Television with a proposal to create a trans-Tasman league, following men's sports such as rugby, rugby league, basketball, and football, where teams from New Zealand and Australia competed in a combined competition that capitalized on the traditionally high television ratings that characterize trans-Tasman rivalries. Sky, which saw netball as a "premium" live sport (Thompson, 2017, p. 35), had been waiting in the wings for an opportunity to lure netball's female audience and sponsors across the paywall. With TVNZ not willing or able to match Sky's outside broadcast and technical capacity, Sky won the rights to broadcast the 2007 Netball World Championships in Auckland, using the event to showcase its intentions toward netball and inject new vigor into live coverage using top-of-the-range technology.

The following year, the "ground-breaking," "game-changing," and "revolutionary" ANZ Championship was launched (Johannsen, 2016a, para. 4) with the intention of creating a professional league that would attract top international players and raise the skill base in other netball countries. The Championship replaced the premiere netball leagues in both New Zealand and Australia by creating an even split of five franchise teams from each country and extending the joint competition across a 17-week season. The ANZ Bank's naming rights deal was reputed "to be the biggest sponsorship deal for women's sport in Australasia, while the significant investment from Sky not only ensured the players got paid, it elevated netball into primetime slots on TV" (Johannsen, 2016a, para. 5). Netball Australia saw it as a vehicle through which Australia could access the quality and quantity of broadcast space that the game had enjoyed in New Zealand for decades. Thus, from the outset, Sky in New Zealand financed the television content with the expectation that Australian broadcasting would contribute to revenue returns within five years (Johannsen, 2013). However, despite early success, with television audience up 52% in both countries during the 2009 season, returns from Australian broadcasting did not materialize (Netball Australia, 2009). Indeed, at the end of the 2012 season, Australia's Channel 10 withdrew from a four-year broadcasting contract, stating that netball was "not a premium sport" and too "insignificant" to receive mainstream media attention (Murdock, 2013, para. 5). Three years later, in 2015, despite what was heralded as a "ground-breaking deal for sports broadcasting," Netball Australia had to underwrite the total cost of production and their major sponsors paid Channel 10 to screen ANZ Championship games to safeguard a strong free-to-air presence (Niall, 2015, para. 1).

Over the final two years, it became increasingly evident that the competition was not meeting Netball Australia's goals. Television ratings indicated a trend for national audiences to follow teams from their own country and region (Mitchell, 2016). The competition increased netball's media profile and public following, but Netball Australia no longer saw the close link to New Zealand broadcasting revenue as compatible with its desire to negotiate and control its own future in Australian broadcasting, and provide more opportunities to showcase its larger player base and elite players. To Netball Australia's ongoing frustration, NNZ held the power in any negotiations, because Sky was "still effectively funding Australia's existing franchises" (Johannsen, 2016a, para. 13). The competition ended when Australia gained an "historic five-year broadcast rights and revenue sharing agreement" that put netball on "prime-time free-to-air television," generated higher player salaries, and set the stage for Australian netball to turn fully professional (Mason, 2016, para. 1). Although the deal was rumored to be lower than Sky's (Johannsen, 2016a), Netball Australia felt it would cement "Australia's reputation as having the prime netball competition in the world" (Mason, 2016, para. 10). Netball Australia declared the new domestic league an "overwhelming success" (Delahunty, 2017, para. 2). Television audiences rose by over 40%, with 850,000 watching the first four free-to-air broadcasts, commercial investment tripled, and match attendance rose by 42% (Delahunty, 2017; Hickman, 2017).

Meanwhile, NNZ re-signed with Sky, offering exclusive rights to broadcast all netball until 2021, a five-year deal that NNZ called "a defining moment for women's sport in New Zealand" and "the most significant broadcast deal" in netball's history (Pullar-Strecker, 2016, para. 5). It meant Sky now had long-term deals with all four major team sports, in an increasingly challenging media environment where "internet-television competitors circle and sporting codes weigh up the option of streaming their events direct to consumers" (Pullar-Strecker, 2016, para. 14). Although the total worth of the contract was not publicly available, NNZ's recent financial statements indicate that the total Sky sponsorship package is in the vicinity of NZ$30 million over five years. In comparison, New Zealand Rugby was estimated to be earning NZ$60–70 million annually (Alderson, 2017). The ongoing commitment from SKY and main sponsor, the ANZ Bank, provided the foundation from which to launch New Zealand's ANZ Premiership, featuring 47 games over a 14-week season, which was touted as the "world's most intensely fought, captivating and innovative female sports league, featuring the world's best players" (Netball New Zealand, 2016, para. 7). NNZ applauded the "recognisable return to playing the game in a more traditional New Zealand style" as one of the successes of the Premiership season (Netball New Zealand, 2017, p. 35). As happened in Australia, there was strong audience interest for the inaugural ANZ Premiership season. According to Nielsen TV ratings, viewership totaled 1,299,064, with a live audience of 60,600 watching the final between the Southern Steel and the Central Pulse. Sky broadcast all games live, and delay-screened highlights packages on its free-to-air channel, Prime. Players were on TV screens three times a week during the season, and highlights packages, created by Sky, were also available on the ANZ Premiership, NNZ, and franchise web pages.

In terms of salaries, New Zealand netballers are among the best-paid sportswomen in the country (Egan, 2018). Historically, the Silver Ferns have always received a higher level of financial reward than their Australian counterparts. Although the increased money coming into Australian Super Netball is addressing this imbalance, it is not yet on par with New Zealand (Egan 2018). However, despite good ratings, and strong broadcasting and commercial sponsorship, Egan (2018, para. 5) explained that "there isn't sufficient money for everyone in the competition to be fully professional." Leading players who hold both a Silver Ferns and a Premiership contract can earn around NZ$130,000 per year, but many who play only in the Premiership train and play like professionals on six-month contracts that range from NZ$22,500 to NZ$80,000 (Egan, 2018). Even the best-paid netballers earn only one-tenth of the annual salary received by the captain of the national men's rugby team (Egan, 2018).

The growth of social media

As the trans-Tasman competition ended, the authors' ongoing ethnography of netball fandom revealed that New Zealand fans were concerned about their ability to watch teams and individual players from other countries, especially but not exclusively Australia. Although the total New Zealand television audience for all netball in 2017 was 2.6 million viewers in a country of 4.7 million, the most rapid growth has been the digital audience, which reached 1.5 million in 2017, including a 48% increase in web hits and 21% increase in Facebook activity (Netball New Zealand, 2017). In a "landmark global streaming arrangement," fans *outside* but not *inside* New Zealand were given free, live access to all 47 ANZ Premiership matches via Facebook for an extended period to accommodate different time zones (ANZ Premiership, 2017, para. 1). Over 21.4 million Facebook feeds received details about the live streaming, providing an indication of the game's potential international following (Netball New Zealand, 2017). No such access was available to New Zealand audiences for the Australian competition.

Pegoraro's (2014) research on Twitter recognized that social media gave sport fans a new way of "consuming and communicating about sport" (p. 133). Social media platforms therefore have the potential to significantly address the lack of traditional media coverage historically allocated to women's sport, and potentially to overcome geographical boundaries. Surprisingly, netball in New Zealand has been relatively slow to develop its social media potential (Needs, 2017; Vann, 2014), which may reflect the historically stronger investment in television broadcasting. In a comparison of Twitter activity in New Zealand and Australia, raw numbers of tweets were three to four times higher in Australian netball, but Vann et al. (2015, p. 117) reported "significantly more engagement per capita with netball in the New Zealand Twittersphere." Overall, based on 2013 data, Vann et al. (2015, p. 117) proposed that:

> it is reasonable to conclude that New Zealand *teams* do not need to rely on social media tools as much as Australian teams do, causing them to overlook the benefits and increased publicity that can come from active use of social media,

although they noted that "New Zealand *fans* are already using social media quite actively even in the absence of orchestrated official campaigns aimed at getting them to do so" (Vann et al., 2015, p. 117). In relation to netball's future, a key finding is that social media activity coalesces around live broadcasts, with most activity during breaks in play because "fans are largely focusing on the match during the playing periods" (Vann et al., p. 113; see also Needs, 2017). In the New Zealand context, Needs (2017) concluded that live updates on franchise and ANZ Championship pages were "important for those fans without subscriptions to SKY Sports" (Needs, 2017, p. 74), many of whom were dissatisfied with lack of access to live broadcasts, such as the fan who wrote, "There should be one free-to-air broadcast with one-hour delay each week. Rugby manages this. It is an insult to women that netball management shows little respect for the majority of its supporters by not negotiating for this" (Needs, 2017, p. 53). As a result, almost half used social media, particularly Facebook, as their preferred source for information and "to talk to friends, family and fellow fans about the game as it happens" (Needs, 2017, p. 71).

However, although social media use is growing in response to fan demand and the commercial needs of the elite national and provincial competitions to reach and maintain their fan base, the development of social media is largely due to the efforts of netball, its sponsors, and the community-oriented provincial franchises, rather than the broadcaster that does not offer social media options to complement the domestic elite competition. The Southern Steel franchise, located in New Zealand's southernmost region, is leading the way in leveraging social media to engage its passionate and parochial fans.

The Southern Steel won the inaugural ANZ Premiership in 2017. That success was built on a solid foundation provided by its predecessor franchise, the Southern Sting, which emerged in 1998 after NNZ revamped the national elite competition to offer its broadcast partner and fans a longer, made-for-television season. The Sting rapidly became the most successful franchise in the country winning seven titles during the ten years of the National Bank Cup series, despite the region's relative geographical isolation and low population base. The team came to epitomize a mind-set of a region punching above its weight, and its fans became renowned for donning "tinsel wigs and face paint and tattoos" and going "crazy" (Doherty, 2004, p. 170).

With the introduction of the trans-Tasman ANZ Championship in 2008, the Sting combined with the Otago Rebels to become the Southern Steel, representing the Netball South zone as one of the five New Zealand franchises. The Steel benefitted from the well-established sponsor relationships with the previous Sting franchise, which was described as having "the most savvy franchise board" and the "deepest pocketed and biggest handed sponsors" (Dougherty, 2004, p. 169). Today, the Steel franchise is "well-known throughout New Zealand for their close and loyal following" which comprises a "tight-knit" and "netball-centric" local community (Needs, 2017, p. 121). The team's "unique" social media content "explicitly draws on the community-driven values of the team," and its Facebook posts attract high numbers of responses (likes, emojis, comments) (Needs, 2017, p. 122). Due to the team's social media success, we profile the Steel's corporate and communications manager Kate Buchanan to highlight how she has galvanized sponsor and fan engagement with the franchise.

Conclusion

So, where does this leave netball as a business moving into the future? At the time of writing, we argue that netball is at a crossroads. Having negotiated its way into a solid financial position, with guaranteed live coverage and strong sponsorship arrangements, netball faces an unprecedented set of circumstances that have the potential to threaten its success and dominance of New Zealand women's sport. These include the rapidly changing landscape for women's rugby and other historically male-dominated sports that have begun to pay their top female players' salaries commensurate with domestic-league netballers (Bidwell, 2018; Macdonald, 2017), the end of the trans-Tasman netball competition, and increasing challenges to traditional broadcast delivery systems, with associated issues of access to, quality of, and control over live content.

Netball's success to date has been built on the sport's gender acceptability and exclusivity, which means it offers a unique sporting product in an increasingly congested and competitive sports business space. Yet the growing interest in rugby Sevens, which achieved Olympic status in 2016, may allow women's rugby to leverage longstanding and lucrative sponsor relationships that already exist in men's rugby, putting them in more direct competition with netball. The potential is that netball could be increasingly shut out of valuable sponsorship agreements. Julie Paterson, former CEO of a major netball franchise, sees this as a significant challenge, arguing that more businesses need to "see the value" in the "very high professional product" that is netball, especially the buying power associated with its high female audience (personal communication, March 16, 2018).

Domestic television audiences may have increased after the end of the trans-Tasman competition but the national team, the Silver Ferns, had one of its worst years on record in 2017, losing to Australia and England in key international matches and, for the first time ever, they failed to win a medal in the 2018 Commonwealth Games. Thus, if New Zealand cannot maintain its international dominance, drawing from its domestic competition to effectively develop elite talent, the "very high professional product" may start to lose its luster and attractiveness to broadcasters and sponsors.

Netball's current broadcasting contract is the most lucrative ever achieved by a women's sport with a New Zealand broadcaster, and has provided significant income for NNZ. Yet, a danger lies in the rapid decrease in households subscribing to Sky Sport (Pullar-Strecker, 2017). With less than 35% of households having access to live broadcasts, netball's dominance in television ratings and ability to reach its national audience may be under significant threat, with potential down-stream effects in its ability to attract major sponsors. Although franchises like the Steel, and the ANZ Championship and NNZ, are stepping up their social media activity to fill the gap, the current broadcast agreement prevents live streaming games to New Zealand audiences, although they are available to select international territories, and netball organizations have no access to additional game footage beyond the Sky-produced highlights packages. A key challenge will be to negotiate an ongoing level of broadcaster support in the 2021 rights renewal round that broadens the sport's ability to connect with its audiences, whose fandom revolves around live matches. If this cannot be achieved, netball may find itself—like increasing numbers of sports organizations—needing to explore ways to gain control over the medium and the message—as football's Manchester United or basketball's National Basketball Association have done—to fully service the needs of their fans and sponsors.

Leader profile: Kate Buchanan

Kate Buchanan was appointed to her position as corporate and communications manager at the newly formed Southern Steel at the start of the trans-Tasman competition. Her sports journalism background, predominantly with the local newspaper, *The Southland Times*, gave her a finely tuned understanding of the significance of the netball team to the Southland community, and the nose to seek out and leverage good stories. This ability became increasingly important after retrenchments led to the loss of both *Times* sports reporters. Buchanan's Facebook post on November 9, 2017 highlighted the loss of locally sourced media coverage but strategically reinforced the importance of the Steel's social media posts for fans: "Rest assured, we will be doing everything we can to keep you up to date on news from Your Steel—both here and on

Figure 38.1 Kate Buchanan
Photo: Dianne Manson

our Steel website." The impact on regional communities of the increasingly familiar strategies of print media retrenchment was noted by many fans in the discussion thread from Buchanan's post and reinforced the vital social function of providing an outlet for community opinion, as in the post shown in Figure 38.2 on the Steel's Facebook page the next day:

For Buchanan, her role is all about communication and building relationships: the ability to talk to the sponsors, "listen to their stories," and "listen to what they want." She sees this as the starting point through which to broker unique partnerships between the franchise and its sponsors, and engage clients in a more constructive and ultimately rewarding association.

Buchanan is very aware of the need to draw on but also protect the heritage of the franchise, remain "absolutely true to that brand," and to deliver on and off the court for the commercial partners and fan base. For Buchanan, there are two major benefits from having such a loyal, fiercely parochial, and often fanatical fan base. First, despite representing one of New Zealand's most sparsely populated regions, the Steel have the "biggest membership of all the netball franchises in the country" who are rewarded by a remarkable history of

> It's so sad that our local paper is no longer interested in what is happening in our local community. How are we meant to promote all our wonderful sports and not all families have access to computers in their homes. Bye bye to our local sports reporting and promotions. But the biggest questions is what is next are they going to axe, the only news we are going to see is the rest of country we aren't going to court in the end. This is how communities start to loose their identities.

Figure 38.2 The post on the Steel's Facebook page

success. These factors are also a strong drawcard for sponsors, and Buchanan is constantly looking for "money can't buy experiences" to offer them above the usual contractual obligations such as signage, TV partnership exposure, and branding on the uniforms. Contrary to expectations, the termination of the trans-Tasman competition proved to be a boon for sponsors whose prime focus was the local New Zealand audience. Buchanan found that sponsors' most sought-after activity is the chance to interact informally with the Steel players. One year, she enticed one of their major national sponsors to move its franchisee meeting to Dunedin—the first time it had ever been held outside Auckland—to coincide with a Steel home game in the city. The initiative had high client appeal with a southern touch as delegates were the first ever permitted to join the team at Captain's Run, which made them feel "really connected" with the team and concluded the day with another southern experience—a curling competition.

Another major benefit for Buchanan is the fans' willingness to actively engage with the franchise's social media platforms. She solely controls the franchise's Facebook, Instagram, Snapchat, and Twitter accounts in order to maintain a consistently high standard of content and give the pages a "similar voice and feel to them.. In 2017, the Steel Facebook page had a direct following of around 23,000 and a reach of 2.7 million, which increased by nearly 1 million from the previous year. The fans are protective of "their" team and players, and rarely let a negative comment go unchallenged. For Buchanan, this is a "lovely position to be in when you are in marketing." The most time-consuming but successful social media strategy created by Buchanan is saved for the Southern Steel's most devoted fans. Before and after each game, an SMS text message from the coach is sent out by Buchanan individually to approximately 700 VIP members. Despite the high labor cost, the feedback shows the value of creating a sense of a special connection with the coach, which sometimes results in SMS text message replies from fans apologizing if they cannot attend a game. To be able to report to others the content of a coach's SMS text messages is high sporting capital and intimately personalizes the fans' deeply felt affinity with their regional team.

Player engagement at the community level is a crucial element needed to maintain the feeling of ownership and identification between the team and its franchise zone. Buchanan believes an "absolutely vital part of what we do as a franchise" is the execution of a new community engagement plan each season. She takes a leadership role in educating the players about the "commercial realities" of their position so they understand the "investment" each needs to make toward the collective effort of keeping the team relevant and admired within the community. Although player contracts do not require social media engagement, Buchanan provides guidelines and ongoing support. Netball South attributes the high fan turnout for Steel games and the "unwavering support the team generates" to the "400-plus hours the players spend in the community each season" (Netball South, 2016, p. 6). Buchanan's sense of the local community's close engagement is supported by a range of different measures. First is 2017 data gathered by Nielsen's monthly tracker, *Sportslink New Zealand*, which indicates the Steel, at 81%, have the second-largest avid fan share of all club teams in all sports in New Zealand. The second is a 2017 NNZ match satisfaction survey that revealed a high level of approval from the Steel fans, well above usual benchmarks used by Nielsen across all sports (R. Barr, personal communication, January 25, 2018). Television ratings tell a similar story, of higher than expected numbers watching the ANZ Premiership in the southern zone. Finally, Needs' (2017) social media survey found that Steel fans were notable for self-identifying as part of a "community formed online" (Needs, 2017, p. 122). However, Buchanan worries that younger players stepping straight into a professional environment may not have the same understanding of their accountability to the commercial needs of the franchise as those who have straddled the

Figure 38.3 A devoted Southern Steel fan

transition into the professional era. Ultimately, for Buchanan the future success of the Steel will depend on how "we commit to advancing all facets of the franchise while staying true to our values as a team, an organization and a region" (personal communication). The ongoing adherence to these core values is the secret ingredient that she believes makes the franchise unique and will ensure its ongoing success.

Note

1 New Zealand and Australia are geographically separated by the Tasman Sea. Thus, competitions that include teams from both countries are commonly referred to as trans-Tasman leagues.

References

Alderson, A. (2017). Spark and TVNZ tipped to bid for rugby rights. *New Zealand Herald*, November 22. Retrieved from www.nzherald.co.nz/sport/news/article.cfm?c_id=4&objectid=11946689.

Andrew, G. (1997). "A girl's game—and a good one too": A critical analysis of netball. Unpublished Master's thesis, Christchurch, The University of Canterbury.

ANZ Premiership (2017). ANZ Premiership goes global, March 31. Retrieved from http://anzpremiership.co.nz/news/article/anz-premiership-goes-global.

Bidwell, H. (2018). 30 Black Ferns set for professional contracts as New Zealand Rugby agrees to landmark deal. Stuff.co.nz, March 12. Retrieved from https://www.stuff.co.nz/sport/rugby/102181596/30-black-ferns-set-for-professional-contracts-as-new-zealand-rugby-agrees-landmark-deal.

Bruce, T. (2009). Winning space in sport: The Olympics in the New Zealand sports media. In P. Markula (ed.), *Olympic Women and the Media: International perspectives* (pp. 150–167). London: Palgrave Macmillan.

Bruce, T. (2013a). Communication and sport: Reflections on women and femininities. *Communication and Sport*, **1**(1/2), 125–137.

Bruce, T. (2013b). New Zealand. In T. Horky & J.-U. Nieland (eds), *International Sports Press Survey 2011, Sport & Communication*, Vol. 5 (pp. 245–264). Noderstedt, Germany: Books on Demand GMbH.

Charbonneau, J., & Garland, R. (2006). The use of celebrity athletes as endorsers: Views of the New Zealand general public. *International Journal of Sports Marketing and Sponsorship*, **7**(4), 31–38.

Delahunty, E. (2017). Super netball set for final denouement to "overwhelmingly successful" season. *The Guardian*, June 15. Retrieved from https://www.theguardian.com/sport/2017/jun/16/super-netball-set-for-final-denouement-to-overwhelmingly-successful-season.

Dougherty, I. (2004). *Southern Sting: The team that inspired a region*. Titirangi, Auckland: Exisle Publishing.

Egan, B. (2018). Leading Silver Ferns earn a 10th of salary of millionaire All Black Kieran Reid. Stuff.co.nz, January 3. Retrieved from https://www.stuff.co.nz/sport/netball/100028462/semiprofessional-pay-for-professional-play-thats-the-life-of-a-netballer.

Garland, R. & Ferkins, L. (2003). Evaluating New Zealand sport stars as celebrity endorsers: Intriguing results. *ANZMAC 2003 Conference Proceedings 1–3 December* (pp. 122–129). Adelaide: ANZMAC and University of South Australia.

Henley, M. (2004a). Sports media: Our world on their shoulders? In L. Goode & N. Zuberi (eds), *Media Studies in Aotearoa/New Zealand*. Auckland, NZ: Pearson Longman.

Henley, M. (2004b). Going mainstream: Women's televised sport through a case study of the 1999 Netball World Championships. In R. Horrocks & N. Perry (eds), *Television in New Zealand: Programming the Nation*. Melbourne: Oxford University Press.

Henley, M. A. (2012). A whole new ball game: the symbiotic relationship between broadcast media and netball in New Zealand from cinema newsreels to high definition pay television. Unpublished PhD thesis, University of Auckland.

Hickman, A. (2017). "A success on all fronts"—Netball Australia, Nine and Suncorp hand down netball verdict. *AdNews*, June 21. Retrieved from www.adnews.com.au/news/a-success-on-all-fronts-netball-australia-nine-and-suncorp-hand-down-netball-verdict.

Johannsen, D. (2013). Netball strikes a late TV deal. *New Zealand Herald*, March 19. Retrieved from www.nzherald.co.nz/sport/news/article.cfm?c_id=4&objectid=10872087.

Johannsen, D. (2016a). Anatomy of a netball split, *New Zealand Herald*, May 14. Retrieved from www.nzherald.co.nz/sport/news/article.cfm?c_id=4&objectid=11639010.

Johannsen, D. (2016b). Netball NZ should walk away. *New Zealand Herald*, March 1. Retrieved from www.nzherald.co.nz/sport/news/article.cfm?c_id=4&objectid=11598201.

Macdonald, N. (2017). Girls just wanna get paid: Calling time on the undervaluing of women's sport. Stuff.co.nz, September 2. Retrieved from https://www.stuff.co.nz/sport/rugby/96239745/calling-time-on-the-undervaluing-of-womens-sport.

Marfell, A. E. (2011). Netball in the lives of New Zealand women: An intergenerational study. Unpublished Master's thesis. Hamilton, University of Waikato.

Marfell, A. E. (2016). Understanding "the national sport for New Zealand women": A socio-spatial analysis of netball. Unpublished PhD thesis, Hamilton, University of Waikato.

Mason, M. (2016). Nine and Telstra sign Netball Australia broadcast deal. *Sydney Morning Herald*, May 16. Retrieved from www.smh.com.au/business/media-and-marketing/nine-and-telstra-sign-netball-australia-broadcast-deal-20160518-goyknu.html.

Mitchell, B. (2016). Why Netball Australia had to separate from New Zealand to secure dominant future. ESPN.com.au, August 26. Retrieved from www.espn.com.au/netball/story/_/id/15730409/why-netball-australia-was-right-ditch-new-zealand-netball.

Murdock, A. (2013). Netball still looking for TV deal for ANZ Championship. *News Corp Australia Network*, February 10. Retrieved from www.news.com.au/sport/netball/netball-still-looking-for-tv-deal-for-anz-championship/story-fndl0424-1226574513529.

Nauright, J. & Broomhall, J. (1994). A woman's game: the development of netball and a female sporting culture in New Zealand, 1906–70. *The International Journal of the History of Sport*, **11**(3), 387–407.

Needs, B. A. (2017). #welivethisgame: Social media, online communities and the ANZ Netball Championship 2016. Unpublished Master's thesis, Auckland: University of Auckland.

Netball Australia (2009). *Netball Australia Annual Report 2009*. Melbourne, Victoria: Netball Australia. Retrieved from: https://netball.com.au/about-netball-australia/annual-reports.

Netball New Zealand (2016). ANZ backs new NZ netball elite league. *Netball New Zealand*, July 29. Retrieved from www.netballnz.co.nz/news/detail/anz-backs-new-nz-netball-elite-league.

Netball New Zealand (2017). *Ninety-third Annual Report 2017*. Netball New Zealand. Retrieved from https://issuu.com/netballnz/docs/nnz_annual_report_-_2017.

Netball South (2016). *Netball South Annual Report 2016*. Retrieved from https://www.netballsouth.co.nz/images/zones/south/documents/2016/2016-annual-report.pdf.

New Zealand Secondary Schools Sports Council (2017). *NZSSSC Representation Census 2017*. Oakura, NZ: NZSSSC. Retrieved from www.nzsssc.org.nz/school-sport-data/nzsssc-census-reports.

Niall, J. (2015). Netball pays Channel Ten to televise games in ground-breaking deal. *The Sydney Morning Herald*, February 26. Retrieved from www.smh.com.au/sport/netball/netball-pays-channel-ten-to-televise-games-in-groundbreaking-deal-20150226-13q5aj.html.

Pegoraro, A. (2014). Twitter as destructive innovation in sport communication. *Communication & Sport*, **2**(2), 132–137.

Pullar-Strecker, T. (2016). Sky TV lines up rights for new NZ netball league for next five years. Stuff.co.nz, May 19. Retrieved from https://www.stuff.co.nz/business/industries/80163561/Sky-TV-lines-up-rights-for-new-NZ-netball-league-for-next-five-years.

Pullar-Strecker, T. (2017). Sky TV loses 33,880 satellite subscribers. Stuff.co.nz, August 22. Retrieved from https://www.stuff.co.nz/business/industries/96015124/Sky-TV-loses-33-880-satellite-subscribers.

Russell, K. (2007). Queers, even in netball? In C. C. Aitchison (ed.), *Sport and Gender Identities* (pp. 106–212). New York: Routledge.

Sport New Zealand (2015). *Sport and Active Recreation in the Lives of New Zealand Adults: 2013/14 Active New Zealand survey results*. Wellington: Sport New Zealand.

Tagg, B. (2014a). Changing hegemonic masculinities in men's netball. *Sport in Society*, **17**(6), 689–705.

Tagg, B. (2014b). Men's netball or gender-neutral netball? *International Review for the Sociology of Sport*, **51**(3), https://doi.org/10.1177/1012690214524757.

Taylor, T. (2001a). Gendering sport: the development of netball in Australia. *Sporting Traditions*, **18**(1), 57–74.

Taylor, T. (2001b). Netball in Australia: A social history. In A. J. Veal (ed.), *Working Paper No. 2* (pp. 1–20). Sydney: School of Leisure, Sport and Tourism, University of Technology.

Thompson, P. A. (2017). Pie in the sky? The political economy of the failed Vodafone–Sky merger. *MEDIANZ*, **17**(1), 28–73.

Treagus, M. (2005). Playing like ladies: basketball, netball and feminine restraint. *International Journal of the History of Sport*, **22**(1), 88–105.

Vann, P. (2014). Changing the game: The role of social media in overcoming old media's attention deficit toward women's sport. *Journal of Broadcasting & Electronic Media*, **58**(3), 438–455.

Vann, P., Woodford, D., & Bruns, A. (2015). Social media and niche sports: The Netball ANZ Championship and Commonwealth Games on Twitter *Media International Australia*, **155**(1), 108–119.

39
Deserving of attention
Traditional media coverage and the use of social media by female athletes with disabilities

Erin McNary and Michael Cottingham

Imagine being a woman having just competed in the largest mega sporting event contest in the world, the Paralympics. Then, imagine winning a medal! A reporter walks up to you with a line of questioning that begins with asking how you were able to have children or how you ended up in a wheelchair with no mention of your major accomplishment: winning a medal at the Paralympics. Although this does not occur all the time, many times this is a narrative created by the media for a female athlete with a disability. The emphasis becomes less about athletic achievement and more about the athlete being a woman or disabled.

Other chapters in this handbook have provided insightful information about various aspects of women in the sport industry, including media portrayals of athletes. This chapter examines media coverage of female athletes with disabilities who compete at a national and/or international level. Women face unique challenges as it pertains to sport media coverage, and female athletes with disabilities face these same challenges along with others such as less media coverage, discriminatory narratives, and reduction of performance compared with their male counterparts. The scholarly research is limited in this area, which suggests the need to further examine present-day depictions of these athletes. Much of the research focuses on that of Paralympic athletes with very few articles specific to women who compete in Paralympic events. Individuals with a wide range of physical disabilities compete in various levels of sport, but little research exists outside of elite competition. The last part of the chapter provides specific examples of how female athletes with disabilities overcome some of the challenges posed by limited media coverage and use social media to their advantage to further promote their brand and strengthen fan followings.

Framing of athletes with disabilities

In the United States, researchers have identified two major paradigms to study athletes with disabilities. The first is the "medical" model, in which disability is viewed as a deficit or a condition that needs to be cured (Barnes & Mercer, 1996). In essence, the person with a disability is broken, or at least not whole. The second framework centers on the idea that the disability should be viewed as a social construct (Hughes & Paterson, 1997). Instead of modifying the person or addressing their perceived condition, this model suggests considering disability no differently from other demographic characteristics. Rather than "fixing" the disability, we should simply modify the environment to make it more inclusive. For example, the spinal cord injury is not the issue; the use of stairs rather than a ramp is what needs to be fixed. When an environment is modified, the impact of a disability becomes nullified.

As the medical model, which focuses on disability as a deficit, is our primary frame of reference, society tends to view people with disabilities—and in turn, athletes with disabilities—as automatically inferior to able-bodied people. The medical model has promoted the inspirational, supercrip image as the primary media presentation of athletes with disabilities (Silva & Howe, 2012). A "supercrip" is a person with a disability who is perceived as constantly having to "overcome" her disability every time she succeeds. Her ability to perform even menial tasks is viewed as an "inspiration" to able-bodied people who view disability as an inherently insurmountable deficit. In short, the athlete seems to exist only as an object of inspiration to the able-bodied audience, rather than simply as a competitive athlete. Although the supercrip image may seem complimentary, the impact is that the media often do not seriously cover an athlete's scores, results, times, and accomplishments. Instead, it becomes preoccupied with the disability itself and uses coverage time to retell the story of how the athlete acquired the disability in the first place, even if this occurred decades before. The overworked tale of inspiration ignores the fact that main goal of athletes with disabilities is not to inspire spectators; they are doing so to engage in competition at the highest levels, for prize money, sponsorships, and the thrill of the sport.

The predominance of the supercrip image presents a serious challenge for promoters of disability sport because of the fact that promoting the inspirational stories rather than the scores and athletic accomplishments sells, at least for new spectators (Cottingham, Byon, Chatfield, & Carroll, 2013; Cottingham, Carroll, Phillips, Karadakis, Gearity, & Drane, 2014). For women, this quandary is not lost on athletes with disabilities who are frustrated with being promoted as inspirational stories and sexually objectified (Hargreaves & Hardin, 2009). These athletes understand that the very images and presentations that produce funding also devalue their accomplishments to society. Disability sports promoters have elected to walk a narrow line of using the inspirational supercrip trope to draw people to the sport while attempting at the same time to refocus the spectators' attention on the participants' athleticism (Cottingham, Gearity, & Byon, 2013).

Characterizations of women athletes with disabilities

Historically, women athletes have been characterized in the media as "other" and challenging to stereotypical representations through a hegemonic masculine lens (Duncan, 1990; Messner, 1988). Sport has typically been reserved for heterosexual, able-bodied males (Hardin & Hardin, 2003). Hegemonic masculinity asserts that women exist in positions below men and masculine qualities such as heterosexuality, aggression, and assertiveness are the most accepted in sport in western society (Connell, 1990). Hughes (2009) summarizes historical coverage from this viewpoint by saying "strong, well-formed, non-disabled, masculine body is the benchmark and against this benchmark a woman is found wanting and a disabled person—man or woman—is weak and vulnerable" (Hughes, 2009, p. 400). There are similarities between the media coverage of males and females with disabilities. However, as sport is gendered in nature (Hums, 2016), women with disabilities are covered by the media through the gendered lens first. This is further compounded by the fact that women make up a smaller proportion of people with disabilities than men do. The gender imbalance is true regardless of whether disabilities are caused by traumatic (National Spinal Cord Injury Statistical Center [NSCISC], 2016) or non-traumatic injuries (Center for Disease Control and Prevention [CDC], 2016; Myotonic Dystrophy Foundation, 2017).

The intersection of gender and disability challenges widely accepted notions about sport where the media have framed content. Ashton-Shaeffer, Gibson, Autry, and Hanson (2001) noted the same issues that women without disabilities face in our society are also experienced by people with disabilities. This means that women athletes with disabilities must experience oppression both for being female and for being disabled, a double oppression. Women athletes are clearly aware of this, and they express frustration about being disrespected by the non-disabled community but also by the male disability sport community (Cottingham, Hums, Jeffress, Lee, & Richard, 2018; Hargreaves & Hardin, 2009). When issues of condescension and de-legitimization of athletic accomplishments are directed at an athlete due to gender and disability, athletes find unique ways to address this.

For example, consider the story of Hope Lewellen, a former top 10 wheelchair tennis player and Paralympic Silver medalist known for her fearless forehand and outstanding chair skills. When she was competing in the early 1990s through the mid-2000s she had to battle social stigmas of being a Mexican–American female athlete with a disability, as well as identifying as a lesbian. Understanding this, Lewellen embraced the attention, developing her fearless game style and confident court presence, attracting photographers by shaving her head and dyeing her hair bright yellow, the shade of a new tennis ball. Although her on-court skills should have been enough to garner media attention, Lewellen understood that the media would focus on her inspirational story and her challenge to traditional femininity rather than just her fearless court presence. She was able to parlay her efforts into being a focal point of the limited but valuable coverage CBS provided on the 1996 Paralympic games. As expected, the media attention was problematic, with minimal attention focused on her on-court performance and a substantive focus on the supercrip narrative (Schell & Rodriguez, 2001). A keen observer could see Lewellen actively challenging this dogma. She understood that coverage was important for an industry struggling for sponsors and audience attention. According to Schell and Rodriguez, her efforts produced a presentation "of her disabled athletic body as representing a freedom from, or transcendence over, the female body and its stereotypes of weakness, passivity, and dependence" (Schell & Rodriguez, 2001, p. 131). Lewellen's efforts to promote herself, advance her sport, and work within the framework that society held disability sport were admirable. Now, female athletes with disabilities have unique mechanisms to combat the social stigmas, those of social media. This provides athletes more control of their image and their athletic framing, and is addressed later in the chapter.

Paralympic Games and coverage of athletes with disabilities

The Paralympics are commonly noted as the second largest sporting event in the world. The Paralympic Games feature athletes with a physical impairment. The first Paralympic Games took place in Rome, Italy in 1960. Individuals trained and certified by the International Paralympic Committee (IPC) classify Paralympic athletes using a series of three questions: (1) Does the athlete have an eligible impairment for this sport? (2) Does the athlete's eligible impairment meet the minimum disability criteria of the sport? (3) Which sport class describes the athlete's activity limitation most accurately? Many times, athletes are classified repeatedly throughout their careers depending on the nature of their impairment and medical advances surrounding the condition (Paralympic Movement, 2018).

Held at the same facilities and following the Olympic Games, the Paralympic Games represent the pinnacle of disability sport competition. With over 150 countries competing in the 2017 Summer Rio Paralympic Games—often to sold-out crowds—the best athletes in the world are truly on display. The Games also represent divergent views of how disability sport should be presented. Beacom, French, and Kendall (2016) note the complexity of the Paralympic Games presentation. For example, host nations often use the Paralympic Games to educate the public on disability. Media outlets struggle with promoting sports that the public may not have previous exposure to, and sponsors want to affiliate with feel-good stories that, at times, cross over into inspirational objectification. Until recently, the Paralympic Games received minimal television coverage in the United States. This started to change with the XX Games, and media coverage continues to increase (PyeongChang, 2018a). Although more media attention is valuable, the coverage has not frequently been aired on NBC's most viewed stations. However, streaming opportunities have become one of the greatest advancements the Paralympic Games have seen, causing an increase in promotion and viewership with an active YouTube channel, the NBC Sports App, and streaming through the NBC website. The Paralympic Games can now be seen by the millions of fans seeking them out. NBC's coverage of the Summer 2017 Rio Paralympics increased to more than 70 hours across NBC's network and sports app, compared with just six hours of coverage for the London Paralympics (Whiteside, 2016).

It is reasonable to assume that the strides made in viewership of the Paralympics is due in large part to the two-way communication social media allow. According to the IPC, the Rio Olympics set a record for the most watched games and saw a global audience increase of 7% when compared with the London 2012 Paralympic Games (Paralympic Media Centre, 2017). A brief review of scholarly literature on Paralympic coverage shows the evolution of the Paralympic Games in the media. Schantz and Gilbert (2001) described the media coverage of the games as problematic and objectifying. Golden (2003) described the newsroom from the 2002 Paralympics as relatively empty. Howe (2008) believed the quality of coverage was due at least in part to the lack of disability in the Paralympic newsrooms. The sport coverage now more reflects the nationalism that is common in Olympic coverage (Bruce, 2014). In short, coverage of the Games was an echo chamber of able-bodiedness with a lack of understanding on how to adequately cover athletes with a disability. In addition, many of these reporters have been male, so there is a double layer of lack of empathy in both of these areas.

A new era of technology and social media has enabled athletes' direct access to their fan base as well as other individuals with disabilities. Paralympic medalist Amy Purdy has spoken about the lack of coverage of Paralympians when she first had an amputation of both legs below the knees at age 19. Now, at age 38, she is able to connect with young athletes going through similar feelings that she experienced when she lost her legs. Purdy said this of the most current Olympics: "I was watching the Olympics and I think there's more Paralympic athletes being represented than Olympic athletes in the advertising campaigns" (Williams, 2018, para. 5). She has also embedded herself in American pop culture appearing on "Dancing with the Stars," a popular dance show in the United States, as well as "The Amazing Race," a successful television show in the United States. These appearances bring awareness and provide a platform for Purdy to serve as a role model for other individuals with disabilities.

With more two-way communication, stakeholders such as the IPC have been able to leverage fans to communicate their concerns with not only the amount of coverage but also the quality of coverage and the way disability is presented (Beacom et al., 2016). However, it should be noted that the issues of an inspirational frame rather than one of athleticism have not gone away. Rather than focusing on the quality of the athleticism or the intensity of the competition, Gary Zenkel, president of NBC Olympics, was quoted as saying, "There is arguably no event in the world more inspiring than the Paralympics, and it's our privilege to tell the captivating stories of these world-class athletes" (NBC, 2018, para. 3). With well-intended but problematic framing of the Games, spectators and fans engaging online and through social media will need to work with athletes to continue to educate formal media outlets on the Paralympic Games and the value of disability sport.

Female athletes competing in the Paralympic Games

Although Title IX has encouraged participation in sport by girls and women, and the numbers are increasing, female Paralympians are still not privy to the same number of events or participation numbers as their male Paralympian counterparts (University of Michigan Sharp Center/Women's Sports Foundation, 2013). In the 2017 Rio de Janeiro Summer Olympic Games, women were outnumbered 2,657 to 1,671. However, in the 2020 Tokyo Olympics, 1,756 slots will be available to women, which is a 17% increase from the 2012 London Olympics (BBC Sport, 2017). The IPC President, Sir Philip Craven, said, "We wanted to increase the number of slots for female athletes and athletes with high support needs" (BBC Sport, 2017, para. 4). There are barriers of entry for many wanting to participate in sport, which is even more true in para sport, especially when examining gender equity among wealthy countries and lesser-financed countries. More developed nations tend to be the countries offering greater access to individuals with disabilities (University of Michigan Sharp Center/Women's Sports Foundation, 2013).

Several studies have examined the Paralympic Games, although few have examined the media coverage of Paralympic women athletes explicitly. As stated in a report by University of Michigan's Sharp Center/Women's Sport Foundation (2013), in the 2012 London Paralympic Games, the top 5 delegations by number of women included China (128), Great Britain (113), United States (94), Australia (71), and Brazil (68). Few researchers from these respective countries have examined the media coverage of Paralympians. Female Paralympians must be studied independently of their male counterparts given the gendered nature of sport. In a study focused on *The New York Times*, Tynedal and Wolbring (2013) found there was minimal coverage of Paralympians, and the stereotype of supercrip or suffering entity was perpetuated. The reality is that females with disabilities have received the most coverage during years in which a Paralympic Games takes place. With that being said, research focuses on overall coverage of the Paralympic Games, not specifically taking into account race, gender, sexual orientation, etc., which highlights a gap in the literature.

Financial concerns for women athletes with disabilities

As female athletes, especially those with a disability, are under-represented in media coverage, fewer marketing and sponsorship opportunities exist. There are specific challenges in promotion and sponsorship along with the fact that disability sports receive disproportionate and lesser resources (Cottingham, Vineyard, Velasco, & Asias, 2017). In contrast, it has been noted that disability sport is expensive. For example, think of an athlete competing on a national rugby wheelchair team. Travel expenses include transportation and lodging as well as meal expenses and competition-associated costs. Costs for a rugby wheelchair can range from US$2,000 to US$3,000 for a chair that will last only a few years due to the nature of physical contact in the sport. Some athletes receive financial support via their sponsors, which helps to offset these costs, but some do not. For those whom do not receive the same level of support, these athletes must find alternate ways to build their brand.

Women athletes with disabilities' use of social media

Social media platforms (SMPs) have the potential to build the brand of an athlete and potentially generate interest from a company looking for athletes to sponsor. SMPs also serve as a way to garner and increase fandom. Although, on the surface, it seems that female athletes with disabilities may benefit from social media, it must be noted that this is still an area of research that needs attention. For example, marketing and sponsorship approaches have not evolved to the same extent for athletes with disabilities as they have for able-bodied athletes. In a study of wheelchair athletes, it was revealed that most athletes were not successfully developing their online presence and not capitalizing on the opportunities that social media outlets provide in terms of building the brand of the athlete (Cottingham et al., 2017). The authors speculated that the lack of this online presence was due to fewer resources and limited knowledge on how to effectively build their individual brand using SMPs. With this finding, more research, focus, and attention should be directed toward developing strategies that assist athletes with disabilities in branding themselves via an effective social media campaign. Many women Paralympic athletes are proactively engaged and successful at building their brands, and the next section highlights some of these athletes.

Tatyana McFadden is a US wheelchair-racing Paralympian who has won seven gold, seven silver, and three bronze medals in various Games, which include Athens 2004, Beijing 2008, London 2012, Sochi 2014, and Rio de Janeiro 2016. She has also won 20 medals in multiple World Championships participating in Track and Field in 2006, 2011, 2013, and 2017, Marathon in 2015, and Nordic in 2015. She has also served as an advocate for equal access for people with disabilities. She uses social media, especially Twitter, to talk about her athletic career, and she has a website, which details her accomplishments and includes various sections, including one thanking her sponsors. McFadden says, "We're on the cusp of breaking the barriers for Paralympic sport. It has taken a lot of hard work and dedication, trying to teach society what it means to a Paralympian, that we're not any different, that we're just like the Olympians, with the same training sites, sponsorships, medal and venues" (Whiteside, 2016, para. 12). However, it must be noted that there is a difference for money given to the winner of an Olympic medal versus a Paralympic medal. For example, gold medals are worth US$5,000 for Paralympians whereas Olympians receive US$25,000 (Garcia, 2016). It is the same for silver medals, which are worth US$15,000 for Olympians and just US$3,000 for Paralympians, as well as bronze medals worth US$10,000 for Olympians and US$2,000 for Paralympians (Garcia, 2016). Similarly, the purse money is less for major marathons. In 2018, the payout for Desiree Linden, the first American woman to win the Boston Marathon since 1985, was US$150,000, whereas the payout for Tatyana McFadden, winner of the women's push rim wheelchair, was US$20,000 (D'Andrea, 2018). There is a disparity in payouts, stressing the fact that more media attention needs to be afforded to the athletes that would incentivize sponsors to increase their support.

Kelly Cartwright, an Australian World Champion and 2012 London Paralympic gold (long jump) and silver medalist (100-meter sprint), uses Facebook and Instagram as platforms to share her sporting experiences and personal life. Her Instagram account has generated over 26,500 followers. She was diagnosed with a rare form of cancer at age 15 and faced with the difficult decision of having her leg amputated, and has shared her personal journey. She frequently posts about training for competition as well as being a mother. Serving as a cancer advocate, she has taken on motivational speaking roles collaborating with Rare Cancers Australia. This is documented on her social media platforms. Her other partners include Tradie Workwear, an Australian-designed underwear and workwear company. Cartwright is also sponsored by Reebok and has appeared in their #BeMoreHuman campaign, Reebok's largest women's campaign empowering women and encouraging positive change for oneself. The campaign features several women from the sport and entertainment sectors. Although many of these women have crafted successful brand-building social media campaigns, data needs to be collected to assess the impact of using SMPs and outcomes achieved.

The IPC's digital media guidelines (IPC, 2017)

Although many competitions do not restrict social media posts, it must be noted that. during a time period surrounding Paralympic competition, athletes like Cartwright must be aware of the IPC social media guidelines. The organization has encouraged athletes to have a social media presence but cautioned athletes at the same time. Through athletes' online presence, they hope to generate more attention for the IPC. However, there are restrictions on what can and cannot be posted during Olympic competition. According to the IPC's digital media guidelines (PyeongChang, 2018b, p. 3), athletes can:

- Use social media to share your experience;
- Post information directly relating to your performance;
- Answer questions from the media via social channels;
- Upload video that is not live stream and does not show the competition.

The document states that athletes cannot:

- Commercialize posts;
- Publicize sponsors;
- Show moving images of competition, e.g., races, matches, games, etc.;
- Live stream video from venues;
- Share private information about fellow athletes;
- Film in the Residential Zone, except for your own private athlete accommodation.

These guidelines exist because of Rule 40, which was created to protect Olympic sponsors who spend millions of dollars in sponsorship dollars. Chris Chavez, a *Sports Illustrated* journalist who covers track and field, marathons, and the Olympics, wrote about the intricacies of social media relating to athlete sponsorships and how Rule 40 means no unofficial sponsors can associate with the Olympics on any social media platforms (Chavez, 2016). This could pose challenges to a woman athlete with a disability if she wants to thank or credit her sponsors for supporting her journey to the games. For example, if the Reebok #BeMoreHuman campaign would have launched around the time of Olympic competition and Reebok was not an Olympic Partner, then Cartwright would not be allowed to share videos or information at certain points during the Paralympic competition or thank any unofficial sponsors that supported her journey.

The future

Even in the most recent media coverage of the Paralympic Games, there has been criticism. Legendary Paralympian, Louise Sauvage, who won one gold medal and two silver medals at the 2000 Sydney Paralympics, says this about Australian news coverage:

> Any athlete [Paralympian or Olympian] who is competing at the highest level of their chosen sport deserves the recognition for all the hard work they have gone through to get

the results they achieve. We have come such a long way in terms of public awareness and education about sport for athletes with disabilities. Why are we taking a step back with this very woeful coverage?

(Spits, 2018, paras. 8 and 9)

The Canadian Paralympic Team is hoping to capitalize on sharing unique stories. Andrew Greenlaw, senior director of sponsorship at Canadian Imperial Bank of Commerce (CIBC), a sponsor of the Canadian Paralympic Team since 2013, believes the Paralympic Games are a platform that serve to shift societal perceptions of disability. He says, "These athletes are a great visual representation. From a marketing perspective, storytelling is our greatest asset" (Dembe, 2018, para. 9). More national teams should share unique stories and continue educating athletes on strategies to engage in SMPs and increase awareness of the competition to help grow fandom around Paralympic competitions.

As professors in the field of sport management, it is our hope that, when we ask this question in class, "Who knows about the Paralympics?" every student raises their hand. Then, if we ask a follow-up question, "Can you name some famous Paralympians?," we would then engage in a lively discussion about some of the influential women discussed in this chapter. As discussed in the chapter, several current and former women athletes are paving the way for future athletes with disabilities so that they may successfully train and compete at their desired level of competition. Work needs to continue to positively represent marginalized athletes in the media, especially women athletes competing in disability sport. With more media exposure comes more recognition and increased opportunities for sponsorship as well as growing fandom of athletes and para sports. Athletes with a disability should also continue storytelling via streaming and SMPs to increase their exposure and share their uniqueness in the sporting world. It is our hope that, with the continuation of media exposure, continued use of SMPs by disability sport organizations at the national and international levels, and individual athlete SMP usage, more attention will be directed to women athletes with disabilities at all levels of sporting competition.

Leader profile: Alana Nichols

Another example of an athlete using social media is Alana Nichols. She is a three-time Paralympic gold medalist; she represented the United States in basketball, sprint-kayaking, and alpine skiing, taking home a gold medal in wheelchair basketball, as well as three golds, a silver, and a bronze in skiing. Nichols serves on the board at espnW, the Women's Sports Foundation, and the Christopher and Dana Reeve Foundation. She has also earned three nominations for ESPY Awards (Excellence in Sports Performance Yearly) in the category of female athlete with a disability. As remarkable as her accomplishments are, the way in which Nichols has developed her brand and utilized the role social media plays in that brand is equally impressive.

Nichols manages all her social media efforts and much of her self-promotion. She is admittedly not comfortable with the present-day selfie culture, but has come to embrace the need for it:

> Pictures with my face just get more interaction, so I have had to get comfortable with it. I have worked to find authentic ways of presenting myself. I like to share advocacy work, but to get that across I often need to attach an engaging photo.

Her guiding principal in selecting photos, however, is to post only what her grandmother is comfortable seeing: "She is my biggest supporter, and it's a good guide for me to reflect on."

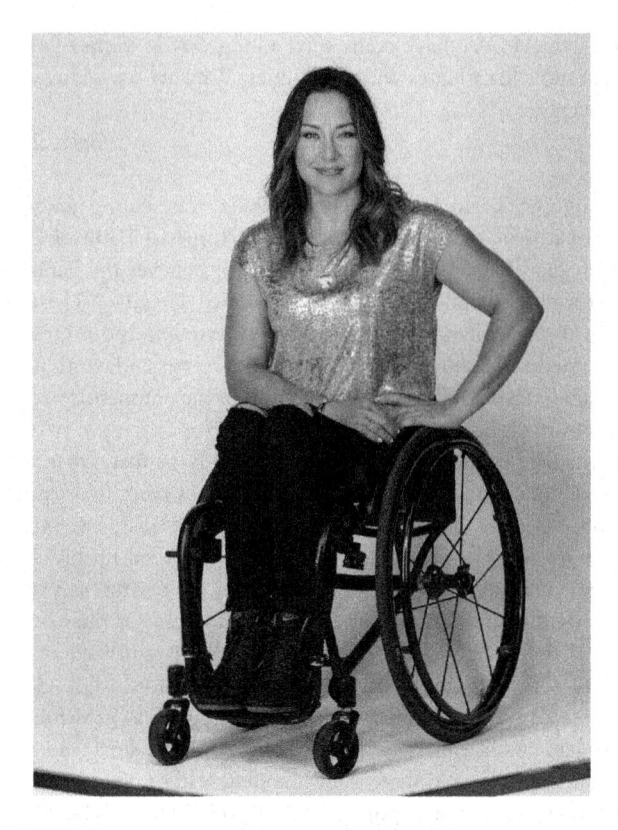

Figure 39.1 Alana Nichols

Her branding, therefore, has caused her to eschew opportunities such as ESPN's Body Issue and more provocative media promotions, instead focusing on what she refers to as an "authentic presentation."

Nichols strives to show an authentic view of what she believes is self-love and beauty. She believes that this image is, in part, a strong capable woman in a wheelchair. Some may be unaccustomed to this depiction, and Nichols is keenly aware that those who follow her and engage with her on social media are at different points in their understanding of what she does and who she is. She addresses these in what she refers to as layers. In the images she chooses to share with the world, certain layers of her image may strike people in different ways. For example, Nichols would be naive to deny that some people engage with her on social media partly because she is a highly photogenic and beautiful woman. She also understands that an inspirational element may be present in her imagery simply because being in a wheelchair may inherently invoke inspiration among others. Still, the images she chooses to promote herself are designed to actively feature power, athleticism, strength, and performance.

This model of effective self-promotion, coupled with her passion for helping people with disabilities get active, ties in nicely with Nichols' personal mantra of, "Do the best you can with what you have, right now!" When asked to confirm this quote in a message, Nichols always included an exclamation point. Her enthusiasm, however, is clearly channeled towards meaningful advertising, because she is selective in what she shares: "I don't share every story that comes across Google news about me, but if it promotes people being active with disabilities, I do."

Admittedly, there are substantial challenges that come with managing her brand. Disability sport is a small community, and Nichols has a number of publics to consider, including those within the community, corporate sponsors, fans, curious casual onlookers, the United States Paralympic Committee, and those in her personal circle. Although the disability sport community wants her to be an advocate for athletics and elite athleticism, the mainstream media often pressure her for an inspirational angle. Although she knows the camera angle has to be different for a wheelchair user, Nichols' "angle" has more to do with her athletic mindset than the cliché inspirational backstory that the mainstream media would rather gobble up. To that end, she has gotten crafty at redirecting interviews to better focus on how she truly wants to represent her brand:

> I used to give them what they wanted, but now I am able to help them [those conducting interviews] to see beyond the challenges to focus on an athlete mindset. To help them look at the facts, to how well I or other athletes are executing.

References

Ashton-Shaeffer, C., Gibson, H. J., Autry, C. E., & Hanson, C. S. (2001). Meaning of sport to adults with physical disabilities: A disability sport camp experience. *Sociology of Sport Journal*, **18**(1), 95–114.

Barnes, C. & Mercer, G. (eds) (1996). *Exploring the Divide: Illness and disability*. Leeds: Disability Press.

BBC Sport (2017). 2020 Paralympics to feature more female athletes than any previous Games, September 4. Retrieved from www.bbc.com/sport/disability-sport/41149890.

Beacom, A., French, L., & Kendall, S. (2016). Reframing impairment? Continuity and change in media representations of disability through the Paralympic Games. *International Journal of Sport Communication*, **9**(1), 42–62.

Bruce, T. (2014). Us and them: The influence of discourses of nationalism on media coverage of the Paralympics. *Disability & Society*, **29**(9), 1443–1459.

Center for Disease Control and Prevention (2016). Data and Statistics for Cerebral Palsy, May 2. Retrieved from https://www.cdc.gov/ncbddd/cp/data.html.

Chavez, C. (2016). What is rule 40? The IOC rule on non-Olympic sponsors, explained. *Sports Illustrated*. Retrieved from https://www.si.com/olympics/2016/07/27/rule-40-explained-2016-olympic-sponsorship-blackout-controversy.

Connell, R. W. (1990). An iron man: The body and some contradictions of hegemonic masculinity. In M. A. Messner & D. F. Sabo (eds) *Sport. Men, and the Gender Order: Critical feminist perspectives* (pp. 83–114). Champaign, IL: Human Kinetics.

Cottingham, M. P., Byon, K., Chatfield, S., & Carroll, M. (2013). Examining the influence of relationship to disability on the motivations of wheelchair basketball spectators. *Disability Studies Quarterly*, **33**(3). http://dx.doi.org/10.18061/dsq.v33i3.3345.

Cottingham, M., Carroll, M. S., Phillips, D., Karadakis, K., Gearity, B. T., & Drane, D. (2014). Development and validation of the motivation scale for disability sport consumption. *Sport Management Review*, **17**(1), 49–64.

Cottingham, M., Gearity, B., & Byon, K. (2013). A qualitative examination of disability sport executives' perceptions of sport promotion and the acquisition of sponsors. *Sport Marketing Quarterly*, **22**(2), 92–101.

Cottingham, M., Hums, M., Jeffress, M., Lee, D., & Richard, H. (2018). Women of power soccer: exploring disability and gender in the first competitive team sport for powerchair users. *Sport in Society*, 1–14.

Cottingham, M., Vineyard, A., Velasco, F., & Asias, B. (2017). Meeting expenses of Wheelchair rugby: Strategies employed to procure funding and promotion by teams and Players. *Palaestra*, **31**(1).

D'Andrea, Ch. (2018). How much did Des Linden and Yuki Kawauchi earn for winning the 2018 Boston marathon?, April 16. Retrieved from https://www.sbnation.com/2018/4/16/17243356/boston-marathon-prize-money-2018-des-linden-yuki-kawauchi-earn-win.

Dembe, J. (2018). Struggle with Paralympic exposure in Canada nothing new, March 10. Retrieved from www.cbc.ca/sports/paralympics/struggle-with-paralympic exposure-in-canada-nothing-new-1.4565864

Duncan, M. C. (1990). Sport photographs and sexual differences: Images of women and men in the 1984 and 1988 Olympic games. *Sociology of Sport Journal*, **7**, 22–43

Garcia, A. (2016). Paralympians gold medals are worth less than those of Olympians. Retrieved from https://money.cnn.com/2016/09/02/news/paralympians-medals-worth-less/index.html.

Golden, A. (2003). An analysis of the dissimilar coverage of the 2002 Olympics and Paralympics. *Disabilities Studies Quarterly*, **23**(3/4).

Hardin, B. & Hardin, M. (2003). Conformity and conflict: Wheelchair athletes discuss sport media. *Adapted Physical Activity Quarterly*, **20**(3), 246–259.

Hargreaves, J. A. & Hardin, B. (2009). Women wheelchair athletes: Competing against media stereotypes. *Disability Studies Quarterly*, **29**(2). Retrieved from www.dsq-sds.org/article/view/920/1095.

Howe, P. D. (2008). From inside the newsroom: Paralympic media and the production of elite disability. *International Review for the Sociology of Sport*, **43**(2), 135–150.

Hughes, B. (2009). Wounded/monstrous/abject: A critique of the disabled body in the sociological imaginary. *Disability and Society*, **24**, 399–410.

Hughes, B. & Paterson, K. (1997). The social model of disability and the disappearing body: Towards a sociology of impairment. *Disability & Society*, **12**(3), 325–340.

Hums, M.A. (2016). Women with disabilities in sport. In E. Staurowsky, *Women in Sport: From liberation to celebration*. Champaign, IL: Human Kinetics.

International Paralympic Committee (IPC) (2017). IPC digital media guidelines. Retrieved from https://www.paralympic.org/sites/default/files/document/120208111714089_2011_11_24_IPC_Social_Media_Guidelines_FINAL_update.pdf.

Messner, M. A. (1988). Sport and male domination: The female athlete as contested ideological terrain, *Sociology of Sport*, **5**(3), 197–211.

Myotonic Dystrophy Foundation (2017). Types of DM. Retrieved from www.myotonic.org/node/181.

National Spinal Cord Injury Statistical Center (2016). *Facts and Figures at a Glance*. Birmingham, AL: University of Alabama at Birmingham.

NBC (2018). Olympics to present unprecedented 94 hours of Paralympic television coverage in march, January 29. Retrieved from https://www.teamusa.org/News/2018/January/29/NBC-Olympics-To-Present-Unprecedented-94-Hours-Of-Paralympic-Television-Coverage-In-March.

Paralympic Media Centre (2017). Rio 2016 Paralympics smash all TV viewing records, March 16. Retrieved from https://www.paralympic.org/news/rio-2016-paralympics-smash-all-tv-viewing-records.

Paralympic Movement (2018). Paralympic Classification. Retrieved from https://www.paralympic.org/classification.

PyeongChang (2018a). NBC announces Paralympic coverage, February 2. Retrieved from https://www.paralympic.org/news/pyeongchang-2018-nbc-announces-paralympic-coverage.

PyeongChang (2018b). Social and Digital Media Guide. Retrieved from https://www.paralympic.org/sites/default/files/document/171019144643083_2017_08_25+IPC+Social+and+Digital+Media+Guidelines+FINAL.pdf.

Schantz, O. J. & Gilbert, K. (2001). An ideal misconstrued: Newspaper coverage of the Atlanta Paralympic Games in France and Germany. *Sociology of Sport Journal*, **18**(1), 69–94.

Schell, L. A. & Rodriguez, S. (2001). Subverting bodies/ambivalent representations: Media Analysis of Paralympian, Hope Lewellen. *Sociology of Sport*, **18**, 127–135.

Silva, C. F. & Howe, P. D. (2012). The (in) validity of supercrip representation of Paralympian athletes. *Journal of Sport and Social Issues*, **36**(2), 174–194.

Spits, S. (2018). "They should be all over the media right now": Seven to task for Paralympics coverage, March 14. Retrieved from https://www.smh.com.au/sport/they-should-be-all over-the-media-right-now-seven-taken-to-task-for-paralympics-coverage-20180314-p4z4dj.html.

Tynedal, J. & Wolbring, G. (2013). Paralympics and its athletes through the lens of the *New York Times*. *Sports*, **1**(1), 13–36.

University of Michigan Sharp Center/Women's Sports Foundation (2013). Women in the Olympic and Paralympic games: An analysis of participation and leadership opportunities, April. Retrieved from http://sharp.research.umich.edu/wp-content/uploads/2017/03/olympic_report_2012_final-4-11-13.pdf https://www.paralympic.org/rio-2016.

Whiteside, K. (2016). A Paralympian races to remove obstacles for the next generation. *The New York Times*, September 1. Retrieved from https://www.nytimes.com/2016/09/04/sports/olympics/paralympics-tatyana-mcfadden-wheelchair.html.

Williams, D. (2018). Increased interest in Paralympic games shines a light on athletes, March 6. Retrieved from https://www.teamusa.org/News/2018/March/06/Increased-Interest-In-Paralympic-Games-Shines-A-Light-On-Athletes.

40
Sport, sponsors, and sponsor fit
Media presentations of Norwegian women athletes in Olympic events

Elsa Kristiansen, Birgit Andrine Apenes Solem, and Mikael Lagerborg

Introduction

The day before the first cross-country ski event at the 2014 Sochi Winter Olympic Games, the brother of one of the Norwegian Olympic women skiers died. The following day this athlete did not compete, but, that day, all Norwegian female cross-country skiers wore black mourning bands in honor of, and in support for, their teammate's brother. This collective spirit deeply moved the Norwegian people, but not the International Olympic Committee (IOC)—who sent a letter to the Norwegian Olympic Committee of the IOC to complain about these athletes' breaking regulations with "political protest." The following public debate damaged the IOC's popularity in Norway, because few were left untouched by the emotional (and tearful) collective spirit of the women's cross-country team, which was given much attention in the media (Figure 40.1).

In this chapter, we compare how women athletes were portrayed in the media during the Youth Olympic Games (YOG) and the Olympic Games (OG), and discuss how these presentations impacted sponsors of the female athletes (as teams) in terms of the sponsors' brand values. The OG are well known, but YOG events have received limited media coverage (Hanstad, Parent, & Kristiansen, 2013) and there is minimal public awareness regarding the YOG (Judge et al., 2015). The IOC and local hosts of the YOG events—Singapore in 2010, Innsbruck in 2012, Nanjing in 2014, and Lillehammer in 2016—use social media to target stakeholders. The YOG received more attention after the 2014 and 2016 OG (Yoon, 2017), but, compared with the OG, the media coverage of YOG continues to be minimal.

We focus on *cross-country skiing* and *handball* and compare both amount and content of *media presentations* from *four* events:

- Handball, with a focus on media representation of women athletes during the 2014 Nanjing Summer YOG and the 2016 Brazil Summer OG;
- Cross-country skiing with a focus on media representation of women athletes during the 2016 Lillehammer Winter YOG and the 2014 Sochi Winter OG.

Figure 40.1 Example 1: *Dagbladet*, February 9, 2014 with heading "This one was for you, Astrid!"

Handball and cross-country skiing are not overly popular sports worldwide, but they, and their women athletes (and teams), are tremendously popular in Norway. First we introduce the Norwegian sport context and sponsorship opportunities for women athletes in Norway before elaborating on how the media cover women athletes. Next, we discuss whether women athletes contribute to sponsor awareness and brand image transfer for the holding company Aker ASA and the insurance company Gjensidige, and whether there is a fit between sponsor values and media representation.

The Norwegian sport context

To understand the context of women's presentation in Norway, a few words about the sport context would seem to be an appropriate point of departure. Norway is a democratic country with an egalitarian culture and five million inhabitants. Norway is a successful Olympic country when it comes to winter sports (more than the summer sports). Results at the Rio 2016 Summer Olympic Games were at an almost all-time low with only four bronze medals and a 74th place ranking out of all nations in the medal count.

Before the closing ceremony in Rio, the debate about the Norwegian model for elite sport started. One argument was that the egalitarian nature of Norwegian society does not foster an elite culture because everyone is treated as entitled to the same opportunities and, as a consequence, federations are reluctant to embrace talent development at an early age. Support systems and the lack of sponsor money for athletes were also scrutinized (Bugge, 2016; Ekeli, 2016). Currently, there are two different ways of being funded in Norway, either as an athlete by the Norwegian Top Sports Program—Olympiatoppen—or as a student by the State Educational Loan Fund. Unfortunately, athletes tend to choose one of the two options to avoid a dual workload. Hence, the pool of talent is reduced because many withdraw from sport to focus on school or early work career (Kristiansen, MacIntosh, Parent, & Houlihan, 2017). The approximately 500 elite athletes who chose to stay in sport after ending high school (Tvedt, Røste, Smith, Høgmo, Haugen, & Ronglan, 2013) need sponsors.

The best-paid athletes in Norway do not earn as much as the top 50 athletes on the Forbes list such as LeBron James, who made US$31.2 million in salary/winnings and US$55 million in endorsements in 2017 (Badenhausen, 2017). The first woman on this list was Serena Williams at number 51, and the only woman among 49 men with US$8 million in salary/winnings and US$19 million in endorsements in 2017. No Norwegian made it to the top 100 list. Looking into the sports we focus on here, cross-country skier Petter Northug earned US$1.8 million in 2016, whereas cross-country skier Therese Johaug made US$565,000 (Rye, 2016). Handball players make less money generally, with one high-profile player on the national team, Nora Mørk, for example, making US$92,570 in 2016.

Norway has few "wealthy" athletes. For years, the women's Norwegian football team (soccer) was among the best in the world and winning an Olympic gold medal encouraged sponsors to support them. Today an average male player earns 10 times what a woman player earns in the top league (Day & Kristiansen, 2017), despite the Norwegian Equal Status Act (passed in 1979) and despite Norway being a leader in gender equality (i.e., performance in women's political participation). Media producers in Norway devote more time and resources to male sports (Cooky, Messner, & Hextrum, 2013), which is supported by previous media content analyses (see, for example, Christopherson, Janning, & McConnell, 2002). To obtain sponsorship, athletes need impressive competition results and personalities. Cross-country skiers are national stars in Norway, which helps them in terms of the business aspect of sports—they can draw in huge audiences (Boyle & Haynes, 2009), and arguably, both women's handball and cross-country athletes are attractive sponsor subjects for powerful Norwegian companies.

Sponsorship

Corporate sponsorship is growing in importance as an element of companies' brand building and communications strategies. The number of companies participating in sponsorship, as well as corporate expenditure for sponsoring sport events, teams, and athletes, has been on the rise as organizations seek new ways to reach audiences and enhance their image (Javalgi, Traylor, Gross, & Lampman, 1994).

Sponsorship is an indirect form of persuasion that works through the mental link between a company/brand and an athlete (Skard & Thorbjornsen, 2017). Due to the sponsorship's indirect nature, this form of communication is fundamentally different from traditional advertising, where the persuasive message is verbal and controlled (Bennett, Henson, & Zhang, 2002; Cornwell, Humphreys, Maguire, Weeks, & Tellegen, 2006). A sponsor connects with an event, athlete, or team that is highly valued by the target audience, in the hope that this association will reflect positively on their brand. By linking a brand to athletes or teams, the audience may *infer* that the brand shares associations with those teams or athletes, hence producing secondary associations (Keller, Apéria, & Georgson, 2008).

Sponsorship managers of companies select sponsorship objects that *fit* features of their brand, yet fit is an uncontrollable variable (Musante, Milne, & McDonald, 1999), because it is hard to plan for and measure. Empirical findings in the sponsorship literature support the notion that high fit is associated with positive sponsorship effects, such as enhanced image transfer (Grohs, Wagner, & Vsetecka, 2004; Gwinner, Larson, & Swanson, 2009), enhanced awareness (Cornwell et al., 2006), improved attitude toward the sponsor (Speed & Thompson, 2000), and increased willingness to consider the sponsor's products (Speed & Thompson, 2000). Cornwell, Roy, and Steinard (2001) argue that sponsorships should be leveraged through *traditional* advertising channels (TV, radio, newspapers) and more *explicit* channels such as public relations (PR) in the media to achieve marketing objectives.

The main sponsors for cross-country skiing and handball

The two chosen sports have different main sponsors, but they are both major and visible companies/brands in Norway. At the time of the different OG and YOG events we looked into, Aker ASA was one of the main sponsors for the cross-country ski team whereas Gjensidige was one of the main sponsors for the handball team.

Aker ASA is a Norwegian holding company engaged in offshore fishing, construction, and engineering. The company signed an agreement with the Norwegian Ski Federation in the 2010–2011 season, and originally wanted to be part of the team until after the 2014 Sochi OG. At the time, it was the biggest sponsorship agreement ever for the national ski federation, worth US$7.2 million over four years (Åsali & Bøthun, 2010). Another novel feature was the large amount of money that was paid directly to athletes on the national team as well as to their local clubs. Altogether they would allocate over US$120,760 each season.

Aker ASA's vision is "proud ownership," meaning that they want to cultivate and promote a company culture in which people deliver good results in a responsible manner. The company issued the following statement as a guideline for their values: "Together, we make each other better" (see https://www.akerasa.com).

Gjensidige, on the other hand, is a Norwegian insurance company with old roots and reputation, which is also in neighboring countries. The vision of Gjensidige is "We shall know the customer best and care the most." To enhance employee engagement, the phrase "vibrant soul" is highlighted as central to delivering the Gjensidige experience. Furthermore, the brand values communicated to the market are that "it is good to be prepared" and that Gjensidige is engaged in people's and companies' lives—both before and after an injury. Gjensidige's goal is for people to feel known, cared about, and helped.

Gjensidige has been the sponsor of the women's handball team for 25 years—they see the team as one of the most popular teams in Norway (Nyman, 2016). This well-established sponsor deal makes the company more visible (i.e., through logo labeling and online, TV, and radio commercials) and is an important part of the company's marketing strategy (S. Grøstad, personal communication, November 20, 2017). In the interview it was highlighted that Gjensidige considered the Summer Olympics a good opportunity to profile their brand—and there was a lot of media coverage in the period leading up to the Games. In this coverage, the insurance company stressed the importance of injury prevention—which is in line with their company vision (Nyman, 2016).

We now turn to the media coverage of the women athletes and teams during the YOG and OG to explore whether this coverage enhanced sponsor fit.

The media presentation of women athletes and teams during four events

We examined 837 articles from four sources—three of the four largest printed national newspapers (the fourth being a business newspaper) were chosen: *Aftenposten, Dagbladet*, and *VG*, and the largest online Norwegian news site, NRK.no. The articles were downloaded from a Norwegian database called Atekst. We included articles that were published within the period of a day before to a day after the 2014 and 2016 OG and YOG women's competitions. The articles in *Atekst* media archive are not indexed with keywords, so we searched by words (truncated) describing the two sports. The articles were sorted and examined in chronological order.

When comparing the four events, we found a significant difference in amount of coverage of women athletes within the two sports (Table 40.1) and between YOG and OG. Even though knowledge about and interest in the YOG is increasing (Yoon, 2017), junior athletes are not famous or brand material, and media coverage of YOG is sparse. When Norway hosted the 2016 Games in Lillehammer, this changed slightly, but the news was not focused on athletes—instead they covered results or other aspects of the event. It is also interesting to see the significant difference between coverage of handball and cross-country skiing, which also underlines the enormous popularity that the winter versions of OG have in Norway.

Table 40.1 The coverage of women athletes in four events

Name of event	Number of articles
Handball YOG Nanjing 2014	13
Handball OG Rio 2016	222
Cross-country skiing OG Sochi 2014	534
Cross-country skiing YOG Lillehammer 2016	68
Total	**837**

Collective smiles and tears: Handball YOG 2014 and OG 2016

Until the recent success of Norwegian men, who won a silver medal in the World Championship in 2017, handball was mostly seen as a women's sport because the Norwegian women's team has been successful internationally (Goksøyr, 2008; Lippe, 2010). Women handball players were exemplary models for both girls and boys (Kristiansen & Broch, 2013), which created a huge pool of new talent. However, the Norwegian women's team did not qualify for the YOG; only the men's team qualified and represented Norway in the 2014 Nanjing YOG. When questioning the Norwegian Handball Federation about this issue, they responded that. during the European Youth Olympic Festival (EYOF) in 2013, they sent both a women's and a men's junior team, but the girls also had a European Junior Championship to attend. To protect the best athletes from exhaustion, which is a big Norwegian concern and reason for the reluctance to develop talent early on (Kristiansen et al., 2018), the best players rested during EYOF and participated only in the European Championship. The women junior team sent to EYOF to qualify for YOG had hardly played together before departure and did not qualify. Hence, the 13 articles reflected only the junior men's games.

At the elite level, Norway always sends their best team. Norwegians are accustomed to these women winning almost every competition (European, World. and Olympic Championships) over the past decades. Their smiles and laughter stand out and are well recognized. This has become the team's brand value, which attracts the sponsors. The concept of handball-girl (Hovden, 2003) has actually for years been branded successfully by the Norwegian Handball Federation. The Norwegian people love the team and everything it stands for. Both the team and its star players represent a collective winning culture that the Norwegian people, as well as their sponsor Gjensidige, embrace, identify with, and support.

Having said that, things did not go as smoothly as usual for the "smiley girls" during the Rio 2016 OG. The handball team had a tough opening in the tournament, losing against Brazil. In the following debate in the media, the handball players stressed that they had done the best they could, but it had not been good enough. Detailed questioning followed the first game, and words such as "defeat," "nightmare," and "tears" colored the headlines in the news—and some of the girls had indeed cried after the game. It is of interest that the goalkeepers were the ones who were identified as most in need of improvement, and articles focused on how they could do so before the next game. As reigning Olympic, World, and European Champions, the people wanted more. After the next game, the news media used the word "magical" when they defeated Spain, and the best individual players in that game were quoted saying that it had been a fun game. The team seemed restored and carried on with the collective effort. The following days saw headlines such as "help from her little sister" and "the mom-team," referring to four team members who were mothers. Some headlines focused on the spectators in Brazil, because they were very nationalistic and booed teams they did not like—which became an issue when Norway played former Portuguese colony Angola. With each win, the news included photos of the players smiling again, and the players thanked the people for the tremendous support on social media.

Despite this recovery, the 2016 OG was disappointing in the eyes of Norwegians, and the team "only" brought home a bronze medal. The usual photos of smiley players were replaced with photos of reflective and tearful faces. The semifinal between Norway and Russia took place in the middle of the night, yet some 460,000 of Norway's five million stayed awake to watch this game.

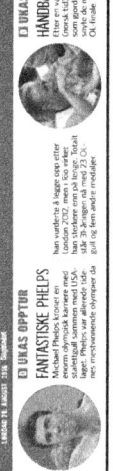

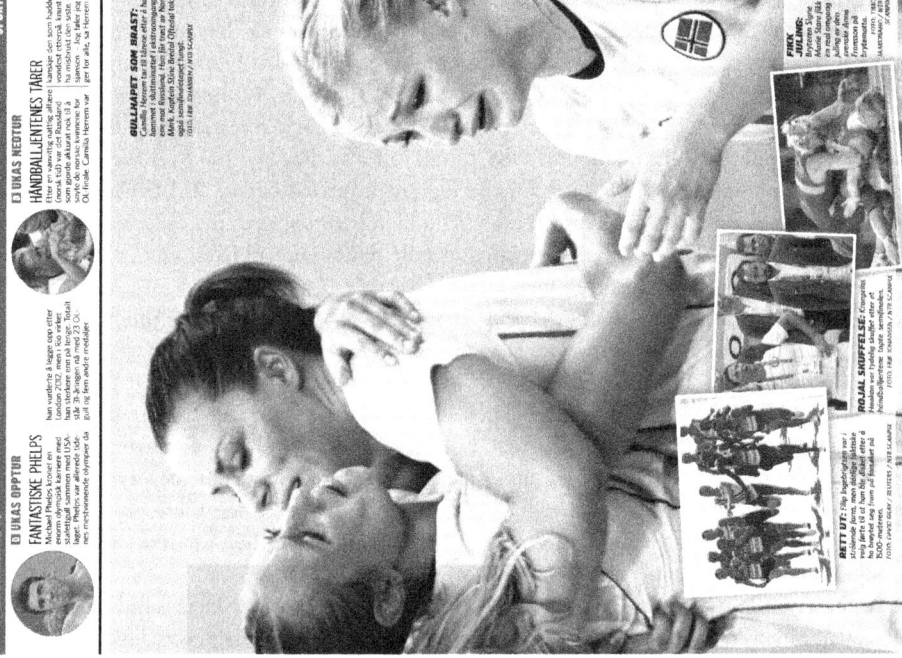

Figure 40.2 Example 2: *Dagbladet*, August 20, 2016 with the heading (discussing the Norwegian Olympic disaster) "Find comfort in Finland being worse"

Medals and tears: Cross-country skiing YOG 2016 and OG 2014

Cross-country skiing originated in Scandinavia, with skiing battalions used in the army since the seventeenth century. One of the main objectives for the Federation is to maintain its status as *the* national sport (Skiforbundet, 2015), and Table 40.1 confirms that they are succeeding in this endeavor. Helpful to this aim is a budget almost on the same level as that of Olympiatoppen (Ronglan, 2015)—due to contracts signed after the 2010 Olympic Winter Games (Hansen, 2014). Of the ski federation's income 90% comes from commercial partners, and the budget for 2015 was US$9.7 million. Of this amount, US$7.2 million was allocated to cover the expenses for the national team and US$5.4 million for the regional teams (Vesteng, 2014). Among the sponsors is Aker ASA. For the 2015–2016 season, 47 athletes were part of the different national teams (NSF, 2015). The resources are mostly spent on the senior elite athletes, who, in addition to this, often have individual sponsors as well.

With the above in mind, one might also expect some media interest for the junior athletes who participated in YOG 2016. One woman medal winner was mentioned by name after the results listed in the articles. However, after one of the junior men won a medal, half a page was dedicated to this win in a major newspaper. The only coverage of women athletes was of two women participants, who did not win a medal, but their fathers were former Olympic medal winners. The theme for the article was quite a paradox because it covered the psychological pressure that might exist from following in your parents' footsteps when there are Olympic expectations. Such an article may actually create stress if the athlete her- or himself had not reflected on it before the event (Figure 40.3).

The amount of media coverage of the Olympic women cross-country skiers is influenced by the status of and interest in the sport and in the Winter Olympics. Coverage was also increased and changed in focus due to the one athlete losing her brother the day before the championship started, and also due to the team rallying behind her in showing support with the mourning bands (see Example 1). Although Norway won gold and bronze medals in cross-country, only the Swedish silver medalist looked happy during the ceremony—the other two medalists were overwhelmed with sadness and emotions.

The cross-country's strong team spirit was emphasized again, as was the observation that they were so strong because they always had each other's backs. The crying after the first race and during the following press conference impacted the entire nation back home throughout the extreme medal tally that took place the following weeks. The grief, tears, and "fight" with the IOC were followed by some disappointing results due to waxing issues. But again, the women athletes defended the wax tech team in the news—and again they succeeded. In contrast to the coverage of the collective spirit of the women's cross-country skiers, the men's coverage focused more on medals and internal rivalry.

Women athletes, team values, (lack of) coverage, and sponsors

The massive media coverage of the women profiled within handball and cross-country skiing in their respective OG is not mirrored in the coverage of top junior athletes in the YOG. This must be understood from the Norwegian context where having juniors qualify for YOG or winning a gold medal is not a main priority for national federations (Kristiansen, 2017a). Instead the *learning experience* is emphasized for young athletes (Kristiansen, 2017b), and sport leaders focus on collective framing in order to avoid a media focus on the individual athletes. This protective attitude may also be a reason for the lack of coverage of youth Olympians (as referred to in

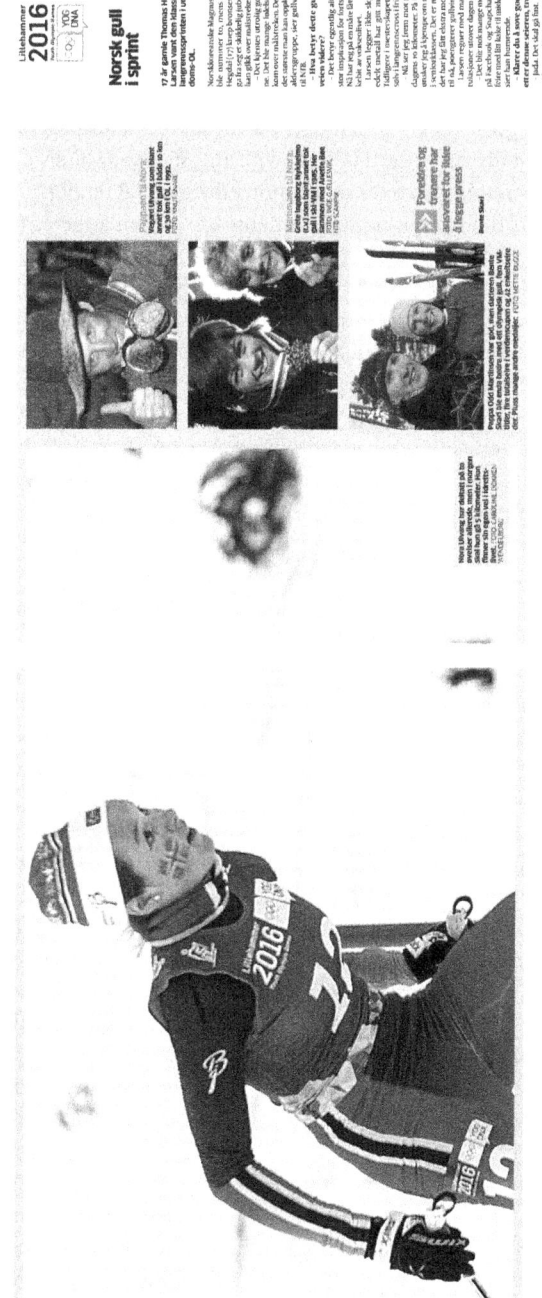

Figure 40.3 Example 3: *Aftenposten*, February 17, 2016 with the heading "Gold winning parents might become a source of pressure" with a focus on one of them (major picture in the newspaper) where both parents are former gold medalists (little pictures)

Table 40.1). Within this framework, the focus on the daughters of former Olympic winners in cross-country skiing also makes sense.

When looking into media presentations of women athletes, it is the senior Olympic participants we need to scrutinize because media coverage also makes them attractive to sponsors. It is interesting that both sports are covered as team sports, even though only one is a team sport. The *collective helping and caring values* are emphasized in both tearful "loss" stories (losing a game versus losing a brother). It is the collective that helps the cross-country skiers ski and it is the collective that helps the goalkeepers in handball (who served as scapegoats for a day) get back on the winning track. This coverage fits well with the sponsor values and indicates high levels of sponsor fit. Furthermore, the coverage supports the general tendency to focus on their emotions and not always on the many accomplishments of women athletes (Kristiansen, Hanstad, & Roberts, 2011).

During Aker ASA's six-year-long commitment to cross-country skiing, the national team's medal tally ended with 57 Olympic and World Championship medals—2014 Sochi OG alone yielded 11 medals (five of them being Gold medals). Communication director Atle Kigen emphasized that "no one can beat the women cross-country skiers when it comes to representing the value of *making each other better*" (A. Kigen, personal communication, October 10, 2017). These values were transferred and emphasized within Aker ASA as well, because they hoped to create more pride and strive for achievements, together with promoting a healthy lifestyle among employees. When ending their support, Aker summed up their contribution as a win–win relationship, and the togetherness and team spirit branded by the skiers felt internalized by the company.

Gjensidige's long-term commitment to handball is unique within Norwegian sponsoring history. Gjensidige wants to be associated with the women's handball team because they are great role models and stand for a relational, proud. and caring culture, which provides positive external effects in the market, as well as positive internal effects among employees. To create powerful ties between the company and the team, a number of tickets to the OG and World Championships were dedicated to employees and their peers. Also, in close cooperation with the team players, the sponsorship opens up the possibility of creating societal and sustainable community projects (S. Grøstad, personal communication, November 20, 2017).

From the brand values highlighted by Aker ASA and Gjensidige we recognize that there is a "natural" fit between those companies as sponsors and the teams sponsored. The "proud ownership" and "cooperation" values of Aker ASA fit well with the values of the women's cross-country team. Without a doubt, the women cross-country skiers are collectively oriented, working together to make each other better. The "vibrant soul" and "caring" and "preparing" values of Gjensidige may also be easily recognized as main characteristics for the women's handball team. Arguably, by sponsoring the teams of cross-country skiing and handball, Aker ASA and Gjensidige obtain positive sponsor fit and enhance company awareness, attitude, image transfer, brand value, and increased sales (Grohs et al., 2004; Gwinner et al., 2009; Skard & Thorbjornsen, 2017).

Although these companies embrace the aforementioned values, there is a lack of awareness among sport sponsors to see this, or only a few are aware of it. Recently, the representative for one sponsor came forward and *he* received headlines when he, on behalf of OBOS (the largest Nordic cooperative building association), as a CEO, made a deal with the national women's soccer team. When the CEO "learned" that women's football had *no commercial value* (Berntsen & Hove, 2017), he offered the team around US$7.2 million. The CEO emphasized that this was his contribution to equality and support for women leaders and women's football. By sponsoring women and encouraging others to follow, things may slowly change in Norway.

Sport, sponsors, and sponsor fit

In conclusion, companies that need to emphasize the usefulness of collective values and team spirit should be encouraged to sponsor and be aware of the positive effects of sponsoring women athletes. This was also emphasized in an interview with Jorunn Horgen, CEO, Olympiatoppen[1] Southeast—women more than men (at least in Norway) focus on team work and on making each other better. Returning to the opening story of this chapter, the 2014 Sochi OG story captures the team values that Aker ASA supports. As such, women's sport offers a unique business proposition for companies that would like to strengthen these values among their employees and in the public sphere. Arguably, women athletes could be better in building their personal brand, and thus should develop an understanding of how to work with the media as a communication and marketing asset (Geurin-Eagleman & Burch, 2016). Furthermore, companies should be encouraged to dedicate sponsorships to "build" the brands of women athletes in addition to supporting women's teams, given the unique sponsor fit offered by supporting their endorsements. This is a take-home message to potential sponsors—despite men's sport receiving more media coverage, women athletes represent more collective than individual values, which is in accordance with Norwegian egalitarianism and with significant Norwegian companies' values as well.

Leader profile: Jorunn Horgen

Jorunn Horgen is a former Norwegian windsurfer who became a six-time World Champion between 1984 and 1992, and who participated in the 1992 and 1996 Summer Olympic

Figure 40.4 Former windsurfer and current section leader (CEO) of Olympiatoppen Southeast, Jorunn Horgen. © Magne Klann

Games. During her career she won 19 medals while at the same time graduating as an engineer and with a Master's degree in Management. Her first job after retiring from sport was in the private sector. Here she experienced discrimination for the first time, in boardrooms where she was the only woman. Somehow it was unexpected that, and questioned whether, she had the right educational qualifications. Horgen is currently the section leader (CEO) of Olympiatoppen Southeast. Olympiatoppen is part of the Norwegian Olympic and Paralympic Committee and Confederation of Sports (NIF) with the responsibility for training elite athletes. Horgen's goal is to improve organizational structures and women's opportunities by combining sport with education.

In the interview, women, sport, and sponsors were debated, and Horgen emphasized that men are more visible in the media, which makes them more attractive to sponsors. From her experience with sponsors since the 1980s, she feels that most companies' sole focus is now on branding and has shifted to corporate values and a business culture. Today there is an expectation from companies that the internal impact from sponsorship should almost equal the external. This means that the world of business may have something to learn from *women* athletes—and what is often referred to as feminine values. She further emphasizes that the companies must consider what they get back from sport sponsorship. What is the added value and what needs do the sponsors have that the teams and athletes can impact? The key is to create win–win situations for both parties, the athletes, and the company. Naturally, it also matters how much money a sponsor can invest in sport sponsorship, to obtain a return on their investments.

For Horgen, it is important to see the women athletes as an asset and to acknowledge that they may even have an advantage in this new sponsorship market due to their experiences with team processes. Actually, to run team processes is one of the core methods Olympiatoppen tries to implement in the different national federations, and Horgen admits that maybe women athletes and their (often) women coaches may be more open to seeing that team spirit is key to success. In male-dominated environments, spending time on team processes is not prioritized. Handball is particularly known for its collective attitude, which is a result of one woman coach (Marit Breivik) implementing these collective strategies.

Horgen has broken many barriers herself—and one of her hopes as the leader for Olympiatoppen Southeast would be to challenge the men's team with what they can learn from women.

Note

1 Olympiatoppen is an organization that is part of Norwegian Olympic and Paralympic Committee and Confederation of Sports with responsibility for training Norwegian elite sport.

References

Åsali, B. B., & Bøthun, G. (2010). Røkke sponser langrennslandslaget med 60 mill [Røkke sponsors the ski federation with 60 millions]. *VG*, January 21. Retrieved from https://www.vg.no/sport/langrenn/langrenn/roekke-sponser-langrennslandslaget-med-60-mill/a/591125.

Badenhausen, K. (2017). The world's highest paid athletes 2017: Behind the numbers. Retrieved from https://www.forbes.com/athletes/#676b75a655ae.

Bennett, G., Henson, R., & Zhang, J. (2002). Action sports sponsorship recognition. *Sport Marketing Quarterly*, **11**(3), 174–185.

Berntsen, P. A. & Hove, L. B. (2017). OBOS-sjefen ble forbanna. Det førte til historisk god avtale for kvinnefotballen [CEO of OBOS gets upset: Historical sponsor agreement for women's football]. *TV2 Sporten*, November 16. Retrieved from www.tv2.no/a/9492047.

Boyle, R. & Haynes, R. (2009). *Power Play. Sport, the media and popular culture*. Edinburgh: Edinburgh University Press.

Bugge, M. (2016). Frykter at Norge gjør idrettsutøvere til gjeldsslaver [Fear of Norway making athletes into "debt-slaves"]. Retrieved from www.aftenposten.no/article/common-809043.snd (accessed August 25, 2016).

Christopherson, N., Janning, M., & McConnell, E. D. (2002). Two kicks forward, one kick back: A content analysis of media discourses on the 1999 Women's World Cup Soccer Championship. *Sociology of Sport Journal*, **19**(2), 170–188.

Cooky, C., Messner, M. A., & Hextrum, R. H. (2013). Women play sport, but not on TV: A longitudinal study of televised news media. *Communication & Sport*, **1**, 203–230.

Cornwell, T. B., Humphreys, M. S., Maguire, A. M., Weeks, A. M., & Tellegen, C. L. (2006). Sponsorship-linked marketing: The role of articulation in memory. *Journal of Consumer Research*, **33**(3), 312–321.

Cornwell, T. B., Roy, D. P., & Steinard, E. A. (2001). Exploring managers' perceptions of the impact of sponsorship on brand equity. *Journal of Advertising*, **30**(2), 41–51.

Day, S. & Kristiansen, E. (2017). All stressed out? Managing stress among football players. Retrieved from http://idrottsforum.org/wp-content/uploads/2017/04/day-kristiansen170428.pdf.

Ekeli, E. (2016). Toppidrett og høyere utdanning: En kvalitativ case studie av elitesyklisters opplevelser av å kombinere toppidrett og høyere utdanning [Elite sport and higher education: A case study of dual careers among elite cyclists]. Retrieved from http://hdl.handle.net/11250/2399251.

Geurin-Eagleman, A. N. & Burch, L. M. (2016). Communicating via photographs: A gendered analysis of Olympic athletes' visual self-presentation on Instagram. *Sport Management Review*, **19**(2), 133–145.

Goksøyr, M. (2008). *Historien om norsk idrett* [Norwegian Sports History]. Oslo, Norway: Abstrakt Forlag.

Grohs, R., Wagner, U. M., & Vsetecka, S. (2004). Assessing the effectiveness of sport sponsorships-an empirical examination. *Schmalenbach Business Review*, **56**(2), 119–138.

Gwinner, K. P., Larson, B. V., & Swanson, S. R. (2009). Image transfer in corporate event sponsorship: Assessing the impact of team identification and event-sponsor fit. *International Journal of Management and Marketing Research*, **2**(1), 1–15.

Hansen, P. Ø. (2014). Making the best even better. Fine-tuning development and learning to achieve international success in cross-country skiing. Norwegian School of Sport Sciences. Retrieved from http://hdl.handle.net/11250/223368.

Hanstad, D. V., Parent, M. M., & Kristiansen, E. (2013). The Youth Olympic Games: The best of the Olympics or a poor copy? *European Sport Management Quarterly*, **13**, 315–338.

Hovden, J. (2003). From equality and justice – to difference and profitability? Gender political discourses in market-oriented sport bodies. In Gender and Power in the New Europe, the 5th European Feminist Research Conference, August 20–24, Lund University, Sweden.

Javalgi, R. G., Traylor, M. B., Gross, A. C., & Lampman, E. (1994). Awareness of sponsorship and corporate image: An empirical investigation. *Journal of Advertising*, **23**(4), 47–58.

Judge, L. W., Petersen, J., Bellar, D., Wanless, E., Leitzelar, B., & Gilreath, E. (2015). Visibility and recognition of the inaugural Youth Olympic Games. *Applied Research in Coaching and Athletics Annual*, **30**, 59–82.

Keller, K. L., Apéria, T., & Georgson, M. (2008). *Strategic Brand Management: A European perspective*. Harlow: Prentice Hall.

Kristiansen, E. (2017a). Norway. In E. Kristiansen, M. M. Parent, & B. Houlihan (eds), *Elite Youth Sport Policy and Management: A comparative analysis* (pp. 80–95). Abingdon: Routledge.

Kristiansen, E. (2017b). Walking the line: How young athletes balance academic studies and sport in international competition. *Sport in Society*, **20**(1), 47–65.

Kristiansen, E., & Broch, T. B. (2013). Athlete-media communication: A theoretical perspective on how athletes use and understand gendered sport communication. In P. M. Pedersen (ed.), *The Routledge Handbook of Sport Communication* (pp. 97–106). New York: Routledge.

Kristiansen, E., Hanstad, D. V., & Roberts, G. C. (2011). Coping with the media at the Vancouver Winter Olympics: "We all make a living out of this." *Journal of Applied Sport Psychology*, **23**(4), 443–458.

Kristiansen, E., MacIntosh, E., Parent, M. M., & Houlihan, B. (2018). The Youth Olympic Games: a facilitator or barrier of the high-performance sport development pathway? *European Sport Management Quarterly*, **18**(1), 73–92.

Lippe, G. v.d. (2010). *Et kritisk blikk på sportsjournalistikk* [A critical view on sports journalism]. Kristiansand, Norway: IJ-forlaget.

Musante, M., Milne, G. R., & McDonald, M. A. (1999). Sport sponsorship: Evaluating the sport and brand image match. *International Journal of Sports Marketing and Sponsorship*, **1**(1), 24–39.

NSF (Norwegian Guide and Scouting Association) (2015). 23 utøvere på rekrutt-og juniorlandslaget [23 athletes on the recruit and junior team]. Retrieved from www.skiforbundet.no/langrenn/nyhetsarkiv/rekrutt-og-junior (accessed July 28, 2015).

Nyman, H. (2016). Derfor sponser Gjensidige våre største OL-håp [That is why we sponsor the biggest OG hopes]. *Kampanje*, August 5. Retrieved from http://kampanje.com/markedsforing/2016/08/derfor-sponser-gjensidige-norges-storste-ol-hap.

Ronglan, L. T. (2015). Elite sport in Scandinavian welfare states: Legitimacy under pressure? *International Journal of Sport Policy*, **7**(3), 345–363.

Rye, J. M. (2016). Dette tjente Norges største idrettsstjerner [This is what Norway's best elite athletes earned]. *Tv2.No*, October 5. Retrieved from www.tv2.no/a/8656045.

Skard, S. & Thorbjørnsen, H. (2017). Closed-ended and open-ended fit articulation: Communication strategies for incongruent sponsorships. *European Journal of Marketing*, **51**(7/8), 1414–1439.

Skiforbundet (2015). Verdigrunnlag og hovedmål [Values and aims], July 14, 2015. Retrieved from www.skiforbundet.no/norges-skiforbund/verdigrunnlag-og-hovedmal.

Speed, R. & Thompson. (2000). Determinants of sports sponsorship response. *Journal of the Academy of Marketing Science*, **28**(2), 226–238.

Tvedt, T., Røste, E., Smith, M., Høgmo, P. M., Haugen, K., & Ronglan, L. T. (2013). Den norske toppidrettsmodelen-norsk toppidrett fram mot 2022 [The Norwegian top sport model—Norwegian sport towards 2022]. The Norwegian Olympic and Paralympic Committee and Confederation of Sports (NIF). Retrieved from www.idrett.no/nyheter/Documents/Toppidrettsrapporten_2022.pdf.

Vesteng, C. (2014). Langrenn øker budsjettet til 80 mill [Cross-country skiing increases the budget to 80 millions]. *VG*, August 29. Retrieved from www.vg.no/a/23284606.

Yoon, J. (2017). A network approach to the use of social media in the Youth Olympic Games and the Olympic Games. Doctoral dissertation, Bloomington, IN: Indiana University, Bloomington, Indiana.

41
Media coverage of women athletes during the Olympic Games

Andrea N. Geurin

Introduction

Women athletes have competed in the Olympic Games since 1900, when 22 women (2.2% of all competitors) participated in tennis, sailing, croquet, equestrian, and golf at the Paris Olympics. These numbers steadily climbed over time and, by 2016, women made up 45% of all competitors at the Rio de Janeiro Summer Olympic Games (Crockett, 2016). In addition, at the 2018 Winter Olympics in PyeongChang, South Korea, 43% of all athletes were women, a record for the Winter Olympics (Taylor, 2018). Despite the increase in women athletes competing in the Games, male athletes have historically received more media coverage during the Games (e.g., Billings, Angelini, & Duke, 2010; MacArthur, Angelini, Smith, & Billings, 2017), and indeed male athletes have consistently been shown to receive far more media coverage than their female counterparts in general (e.g., Bishop, 2003; Eagleman, Pedersen, & Wharton, 2009; Fink & Kensicki, 2002; Greer, Hardin, & Homan, 2009; King, 2007).

As one of the only major international multisport events to feature both men and women competitors, the Olympic Games are unique in that they provide an opportunity for more equitable media coverage between men and women athletes. For the vast majority of sport fans and consumers, the Olympic Games are consumed via media rather than in person, which underscores the importance of equitable coverage during this event to present sport consumers with an accurate picture of the Games (Billings, 2007). According to Eagleman, Burch, and Vooris (2014), providing equitable coverage can result in accurate historical records being kept and preserved. In addition, when news outlets consistently provide equitable coverage of male and female athletes, shifts in societal biases and stereotypes can occur. For example, when coverage highlights the accomplishments and performances of both men and women athletes, potential outcomes include a greater societal respect for women's sport and women athletes, greater participation by women in sport, increased media coverage for women athletes in non-Olympic years, and "ultimately greater acceptance of and respect for women in all areas of society" (Eagleman, Burch et al., 2014, p. 465).

This chapter seeks to present an historical overview of both the amount and quality of coverage devoted to women athletes during the Olympic Games, while also discussing the emergence of new media and the potential benefits internet-based media coverage holds for women athletes, and the power that social media afford women athletes in terms of promoting their careers and seeking commercial opportunities. The chapter concludes with a profile of Olympic gold medal-winning gymnast, Nastia Liukin, who is now a member of US-based broadcaster NBC's Olympic broadcast team and who founded a company focused on empowering young female athletes via the use of a mobile app.

Olympic media coverage devoted to women

Amount of coverage

Myriad studies have examined the amount of coverage devoted to men and women during the Olympic Games. Time and time again, these studies have shown discrepancies in the amount of coverage, with the men often receiving significantly more than the women. For example, several scholars have examined coverage in terms of clock time devoted to male and female athletes. As far back as the 1992 Barcelona Summer Olympic Games, Higgs and Weiller (1994) found that US broadcaster NBC devoted more of its coverage to men than to women. The focus on NBC's coverage has continued, with Billings et al. (2008) finding that men received 60% of the clock time during NBC's television coverage of the 2006 Torino Winter Olympics, and men also constituted the majority (60%) of the top 20 most mentioned athletes. Two years later, Billings et al. (2010) examined NBC's television coverage of the 2008 Beijing Summer Olympics, finding a greater disparity in clock time between men and women than at the previous Summer Games in Athens, with men receiving significantly more coverage. The focus on NBC is warranted, because the network has had exclusive rights to broadcast the Games in the United States since 1992, and extended its deal with the International Olympic Committee in 2014, paying an astronomical US$7.75 billion for rights to broadcast the Games from 2022 to 2032 (Sandomir, 2014). Thus, it is the only televised coverage available to Olympic consumers in the United States, and its coverage paints a picture of the Games for those who cannot attend the three-week-long event in person. The sports and athletes shown on NBC's broadcasts shape US media consumers' perceptions of the event and which sports and athletes are most important.

The issue of inequitable coverage is not limited to television, as many scholars have found the same to be true of print coverage as well. For example, Zurn, Lopiano, and Snyder (2006) examined *The New York Times'* coverage of the 2006 Winter Olympics and found that nearly 62% of the outlet's coverage focused on men's sport, whereas just 38% focused on women. The percentage of photos featuring men was even higher at 64%, to women's 36%. Similarly, Smith and Wrynn (2010) examined US newspaper and website coverage of the 2010 Winter Olympics in Vancouver, Canada, and found that all outlets examined (*New York Times, USA Today, Sacramento Bee*, NBC Olympic website, ESPN website) afforded far greater coverage to men than women, with men receiving a combined total of 62.4% of coverage to women's 37.6%. The men also received more favorable article placement and more photographs than women. Arguing for greater coverage for women, the authors wrote that media coverage:

> can play a significant role in exposing girls and women to a variety of sport participation opportunities, as well as shaping our culture's ideas of a wide range of acceptable gender roles worthy of recognition and celebration for both females and males.
>
> (Smith & Wrynn, 2010, p. 41)

Although much attention has been focused on US-based news outlets and their coverage of the Olympic Games, it is important also to understand coverage trends in countries outside of the

United States. One such study was Eagleman, Clavio, and Kwak's (2011) comparison of online news coverage between a US-based online news outlet (*USA Today*) and a Chinese-based online news outlet (*People's Daily*). The researchers found coverage from both countries favored male athletes, but the disparity between the amount of coverage of men and women was much higher for the US-based outlet. Another study focused on China's media coverage examined Chinese Central Television's (CCTV's) coverage of gymnastics at the 2016 Olympic Games, hypothesizing that women would receive more coverage (Xu, Billings, & Fan, 2018). To the authors' surprise, however, the men competing in gymnastics received more clock time, more total name mentions in the broadcasts, and 13 of the top 20 most-mentioned athletes were men. Hedenborg (2013) examined coverage of the 2012 London Olympics from a Swedish media lens, and unsurprisingly found that men received greater coverage from both a daily newspaper and a tabloid newspaper. She argued that media coverage plays an important role in shaping society's views on who is and is not considered a "real sportsman or sportswoman" (Hedenborg, 2013, p. 800), highlighting the need for greater coverage of women athletes in order to legitimize them in the minds of society.

Another study focused on Canada's television coverage of the 2014 Sochi Winter Olympics, on the Canadian Broadcasting Corporation's (CBC's) broadcasts, revealed that men received over 60% of airtime compared with women's nearly 40%, men received more mentions, and men made up 65% of the top 20 most-mentioned athletes list (MacArthur et al., 2017). Still, the authors noted that, outside of Olympic competition, women received only 1.7–3.1% of all television sports coverage in Canada, suggesting that the 40% received during the Sochi Olympics was a marked improvement from non-Olympic coverage. This sentiment was echoed in Packer et al.'s (2014) examination of British media coverage of women's sport in the five months leading up to and the five months after the 2012 London Olympic Games. The authors found no evidence that the United Kingdom's hosting of the 2012 Games led to improved coverage of women's sport, with women receiving just 4.5% of coverage before the Games and an even lower 2.9% of coverage after the Games. Packer et al. (2014) also found that, for every photo of a woman athlete featured in British newspapers, there were 25 photos of men athletes. The authors cautioned of potential negative consequences of this dismal coverage, such as lower sport participation rates for women and girls in the United Kingdom, which could lead to adverse health implications.

Despite these discouraging findings relating to the amount of coverage devoted to women athletes during the Olympic Games, the proportion of women athletes competing in the Olympic Games has steadily risen over time. In 2016, not only was the percentage of women the highest ever at 45% of all competitors, but women were touted as being the stars of the Games in many media accounts. US-based news outlet NPR dubbed the American women as "the biggest winners" at the Rio Games (Myre, 2016, para. 1), and *The New York Times* reported that, in 29 of the nations competing in the Games, women won more medals for their country than the men, including traditional powerhouse countries such as the United States, China, and Russia (Lai & Lee, 2016). Although a great deal of the research presented to this point in the chapter shows inequitable coverage for women during the Olympics, a more optimistic body of research has begun to emerge, which reveals improvements in equity of coverage. One such example is Eagleman, Burch, et al.'s (2014) comparison of online media coverage of the 2012 Olympic Games from outlets in Australia, Brazil, China, the United Kingdom, Kenya, and the United States, which found that all six countries afforded a greater percentage of coverage to male than to female athletes, but the difference was not statistically significant when tested against the independent standard of the number of participants from each gender. In terms of article placement on the news website, only Kenya's *Daily Nation* afforded significantly better placement to male athletes. This finding was one of the first of its kind, in which Olympic media coverage was found to be equitable between men and women. The authors concluded that the internet may allow for more equitable coverage than traditional media in terms of the amount of coverage, and that "the relative absence of time and space restraints on news websites helps to facilitate more equitable and representative coverage" (Eagleman, Burch, et al., 2014, p. 466).

Lending credence to the notion that the internet may represent a step forward in the direction of gender equity, Burch, Eagleman, and Pedersen (2012) found that, although men received more coverage on the NBC Olympics website, Yahoo! Sports website, and USA Today website during the 2010 Vancouver Winter Olympics, the amount of coverage was not statistically significant when compared with the independent standard of the number of athletes of each gender participating in the Games. Burch et al. (2012) noted that this was a departure from traditional media trends, because previous research showed statistically significant differences in the amount of coverage devoted to men and women during the 2000, 2002, 2004, and 2006 Olympic Games. Finally, Billings, Angelini, MacArthur, Bissell, and Smith (2014) found that, in 2012, NBC devoted more coverage to women athletes than men in the London Olympic Games. Although the work by Eagleman, Burch, et al. (2014), Burch et al. (2012), and Billings et al. (2014) indicates marked improvements in terms of equitable coverage, more quantitative analyses are necessary, specifically focused on the 2014, 2016, and 2018 Olympics and beyond, in order to understand whether the trend of more equitable coverage continues.

Quality of coverage

Along with the amount of coverage afforded to women athletes, the *quality* of coverage is also very important in terms of equity and shaping societal views of women athletes. Fink (2015) wrote that what was even more disturbing than the lack of coverage afforded to women athletes was "the fact that when female athletes are provided coverage, it is disparagingly different than that afforded to male athletes" (Fink, 2015, p. 333). Furthermore, Cooky and Antunovic (2018) cautioned scholars to be careful in celebrating greater equity in terms of the *amount* of coverage afforded to women, stating that "these indicators of progress exist alongside forms of blatant sexism, racism, and discrimination" (Cooky & Antunovic, 2018, p. 946). That is, just because the amount of coverage of male and female athletes during the Olympic Games is reaching a level of equity, the language and portrayals used to describe women athletes still need improvement.

Research has shown a long history of coverage in which the size and strength of men's bodies is a central focus, and they are often portrayed as being powerful and strong (e.g., Billings, 2003; Billings & Eastman, 2003), whereas, when women receive coverage, it often seeks to diminish their athletic accomplishments by focusing on their attractiveness, femininity, and sexuality (e.g., Bissell & Duke, 2007; Eastman & Billings, 1999). In her review of media coverage of women's sport, Fink (2015) identified five common practices employed by the media when reporting on women, which are used so often that they are deeply embedded in our cultural psyche and many consumers do not even notice or question them.

The first practice Fink (2015) identified was a term Messner, Duncan, and Jensen (1993) coined "gender marking." This is the practice of presenting male athletes as the norm, whereas female athletes are relegated to second-class status. One way in which this is accomplished is through the use of the word "Women" in the title of sporting events such as the FIFA Women's World Cup. Meanwhile, the men's competition is simply the FIFA World Cup, with no mention of their sex in the title.

Next, Fink (2015) identified the practice of infantilizing women athletes, a process by which women are often referred to as "girls" or "young ladies." Eagleman, Rodenberg, and Lee (2014) examined this concept in the context of women's Olympic gymnastics, studying language used to describe women gymnasts from the 1984 Olympic Games through the 2008 Olympic Games. They found that, over time, less infantilizing language was used by the journalists to describe the female gymnasts, but the coaches and other gymnastics officials routinely used such language in their quotes when speaking about the gymnasts, illustrating the earlier point that these gendered language practices are deeply embedded in our culture. Another method of infantilizing is by referring to women only by their first names, but not doing so when discussing male athletes. Messner et al. (1993) indicated that this serves to diminish the reputations of female athletes. It may also be a method for reinforcing ambivalent attitudes, which is the third practice Fink (2015) identified. According to Eagleman (2015), it is a practice by which the media present information that at first seems positive, but on further investigation is actually used to subtly belittle women athletes. An example from Eagleman's (2015) study on newspaper portrayals of male and female gymnasts from the 2012 Olympics was journalists' displeasure with the women gymnasts' frowning and concentration on their faces while performing more difficult skills than had ever been done before. Eagleman (2015, p. 244) said, "This desire for pleasant facial expressions serves to objectify gymnasts as pretty things meant to bring joy to the audiences and further stereotypes gymnastics as a female appropriate sport."

Along those lines, the fourth practice identified by Fink (2015) was a focus on femininity and heterosexuality. By focusing on the athletes' femininity, sex appeal, and aspects of heterosexuality such as their families, romantic partners, or roles as mothers, these portrayals serve to diminish their athletic accomplishments. Indeed, an examination of NBC's coverage of women athletes in the 2016 Rio Olympic Games revealed that the broadcast network focused on heterosexualizing athletes and highlighting their roles as wives and mothers (Villalon & Weiller-Abels, 2018). In one example from Villalon and Weiller-Abels' study, an NBC announcer referred to a lesbian volleyball player's female partner as her "husband," seeking to heterosexualize the athlete. In another example, an announcer referred to a Hungarian swimmer's husband as "the guy responsible" for her success, belittling her abilities and suggesting she needed a man to achieve success in her sport.

Finally, Fink (2015) explained that the production techniques used for men's and women's sport are different, and research has shown that this results in women's sport being perceived as less exciting than men's. Fink (2015) pointed out several examples of this, including more camera angles/shots used in men's sport, more on-screen graphics in broadcasts of men's sport, camera angles that highlight women's buttocks and chests, and selective gender comparisons in which women are compared only with men who outperform them, but no mention is made of how many men the woman is superior to, such as in marathon coverage where a women's race winner is faster than the vast majority of men participating in the same race. Yet, in most marathon coverage, the women's race winner is only compared with the men's race winner (Kane, 1995).

The results of recent studies focused on quality of coverage, such as those by Villalon and Weiller-Abels (2018), Eagleman (2015), and Eagleman, Rodenberg, et al. (2014) point to the continuation of problematic portrayals of women athletes, which seek to diminish their accomplishments and perpetuate the notion of male dominance in sport.

Opportunities for women Olympic athletes via social media

Although it is well documented that both the quantity and quality of mainstream media coverage of women athletes need improvement, several scholars (e.g., Geurin, 2017; Geurin-Eagleman & Burch, 2016; Lebel & Danylchuk, 2012) have pointed to social media as a potential equalizer for women athletes, because social media platforms allow the athletes to post news and updates themselves, thus directly promoting their performances and careers without reliance on traditional media. In addition, social media allow athletes to build their personal brands and craft their desired images in the minds of fans and sport consumers (Arai, Ko, & Ross, 2014). Social media are thought to be an especially useful tool for Olympic athletes, who often do not benefit from being part of teams/organizations that receive a great deal of social media and traditional media coverage in non-Olympic years (Eagleman, 2013).

Geurin-Eagleman and Burch (2016) examined Olympic athletes' Instagram posts and found that photos of athletes engaged in their sport (e.g., action shots) elicited greater engagement from followers. Despite this, however, women athletes posted more photos of themselves in personal life settings, thus missing an opportunity to establish larger fan followings and elicit greater engagement with their posts. The authors concluded: "The prevalence of personal life photos posted by female athletes reflected the traditional practices of mainstream sports media outlets, which can have implications for these athletes in terms of the followers they attract and the brand image they project" (Geurin-Eagleman & Burch, 2016, p. 142). In addition, the women athletes were found to post more sexually suggestive images of themselves than the men, and the authors cautioned that "athletes should be careful when posting such photos, as they could have long-term consequences on the public's perceptions of the athlete. It is imperative that the types of photos posted align closely with the brand image the athlete wishes to build" (Geurin-Eagleman & Burch, 2016, p. 142). Interestingly, Kane and Maxwell (2011) found that sexually suggestive images of women athletes did not elicit more interest in women's sport from either men or women, who were more interested in photos displaying athletic competence.

Geurin (2017) sought to build on the content analysis conducted by Geurin-Eagleman and Burch (2016) by speaking directly with women athletes to better understand their perceptions of using social media as a marketing communication tool related to their careers. Although the athletes, all of whom were training for the 2016 Summer Olympics, appeared to have goals for their social media use (e.g., sharing their lives, developing connections, sponsorship, and self-promotion), none employed specific strategies to achieve these goals, nor did they attempt to use any measurement mechanisms by which to assess whether their goals were met. Social media offer the potential to help women athletes build their profile, which could lead to positive outcomes such as larger fan bases, sponsorship/endorsement opportunities, and overall greater recognition for and interest in themselves and their sports. Despite these potential benefits, however, evidence such as that from Geurin's (2017) study points to women athletes under-utilizing this tool. This reveals an opportunity for women athletes and those who work with them (e.g., agents, publicists, national governing bodies) to develop specific strategies for their social media use to build their personal brands and develop greater recognition for themselves, their achievements, and their sport in the public eye.

Despite the potential benefits social media provide women athletes, especially those in Olympic sports, there are also documented risks associated with social media use that extend beyond posting something that may negatively affect public perception of the athlete. In speaking with women Olympic athletes, Geurin (2017) found that each athlete described receiving unwanted direct private messages from "fans" and followers on social media platforms. These unwanted communications were highly inappropriate and some bordered on the act of stalking. For example, one woman boxing athlete described the messages she received in the following quote:

> I've had a few people tell me that they want to be married to me and they send me inbox messages. One guy told me once that he dreams of me every day and another guy told me

once that he knows everything about me. Like he's Googled every last thing about me. And then I've had a few guys send me pictures of their private areas through Facebook messages. I have a very long "block" list of people who cannot contact me.

(Geurin, 2017, p. 351)

Challenges such as this one, in which some athletes fear for their personal safety, can seek to turn women athletes away from social media, thus denying them the potential benefits social media afford them. Given that traditional media still lag in equal and equitable coverage of women athletes and women's sport, it is disheartening that some women athletes are also unable to utilize social media as a marketing communication tool due to "a combination of hegemonic masculinity, sexism, and harassment" (Geurin, 2017, p. 354), which "highlights a larger societal problem with regard to women's equality" (Geurin, 2017, p. 354).

Still, some athletes have recently begun to use social media as a means for speaking out about injustices, harassment, and abuse. In October 2017, the "#MeToo Movement" took over social media in all areas of life – not just sport – with over 12 million Facebook posts featuring the hashtag within 24 hours of actress Alyssa Milano encouraging people, especially women, to share their stories of sexual assault and harassment (Smartt, 2017). #MeToo spurred a movement in which women in all sectors of society began speaking out about their experiences, and it seemed to give women an unprecedented confidence, platform, and voice to speak out about gender-related injustices, build awareness for these issues, and demand change. As a result, some Olympic athletes and their fans/followers began using social media as a way to draw attention to situations that may never have reached public consciousness otherwise, and have been able ultimately to influence positive change in some instances.

One high-profile example came in October 2018 when five-time Olympic medalist in gymnastics, Simone Biles, posted a tweet that was critical of Mary Bono, the newly appointed interim CEO of USA Gymnastics, the sport's national governing body. Before Bono's appointment, USA Gymnastics had been roiled by a sexual abuse scandal in which the national team doctor, Larry Nassar, was found to have abused hundreds of gymnasts, including several national team members, in the 20 years he was in his position. When Bono took over for the recently resigned and widely criticized CEO Kerry Perry, Biles took to Twitter to retweet a post by Bono that was critical of Nike-sponsored athlete Colin Kaepernick, along with a photo showing Bono blacking-out the Nike logo on her shoes with a Sharpie marker. Biles wrote, "*mouth drop* don't worry, it's not like we needed a smarter USA gymnastics president or any sponsors or anything" (Hill, 2018, para. 15). Biles' Olympic teammate from 2016, Aly Raisman, a five-time medalist herself, also tweeted about Bono, writing, "My teammates & I reported Nassar's abuse to USAG in 2015. We now know USOC & lawyers at Faegre Baker Daniels (Mary Bono's firm) were also told then, yet Nassar continued to abuse children for 13 months!? Why hire someone associated with the firm that helped cover up our abuse?" (Hill, 2018, para. 6). Just four days later, only five days into her term as interim CEO, Bono resigned from the position due to the pressure from the athletes and their fans, thousands of whom "liked," "retweeted," responded to the tweets, and tweeted their disapproval directly to Bono's account (Adams, 2018). The support shown by fans and followers in this example helps to highlight the power of what Cooky and Antunovic (2018) described as "'call out' culture" (p. 947), which they argued "challenges conventional forms of male-dominance and masculine hegemony in sports media" (Cooky and Antunovic, 2018, p. 947). Women's newfound empowerment stemming from the #MeToo movement is only just beginning to be felt in society, and is a movement ripe for women athletes to use to highlight the inequalities and injustices they have faced for decades in sport.

Conclusion

The lack of coverage for women athletes is well documented and, although women athletes receive much more equitable coverage during the Olympic Games, the need for greater coverage in non-Olympic years remains. Perhaps more important than the *amount* of coverage devoted to women is, however, the need for more equitable coverage in terms of *quality*. As discussed in this chapter, several antiquated practices persist in sports media with regard to the portrayals of women athletes and the language used to describe them. In order for women's sport to reach a level where it is legitimized in society, the language used to describe women athletes and women's sport must be free of the five gendered practices identified by Fink (2015).

Social media use offers women athletes, especially those in Olympic sport, the opportunity to build their own brand and desired public image, but, to take advantage of social media's opportunities, women athletes must develop social media goals, strategies to achieve those goals, and measurement techniques to understand whether they are truly reaching their goals. Unfortunately, the harassment felt by some women athletes on social media by their male "fans" may prove to be a deterrent to the otherwise equalizing opportunity that social media use provides. This points to a larger, problematic societal belief in male hegemony, or the idea that men have the power to dominate others (namely, women) and can therefore treat them in ways that are disrespectful and harassing in nature. Women's empowerment movements such as #MeToo will help women athletes to conquer some of these situations, but it is obvious that a larger shift in our societal mindset, when it comes to views on men and women, is necessary for this issue to truly improve. One interesting mechanism by which to bring women together for greater unity and empowerment may be through the use of technology, such as mobile device apps that connect women athletes to each other for support and friendship. One such example is provided in the following leader profile on five-time Olympic medalist Nastia Liukin.

Leader profile: Nastia Liukin

Born in Moscow, Russia, to a father who was an Olympic champion in men's gymnastics and a mother who was a World Champion in rhythmic gymnastics, Anastasia "Nastia" Liukin grew up learning the sport of gymnastics in her parents' gym in Plano, Texas, where they moved when she was two and a half years old. By age 18 she was a five-time Olympic medalist and just the third American woman to win the coveted Olympic All-Around gold medal at the 2008 Beijing Olympic Games. The same year, she was named the Women's Sports Foundation's "Individual Sportswoman of the Year," USA Gymnastics' "Sportswoman of the Year," and won "Best Female Athlete" at the 2009 ESPY Awards.

While completing her Bachelor's degree in Sports Management at New York University, Liukin entered the world of sports broadcasting, joining the NBC Sports Group as an analyst during the 2012 Summer Olympics in London, then serving as a special correspondent for NBC during the 2014 Sochi Winter Olympics in Russia. She has since become a regular member of the NBC Sports broadcast team for national, world, and Olympic gymnastics competitions as a gymnastics analyst, providing a unique perspective as a former athlete and as someone who has close ties to many of the athletes she covers, leading to the sharing of interesting facts and insights about the gymnasts who were not covered before her tenure at NBC.

Along with her role as a gymnastics analyst for NBC, Liukin founded an organization in 2016 called "Grander," which is "an inspirational Mobile App for motivated gymnasts to be mentored by their biggest role models. They can connect and communicate with them, learn valuable lessons for their sport and receive exclusive content" (Duffy, 2018, para. 5). By connecting

Figure 41.1 Nastia Liukin

with young girls and women primarily through a mobile app, Liukin is meeting these athletes where they most often consume sport and interact with their peers. Her goal for the app is to empower young women by assisting them in acquiring the tools they need to succeed in all aspects of their lives: athletically, personally, and professionally.

In addition to the app, Liukin has hosted several Grander Summits in cities around the United States, where she and other former world-caliber gymnasts connect with young female athletes. Liukin said, "Even when I was competing, there was always the importance of having a mentor in my life. Regardless of what you want to be, whatever your dreams or goals are, to get connected, to gain knowledge and inspiration from the people you look up to is so important" (Gardner, 2018, para. 2). Although the Grander app is currently limited to a community for gymnasts, Liukin hopes to expand it to additional sports in the future so that other athletes can also benefit from the mentorship connections it establishes for young athletes.

References

Adams, D. (2018). Here's everything we know about Mary Bono and her abrupt departure from USA Gymnastics. *Indianapolis Star*, October 17. Retrieved from https://www.indystar.com/story/news/2018/10/17/mary-bono-resigns-usa-gymnastics-sonny-bono-nike-tweet-simone-biles-everything-we-know/1669213002.

Arai, A., Ko, Y. J., & Ross, S. (2014). Branding athletes: Exploration and conceptualization of athlete brand image. *Sport Management Review*, **17**, 97–106.

Billings, A. C. (2003). Dueling genders: Announcer bias in the 1999 U.S. Open tennis tournament. In R. S. Brown & D. O'Roarke (eds), *Topics in Sport Communication*. Westport, CT: Praeger.

Billings, A. C. (2007). From diving boards to pole vaults: Gendered athlete portrayals in the "big four" sports at the 2004 Athens Summer Olympics. *Southern Communication Journal*, **72**(4), 329–344.

Billings, A. C., Angelini, J. R., & Duke, A. H. (2010). Gendered profiles of Olympic history: Sportscaster dialogue in the 2008 Beijing Olympics. *Journal of Broadcasting & Electronic Media*, **54**(1), 9–23.

Billings, A. C., Angelini, J. R., MacArthur, P. J., Bissell, K., & Smith, L. R. (2014). (Re)calling London: The gender frame agenda within NBC's primetime broadcast of the 2012 Olympiad. *Journalism & Mass Communication Quarterly*, **91**(1), 38–58.

Billings, A. C., Brown, C. L., Crout, J. H., McKenna, K. E., Rice, B. A., Timanus, M. E., & Ziegler, J. (2008). The games through the NBC lens: Gender, ethnic, and national equity in the 2006 Torino winter Olympics. *Journal of Broadcasting & Electronic Media*, **52**(2), 215–230.

Billings, A. C. & Eastman, S. T. (2003). Framing identities: Gender, ethnic, and national parity in network announcing of the 2002 Winter Olympics. *Journal of Communication*, **53**(4), 569–586.

Bishop, R. (2003). Feature coverage of women's sports in Sports Illustrated. *Journal of Sport & Social Issues*, **27**(2), 184–194.

Bissell, K. L. & Duke, A. M. (2007). Bump, set, and spike: An analysis of commentary and camera angles of Women's Beach Volleyball during the 2004 Summer Olympics. *Journal of Promotion Management*, **13**(1/2), 35–53.

Burch, L. M., Eagleman, A. N., & Pedersen, P. M. (2012). New media coverage of gender in the 2010 Winter Olympics: An examination of online media content. *International Journal of Sport Management*, **13**, 143–159.

Cooky, C. & Antunovic, D. (2018). The visibility of feminism in the Olympic Games: Narratives of progress and narratives of failure in sports journalism. *Feminist Media Studies*, **18**(5), 945–948.

Crockett, Z. (2016). More women will compete in Rio 2016 than in any other Olympics. *Vox*, August 5. Retrieved from https://www.vox.com/2016/8/5/12386612/rio-olympics-2016-women.

Duffy, P. (2018). Industry insider: Grander. *Inside Gymnastics Magazine*, January 31. Retrieved from https://www.insidegymnastics.com/news-features/industry-insider-grander.

Eagleman, A. N. (2013). Acceptance, motivations, and usage of social media as a marketing communications tool amongst employees of sport national governing bodies. *Sport Management Review*, **16**(4), 488–497.

Eagleman, A. N. (2015). Constructing gender differences: Newspaper portrayals of male and female gymnasts at the 2012 Olympic Games. *Sport in Society*, **18**(2), 234–247.

Eagleman, A. N., Burch, L. M., & Vooris, R. (2014). A unified version of London 2012: New-media coverage of gender, nationality, and sport for Olympics consumers in six countries. *Journal of Sport Management*, **28**(4), 457–470.

Eagleman, A. N., Clavio, G., & Kwak, D. H. (2011). Treading the political media waters: Coverage of the 2008 Olympic Games in U.S. and Chinese news outlets. *International Journal of Sport Management*, **12**(4), 471–485.

Eagleman, A. N., Pedersen, P. M., & Wharton, R. (2009). Coverage by gender in *ESPN The Magazine*: An examination of articles and photographs. *International Journal of Sport Management*, **10**(2), 226–242.

Eagleman, A. N., Rodenberg, R. M., & Lee, S. (2014). From "hollow-eyed pixies" to "team of adults": Media portrayals of Olympic women's gymnastics before and after an increased minimum age policy. *Qualitative Research in Sport, Exercise and Health*, **6**(3), 401–421.

Eastman, S. T. & Billings, AC. (1999). Gender parity in the Olympics: Hyping women athletes, favoring men athletes. *Journal of Sport & Social Issues*, **23**, 140–170.

Fink, J. S. (2015). Female athletes, women's sport, and the sport media commercial complex: Have we really "come a long way, baby"? *Sport Management Review*, **18**(3), 331–342.

Fink, J. S. & Kensicki, L. J. (2002). An imperceptible difference: Visual and textual constructions of femininity in *Sports Illustrated* and *Sports Illustrated for Women*. *Mass Communication & Society*, **5**, 317–339.

Gardner, I. (2018). Olympic gold medalist Nastia Liukin on her empowerment app Grander & the importance of inspiring women. *Boston Common*, July 31. Retrieved from https://bostoncommon-magazine.com/nastia-liukin-on-empowering-women.

Geurin, A. N. (2017). Elite female athletes' perceptions of new media use relating to their careers: A qualitative analysis. *Journal of Sport Management*, **31**(4), 345–359.

Geurin-Eagleman, A. N. & Burch, L. M. (2016). Communicating via photographs: A gendered analysis of Olympic athletes' visual self-presentation on Instagram. *Sport Management Review*, **19**(2), 133–145.

Greer, J. D., Hardin, M., & Homan, C. (2009). "Naturally" less exciting? Visual production of men's and women's track and field coverage during the 2004 Olympics. *Journal of Broadcasting & Electronic Media*, **53**(2), 173–189.

Hedenborg, S. (2013). The Olympic Games in London 2012 from a Swedish media perspective. *The International Journal of the History of Sport*, **30**(7), 789–804.

Higgs, C. T. & Weiller, K. H. (1994). Gender bias and the 1992 Summer Olympic Games: An analysis of television coverage. *Journal of Sport and Social Issues*, **18**(3), 234–246.

Hill, C. (2018). USA Gymnastics interim president faces scrutiny from Simone Biles, Aly Raisman. *Indianapolis Star*, October 15. Retrieved from https://www.indystar.com/story/news/2018/10/15/usa-gymnastics-under-fire-biles-raisman-mary-bono-hire/1652340002.

Kane, M. J. (1995). Resistance/Transformation of the oppositional binary: Exposing sport as a continuum. *Journal of Sport and Social Issues*, **19**(2), 191–218.

Kane, M. J. & Maxwell, H. D. (2011). Expanding the boundaries of sport media research: Using critical theory to explore consumer responses to representations of women's sports. *Journal of Sport Management*, **25**, 202–216.

King, C. (2007). Media portrayals of male and female athletes: A text and picture analysis of British national newspaper coverage of the Olympic Games since 1948. *International Review for the Sociology of Sport*, **42**(2), 187–199.

Lai, K. K. R. & Lee, J. C. (2016). The countries where women won more medals than men in Rio. *The New York Times*, August 24. Retrieved from https://www.nytimes.com/interactive/2016/08/24/sports/olympics/countries-where-women-won-more-medals-than-men-in-rio.html.

Lebel, K. & Danylchuk, K. (2012). How tweet it is: A gendered analysis of professional tennis players' self presentation on Twitter. *International Journal of Sport Communication*, **5**, 461–480.

MacArthur, P. J., Angelini, J. R., Smith, L. R., & Billings, A. C. (2017). The Canadian state of mind: Coverage of men and women athletes in the Canadian Broadcasting Corporation's prime time broadcast of the 2014 Sochi Winter Olympic Games. *Journal of Broadcasting & Electronic Media*, **61**(2), 410–429.

Messner, M., Duncan, M. C, & Jensen, K. (1993). Separating the men from the girls: The gendered language of televised sport. *Gender and Society*, **7**, 121–137.

Myre, G. (2016). U.S. women are the biggest winners at the Rio Olympics. *NPR*, August 21. Retrieved from https://www.npr.org/sections/thetorch/2016/08/21/490818961/u-s-women-are-the-biggest-winners-in-rio-olympics.

Packer, C., Geh, D. J., Goulden, O. W., Jordan, A. M., Withers, G. K., Wagstaff, A. J., et al. (2014). No lasting legacy: No change in reporting of women's sports in the British print media with the London 2012 Olympics and Paralympics. *Journal of Public Health*, **37**(1), 50–56.

Sandomir, R. (2014). NBC extends Olympic deal into unknown. *The New York Times*. , May 7 Retrieved from https://www.nytimes.com/2014/05/08/sports/olympics/nbc-extends-olympic-tv-deal-through-2032.html.

Smartt, N. (2017). Sexual harassment in the workplace in a #MeToo world. *Forbes*, December 20. Retrieved from https://www.forbes.com/sites/forbeshumanresourcescouncil/2017/12/20/sexual-harassment-in-the-workplace-in-a-metoo-world/#79ae25f55a42.

Smith, M. M. & Wrynn, A. M. (2010). *Women in the 2010 Winter Olympic and Paralympic Games: An analysis of participation, leadership, and media opportunities, a Women's Sports Foundation Research Report*. East Meadow, NY: Women's Sports Foundation. Retrieved from https://www.womenssportsfoundation.org/wp-content/uploads/2016/08/2010_olympic_report.pdf.

Taylor, L. (2018). Female athletes race towards gender equality at Winter Olympics. *Reuters*, February 12. Retrieved from https://www.reuters.com/article/us-olympics-2018-women/female-athletes-race-towards-gender-equality-at-winter-olympics-idUSKBN1FW1M7.

Villalon, C. & Weiller-Abels, K. (2018). NBC's televised media portrayal of female athletes in the 2016 Rio Summer Olympic Games: A critical feminist view. *Sport in Society*, **21**(8), 1137–1157.

Xu, Q., Billings, A., & Fan, M. (2018). When women fail to "hold up more than half the sky": Gendered frames of CCTV's coverage of gymnastics at the 2016 Summer Olympics. *Communication & Sport*, **6**(2), 154–174.

Zurn, L., Lopiano, D., & Snyder, M. (2006). *Women in the 2006 Olympic and Paralympic Winter Games: An analysis of participation, leadership and media coverage*. East Meadow, NY: Women's Sports Foundation. Retrieved from https://www.womenssportsfoundation.org/wp-content/uploads/2016/08/2006_olympic_report.pdf.

Conclusion

Andrea N. Geurin and Nancy Lough

> The strength of the women's sector of the sport industry is an indicator and harbinger of the strength of the industry itself.
>
> *(Quote from E. Staurowsky, Chapter 2)*

As we reflected on the development of this work and considered the key takeaways drawn from the culmination of all 41 chapters, several core ideas became clear. The deficit perspective and long-held limiting beliefs that have plagued women's sport need to be replaced by a fact-based perspective that relies on data showing the significant opportunity awaiting those who choose to invest in women's sport. Although the challenges that remain are daunting and unique, in that they are not challenges for mainstream men's sport, we believe these challenges can be overcome. The future of women's sport and women athletes will increasingly look very different. We invite you to consider each of our takeaways and commit to doing your part to advance opportunities for women's sport and women in sport.

Media

Women are still excluded to a large extent in sport media coverage. Although social media offer opportunities for women's sport properties and athletes to promote their brands and engage with current fans, social media do not necessarily create the *awareness* needed for sport properties and athletes among potential fans. To truly legitimize women's sport societally, expanded and improved mainstream media coverage of women's sport is necessary. In addition to *more* coverage of women's sport, a shift is necessary in the ways in which the media speak about and present women's sport. For example, eliminating gender marking, as illustrated in FIFA's use of "World Cup" for men and "Women's World Cup" for women, is necessary to achieve true legitimacy. Expanded and more authentic media coverage is also necessary to achieve greater endorsements, sponsorships, salaries for athletes, and sales/revenues for women's sport teams/properties.

Studies cited in this text have demonstrated that interest in women's sport does exist, and it grows when fostered. In some cases, like the NCAA Women's College World Series for softball, interest in the form of viewership eclipses the comparable men's sport competition, the College World Series for baseball. When more coverage is provided, it typically equates with positive results for the media outlets as well as the women's sport properties. Initiatives on social media, such as the hashtag "If you can see her, you can be her," work as strategic efforts to overcome the challenges of limited media coverage.

Marketing

There is an opportunity for further utilization of women athletes as endorsers for products and brands, and for brands to expand their presence in women's sport through partnerships and sponsorships. Women hold much greater purchasing power than men in most developed nations. Companies who fail to engage with women via relatable endorsers, and sport properties that neglect women as consumers, are missing a tremendous opportunity for growth and revenue generation.

New approaches to marketing women's sport are essential, including new theories to validate the notion that, if more fans are created through effective marketing, investment will grow. Equity has been defined as investment over time. In the case of women's sport, the investment is needed upfront, to create effective marketing to generate equitable awareness, interest, desire, and eventual fandom of women's sport. Similarly, unique opportunities exist for marketers to use women athletes in endorsements, distinct from the ways male athletes are used.

The time is long overdue to retire the old adage of "sex sells." To persuade consumers through marketing, messages associated with the competence of the athlete and the reputation or credibility of the athlete are more beneficial and more likely to relate specifically to female athlete endorsers. Innovative sport marketers that position women athlete endorsers toward underserved markets will reap substantial rewards, by cutting through clutter and communicating more authentically with core consumer groups.

Finally, marketers must stop comparing women's sport with men's sport. Typically, comparisons work in favor of men's sport because investments favor men over women. For example, much more time (in decades), far more money (in marketing and sponsorship), and more media attention have built audiences and created fans in a manner that is incomparable. Relatedly, analytics and data-driven decision-making are increasingly critical to competing in sport. Women's sport organizations tend to lack the data they need, and few have the resources to employ analytics experts to drive future success. Scholars can assist women's sport and women athletes with more research focused on the gender that comprises 50% of the global population.

Consumers

Related to marketing, people, *not just women*, are interested in women's sport – there is a market for it! The recent report by Nielsen focused on the business of women's sport points to the global growth of women's sport fans (Nielsen, 2018). As such, it is incumbent on women's sport properties to develop marketing strategies to further engage those interested in women's sport in order to develop deeper identification and loyalty to these properties. Doing so will also theoretically assist in achieving the marketing potential illustrated in the previous section (women athletes as endorsers; brands sponsoring women's sport), because expanded fan bases provide a greater motivation for brands to engage with women's sport.

Research presented in this text showed how women remain undervalued as a market, which means that both opportunity and opportunity costs exist in all sport organizations. Statistics provided in this text also illustrated the depth of female sport fandom and the pressing need for sport organizations to understand their female fans to increase their sport consumption. However, several authors demonstrated how many leagues and teams miss or fail to meet the needs of this key customer segment because they do not understand the communication and marketing preferences of their female fans. Research on women as sport consumers is not only warranted, but is also critical to the growth of the sport industry globally. Scholars and educators have largely ignored women as sport consumers, women's sport as a product, and the market potential of women athletes, as evidenced by only 3 scholarly articles out of 157 focused on team identification and women's sport.

Management

There is an opportunity to utilize women to a much greater extent in several areas of sport, such as in coaching roles, as leaders/managers, and on governing boards within sport organizations. Several of the chapters in this book identified the positive outcomes associated directly with having women on boards and in leadership positions. A more diverse workforce benefits the organization and the employees, and gender composition is one area that needs more intentional focus to increase diversity within the sport industry.

Some promising steps are being taken to increase women's representation, largely in response to the growing research and awareness generated. Cultural change takes time, persistent effort, and accountability. Tools like the Gender and Race Report Cards from the University of Central Florida and the Tucker Center's Report Card on Women in Coaching stand as examples of what public accountability can do to create awareness needed to change behavior, and eventually change the sport culture. Additional measures to create visible change include removing gender differentiation or marking. We suggest that sport-organizing bodies begin to add the word "men's" to monikers such as the FIFA World Cup or remove "women's" from these titles to avoid depicting the women's competition as a separate championship/competition, when a sport both genders compete in is involved.

Real change in the business of women's sport requires consideration of innovative thinking and new leadership models. Increasingly, we have the research to make the case that increasing inclusion of women on boards and in leadership positions creates a positive result for organizations, the work climate, and the financial bottom line. Research shows improving financial returns are more likely with greater gender diversity, and a 30% threshold in the representation of women is the recognized tipping point that results in significant change. Specific strategies are needed to improve movement toward 30% representation as a measurable goal in various aspects of the sport industry.

Academia

There is a greater need for women faculty in sport management academic programs, as well as a greater need for research focused on women's sport. In terms of faculty composition, women bring diverse viewpoints to sport management departments, and can also serve as valuable mentors and role models for women students. Women enrolled in sport management programs are often under-represented in the classroom and may feel intimidated by the male dominance (from both a student and a faculty perspective) prevalent in the academic field of sport management. Although men in sport management faculty roles can certainly provide strong mentorship and serve as role models to women students, it has been proven time and time again that, when a person sees someone with whom they can identify in a specific position or role, it allows that person to realistically view themselves in the same role or position. Therefore, women faculty have the ability to offer this inspiration to women who are considering entering the sport management field. In addition, as evidenced by some of the authors in this book, research on women's sport is not and should not be limited to women scholars. It is incumbent on men to realize and understand the importance and value of women's sport, and to engage in research on this topic, and/or partner with women faculty on such research projects.

Perhaps the most important takeaway from this entire compilation is the notion that sport management programs can affect a significant and meaningful cultural shift by educating students about women's sport, and the possibilities that exist working in women's sport, conducting research on women's sport, and changing the practices that have limited women athletes and women's sport for too long. Education is the key to real change, and to a more equitable future for everyone who cares about the sport industry.

Final thoughts

Sport is "one of the most powerful economic, social, and political institutions on the planet" (Kane & Maxwell, 2011, p. 204). As a result of sport's global appeal across age groups, social classes, and cultures, it can be a powerful tool for challenging gender-based power differentials. The work presented in this book confronts assumptions and long-held beliefs to create a more accurate depiction of how sport impacts women's lives. This critical analysis of the sport industry should be used to advance women's status in society by utilizing the thought leadership provided to create strategies that will result in overcoming the social, economic, and political constraints that can lead to greater opportunities for all who aspire to work in women's sport.

By implementing an interdisciplinary approach to the study of the business of women's sport, this Handbook has delivered a contemporary view of the "state of women's sport" from a business perspective. Analysis of scholarly work in each of the combined areas points toward strategic approaches to continue the advancement of theory, the development of women's sport as a commodity, and women as leaders in the business of sport.

References

Kane, M. J. & Maxwell, H. D. (2011). Expanding the boundaries of sport media research: Using critical theory to explore consumer responses to representations of women's sports. *Journal of Sport Management*, **25**, 202–216.

Nielsen (2018). The rise of women's sports: Identifying and maximizing the opportunity, October 3. Retrieved from https://www.nielsen.com/us/en/insights/reports/2018/the-rise-of-womens-sports.html.

Index

Locators in *italics* refer to figures and **bold** to tables.

#LikeAGirl 375
#MeToo movement 375, 535, 536

academia *see* scholarship
access discrimination 87, 262–263
accessory fans 395
accountability, Canadian sports system 117
Ackerman, Val 50–51, 336, 338
Adidas 374, 375, 410, 449
administration *see* sports governance
admissions, sex discrimination 25
adult-onset athleticism (AOA) 104
advertisement *see* celebrity athlete endorsement; marketing; sponsorship
advocacy, women-only sport events 100–101
African-American consumers 369
Agenda 2030 281
agents 58–59
AIDA framework (awareness, interest, desire, and action) 435, *446*, 446–447
Aker ASA 518, 524
All-American Girls Professional Baseball League (AAGPBL) 16
Allaster, Stacey 403–404, 413
all-women *see* women-only sport events delivery and management; women-only sport programming
amateur athletes: Brazilian Olympic women migratory processes 151–159; gender equity in sports organizations 275; *see also* college sports; school sports
Amateur Athletic Union (AAU) 275
Amateur Sports Act 220–221
Ambient Sexism Inventory 74–75
analytics *see* business analytics
appearance: emphasis on for female athletes 406, 407–408; evolution of women's professional sport 15–16, 17; girl power 486–487; self-presentation 468–476; sex appeal in marketing 407–408, 420–425; sexualized images 420–425, 457, 458, 460, 468, 534; social media portrayal 457, 458, 460, 534; *see also* attire
Applebee, Constance 24–25
apps 247, 536–537
Association for Intercollegiate Athletics for Women (AIAW) 14–15
Athleisure apparel 374–375
athletes' perspectives: identity 422–423; self-presentation 468–476; social media portrayals 410–412, 457–459
athletic departments: gender equity as ongoing challenge 31–32; participation rates 27
athletic directors: family-work interface 261; gatekeeping theory 39; gender balance 18; hiring practices 258; informal networks 262; operations and functional practices 260; Phillips, Patti 235; stereotypes 262
attendance at games: baseball 194; basketball 193–196; football 194–195; National Basketball Association (NBA) 195–196; team identification 384–386; women's sport 448; *see also* fandom; viewership
attire: emphasis on for female athletes 406; historical foundations of women's sport 12; Lululemon Athletica Inc. 374–375
attractiveness: celebrity athlete endorsement 430–433; sex appeal 407–408, 420–425, 541
audiences *see* attendance at games; fandom; viewership
Australia: 2017 successes 124; basketball 126; club-based system 292–293, 296–297; cricket 127; football 125–126, 297–298; history of professional sport 124–125; individual sports 128–129; leader profiles 131–132; netball 127–128, 493; new leagues in 2018 and beyond 129–130; participation in women's sport 292, 294–296, 298–299; soccer 128; sports organizations 276, 295–297, 295–299; Sydney Paralympics 510–511; trans-Tasman ANZ Championship 494–496, 497

Index

Australian Broadcasting Corporation (ABC) 126
Australian Football League (AFL) 297–299
Australian Rules Football League - Women (AFLW) 125–126, 129, 297–299
Austrian Ministry for Sport, public expenditure 205–206
authentically communicating with women consumers 367–368, 376; culture 368–369; failure to communicate 369–370; fandom 397–399; leader profiles 376–377; properly targeting women 371–375; research and staffing 370–371
Aymar, Luciana 286

Barbour, Sandy 26, 33
barriers to women athletes as endorsers 430–436
barriers to women in leadership roles: bias 83–84, 87–89; Canadian sports system 113–114; discrimination 86–87; gendered space 319–320; Leadership Labyrinth 255–257; prejudice 85–86; stereotypes 84–85
baseball: attendance at games 194; evolution of women's professional sport 16; Major League Baseball 193–194, 239, 259–260; trailblazers in sport business 48–49
Basilio, Enriqueta "Queta" 285
basketball: attendance at games 193–196; Australian professional sport 126; Brazilian Olympic women migratory processes 155, 157; college sport 335–336; gender equity as ongoing challenge 30–31; gender-wage gap 196–197; historical context 12; Title IX, Educational Amendments Act (1972) 219–220; trailblazers in sport business 49–51; *see also* Women's National Basketball Association
basking in reflected glory (BIRGing) 383
Becher, Scott 420
Bell, Mike 462
Beltrame, Stephanie 131–132
Berenson, Senda 12
bias, role in leadership under-representation 83–84; discrimination 86–87; impact of 87–89; leader profiles 90–91; Leadership Labyrinth 257; prejudice 85–86; stereotypes 84–85
Big Bash League (BBL) 127
Biles, Simone 535
blogs 459
board members: equestrian sport 143–147; gender equity 209, 318–319; International Olympic Committee 271–273; New Zealand Rugby 319, 322–323; rugby 346–347; *see also* careers in sport; sports governance
body: equestrian sport 137; muscular development 342–343; sexual difference 484; *see also* appearance
Bond, Amanda 147–148
Bono, Mary 535

Bouchard, Eugenie 406
Bradley, Pat 179
brand communities 408; *see also* fandom
brand image: celebrity athlete endorsement 429–436; golf 169; match-up hypothesis 434–435; social media 410–411
Brazilian Olympic women migratory processes 151–153; leader profiles 159; methods 153; migration outcomes 157–158; results 153–156
British Cycling 360
British Equestrian Federation (BEF) 144–145
Browning, Heidi 52–53
Buchanan, Kate 498–501
Budge, Karl 413–414
budgets *see* economic aspects of women's sport; public expenditure
business acumen: social entrepreneurship 229; trailblazers in sport business 60
business analytics: fandom 399; men's professional sports 244–248; sponsorship 444–445
business analytics in women's professional sports 239; contemporary context in US 240–243; growing use of 239–240; leader profile 248–249; types used 243–244

Canada's television coverage 531
Canadian Association for the Advancement of Women and Sport and Physical Activity (CAAWS) 109–110
Canadian Sport Institute (CSI) Pacific 120
Canadian sports system 106–107; future prospects to achieve gender equity in 115–119; gender-based violence 114–115, 117; government actions and organizations 107–110; leader profiles 119–120; leadership of women 106–107, 110–114, *112*, 117–119; women's rugby 343
Canales, Andrea 476–477
careers in sport: bias 87, 88–89; double standards 61; equestrian sport 143–147; family-work interface 261, 308, 310; gender balance 18; gender equity as ongoing challenge 31–32; self-confidence 348; sociological perspectives 38–39; *see also* leader profiles; sports governance; trailblazers in sport business
Carter, Kathy 55
Cartwright, Kelly 509–510
celebrity athlete endorsement 429–430; barriers to women as endorsers 430–436; match-up hypothesis 434–435; netball 494; source attractiveness 432–433; source credibility 430–432; transfer of meaning process 433–434
Chastain, Brandi 486
chief executive officers (CEOs) 107, 111–113, 209
Chinese governance of women's sport 303; girls and women in history 304–305; leader profile 312–313; Olympic Games strategy 308–310;

545

Index

rise of sports consumption 310–312; sports organizations 305–308
Choi, Kyoungju (K. J.) 179, 184
Civil Rights Act (1964) 13
Civil Rights Restoration Act (1987) 13
Claudino, Fabiana 287
clothing *see* attire
club-based system, Australia 292–293, 296–297
coaching: Canadian sports system 110–111; framing theory 40; gender balance 17–18; gender equity as ongoing challenge 32; Gender-Equity Task Force 333; New Zealand elite coaching 352–361; pay equity 211–212; public expenditure 211–212; qualifications 212; sociological perspectives 38–39; WeCOACH 448–449; Women's National Basketball Association 200
Coaching Association of Canada (COC) 360
Cohen v. Brown University 219
college sports: basketball 335–336; female physical education 25; financial streams and fan support 334–337, 338; gender equity 30, 332; Gender-Equity Task Force 332–334; governance 329–332; growth of women's sport 337–338; historical context 13–15; Korean professional golf 181–185; leader profiles 338; leadership by women 260–261, 329–332; participation rates 329, 334–336; Senior Woman Administrator 330–332; softball 336–337; Title IX, Educational Amendments Act (1972) 28–30; *see also* National College Athletic Association (NCAA)
commercialization: Australia 293; Korean golf 183–184
Commission on Intercollegiate Athletics for Women (CIAW) 14
Commission on Sport Management Accreditation (COSMA) 66–67, 388–389
communication *see* authentically communicating with women consumers
competence, female stereotypes 84–85
competition: Chinese history 305; gendered space 320; 'winning at all costs' 358–359
consumption of women's sport 4, 5; authentically communicating with women consumers 367–371, 376; celebrity athlete endorsement 429–436; China 310–312; college sport 334–337; conclusions 541–542; demographics 1–2, 541–542; differences between men and women 396–397; fandom 391–392, 397–399; media types 2; properly targeting women 371–375; team identification 382–386; transfer of meaning process 433–434; *see also* media consumption
contrapower harassment 71–75
credibility, celebrity athlete endorsement 430–432

cricket: Australian professional sport 127; Beltrame, Stephanie 131–132; New Zealand 356–357
Cricket Australia 295–297
Cronan, Joan 19–20
cross-country skiing, Norwegian Olympic athletes 515–516, 519–525
CrossFit 97, 99
Cultural Revolution, China 305
culture: fandom 392–394; meaning of 368–369; speaking to 367–368
Curtin, Kerrilyn 387–389
cycling, women-only sport events 97

da Silva, Marta Vieira 286
data *see* business analytics
Davidson, Jacqueline 51–52
de Coubertin, Baron 271
decision-making *see* leadership; sports governance
DeFrantz, Anita 54–55
demographics: attendance and viewership 384–386; business analytics 245; consumption of women's sport 1–2, 541–542; Ladies Professional Golf Association viewership 165–166; sport leadership 259–260; subcultures 369
Deng Yaping 309
Denmark, sports organizations 274–275
depression 232–233
DeSensi, Joy 76–77
development, sports organizations 294–295, 299–300
DiCaro, Julie 461–462
digital media: business analytics 246–247; gender equity 531; journalists' experiences 460–462; trends 37; user-generated content (UGC) 459–460; *see also* social media
disabled athletes 504; characterizations 505–506; financial concerns 508; framing 504–505, 506; future of media coverage 510–511; IPC's digital media guidelines 510; leader profile 511–512; Paralympic Games 504, 506–508; social media 507, 509–510
discrimination 86–87; access and treatment 87, 262–263; China 308; Latin America 281, 284; legal context 218–221; and pay equity 222; sponsorship 442; Title IX, Educational Amendments Act (1972) 26; *see also* bias, role in leadership under-representation
diversity: board members 318–319; coaching at elite level 357–358; Latin America 281; media coverage 323; organizational culture 261; United States professional golf management 169–170
Driessen, Christine 56
dropout, social entrepreneurship 232–233
Duffy, Amanda 55–56
Duncan, Jane 320–321

Ecological-Intersectional Model 358–359
economic aspects of women's sport 5; *see also* commercialization of sport; financial assistance; pay equity; public expenditure; revenues
economic exploitation 197–200
Educational Amendments Act (1972) *see* Title IX
elite *see* professional sport
email marketing 247
emotional relationships 209
employment: China 309–310; family-work interface 261, 308, 310; history and treatment of women in higher education settings 67–75; sex discrimination 25; *see also* careers in sport
empowerment: #MeToo movement 535, 536; female consumers 374–375, 398; girl power 487; Millennium/Sustainable Development Goals 281, 284; social entrepreneurship 231
endorsement *see* celebrity athlete endorsement
Entertainment and Sports Programming Network (ESPN): digital platform 264; Driessen, Christine 56; media coverage 336–337, 482; Mowins, Beth 257; Navratilova and Evert 17; Overholt, Alison 57; sex appeal 420; softball 336–337; women's sport coverage 433, 447
entrepreneurship, China 310–311; *see also* social entrepreneurship
Equal Pay Act (EPA) 221–222
equestrian sport: gender 136–137, 147; leader profiles 147–148; participation, presence and power 137–147
ethics, sports governance 318–319
etiquette training, evolution of women's professional sport 16
Europe *see also individually named countries*; Eurocentrism in equestrian sport 136–137; public expenditure 204–206; sport organizations 269–270, 273–275
event delivery *see* women-only sport events delivery and management
Evert, Chris 17
expenditure *see* economic aspects of women's sport; public expenditure; revenues

Facebook: athlete's use 412, 469, 470; netball in New Zealand 496; Steel franchise 497, 498–499, 500; trends in use 408
facilities for women's sports: Australia 125–126, 130, 292–293, 294–295, 301; budgets 28; sport dropout 232
familiarity, celebrity athlete endorsement 432
family-work interface: China 308, 310; women in leadership roles 261
fandom: analytics 399; business analytics 245–246; cultural shifts 392–394; definition 392; demographics 1–2, 541–542; female fans 391–392; female stereotypes 395; gender differences 396–397; inappropriate comments 534–535; leader profile 399–401; marketing to 371–372; netball in New Zealand 496–497; social media 410–412, 455, 457–460; and sponsorship of women's sport 442, 447–448; sport industry implications 397–399; team identification 380, 382–386; transformation of the female sport fan 394–395; user-generated content (UGC) 459–460; women as equal 'fans' 396; women not watching women 395–396; *see also* attendance at games; consumption of women's sport; viewership
Federer, Roger 429
female frailty myth 11, 269–270
female participation *see* participation (women's sport)
female-appropriate sports 420, 441, 456
femininity: celebrity athlete endorsement 430–432; evolution of women's professional sport 15–16, 17; fandom 394, 395; media coverage 483–484, 533; muscular development 342–343; social media portrayal 457; sporting spaces 484
feminism: girl power 486–487; liberal feminism 134–136, 481; sex-integrated sport 138; social media 460; theoretical perspectives 115–116
FIFA World Cup 440
financial assistance: college sport 334–337, 338; historical context 14; social entrepreneurship 230; Title IX, Educational Amendments Act (1972) 28, 29–30; *see also* public expenditure; sponsorship
football: attendance at games 194–195; Australian professional sport 125–126, 128, 297–299; Carter, Kathy 55; Chan, Yuen Ting 90–91; Davidson, Jacqueline 51–52; Duffy, Amanda 55–56; gender equity next frontier 222–223; Latin America 285–286, 287–289; New Zealand 355–356; Title IX, Educational Amendments Act (1972) 220; Trask, Amy 51; *see also* National Football League; National Women's Soccer League
Foundation, Talent, Elite, Mastery (FTEM) framework 294–295
Fowles, Sylvia 199
frailty myth 11, 269–270
framing: disabled athletes 504–505, 506; media coverage 486; social media 407, 412; theoretical perspectives 39–40
funding *see* financial assistance; public expenditure; sponsorship

gatekeeping theory 39, 41, 486
Gazelle Girls 96
gender: careers in sport 18; equestrian sport 136–137; fandom differences for men and women 396–397; leadership 4; liberal feminism 134–136; sports organizations 273–275, 305–308; team identification 382–384;

547

see also femininity; masculinity; sex differences; women-only sport events delivery and management
gender balance zone 206, 207–208
gender equity: board members 209, 318–319; Canadian sports system 106–110, 113–119; college sport 30, 332; disabled athletes 508; double standards 61; fandom 396; legal context 217–224; marketing women's professional tennis 403–406; media coverage 3, 530–533; New Zealand 352–353; as ongoing challenge 30–33; public expenditure 206–213; sex-integrated sport 137–147; sports organizations 273–275, 305–308, 318–319; Title IX, Educational Amendments Act (1972) 26, 27–29
gender marking 397–399, 485, 532, 540, 542
gender regime 209
gender roles: China 304–305; fandom 392–394; female frailty myth 11, 269–270; Latin America 281–284; marketing implications 397–399; social role theory 343
gender-appropriate sports 420, 441, 456
gender-balanced audiences 1–2
gender-based violence 114–115, 117
gender-bland sexism 434
gendered space, sport as 319–320
Gender-Equity Task Force 332–334
gender-specific sport programming 230–231, 234
German Olympic Sports Confederation (DOSB) 210
Germany: gender equity 208, *208–209*; sports organizations 274–275
Gil, María José Soto 288–289
girl power, media coverage 486–487
Girls Athletic Leadership Schools Inc. (GALS) 228
Girls on the Run (GOTR) 96–97, 231–232
girls' sport participation 2; Australia 298–299; events delivery and management 96–97; Korean golf 182, 185–186
Gjensidige 519, 524
glass ceiling 255–256, 319, 320–321, 322–323; *see also* barriers to women in leadership roles
glass wall 320–321, 322–323
globalization, tennis 403
Goffman, Erving 469
golf: Australian professional sport 129; history of women's golf 161–163; Korean professional golf 178–186; sexism in marketing 418–419; Zaharias, Babe Didrickson 15–16; *see also* Ladies Professional Golf Association; United States professional golf management
Golf Channel 57–58
Gorgone, Angela 52
government: Chinese governance of women's sport 306–308; gender equity in Canadian sports 107–110; Latin America's socio-political context 282–284; *see also* public expenditure; sports governance
Gramsci, Antonio 40–41
Grand Slams, golf 178–179
Grander (app) 536–537
Gray, Jennifer 347–349

handball, Norwegian Olympic athletes 515–516, 519–525
harassment *see* contrapower harassment; online harassment; sexual harassment
Hardy, Stephen 65–66
Harrolle, Michelle 394
hashtags 459–460, 473, 476
head coaches: Canada 110; gender equity as ongoing challenge 32; masculinity 18; self-limiting behaviors 88; trends 38, 83, 333
health, physical activity 231–232
hegemonic masculinity: disabled athletes 505; equestrian sport 137; gender equity 209; traits 41
hegemony theory 40–41
Henderson, Brooke 167
heteronormativity 40, 41
heterosexism 40, 41, 73–74
Higgs, Sandi 174–175
High Performance Sport New Zealand (HPSNZ) 354, 359
higher education, history and treatment of women 65–75
hiring practices 258, 334
historical context: Australian professional sport 124–125; Chinese women's sport 304–305; Korean professional golf 179–181; Latin America 280–281; marginalization of women's sports 483–484; rugby 341–342; sponsorship 439–441; sport management programs 67–75; sports organizations 269; women's golf 161–163
historical foundations of women's sport 5, 18–19; evolution of women's professional sport 15–18; leader profiles 19–20; philosophical context 11–15
history of business 67
hockey: Applebee, Constance 24; Aymar, Luciana 286; gender equity next frontier 223–224; New Zealand 355; trailblazers in sport business 52–53
homologous reproduction: gender 42; institutionalization 321; sport management programs 68
homophobia 41
Hong Kong Premier League (HKPL) 90–91
Hookit 457–458
Horgen, Jorunn 525–526
horse ownership, equestrian sport 142–143
Huchthausen, Amy 264–265
human capital 263

Ibargüen, Caterine 286
ice hockey 225–226
identity: female athletes' perspectives 422–423; match-up hypothesis 434–435; media representations 407; self-presentation 468–476; social identity theory 380, 397; team identification 380–387
ideological work of sports journalism 481
Impey, Brent 323
incivility, women in academia 70–71, **72**
inclusion, Canadian sports system 117
individual perspectives, women in leadership roles 263–264
individual sports *see also individually named sports*; Australian professional sport 128–129; Brazilian Olympic women migratory processes 158; female leadership 273, 274; female-appropriate sports 420
inequality *see under* leadership *see* gender equity; pay equity
infantilizing women athletes 397–398, 532–533
in-group members: bias 85–87; influence of power 258–259; team identification 380
Inkster, Julie 179, 418–419
Instagram: disabled athletes 509–510; Olympic athletes 534; personal branding by female athletes 458–459, 468–476; Steel franchise 500; trends in use 408
institutional theory 116, 318
institutionalization: challenges to 321–323; masculinity 47; New Zealand Rugby 319–323
intercollegiate sport *see* college sport
interdisciplinary approach 5, 543
international federations (IFs) 138, 143–147
International Olympic Committee (IOC): 20% minimum threshold 47, 143; as autocratic and centralized system 152–153; DeFrantz, Anita 54–55; equestrian sport 143–145; Norwegian Olympic athletes' protest 515; Ruggiero, Angela 225; Women and Sport Trophy 272; women in leadership roles 271–273, 276
International Rugby Board (IRB) 343–344, 352
international sports organizations, women in leadership roles 271–273, 276
International Triathlon Union (ITU) 144
internet use 2
Inter-Parliamentary Union (IPU) 283
intersectionality: Canadian sports system 117, *118*; Ecological-Intersectional Model 358–359; sociological perspectives 36, 40
intimidation factor 98–99
investment *see* financial assistance; public expenditure; sponsorship
IPC's digital media guidelines 510

Jackson, Terri 200–201
Jones, Jonquel 199

journalism: Driessen, Christine 56; ideological work of sports journalism 481; Overholt, Alison 57; Solomon, Molly 57–58; women working in 460–462, 464; *see also* media coverage
judo 286

Kahn, Megan 448–450
Kane, Mary Jo 37, 39, 42–44
Karefa-Johnson, Anna 376–377
Kempf, Cheri 421, 425–426
Kennedy, Lesa France 53–54
Kim, Chloe 433–434
King, Billie Jean 16–17, 59–60, 222
Knapp, Shannon 53
Korea Elementary School Golf Association 182
Korea Golf Association 180–181
Korea Junior Golf Association 182
Korea Ladies Professional Golf Association 182–185
Korean College Golf Federation 181
Korean professional golf 178–179, 186; evolving social issues 185–186; historical context 179–181; junior and college golf 181–185; Korea Golf Association 180–181
Kurdas, Chyloe 300–301

lacrosse 24
Ladies Golf Union (LGU) 162
Ladies Professional Golf Association (LPGA) 16; business analytics 240, **242**, 243; current state of 163; diversity on tour 169–170; history of 161, 163; history of growth 163–164; Korea Ladies Professional Golf Association 182–185; language controversy 171–172; leadership 170–171; market research 387–388; media coverage 166–169; Park, Inbee 178; sponsorship 441; Tour 164, 173; viewership 165–166
language: controversy in golf 171; fan engagement 397–398; gender marking 397–399, 485, 532, 540, 542; infantilizing women athletes 397–398, 532–533
Latin America's socio-political context 280–281, 287–288; historical context 280–281; leader profiles 288–289; women and sport 284–287; women in society 281–284
LaVoi, Nicole 264, 357–358, 359
leader profiles: Ackerman, Val 338; Barbour, Sandy 33; Beltrame, Stephanie 131–132; Bond, Amanda 147–148; Buchanan, Kate 498–501; Budge, Karl 413–414; Canales, Andrea 476–477; Chan, Yuen Ting 89; Cronan, Joan 19–20; Curtin, Kerrilyn 387–389; DeSensi, Joy 76–77; Doll-Tepper, Gudrun 277–278; Gil, María José Soto 288–289; Gray, Jennifer 347–349; Higgs, Sandi 174–175; Horgen, Jorunn **525**–526; Huchthausen, Amy 264–265; Jackson, Terri

549

200–201; Kahn, Megan 448–450; Kane, Mary Jo 42–44; Karefa-Johnson, Anna 376–377; Kempf, Cheri 425–426; Kurdas, Chyloe 300–301; Liukin, Nastia 536–537; Meyer, Laura 248–249; Michaelis, Vicki 488–489; Nichols, Alana 511–512; Palmer, Farah 324–325; Pattenden, Wendy 119–120; Phillips, Patti 234–235; Reinisch, Nancy 103–104; Rubio, Katia 159; Ruggiero, Angela 225–226; Steinhaus, Bibiana 213–214; Summitt, Pat 19–20; Tiffen, Haidee 360–361; West, Tracy 399–401; Xu, Lijia (Lily) 312–313; *see also* trailblazers in sport business

leadership: Canadian sports system 106–107, 110–114, *112*, 117–119; college sport 260–261, 329–332; conclusions 542; discrimination 87–88; gatekeeping theory 39; rugby 345–346; self-limiting behaviors 88, 263–264; sociological perspectives 38–39; sport governing bodies 206–209, 210; sport organizations 269–275; stereotypes 38, 85, 262; Title IX, Educational Amendments Act (1972) 32, 38; under-representation as continuing challenge 4, 83–84, 255, 257–264; United States professional golf management 170–171; Women in Sports Leadership Council 249; *see also* athletic directors; barriers to women in leadership roles; bias, role in leadership under-representation; head coaches; sports governance

Leadership Labyrinth 255–257

leagues *see also individually named associations e.g. Women's National Basketball Association*; attendance and viewership 384–385; Australia 293; business analytics 239–241; fan demographics 2; first significant professional sport league for women 16; niche sports 443–445; recent launches of women's leagues 191; sport leadership 259–260

legal context: Amateur Sports Act 220–221; college sport 329–330; Equal Pay Act 221–222; female physical education 25; gender equity in Canadian sports 108–109; historical foundations of women's sport 13–14; pay equity 221–224; *see also* Title IX, Educational Amendments Act (1972)

Lewellen, Hope 506

liberal feminism 134–136, 481

Licht, Jason 373

life cycle, business analytics 242–243

lifestyle: 'active women' 96; brand image 169; Lululemon 374–375; marketing 367–368; *see also* family-work interface

likability, celebrity athlete endorsement 432

likes (social media) 473

limiting the pool 88–89

Liu Fei 309

Liukin, Nastia 536–537

London Olympics: female participation 134; media coverage 531, 532

Longoria, Paola 286

Lululemon Athletica Inc. 374–375

luxury sport, golf as 185

Major League Baseball (MLB): business analytics 239; history of 193–194; sport leadership 259–260

Major League Soccer (MLS) 55

management *see* leadership; United States professional golf management; women-only sport events delivery and management

Manley, Effa 48

Mao Zedong 304–305

marathoners, gender differences 102

market research 388–389

marketing 5; authentically communicating with women consumers 367–371, 376; barriers to women as endorsers 430–436; business analytics 246–247; celebrity athlete endorsement 429–436, 494; conclusions 541; gender equity 403–406; leader profiles 413–414; media representations 407–408; properly targeting women 371–375; sex appeal 407–408, 420–425, 541; sexism 418–425; social media 408–413; speaking to a culture 367–368; and sponsorship 439–440, 442–445; understanding fandom 391–392, 397–399; women-only sport events 101–102; women's professional tennis 403–413

married sportswomen: Chinese society 304, 308, 310; personal rebranding of Zaharias 15–16

martial arts 53, 424

Mary, Queen of Scots 161–162

masculinity: and athleticism 483, 485; disabled athletes 505; fandom 394, 395; head coach 18; hegemonic 41, 137; institutionalization 47; muscular development 342–343; 'old boys' networks 68, 261–263, 358; rugby 341–342; sport leadership 257–259, 262; sporting spaces as male 484–485; sports organizations 275–276

match-up hypothesis 434–435

McFadden, Tatyana 509

medals: Chinese strategy 308–309, 311; equestrian sport 137–138, 141; Norwegian Olympic athletes media coverage 522–523

media *see* digital media; journalism; media coverage; social media

media consumption 2; *see also* consumption of women's sport

media coverage: Australian professional sport 125, 126, 128; Canadian sports system 117; celebrity athlete endorsement 433; college softball 336–337; conclusions 540–541; connecting content to the producers 485–486; constructing women as the athletic other 481–483; disabled athletes 504–511; diversity in New Zealand

Rugby 323; exposure 426; femininity 483–484, 533; framing theory 40, 407, 412, 486; future research 488; gender equity 3, 530–533; girl power 486–487; golf 166–169; ideological work of sports journalism 481; journalists' experiences 460–462; leader profile 488–489; marginalization and historical connections 483–484; marketing women's professional tennis 407–408; New Zealand netball 492–501; Norwegian Olympic athletes 515–517, 519–525; Olympic Games 3, 151, 483, 529–536; quality 532–533; rugby 345; sexualized images 420–425, 457, 458, 460, 468; social media 456–457; sociological perspectives 37; sporting spaces as male 484–485; Staley's championship success 480, 481, 488; top-rated women's sport events 167, **168**; women not watching women 395–396; Zaharias, Babe Didrickson 15–16
media engagement, business analytics 246–247, 248
medical context: disabled athletes 504–505; female frailty myth 11, 269–270
Mendoza, Jessica 462
menstruation 11
mental health 232–233
Mexico, "Queta" (Enriqueta Basilio) 285
Meyer, Laura 248–249
Michaelis, Vicki 488–489
migration, Brazilian Olympic women migratory processes 151–159
military roots, equestrian sport 137
millennials 369
Millennium Development Goals (MDGs) 281, 284
Miranda, Francisco de 283
mixed martial arts 53, 424
Moore, Maya 196
Moore, Raymond 405
Motivation Scale for Sport Consumption 383
motorsports trailblazers 53–54
Mowins, Beth 264
Multi-Sport Organizations (MSOs) 111–113
Murray, Lisa 58

Naismith, James 12
National Amateur Athletic Federation (NAAF) 12–13
National Association for Girls and Women in Sport (NAGWS) 12–13
National Association for Sports and Physical Education (NASPE) 66
National Association for Stock Car Auto Racing (NASCAR) 53–54, 248
National Association for the Advancement of Colored People (NAACP) 48
National Basketball Association (NBA): Ackerman, Val 50, 338; attendance at games 195–196; history of 193–194; O'Malley, Susan 49–50; sport leadership 259–260; television revenue 67
National College Athletic Association (NCAA): female physical education 25; financial streams and fan support 334–336, 338; gender balance 18; gender equity 30, 275; Gender-Equity Task Force 332–334; growth of women's sport 337–338; historical context 15; history of sport business 67; Huchthausen, Amy 264–265; role of bias 83; rugby 345; Senior Woman Administrator 330–332; structure and functions 330; women in leadership roles 260–261
National Football League (NFL): attendance at games 194–195; female physical education 25; marketing 398–399; marketing to women 372; television revenue 67; trailblazers in sport business 51–52
National Hockey League (NHL) 52–53
National Netball League (NNL) 127–128
national Olympic committees (NOCs) 47, 83–84, 143
National Rugby League (NRL) 130
National Soccer League 128
National Sport Organizations (NSOs): Australia 293, 294–295; Canada 111–113; China 305–308; gender equity 318–319
National Women's Soccer League (NWSL): business analytics 240, 241, **242**, 243–244; Duffy, Amanda 56; marketing campaign 398; team identification 384
Navratilova, Martina 17
Neal v. Bd. Of Trustees of Cal. State Univs 219
Negro Leagues 48
netball: Australian professional sport 127–128; New Zealand media coverage 492–501
New Zealand: amateur rugby 344; coaching benefits 357–358; coaching challenges 358; coaching current state of play 353–357; coaching strategic approach 359–360; coaching success measures 358–359; elite coaching 352–361; leader profiles 360–361; netball media coverage 492–501; participation in women's sport 352, 493; trans-Tasman ANZ Championship 494–496, 497
New Zealand Cricket 356–357
New Zealand Football 355–356
New Zealand Rugby 319–325, 355, 495
Ng, Kim 49
niche sports, sponsorship 443–445
Nichols, Alana 511–512
Noceda, Paloma 286
non-profit sport organizations: European sport systems 204, 210; gender equity in Canadian sports 107–110; Girls on the Run 96–97, 231–232; governance 316–317; and Lululemon Athletica Inc. 376–377; Sport for Life Society 120

551

Index

North American Society for Sport Management (NASSM) 65, 66–67, 76–77
Norwegian Olympic and Paralympic Committee and Confederation of Sports (NIF) 210
Norwegian Olympic athletes in the media 515–517, 519–525
Norwegian sport context 517–518

obesity 231–232
Octagon Sports and Entertainment Network 58
Office for Civil Rights (OCR) 26–27, 219–220
officials, Canadian sports system 111, *112*; see also sports governance
'old boys' networks 68, 261–263, 358
Olympic Games: Australian professional sport 124; Brazilian Olympic women migratory processes 151–159; Canadian sports system 106; Chinese strategy 308–310; equestrian sport 136, 138–147; female participation 134, *135*, 270; gender equity as ongoing challenge 30–31; Korean professional golf 178; media coverage 3, 151, 483, 529–536; Solomon, Molly 57–58; sponsorship 440; Title IX, Educational Amendments Act (1972) 220–221; trailblazers in sport business 54–55; see also International Olympic Committee
Olympic movement 220–221, 224–225, 273
O'Malley, Susan 49–50
online coverage see media coverage; social media
online dating sites 469
online harassment 461–462
opposite-sex referees 213–214
organizational change 115–116
organizational culture 261–262, 318
organizational demography 259–260
organizational perspectives, women in leadership roles 260–263
organizations see sports organizations
Ortiz, Idalys 286
out-group members 85–87
Overholt, Alison 57

Pajón, Mariana 286
Pak, Se Ri 169, 179, 182, 183, 184
Palmer, Farah 324–325
Paralympic Games 504, 506–508
Pareto, Paula 286
Park, Inbee 178, 179
participation (women's sport): advocacy 100–101; athletic departments 27; Australia 292, 294–296, 298–299; Canada 107, 116–117; college sport 329, 334–336; and discrimination 218–221; events delivery and management 96–97; and fandom 371–372; intimidation factor 98–99; Latin America 284–286; and media coverage 456–457; New Zealand 352, 493; Olympic Games 134, *135*, 270, 531–532; presence and power 137–147; promotion 101–102; rates of female participation in sports 2; rugby 344; social community 99–100, 104; social norms 217–218; sports governance 318–319; Title IX, Educational Amendments Act (1972) 28–29; see also girls' sport participation
paternalistic stereotypes 84–85
patriarchy, equestrian sport 137
Pattenden, Wendy 119–120
pay equity: basketball 196–197; coaching 211–212; disabled athletes 508, 509; Equal Pay Act 221–222; evolution of women's professional sport 17; golf 166; legal context 221–224; next frontier 222–224; tennis 405, 407; see also salaries
Pennsylvania State University 33
per game attendance see attendance at games
Performer Q-Rating 432–433
Phillips, Patti 234–235
philosophical foundations of women's sport 11–15
physical activity: Chinese history 304–305; female frailty myth 11; historical context 269–270; mental health 232–233; obesity and health 231–232
pink-and-proud fans 395
player associations see individually named associations e.g. Women's National Basketball Association
Poland, gender equity 208
policy see legal context
post-structuralist feminism theories 115–116
power: contrapower harassment 71–75; framing theory 39–40; gatekeeping theory 39; girl power 486–487; hegemonic masculinity 41; homologous reproduction 42; participation as distinct from 137–147; sport leadership 258–259; see also empowerment; sports governance
power relationships 209
pragmatic approach 116–117
pregnancy, history and treatment of women in higher education settings 69–70
prejudice 85–86; see also bias, role in leadership under-representation
presence 137–147; see also participation
Proctor and Gamble marketing 375
production relationships 209
production techniques, media 533
Professional Golf Association (PGA) 164, 166, 169–170, 400–401; see also Ladies Professional Golf Association (LPGA)
professional sport: attendance and viewership 384–385; China 310–311; gender equity and the legal context 217–224; history in Australia 124–125; public expenditure 212–213; see also individually named sports; trailblazers in sport business
professionalization: Brazilian Olympic women migratory processes 151–159

promotion *see* marketing; sponsorship
psychographics, business analytics 245
psychological connection, team identification 386–387
psychological continuum model (PCM) 98
public expenditure: gender equality 206–213; leader profiles 213–214; Title IX, Educational Amendments Act (1972) 28; women's rugby 346–347; women's sport 204–206
public relations, business analytics 248
Puig, Mónica 286

Qin Xiaowen 311
qualifications, coaching 212
"Queta" (Enriqueta Basilio) 285

race *see* women of color
radical feminism 138
recruitment practices 258, 334
Reebok #BeMoreHuman campaign 509–510
Reed-Francois, Desiree 255
refereeing: Latin America 287; Steinhaus, Bibiana 213–214
Regina, Silvia 287
Reinisch, Nancy 103–104
research *see* scholarship
retention: business analytics 244–245; college sport 334
return on investment (ROI): business analytics 246, 248; gender equity 421; sponsorship 445
revenues: business analytics 242–245; college sport 334–336; history of sport business 67; netball in New Zealand 495–496; sponsorship 440, 441, 444
rights *see* legal context; women's rights
Rio Olympics: Brazilian Olympic women migratory processes 152; female participation 134, 139, 529; Korean professional golf 178
Robson, Laura 410
role models: academia 542–543; advancing women's sport 450; Canadian sports system 109; coaching at elite level 357–358; Latin America 287; *see also* trailblazers in sport business
Rothenberg, Ben 410
rowing 54
Rowling, J. K. 455
Rubio, Katia 159
rugby: evolution of women's rugby 341–346; future of 349; investment in 346–347; leader profile 347–349; *see also* New Zealand Rugby
Rugby Australia 129–130
Ruggiero, Angela 225–226
running, women-only sport events 96–97

salaries: Australian professional sport 129–130; basketball 196–197, 199–200; Korean professional golfers 184; netball in New Zealand 496; Norwegian sport context 517–518; *see also* pay equity
Sauvage, Louise 510–511
scholarship 3; conclusions 542–543; history and treatment of women 65–75; institutional theory 116; post-structuralist feminism theories 115–116; sociological perspectives 36–37; sports governance 316–318; *see also* sport management programs
school sport, Title IX 26–29; *see also* college sport
season tickets 245
self-limiting behaviors 88, 263–264
self-presentation, social media 468–476
Senior Woman Administrator 330–332
Seoul Country Club 180
sex appeal in marketing 407–408, 420–425, 541
sex differences: fandom 396–397; sex-integrated sport 137
sex-integrated sport: equestrian sport 136–137; liberal feminism 134–136; participation, presence and power 137–147
sexism: Ambient Sexism Inventory 74–75; focus on appearance of female athletes 406; gender-bland 434; Latin America 284; marketing 418–425; prejudice 86; sponsorship 441–442; sport leadership 257–258; Title IX, Educational Amendments Act (1972) 26; women in academia 68–69; *see also* discrimination
sexual assault, college sport 333–334
sexual harassment: #MeToo movement 375, 535; gender-based violence 114–115; women in academia 68–72, **73**
sexual orientation: contrapower harassment 74; golf 170; heteronormativity 41; Navratilova, Martina 17
sexualized images 420–425, 457, 458, 460, 468, 534
Sharapova, Maria 411, 412
similarity, celebrity athlete endorsement 432
skiing, Norwegian Olympic athletes 515–516, 519–525
Sky 495–496, 498
SMART Girls 233
Smoller, Jill 58–59
snowboarders 485
Soccer United Marketing (SUM) 55
social capital 263
social community: women in leadership roles 261–262; women-only sport events 99–100, 104
social entrepreneurship: challenges 229–230; characteristics 229; critiquing 233–234; gender-specific sport programming 230–231, 234; issues impacting women and girls 231–233; leader profiles 234–235; meaning of 228–229; Wolfson, Liz 228
social identity theory 380, 397
social issues: Chinese history 304–305; Korean professional golf 185–186; Latin American

553

socio-political context 280–288; social entrepreneurship 230; women's rugby 342, 347
social media 455–456, 462–463; athlete-fan interactions 410–412, 457–459; business analytics 247; disabled athletes 507, 509–510; fandom 410–412, 455, 457–460; The GIST 463–464; golf 168, 169; inappropriate comments 534–535; journalists' experiences 460–462; marketing women's professional tennis 408–413; media coverage of women's sport 456–457; netball in New Zealand 496–497; Olympic athletes 533–535; self-presentation 468–476; trends in use 408; *see also individually named platforms e.g. Twitter*
social norms: China 304–305; fandom 392–394; female participation 217–218; Latin America 281–284; marketing implications 397–399
social role theory 343
socialist feminism 135
sociocultural perspectives: Ecological-Intersectional Model 358–359; sport leadership 259–260
sociological perspectives of women in sport 5, 33–34, 42; leader profile 42–44; leadership and coaching 38–39; media coverage 37; theoretical perspectives 39–42
Sociology of Sport Journal (SSJ) 37
softball: college sport 336–337; Gil, María José Soto 288–289; Kempf, Cheri 425–426; Mendoza, Jessica 462
Solheim Cup 418
Solomon, Molly 57–58
Sorenstam, Annika 179
source attractiveness, celebrity athlete endorsement 432–433
source credibility, celebrity athlete endorsement 430–432
sponsor fit 524–525
sponsorship: barriers to women athletes as endorsers 430–436; business analytics 244, 248–249; celebrity athlete endorsement 429–436, 494; company participation 518; conceptual framework 446–448; conclusions 541; gender equity 421; history of in sport 439–441; Korean professional golfers 184–185; Ladies Professional Golf Association 172; leader profiles 448–450; and marketing 439–440, 442–445; Norwegian Olympic athletes 518–519, 522–524; objectives 442–445; revenues 440, 441, 444; rugby 344; sexism 441–442; tennis 403; Title IX, Educational Amendments Act (1972) 28; women's sport 442, 445, 447–448; *see also* financial assistance
Sport Canada 107–108
sport dropout, social entrepreneurship 232–233
sport events, public expenditure 205–206; *see also* Olympic Games; women-only sport events delivery and management

Sport for Life (SFL) Society 120
sport management programs: conclusions 543; creation and growth 65–67; history and treatment of women 67–75; history of business 67; leader profiles 76–77
Sport New Zealand (SNZ) 353–354, 359
sport programmes: Gender-Equity Task Force 333; gender-specific 230–231; women coaches 359–360
Sport Spectator Identification Scale (SSIS) 381
Sporting Intelligence website 124–125
sporting spaces as male 484–485
sports agents 58–59
sports facilities *see* facilities for women's sport
sports governance: Canadian sports system 111–113; challenges to institutionalization 321–323; Chinese governance of women's sport 303; college sport 329–332; conclusions 542; equestrian sport 143–147; leadership 206–209, 210; national Olympic committees 47, 83–84, 143; New Zealand Rugby 316, 319–325; rugby 345–347; scholarship 316–318; sport governing bodies 206–209; sports organizations 269–275; women's involvement 318–319; *see also* board members; careers in sport; International Olympic Committee
sports organizations: Australia 276, 292–299; China 305–308; development 294–295, 299–300; European 269–270, 273–275; gender arrangements 273–275, 305–308, 318–319; gender equity 318–319; international 271–273, 276; leader profiles 277–278, 300–301; as a male preserve 275–276; New Zealand Rugby 319–325
Staley, Dawn championship success 480, 481, 488
state governing bodies (SSOs) 294–297
Steel franchise 497, 498–501
Steinhaus, Bibiana 213–214
Stephens, Sloane 410, *411*
stereotypes 84–85; fandom and gender 395; social media portrayal 460; women in leadership roles 38, 85, 262; *see also* bias, role in leadership under-representation
Stern, David 50
Structure-Agency model 359
student-centered educational model 14–15
students, history and treatment of women 67–75; *see also* college sport; school sports
subcultures 368–369
success measures 358–359
Suggs, Louise 178
Summitt, Pat 19–20
surfing 129
Sustainable Development Goals (SDGs) 281
Sweden, gender equity 207–208
Sydney Paralympics 510–511
Sydney Scoreboard Global Index of Participation (SSGIP) 318

symbolic annihilation 461
Symthe, Pat 140

Tampa Bay Buccaneers 372–373
Taurasi, Diana 199–200
team identification: attendance and viewership 384–386; definition 381–382; future research 386–387; leader profile 387–389; theoretical perspectives 380; in women's sport 380, 382–384
Team Identification Index (TII) 383
team sports, attendance at games *see also individually named sports e.g. basketball*, 193–195
TEAM.ID 381
technology *see* business analytics; digital media
televised sports coverage: framing theory 40; gender equity 531; history of sport business 67; netball in New Zealand 494, 495–496; Olympic Games 151; trends 37; viewership 384–385
Tennessee University 19–20
tennis: Australian professional sport 129; evolution of women's professional sport 16–17; gender equity 403–406; media representations 407–408; social media 408–413; trailblazers in sport business 59–60; *see also* Women's Tennis Association
terminology *see* language
"Thank you Mom Campaign" 375
The GIST 463–464
three-part test, participation 27–28
ticket prices, business analytics 243–245
Tiffen, Haidee 360–361
Title IX, Educational Amendments Act (1972): Applebee, Constance's entrepreneurial influence 24–25; college sport impacts 29–30; disabled athletes 508; female participation 134; gender balance 17–18; gender equity and the ongoing challenge of 30–33, 217–220; intention and impact 13–15, 23; Kane, Mary Jo 43; leader profile 33; Leadership Labyrinth 256–257; liberal feminism 134–136, 481; media coverage 482, 486; as a response to sex discrimination 26; school and college level participation 28–29; school sports impact 26–28; sociological perspectives 36; US Olympic movement 220–221; women in leadership roles 32, 38
tobacco advertising 439–440
tokenism 324–325
tomboy fans 395
Torres, Regla 286
tournament titles 397–399
track and field 286
trailblazers in sport business 47–48, 60–61; agents 58–59; baseball 48–49; basketball 49–51; football 51–52; hockey 52–53; media 56–58; mixed martial arts 53; motorsports 53–54; Olympics 54–55; soccer 55–56; tennis 59–60
transfer of meaning process 433–434

transnationalism 153
trans-Tasman ANZ Championship 494–496, 497
Trask, Amy 51
treatment discrimination 87, 262–263
triathlon, women-only sport events 95–96, 99, 104
trustworthiness, celebrity athlete endorsement 430–432
Twitter: athlete-fan interactions 410–411; athletes' perspectives 470; disabled athletes 509; fandom of Serena Williams 455; journalists' experiences 461–462; netball in New Zealand 496; Olympic athletes 535; Steel franchise 500; user-generated content 459–460

Umpiérrez, Claudia 287
United Kingdom, public expenditure 210–211
United States: business analytics 240–243; sports organizations 275
United States Olympic Committee (USOC) 54–55, 220–221
United States professional golf management 161; diversity on tour 169–170; history of growth 163–164; history of women's golf 161–163; language controversy 171–172; leader profiles 174–175; LPGA leadership 170–171; LPGA Tour 164, 173; LPGA viewership 165–166; media coverage 166–169
United States Soccer Federation (USSF) 222–223, 224
upselling, business analytics 244–245
US Lawn Tennis Association Tour (USLTA) 16–17
USA Cycling (USAC) 97
USA Triathlon (USAT) 96
user tags 473
user-generated content (UGC) 459–460

Venezuela, female participation in sports 285–286
viewership 1–2; media coverage 3; team identification 384–386; tennis 403; United States professional golf management 165–166; women not watching women 395–396; *see also* fandom
VOCASPORT (Vocational Education and Training related to Sports in Europe) typology 204
volleyball 155, 157
Votaw, Ty 170–171

wages *see* pay equity; salaries
warmth, stereotypes 84–85
Washington Sports Entertainment (WSE) 49–50
Webb, Karrie 129
Werner, Johann Adolf Ludwig 270
West, Tracy 399–401
Whan, Michael 163–164, 170–171

555

Wideman, Jamila 255
Williams, Carla 255
Williams, Serena 368, 406, 455
'winning at all costs' 358–359
Winter Olympics 221, 522, 529, 530–532
Wolfson, Liz 228
Women in Sports Leadership Council 249
women of color: golf 169; Latin America 286, 287; Negro Leagues 48; sociological perspectives 40
"Women of Red" campaign 372–373
women-only sport events delivery and management 95–96, 102–103; leader profiles 103–104; participation rates 96–97; research on 98–102
women-only sport programming 230–231
Women's Big Bash League (WBBL) 127
Women's College World Series (WCWS) 336–337
Women's National Basketball Association (WNBA): Ackerman, Val 50; attendance and viewership 385; business analytics 240–244, **242**; economic exploitation 197–200; future of 200; gender-wage gap 196–197; history in perspective 191–196; leader profile 200–201; marketing campaign 398; sponsorship 444, 447; sport leadership 259–260; success of 191; Title IX, Educational Amendments Act (1972) 31
Women's National Basketball League (WNBL) 126
Women's National Hockey team 223–224, 225

women's participation *see* participation (women's sport)
women's rights: fandom *393*, 393; Latin America 281, 282–284
Women's Rugby World Cup (WRWC) 343–344
Women's Tennis Association (WTA): appearance of female athletes 406, 408; Budge, Karl 413–414; business analytics 240, **242**, 243; provocative marketing 420–421; tobacco advertising 439; viewership 403–404
Wonsan Golf Course 179–180
Woods, Tiger 169–170
work *see* careers in sport; employment; family-work interface
World Cups: gender equity next frontier 223; gender marking 532, 540, 542; pay equity 213, 223; rugby 343–344, 347, 349; soccer 1, 128, 220, 440, 460
World Rugby 322, 344, 345–349
World Surf League (WSL) 129
World Tennis Association (WTA) 129
Wright, Mickey 178
Wrigley, Philip K. 16

Xu, Lijia (Lily) 312–313

Yang, Y. E. 179, 184
Yang Yang 309
Youth Olympic Games (YOG) 515, 519–525

Zaharias, Babe Didrickson 15–16
Zeigler, Earle 65